LIBRARY

In Memory of

Barbara Catton
Class of 1929

The American Way

The American Way

A Geographical History of
Crisis and Recovery

CARVILLE EARLE

ROWMAN & LITTLEFIELD PUBLISHERS, INC.
Lanham • Boulder • New York • Oxford

ROWMAN & LITTLEFIELD PUBLISHERS, INC.

Published in the United States of America
by Rowman & Littlefield Publishers, Inc.
A Member of the Rowman & Littlefield Publishing Group
4501 Forbes Boulevard, Suite 200, Lanham, Maryland 20706
www.rowmanlittlefield.com

P.O. Box 317, Oxford OX2 9RU, United Kingdom

British Library Cataloguing in Publication Information Available

Library of Congress Cataloging-in-Publication Data

Earle, Carville.
      The American way : a geographical history of crisis and recovery / Carville Earle.
         p.   cm.
      Includes bibliographical references and index.
      ISBN 0-8476-8712-0 (alk. paper)
         1. United States—Historical geography.   2. United States—Politics and government.
      3. Political culture—United States—History   4. United States—Economic conditions.
      5. Crisis management—United States—History.   6. United States—Territorial expansion.
      7. Regionalism—United States—History.   I. Title.
      E179.5 .E36   2003
      911'.73—dc21   2002013413

Printed in the United States of America

Contents

Figures

Tables

Acknowledgments

I have come to see *The American Way* as a collaborative project, a collaboration between author and contributors both near and far in time and space. The collaboration begins with the scores of references listed at the end of the volume and with others too numerous to be cited. *The American Way* is above all a macrohistorical and multiscalar synthesis of perspectives arising out of the literatures of American history, geography, and interdisciplinary history. Not a few of these references were brought to my attention in critical essays, research papers, and bibliographies prepared by graduate students past and present. For these references as well as for important insights on a variety of issues taken up in this volume, I'm grateful to Robert Aguirre, Roger Hamilton, John Heppen, Keumsoo Hong, Sam Otterstrom, and Meg Strieff. I'm also grateful for the critical commentaries of colleagues in geography and history at Louisiana State University and elsewhere, most notably John Agnew, Steve Hoelscher, Paul Paskoff, and Gregory Veeck. An invited paper at Johns Hopkins University proved especially valuable in consolidating my thoughts on ideology, geography, policy regimes, and their non-Marxian dialectical alternations. Refinements in these theoretical linkages found their way into my lecture as Distinguished Scholar in Historical Geography presented at the meetings of the Association of American Geographers and, once again, into my reflections on the empirical and theoretical criticisms of the commentators: Edward Muller, Van Beck Hall, Anne Knowles, and James Lemon.

Visual graphics play an important role in *The American Way*. The key spatial variables and their periodic alternations are mapped and graphed at multiple scales: local, regional, national, and global. To produce these many maps in camera-ready form in both digital and hard-copy versions and in short order, I have relied on the extraordinary talents of Clifford Duplechin and Mary Lee Eggart in the Department of Geography and Anthropology at Louisiana State University. They have transformed the crudest of sketch maps into the finest of visual aids.

Louisiana State University has also contributed to this volume in other important ways. The department under Bill Davidson and Craig Colten has provided occasional student assistance and copying; the College of Arts and Sciences under Dean Jane Collins provided copying assistance when department funds were tight; and, lastly, the university generously provided sabbatical leave that enabled me to finish the manuscript and move toward publication.

I cannot find enough kind words for the supportive assistance and the fine work of the staff at Rowman & Littlefield. I am especially indebted to executive editor Susan McEachern for her encouragement, her good judgment, and her editorial wisdom at a critical phase in the manuscript's preparation.

In the end I reserve my deepest appreciation for the indispensable contributions of three very special persons: to Elizabeth Earle for reconfiguring my tables, reformatting the text, and generally preserving good cheer when times were tough; to Dr. Karen Miller for helping keep pain at bay and rationality more near at hand; and, above all, to Mary Louise Earle for sharing her joy in life along with her unswerving faith in the life of the world to come. Theirs is the kind of optimism that sets the United States apart, that is embedded in the American past and in the American Way of periodic crises and the dialectic of response and recovery.

Introduction

The Whig Perspective: Dialectical Strategies, Enlarging States

The American Way offers, I believe, a fresh approach to past American geographies. While sharing much in common with Donald Meinig's *The Shaping of America* series (1986, 1993, 1998, and forthcoming) and John Agnew's *The United States in the World-Economy* (1987), my perspective is dialectical and optimistic as compared to Agnew's jaded presentism or Meinig's celebratory particularism. Moreover, my political persuasion is Whiggish as compared to the social-democratic politics of Agnew or the Tory politics of Meinig. By Whiggish, I mean that *The American Way* is predicated not on mindless celebration of victorious institutions (e.g., as imagined by Taylor 1999) but rather on institutionalized continuities with the past even in the midst of change (as imagined instead by Thomas Macaulay or his American variant, Louis Hartz [1955]; Key 1998, II: 941–42; Pocock 1985). These continuities consist of a repertoire of responses to recurrent crises that date back over two centuries in their current form and over three centuries to their English origins in the crucibles of the English Civil War and the Glorious Revolution. From the former emerged English republicanism with its curious blend of nationalist protectionism and puritan egalitarianism and its geographies of spatial expansion, demographic concentration, and regional volatility and diversification. From the latter emerged English liberalism with its Lockean blend of internationalist free trade and elitist biases and its geographies of spatial consolidation, demographic dispersion, and regional stability and specialization.

This repertoire is also dialectical in its periodic alternation of policy regimes and their associated geographies. Prior to the 1780s, these regimes alternated between republicanism and liberalism; but since the establishment of the United States, they have alternated between elite nationalist *republics* and egalitarian internationalist *democracies* and between their domestic and foreign policy preferences, their geographic reconstructions, and their producer or consumer biases. And thus far these alternations have enabled Americans to cope with these recurrent crises (occurring at half-century intervals), to preserve equilibrium in the American polity, to sustain economic growth, and to maintain an expansive political economy. They have functioned effectively in eight crises over three centuries. In so doing they have tended

1

to affirm the spirit of Edward Everett's words "that in this country the wheel of fortune is in constant revolution, and the poor in one generation [regime] furnish the rich in the next" (quoted in Hartz 1955: 112; on reformed Whiggery more generally, 89–113).

The American Way assumes a similarly Whiggish approach to empire, expansion, and the American state. Whereas Meinig and Agnew share the view of empire as a materialist function of territorial expansion and/or the extension of American economic influence abroad, I here regard empire as an idealist function of the dynamics of jurisprudence and the territorial and extraterritorial extension of American jurisdiction. The focal point of empire is the enlargement of American territorial jurisdiction via constitutional interpretation and reinterpretation (by way of contrast, Ackerman 1991; Hardt and Negri 2000: 160–82). Our juridical definition results in three fairly distinctive stages in American constitutional history—stages that partition the American state into its three scalar dimensions: the Sectional State, 1780s–1877; the National State, 1877–1970s; and the Transnational State, 1980s to date. The Sectional State and its principles of dual federalism gave way to the National State predicated on the Fourteenth Amendment and the ensuing nationalization of the Bill of Rights. The National State was especially well suited to the American engagement with the Soviet Union in the bipolar Cold War. It was less well suited, however, to the post-1980 globalization of the world economy. But even before 1980, steps had been taken to enlarge the jurisdiction of American federal courts abroad and to establish the Transnational State. These included the Civil Rights Act of 1964, which entitled employees of American companies overseas to equal protection; the court's extraterritorial extensions of American jurisdiction overseas in economic litigation involving cartels and dumping; and, more recently, in cases of state-sponsored terrorism. These jurisdictional enlargements of the American state in concert with expanding free-trade areas such as the North American Free Trade Agreement (NAFTA) and the Free Trade Area of the Americas (FTAA) suggest that empire remains a vibrant and growing component of the American political economy (for a more conspirational critique from the left, see Hardt and Negri 2000).

Time

Historical time can be defined variously so as to match distinctive interpretations of the past. Meinig's time, for example, is linear, particularistic, and descriptive; it consists of an orderly array of imperial regimes and periods. Agnew's is presentist, overlain with an elaborate hierarchy of cycles, periods, and eras associated with world-systems theory. My concept of time engages a half-century dialectic of economic crisis and response in conjunction with constitutional crises and successive enlargements in the American state at intervals of about a century.

DIALECTICAL RHYTHMS FROM CROMWELL TO REAGAN

"The American Way" is defined by its periodic structure. This structure traces its origins to the seventeenth century and the emergence of the English ideologies of liberalism and republicanism. These ideologies and their American variants are foundational; they would soon serve as alternative solutions for capitalism's most vexing problem—namely, the severe and protracted economic crises that erupted at recurrent intervals of forty-five to sixty years. That is to say that the responses to these recurrent crises are periodic and dialectical; that they are defined by an institutionalized repertoire of alternating (1) historical periods, (2) policy regimes, (3) geographical reconstructions, (4) producer and consumer revolutions, and (5) a series of scalar enlargements in the jurisdiction of the American state.

This periodic structure consists of seven and a fraction historical periods beginning in the 1640s and extending through the Reagan Revolution. The first of these periods is predicated on the republicanism that emerged out of the English Civil War and the nationalist policies of Oliver Cromwell and the egalitarian philosophies of James Harrington. These policies, albeit bruised, battered, and misshapen by the Restoration, managed to endure until the political and economic crisis of the 1680s. The second period extends from the 1680s to the early 1740s. It arises out of a cascade of economic and political problems—the depression of commodity prices and the rise of unemployment; James II's abortive attempt to restore Catholicism to the throne; the coup known as the "Glorious Revolution"; the installation of a protestant monarchy (William and Mary) and the political supremacy of Parliament—all underlain by the origins of English liberalism. Under the guidance of John Locke and later of Robert Walpole and the Whigs, liberalism nurtured domestic policies of stability, tranquility, and financial surety and colonial policies of "salutary neglect" (tantamount to free trade). All of this leads to the third and final of the colonial periods: the era of neomercantilism or "the age of empire" established on the resignation of Walpole in 1742. The new age reestablished many of Cromwell's protectionist principles and statutory practices. The Navigation Acts, the Sugar Act, the Currency Act, and so on aimed at tightening and centralizing English control over the empire and trumping the power of the French much as their predecessors had trumped the Dutch.

Americans, of course, did not concur with Britain's restrictive imperial policies, and these conflicts soon led to the war for independence and an improbable American victory. In this unique moment, Americans faced such long odds of success as to warrant a trade-off of ideological purity on behalf of more practical concerns. Americans wanted above all else their freedom from an oppressive government, and it was this desire for freedom that led them in the 1780s to liberalism. Yet at the same time, they wanted a powerful nation capable of defending these liberties, and it was this desire for security that led them toward republicanism. Henceforth, American revolutionaries split the atoms of liberalism and republicanism and the Founding Fathers recombined their constituents as republics and democracies—republics joining republican nationalism and liberal elitism, and democracies joining liberal internationalism (and free trade) and republican egalitarianism. The atoms of ideology had been split and recombined in the distinctively American Way.

And thus it was when crisis arrived in the 1820s and 1830s, Americans set aside the First Republic and its discredited ideology of elite nationalism and turned toward the alternative of egalitarian internationalism (i.e., of Jacksonian democracy and the

First American Democracy). Or again in the 1870s, Americans reverted to elitist nationalism and launched the Second American Republic during the Gilded Age and Progressive Era. The alternation persisted in the Great Depression of the 1930s with the New Deal, the restoration of egalitarian internationalism (free trade), and the Second American Democracy; and in the 1980s with the switchover to the Third Republic and the elitist nationalism of Reagan's revolution.

In addition to these dialectical alternations of policy regimes in response to economic crises, the American Way has also involved successive enlargements in the American state at intervals of a century more or less. These enlargements arose out of civil dissent over the rights of individuals in the 1770s, 1850s, 1960s, and 1970s and the ensuing enlargements in the territorial jurisdiction of federal courts via the Constitution (the Sectional State), the Thirteenth through Fifteenth Amendments (the National State), and the Civil Rights Act of 1964 (the Transnational State).

Space

Time moves through space, an equally powerful conceptual tool. Meinig accents the interplay between schematic spatial models and powerful narratives of conquest, colonization, and regional development. Agnew positions the United States within the core–periphery structures of the world economy and the alternations in regional competition and dominance since the 1750s. I have chosen to explore the dialectical alternation of geosophies—of geographical ideals and ideologies—and geographical reconstructions from the 1640s to the present in the context of successive enlargements in the American state.

THE AMERICAN WAY: GEOGRAPHICAL RESPONSES TO CRISIS

The geographies of *The American Way* unfold in three systematic parts. First are the geographical responses to recurrent economic crises (i.e., the Kondratieff cycle with economic crisis at intervals of forty-five to sixty years). Second are the alternations between producer and consumer geographies and their revolutionary impacts on the landscape. And third are the periodic enlargements (every century or so) in the jurisdiction of the American state—in the 1780s, the 1870s, and the 1980s.

Americans have long been beset by economic crises recurring at intervals of a half century more or less. And their responses to these crises have been contingent on the prevailing policy regime and its affiliated geographies. The latter vary on one of four dimensions: spatial expansion/consolidation, demographic concentration/dispersion, regional specialization/diversification, and regional stability/volatility. Before the American Revolution, Anglo-Americans responded to these crises by alternating between two policy regimes—republican and liberal—and their four-dimensional geographies. Republican regimes (1640–1680s and 1742–1780s) promoted nationalist/protectionist foreign policies and their geographies of spatial expansion and demographic concentration along with egalitarian domestic policies and their diversified and volatile regional geographies. Liberal regimes (1689–1742) promoted the converse in policies and geographies. Locke and the Whigs favored a colonial policy of "salutary neglect"—a policy that was tantamount to colonial free trade—and their geographies of spatial consolidation and demographic dispersion along with an elitist domestic policy of regional specialization and stability.

After the Revolution, Americans reconfigured both policy regimes and geographies. Liberalism and republicanism gave way to republics, democracies, and their geographies. Republics were predicated on a nationalist foreign policy—with national-scale geographies of spatial expansion and demographic concentration—and an elitist domestic policy—with regional geographies of specialization and stability. And democracies were predicated on the opposites: an internationalist/free trading foreign policy—with national geographies of spatial consolidation and demographic dispersion—and an egalitarian domestic policy—with geographies of regional diversification and volatility.

From this perspective, the periods of American history are a coaxial bundle of periods, policy regimes, and multiscalar geographies. Seventeenth-century America becomes a republican period of frontier spatial expansion, demographic concentration in Greater New England and Greater Virginia, regional diversification and volatility (underscored by the tensions expressed in Bacon's Rebellion, among other events). The ensuing period (1680s–1740) responds to the earlier headlong expansion and volatility by slowing the pace of expansion, consolidating settlement, and promoting both regional specialization and stability. During this liberal regime, a fluid immigrant society steadily gave way to a more stable Creole American society.

English Whigs were not displeased with the loose-knit society created on their watch, but others in England insisted on much tighter control over colonial trade, commerce, settlement, and, more generally, the empire as a whole. After 1763, following the French and Indian War, these neomercantilists exercised greater control over the formulation and implementation of colonial policies. Britain's screw-press policies of orderly Anglicization invited first a reasoned American response, and when that failed, rebellion and independence ensued. In the 1780s, revolutionaries confronted an economic depression that soon turned into a broader social and political crisis. They soon set about reconstructing a new nation, a federal republic—one that was centralized and powerful enough to protect the nation in both war and peace yet sufficiently restrained by the federation's sovereign states to preserve both liberty and property. Their creation of an elitist/nationalist regime was novel indeed; it was one part liberalism (elitist bias) and one part republicanism (nationalist/protectionist). This First American Republic constituted a new synthesis and occasioned new geographies: nationalism giving rise to rapid spatial expansion (the Louisiana Purchase and the fastest rate of frontier expansion in American history) and demographic concentration (an incipient megalopolis; Pred 1973) and to elitist domestic policies fostering regional specialization (the Northeast, Old South, Old Northwest, and the New South) and regional stability.

Economic crisis returned in the late 1820s and 1830s. The Jacksonians responded by abandoning the policies of the First Republic in favor of the new policies of the First American Democracy. More precisely, the Jacksonians fostered a foreign policy of free trade and a domestic policy that promoted a more egalitarian, mass distribution of resources. And thus did the First American Democracy pass from a common epithet to a point of pride. Geographies changed as well. Spatial expansion ebbed to an historic low as the nation consolidated the gains made in the eastern third of the nation. Within that area, Americans became more evenly dispersed thanks in part to more equitable policies of land distribution and more widespread and readier access to bank capital. These policies resulted in regions that were more diversified and self-sufficient as well as more volatile, with poorer regions rising in status and richer regions falling. By 1840, the American variants of crisis and recovery, of alternating Republics and Democracies and their geographies, were in place.

And this alternation would persist *ad seriatim* as follows:

Crisis	Regime	Geographies
1870s	Second American Republic	Spatial expansion; demographic concentration; regional specialization; regional stability
1930s	Second American Democracy	Spatial consolidation; spatial dispersion; regional diversification; regional volatility
1970s–1980s	Third American Republic	Spatial expansion; demographic concentration; regional specialization; regional stability

The second geographical component of the American Way is the half-century alternations between consumer and producer revolutions. These revolutions are a function of two factors. First, they are inextricably linked with the domestic policies of prevailing regimes: with consumer revolutions prevailing during mass, egalitarian policy regimes, and producer revolutions prevailing during elitist regimes. Second, their alternation responds to excesses and shortfalls in production and consumption, with consumer revolutions leading to overconsumption (underproduction) and triggering a producer revolution that a half century hence leads to overproduction (underconsumption), and so on.

The first notable consumer revolution took place in the 1750s and 1760s. In this neomercantile era, consumers purchased assorted household goods such as ceramic ware, cutlery, cloth, and a mix of luxury items such as tea, chocolate, wine, wigs, and books all distributed via a thickening hierarchy of central-place retailers in England and in America. Much of this can be laid at the foot of a vast expansion in credit provided by manufacturers and wholesalers as a result of falling returns on government securities. The second consumer revolution came in the middle third of the nineteenth century thanks to Jacksonian domestic policies that eased credit and protected debtors and a foreign policy of free trade that meant cheaper prices for imported goods. In short order, the American household was "mechanized." Machines at home facilitated bottling, canning, pressing, ironing, paring, squeezing, grass cutting, and music making. And last, the third consumer revolution began in the 1920s and 1930s. Innovations in installment credit and advertising stimulated a rapid expansion in consumer durable purchases and the electrification of the home. Americans splurged on heavy-duty items ranging from washing machines to automobiles, from electric ranges to entire houses; and debt became a way of life. In all of these revolutions, Americans, their goods, and their regions became more diversified and hence more alike; wholesalers and retailers increased in numbers as central places became more frequent especially at lower levels in the urban-system hierarchy. All these factors contributed to the assimilation and cultural homogenization of natives and immigrants in both the core and the periphery.

These consumer revolutions have alternated with three producer revolutions. All of the latter were initiated by crises of underproduction (overconsumption) in the final third of the past three centuries; all were facilitated by protectionist tariffs or currency devaluation; all were sustained by new and cheaper supplies of labor; all favored the development of certain industries and geographies. The first producer revolution unfolded between 1780 and 1830 in close accordance with Alexander Hamilton's plan using protective tariffs, machines, and the cheap labor available in the northeastern states. The second revolution followed a century later between the 1880s and 1930s. In this case, high tariffs, abundant supplies of cheaper immigrant labor, and lower transport costs fostered mass production in heavy industries, assembly-line fabrication (Fordism), vertical integration of firms, and the emergence of the American manufacturing belt. The third and most recent producer revolution has unfolded since the 1970s. Fordist production gave way to flexible specialization, small-batch production, contracting and outsourcing, and the relocation of firms from the cities to the suburbs and edge cities and from the core to the periphery.

Together these six revolutions have helped transform American regional landscapes. Consumer revolutions have tended to make regions more alike by providing them with similar arrays of goods and services and by bulking up central-place systems. Producer revolutions, by contrast, have tended to sharpen regional differences as firms exploited localized factor endowments and promoted regional specialization in mining, manufactures, and, more recently, producer services.

The third geographical routine has to do with successive enlargements in the jurisdiction of the American state—to the Sectional State in the 1780s, the National State in the 1870s, and the Transnational State in the 1980s. In each case, to reiterate, these enlargements arose out of periodic conflicts over civil rights and their constitutional resolution. The first of these enlargements came in the 1780s. The Constitution defined the Sectional State (1780s–1870s) with its emphasis on a compound republic, the allocation of power between the national government and the sovereign states, and the central role of sectional coalitions and conflict within the political process. Secession and the Civil War brought an end to the Sectional State, and a

series of constitutional amendments paved the way for the extension of federal jurisdiction to the nation at large and for the rise of the National State (1870s–1970s).
Federal courts routinely intruded upon the jurisdiction of state courts, offered more
favorable venues for national-scale firms, and firmed up the political power of the
urban-industrial Northeast and Midwest. The National State, in turn, gave way to
the Transnational State in the 1970s and 1980s (see chapter 6). The Civil Rights Act
of 1964 initially extended the jurisdiction of the federal courts to cases involving
overseas American firms and their workers. Their jurisdiction has continued to expand in matters involving international economic litigation (e.g., foreign cartels and
the dumping of foreign goods on American markets) as well as in civil suits success-
fully seeking damages against the state sponsors of terrorism. But the enlargement of
the American state is not restricted to unilateral actions; concurrently, the agents of
the Transnational State have advanced the course of empire via regional (NAFTA,
NATO) and multilateral agreements (the World Trade Organization, United Nations) in both economic and political-strategic spheres.

Collectively, *The American Way*, *The Shaping of America*, and *The United States in the
World-Economy* constitute a renaissance in a distinctive genre of scholarship in historical geography. Collectively, they represent a regional historical geography on a
sweeping scale. And collectively, they also represent the distillation of several generations of inquiry—from Derwent Whittlesey's sequent occupance to Allen Pred's
notion of urban growth via interdependence and cumulative causation, from James
Vance's mercantile model of colonization and settlement to central-place theory, and
from the history of economic cycles to cultural geographies of acculturation (for
other perspectives on past American geographies, see Dennis 1994; Conzen, Rumney, and Wynn 1993). Each represents a serious engagement with the American
past; each offers a sustained and coherent interpretation of American historical geography from colonization in the seventeenth century to globalization in the late twentieth century. Yet together they serve less as an end than a promising beginning, less
as a definitive conclusion than a significant advance in our understanding of the
American past. Wedding history with geography as these volumes do affords new
angles of vision on the origins and the evolution of American human geographies
and the centrality of these geographies for the American experience. Most of all,
they underscore the inseparability of geographies, ideologies, empires, and policy
regimes—from the republicanism of Harrington to the liberalism of Locke, from
the elite nationalism of Madison, Hamilton, and Ronald Reagan to the egalitarian
internationalism of Andrew Jackson and Franklin D. Roosevelt.

The American Way divides into three parts. The first of these lays out the theoretical arguments; the second reconstructs the colonial foundations of historical periods,
policy regimes, and geographies between 1560 and 1783; and the third describes the
changes between the 1780s and the present. Part I presents in six chapters the theoretical foundations of the argument—that is, the way in which Americans have responded to (and repeatedly overcome) recurrent economic and social crises at
intervals of a half century more or less. Chapter 1 offers an overview of the American
way of crisis, response, and recovery. Chapter 2 describes the periodic structure of

the American past; this structure is based on seven and a fraction historical periods each lasting a half century more or less with the first period beginning in the 1640s and the last in the 1980s. These periods likewise consist of a conjunctural association of long-wave price cycles, economic innovations and their half-century diffusion, religious awakenings and revitalizations, and critical elections and policy regimes. Chapter 3 identifies the principal policy regimes and the alternations in their domestic and foreign policies. For nearly a century and a half, between the English Civil War in the 1640s and the Revolution in the 1780s, these regimes alternated between republicanism and its egalitarian nationalist policies, on the one hand, and liberalism and its elite internationalist policies, on the other. At that point, American revolutionaries introduced a more fundamental change in American regimes and ideologies. Henceforth, they split the atoms of liberal and republican ideologies and recombined them in a novel way. And henceforth, American regimes alternated between the elite nationalist policies of American republics (e.g., 1780–1830, 1880–1930, and 1980s–present) and the egalitarian internationalist policies of American democracies (e.g., 1830–1880 and 1930–1980).

Chapter 4 describes the geographical reconstructions associated with the alternations in policy regimes and their domestic and foreign policies. Consider the relations between geography and foreign policy. Geographies of spatial expansion and demographic concentration are invariably associated with nationalist/protectionist foreign policies. Conversely, spatial consolidation and demographic dispersion are the heirs of a foreign policy of internationalism and free trade. On matters of domestic policy, regional geographies of diversification and volatility are invariably associated with egalitarian domestic policies; and conversely, regional specialization and stability are the heirs of elitist domestic policies. Over time, these geographies were combined in various ways. Before 1780, it was the republicans who united spatial expansion, demographic concentration, and regional volatility and diversification; and it was the liberals who regularly insisted on spatial consolidation, demographic dispersion, and regional specialization and stability. But all that changed after 1780 as Americans split along ideological and policy lines. Henceforth, republics promoted nationalist foreign policies and their geographies of spatial expansion and demographic concentration, as well as elitist domestic policies and their geographies of regional specialization and stability. Meanwhile, democracies promoted their opposite numbers in policy and geography.

Chapter 5 turns to the alternating revolutions in consumption and production (three of each and six in all). The first of three consumer revolutions emerged in the middle third of the eighteenth century and was predicated on a healthy expansion of credit in Britain and then in its colonies that enabled consumers to embark on a binge of consumption. Terms of trade were highly favorable for the purchase of large quantities of British manufactured goods from a phalanx of merchants, wholesalers, and retailers in a hierarchy of central places. Other consumer revolutions followed, in the middle of the nineteenth century (the so-called mechanization of the household) and once again in the middle third of the twentieth century (the "electrification of the household," the emphasis on consumer durables, and the growing role of government in high-mass consumption). Meanwhile, three producer revolutions alternated with these three consumer revolutions. The first emphasized machines and factory production and came at the end of the eighteenth century; the second emphasized the vertical integration of mass production and throughput and came at the end of the nineteenth century ("Fordism"); and the third emphasized flexible production, lean manufacturing, and producer services and came at the end of the twentieth century ("post-Fordism"). These revolutionary alternations in production and consumption systems have played a key role in maintaining the vibrancy of the American economy and the equitable nature of economic returns.

Finally, chapter 6 depicts the successive enlargements in the territorial jurisdictions of the American state—in the 1780s with the drafting of the Constitution and the creation of the Sectional State; in the 1860s and 1870s with the passage of the Thirteenth through the Fifteenth Amendments and the creation of the National State; and in the 1980s and 1990s with the passage of the Civil Rights Act of 1991 and NAFTA and the creation of the Transnational State.

Part II describes in four chapters the colonial foundations of the American Way, circa 1560s–1780s. Chapter 7 chronicles the English backing into empire between the reign of Elizabeth (1558–1603) and the English Civil War in the 1640s. The result was a highly decentralized imperial system consisting of five to ten colonies variously chartered to the king or queen, proprietor, or company and variously inspired by profits, fame, or faith.

Chapter 8 traces the origins and development of English republicanism. The first it attributes to Oliver Cromwell, James Harrington, and the English Civil War; the second to the continuities linking republicanism and the Restoration policies of Charles II and his ministers (e.g., the continuing wars with the Dutch, the expansionary thrust of Cromwell's "Western Design," the demographic concentration in Greater New England and Greater Virginia, and the high rates of frontier expansion—and of social mobility).

Chapter 9 examines the devolution of Restoration republicanism, liberalism's gradual emergence out of the Glorious Revolution, and that ideology's eventual coronation in the establishment of the Whig Party between 1689 and 1720. This policy regime promoted above all else the rights of producers and of property holders in ways that favored stability in domestic politics as well as "salutary neglect" in the American colonies—a neglect that left to the "invisible hand" of the Atlantic market the slower pace of spatial expansion, the widening fronts (in twelve or more sociocultural regions) of demographic dispersion, and the promotion of regional specialization and regional economic stability in the mainland colonies of British North America.

Chapter 10 draws to a close the colonial periods of the American past in its chronicle of the renaissance of mercantilism, nationalism, and an "Age of Empire" between 1740 and the 1780s. In this regime, the neomercantilists reasserted English power in the form of their bold American expansion at the expense of their French adversaries and their retaliatory Anglicization in the Scottish Highlands. Concurrently, these neomercantilists restored the concentration of social, economic, and demographic power in London and in Greater Virginia and Greater New England; promoted the expansion of consumer culture, credit, and a profusion of retailers in a hierarchy of central places in Britain and the colonies; and fostered regional diversification and volatility that tended to modulate regional inequalities on the eve of the Revolution.

Part III offers one short chapter and one long on national geographies, 1780s–present. Chapter 11 sketches the ideological and political transformations that, owing to loyalism, foreshortened the Tory wing of American politics, gave rise to the American Constitution, and established a political regime consisting of alternating republics and democracies. Chapter 12 distills the multiscalar geographies created during five policy regimes (three republics and two democracies). During the three republics, elite nationalist regimes promoted geographies of spatial expansion, demographic concentration, and regional specialization and stability within the context of producer revolution and scalar enlargement in the American state (machine and factory production during the Sectional State, 1780s–1830; Fordist mass production during the National State, 1880–1930; and post-Fordist flexible production during the Transnational State, 1980–present). In proper dialectical fashion, the nation's two democracies have served quite different aims and constituencies. These egalitarian internationalist regimes steadfastly promoted geographies of spatial consolidation, demographic dispersion, and regional diversification and volatility all within the context of consumer revolutions and revolutions in civil rights (the demands for home manufactures and for slave emancipation, 1840s–1860s; and the demands for consumer credit, consumer durables, and black suffrage, 1930s–1960s). For these revolutions of the 1860s and the 1960s, however, there were important origins nearly a century earlier—an egalitarian preamble as it were, one that was voiced in American demands for imports of ceramics and cloth, for CATO and political independence, 1750s–1770s. Subsequently, the English Way of alternating regimes of republicanism and liberalism no longer seemed a sufficient response to periodic economic crisis.

PART I

THEORETICAL
FOUNDATIONS

CHAPTER 1

Space, Time, and the American Way

The roots of American geography—everything from NAFTA to flexible specialization, from edge cities to globalization—run deep into the subsoil of early modern England, to the seventeenth-century origins of liberalism, republicanism, and the half-century crises by then endemic in the capitalist societies of maritime Europe. The problem for the English (and later the Americans) was overcoming these crises while avoiding the political extremes of royal absolutism, socialism, communism, and fascism. The English Civil War and the Glorious Revolution provided the solution—namely, the alternating ideologies and geographies of liberalism and republicanism. Henceforth, the English repertoire of "crisis and recovery" would alternate between these two distant but not bipolar approaches to governance—between republicanism's organic state replete with its nationalist/egalitarian policies and geographies (most notably those of Oliver Cromwell and James Harrington) and liberalism's mechanical state and its internationalist/elitist clockwork of policies and geographies (most notably those of John Locke and Robert Walpole). All of these came into play in the American colonies.

Americans would arrive at a rather different set of solutions. Between 1776 and 1800, they set aside these doctrinaire English ideologies in favor of two new and more supple alloys of liberalism and republicanism. Henceforth, American policy regimes have alternated between republics and democracies—conceptualizations that are at once apt and enduring. Republics (three in all: 1780s–1828, 1880s–1930, and 1980 to date) have fused liberal preferences for elite domestic policies, regional specialization and stability, and producer revolution with republican preferences for nationalist foreign policies, expansion, and demographic concentration. Democracies (1828–1877, 1930s–1980), meanwhile, have fused republican biases of egalitarian domestic policies, diversified and volatile regions, and consumer revolution with liberal biases of internationalist (free trade) foreign policies, geographical consolidation, and demographic dispersion. Lastly, on three separate occasions, Americans have enlarged the geographical jurisdictions of the federal government, expanded the domains of American power, and redefined the nature of the state. First came the *Sectional State* in the 1790s; second, the *National State* in the 1880s; and third, the *Transnational State* in the 1980s. On each of these occasions, Americans enlarged the scale of the new and revised American state, expanded its territorial and jurisdictional reach, and within these boundaries extended the spatial range for implementing the policies and geographies of the ensuing policy regimes. In these new American states, republics now had room for embarking on the geographies of spatial expansion associated with that regime's nationalist/protectionist foreign policies as well as resources for promoting a domestic producer revolution predicated on private property and entrepreneurial elites. And a half century hence, when economic crisis returned, democracies offered a set of alternative solutions—spatial consolidation in place of expansion, demographic dispersion in place of concentration, a revolution in consumption in place of production, regional diversification and volatility in place of regional specialization and stability. There is, in short, a distinctively American way of crisis and recovery.

Continuity, Institutions, and the American Repertoire of Crisis and Recovery

In the 1780s, Americans entrusted their noble experiment to Providence. By the 1840s, they were convinced that continental occupation was their destiny. By the 1890s, with that destiny seemingly fulfilled, they feared that the closure of the frontier would undermine American democracy by closing the safety valve of "free land" and opening the valve to federal power. By the 1950s, they buoyantly acknowledged American mastery in military and civilian affairs and attributed these to the national consensus forged by two-party politics in a liberal democracy. By the 1990s, momentary doubts in themselves and their institutions as the most appropriate for a multicultural nation adrift in a global economy and polity were swept aside in the rising tides of confidence welling up first out of prosperity and then, in September of 2001, out of a floodtide of nationalism. In this U-shaped transit from hope to disillusion and back, from sacred Providence to secular nihilism to the Manichaean ethics of real politic, the most reassuring fact is that American society has endured, and endured, and endured. To have logged nearly four centuries is no small achievement for any society, and to have survived a revolution, a civil war, two world wars, assorted other conflicts, a Cold War, and at least eight serious economic crises is all the more impressive. But longevity is no guarantor of a society's survival into the future. It will not tell us if we are, as some have claimed, at the end of American history or if we are merely at one of its recurrent punctuations. The future will depend instead on the historical sources of American social continuity and the likelihood of their continuation.

The longevity of American society provides circumstantial evidence of continuity, but it is silent on what matters most: the institutional means that Americans have employed for ensuring continuity, for coping with and adapting to social, economic, and geographical change. Historians, of course, regard continuity as a central issue, and their institutional interpretations of the American past, which are by now commonplace, provide a natural place to begin. These interpretations have emphasized variously the critical contributions made by discrete institutions—by, for example, the Constitution and constitutional law, by two-party politics, by a relatively unfettered market economy, as well as by the variety of religious institutions and voluntary associations. These institutions form a necessary part of any explanation of American social continuity, but they are not in themselves sufficient. In the first place, some of these institutions are relatively new on the American scene, and most of them are not coterminous with the full span of American history. By focusing primarily on institutions within the national period of American history, these interpretations tend to overlook the importance of colonial sources of social continuity. Equally important, these interpretations tend to isolate the institutional roles of American law, economy, politics, and so forth, with the result that each interpretation assigns its peculiar periodizations and its distinctive dynamics, and each emphasizes the differentiation of institutional roles at the expense of their interrelationships with other institutions. There is, however, an institution that encompasses this span of nearly four centuries, which subordinates the several institutional trajectories just noted, and which, more important, has proven capable of surmounting most, if not all, of the threats to American society *without* exceeding the narrow tolerances imposed by a liberal democracy and *without* succumbing, as others have, to the ideological alternatives of tory aristocracy, monarchy, and more recently socialism, communism, or fascism. This institution consists of a series of geohistorical strategies and structures—a repertoire, as it were—that Americans have deployed in response to the periodic crises endemic to a capitalist market economy.

An *institutional repertoire* is, for our purposes, a way of conserving the knowledge that we gain in solving one social problem so that it can be used when that problem arises at a later date. More precisely, it is a sequential set of routines that result in enduring principles of conduct or behavior governing important spheres of social activity. In this fashion, problems that are identical or nearly so are solved in a regular way. In the case of the American past, perhaps the most pressing problem has to do with the capitalist market economy and the periodic crises to which it is susceptible. While this problem has eluded institutionalization in many other societies, Americans were fortunate to have hit upon a set of routines that enabled them to respond to these crises, revitalize their economy, and, on rarer occasions, expand its limits while remaining within the bounds of a liberal democracy.

This geohistorical repertoire of crisis-and-recovery, when traced from its origins in the seventeenth century to the present, consists of five roughly sequential and more or less institutionalized routines. The first of these is a periodic structure that encompasses over three and a half centuries and is composed of seven and a fraction periods set apart from one another at intervals of a half century more or less by protracted economic depressions and social malaise. Second is a dialectical dynamic in which the political philosophies of liberalism and republicanism are brought to bear on the domestic and foreign policies and problems of alternating periods and out of which emerges a series of policy regimes that alternate between liberalism and republicanism before 1776 and between republics and democracies thereafter. Third is a series of collateral geographical reconstructions (likewise periodic and dialectical) arising from the geosophical foundations of liberalism and republicanism, deploying spatial strategies consistent with these foundations (to wit, on these dimensions republicans invariably preferring the first, and liberals, the second: spatial expansion/ consolidation, spatial concentration/dispersion; regional diversification/specialization; and regional volatility/stability), and extending these across the multiple scales of nation (state), region, and locale. Fourth is an alternating series of producer and consumer revolutions that begins with the consumer revolution that spread across the colonies on the eve of the American Revolution and continues down to the producer revolution of flexible specialization, virtual production, and lean manufacturing currently under way. And fifth, at longer intervals of a century more or less, is a series of enlargements in the spatial domains of American power (from dependent provinces to sovereign states, sections, and the Sectional State in the 1780s, to the National State in the 1880s, and to the extraterritorial or Transnational State in the 1990s)—enlargements that arise from the sectional stresses of geographic reconstruction and the convulsive civil conflicts that ensue, which are enabled by the triumphant section(s)'s redefinition of the territorial jurisdictions of the state, and that culminate in the long-run viability of American society. In drawing upon these distinctively American routines for crisis and recovery, Americans have met and overcome the recurrent problems of economic crisis; they have transformed American space through the periodic alternation of geographical processes—of spatial expansion and consolidation, demographic concentration and dispersion, regional specialization and diversification, and regional stability and volatility, of republics and then democracies; they have resolved the sectional conflicts that recovery invariably spawns; they have enlarged the spatial domains of American power and social opportunity; and, not least, they have maintained social continuity within a liberal democracy. This, in a word, is the American Way.

The Periodic Structure of the American Past

The periodic structure of the American past serves as the foundation for the institutional repertoire of crisis and recovery (figure 1.1). This structure, in accordance with the periodizations formulated by traditional American historians, consists of a series of historical periods, seven and a fraction to date, and is punctuated at intervals of a half century more or less by the periodic crises in a market economy (Earle 1992). The colonial era provides three of these periods: the mercantilist between the 1630s and 1680, the era of "salutary neglect" from the 1680s to the 1730s, and the neomercantilist revival known as the Age of Empire from 1740 through the American Revolution. The national period provides the rest: the early nationalist era between the 1780s and Andrew Jackson (1828); the middle period, encompassing the Age of Jacksonian Democracy, the Antebellum Years, and Radical Reconstruction to 1877; the corporatist period, more commonly known as the Gilded Age and the Progressive Era (into the 1920s); New Deal Liberalism from 1932 to the 1970s; and, lastly and for lack of a better term, "the end of the era of big government" from Ronald Reagan to the present. If, as seems obvious, each of these periods is different,

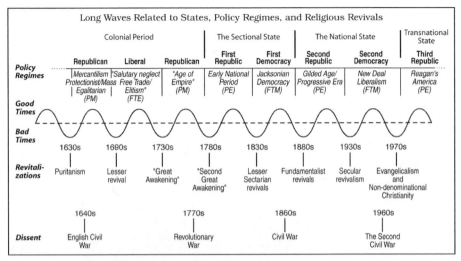

Figure 1.1.   The periodic structure of the American past.

if each distinguishes a unique configuration of particulars—ideas, attitudes, social forms, and economic arrangements—and baptizes them in the name of equally distinctive policies and politics, they are also laced with commonalities and similarities. One must come to grips with the uncanny resemblances between one period and another, with durations that are strikingly alike, with a cascade of social problems that are so familiar and recurrent as to be generic, and with the repeated conjuncturings of key variables—the economic variables of prices and long waves; the half-century-long logistic curves of key inventions, innovations, and their diffusion; the explosive awakenings and revitalizations in religious life; and the rise and fall of a string of American policy regimes. These resemblances across historical periods—of recurrent and generic problems and the often novel solutions to them—provide a scaffolding, as it were, for comparative inquiry and, more particularly, for a natural history of the historical period. Suffice to say that this natural history partitions the period into six distinctive, if often overlapping, phases—those of Crisis, Creativity, Conflict, Diffusion, Dissent, and Decline—and that it is the first of these, the phase of economic Crisis, which holds the key to the rest (figure 1.2).

Policy Regimes

The phase of economic and social Crisis is at once an end and a beginning, a joint announcement that one period has passed away and another has been born. When these periodic crises are as grave and protracted as the economic depressions of the 1680s or the 1930s or, more recently, the 1970s, the social effects are catalytic. Since the mid–seventeenth century at least, hard economic times have set into motion a dialectical alternation in historical periods cum policy regimes. In this dynamic—the second of our five institutional routines—the onset of economic crisis has repeatedly

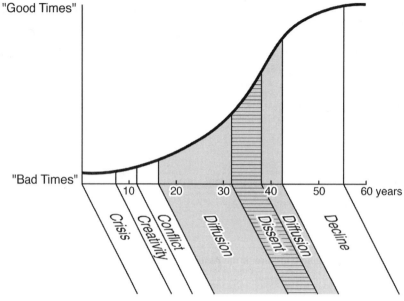

Figure 1.2.   The phases of a macrohistorical period.

discredited the domestic and foreign policies prevailing under one regime and prepared the way for their opposite numbers. Beginning in the 1640s, English regimes
began the alternation between republican and liberal ideologies that had been mol-
ded in the respective crucibles of the English Civil War and the Glorious Revolution
(figure 1.3). Republicans, with their commitments to the organic state and its citizenry, promulgated an intensely nationalist and protectionist foreign policy side by
side with a domestic policy that fostered a broadening of economic and social opportunities for the English citizenry (i.e., a mass egalitarian policy, as it were). Liberals,
by contrast, envisioned a radically different kind of regime. In the view of liberals
such as Locke, Newton, and Mandeville, the strength of the nation was predicated
on liberty, property, and greater freedoms for trade both at home and abroad; on
unfettered individual ingenuity and energy; on unleashing England's entrepreneurial
elite and the nation's productive might on the world at large. In 1776, however,
Americans embarked on a new course. American regimes subsequently have alternated between one set of domestic policies—either the elite or the mass distribution
of domestic resources—and one set of foreign policies—either protectionism (nationalism) or free trade (internationalism). More precisely, these regimes are one part
republican and one part liberal; they have, in other words, alternated between republics, with their commitments to republican nationalism abroad and liberal elitism at
home, and democracies, with their commitments to liberal internationalism and free
trade abroad and republican egalitarianism at home. In this fashion, American regimes have afforded periodic, if often impure and alloyed, expression to the ascendant American philosophies of liberalism (elite and free trade) and republicanism
(mass and protectionist). If over the long run of American history these periodic

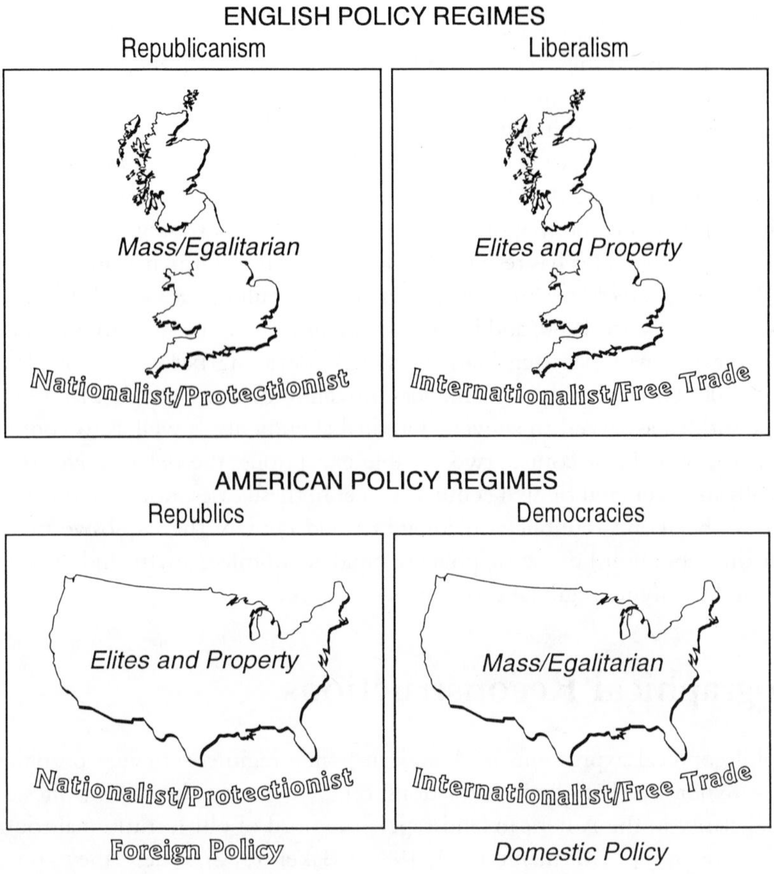

ENGLISH POLICY REGIMES

Republicanism   Liberalism

Mass/Egalitarian   *Elites and Property*

Nationalist/Protectionist   *Internationalist/Free Trade*

AMERICAN POLICY REGIMES

Republics   Democracies

Elites and Property   *Mass/Egalitarian*

Nationalist/Protectionist   *Internationalist/Free Trade*

Foreign Policy   *Domestic Policy*

Figure 1.3. Anglo-American policy regimes.

ventings of divergent philosophies have served to moderate policy excesses, in the short run they have often entailed wrenching shifts from one policy regime to another.

This was especially the case during the colonial era when policy regimes tended to be unusually doctrinaire and the transitions between them unusually rocky. With a philosophical consistency that was more nearly a caricature of the murky realities of British politics, colonial regimes tended to alternate between policies that were more purely liberal (elite/free trade) and more purely republican (mass/protectionist); but policies so pure and unalloyed proved to be too brittle to accommodate the tensions in a sprawling colonial society—tensions that invariably erupted in social movements of rebellion, revitalization, or revolution (e.g., Bacon's Rebellion in 1676, the Great Awakening in the 1740s, the Regulator Movement in the 1750s, and, lastly, the American Revolution itself; see Zuckert 1994; Greene 1998; Bailyn 1967a, 1967b; Armitage 2000: 100–198). This brittle dialectic failed to survive the last of these social movements, and with independence secured from Britain, Americans proceeded to make radical revisions in their ideologies and their politics. American regimes subsequently combined various strands of liberal and republican philosophy in a way that defused their tensions and softened the ideological differences between the political "outs" and "ins" (Kramnick 1988).

What this has meant in practice is that American policy regimes since the 1780s have been reconstituted; they have combined *either* the republican strategy of protectionism/nationalism and the liberal strategy of elite resource distribution *or* the liberal strategy of free trade/internationalism and the republican strategy of egalitarian resource distribution. This has resulted in the first instance in the nation's three republics—the elite protectionist/nationalist regimes prevailing between 1790–1830 and 1880–1930, and since 1980; and in the second instance, in its two American democracies—the internationalist egalitarian regimes prevailing between 1830–1880 and 1930–1970s. This dialectical dynamic has proven to be more supple than its colonial predecessor. It has served to subvert doctrinal alignments as well as to cool revolutionary fervor with, of course, two notable exceptions: the debates over slavery in the 1850s and over civil rights a century hence. In these cases, not even the pragmatic fusion of liberal and republican ideologies could contain the explosive mixture of egalitarian (republican) domestic policies, rapid economic growth, and the hypervolatility of diversifying regional economies.

Geographical Reconstructions

The philosophical expressions of American policy regimes—their geosophies, as it were—are not merely hollow abstractions; on the contrary, they are manifested with unusual clarity in the American landscape—the third of our institutional routines of crisis and recovery (Gottmann 1973, 1980a; Baker 1982). There they appear as a series of geographical reconstructions (likewise periodic and dialectical) across the multiple scales of nation (state), region, and locale. These geographies emerge out of the recurrent crises in the American economy. Reconstruction gets under way with the emergence of each new policy regime; in the interest of revitalizing a stagnant economy, old regimes and their geographies are discredited and displaced and new ones installed. In due course, the agents of the new regime boldly reconfigure the territorial arrangements within the nation, its regions, and politically subordinate locales; and, more to the point, they do so in ways that reaffirm the ideological and geosophical biases inherent within the prevailing regime. In ways envisioned long ago by liberals such as John Locke and Adam Smith or republicans such as Oliver Cromwell and James Harrington, peoples, economies, and social institutions are reshuffled and rearranged along one of four spatial dimensions. Arrayed along the republican/liberal spectrum, these are expansion/consolidation, demographic concentration/dispersion, regional volatility/stability, and regional diversification/specialization (figure 1.4). These are far from casual options since the choices among these opposing spatial processes largely define a policy regime. Which of these strategic interventions are implemented depends largely on two considerations: the philosophical principles of the prevailing policy regime and the extent of its ideological purity or (after 1776) fusion. With respect to foreign policy, the republican principle

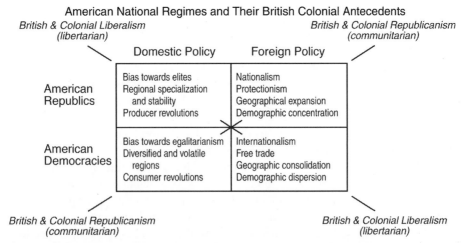

Figure 1.4.   **American policy regimes and their associated geographies: Post-1776.**

of nationalist protectionism is manifested as organic spatial expansion on the periphery and demographic concentration at home; the liberal principle of free trade, as the consolidation and coordination of the domestic space economy and demographic dispersion within that more efficient space. Turning toward domestic policy, the republican principle of mass egalitarianism (in one form or another) is manifested in geographies of regional diversification and regional economic volatility; the liberal principle of domestic elitism, in geographies of regional specialization and stability among regional economies.

A case in point is the geography of the colonial American frontier. The pace of frontier expansion was very rapid under the republican mercantilism that began with Cromwell in the 1650s and lasted into the 1680s, considerably slower in the more liberal era of Whiggery and "salutary neglect" from 1680 to the 1730s (a period of consolidation rather than expansion), and rapid once again in the course of the neomercantilist "Age of Empire" from 1742 to the Revolution. As with spatial expansion/consolidation, so, too, with the colonial geographies of population and regional economies. Thus, we may speak of the stark alternations in colonial geographies, between the republican geographies of expansion, concentration, diversification, and volatility lasting from the 1640s to the 1680s and again from the 1740s to the 1780s, on the one hand, and liberal geographies of consolidation, dispersion, specialization, and stability lasting from the 1680s to the 1740s, on the other.

While these oscillations in colonial geography served the useful purpose of blunting one set of ideological extremes with those of another, they did little to moderate the wild and often wrenching swings from one doctrinaire regime to another. It was the Revolution that clearly demonstrated the need for some modulation in these doctrinal geographic swings, and it was the post-Revolutionary era that completed the task of rewiring the ideological circuitry of American policy regimes (figure 1.3). One set of regimes (the republics), by fusing a republican foreign policy of protectionism and economic nationalism with a liberal domestic policy of entrepreneurial elitism, has promoted a geographical regime characterized by spatial expansion and demographic concentration at the scale of the state and locale (cities, in particular), economic stability and specialization at the regional scale, and a producer revolution in the economy at large (the regimes prevailing during the 1780s–1830, 1880–1930, and since 1980). The other (the democracies), by fusing liberal principles of free trade with republican egalitarianism, has promoted precisely the opposite, a geographical regime of spatial consolidation and dispersion (again at the scale of the state and city), regional volatility and diversification, and a series of consumer revolutions aimed at elevating the standard of living among the masses (the regimes prevailing during the 1830–1870s and 1930–1970s).

Intuition alone would not imagine the possibility of uniting, for example, the spatial processes of expansion (republican) and regional stability (liberal) or even of spatial consolidation (liberal) and regional volatility (republican). Such prospects are more likely if we regard the American landscape as an amalgam compounded out of the volatile materials of Anglo-American philosophy and policy and remixed periodically by dialectical regimes. Of course, landscapes created of such volatile materials could hardly have been inert. Repeatedly these new geographies imposed new conditions and new constraints on American life—and not least on the courses of the American economy and the contours of American power.

Consumer and Producer Revolutions

Geographies are also at stake in the periodic alternation between consumer and producer revolutions—the fourth of our routines. In response to recurrent economic crises, American regimes since the 1740s have alternated between the consumer revolutions of more egalitarian regimes and the producer revolutions of the nation's more elitist regimes. Egalitarian regimes define the crisis as arising out of underconsumption (or, to put it another way, overproduction); they thus adopt a grand strategy that is aimed at expanding aggregate demand (i.e., of expanding consumption among the masses of the citizenry). Toward these ends, their tactics include expanding credit by lowering interest rates on government securities (thereby shifting funds toward the private sector and retailing and wholesaling systems in particular), lowering the prices of land, promoting internal improvements for the purpose of lowering transport costs, providing federal or state guarantees on private housing mortgages, lowering the costs of education via the GI Bill, and so on. Elite regimes, in contrast, regard the crisis as a problem of underproduction arising out of the diminishing outputs and the falling rates of productivity among American farms and factories and offices. Their solutions involve a grand strategy aimed at increasing the size and pace of American production and a series of tactics directed toward eliminating inefficiencies in existing production systems (e.g., Taylorism, lean production, etc.); fostering the introduction of new products and processes (e.g., patents, copyrights, etc.); lowering the costs of capital (e.g., reducing interest rates, lowering capital gains taxes, etc.); facilitating scale economies (e.g., via litigation favoring national-scale enterprise over regional-scale); and promoting increasing returns to scale via spatial-corporate concentration.

In these complementary swings of demand and supply, consumer revolutions have prevailed in the middle third of the past three centuries. On these three occasions—"the transatlantic revolution in consumer tastes" between 1730 and 1780 (Main and Main 1988: 44); "the mechanization of the household" between 1834 and 1878 (Vatter 1967: 9); and the "age of high mass consumption" between the 1930s and the 1970s—egalitarian regimes sought to reduce the inequalities among American income distributions, to socialize consumer risk, and to stimulate consumer spending. Producer revolutions have prevailed in the ensuing three rollovers from one century to the next. On these three occasions in the 1780s–1790s (the first industrial revolution: factory production), 1880s–1890s (the second industrial revolution: mass production), and 1980s–1990s (the "new economy"), elitist regimes sought to tap sources of cheap labor (tapping variously new supplies of women and children—the New England mills; slaves, and immigrants), raise technical productivity, stimulate capital investment, protect property rights, and discover and implement new products and processes.

Scalar Enlargements in the American State

The fifth and final routine in the American repertoire is the series of enlargements in the American state in the late eighteenth, nineteenth, and twentieth centuries. In each case, these enlargements were pursuant to certain redefinitions in the fundamental rights of American citizens and to the expanded jurisdiction of the state. The first of these enlargements—the *Sectional State*—emerged out of the Revolution, the Constitution, and the framers' creation of a concurrent republic in which sovereignty was divided among each of the several states, on the one hand, and the federal government (and "the people"), on the other. The second enlargement—the *National State*—emerged out of the Civil War; the ratification of the Thirteenth, Fourteenth, and Fifteenth Amendments; and the ensuing extension of federal jurisdiction and the Bill of Rights to the several states. The third enlargement—the *Transnational State*—traces its origins to the civil rights legislation of the mid-1960s and to the extraterritorial extension of civil rights to American firms operating abroad.[1]

Of the several routines in our institutional repertoire of crisis and recovery, these periodic enlargements in the domain of American power may be the most important for social continuity. The function of these enlargements is straightforward: to eliminate the existing territorial constraints of a zero-sum game and thereby expand the range of American economic and political opportunity. Occurring at long intervals of a century more or less, these enlargements involve the ratcheting of American power to ascending scales—from provinces/states to sections in the 1780s, from sections to the state in the 1890s, and from the state to the continental trading bloc in the 1990s. The paradox of these enlargements of power is that while they culminate in the long-run viability of American society, their origins reside in the sectional stresses of spatial reconstruction (and more specifically in conjunction with the regional volatilities associated with egalitarian regimes). As noted, these sectional stresses have erupted on three occasions—the American Revolution, the Civil War, and the civil rights movement (and the attendant rise of the Sunbelt)—and on each of these occasions, three sequential outcomes have ensued: First is the reconfiguration of sectional power; second is the triumphant section(s)'s expansive redefinition of the territorial jurisdictions of American law (i.e., via the Constitution, which reserved considerable power for states and sectional alliances; the Fourteenth Amendment, which extended the application of the Bill of Rights and federal law to the several states; and, more recently, the civil rights legislation of the 1960s, which has provided the foundation for a developing body of extraterritorial law); and third is the implementation of policies (and geographical reconstructions) within these newly enlarged domains (jurisdictions) of American law and power. These spatial ratchetings of American power (de facto and de jure) did not just happen, however; nor were they the serendipitous consequences of episodic social movements. On the contrary! These enlargements in the domain of American power were (and are) rooted in and enabled by the other routines in the American geohistorical repertoire—by the periodic structure of the American past, by the dialectical dynamic of liberal and republican ideology, and by the periodic reconstructions of American space. Taken together, these institutionalized routines have provided Americans with a geohistorical repertoire—one that has enabled them to overcome recurrent economic crisis, to expand the domain of American opportunity, and to maintain the social continuity of a liberal democracy. More succinctly, they constitute the American Way of "crisis and recovery."

Note

1. Although civil rights legislation represents one of the earliest and most important illustrations of the extraterritorial extension of American law and jurisdiction, it is not alone. American litigation in matters of international economics, most notably on dumping and securities trading, is increasingly significant, as are other scalar enlargements such as NAFTA or private litigation against states sponsoring terrorism.

CHAPTER 2

The Periodic Structuring
of the American Past

The periodic structure of the American past, by which I mean the United States and its colonial antecedents since 1600, provides the scaffolding for American policy regimes, their dialectical dynamics, and their geographical reconstructions. This structure, when assembled from the various periodizations advanced by American historians, consists of a series of historical periods (seven and a fraction to date) with a range of forty-five to sixty years in length and an average of a half century (table 2.1). These periods, whether in the seventeenth century or the twentieth, have much in common. All originate in the conjuncturings of recurrent social processes—in a coaxial bundling, as it were, of long waves in the economy, policy cycles, periodic religious revitalizations and "awakenings," innovation diffusion, and cycles of settlement expansion—and all consist of a series of internal phases—of Crisis, Creativity, Conflict, Diffusion, Dissent, and Decline (and then Crisis once again). Stepping into any one of these periods invokes a sense of familiarity that goes beyond the commonalities of language, religion, politics, and economy. Though the particulars will vary from one period to another, the bundle of processes and the sequence of phases are reassuringly generic.

The historical period is a synthesis of economy, society, and polity. Each of these

Table 2.1. Historical Periods and Approximate Dates

1630s–1680s	Mercantilism, Civil War, and Restoration
1680s–1740s	"Salutary Neglect" (Free Trade) and the Whig Oligarchy
1740s–1783	Neomercantilism and the "Age of Empire"
1780s–1830	The Early Nationalist Period
1830s–1877	The Middle Period, Civil War, and Reconstruction
1880s–1930s	The Gilded Age and the Progressive Era
1930s–1980s	New Deal Liberalism and its Legatees
1980–date	The Reagan Revolution and Conservative Centrism

Sources: These historical periods are based on a wide range of sources and experiences that date back to when I was an undergraduate in the introductory surveys of American history and that continue in my current research. The datings of these periods are regularly corroborated by the inclusive datings in monographs on American history. See, for example, the datings in the titles of books reviewed or advertised in any issue of the *Journal of American History.* It is worth noting that these half-century periods subsume the public-private political cycle of Schlesinger (1986) and the twenty-two-year business cycles of Kuznets (1930). See also Eisenach (1990), Berry (1992), and Earle (1992: 446–540).

domains provides the period with a recurrent set of processes, with, as it were, an anchoring set of structures. The economy contributes two of these structures: The first is the long wave in commodity prices; the second, the S-shaped curve in the diffusion of innovations. Economic historians have long used commodity prices as an index of the healthiness of an economy. Rising prices generally indicate prosperity; falling prices the converse. Studies of price series in the market economies of the United States and Western Europe strongly suggest that prices move in a series of shorter and longer cycles. The most interesting cycle for the historical period is what has been called the "long wave" or, in honor of its founder, the Kondratieff wave (1935)—a forty-five- to sixty-year span in which commodity prices rise and then fall (figure 2.1). In a typical long wave, prices move from one trough to another with a peak roughly midway in between. From the initial trough or low point, prices tend to rise for a quarter century more or less and then to fall for a roughly equal period of time to the terminal trough—sometimes called A and B phases. The great French historian Fernand Braudel (1979–1984) maintains that the long wave arises with the emergence of capitalism in Europe during the late fifteenth and early sixteenth centuries and persists to the present. Be that as it may, the long wave seems to have been present in England and the United States—the relevant units for this study—since sometime in the seventeenth century. Much more controversial are the precise datings of the long wave's peaks and troughs; certitude on these matters is a fool's errand, and it suffices for our purposes if we are in the general neighborhood of the troughs and, to a lesser extent, the peaks.

In this connection, Goldstein's (1988) base-dating scheme is a useful place to begin. His post-1600 survey of the North Atlantic rimland reports seven price troughs: 1621, 1689, 1747, 1790, 1848, 1893, and 1940. Confining attention to

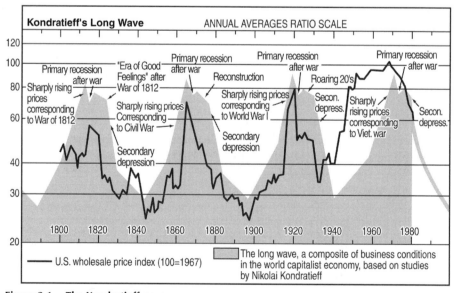

Figure 2.1. The Kondratieff wave.

prices in the United States and its colonial antecedents, Harris (1996), David and Solar (1977), and McCusker (1992) document price troughs in the neighborhoods of the 1630s, 1690s, 1730s, 1740s, 1780s, 1820s, 1870s, 1930s, and 1970s (figure 2.2). For the period since 1800, Berry (1991) identifies four primary Kondratieff troughs in U.S. prices: 1825, 1873, 1933, and 1987.[1] The datings of these long-wave troughs closely resemble (astonishingly so, in several cases) the historians' somewhat fuzzier turning points in the periods of American history—namely, the 1630s, 1680s, 1690s, 1730s, 1780s, 1830s, 1880s, 1930s, and 1970s.

There may be more to these long waves than a series of discrete cycles of rising and falling prices. As Fischer (1996) points out in his comprehensive survey of Western price history, these cycles are paired with the trend in prices rising across two cycles and falling across two successive cycles. The former are associated with the price revolutions that unfolded in the sixteenth, eighteenth, and twentieth centuries; the latter with the long deflations of the seventeenth and nineteenth centuries. The trend in American prices since 1630 (figure 2.2) offers provisional support for Fischer's hypothesis of cyclical pairing. In the upswings in even-numbered centuries, prices tend to increase at decreasing rates; in the ensuing pair of downsprings, prices tend to do the reverse (i.e., decreasing albeit at decreasing rates). It is worth noting that the turnaround constitutes a significant if remarkably prosaic conjuncturing—one that has been invariably associated with the introduction of somewhat more egalitarian policies, the mass distribution of domestic resources, and the hallmarks of consumer revolution—in the 1740s, 1830s, and 1930s. In the first and last of these, entrepreneurs vastly extended the tissue of credit in ways that provided market access to ceramics, household fineries, and tropical exotica in the one case, and to electrified durables in the other. And in the interim, metal manufactures in the mid–nineteenth century continually lowered the costs of an endless supply of machines aimed at reducing the drudgery of household chores. If the reasons for the pairing of these price cycles remain unclear, we know a bit more about their constituent long waves—their discrete cycles of forty-five to sixty years.

Long waves behave as they do for a variety of reasons, not the least of which is the kindred trajectory of innovation diffusion. The points to remember are that both

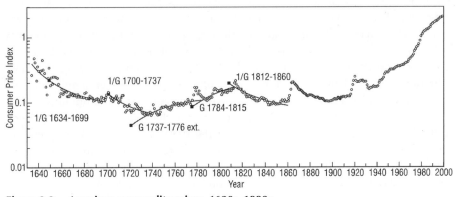

Figure 2.2.   American commodity prices, 1630s–1990s.

of these processes run their course in forty-five to sixty years and that both price and diffusion curves exhibit critical turning points one-half to two-thirds of the way into their cycles. In short, they operate in tandem. Beginning at the trough of the long wave in the midst of protracted economic depression, the curve of prices—and economic prosperity—rises slowly at first as fundamental innovations are devised, introduced, and adopted by risk takers. The curve rises much faster as profitable innovations are diffused more widely; it then begins the long decline toward economic crisis (the end trough) as the diffusion process reaches its point of saturation (i.e., the proportion of potential adopters falls toward zero). The half-century rise and fall of commodity prices (the long wave) thus corresponds quite closely with the inflections and deflections in the S-shaped (logistic) curve of innovation diffusion (for examples past and present, see figures 2.3 and 2.4). While the particulars charted in these curves may change dramatically over time (e.g., the commodities that make up the price series of the long wave, the specific innovations that emerge, or the class bias or neutrality of innovations), the structures endure from one period to the next. One could hardly mistake the innovation of large-scale slavery in the Chesapeake colonies between 1680 and 1720 with the rise of textile manufacturing in New England between 1790 and 1820, or, for that matter, the reaper in the Midwest, crop rotation in the cotton South, and the railroad more generally in 1830s and 1840s with telecommunications and computer technologies in the 1980s and 1990s. Yet these very different innovations, among others, perform the same function—the stimulation of economic recovery and the subsequent rise and fall of commodity prices—and chart a similar course in time.

American society provides the historical period with an equally novel and enduring structure—the religious revitalizations on the period's outset. In matters of faith, McLoughlin (1978) has identified five major religious revitalizations in the American past: the Puritan moment in the 1630s, the Great Awakening in the 1740s, the evangelical revivals at the end of the eighteenth century, the fundamentalist reaction a century hence, and the politically conservative fundamentalism of the 1970s and 1980s. In their timing, these revitalizations dovetail nicely with the economic crises (troughs) that constitute the turning points for five of American history's eight periods. As for the missing turning points, two of them—the 1680s and the 1830s–1840s—seem to qualify as lesser-intensity runner-ups. Certainly the 1680s experienced more than its share of religious ferment: the migration of Quakers, Huguenots, and other dissenting groups; the establishment of the episcopacy in many colonies; and the recrudescence of witch trials in Salem, Massachusetts. Likewise, the 1830s and 1840s were filled with religious dispute, schism, and evangelical revitalization: the turbulent rise of Mormonism, Quaker schism, Millerite millennialism, and Protestant revivalism (Thomas 1989; on the peaks of utopian community foundings in the 1790s, 1840s, and 1890s and subpeaks in the 1820s and 1870s, see Berry 1992: 16–26). That leaves only one vacancy, the 1930s, which, for reasons presented later, probably qualifies as a secular if not a sectarian revitalization movement (Burns 1956: 291–315). In each of these points of transition, when Americans moved from one period to the next, religious revitalization offered a powerful antidote for a body ravaged simultaneously by economic depression and a crisis in faith. In their reckless

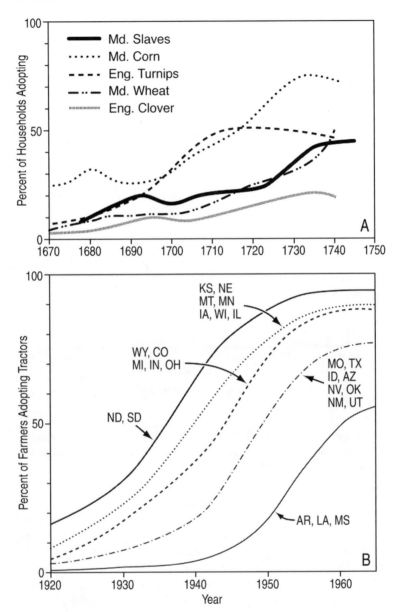

Figure 2.3. Agrarian innovation diffusion.

conviction that faith alone could move mountains, evangelicals carried forth the word of Christian idealism, energized the spirits of those who were beaten down, lifted the hopes of the downtrodden, and, which was not their intention, legitimated an equally radical if vastly wider range of creative experimentations in society at large.

Polity provides the period with the last of its enduring structures—the policy

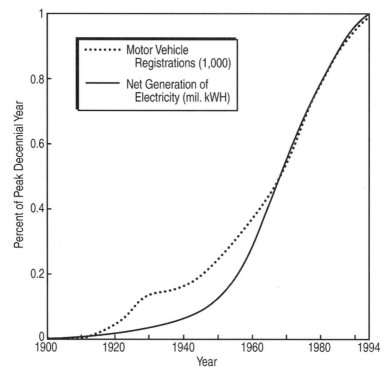

Figure 2.4.   The diffusion of motor vehicles and electricity in the United States.

regime (I, of course, am momentarily setting aside geography's contributions). Policy is an innovation. It is to politics what profitable innovations are to economy and religious revitalization is to society. But unlike Christian idealists, policymakers presume that God helps those who help themselves; and unlike entrepreneurs, they presume that economic crisis warrants a proportionate response—one that is swift, forceful, and collective or, in other words, political. Those who would resolve economic crisis through policy revision and political reform, for all of their bravado, usually end up following a fairly conventional course. They come to power by discrediting policies that have failed; they settle their nerves with cut-and-paste revisions; and in the end, these revisions having failed, they discard the old policies and install new ones in their place (Krasner 1983; Kramnick 1988; Bailyn 1967b; and Zuckert 1994, among others).

This fitful genesis of policy regimes is twice illustrated in the twentieth century. The path taken by New Deal liberalism out of the Great Depression in the 1930s was hardly a smooth one. Only gradually did the Democratic administration of Franklin Roosevelt abandon the policies of the Second Republic. Indeed, it was not until 1935, over two years after FDR's election, that "the symptoms of a pronounced change in the political orientation of the Administration" were fully evident.

> The meagre success of NRA [the National Recovery Administration] and
> its ultimate invalidation by the Supreme Court meant that active co-oper-

> ation of government and business in the process of recovery was at an end; and the mounting opposition from the Right to the New Deal as a whole meant that the Administration would have to enlist its support in other quarters. Moreover the demand for reform which may have been numbed by the rigors of full depression was excited by the mildness of recovery. While the policies of the first New Deal aimed at relief and recovery those of the second were directed to recovery and reform. (Smithies 1946: 13–14)

But if there was no clear and immediate break in the administration's domestic policies, there can be little doubt that the first New Deal provided pretty clear signals of a regime change on matters of foreign policy and overseas trade. The bold devaluation of 1933, the abandonment of protectionism, and the wholesale adoption of free trade (i.e., the reciprocal trade agreements under Cordell Hull) are cases in point. All represented sharp departures from the trade policies of the Second Republic, albeit departures that may have been clearer to observers abroad than to Americans besieged by unemployment and deflation at home (Eckes 1995; Temin 1990).

Similarly, in the 1980s, the Reagan administration valiantly attempted to preserve the free-trade legacy of the New Deal in the face of all reason, not to mention mounting U.S. deficits. But by 1985, as deficits worsened and demands for protectionism resounded in the halls of Congress, the administration quietly reversed its course. Intervening in the global economy, the administration in consort with the central banks of Japan and Germany engineered a sizable devaluation of the American dollar. Under the terms of the Plaza Agreement in September 1985, the value of the dollar fell from near 260 yen to around 160 yen in late 1986. Further agreements on coordinated exchange pushed the dollar down into the vicinity of 120 to 130 yen in 1988 and 1989; similar trends are evident in the falling value of the dollar relative to the German mark (Destler and Henning 1989: 23, 42; Funabashi 1985). By the end of 1985, the Reagan administration had uncovered a new mechanism that paved the way for the abandonment of New Deal–style free trade in favor of coordinated exchange rate agreements among the G-7. The new mechanism offered all of the virtues of protectionism for all producers without all of the untidy wheeling and dealing in the halls of Congress. Indeed, Congress was largely sealed off from a process that required the concurrence of a very few principals: namely, the executive branch, the Federal Reserve, and their counterparts abroad. But if this new version of protectionism was more efficient than its classical antecedents, it was no less biased; exchange-rate coordination had its winners (notably producers for the domestic market such as automakers) and its losers (mostly firms built on imports and, perhaps, consumers).

The policy transformations within the Reagan Revolution and the New Deal are exemplary. The fitful emergence of distinctively new historical periods and policy regimes in the 1930s and the 1980s, as well as in six other cases at earlier dates, underscores the cautious, empirical, and pragmatic approaches of policymakers in times of social and economic crisis. A new regime could emerge when, and only when, the inertia of older policies had been overcome, the blinders on policy possibilities—both domestic and foreign—had been removed, and strikingly new domestic and foreign policies were being brought on line.

Policy regimes are founded on policies that succeed and, more critically, that serve as the keystones in the arch of economic recovery (on these crucial points, see McCormick 1979, 1982). These stringent criteria narrow the field from the hundreds of policies that Americans have pursued to just two: a regime's policies on foreign trade (protectionist or free trade) and on the domestic distribution of resources (elite or mass/egalitarian). In practice, colonial historians have emphasized the former (in this case, British overseas trade policies) and national historians the latter. Colonial historians thus distinguish three regimes. The first of these centers on the nationalist-protectionist ideology of mercantilism as manifested in the Commonwealth's Navigation Acts of 1650 and 1651, its war with the Dutch (1652–1654), and Oliver Cromwell's ambitious expansionist plan of American colonization, his "Western Design" (Hill 1980: 94–100)—all of which emerge out of the English Civil War and the Interregnum (1641–1659) and survive in one form or another until the 1680s in the policies of Charles II and the Stuart Restoration (on the series of social and political continuities between 1640 and 1680, see Stone 1980: 46–57; Malcolm 1999, 2: ix–xxxi). This may seem an odd continuity to be taken up by an adversary, and particularly by someone such as Charles II whose father in 1649 lost his head at the hands of Cromwell and the puritan revolutionaries. But however intense his hatred of Parliament's restraints on royal prerogatives after 1660, Charles II managed to build on the Commonwealth's policies on overseas trade and colonization, and at points even to reinforce them. Even as Charles consorted secretly with the French king, he managed to stiffen the Commonwealth's Navigation Acts, to embark on a second and then a third war with the Dutch, and to assume a more active role in the strategic affairs of the American colonies. While Charles and his nonconformist republican adversaries may have disagreed as to England's real foreign menace, "they knew . . . that England's proper role was to prevent universal dominion"—be it Protestant or Catholic, Dutch or French, republican or monarchist (Pincus 1996: 450–52).

The issues of continuity that arise in defining the mercantilist regime from the 1640s to the 1680s are less apparent during the two succeeding colonial regimes. The second of these regimes is the era of "salutary neglect"—a policy tantamount to free trade that arises out of the economic and political turmoil of the 1680s, the Glorious Revolution and the ascendance of parliamentary power, and the triumph of "secure property rights, [the] protection of . . . wealth, and the elimination of confiscatory government" (i.e., of economic liberalism) and that lasts until the 1730s (North and Weingast 1989: 803). The third and last of these regimes is the "Age of Empire," which begins in (and is defined by) the neomercantile revival that replaces Robert Walpole and Whig liberalism in the 1740s and which lasts until American independence in 1783 (on the Age of Empire, see Gipson 1936–1970). The American colonial era thus provides us with three cases in which the affinity between periods and policy regimes is so close as to affirm Herbert Baxter Adams's axiom that, in the end, "history is past politics."

This identity of history and politics likewise persists after the Revolution, but with a difference. Thereafter, political historians shift the emphasis from foreign trade to domestic policy, and, more specifically, to elite or egalitarian biases in the distribution/redistribution of domestic resources (see especially McCormick 1979, 1982; Lowi 1964, 1972). On this basis, they distinguish two elite and two mass/egalitarian policy regimes—regimes that are ratified by the citizenry in critical elections (Burnham 1967, 1970). Elite regimes prevail during the "early national period" (the 1780s–1830) and the Gilded Age and Progressive Era (1880–1930)—both of which are protectionist/nationalist in matters of foreign policy. And egalitarian regimes prevail during the "Age of Jackson" and the Middle Period (1830–1880) and New Deal liberalism (1932–1970s)—both of which are internationalist and free traders in their foreign policy.

To these American policy regimes I would append a fifth—one that President Bill Clinton acknowledged when, in his State of the Union message, he conceded that the age of big government was over. The larger conclusion was perhaps too obvious for words: a half century or so after it had begun, New Deal liberalism (and its egalitarian commitments to centralized redistribution) was in full retreat and the routed remnants (i.e., the New Democrats) were suing for peace; Reagan's "revolution" (and its elite predispositions) had won the day. Like its predecessors, this newest of regimes has made the oldest of choices. It has chosen between a foreign policy of internationalism and free trade or nationalism and protectionism, on the one hand, and a domestic policy of egalitarian or elite resource distribution, on the other. Elite nationalists have opted for creating one of our three republics; egalitarian internationlists, one of our two democracies. There are, of course, several ways of looking at these sorts of choices. The humanist would highlight what Henry Kissinger has called the necessity for choice; regimes must make crucial policy decisions and these matter greatly. The materialist would point out how little has changed; today's choices are essentially the same as those in the past, and the range of options are as sharply constrained by classical liberal and republican principles. The realist would agree with neither and both; it is possible (and, I would add, probable) that constrained choice is more nearly at the heart of policy regimes and their periodic alternations. But policy choices are only half of the story—and the lesser half at that. In order for a full-fledged regime to emerge, the policies that it chooses must succeed in stimulating, and then sustaining, economic and social recovery.

Policy regimes play an especially prominent role in defining the periods of American history, but in the larger scheme, they are merely the first among equals. In the first instance they must be affirmed by American voters in what are known as "critical elections" (Burnham 1967, 1970). Insofar as the historical period is a synthesis or conjuncturing, the contributions of social and economic processes are as important as the contributions of policy and electoral politics. And insofar as the period is a source of continuity in American history, what matters most is the unions of these covariant and recurrent processes—in the economy's long waves and the related logistic trajectories of innovation diffusion, in society's movements of religious revitalization, and in the polity's policy regimes. Taken at any particular moment, these processes define the spirit of the times, the zeitgeist, and the prevailing "rules of the game"; taken together, they delineate the several periods of American history;

and taken as a temporal series, they constitute the periodic structure of the American past.

With the periods of American history in hand, it is a short step from the historical particulars to a comparative history of the American repertoire of crisis and recovery. Using the period as the unit of analysis, we find that "crisis and recovery" unfolds in a series of six distinctive phases—Crisis, Creativity, Conflict, Diffusion, Dissent, and Decline (for a full account, see Earle 1992: 446–540 and sources cited therein). Any given phase within this sequence presents a similar set of problems and imposes a similar set of conditions and constraints. But if phases are invariably recurrent, the ways in which Americans have responded to them varies dramatically from one period to the next. Behavioral outcomes are rarely, if ever, foreordained. The fact that a given phase may last only a few years or for over a decade is merely the first and most obvious clue to this impressive variability.

Every period in American history begins in the phase of Crisis. In these years of protracted economic depression, problems abound. Unemployment is rampant, prices and profits continue to fall, anxiety intensifies, and social malaise becomes epidemic. Out of the mire of hard economic times, a few Americans grasp for solutions to their dilemma. In the phase of Creativity, they embark on a series of novel experimentations that touch on every sphere of daily life: entrepreneurs experiment with economic innovations; politicians debate policy revisions and reform; spiritual men and women seek to revitalize their faiths. Although many of these experiments are silly, harebrained, or simply ahead of their time, a few are practical enough for wider application. These more practical innovations provide the foundations for economic recovery, policy reform, and religious revitalization.

Just as the society begins to flex its muscles, usually ten to fifteen years into the period, it is convulsed by international war—the Conflict phase. Although warfare may be early or late, longer or shorter, or higher or lower in magnitude, there is always war—war with the Dutch in the 1650s, the French in the 1750s, the Barbary pirates and the English between 1800 and 1815, Mexico in the 1840s, Spain in the 1890s, the Germans and Japanese in the 1940s, and Iraq and terrorists in the 1990s and the new century.

With the muffled sounds of gunfire in the background, Americans step into the buoyant phase of Diffusion. Over the course of the next twenty to twenty-five years, the economy enters into a sustained recovery, profitable innovations are widely and rapidly adopted, and new policies are implemented by the prevailing regime. Prosperity reigns.

Midway into the Diffusion phase, however, American confidence is shaken by domestic controversies over civil rights and the boundaries of citizenship—not to mention the fall in commodity prices from their long-wave peak. In the Dissent phase, mounting tensions are released in superheated rhetoric, rumblings of violence and, on several occasions, in the explosive eruptions of internal war. Of such wars there are two clear-cut cases—the American Revolution and the Civil War—and a near case—the civil rights movement of the 1950s and 1960s; and in all three cases, the battles erupt in the course of regimes that are more egalitarian than elitist.

Scarcely noticed in the din of Dissent is the fact that American society has slipped quietly into the final phase of economic and social Decline. As the ailing economy makes its long descent, the symptoms accumulate: prices in real dollars fall; productivity lags; recessions deepen and widen; profits dwindle; unemployment mounts; and with the market for innovations now saturated, the S-shaped curves of logistic diffusion flatten out once and for all. Americans discount these symptoms, or dismiss them altogether, until, on the eve of Crisis, they are themselves stricken by recurring bouts of Malthusian pessimism, "nervousness," and anxiety. The period's forty-five- to sixty-year circuit is now complete.

For all of the commonalities across the periods and phases of American history, this periodic structure accommodates a remarkably wide range of behaviors. Historical periods are hardly slavish copies of one another since each of them is likewise the distinctive product of its times and the particular problems that these present. Historical outcomes within periods and phases thus are as invariant in their variability, in their contingency upon particular events, as periods and phases are invariant in their recurrence. Consider, for example, just a few of the immense differences in American behavior across historical phases: that Crises may be shorter or longer; that religious revitalizations (Creativity) may be lower or higher in intensity; that international Conflicts may be quick or deferred; that Diffusions may be faster or slower; that domestic Dissent sometimes rumbles and other times erupts into internal war; and that Declines may be abrupt or painfully drawn out. Comparative perspective helps in putting a finer point on what is distinctive—and what is not—in the seven periods of the American past; but it is the dialectical dynamic that sharpens our interpretation of the causes of these behavioral variations. And it is to these that we now turn.

Note

1. In his comprehensive survey of prices in capitalist economies, David H. Fischer (1996) describes century-long price revolutions alternating with century-long price equilibria: the former in the sixteenth, eighteenth, and twentieth centuries; the latter in their odd-numbered successors (the Enlightenment equilibrium of the seventeenth century and the Victorian equilibrium of the nineteenth). These also appear in the semilogarithmic graph of American prices between 1630 and 1974 with the equilibria depicted as successive downtrends of forty to sixty years (1634–1699/1700–1737 and 1812–1860s/1860–1920s) and the revolutions as successive uptrends of similar length (1737–1776/1784–1815 and 1930s–1970s). In the former, prices trend downward but at a decreasing rate; in the latter, prices trend upward but again at a diminishing rate (i.e., the trend in prices, whether up or down, is exaggerated in the first half of the Kondratieff and dampened in the second half). Lastly, note that each of these long waves, save one (here I exclude the first wave since data on colonial prices before 1630 are nonsystematic), seems to be signaled by several years of rapid price inflation followed by a slump in prices toward the trend line of the ensuing wave. The exception, for reasons not entirely understood, is the long wave beginning in the late 1730s and into the 1740s; the transition from the Enlightenment price equilibrium to the eighteenth-century price revolution appears to have been fairly smooth (i.e., unaccompanied by a bump in prices). Subsequently, the inflationary signal has appeared at the end and the beginning of every ensuing long wave. See figure 2.1, Harris (1996), McCusker (1992), David and Solar (1977), and *Statistical Abstract 2000.*

CHAPTER 3

The Dynamics of Policy Regimes

LIBERALISM, REPUBLICANISM, AND THEIR VARIANTS

Since the mid–seventeenth century, the advent of hard times in the American past has set in motion a periodic alternation of historical periods and policy regimes. The onset of economic crisis has repeatedly discredited the domestic and foreign policies prevailing in one regime and prepared the way for its successor. In this fashion, English, British, and then American regimes have alternated between one set of domestic policies—either the elite or the mass/egalitarian distribution of domestic resources—and one set of foreign policies—either protectionism or free trade. The results have been impressive. For over three centuries, policy regimes have facilitated recovery from capitalism's recurrent crises even as they have managed to steer between the political extremes of royal absolutism, socialism, communism, and fascism—thanks in no small measure to the ideological alternations of liberalism, republicanism, and their American variants.

These ideological and philosophical alternatives have their origins in the seventeenth century, in the narrow span extending from the English Civil War in the 1640s and *the birth of English republicanism* to the Glorious Revolution in 1689 and *the birth of liberalism*. Similarly narrow, as one might expect, is the span in these ideological positions. Republicanism and liberalism are "not polar opposites," to quote Garry Wills on a related matter (1999: 18), "but distant points on the continuum of approaches to government." The reason why they are distant points and not polar opposites is because liberals and republicans, whatever their other differences, share two core convictions: first, that government should (more or less) ensure the property rights of its citizens; second, that overseas trade and commerce are (more or less) important components of a republic's economy. The differences in these cases are ones of degree rather than of kind.

That said, liberalism and republicanism are sufficiently different in their underlying principles for us to regard them as "distant points on the continuum of approaches to government." Consider liberalism. It is predicated on the precepts of liberty, individualism and the sanctity of property rights (insofar as these are derived from work and labor); on unfettered markets at home and abroad; and on toleration, the common law, and the minimalist state. Republicanism, by contrast, is predicated on the viability of the republic above all else, on precepts of communitarian obligation, on political equality, economic opportunity, and the general welfare of an independent citizenry, and on ethnocentric nationalism, statutory law, and "princely" interventions into the affairs of the republic. Liberalism is codified in John Locke's mechanical notions of liberty, property, social contract, and Newtonian stability; republicanism, in the commonwealth tradition of the organic state and egalitarian nationalism (of "left patriotism" as a good friend once called it) attributable primarily to Machiavelli, James Harrington, and Cromwell and his New Model Army—it is one part real politic and one part Calvinist puritanism. These enduring precepts are not merely ideological abstractions. Indeed, liberal (libertarian) and republican (communitarian) perspectives are stamped on virtually every aspect of American life, from the prosaic task of naming places in the landscape to arch debates over regional development and trade (e.g., NAFTA). Herein lie the ideological and policy axes on which, in the darkest moments of economic crisis, all else turns (the literature on liberalism and republicanism is massive; for their European origins, see Pocock 1975; Locke 1970, especially the section on property, 303–20; Hill 1970; Appleby 1978; Stone 1980; Zuckert 1994; and Ashcraft 1987; on foreign policy and empire, Armitage 2000; for the American permutations, see Young 1996; Greene 1988; Bailyn 1967b; Kramnick 1988; Rodgers 1992; Elazar 1994).

Free Traders and Protectionists/Egalitarians and Elites: The Battlegrounds of American Policy Regimes

Naturally the sharpest lines of division between these competing ideologies are associated with the most pressing issues of public concern. Principal among these are the state's conduct of foreign trade and the distribution of domestic resources. On the matter of foreign trade, Anglo-Americans appear to have been of two minds. At one extreme is liberalism's preference for economic liberty, free trade, and internationalism; at the other is republicanism's preference for the republic's security, protectionist-mercantilism, and nationalism (table 3.1). Recall, however, that these preferences are not polar opposites. Republican and liberal positions on foreign trade are rarely so extreme as the polarities defined by autarchy (national self-sufficiency) and free trade. Contrary to the hyperbolic criticisms of classical liberals, republican protectionist policies are—and always have been—conditional; tactics such as tariffs, non-

Table 3.1.   Republicanism and Liberalism: Domestic and Foreign Policies

	Domestic Policies	*Foreign Policies*
Republicanism	Mass/egalitarian distribution of resources	Protectionist-mercantilist and nationalist
Liberalism	Elite distribution of resources	Free trade and internationalist

tariff trade barriers, orderly marketing arrangements, coordinated exchange rates, and "strategic trade policy" (Dicken 1992: 148–72) have been deployed only *insofar as is necessary to ensure a secure and powerful republic*. In practice, republican versions of protectionism have always been fairly restrained; no serious American politician (certainly not Alexander Hamilton or even Patrick Buchanan; Jefferson may have come closest) has ever advocated a policy of autarchy, of national self-sufficiency. Nor, for that matter, did Oliver Cromwell and the Puritan revolutionaries who formally installed mercantilism in England in the 1640s and 1650s; they always wanted trade with other nations—provided that it was on English terms (Wilson 1965; Hill 1970; Stone 1980; Armitage 2000). Conversely, Americans of liberal persuasion have openly and unconditionally advocated free trade within a global economy. *Internationalism* is their code word—which seems fair enough; but liberals go too far when they mischaracterize republican trade policy as *isolationism*. Since the middle of the seventeenth century, republicans in the commonwealth tradition have largely accepted the realities of the capitalist economic system (Appleby 1978; McDougall 1997). They have ever since embraced international trade, and, indeed, they have even courted it aggressively when and where foreign trade served the larger security interests of the commonwealth. The point that economic nationalism, not isolationism, is the touchstone of republican foreign policy is one that "little American" internationalists perversely or obtusely have failed to grasp.

Americans are likewise of two minds with respect to the distribution of the nation's domestic resources (McCormick 1979, 1982). The republican view naturally inclines toward an egalitarian (or mass) distribution of resources among the citizenry (table 3.1). Citizens of the republic, being of equal standing, are entitled to correspondingly equitable shares of whatever resources the republic might choose to distribute. The liberal view, by contrast, inclines toward an elite distribution of resources. For liberalism in the classical Lockean sense, inequality is the inevitable and enduring consequence of resource scarcity in a market economy staffed by individuals of unequal talent (Locke 1970: 303–20 regards economic equality as an ephemeral condition associated with a momentary abundance of land). In this context of finite resources and inherent inequality, the most efficient solution is for governments to distribute resources to entrepreneurs who will use them wisely and efficiently for the betterment of society as a whole (this, of course, is what its critics call "trickle-down economics"). The rosy rhetoric on the virtues of market competition notwithstanding, liberalism ultimately subscribes to the notion that the general welfare depends on the very few who are fittest to flourish in a market economy. Liberty's price, one might say, is an enduring inequality—a price that Americans, when judged by their histories of income and wealth, have been more than willing to pay.

Republicanism is not entirely uncomfortable with these inegalitarian liberal assumptions. After some initial hesitation, Cromwell and his puritan lieutenants grudgingly accepted two protoliberal premises and one political reality. The first held that republics are based on property and an economically independent citizenry; the second, that the ownership of property is and would remain unequal; and the third, that radical (in this case, Leveller) appeals for coerced equality would, if implemented, result in renewed civil strife and the recrudescence of the Stuart aristocracy.[1]

Cromwell's concordat with liberalism, as with Franklin Roosevelt's three centuries hence, served to temper and restrain republican policies. Henceforth, republicans would aim their arrows a bit lower, with egalitarians targeting the reduction rather than the elimination of domestic inequality and nationalists targeting the subordination rather than the rejection of international trade. Inequality and international trade thus emerged as the great givens of liberal democracy American style; the debate was over how much or how little of each best served the security of the republic and the welfare of its citizenry (Armitage 2000: 135–42).

The republican concordat with liberalism sharply narrowed the distance between these two philosophical positions. But if English liberals and republicans can be said to have reached an agreement of sorts on first principles—on the sanctity of property, on the inherent nature of inequality, and on the imperatives of international trade—there remained a wide berth for strategic maneuver. On this side of the Atlantic, Americans have not been above taking advantage of the ambiguities and tensions running through these ideological positions, or of exploiting both sets of positions simultaneously, or of cooking up a pragmatic alloy of private (liberal) and public (republican) interventions in the crucibles of economic crisis. Pragmatism accordingly assumed a key role in the American repertoire of crisis and recovery, most especially after 1776.

Moderation and Ambivalence in Anglo-American Policy Regimes

The American temperament for philosophical moderation, which pragmatism did so much to ensure, is an older and largely an acquired taste. Over the long run of the colonial era, the virtues of moderation in the running quarrel of liberalism and republicanism became increasingly apparent. On the positive side, the periodic ventings of liberalism (1689–1740s) and republicanism (1640s–1680s and 1740s–1783) certainly served to moderate policy excesses; but on the negative side, these ventings also entailed wrenching shifts during the short-run transitions from one policy regime to another. This was especially the case during the colonial era when policy regimes tended to be unusually doctrinaire and the transitions between them unusually rocky. With a philosophical consistency that was characteristically British, colonial regimes tended to alternate between policies that were *purely* liberal (elite/free trade) and *purely* republican (egalitarian/protectionist); but policies so pure and unalloyed were too brittle to accommodate the tensions between the political "outs" and the "ins." (This did not preclude revolutionary coalitions—such as between various Whigs and Tories in the 1680s. See Jones 1979; Zuckert 1994.) And toward the end of a regime's half-century-or-so life span, these accumulating tensions invariably erupted in revolutionary or revitalizing social movements—for example, Bacon's Rebellion in the 1670s, the Great Awakening in the 1740s, and the American Revolution itself.

This brittle dialectic failed to survive the last of these social movements, and with independence secured from Britain, Americans proceeded to make radical revisions in the substance of American politics. American regimes subsequently combined various strands of liberal and republican philosophy in ways that defused their tensions and softened the differences between the outs and the ins. In practice, this has meant the alternation between two kinds of regimes—between republics and democracies—since the 1780s (table 3.2). Republics combine republican foreign policy (nationalist protectionism) and liberal domestic policy (elite resource distribution) in the three regimes prevailing between the 1780s–1830s, 1880s–1930, and since 1980; democracies combine liberal foreign policy (free trade) and republican domestic policy (egalitarian resource distribution) in the two regimes prevailing between the 1830s–1870s and 1930s–1970s. This dynamic has proven to be more supple than the liberal-republican alternation of its colonial predecessor. It has served to subvert doctrinal ideological alignments as well as to cool revolutionary fervor with two notable exceptions: the debates over slavery in the 1850s and over civil rights a century hence. In these cases not even the pragmatic fusion of liberal and republican ideologies could contain the explosive mixture of egalitarian (republican) domestic policies, rapid economic growth, and the hypervolatility of regional economies (Scheiber 1975).

The American Revolution fundamentally altered the course of American policy regimes and ideology. Henceforth, the ideological purity of colonial regimes gave way to a pragmatic fusion of republican and liberal positions that was all but secured with the ratification of the Constitution—a document contemptuously described by Clement Atlee as designed for an isolationist state and by Charles Beard (1913, 1923) as the product of a cabal of elite economic interests. In their haste to dismiss the bastardized ideologies inherent in the Constitution, ideologues such as Atlee and Beard vastly underestimate the framers' commitments to moderation and to ambivalence in their fusion of republican nationalism with liberal elitism. The Constitution, as the authors of the Federalist Papers endlessly reminded their readers, represents a rejection of the doctrinaire propensities of British colonial regimes in favor of a pragmatic balance of federalism's ambivalent propensities. Indeed, federalism is by definition a system of governance rooted in ambivalence over the locus of power. It

> is always an arrangement pointed in two contrary directions or aimed at securing two contrary ends. One end is always found in the reason why the member units do not simply consolidate themselves into one large unitary country; the other end is always found in the reason why the member units do not choose to remain simply small, wholly autonomous countries. The natural tendency of any political community, whether

Table 3.2.   American Republics and Democracies: Domestic and Foreign Policies

	Domestic Policy	Foreign Policy
Republics	Elite distribution of resources	Protectionist-mercantilist and nationalist
Democracies	Mass/egalitarian distribution of resources	Free trade and internationalist

large or small, is to completeness, to the perfection of its autonomy. Federalism is the effort deliberately to modify that tendency. Hence any given
federal structure is always the institutional expression of the contradiction
or tension between the particular reasons the member units have for remaining small and autonomous, but not wholly, and large and consolidated, but not quite. (Diamond 1992: 145)

The framers of the Constitution further institutionalized federalism's contradictions and tensions in their peculiar fusings of liberal and republican policies. In their
fusing of republican preferences for a powerful republic with expressed powers and
expressed sources of revenues (most notably the tariff)—Atlee's "isolationist state"—
with liberal preferences for a relatively large and autonomous sphere for individual
liberty within the several states—Beard's elite cabal—the framers accomplished three
aims. First, they laid the foundations for the first of three American republics. Second, they mitigated the "baneful" and "insidious" effects of political factions by
obscuring the ideological differences among them. And third, they established the
dialectical ground rules for ensuing policy regimes. Thus, when Jacksonian Democrats during the economic crisis of the late 1820s and 1830s challenged the ideological hegemony of the early nationalists and their First Republic, they did so by
inversion—abandoning the early nationalist's fusion of republican protectionism and
liberal elitism for the Jacksonian amalgam of liberal free trade and republican egalitarianism (i.e., for the first American democracy). Henceforth, the American policy
regime, like American federalism itself, constituted "an arrangement pointed in two
contrary directions or aimed at securing two contrary ends."

Ambivalence rarely ranks high on the lists of American virtues. Thus, to say that
because Americans could not decide between liberalism and republicanism, they
decided on some of each is to damn with the faintest of praise. But when ambivalence is placed in the service of political moderation, the effect is wondrously paradoxical. We see that the stock of ambivalence rises dramatically in value when, as in
the case of American politics, the pursuit of this dual strategy—of ambivalence and
moderation—enables a society to endure as others are consumed by the fires that
rage in the pure air of doctrinaire ideology. Indeed, it might be said that it is the
ambivalence of American political philosophy that set the nation apart. And, insofar
as our simultaneous attraction to and repulsion from the ideologies of liberalism and
republicanism lie close to the truth of American exceptionalism, we are behooved
to inquire into the origins as well as the consequences of our hybrid ideologies.

Unraveling the Strands of English
Ideology: The Revolutionary Critique

In tracing the course of the American journey from ideological doctrine to ambivalence, the American Revolution and the intellectual conflicts between British and
American ideologies offer the most convenient points of departure. Although

> recent studies of Revolutionary ideology have accustomed us to think of
> republicanism and liberalism as two coherent, competing ideologies, [as]
> "separate tunnels" through the thought of the eighteenth century . . . it
> may be [more] useful to think of Revolutionary thought as a series of
> unstable syntheses of several different but overlapping philosophical
> strands. "Republicanism" and "liberalism" should be considered not so
> much as antithetical doctrines [or more precisely as the distant points on
> the continuum of governance which they occupied prior to 1763], but as
> positions on particular issues, vocabularies to be used for certain situations
> and in special settings. That an individual might draw upon Locke for one
> purpose and Harrington for another demonstrates not simply the com-
> plexity and occasional inconsistency of Revolutionary thought, but the
> array of problems to be addressed and the variety of sites in which those
> discussions took place. *Yet in specific locations, the terms that were used had
> precise meanings and clear implications.* (Lewis 1995: 273; italics added)

But how then did this ideological devolution come about? And why, in one very
specific location and time—the thirteen mainland colonies of British North America
after 1740—did the relatively coherent, competing ideologies of liberalism and
republicanism become unstable and start to unravel into "several different but overlapping strands"? (The unraveling, contra Rodgers 1992, was not merely historio-
graphical; Young 1996.)

Political expediency is part of the answer. In the tumult of the Revolutionary
era, the liberal elites who led the post-1763 attack on Britain's neomercantilist policies were compelled to use whatever ideological weapons were at their disposal. For
men born into the colonial elite who had risen to wealth and power in the era of
"salutary neglect" and had been bred on commerce, contract, and liberty of trade,
liberalism of one form or another was virtually an involuntary reflex. But Lockean
liberalism, whatever its other merits, was ill equipped for the colonial critique of
parliamentary statutes, ministerial and royal policies, and the diminishing political
influence of colonial agents in Britain. Liberalism, with its reliance on reasoned
discourse and its passive metaphors of stability and equilibrium, was simply not up
to the task (Striner 1995). To be sure, liberals might have based their critiques on
colonial self-interest, but this was too grubby and crass; or perhaps on the economic
inefficiencies arising from taxation, but this flew in the face of the enormous expansion of colonial trade after the 1740s and the modest impact of taxation in most of
the colonies; or then again on the violation of a Lockean social contract between
the colonies and Britain, but this, as they all knew, was a fiction. Nor, in revolutionary times, could one expect much blood to be drawn by liberalism's timeworn
metaphor of state and society as "joint-stock company." If indeed society was akin
to the company's shareholders and the state to its board of directors, then the former
had duly delegated the latter (via the social contract) with the authority to do all of
the things that the colonials did not like—taxing, surveillance, customs, ship seizures,
and the like. In sum, liberalism of itself was not sufficient in the political struggle
against the neomercantile version of imperial republicanism.

The trick for colonial elites was to fight fire with fire, to fight the new republicanism with the tactics of the old. Toward that end, these heirs of liberalism appro-

priated and updated the oppositional republican arguments that had been sharpened in earlier attacks on Robert Walpole and the Whig oligarchy. With a style reminiscent of "the bitterness, the virulence, and the savagery of the attacks on Walpole's ministry by the opposition press," liberal colonial elites in the 1760s traduced the corruption of English politics in the Age of Empire (on these intellectual debts, see Bailyn 1967b, especially 38). First they vilified the policies of royal ministers and their agents, next the statutes of Parliament, and, in the end, the king himself. Corruption, they argued, was the root of the problem. Corruption was responsible for reducing Americans to the status of slaves, for withholding from them the rights equally accorded to the citizens of a republic, and then for imposing on them taxations and regulations without republican representation. And from this improbable alliance of superheated republican rhetoric and coolly calculated liberal interest came an equally improbable result—a revolution that blurred American political idioms and, in due course, the very nature of American policy regimes (among many others, see Kramnick 1988, 1992).

Republican words invoked in the heat of battle could not be so easily retracted once independence had been won; their meanings could, however, be trimmed and hedged. Elites hastily attempted to place limits on what they had meant by democracy and republican equality, arguing as did Timothy Ford in 1794 "that *equality of rights* [what he saw as the revolutionary aim] and *equality of conditions* are matters entirely distinct" (quoted in Konig 1995: 189). In liberal language, they defended the naturalness of economic inequality and rejected any thought of redistributing income and wealth, save perhaps for the concession of abolishing entail and primogeniture. But their veneration of private property was possible "only because they attached to it as an inseparable corollary the [republican] notion that private property was a social right whose ultimate purpose was the public welfare of the republic" (Konig 1995: 215). Herein lies an ideology and a form of governance pointed in two cardinal directions: toward the inegalitarian liberalism of propertied elites, at one end, and the egalitarian republicanism of political rights and economic opportunities, at the other. From ambivalences of precisely this sort was the amalgam that we know as a liberal republic compounded (hence the scrambled ideological vocabularies of the revolutionary generation; Kramnick 1988; Hartz 1955; Lewis 1995).

In their repeated fusings of liberal and republican ideologies, American regimes have succeeded in taking the sting out of doctrinaire factionalism, but they also have made nonsense of the political labels we attach to them. Consider the confusion that surrounds the term *New Deal liberalism*. The confusion begins when this policy regime is labeled "liberal" because of egalitarian biases that are, in fact, firmly rooted in classical republican ideology; the confusion is compounded when we simultaneously ignore what is truly liberal about New Deal Liberalism—namely, its steadfast commitment to free trade abroad. When words are used so loosely, political discourse suffers; and this, more than "truth in political packaging," is a point worth considering. The ideological ambivalence of American policy regimes such as New Deal liberalism presents doctrinaire opponents with a dilemma. Consider, for example, the problem of libertarian conservatives. While they reject "New Deal liberalism's" republican egalitarian thrust on domestic policy, on the one hand, they warmly embrace that regime's liberal foreign policy of free trade, on the other. Given their common policy interest (in this case, on behalf of free trade), it is hard for unalloyed libertarians to wage a successful fight against the prevailing policy regime. The fight is not nearly so difficult, however, for nationalist conservatives in the Reagan tradition because they, too, are committed to ambivalence—albeit of a different sort. They turn "New Deal liberalism" on its head by promoting nationalist interventions in foreign trade (republican) and the elitist distribution of resources (liberal) at home. Insofar as Americans in the 1980s and 1990s have chosen the path of elite nationalism—and some evidence suggests that is the case—they ensure the continuance of the periodic alternation of American policy regimes and their peculiar fusions of ambivalent ideologies (albeit often begrudgingly; Skowronek 1993: 409–64; Jones 1988).

Further evidence of these ideological confusions comes from the streets of Seattle and the protests over globalization that attended the meeting of the World Trade Organization in December 1999. Party labels literally dissolved in the course of the protest. Liberal Democrats such as Jesse Jackson and various trade union leaders joined ranks with conservative Republicans such as Patrick Buchanan, antigovernment independents such as Ross Perot, and environmentalists such as Ralph Nader. These unusual alliances were not altogether surprising. Indeed, "some farsighted politicians had long predicted this kind of traffic jam on the ideological highways . . . that globalization was going to put both parties under severe pressure because of their own inconsistencies." The problem with globalization is that it

> unites capitalism and internationalism in a tight embrace [this, of course, is the free trade elitism of classical Lockean liberalism]. The fact is enough to confound both liberals and conservatives. The left side of the Democratic Party leans toward internationalism and away from capitalism [as per egalitarian free-traders]. The right side of the Republican Party leans toward capitalism and away from internationalism [as per elitist nationalists]. Neither is equipped to face a situation where it must jettison one of its prejudices, to accept or reject the capitalist-internationalist package as a unit (they were always connected, though never [at least not since 1783] so inextricably). (Wills 1999b)

In other words, the pressures of globalization have revealed "the double fault lines running transversely across both our parties and all our ideologies. Sorting out the inconsistencies and self-contradictions of our politics is not something we are very good at" (Wills 1999b). Nor, one might add, is it necessarily in the nation's best interest for parties to eliminate the moderating influences of these ideological inconsistencies and self-contradictions. Indeed, modern-day "liberals" managed to avert the crisis of contradiction for as long as they did by using the profits of free trade and globalization to underwrite the perpetuation of democratic socialism at home.

Whatever one's position on these normative issues, it is clear that globalization is imposing new demands on the American political system and, most especially, on the nature of the American state. But the demands of this scalar geographical transformation are not new; twice before they have been met and twice they have been overcome: first with the invention of the Sectional State in the 1780s and second with the reinvention of the National State in the 1870s and 1880s (see chapter 6). The Transnational State now emerging represents the third of these political-geographical innovations. Like its predecessors, the third American state has acknowledged the ascension of new geographical realities at home and abroad, has hitched these realities to the strategic aims of the new state and its framers—that is, the "founding fathers" in the 1780s (Kammen 1972; Beer 1993; Rakove 1996) and the architects of "Yankee Leviathan" after the Civil War (Bensel 1990, 2000)—and is vigorously carrying out the tactical actions that will secure these aims (e.g., routinely insisting on preferential treatment of the United States in matters of international trade and on the uniqueness of the American position in matters of international justice)—all the while preserving the moderating (con)fusions of American policy regimes with all their inconsistencies and contradictions.

But in the end, then, what does one conclude about American political discourse? Is it impoverished by these (con)fusions of ambivalent ideologies and by their periodic alternations, or is it enriched? The answer depends, in part, on one's political biases and, in larger part, on the enduring social and economic accomplishments of American policy regimes—which, so far, have been pretty good.

American Society, Economy, and Policy Regimes over Time

I have thus far resisted defining policy regimes in a formal way for reasons that are now made apparent. In the smallest and most narrow of ways, policy regimes are about ideology and governance; but in the largest and most ample of ways, they are about the host of related changes in society at large. These larger conjuncturings of society and economy proceed in accordance with the alternations in the four classes of American policy regime: namely, the two colonial regimes that alternated between *republicanism* (protectionism and mass or egalitarian resource distribution [PM]) and *liberalism* (elite resource distribution and free trade [FTE]); and the two national regimes that alternated between *republics* (elite protectionist/nationalist [PE]) and *democracies* (egalitarian [mass] free trade/internationalist [FTM]). Table 3.3 presents the sequence of republics and democracies since 1780 along with their common names. The table also takes note of the several American states described briefly in chapter 1 and more amply in chapter 6, their pairings of republics and democracies, their century-long durations, and their prevailing modes of governance.

This history, with its reconfiguration of regime policies after the Revolution, is a stroke of luck because it enables us to compare across historical periods and to isolate certain social and economic associations that are essentially invariant across one or another of the domestic or foreign policy dimensions (see Earle 1992: 446–540 and sources cited therein). The findings, of course, are provisional. On the outset, consider the case of protectionist-nationalist regimes (periods 1, 3, 4, 6, and 8). These regimes are invariably associated with high-intensity religious revitaliza-

Table 3.3.   Republics and Democracies in the American Past

Colonial Era
1. "Republicanism" (1640s–1680s)   (Mercantilism)
2. "Liberalism" (1690s–1740s)   (Salutary neglect)
3. "Republicanism" (1740s–1783)   (Neomercantilism)

The Sectional State (1780s–1870s)—partisan and distributive polities
4. The First Republic (PE) (1780s–1828)   (The Early National Period)
5. The First Democracy (FTM) (1828–1877)   (The Middle Period/Jacksonian democracy)

The National State (1880s–1980)—interest groups, regulatory and redistributive polities
6. The Second Republic (PE) (1880s–1932)   (Gilded Age and Progressive Era)
7. The Second Democracy (FTM) (1932–1970s)   (The New Deal Era)

The Transnational State (1980s–?)—"neoliberalism," neoregulationist at global scale
8. The Third Republic (PE) (1980–?)   (Reagan's America)

tions (in the phase of Crisis), national spatial expansion, and, after 1790, deferred and low-magnitude international Conflicts. Second, free-trade regimes (periods 2, 5, and 7) are regularly associated with protectionism's opposites—lower-intensity revitalizations, spatial consolidation, and again after 1790, international wars that come more quickly and that are higher in magnitude. Third, mass or egalitarian regimes (periods 1, 3, 5, and 7) are routinely conjoined with low-cost economic innovations (often derived from "folk" sources)—for example, tobacco topping, crop rotations, etc.; rapid innovation diffusion; internal war over civil rights in the midst of the Diffusion phase; and an accelerated phase of socioeconomic Decline. Fourth, elite regimes (periods 2, 4, 6, and 8) are affiliated with higher-cost economic innovations, slower diffusions, civil Dissent that is contentious but contained, and an extended phase of Decline.

These associations go a long way in explaining the recurrence of fairly specific historical events and processes across the colonial and national eras. Internal war, for example, invariably arises in association with egalitarian American regimes—the American Revolution and the Civil War are cases in point, and the civil rights movement of the 1960s is a strong candidate—presumably because these regimes are more solicitous of concerns over citizenship and civil rights. Similarly, spatial expansions of settlement—both rural (e.g., the frontier) and urban (e.g., "urban sprawl")—are regularly associated with protectionist/nationalist regimes committed, as they are, to the organic state and centrifugal enhancements in the power of the republic.

Ironically, it is the most important events in the American past—the recurrent phases of economic Crisis—that exhibit the least clear associations with prevailing policies. This is so for two reasons. First, given the fragmentary data currently available for the colonial economy, it is difficult to make a definitive assessment of the severity of colonial economic depressions and, therefore, to associate these variations with particular policy regimes.[2] Second, even when we are able to differentiate the magnitude of these depressions—as we can do after 1776—their transitional positioning confounds interpretation. When we look at the several Crises during the national era, it seems clear that the most severe and protracted depressions came at the end of elite protectionist/nationalist regimes and the beginning of egalitarian free-trade regimes (i.e., in the 1820s and 1830s and again in the 1930s). But who is to blame? Given the variety of agents and policies involved in these Crises (or, for that matter, in the Crises of lesser severity in the 1880s and 1970s), it is virtually impossible to assign causal responsibility. What we can say is that Crises since 1790 have tended to be worse at the end of elite protectionist regimes; but whether the damage that these Crises do is attributable to the stubbornness of elite regimes, to the timidity of their egalitarian successors, or to both is a question worthy of more detailed inquiry.

Toward the American Way: The View from the 1780s

These long-running associations between policy regimes and society are more interesting to the social scientist than the practical politician (or the historian) who, taking the world as it comes, must deal not with these isolated associations, but with their fusion into dialectical policy regimes. These fusings, once established, have proven to be unusually durable, and only once—in the 1780s and 1790s—have Americans been compelled to rearrange the wiring of domestic and foreign policy. To understand the reasons behind this revolutionary reversal in policy regimes, it is useful to return to the 1780s, to put ourselves in the position of Americans who, at that time, had one eye on the future and the other on the past.

Looking back on the colonial era from the perspective of American independence, there was much not to like. Besides the usual complaints over Britain's ill-fated policies of taxation and its overzealous surveillance and interdiction of colonial trade was the disquieting tendency for Anglo-colonial regimes to lurch from one set of doctrinaire and factional policies to another. Colonial regimes, crystallized as they were around the policies of British ideological factions, were unavoidably caught up in the seemingly endless rounds of internal strife in the mother country. In the space of a century and a quarter, colonial policies were tossed and turned by the English Civil War, the Glorious Revolution, and the "legal reformation" that preceded the Revolution itself. Regimes shifted fairly abruptly from the doctrinaire principles of Commonwealth republicanism to the equally doctrinaire Whig principles of Lockean liberalism and, in turn, to the imperial republicanism under the ministries of George III (Pocock 1980). These swings in British colonial policy regimes were compounded by the equally vast swings in the processes that these regimes set in motion. "Frenetic" is the only way of describing the protectionist republican regimes that, between the 1630s–1680s and the 1740s–1780s, crammed rapid spatial expansion, rapid innovation diffusion, internal war, rapid decline, and expanded opportunities for the masses into spans of just forty-five to fifty years. Sandwiched in between these republican frenzies was the apotheosis of calm sliced out by Lockean liberalism and the stabilizing patronage politics of the new Whig oligarchy.

Whig England, it has been said, "held as a self-evident truth that every political man was entitled to life, liberty, and the pursuit of influence" (Pocock 1980: 270). Preoccupied with the domestic tasks of firming up Whig political power, establishing the foundations of a modern aristocracy, and carrying through the financial revolution that ensured the public credit so essential for a liberal economy, the Whig "robinarchy" demonstrated that it "desired stability more than empire, but pursued empire as a byproduct of its means of maintaining stability [at home]" (Pocock 1980: 271). British intrusions into American affairs thus diminished in proportion with the Whigs' programmatic successes in England. All of the colonial processes that were so frenetic before 1700 or so were reversed, expansion gave way to spatial consolidation, diffusion and decline slowed their pace, internal war did not erupt, and colonial elites arose to unprecedented wealth and power. The tranquility that the colonies enjoyed under the Whig oligarchy came to an abrupt end in the 1740s. The era of "salutary neglect," with its trappings of elite liberalism, social class, and deference, was shattered by two decades of "the most bitter tactical and theoretical conflicts over religion, war, the dynasty, and the possession of power within the Whig party" (Clark 1986: 116). Henceforth, "foreign affairs overshadowed those domestic issues which Walpole [the prime minister who resigned in 1742] had made his special concern." (Williams 1939: 227).

The fall of Walpole broke the calm, once and for all. For the string of ministries that followed during the reigns of George II and III, empire was desired at least as much as stability. Republican nationalism was, as it were, back in the saddle. Envisioning a colonial empire welded together by the force of law and, if necessary, the raw force of military power, this new regime charged ahead into three decades of legal activism and aggressive intervention into colonial affairs (Olson 1980). But the imperial law that these ministries sought to enforce was not only "as matter of practice [i.e., the common law], but also as a rational science" (Blackstone 1871, II: 2) that left nothing to discretion. With the hubris that commonly attends those who would reduce society to a science, these republican-nationalist advocates of scientific law formulated the bold hypothesis of law as the instrument of social and cultural change: Given a well-constructed and properly administered body of scientific law, the hypothesis ran, members of a colonial society could be expected to respond in logically predictable—and desirable—ways. History in this case was all too availing for in the 1740s, following the suppression of the Scottish rebellion, it provided these legal activists with a convenient opportunity for testing—and affirming—their hypothesis. Having discovered that parliamentary law could effect dramatic social change even in so implacable a culture as the Scottish Highlands, they were encouraged to take the next step and impose their wonder-working hypothesis on their colonies abroad (on these policies, Olson 1980 is indispensable).

Legal activism did not set well with American colonists so long sheltered from British politics by the negligence of the Whig oligarchy. The renewed and generally unwelcomed attention showered on the colonies was less grating, however, than the substance of the emerging body of parliamentary law. For the recently arrived colonial elites weaned on the ideology of liberalism, the series of statutes enacted after 1750 represented an ideological antithesis, not to mention a threat to colonial liberties. They rightly understood that these statutes summoned up republican precepts on national power that could be traced back through the Old Whigs to the Commonwealth tradition—a provenance that is less remarkable when one considers the comparable foreign threats presented by the Dutch in the 1650s and by the French in the 1740s. Colonial elites were less appreciative of the fact that these statutes would, in ways entirely consistent with republican ideology, ensure equity and justice before the law even as they subordinated colonies to the larger aims of imperial power and welfare. For colonial elites, equity and justice were besides the point. They had little quarrel with scientific law per se; what they could not stomach was the use of parliamentary law as a republican instrument of social and political subordination. And thus it was with the deepest irony that men so thoroughly steeped in liberalism would resort, almost in desperation, to the most radical, and for liberal elites the most dangerous, of republican ideas—the notion of political equality among the citizens of the republic—in service of their rebellion against the empire (for revolutionaries such as Jefferson, in fact, statutory law was preferable to the common law; Konig 2001; more generally, Bailyn 1967a, 1967b).[3]

The road to revolution was paved as much by the instabilities occasioned by British imperial policy as by the colonials' objections to the policies themselves. As we have come to expect of purely republican regimes, the overbearing pace of social and economic change was frenetic. Spatial expansion in the colonies was especially rapid, as was the diffusion of relatively low-cost agrarian innovations (e.g., regional specialization in staple production) to the majority of rural households. And as the wealth that had been so concentrated among the colonial elite in 1740 spilled over to small farmers and tenants, an economy fueled by newly opened markets for wheat and rice in southern Europe, the Low Countries, and Ireland rocketed (McCusker and Menard 1985; Egnal 1998). Social and economic changes so fast and furious were almost impossible to assimilate within colonial societies that were being bombarded simultaneously by a degree of legal activism unprecedented in colonial history. It was only natural perhaps that this frenzied policy regime would invite an equally frenzied colonial response. Rebellion must almost have seemed as a release from the grip of scientific law too ardently applied.

If in looking back on this history Americans found much not to like, they also found much that was instructive. The federalists in particular seem to have learned two important political lessons, and both had to do with political instability. The first of these was that doctrinaire ideological factions (and their equally doctrinaire policy regimes) are susceptible to abrupt lurches from one ideological extreme to another. The second was that doctrinaire regimes tend to amplify these sudden shifts by juxtaposing periods of relative calm (liberal regimes) with periods of frenzy (republican regimes). Armed with these insights—and recoiling from them—the federalists committed themselves to the creation of a more stable political system, one that modulated the lurches and the swings that were so characteristic of Anglo-colonial regimes. This they managed to achieve by splitting the atoms of liberal and republican ideology and creating a new and pragmatic fusion of policy regimes. Henceforth, the ideologically pure regimes of the colonial era gave way to regimes compounded variously of liberal elitism and republican protectionism or republican egalitarianism and liberal free trade, which is, in our shorthand, to republics (PE regimes) and democracies (FTM regimes), respectively.

The fact that these regimes have alternated ever since gives unusual significance to the first of these ideological fusions. How did it arise that the founders of the United States chose to fuse liberal elitism and republican nationalism/protectionism? Elbridge Gerry provided the short answer for nationalism in warning his fellow delegates at the Constitutional Convention, "If we do not come to some agreement among ourselves some foreign sword will probably do the work for us" (*Records,* I: 552 [July 5, 1787]); and George Mason unwittingly did the same for liberal elitism when he reminded them that: "Notwithstanding the oppressions [and] injustice experienced among us from democracy; the genius of the people is in favour of it" (*Records,* I: 101 [June 4, 1787])—and the people should be served provided, however, the Constitutional precautions of an elaborate set of checks and balances and a set of electoral qualifications that only the elite could satisfy. An elite protectionist regime thus spoke to the greatest fears of the founders of the American republic—the foreign sword that would destroy a weak nation from without and the factional "turbulence and follies of democracy" that would destroy it from within. Although later regimes would take somewhat different views on these matters, they would also find that the dialectical outlines of their course had been largely set.

Notes

1. Republican views on property and equality are protean and contested during the two decades embraced by the Civil War, the Commonwealth, and the Protectorate. The issues were joined in the Putney Debates of 1647 between Leveller agitators, the rank and file, and conservative army officers. General Ireton insisted that "the basis of liberty was property, the Agitators that all men are born equal, and have an equal right to consent" (Stone 1980: 36). Republicans ever since have continued this debate, fighting over the appropriate relationship between economic and political equality and between economic condition and opportunity. Liberals took a different tack. Thirty to forty years after the Putney Debates,

> the neo-Harringtonians solved the dilemma by twisting the theoretical argument
> of the Agitators to establish the practical policies of Ireton. They did this by arguing
> that only the economically independent are free; that property confers both politi-
> cal and personal responsibilities and political privilege; that the more the property,
> the greater the privilege; that property is the principal security for liberty; and that
> the duty of the state is therefore carefully to preserve and protect it. This doctrine,
> so convenient to all property owners, and so perfectly adapted to the existing social
> and political situation, was an immediate success, and became the stock political
> cliche of the eighteenth century from John Locke to Thomas Jefferson. (Stone
> 1980: 36–37)

In this brief but stunningly insightful passage, Lawrence Stone captures the continuities between republicanism and liberalism, the centrality of their debate over property and citizenship, and the ongoing divergence in their egalitarian and elitist points of view. I would suggest, however, that Madison or Hamilton rather than Jefferson might better represent the liberal lineage.

2. The prices assembled by Harris (1996), David and Solar (1977), and McCusker (1992)

for the three-century span beginning in 1630 indicate a series of four short to medium "long waves" of thirty-nine to forty-six years bracketed by longer waves of fifty-nine to sixty-four years in the seventeenth (1634–1697) and nineteenth/twentieth (1861–1866 to 1920–1925) centuries. The latter are roughly concurrent with two nationalist-protectionist regimes: Cromwellian-Restoration "mercantilism" (1641–1689) and the Second Republic (1877–1932), respectively. They are also concurrent with extended periods of increasing productivity (and falling prices).

3. I do not share the view that the American commitment to the market before 1776 was so modest as to have fostered a traditional or precapitalist republican society that the Revolution helped to replace with society's opposite numbers—namely, modernity, capitalism, and liberalism. Contrary to the proponents of the discontinuity thesis (most notably, Wood 1969), all of the latter were well along in most of the mainland colonies by 1740 and in all by 1783 (McCusker and Menard 1985; Appleby 1984a).

CHAPTER 4

Policy Regimes and Geographical Reconstructions

What has been called "the acceleration of history" was already under way by the time the English planted the flag on the Atlantic Seaboard of North America. By 1607, the medieval world of "motionless history" with its long demographic swells of two to three centuries and their successive subsistence crises had largely faded from memory, crowded out by the speedup demanded by capitalist history with its half-century rhythms of economic advance and recurrent economic crisis (Ladurie 1977). As with history, so, too, with geography. Whereas "motionless geography" had perpetuated landscapes that seemed static, immutable, and enduring, "capitalist geography" rendered them as dynamic, plastic, and disposable. Marx (1936) captured the essence of geography's newfound evanescence in his chilling observation on sixteenth-century rural England as a place where "sheep ate men." The gentry's eviction of peasants, their enclosures of peasant open fields, and their switch from arable crops to running sheep was merely the first in a painful series of geographical reconstructions that have repeatedly transformed English and American landscapes.

Marx's emphasis on the harsh and exploitive aspects of these reconstructions, though eloquent in defending the rights of those who occupied the bottom rungs of capitalist society, tended nonetheless to oversimplify these complex transformations. It was left to Joseph Schumpeter (1939) to present the other side of the story, to view it from the vantage point of capitalist entrepreneurs and their paradoxical commitment to the processes of "creative destruction." For Schumpeter, capitalism's recurrent crises caught entrepreneurs and policymakers in a double bind. If they did nothing, the economy (and then the society) would come unhinged; conversely, if they implemented creative solutions to the crisis, the society would be changed once and for all; existing structures—social, economic, and geographic—would be revised, revamped, or obliterated altogether. The choice, or so it seemed, was between social chaos and the creative destruction of recurrent economic revolution. But Schumpeter, like Marx, puts the point too starkly. Trapped in their partisan morality play on capitalism's vices and virtues, they largely ignore the enormous variability in the processes of creation, destruction, and exploitation. Consider capitalism's creative innovations. These are far from homogeneous, nor are their impacts always as neutral as Schumpeter supposed nor as immizerating as Marx presumed.

Indeed, the most crucial of innovations are highly variable with respect to class bias that, in some instances, favor elites and, in others, the masses of the population (Earle 1992: 258–345, 519–37; Yapa 1977, 1982). Similarly variable is the extent of "destruction"—or, alternatively, of sociogeographical reconstruction—which typically ranges from modest landscape revisions to extensive geographical reconfigurations. Consequently, we find that innovations that favor the masses (i.e., ones that are low in cost and hence widely adopted) tend to be less destructive of social landscapes than elite-biased innovations (i.e., ones that are high in cost and selectively adopted). Another way of saying this is that it was not inevitable that sheep ate men (an elite innovation) in sixteenth-century England; one can rather easily imagine more equitable and less destructive outcomes under alternative, more egalitarian regimes.

On the presumptions that creative destruction is a variable process, that it is mediated by policy regimes, and that it rearranges space in ways that are consistent with regime biases, we may turn to the American uses of space and to the massive reconstructions periodically engineered by these biased regimes. The philosophical expressions of policy regimes are manifested with unusual clarity in the American landscape. There they appear as a series of geographical reconstructions (likewise periodic and dialectical) across the multiple scales of nation (state), region, and locale. As Gottmann (1980a: 217) reminds us, "the political process develops within the geographical space. . . . However, geography does not simply 'contain politics.' The political process organizes the space within which it develops, and being a dynamic process, it constantly strives to improve the spatial organization in order to adapt it to change and to fit it to better serve the purposes of government." Toward these ends, reconstruction gets under way with the emergence of each new policy regime; in the interest of revitalizing a stagnant economy and in accordance with the regime's ideological biases, old geographies are displaced and new ones installed. Peoples, economies, and social institutions are reshuffled and rearranged along one of four spatial *cum* policy dimensions: expansion/consolidation, concentration/dispersion, regional stability/volatility, and regional specialization/diversification. The first two of these dimensions are associated with foreign (trade) policy and the national scale; the second two, with domestic policies of resource distribution and the regional scale. With respect to foreign trade, republican protectionism is manifested as spatial expansion and population concentration; liberal free trade, as spatial consolidation and population dispersion. Pretty much the same thing happens when regimes turn their attention to domestic policy, but in this case the geographical processes are downshifted from the scale of the state to the scale of the region. Thus, the regional geographies engineered by liberal elite policy regimes are characterized by economic stability and increasing levels of regional economic specialization; conversely, the regions of republican egalitarian regimes are associated with remarkably high levels of volatility and steady increases in economic diversification. But if the empirical evidence on these matters is quite compelling, the theoretical connections between ideology and geography have been somewhat less obvious.

The English Origins of Liberalism, Republicanism, and Their Geographies

The mystery of ideologies, and not the least of the reasons for the confusion over their ramifications for policy and geography, is that they are so seldom taken at their word. If we cut through all of the exegetics, all of the interpretations and reinterpretations of American ideology, we find that republicanism means precisely what it says; it values one thing—the republic—above all others. Liberalism is similarly telegraphic; it, too, values one thing—liberty—over all others. From these core ideological premises, a great deal of foreign policy and geography flows (table 4.1; Gottmann 1978; Dockès 1969). These, we might say, are the inextricable geosophical corollaries of political philosophy.

Consider the case of republicanism. Republican ideology is anchored by a singular and unequivocal commitment: the preservation of the security and integrity of the republic. Defending the republic is at once the highest of republican obligations and the most strategic of republican imperatives in the conduct of foreign affairs. Toward these ends, republican foreign policies seek to strengthen the republic without jeopardizing its security, to move it along the more secure path of expansion at home (both economic and spatial) rather than along the risky and more dangerous path of trade expansion abroad. These, of course, are the kinds of policies—nationalist, protectionist, and expansionist—that we regularly associate with republican regimes, and they are shot through with geography. The republican project turns, as it were, on the hinges of domestic spatial expansion and demographic concentration, the former because domestic expansion is, for republicans, the surest and most secure means of augmenting the power of the republic; the latter, because demographic concentration is the natural consequent of the advantage which protectionist measures confer upon favored (i.e., protected) regions (see Roncaglia 1985: 59–60 for William Petty's views on the advantages of urbanization and spatial concentration).

These are the proximate causes of applied protectionist geographies; their theoretical origins, however, are located in the more distant and more remote milieu of

Table 4.1.   Anglo-American Regimes, Policies, and Geographies

Republicanism		Liberalism	
Foreign Policy	*Geographies*	*Foreign Policy*	*Geographies*
Nationalist	Spatial expansion Demographic concentration	Free(r) Trade	Spatial consolidation Demographic dispersion
Domestic Policy	*Geographies*	*Domestic Policy*	*Geographies*
Egalitarian	Regional diversification Regional volatility	Elitist (property rights)	Regional specialization Regional stability

republican metaphor and analogy. Republican political theory has long been animated by the metaphoric notion of an organic state (as manifested, e.g., in the nineteenth-century notion of *lebensraum*; see also Gottmann 1973: 91–108). Whatever its other origins, the model of republic-as-organism seems to have crystallized into a distinctively modern form during the mid–seventeenth century, inspired by William Harvey's anatomical studies of the heart and the circulation of the blood and their reformulation for the body politic by James Harrington, the most prominent of republican theorists (Cohen 1994). The significance of this analogy between the body and the state, between the human circulatory system and the republic, was that, among other things, it mapped out a distinctively republican geography. In this mapping, the republic, like the human organism, was required to grow (expand) and its muscular heart (the equivalent of populations concentrated in protected core regions) was required to pump fresh blood (economic growth) throughout the organism (the republic), or else it would die. In republicanism's organic model, geography was a matter of life and death—of life through spatial expansion and demographic concentration or death through spatial entropy. These are the classical republican geographies that we know today via their revitalization by the early nationalists in the 1780s and 1790—spatial expansion in the form of James Madison's notions of an "extended republic" and demographic and economic concentration in Alexander Hamilton's proposals for industrial development in the northeastern United States (Beer 1993: 130; McCoy 1987; Onuf 1996).

The organic model of protectionist-nationalism, spatial expansion, and demographic concentration, however gripping its hold on the republican imagination, has rarely stirred much enthusiasm among liberal thinkers and their free-trading regimes. Liberals rally around a very different set of priorities; they value individual liberty and limited government more highly than the organic republican community, the freedom to trade overseas more highly than protectionist coercion and expansion at home. "Securing our Navigation and Trade [is for Locke] more the Interest of this Kingdom than War of Conquest" (Locke, quoted in Arneil 1996: 106–7). Toward these ends, liberal regimes deploy geographical strategies that facilitate the conduct of free and unfettered trade. Whereas republicans expand and concentrate peoples and economies in space, liberals consolidate and disperse them. Or, as Locke (1970, II: para. 42) put it: "Numbers of men are to be preferd to largenesse of dominions, and . . . the increase of lands and the right imploying of them is the great art of government." Consolidation of the space economy via internal improvements is perhaps the surest and most efficient means of promoting the intra- and interregional integrations capable of expediting the flow of commodity exports and expanding overseas trade. Similarly, the dispersion of population (within areas already settled) is the natural consequence of liberal policies—of free trade at home and abroad and of infrastructural improvements that redistributed people as efficiently as they moved commodities. Free-trade liberals thus take their cues from a somewhat more mechanical model of society, a model that is composed of lines (of transport and communication) and vectors (of commodity flows) and, as noted later, of equilibria and specialized regional economies—all predicated on early liberalism's insights on opportunity costs and comparative advantages (Gomes 1987: 94–103; Appleby 1978:

158–279). That said, liberals rarely went so far as to believe that theirs was a machine that could go by itself. The machine required entrepreneurs and politicians, men who were wise to the ways of limited governance and the vital spark that such governance provided (on government's role, see Striner 1995; Pole 1978: 117–30, 1992: 89–92). It was not for nothing that John Locke, the greatest of all liberals, was in the 1690s a member of the Board of Trade, a leading proponent of the recoinage of English silver, and a staunch advocate for reform in Virginia's land system, laws, and tax structure. While Locke's liberalism on these grounds has seemed overly Whiggish and conservative for some of his critics (Appleby 1978: 242–79), it was precisely these sorts of interventions—and not simply the market's—that made the liberal machine go.

Turning to domestic policies, the geographic impacts of liberal and republican regimes are most evident at the scale of the regional economy. Here we have seen that the elite policies of liberal regimes have favored regional economic stability and specialization, while the more egalitarian policies of republican regimes have led to regional economic volatility and the diversification of regional economic activity. But why should this be the case? How, in other words, is ideology translated into regional geography? I begin with stability/volatility. Stability—geographic or otherwise—is, need we be reminded, one of liberalism's central assumptions. From Newton to Locke to Adam Smith and his heirs, liberal thinkers have accorded "equilibrium" (stability by another name) a premier role within their ideological system (Striner 1995; Freudenthal 1986). It is not surprising, therefore, that elite-liberal regimes would accord regional economic stability a similarly prominent place in their geographical reconstructions. Nor is it surprising that egalitarian regimes would do the reverse: that as heirs of the revolutionary republicanism of the English Civil War, they would stir the pot of opportunity by constructing highly volatile regional geographies. The Puritans' plan for a northern university to rival Oxford and Cambridge and, nine score years hence, Andrew Jackson's redistribution of the federal government's budget surplus among the states (Stone 1980; Temin 1969) are cases in point.

But if regional stability and volatility are deeply rooted in liberal and republican ideologies, respectively, what of the even more abstruse notions of regional specialization and diversification? These, too, may be traced to the core precepts of these two ideological systems. As Adam Smith's (1976) famous description of pin making suggests, specialization resides within the realms of liberalism and the production system. Smith's account nicely illustrates the manifold benefits that liberals have envisioned as flowing from economic specialization and the division of labor. Coordinating the small tasks of many men would, in Smith's opinion, vastly increase their total output and their productivity. And it followed that specialized regions, in their pursuit of comparative advantage, would accomplish the same ends at a different geographical scale. All of this points toward a normative model for liberal policy regimes—a model that seeks to construct an unusually stable mechanical system composed of highly specialized and interdependent parts, be they regions or pin makers.

Republicans take a rather different view of regions. To understand their preferences for the diversification of regional economies, we must turn again to republican notions of equality, to what it meant to be a citizen, and to the role of consumption within the republic (Beer 1993, especially 84–131). One of republicanism's central tenets is that a republic of free and equal citizens is predicated on an independent citizenry. And as republicans from Cincinnatus to Jefferson have maintained, an independent citizenry depends, in turn, on one critical precondition: a diversified and productive household economy capable of providing a subsistent consumption system. And what was good for republican households was equally good for republican regions where a free and independent citizenry ran in a straight line to economic diversification. While regional specialization may have been more efficient for elite producers, diversification better served the security of the republic and its citizens.

Variable Geographies at the National Scale: Expansion/Consolidation and Concentration/Dispersion before 1776

Republicanism and liberalism provided Americans, for better or worse, with two fairly distinct models of social geography: (1) an organic republican model of spatial expansion, demographic concentration, and regional volatility and diversification; and (2) a mechanical liberal model of spatial consolidation, demographic dispersion, and regional stability and specialization. Although these models sorely tested the fidelities of colonial Americans on whom they were first imposed, any thoughts of adulteration were, until the 1760s, closely held, in part because Americans persisted in thinking of themselves as Anglo-Americans and in part because of the leniency shown them by the mother country. Colonial geographies thus unfolded in close accordance with liberal and republican models. Consider the expansion of frontier settlement or the lack of it after 1650 (figures 4.1 and 4.2; Earle 2000). Frontier expansion was fairly fast under the two republican regimes, in the 1640s–1680s and 1740s–1780s. Newly settled lands on the frontier were incorporated at rates in excess of 2.5 percent per annum. These high rates of spatial expansion are even more stunning when juxtaposed against the frontier's collapse during the intervening liberal regime (1680s–1730s). Between 1680 and 1720, the rate of frontier expansion dwindled to just 1.2 percent per annum, before rallying in the 1720s and 1730s. Not until the closure of the frontier in the 1840s—during a later free-trade regime—would the process of frontier expansion sink so low.

In a nation accustomed to thinking of frontier expansion as somehow "natural," it is hard to appreciate the effort that went into slowing down the frontier's advance at the turn of the seventeenth century—not to mention the reasoning that prompted these counterfrontier policies. For the liberal regime that emerged in the 1690s, two things were clear (Earle 2000). First unchecked growth on the frontier had created many problems, everything from political instability to Indian hostilities, from social unrest to the burdensome costs of defense. Second the solution entailed a countervailing strategy of spatial consolidation—that is, a set of bilevel policies that would,

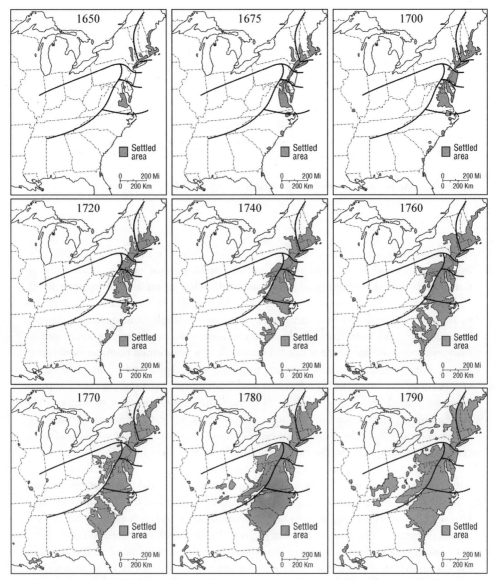

Figure 4.1. Settled areas in the mainland colonies, 1650–1770, and the United States, 1780–1790.

Source: Earle 2000.

at one level, rechannel colonial energies and peoples away from the frontier and into the regions already settled and, at another, expedite the flow of colonial exports and imports. Toward these liberal ends, the principals of this regime—the British Board of Trade, its colonial agents, and the several colonial proprietors—initiated a series of bold moves on behalf of spatial consolidation. Within two decades they managed to abolish the cheap-land policy of head rights that had fueled frontier expansion in

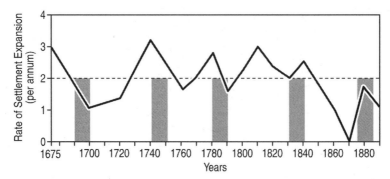

Figure 4.2.   Annual rates of settlement expansion, 1650–1890.

Note: Shaded time spans depict periods of economic depression.

the Chesapeake, create a land market and reduce town size in New England, establish towns as conduits of exports and imports, promote cost-cutting innovations in transportation and marketing (e.g., the unified sailing of an annual tobacco fleet), and facilitate agrarian innovations (e.g., the slave trade with its massive expansions of the slave labor force) that increased the output of staple commodities (e.g., tobacco, sugar, and later rice). These interventions took much of the steam out of frontier expansion and piped it instead into a tripling of colonial population densities (from three to ten persons per square mile) between 1675 and 1720. The "great compaction" had begun (this is evident in the convergence of the curves of population and settled area in figure 4.3). Not until the republican Age of Empire (the succeeding regime) would the frontier resume its heady rate of western expansion and, in keeping with the dialectic of republican expansion and liberal consolidation, revise outward once again the boundaries of American space.

The next order of business was to transform these spaces and rearrange people and resources in accordance with liberal and republican models of social geography. Toward these ends, colonial regimes periodically reshuffled the locations of their populations, concentrating them in republican regimes and dispersing them in their liberal successors. The first republican regime (1630s–1680) managed to concentrate population within preexisting regions while sustaining a very rapid rate of frontier expansion. Most of this expansion involved extensions of settlement from nuclei in the colonies of Virginia and Massachusetts. Indeed, nine of every ten American colonists in 1680 resided within the enlarged domains of "Greater Virginia" and "Greater Massachusetts" (for colonial populations here and below, see *Historical Statistics* 1975, 2: 1168–71). Colonial population thus was nearly as concentrated in these domains in 1680 as it had been in their colonies "proper" in the 1630. The English, of course, had staked out their claims on much of the rest of the Atlantic Seaboard, but as of 1680, these were as figments to the tangible accomplishments in New England and the Chesapeake. Even the one clear-cut case of dispersion away from these initial nuclei—New York in 1664— seems an almost accidental acquisition, one of the tangential spoils of the English wars with the Dutch. And it is owing to the demographic concentrations of a republican regime that the history of the

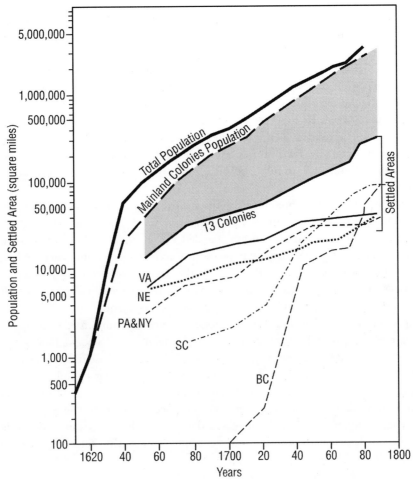

Figure 4.3.   Populations and settled areas of British North America, 1620–1790.

Note: BC refers to the backcountry; *NE,* to New England; *NY,* to greater New York; *PA,* to greater Pennsylvania; *SC,* to greater South Carolina; *VA,* to greater Virginia; and *colonies,* to the English and later British colonies between Maine and Georgia on the Atlantic Seaboard of North America.

American colonies until 1680 is, in large measure, the histories of Virginia and Massachusetts writ large.

That was hardly the case by 1740. At the close of this liberal era of "salutary neglect," nearly one-third of the population of the thirteen colonies—as opposed to ten percent in 1680—resided outside the orbits of Virginia and Massachusetts, in New York, Pennsylvania, Delaware, Georgia, and the Carolinas. Populations that had streamed toward the frontiers of Massachusetts and Virginia before 1680 had been rerouted and debouched in the empty spaces along the Atlantic Seaboard. And in these spaces, the processes of demographic dispersion had spawned a wholly new series of settlement nuclei around which populations grew and, owing equally to the deceleration of the frontier and to liberal policies of spatial consolidation, intensified.

With the onset of the Age of Empire in the 1740s, a new generation of expansionist-minded republicans jettisoned the liberal strategy of population dispersion and reasserted their preference for demographic concentration. Over the next forty years, and despite the near tripling of colonial population (to 2.7 million) and the rapid acceleration in frontier expansion, these neomercantilists held the line. On their watch, the distribution of population among the thirteen colonies remained virtually unchanged. In 1780 as in 1740, some two-thirds of the population of the thirteen colonies resided in the domains of greater Virginia and Massachusetts—which perhaps is why the histories of this revolutionary period, like those of the seventeenth century, are so full of tobacco planters and Yankees, puritans and cavaliers.

The colonial period presents us with two distinctive geographies of settlement and population. Republican geographies in the mid–seventeenth and mid–eighteenth centuries simultaneously expanded the frontier of American settlement while concentrating the mass of peoples and economies within older settlement nuclei. Liberal geographies at the turn of the seventeenth century accomplished precisely the opposite—decelerating the pace of frontier expansion, consolidating the space economy in older regions, and dispersing populations among the colonies along the coast. Republicans thus envisioned power as arising from geographies of interior expansion and coastal concentration; liberals, from geographies of spatial consolidation and the dispersion of peoples and resources. These differences are suggestive of Edward Fox's (1971) useful distinction between the geographies of territorial-administrative regimes and commercial regimes. But whereas Fox's model of France arrays these competing geographies in space in order that he might explore the synchronic tensions of monarchy and democracy, the American evidence leads us to array them in time in order that we might explore the dialectical relations of liberal and republican versions of capitalism.

Variable Geographies at the Regional Scale: Stability/Volatility and Specialization/Diversification before 1776

Colonial policy regimes also present us with several distinctive regional economic geographies. On one dimension, these regions are volatile or stable; on another, they are diversified or specialized. I begin with the latter.

Regional specialization is an enduring theme in American economic history. The theme owes a great deal to economic theory's prediction that regions will always pursue their comparative advantage, will always specialize in the production of commodities which they can produce at the lowest comparative cost. This, of course, is the liberal version of economic theory (North 1955, 1961)—a theory that works pretty well for liberal regimes but not quite as well for republican regimes and geographies.

When we turn to the evidence of regional specialization, colonial history provides us with very few measures. One of the best indicators is the "birthings" of identifiable regional societies (figure 4.4). On this count, the liberal regime between 1680 and 1740 was particularly fecund—which is, as one would expect, in this era of "salutary neglect." As of 1750, Donald Meinig (1986) discerns at least five regional societies (six if we include Canada) along the Atlantic Seaboard of North America. Only two of these had existed sixty years earlier, and only one, at most, would be added in the ensuing thirty to forty years (and even in this case, one could argue that the "backcountry" also had its origins between 1680 and 1740). These regions, both the new ones that had arisen as the specialized offspring of a liberal regime and the old ones, were by 1740 esteemed for their production of specialized commodities

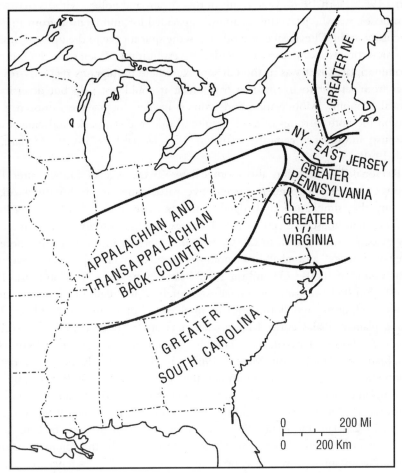

Figure 4.4.   Macroregions on the Atlantic Seaboard of North America, circa 1750.

Source: Adapted from Meinig 1986: 244–54.

and services (Merrens 1964: 4–17). Visitors as well as colonials regularly spoke of the "bread colonies" of Pennsylvania and New York, of the Chesapeake's tobacco coast, of Carolina's rice country, and of Yankee (read merchant) New England. For a liberal regime, these were the specialized parts within the complex machine that was the Atlantic economy—a network of trading lines and vectors connecting points of supply and demand (e.g., the "triangular trade") in the mainland colonies of North America, the Caribbean, Africa, and, the motor of it all, Britain and Western Europe.

On either side of this belching liberal machine of specialized regions, republican regimes took a less sanguine view of regional specialization. For these regimes, a strategy of economic diversification posed fewer risks and promised greater rewards to the security of frontier colonies (Billings 1996; Earle 1992: 158–61; Lockridge 1970). Prior to 1680, the authorities in the Chesapeake and New England were less interested in developing specialized economies than in attracting new settlers to the colonies by making land available to immigrants on the most generous of terms (Harris 1953; Horn 1998). One result of this cheap-land policy, with its mass-egalitarian biases, was the powerful stimulus it provided for immigration from England, particularly to the Chesapeake; the other was the spur it gave to the upward mobility of the newcomers and, in turn, to regional diversification. When social mobility was so commonplace, as it was in the Chesapeake where immigrants regularly rose the ladder from servant to freeman to freeholder, it could not help but diversify the regional economy. Mobile men and women needed to provide subsistence. For those on the bottom rungs of the agricultural ladder, corn, pork, and cider usually came first; and tobacco came later (Bailyn 1959; Menard 1973; Carr, Menard, and Walsh 1991).

Regional diversification also loomed large in the Age of Empire after 1740. Although farmers and planters were active participants in the booming Atlantic economy, they simultaneously hedged against an increasingly volatile market by diversifying their household economies. The new emphasis on diversification is especially evident in one parish in the Chesapeake, where a measure of the "potential for self-sufficiency" among all households increased by over 40 percent between the liberal regime of 1680–1733 and the republican regime of 1734–1766 (Earle 1975: 101–41). Small planters and even tenants throughout the region had the capacity to provide food, drink, and clothing for themselves and their families; and large slave-holding planters like George Mason's father could produce even more—timber, plank, casks, hoops, charcoal, skins, tanning, wool, cotton, flax, spun and knit cloth, fruits, brandy, and on and on (Morgan 1963: 53–54). This tendency toward diversification after 1740 is also evident among the farm households in Pennsylvania and New England, which is a large part of the reason why in 1769 Americans could join together in challenging British trade policies through a nonimportation agreement (Lemon 1972; Main and Main 1988). All of this proved befuddling to British neo-mercantilists who should have known better. Preoccupied by the colonials' commitment to the sustained growth of exports and their seemingly unquenchable appetite for English goods, British policymakers ignored the egalitarian side of American republicanism and its simultaneous commitment to independence, consumerism, and economic diversification (Breen 1986, 1988). They also seem to have ignored the regional volatility that was soon in store.

Change is one of the few constants of capitalist history, and regions are no exception to this rule. Regions may rise or fall, grow or decline, but the way in which they change is not entirely random. In the American case, regions are either stable or volatile. Stability is indicated when the several regions maintain their ranks over time; volatility, when these same regions break ranks, when some advance and others retreat (a condition encompassing both regional divergence and convergence). Stating these concepts is one thing; measuring them is quite another owing to the absence of perhaps the best indicator of regional stability/volatility—estimates of regional income in early American history. In lieu of these estimates (which are unavailable prior to 1774–1840), I use the "next-best" indicator—regional rates of frontier expansion (figure 4.5). The trajectories of these rates suggest a tendency toward regional stability during the era of "salutary neglect"—the liberal regime from the 1680s to the 1730s—and particularly between 1680 and 1720 (Earle 2000). In the republican regimes prior to the 1680s and after 1740, the swings in the regional rates of expansion proved to be more volatile—and more frightening. The increasing volatility of republican regions pushed up to even more dangerous levels the pressures arising from rapidly expanding frontiers, diversifying regional and household economies, and the concentrations of people and power in the two regions that mattered most—greater New England and greater Virginia—and where pressures were almost bound to erupt. And it is precisely this concatenation of republican pressures and processes in the 1670s and again in the 1770s that the great Virginia historian Thomas Wertenbaker (1940) understood so well in elevating Nathaniel Bacon from the failed leader of Virginia's rebellion in 1676 to the much loftier status of torchbearer of the American Revolution.

The Geographies of American Republics and Democracies after 1776

It was Bacon's example and their own that threw fear into the hearts of the framers of the Constitution and that lent a sense of urgency to their deliberations over a system of governance that would, if not eliminate altogether the threat of republican revolution, at least render it less potent. Over the next several decades, their pragmatic fusion of portions of liberal and republican ideologies gave rise to a new configuration of policy regimes and an equally new set of geographies (table 4.2). The first of these distinct regimes (the Republics between 1790–1830, 1880–1930, and since 1980) fused a republican protectionist geography of spatial expansion and demographic concentration with a liberal elitist geography of regional stability and regional specialization. The second (the democracies between 1830–1880 and 1930–1970s) fused a liberal free-trade geography of spatial consolidation and demographic dispersion with a republican egalitarian geography of regional volatility and regional diversification. In this fashion, regimes have imposed their geographical biases on all

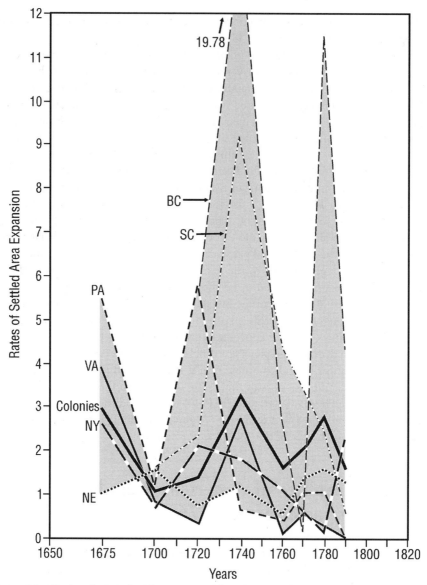

Figure 4.5.   Regional rates of settlement expansion, 1650–1790.

scales of daily life; moreover, they have repeatedly created new geographies the likes of which are rarely imagined, let alone comprehended, by spatial theoreticians.

Not all spatial theory entirely misses the mark. When it comes to the three American republics—the elite protectionist/nationalist regimes (PE) of the 1780s–1830, the 1880s–1930, and the 1980s to date—perhaps our best theoretical guides are Douglass C. North's (1955, 1961) model of American economic development, Allan Pred's (1966: 12–85) dynamic of manufacturing agglomeration, and Friedrich Ratzel's (Agnew 1998: 68, 100–3) model of the organic state. The North–Pred

Table 4.2. American Ideologies, Policy Regimes, and Geographies

Republics Elite National Regimes (PE)		Democracies Egalitarian Free-Trade Regimes (FTM)	
Foreign Policy	*Geographies*	*Foreign Policy*	*Geographies*
Nationalist/ protectionist	Spatial expansion Demographic concentration	Free Trade	Spatial consolidation Demographic dispersion
Domestic Policy	*Geographies*	*Domestic Policy*	*Geographies*
Elitist/property rights	Regional specialization Regional stability	Equality of opportunity	Regional diversification Regional volatility

model fits reasonably well with the geographical aims of elite-protectionist regimes—namely, fostering regional specialization and selective demographic concentration in favored (tariff-protected) regions as a means of stimulating interdependence, interregional trade, the interregional transmission of economic growth, and stability among the various regional economies. The irony here, of course, is that these models of regional specialization and agglomeration work best under the kinds of protectionist policies of which North and many other economists (most notably, Paul Krugman 1991a, 1991b) so thoroughly disapprove. As for Ratzel, his organic theory of the state helps clarify the expansionist tendencies inherent in American Republics as well as their inextricable association of national security, the spatial growth in the ecumene, and revolutions in economic production.

Spatial theory fits even more loosely when applied to the geographical creations of the two American democracies—the egalitarian free-trade (FTM) regimes from the 1830s to the 1870s and the 1930s to the 1970s. There simply is no "off-the-rack" theory for a geographical regime that promotes regional diversification, spatial consolidation, and demographic dispersion and that stimulates, in turn, regional autonomy, involutional regional economic growth, and volatility in regional economic performance. The theory that fits better than most is an amalgam of the hypothesis of balanced regional growth, with its emphasis on egalitarian distributional/redistributional policies (e.g., internal improvements and capital-market integrations on behalf of spatial consolidation), Mrydal's "spread" effects (i.e., spatial dispersion), and the consumer-oriented principles of central-place systems (Hirschman 1958; Myrdal 1957; Berry 1970). The fact of the matter is that these geographies of American republics and democracies are as much the outcome of ideology and policy regimes as of economic forces and invisible hands. Better theory will, in either case, require somewhat more attention to political economy, to the peculiarly ambivalent character of American ideology and policy regimes, and to the ideological biases implicit in geographical theories of production and consumption, industry and retailing/wholesaling services, and agglomeration and dispersion.

If the evidence is clear and, in some cases, resounding on every one of these spatial dimensions of regime geography since the 1780s, their larger social implications are neither self-evident nor readily apparent. Intuition alone would not imagine the possibility of uniting, for example, the processes of spatial expansion, demographic concentration, and regional stability and specialization or, alternatively, of spatial consolidation, demographic dispersion, and regional volatility and diversification; nor, for that matter, has geographical theory. Such prospects are more likely if we regard the landscape as an amalgam compounded out of the volatile materials of American philosophy and policy and remixed periodically by dialectical regimes. Of course, landscapes created of such volatile materials could hardly have been inert. Repeatedly these new geographies imposed new conditions and constraints on American life—on the workings of regional economies and labor markets, on social movements, and, not least, on the periodic enlargements in the spatial domains of American power.

The past two centuries provide ample evidence of these alternating regimes and geographies. Consider the alternating spatial cycles evident in three quick examples and figures: (1) urban spatial expansion and consolidation, (2) demographic concentration and dispersion at the national scale, and (3) regional economic stability and volatility. What follows, then, amounts to a preview of the several post-1780 spatial cycles featured in chapter 12.

The changing geography of American cities provides a good illustration of these spatial cycles and the social ramifications of spatial change. Spatial alternations at the city scale have exercised sizable effects on urban labor markets, wages, and, ultimately, the distribution of income and wealth (inequality). Most interesting are the alternating expansions and consolidations in the structure of American cities as depicted in the schematic maps in figure 4.6 (Baerwald 1984; Harris and Ullman 1945; Earle 1992: 206–25; Gordon 1984). Within cities, the expansionist policies of elite protectionist regimes (PE republics) have invariably extended the built urban environment into "suburban" hinterlands on the rural-urban fringe. Just as invariably, entrepreneurs have tapped (exploited) imperfectly competitive suburban labor markets on behalf of lower wages, higher rates of return on their capital, and, in the long run, income inequality. The great pushes outward have come in conjunction with the nation's three producer revolutions and the associated waves in the suburbanization of leading-sector employment (figures 4.7 and 4.8). These included the decentralization of manufacturing from 1780 to 1830 and again from 1880 to 1930 and most recently in producer and quaternary services (in edge cities) between 1980 and 2000. Conversely, in these same cities, the consolidationist spatial policies of egalitarian free traders (FTM democracies) promoted urban accessibility within the bounds of the urbanized area. These improvements in intraurban movement helped to erase labor market imperfections, increase wages, reduce exploitation, and, in the span of a historical period, sharply lower the levels of income inequality. For FTM regimes, improvements such as street railways and urban beltways represented sizable achievements; but for the PE regimes that followed, these structural additions were more nearly economic obstacles to be overcome via spatial expansion and the centrifugal installation of new production regimes. These alternations are nicely revealed in the distance–density curves of three cities (Philadelphia, Chicago, Atlanta) between 1890 and 1970. In the Second Republic (1880–1930), expansion prevailed with high growth rates both downtown and in the suburbs (ten to thirty miles from city cen-

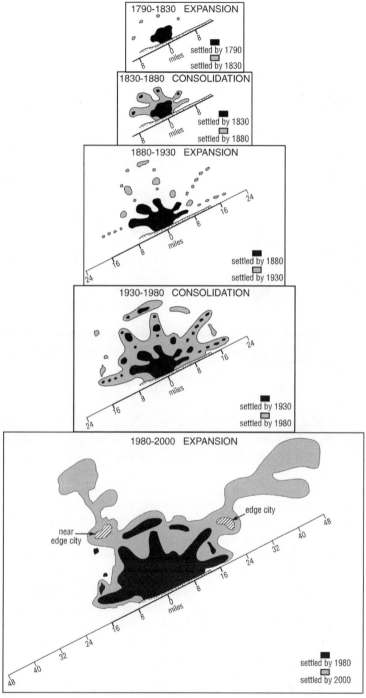

Figure 4.6. A model of the evolution of American cities through macrohistorical time.

Note: The expansionary phases in the life of American cities unfold during the First, Second, and Third Republics, 1790–1830, 1880–1930, and 1980–2000. The consolidationist phases prevailed during the First and Second American Democracies, 1830–1880 and 1930–1980.

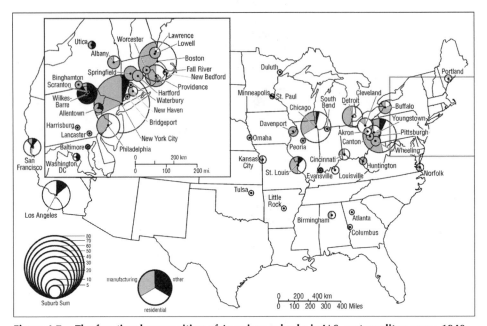

Figure 4.7.   The functional composition of American suburbs in U.S. metropolitan areas, 1940.

Note: The fifty-three metropolitan areas reported 340 distinct suburbs of which the manufacturing function predominated in 148 and the residential function in 174.
Source: Harris 1940.

ter). The locus of growth shifted thereafter. In the Second Democracy (1930–1980), growth rates peaked in intermediate areas between the far suburbs and downtown. In this urban regime, consolidation rather than expansion was the rule (Krakover and Morrill 1992).

Figure 4.9 describes the changes in the spatial concentration and dispersion of American populations between 1790 and 1990. The curve is based on an index (1860 = 0) of Moran's I—a measure of concentration and dispersion that ranges between +1 and −1. The higher the value of the index, the higher the level of spatial concentration and vice versa (Getis and Ord 1992; Anselin 1995; Ord and Getis 1995). In practice, American populations have always been fairly concentrated as Moran's I has oscillated between +1 and 0 (i.e., between more and less concentrated). Levels of concentration are highest in the first and second republics and least in the First and Second Democracies. From its historic high in 1790, the index plunges to its historic low (greatest dispersion) between 1860 and 1880; it then rises in the 1880s (though not nearly so high as in the early National Period) and levels off until the 1910s. The index then falls again during the era of New Deal liberalism (as it did in the era of Jacksonian democracy) as egalitarian policies worked in favor of demographic dispersion. As for the post-1980 Third Republic, the verdict is not yet in. The level of concentration seems to have increased slightly, though noticeably, since the 1960s and 1970s. What is more apparent is that the long-run oscillations in spatial concentration and dispersion are much less extreme in this century

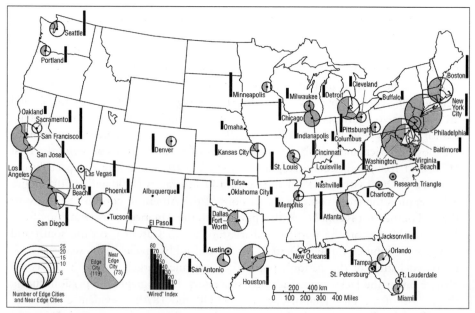

Figure 4.8.   Edge cities and near-edge cities, circa 1990, and the "Wired Index" of larger metropolitan areas, circa 1998.

Note: One hundred ninety-two edge cities and near edge cities were distributed among thirty-five metropolitan areas. Los Angeles, Washington, and New York led the way with twenty-four, twenty-three, and twenty-one, respectively. The Wired Index incorporates various indicators of computer integration—namely, Internet users, hosts/capita, domain density, backbone traffic, and directory density.
Sources: Garreau 1991; Greenman 1998.

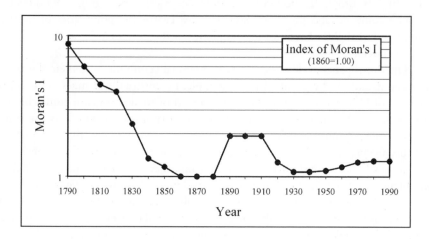

Figure 4.9.   Historical trends in the spatial concentration of American populations, 1790–1990.

Note: The graph depicts Moran's *I* in the form of an index in which 1860 equals an *I* of one. The highest levels in the spatial concentration of American populations came before 1830, the next highest between 1890 and 1910, and the third highest in the slight resurgence since 1980.
Sources: Earle and Cao 1993; Otterstrom 1997.

than in the nineteenth century. One might wonder why that is the case and, perhaps more importantly, if that trend will persist.

Figure 4.10 offers a spatial perspective on these cycles of demographic concentration/dispersion between 1790 and 1950 (Warntz 1967; Stewart 1947). Concentration is here measured by the extent and the compactness of American demographic core regions over time. These core regions, as depicted by the shaded areas in the two figure parts, are defined by the median isolines of population potential for selected years between 1790 and 1950. As expected, American core regions are most compact (and population most concentrated) during the courses of the First (1790 and 1820) and Second Republics (1870 and 1930) and least compact during the First (1820–1840 and 1870) and Second Democracies (1930 and 1950). Figure 4.10 captures the fairly compact dimensions of the American core in 1820 toward the end of the First Republic. At that point, with the American core stretching from Portland, Maine, on the north to Charleston, South Carolina, on the south and along an arc running through Detroit, Michigan, and Nashville, Tennessee, the concentrated nature of the nation's population remained largely intact. That would change under the Jacksonians and their successors. Demographic dispersion during the course of the First Democracy (1820–1840 and 1870) is evident as the core expands and spills over into the Upper South by 1840 before rotating slightly toward the Northwest by 1870. But after the Civil War, the forces of agglomeration are reinvigorated. Between 1870 and 1930—during the Second Republic—the core region steadily contracts; the Upper South and northern New England are ruled out of the core, and population becomes more concentrated. These shrinkages in the American core are halted and then reversed between 1930 and 1950. With the installation of New Deal liberalism (the Second Democracy), the core explodes outward. In short order, the most compact of all American core regions (1930) becomes the least compact (and the most dispersed) by 1950—the boundaries of the latter extending just slightly beyond the boundaries of the core in 1870 at the end of the First Democracy.

The third spatial cycle has to do with regional economies and their alternations between stability and volatility. In this example, I compare the changes in the relative incomes of U.S. census regions (as a proportion of total national income) between years with reliable income estimates. Stability/volatility is measured as the sum of the percentage point deviations of the several regions between two time periods. Stability occurs when there are few changes in the proportions of income held by the various U.S. regions; volatility occurs when there are many changes. Table 4.3 and Figure 4.11 make the key points. First, and most obvious, are the cyclical swings in regional economies. In these cases, Republics are invariably more stable than Democracies. Second, and unlike the cycling of spatial concentration and dispersion, the cycling of regional stability/volatility shows no sign of weakening. Whereas the First Democracy was roughly twice as volatile as the First Republic, the Second Democracy was nearly three times as volatile as the Second Republic. And the trend seems to be continuing. If current rates of stability/volatility prevail (for 1980–1994), the Third Republic promises to rival the record levels of stability registered during the Second Republic (1880–1930). Third is that all of this cycling of regional income

1820–1870

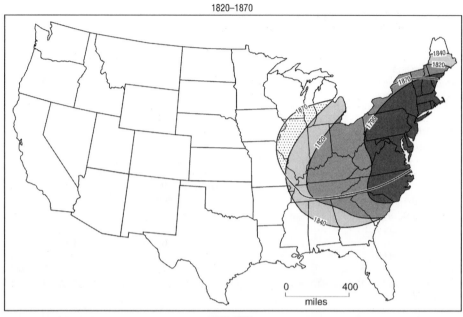

1870–1950

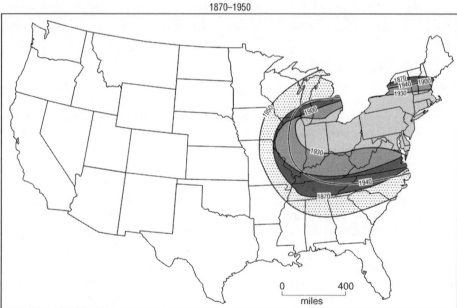

Figure 4.10.   Cycles of demographic concentration and dispersion, 1790–1950.

Notes: Median isolines of population potential for the given years are indicated on the maps. The shaded area depicts the areas that exceeded the median isoline values. The most compact ("concentrated") periods fall in 1790, 1820, 1900, and 1930 (i.e., within the First and Second Republics). The most dispersed periods fall in 1840, 1870, 1940, and 1950 (i.e., within the First and Second American Democracies).
Sources: Warntz 1967; Stewart 1947.

Table 4.3. Regional Stability/Volatility: Regional Shares of Personal Income in the United States, 1840–1996, and the Net Changes in Regional Shares

Census Region	1774	1840	1880	1930	1970	1980	1994
New England	25%	21%					
Middle colonies/states	38%	49%					
Southern colonies/states	37%	44%					
New England (NE)		17%	11%	9%	6%	6%	6%
Mid-Atlantic (MA)		41%	33%	32%	24%	18%	17%
East North Central (ENC)		12%	23%	23%	21%	19%	17%
West North Central (WNC)		2%	11%	9%	8%	7%	7%
South Atlantic (SA)		14%	6%	6%	11%	15%	17%
East South Central (ESC)		11%	6%	4%	5%	5%	5%
West South Central (WSC)		4%	4%	6%	8%	10%	10%
Mountain (MTN)			2%	2%	4%	5%	5%
Pacific (PAC)			4%	9%	14%	16%	16%

Net change in regional shares	1774–1840 (22)*	1840–80 (45)*	1880–1930 (14)	1930–1970 (29)	1930–1980 (47)	1980–1994 (5)

Note: *The tabulation of changes in regional shares 1840–1880 excludes regions not present in 1840; were these two included, volatility would rise from forty-five units to fifty-one units. The comparison of incomes in 1774 and 1840 matches Easterlin's (1961) states with Jones's (1980) colonial regions. The comparison excludes new regions added to the United States between 1774 and 1840; income shares in 1840 are adjusted accordingly. If we include new regions, regional shares in 1840 equal New England 17 percent; Mid-Atlantic, 41 percent; South Atlantic, 25 percent; and New Regions, 17 percent. Regional shares do not always sum to 100 percent owing to rounding.
Sources: Jones (1980); Easterlin (1961); *Historical Statistics* 1975, 1: 242.

has occurred while the inequalities in *regional incomes per capita* have fallen for the past century and a quarter (following a rise in inequality between 1840 and 1880; Williamson 1965). The latter are a third of what they were between 1880 and 1920, and they show no signs of rearing up again.[1] Thus, whether we see convergence in regional incomes per capita today (and since the 1920s) or divergence in the nineteenth century (1840–1880), regional shares of aggregate income continue to be steadfastly cyclical. These shares are highly volatile during the life spans of American democracies and remarkably stable over the courses of American republics.

In ways such as these, the alternating geographies of policy regimes facilitate and then restrain the growth and development of American society, economy, and polity. Near the end of every period in American history, two sets of constraints begin to appear in the prevailing spatial arrangements. For the outgoing policy regime, it is the inexorable constraint of diminishing returns that challenges the regime's capacity to sustain economic growth; for the incoming policy regime, it is the constraints of "built environments" and fixed investments that must be revised or eliminated altogether in order to restore economic prosperity. It is these constraints that Schumpeter had in mind in speaking of "creative destruction" as capitalism's *modus operandi* for economic recovery in times of crisis. To be sure, "creative destruction" is an especially apt characterization of the geographies of the first and second Democracies. By and large, these consolidationist regimes engage in an energetic reengineering of

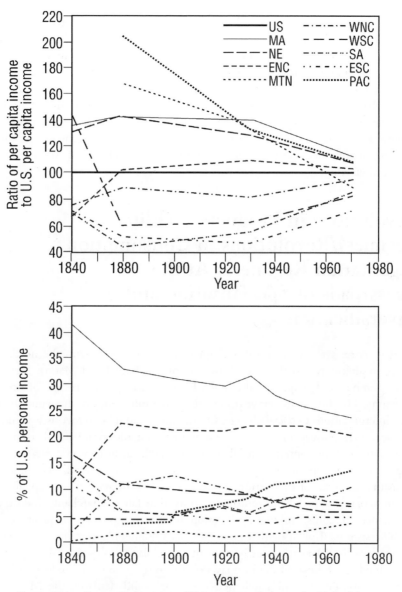

Figure 4.11.   Per capita incomes of U.S. regions relative to the United States as a whole (top); and regional incomes as a proportion of U.S. personal income, 1840–1980 (bottom).

Note: See table 4.3 for abbreviations key.
Sources: See text.

existing spaces (i.e., there was perhaps as much destruction as creativity). But "creative destruction" is much less apt as a characterization of spatial processes in the First and Second Republics. These expansionist regimes, preoccupied as they are with engineering new spaces for the specialized productions of entrepreneurial elites, routinely leapfrog over older occupied spaces in favor of lower-cost frontier and/or suburban sites. In either case, be they the "creative destructions" of American democracies or the "creative expansions" of American republics, these periodic alternations have had profound effects on labor markets and movements, production regimes, income inequality, and, not least, the dual trajectories of American power and social viability.

Revolutions in Production (Elite Regimes)/Revolutions in Consumption (Egalitarian Regimes): At the Crossroads of Specialization and Diversification

On that score, we might end this chapter where it began, with the need for an American alternative to the flawed assumptions of liberal and Marxist theories of innovation bias and geographical change. Even the most casual review of American geographical history invites grave doubts about the sufficiency of these unduly materialist interpretations of social change. On the one hand, liberal theorists would have us believe that innovations are class-neutral, that their adoption has little or no effect on welfare, and, in consequence, that the geographical history of capitalism is one of sustained and more or less equitable progress. On the other hand, Marxist theorists tell us that the dice of innovation are always loaded in favor of the capitalist elite; that the greater share of the returns to innovation fall to merchants, industrialists, and finance capitalists; and that exploitation, immizerization, and inequality are fated for the rest of us. But in neither case—neither the liberal's rosy view of inexorable progress nor the Marxist's dour portrait of class polarization—does the argumentation extend much beyond the iron laws of economy. The liberal reduces economic crisis to a momentary mismatch between supply and demand, the Marxist to a deeper, if still transitory, structural contradiction between accumulation and consumption. And similarly, just as crisis is endogenous to the capitalist economy, so, too, is the process of economic recovery. For liberals, innovation eliminates the mismatch between supply and demand; for Marxists, it alleviates overaccumulation (or underconsumption) by installing a new mode of production. Liberal history marches on, and Marxist history enters its latest stage—all of which would be well and good if these theories bore more than the faintest resemblance to the American way of crisis and recovery.

Theoretical reflections on the geographies of American society might better begin with the mind, with the class-biased ideologies of elite and egalitarian regimes.

We may concede on the outset that material conditions matter, that policy regimes no less than the liberal's entrepreneurs and the Marxist's capitalists are propelled into action by economic crisis. The difference is that the policies that regimes choose have more to do with ideology than with economic conditions and constraints. It is ideology that largely determines how a class-biased regime will deal with crisis, whether the problem will be regarded as a crisis in the *system of production*—as elite regimes tend to do—or in *the habits of consumption*—as is the wont of egalitarian regimes. On this ideological diagnosis, much else hinges—geographies included.

For elite regimes, economic crises are invariably production crises, and their resolution just as invariably entails policies that revamp the ways in which Americans produce goods and services. It is liberal ideology that defines these policies, that impels elite regimes to focus on producer problems, on the geography of production systems, and on ways of freeing up the supply-side factors of land, labor, and capital—to embark, as it were, on a producer's revolution. This is as true of liberal elites in the 1680s and 1690s as of their successors in the 1790s, the 1880s, and the 1980s. Production was the central problem for liberal elites in both England and America during the crisis of the 1680s and 1690s (and rightly so, contra Appleby 1978). One of their solutions, and by far the most consequential, was the massive importation of labor to the colonies—of slaves to colonies in the Chesapeake and the Carolinas after 1680 and of continental immigrants to the Middle colonies a few years hence (Menard 1977; Lemon 1972; Bailyn 1986).

And a century hence, it was labor costs—the lesser the better—that once again preoccupied economic elites in the early national period. As Alexander Hamilton believed and history affirmed, industries and factories were indeed possible in America provided that manufacturers, protected by high tariffs, were able to tap the pools of cheap labor that existed among seasonally unemployed farm workers, women, and children (Cooke 1975). The textile-manufacturing "industrial suburbs" on the edge of Boston (Waltham), Philadelphia (Manayunk), and Baltimore (Hampden) were, of course, the result (Earle 1992: 212–25). Supply-side issues reemerged again after 1880 as elites turned their attention to cheap and abundant immigrant workers, industrial protection, economies of scale and massive throughputs in the so-called "heavy industries," and the "gospel of efficiency" according to Frederick Taylor, Henry Ford, and the New Nationalists. "Time-and-motion" studies, mass production, industrial "suburbs" and "urban decentralization," trusts, interlocking directorates, and the vertical organization of industries were all aimed at mobilizing land, labor, and capital (Gutman 1976; Roy 1997; Chandler 1977, 1990; Earle 1993). And this producer revolution was attended by sharp gains in the regional specialization of manufactures as firms exploited regional comparative advantages. Levels of regional specialization in manufactures began their move upward soon after the Civil War, in conjunction with the national integration of the American railway system, and reached a peak between the outbreak of World War I and the Great Depression (regional specialization also prevailed in other economic sectors in the course of the Second Republic; see Kim 1995, 1998: 666–67).

Production is once again in the news, or more precisely has been since the 1980s and the promulgation of supply-side economics (Harvey 1990; Storper and Walker

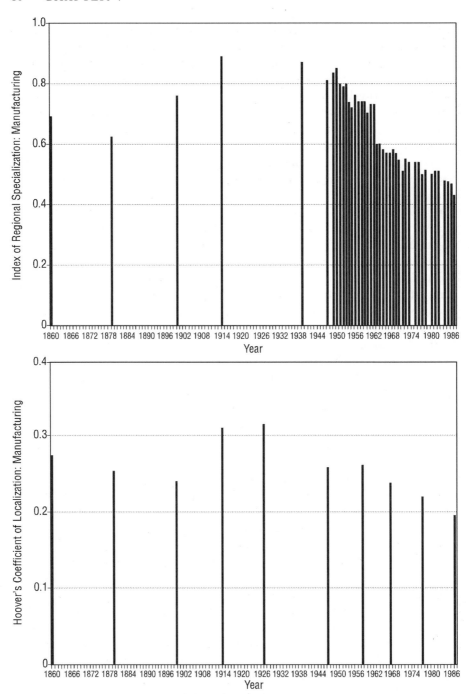

Figure 4.12.   Regional specialization in manufactures, 1860–1987 (top); and the locational concentration of manufactures, 1860–1987 (bottom).

Sources: Kim 1995, 1998.

1989; Sabel 1994). The miniaturization of big business and big technology is well under way what with "lean manufacturing," flexible specialization, and the reductions in inventories and turnover time via "just-in-time delivery" (Sabel 1994). And cheap labor is once again a main theme, particularly in the southern "right-to-work" states, in the profusion of rural and small-town manufacturing plants, and in newly industrialized countries and less developed countries abroad. These changes are especially noteworthy on "Main Street," where the American small town is being "transformed from a central place serving an agricultural hinterland [consumers] into a minor cog in the nationwide [and global] network of manufacturing centers" (Hart 1988: 272). These preoccupations with the production system, with the geography of commodities, productivity, factors of production, factor costs, factor efficiency, and scale economies, are precisely what one would expect of liberal elites and elite regimes. They are likewise what one would suspect as the liberal causes of increasingly specialized regional economies in dynamic equilibrium.

The geographical story becomes somewhat more complicated after 1789, however, owing to the pragmatic fusion of liberal elitism and republican nationalist/protectionism. By and large, capitalist elites with their "production bias" have welcomed the gifts of protectionism, and most notably its generous present of preferential access to a growing national market, and they have accepted its corollary of spatial concentration as reinforcing elite (liberal) commitments to regional specialization. The virtues of this elite-protectionist alliance are cast in doubt, however, by recent events. As the American economy in the 1990s ratcheted upward to continental and global scales, the world marketplace envisioned by capitalist elites seem to have drifted ever further from the nationalist aims of nationalist protectionists. In this increasingly transnational world,

> the conventional distinctions between [what is] internal and external [to the State] . . . are exceedingly problematic, and any given state is but one constraint in corporate strategic calculations. This is the world in which Brothers Industries, a Japanese concern assembling typewriters in Bartlett, Tennessee, brings an antidumping case before the U.S. International Trade Commission against Smith Corona, an American firm that imports typewriters into the United States from its offshore facilities in Singapore and Indonesia. . . . [It] is a world, in short, that is premised on what Lattimore described as the "sovereign importance of movement," not of place. (Ruggie 1993: 172–73)

But it would be a mistake to assume that this latest of production systems is uncontested or, even, that it will triumph. What can be said is that the strains of these changes in the global economy promise a stiff test of America's ambivalent ideologies, not to mention of the allegiances of American elites to nationalism or the market. The issues are large indeed (Agnew and Corbridge 1995). Will American nationalists concede victory to the global market (i.e., to free trade)? Or will they counterattack with relentless assertions of extraterritorial jurisdiction over this "extraterritorial transnational world?" Or yet again, will they trump the autonomy of global capitalism and "the sovereignty of movement" by encroaching on the domains of globalization—that is, by ratcheting American power (and sovereignty) upward from the state to the continental trading bloc? The answer, of course, will go a long way in defining the geographical futures of the American Way and the world order that is emerging.

For egalitarian regimes, economic crises are invariably consumption crises, and their resolution just as invariably involves a "consumer revolution." In these cases, the policies of an egalitarian or mass regime are directed toward the masses of the American population and, in the economic sphere, toward consumers rather than producers. Economic crises are defined as problems of consumption, as failures in aggregate demand, and as opportunities for stimulating demand by broadening and increasing the base of purchasing power. Perhaps the best-known, and certainly the most formal, illustration of demand management is New Deal liberalism's application of Keynesian economics from the late 1930s through the 1970s. Consumer demand was propped up by a host of direct and indirect government expenditures—for the defense industry, highway construction, airports, the college education of returning soldiers, and subsidized home mortgages that stimulated the housing construction industry (Lebergott 1993, 1996; Patterson 1996: 3–81, 137–64, 243–75, 311–74, 524–92; Brinkley 1995). Some have gone so far as to speak of these prosaic changes as heralding the advent of an age of "high-mass consumption," of an age in which consumers rather than producers provided the leading sector in the growth of American capitalism.

Be that as it may, it seems safe to say that the demand for consumer durables shifted upward after World War I. Fueled by consumer credit (installment buying), sharp reductions in excise taxes, the electrification of home appliances, and the Model T Ford, consumers in the 1920s increased their purchases of a host of consumer durables at rates in excess of increases in their incomes (Olney 1987, 1990; Calder 1999; Vatter 1967; Rostow 1960). But this rise in income elasticity that was cause for such happiness and prosperity in the 1920s turned sour with the onset of the vast deflation in incomes during the 1930s. Consumer demand once again outpaced income changes, but this time in the wrong direction. Rescuing the burgeoning industries in consumer durables, not least the makers of automobiles and electrical appliances, required fresh policies. In place of stale arguments for tariff protection and shopworn appeals for industrial efficiency, New Deal "liberalism" turned (as egalitarian regimes generally and eventually do) to consumer-oriented policies— policies that would simultaneously broaden the base of consumers and deepen their incomes. Keynesian policies of "full employment" and demand management through fiscal and monetary policy were well suited to the task (particularly after World War II). So, too, were the spatial theories of retailing with their emphasis on the provisioning of consumer goods and services in central-place urban systems.

Geographers may be less familiar with the earlier incarnations of the consumer revolution that arose in conjunction with egalitarian regimes in the middles of the eighteenth and nineteenth centuries. The first of these was part of the "transatlantic revolution in consumer tastes" that unfolded between 1730 and 1780 (Main and Main 1988: 44; Breen 1986, 1988). With the blessings of a booming economy, rising incomes per capita between 1745 and 1760, a flood of credit, and improved terms of trade (aided by falling or stable prices for imported goods, especially semidurables such as earthenware and coarser cloths), Americans in all regions and ranks embarked on a binge of consumption (Egnal 1975; Price 1980). Beginning in the 1740s, imports per capita rose sharply and the property listings ("inventories") of deceased colonials recorded the rising appeal of tea, earthenware, forks, finer furniture, imported cloths, wigs, wine, beer, books, and assorted consumables. In the households of southern New England recorded (as elsewhere), the variety of amenities present doubled between 1675–1699 and 1745–1759 (Main and Main 1988). And in the average household on the eve of the Revolution, coarse earthenware, imported foods, linenware, and religious books were a commonplace. Richer households added forks, fine earthenware, and finer furnishings. Moreover, the "good life," previously available only to the richest of colonials, spread among the middling and lower sorts. It is not coincidental, I suspect, that the democratization of consumption was also accompanied by democratizations of religious and political life. Just as English and continental goods were entering into most American households, we see that the Arminian and postmillennialist preachers of the Great Awakening were easing the way into God's kingdom and colonial legislatures were relaxing their restrictions on suffrage. In what might seem an odd concatenation, Americans had more goods, more faith, and somewhat more power in the approaching sunset of Britain's American empire.

The last of our "consumer revolutions" is positioned squarely in between the consumerist vision of twentieth-century Keynesianism and the eighteenth century's "empire of goods." In what has been called the "middle period," American expenditures on consumer durables rose from 2 percent of the total flow of goods to consumers in 1834–1843 to 4 percent in 1844–1853, to 8 percent in 1869–1878, to 11 percent in 1884–1893. "Thus in the space of twenty-five years in the nineteenth century [1844–1853 to 1869–1878] we find the best candidate for a consumer equipment revolution. It seems remarkable, by way of contrast, that the proportion achieved over three-quarters of a century has scarcely changed since" (Vatter 1967: 9). These expenditures are less abstract when translated into the nineteenth-century newspaper advertisements that some years back adorned the laminated tables of Wendy's Restaurants (themselves the product of another "consumer age"). Yet these advertisements only hint at the ways in which farm and plantation life was altered by the addition of consumer durables. Americans used machines to do what had previously been done by hand. Rural and urban homes added potbelly stoves, cooking ranges, oil lamps, spring alarm clocks, food grinders, reed organs and melodeons, treadle sewing machines, iron clothes pressers, egg beaters, ice boxes, washing machines, wash ringers, lawn mowers, and buggy wagons, to mention only the more prominent of these additions (Brady 1964: 175–88). All this consumption—what Vatter has called "the mechanization of the household"—resulted in a sevenfold increase in the stock of consumer durables between 1850 and 1880—"a rate much exceeding the rate for total reproducible tangible wealth and for nonfarm residences, and possibly exceeding that for producer durables" (Vatter 1967: 9–10). This rapid expansion in expenditures on consumer durables presumes certain inexorables—an increasingly elaborate marketing system of retailers linked in a hierarchy of central places, markets enlarged in geographical scope, longer lines of credit, and the capital that made them possible—which, as we shall soon see, were there in abundance.

Note

1. In his analysis of regional inequalities in per capita incomes in the United States between 1840 and 1960, Williamson (1965: 36–39) shows that the effects of population redistribution are trivial save for the period 1880–1920 (i.e., the Second Republic), when they are very large. In these years, regional income inequality per capita is high and relatively unchanging. In other words, the impacts of population redistribution on the latter are greatest during the course of a spatial regime characterized by demographic concentration in the core of the American manufacturing belt and a remarkable stability in aggregate regional incomes.

CHAPTER 5

Regulatory Regimes and the Geographies of Producer and Consumer Revolutions

It is tempting to regard these six revolutions as a complementary process, an equilibrating alternation between egalitarian regimes of consumption and elite regimes of production. One regime (elite) channels investments into the production system and expands industrial capacity to the point of overaccumulation (or, more precisely, underconsumption); the ensuing regime (egalitarian) channels investments into the distribution of consumer goods and expands (and at times alters) aggregate demand to the point of underaccumulation (i.e., overconsumption). The deficiencies of the former are thus compensated by the strengths of the latter in an ongoing iteration. It follows that these two sorts of regimes will accent quite different strategies. In the regimes of production, elite capitalists "try to increase the rate of surplus value (improve labor productivity in several ways; intensify labor effort), reduce constant capital (materials saving), [and] reduce the turnover time of capital (eliminate idle time of labor, materials, machines, and finished products)." In consumption regimes, by contrast, firms attempt to "improve realization (better distribution, tighter links to consumers, better product performance) and open up new areas of value production and realization (offer up new commodities)" (Walker 1995: 174–75).

Three Producer Revolutions

These divergent economic strategies had their spatial counterparts in equally divergent geographies of production and consumption. In the case of production regimes, these geographies are most clearly enunciated in the writings of contemporary theorists, observers who sought to mould as well as describe the trajectory of an emerging spatial economy. This was the intent of Alexander Hamilton's model of American industrialization (Cooke 1975; Banning 1995; Earle 1992: 212–25) and of Johann von Thunen's (1930, first presented in the early nineteenth century) theory of agricultural land use within market economies. Each in his own way took the measure of the production regime that was emerging in America and in Europe during the Napoleonic era. Hamilton's normative model challenged the prevailing orthodoxies in European political economy; he demonstrated that manufacturing was possible in the United States and that some American regions—those endowed with an abundance of cheap labor (Earle 1980; Goldin and Sokoloff 1982)—*could,* with the regulatory assistance of protective tariffs, subsidies, and bounties, *industrialize* their economies and thereby reduce American dependence on European markets. Industrial specialization in these regions (most notably in New England and the Middle States), he implied, would complement the production of agricultural staple commodities in the rest of the nation (especially the South) and thus foster American economic growth through regional interdependence. In ways that were typical of the leading American thinkers of his time, Hamilton fused empirical realities and liberal and republican ideologies into a set of guiding principles—in this case, into a theory of interdependent economic growth and regional development based on modest regulatory intervention in lagging economic regions and nonintervention in regions that were doing well enough on their own. On the heels of Hamilton's macroregional theory of industrial development, the German farmer-economist Thunen provided a theoretical guide to spatial processes within capitalist agricultural regions. Beginning with certain givens—a region of rational farmers, the presence of a central market (town or city), commodity prices, and commodity production and transport costs—Thunen calculated the variable rates of return on the region's several commodities and arrayed them into a series of specialized concentric zones around the market. There is in Thunen's theory and in Hamilton's as well a larger point: Regional economies in the early nineteenth century were becoming ever more specialized—which is precisely what one would expect of elite production regimes.

With the exception of David Ricardo's formulation of the notion of comparative advantage—itself a generalization deeply indebted to the insights of Hamilton and Thunen—the geographic theory of production made little headway during the rest of the nineteenth century. It would not be called upon again until the turn of the twentieth century when the need for a theory describing the locations of large industrial firms became obvious. In this case, American geographers and land economists found Alfred Weber's model of industrial location particularly well suited to the American scene (1969; the original German version was published in the first decade of the twentieth century). Weber's mechanical model of prices and costs enabled analysts to predict whether an industrial establishment would be located near the resource, near the market, or indifferently to both (i.e., footloose). In practice, plugging in real prices and costs into the model underscored one central empirical fact: the increasing superiority of market locations as a consequence of continuing reductions in the costs of transporting raw materials over long distances. Weber's theory thus provided American scholars with a ready-made explanation of the spatial concentration of industry near the northeastern market, in what came to be known after 1915 as the "American Manufacturing Belt" (DeGeer 1927; Meyer 1983). And just as Hamilton's infant industries had grown up in "industrial suburbs" outside the city, the vastly larger firms of the late nineteenth and early twentieth centuries mushroomed in the "rural-urban fringes" in the manufacturing belt (Earle 1993; Gordon 1984; C. Harris 1943; R. Harris 1988). Industries "decentralized," moving further and further into the "suburbs" where land and labor were almost always cheaper and labor was rarely organized by unions or the Knights of Labor.

While it is customary to treat the rise of the American manufacturing belt and urban decentralization as the natural outcomes of Weberian locational economics, a closer inspection of the record indicates that the crucial variables were exogenous to the economic model. The variables that explained the tendency of American firms to locate near the market—the integration of the national rail system, the ensuing decline in freight rates, the rapid rise in freight volume ("throughput")—were the subject of contentious debates and conflicting visions in the late nineteenth century (most notably the Populist critique; Goodwyn 1976; also see Berk 1994; Freyer 1979; and Horwitz 1992). Americans argued passionately over every aspect of transport regulation, from the levels of freight rates to the need for a standard railway gauge, from carload configurations to the apportionment of public and private rights and responsibilities of common carriers. These issues were joined in the political arena, and they were resolved by a tendentious process of "constitutive politics." In this arena "was generated a rate structure that systematically favored the long haul over the short, carload over less-than-carload freight, and the large-scale centralized national market over the moderately sized decentralized regional market. It was in this sense that national system builders were compelled to act upon the exogenous constraint—market structure" (Berk 1994: 17). Had these regulatory results been precisely the reverse, Weberian location theory would have produced a radically different and vastly more decentralized geography. The rise of large-scale, mass-producing, and vertically organized industrial corporations might also have been derailed had it not been for the judicial rescue of an integrated national rail system.

> Having overbuilt and overcapitalized, many huge systems collapsed in the 1880s and 1890s and fell into receivership. . . . Under prevailing norms of corporate doctrine, which granted priority to property (debt) holders, the architects of national railroads would have been divested of authority and their systems threatened by dismemberment into regional parts. . . . However, many on the federal bench were convinced that only incumbent managers were capable of reorganizing these systems. The law, they concluded, would have to adapt, even if this meant stripping debt holders of their traditional property rights in insolvent corporations. . . . The result of the transformation in receivership practice . . . was to institutionalize national systems, the legal doctrine that the corporation was a natural entity, and to reduce the fixed costs of railroad technology on average by one-third. (Berk 1994: 16)

Here, then, are the echoes of Hamiltonian nationalism with its resounding endorsement of regulatory interventions on behalf of capitalist elites, spatial concentration, and regional specialization.

The last chapter in the geography of production regimes is, of course, now in draft form, albeit in the multiple versions of regulation theory, flexible specialization, lean production, and neo-Marxist theories of industrial location (Walker 1995; Harrison 1994; Brenner and Glick 1991; Sabel 1994; Amin 1994). These theories attempt to explain the rise of one mode of production—"post-Fordism," with its leaner corporations, networked firms, flexible methods of small-batch production, and increased reliance on producer-service firms—and the fall of another—"Fordism," with its large corporations, vast throughputs and standardized products, elaborate bureaucratic hierarchies, and vertically integrated production processes. What strikes me as ironic about these theories is that they largely ignore Weberian location theory, dismissing it as something of a Fordist anachronism, precisely when Weber's emphasis on production costs enjoys such a harmonious convergence with the Reagan administration's emphasis on cutting the costs of production—that is, on supply-side economics, economic liberalization, and deregulation. My point is that Weber's model is more relevant now than ever for two reasons: first, because the locational costs of production have shifted dramatically since the 1970s, thanks in no small measure to the policies of this new regime; second, because rational manufacturers have relocated or reorganized their firms in accordance with these new cost geographies (i.e., consonant with Weber's least-cost locational theory) (Harrington and Warf 1995). If Weber's model has a shortcoming in the era of post-Fordism, it is its failure to account for the locations of the new producer-services industries—but then Weber's model, restricted as it was to locations within the secondary sector (manufacturing) of the economy, was never intended to explain the geographies of tertiary and quaternary services.

This reconfiguration of industrial costs, not to mention the concurrent dismantling of the fordist economy, may be traced back to the 1970s and the triple problems of lagging productivity, hyperinflation, and mounting trade deficits in the American economy (for a range of views, see Harvey 1990: 121–97; Bernstein and Adler 1994; Spulber 1995). This volatile compound of stagflation and the fierce competition from foreign imports that followed the abandonment of the gold standard, the switch to flexible exchange rates in 1971, and the ensuing rise in the value of the dollar persisted into the early 1980s. At that juncture, the Reagan administration and the Congress enacted a series of supply-side measures (e.g., various tax cuts and credits, large defense expenditures) aimed at increasing American productivity. In addition to the reduction of corporate tax rates, "business was aided by legislation [in 1981] designed to accelerate the rapid depreciation allowances and investment tax credits were also included in the package that was drafted after much consultation with business lobbyists. All in all, a unified corporate America received a handsome·reward, amounting to $150 billion tax cut over a five-year period" (Berman 1994: 93–94). Business also earned a dividend from Reagan's antiunionism in the form of reductions in strikes, the level of collective bargaining settlements, and labor costs more generally. "This is illustrated by the substantial increase in . . . an index of unfair labor practices which jumped from 95.9 between 1960 and 1968 to 162.9 in 1969–77 to 285.2 between 1983 and 1988. A similar index of employer-sponsored union decertification petitions grew from 158.2 in 1969–77 to 358.0 in 1983–88" (Osterman 1999: 64–65).

These supply-side measures had little effect, however, on reducing double-digit price inflation. Toward that end and with the blessing of the Reagan administration, the Federal Reserve Board implemented a stringent tight-money policy. Although the short-term costs of this "cold bath" were high—not the least of which was the sharp recession of 1981–1982—FED policy, with an assist from the collapse of the

OPEC oil cartel, managed to cut inflation from over 10 percent per year in 1980 to less than 5 percent by 1986 (Niskanen 1988; figure 5.1). As the economy continued to show improvement, the Reagan and Bush administrations could claim, with some justification, that their defense expenditures had created new jobs; their tax cuts had stimulated new investment; their liberalization of the economy had undermined entrenched union power and reduced labor costs (e.g., real hourly wages in manufacturing fell by 15 percent between 1978 and 1990); their deregulation of rail, trucking, and air transport had lowered transport costs (and increased long hauls); and, with somewhat less justification, that their efforts had largely stemmed the decline in American productivity (Berman 1994; Weidenbaum 1988; Madrick 1995; Spulber 1995). The Reagan administration was less eager to claim credit for the rising deficits in trade and on the national account that, by the mid-1980s, seemed to have spiraled out of control. The irony in this case is that improvements in the domestic economy drove up the value of the dollar (as did tight monetary policy), opened the gates for a flood of increasingly cheaper foreign imports, and curtailed the flow of increasingly expensive American exports. With the trade deficit hovering in the range of $150 billion per year, the Reagan administration set aside its laissez-faire principles and in 1986 negotiated the first in a series of coordinated exchange-rate agreements (figure 5.2; Funbashi 1988; Destler and Henning 1989; Klein, Mizrach, and Murphy 1991; for a more skeptical view, Bordo and Schwartz 1991). The Plaza Agreement and subsequent accords had several salutary effects. First, they sharply lowered the value of the dollar; second, they helped to reduce the U.S. trade deficit from $150 billion in 1987 to about $30 billion in 1991—while helping to save the American automobile industry along the way; and third, they stimulated a

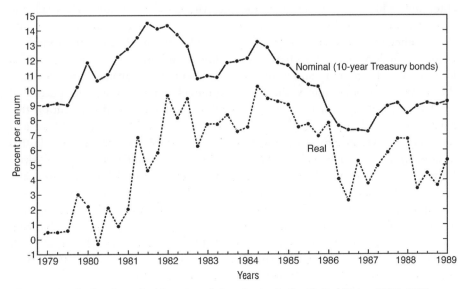

Figure 5.1.   Real and nominal long-term interest rates in the United States, 1979–1989.

Sources: International Financial Statistics, various issues; *Survey of Current Business*, various issues.

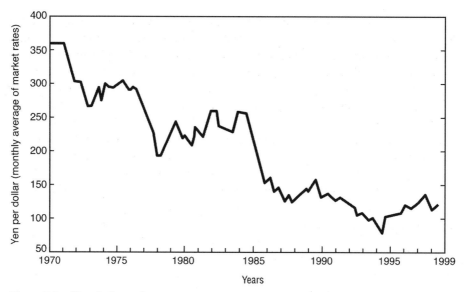

Figure 5.2.   Yen–dollar exchange rate, 1970–1999.

Source: Financial Statistics, various issues.

large volume of foreign investment in the American economy. By 1990, the forces of stagflation and trade deficits had been contained, if not vanquished (Spulber 1995).

It can be said that the Reagan administration revised the course of American history, that it dismantled many of the structures erected by the New Deal and its legatees and laid the foundations for a new policy regime—one that favors business elites and political devolution at home and nationalist-protectionism abroad (the enduring rhetoric of "free trade" notwithstanding). America's "turn to the right" also breathed life into a series of strikingly new industrial geographies, but from these it does not follow that geographers now require an entirely new theory of industrial location. On the contrary and insofar as "liberalization" has managed to turn back the clock of economic history, the Weberian model merely requires an updating of the locational changes in the costs of assembly, production, and distribution that have been wrought by Reagan's "revolution." Indeed, Weber's theory of least-cost sites helps to explain two of the most significant post-Fordist changes in industrial location (Fisher and Mitchelson 1981): (1) the migration of labor-intensive firms from locations near the market toward regions with lower-cost labor (Weinstein and Firestine 1978) and (2) the in situ dismantling of the large, fully integrated corporation in favor of a network of independent firms manufacturing various intermediate goods and subordinated to an "end producer" via subcontracts, competitive bidding, quality control, small-batch production, and fast turnarounds—what I will call "cost shifting" (or, less felicitously, "externalization"; see Harrison 1994; Sabel 1994; Beyers 1996; Beyers and Lindahl 1996; Goe 1991; Osterman 1999).

Consider the cheap-labor migrations of labor-intensive firms to the South and the rural United States. In Weber's day, most of these industries gravitated toward northeastern markets because they provided the least-cost locations for assembling bulky raw materials via the national rail system, accessing cheap labor in industrial suburbs, and distributing the final product to consumers. As the century wore on, the variables in this equation began to change (Noponen, Graham, and Markusen 1993; Storper and Walker 1989; Smith 1988). By the 1960s, labor costs (including benefits) in the northeastern states had shot upward owing to unionization, collective bargaining, strike actions, and a sympathetic National Labor Relations Board (NLRB). What began as a trickle of firms away from the high costs of the northeastern market in the 1960s had become a torrent by the early 1980s. Firms that were able to amortize their plants with the inflated dollars of the 1970s and to accelerate plant depreciation in the 1980s fled from the manufacturing belt, abandoning the region's entrenched unions and high wages and relocating their plants (aided by the subvention of investment tax credits) in the friendlier venues of "right-to-work" states and nonunionized rural areas. These locational shifts were reinforced by the deregulation of rail, truck, and air transport as well as by improvements in production efficiency, the first by lowering freight rates from once-inaccessible rural areas, the second by reducing the quantity of raw materials consumed per unit thereby lowering the transport costs for assembly and distribution. (For the trends toward dematerialization and decarbonization, see figure 5.3; Kates 1995.) In other words, market-oriented locations no longer constituted the optimal sites for labor-intensive industries; inflation, changes in the tax laws, deregulation, and investments in more efficient technologies had shifted the advantage toward regions of cheaper labor. The rural United States, the South, and (because of the high dollar) the newly industrializing countries (NICs) overseas thus emerged as the least-cost sites for labor-intensive firms and, as their pools of skilled labor have deepened, for capital- and knowledge-intensive firms as well (Fisher and Mitchelson 1981).

While Reagan's critics on the left decried the inequalities that his policies of "liberalization" had spawned, not a few on the right lamented that the president had stopped far short of conservative goals. In their view, "the president was a consensus politician, not an ideologue . . . [who] lacked the requisite commitment and passion to undertake the long-term struggle to dismantle the welfare state" (Berman 1994: 97). But if Reagan failed to eliminate many federal intrusions on business activity— everything from the capital gains tax to Occupational Safety and Health Administration and the Environmental Protection Agency, Social Security to workmen's compensation, unions to the NLRB—his administration surely managed to subvert every one of them (save for Social Security) and to provide a freewheeling context for entrepreneurs who would take up the slack. If Reagan could not eliminate these costs, business could by taking a page out of Reagan's text on supply-side economics. And it was the biggest of businesses, the vast corporations that had flourished in a Fordist economy by locating in proximity to the market, that were in the front ranks of the private sector's assault on costs. Finding themselves unable to abandon their extensive inventory of facilities in the northeastern United States, even with accelerated depreciation schedules and investment credits, these firms discovered a way of shifting the burdens of federal and union intrusion onto the shoulders of independent subcontractors (Sabel 1994; Harrison 1994). Drawing on a model long familiar in

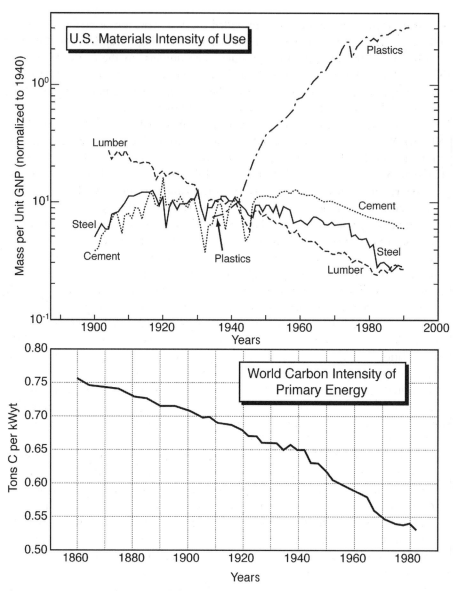

Figure 5.3.   Dematerialization and decarbonization in the United States and the world.
Source: Kates 1995.

the petrochemical industry along the Gulf Coast, large firms "outsourced" increasingly large portions of their in-house production of intermediate goods and services to external contractors and then pitted them against one another in a fierce process of competitive bidding. The result was a new mode of networked production in which the "host" firm established the specifications for "deliverables" and the independent contractors provided these intermediate goods *and* assumed the responsibility for the associated labor costs—for wages, payroll taxes, insurance, Social Security contributions, pensions, health care, leave, and labor negotiations and litigation. This is a mode of production tailor-made for the United States and advanced economies more generally for the simple reason that the host's benefits from shifting the mounting costs of wages, pensions, health care, and associated labor costs in quasi-welfare states far exceed the benefits that accrue from direct control over employees.

The reciprocal of the cost-shifting strategy of host firms was, of course, the breakup of the vertically integrated corporation (Harrison 1994; Sabel 1994; Gowing, Kraft, and Quick 1998). In this process of functional reorganization, bloated bureaucracies were trimmed down; entire units were eliminated as Fordist firms "downsized;" and now-redundant employees were terminated through reductions in force (RIFs). These savings were reallocated, as host firms bulked up their investments in units responsible for "network relations" (e.g., monitoring subcontractors, quality control on intermediate products, competitive bidding processes, the logistics of inventory control, and just-in-time delivery systems).

Networking is one of the most prominent and the most painful features of industrial restructuring within advanced economies during a post-Fordist age. These new systems of production have abolished familiar jobs and entire careers; shifted production costs from big firms that could afford them to smaller subcontractors that usually could not; cracked the whip of competitive bidding so as to ensure evergreater economies from subcontractors; and, more generally, driven down industrial wages and benefits. It is for these reasons that many on the left regard networked production as just another example of the ruthlessness of capitalist economies, but condemning this system sheds little light on the infinite variety of experiments in industrial organization now underway. Beyond the bare minimum on which networking depends—on careful monitoring, attention to quality control, and competitive bidding at fairly frequent intervals—this new mode of production has afforded ample opportunity for novelty and innovation in industrial relations (Ettlinger and Patton 1996). In some networked systems, subcontractors receive thorough training in the host firm's methods, are accorded considerable autonomy in the conception as well as the execution of products, and are ensured of steady work if standards are met. At its best, this "textbook" case of the new industrial relations (flexible specialization) encourages cooperation, fosters trust, and facilitates interactive learning. In other systems, the host firm is more narrowly interested in reaping the benefits of cost-shifting. Subcontractors receive little training, are given little autonomy, are expected to produce to "spec," and are vulnerable to stringent and frequent competitive bidding. Networking in this case "is surely more a matter of perfecting the mass-production system than of abandoning it" (Sabel 1994: 123, also 101–56; see as well Teece 1992; Ettlinger and Patton 1996).

These examples represent the extremes in a continuum of networked production systems. While it is too early to say which of these models will have the greatest impact on American manufacturing in the long run, what does seem clear is that the host will choose a mode of industrial organization that is attuned to the host's market. By and large, host firms will prefer more flexible networks when their consumers insist on frequent changes in and smaller quantities of more specialized products;

they will prefer less flexible Fordist-like networks when their consumers expect reliable deliveries of larger quantities of mass-produced products. All of which points toward several larger conclusions: (1) Networked production is first and foremost a strategy of cost shifting; (2) mass and small-batch production are variants of this grand strategy; and (3) networking arises out of supply-side considerations (cost shifting), while its several variants arise in response to consumer preferences (for standardized or highly variable commodities).

If supply-side strategies occupy center stage in the post-Fordist transition, shifts on the demand side have played an important supporting role. The consensus is that consumer preferences began to change in the 1970s and 1980s when the demand for more specialized products began to outpace the demand for standardized mass-produced commodities. As their markets fragmented, firms were compelled to pare back their divisions of labor and to adopt flexible methods that were better suited to small-batch production. The puzzle, of course, is figuring out why consumers changed. Harvey (1990: 77–82) attributes these changes first to the liberating effects of the 1960s and second to the vain search for status (consumption as symbolic capital) in the ensuing decades. The difficulty with this thesis of conspicuous consumption is that the stagflation-ridden 1970s were not especially generous times for consumers, liberated or otherwise. Just as manufacturers in the 1970s were attempting to cut their costs by cost shifting or relocation, consumers were making valiant efforts to cut household costs and to balance the family budget. Consumers who suffered through the stagflation in this decade will recall that most consumers sought out bargains not status, deep discounts at "killer stores" not pricey goods at upscale shops. It was in this decade, when the prices for gas, coffee, and bread more than tripled, that the cherished notion of "brand loyalty" was shaken to the core. Consumers struggling to make ends meet were more willing to try "inferior brands" and, when (as often happened) they were pleasantly surprised by the quality, to switch brands. The impact of "bargain shoppers" did not pass unnoticed; indeed, their role was officially acknowledged in the early 1980s when the U.S. Bureau of Labor Statistics authorized two comprehensive surveys of consumer behavior and then approved substantial revisions (mostly downward) in its cost-of-living index (Madrick 1997).

Consumers had learned to be more discriminating shoppers during the 1970s, and they put these lessons into practice with the return of prosperity in the 1980s. The new consumer tended to be more receptive to new products and new brands and more inclined to insist on value for price. In this more volatile and more fickle market, manufacturers sought to rebuild brand loyalty with a shotgun approach. They trusted that by peppering the market with a variety of new products in a variety of styles that some of them would win market share. All of this is shaking down in the 1990s as winners are emerging and losers are fading from the scene. Some older brand loyalties have been renewed while newer ones are being forged. In some cases, most notably in the computer software industry, production units are being reintegrated into the host firm. These changes notwithstanding, the pressures on manufacturers to further cut costs persists—not least because the American consumer's assault on costs has been as ruthless and as tough-minded as the assaults that producers have thus far managed to mount.

But what of geography amid all of the high theory of post-Fordism? Students of networked production have generally assumed (wrongly, I think) that this new mode of production requires an equally new theory of industrial location. In making their case, they point to the rise of a new geographical phenomenon, the industrial district with its specialized clustering of networked firms. But these districts, however novel, are hardly evidence against Weber's thesis that manufacturing firms, be they independents, hosts, or subcontractors, will seek least-cost locations for their production facilities. Indeed, networking and competitive bidding make it all the more likely that subcontractors will behave rationally; that having assumed responsibility for the costs of labor and most of the costs of plant and equipment, they will choose the most efficient locations (i.e., locations that minimize the total costs of the products delivered to a given host plant). Some of these subcontractors will locate at some distance from the host firm in order to take advantage of lower labor costs in the production of standardized components such as auto headlamps. Others will locate in the industrial district surrounding the host firm in order to facilitate interactions (and lower transaction costs) with the host in the course of producing customized components subject to swift changes in consumer tastes and preferences (Teece 1992). In both of these cases, firms adhere quite closely to the rules of Weberian location theory.

But it is also possible for firms today as in the past to contravene Weber's rules. Consider first the case of the host firm which, in the interest of promoting face-to-face interaction and synergistic gains in productivity, accepts the higher bid of a subcontractor located within the host's industrial district. In this case, the host firm opts for the promise of higher output in the future, whereas Weber's model opts for the hard reality of lower costs in the present. Weber's rules are similarly contravened by governmental subventions that lower the production costs of particular firms or of regional districts. Note, however, that these exceptions to Weber's rules are venerable ones, applying as much to the firms of a Fordist age as to those in an era of post-Fordist production.

Much of the mystery surrounding the geography of post-Fordist production disappears when industrial restructuring is conceptualized as a series of cost-shifting policies and strategies within high-wage advanced economies. Taking advantage of the stagflation crisis of the 1970s and Reagan's probusiness policies of the 1980s, some manufacturers shifted their cost structures. They abandoned market-oriented high-wage sites in the northeastern United States and relocated their facilities in regions with cheaper labor and lesser union activism (for the state variations in the changes in manufacturing employment, see figure 5.4). Others, unable to abandon market locations, cut their costs in situ by shifting component production onto a network of independent subcontractors and using competitive bidding among these subcontractors as a means of driving down the price of component parts and downsizing the host firm. In the shuffle, workers' wages and benefits eroded, large firms downsized, small firms grew more numerous, labor-intensive firms gravitated away

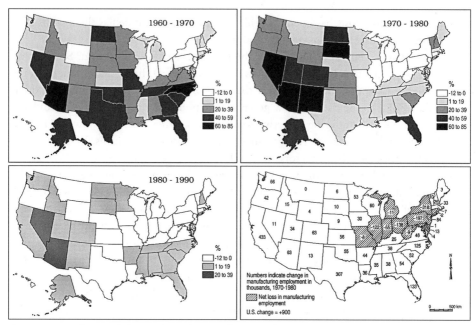

Figure 5.4. Changes in manufacturing employment by state: Relative changes, 1960–1970, 1970–1980, and 1980–1990; absolute changes, 1970–1980.

Source: U.S. Bureau of the Census 1960, 1970, 1980, and 1990.

from the market, and host firms and small-batch subcontractors formed production networks within market-oriented industrial districts.

Weberian location theory goes a long way in explaining the centrifugal and centripetal geographies of post-Fordist manufacturing. The outward trend, on behalf of cheaper supplies of labor, has enlarged the American manufacturing belt by extending it into the countryside and the Sunbelt, especially the southeastern United States; the inward trend, on behalf of cost-shifting economies, has concentrated networked producers within industrial districts. Both of these geographies have arisen, however, out of a common goal—a Weberian commitment to least-cost production.

What is not explicable by Weber's theory, however, is the steady decline in American manufacturing employment since the 1970s and the concurrent rise of employment in the producer-services sector. Manufacturing has taken a severe beating. Between 1974 and 1991, when total employment in the United States rose by 36.7 percent, employment in manufacturing fell by 8.2 percent—over 1.5 million jobs—and its share of total employment fell from 24.7 percent to 16.5 percent (Beyers 1996: 41). Every region save the Mountain West lost manufacturing jobs between 1979 and 1992, with the worst losses in the Northeast and the Midwest (Howes and Markusen 1993: 9).

These figures are, by turns, malignant or benign depending on one's view of manufacturing's role in economic growth. They are frightening symptoms of America's decline for those who regard manufacturing as the crucial sector in the American economy; the numbers are less worrisome for those who see them as something of a statistical artifact, a figment of the processes of industrial restructuring, cost shifting, and networked production. For the latter, manufacturing jobs have not so much been lost as rearranged and reclassified. As manufacturing firms have shed their functions to subcontractors, jobs once listed under "manufacturing" have been reclassified as "business or producer services." Manufacturing jobs in accounting, billing, real estate, finance, legal services, engineering, management, maintenance, and communication services have been outsourced and reclassified, and these changes have contributed to the spectacular growth of the producer-services industry—reaching upward of 17,350,000 workers in 1991, or roughly 15 percent of U.S. total employment. Employment in this sector grew by 115 percent between 1974 and 1991—three times the national rate; accounted for one-sixth of nonfarming earnings in the late 1980s; and generated exports nearly equal in value to agriculture during that decade (Drennan 1992). If as few as 10 percent of these producer-service jobs are credited to manufacturing (probably the most conservative of estimates based as it is on interview data from the rural Midwest; see Beyers 1996: 52), then manufacturing employment would have held steady (at about twenty million) between 1974 and 1991 instead of declining by 8.2 percent. At the opposite extreme, if we credit all producer-services employment (directly and indirectly) to manufacturing, then their combined employment rises from 28 million in 1974 to 35.8 million in 1991 while their share of total U.S. employment falls only slightly (from 34 to 32 percent).

In these trends there is good news and bad news. The good news is that rumors of America's industrial decline are greatly exaggerated; the bad news is that the good news on producer services presents serious problems for Weberian locational theory. The main problem has to do with the distinctive properties of the producer-services industry—with services that are frequently performed by a highly educated workforce, with products that are typically high in value and low in bulk, and with deliverables that are oftentimes transmitted by electronic media. Firms with these properties may locate their facilities almost anywhere. Weber understood as well as most the difficulties of predicting the locations of these sorts of firms, which is perhaps why he set them apart. He defined this class of firms as "footloose" in their locational orientation, which, of course, is a handy euphemism in cases when we have no theory at all. But then in Weber's day, the footloose firm was hardly a problem since there were so few of them. Conversely, in today's superefficient space economy for producer services, the number of footloose firms increases daily and renders the conventional determinants of location increasingly irrelevant.

What is required in these circumstances is a new locational theory of producer services firmly grounded, as were those of Hamilton, Thunen, and Weber, in practical experience. Some headway has already been made. The empirical evidence on the location of producer services suggests that employment is most concentrated in the largest metropolitan centers (65.5 percent in 1986; see figure 5.5 for the spatial concentration of producer-services workers among large metropolitan areas), that concentration diminishes as one moves down the urban hierarchy, that these services are filtering down the urban hierarchy to smaller cities and nonmetropolitan areas, and that the rates of growth in the latter areas exceed those in the larger metropolitan

Figure 5.5. Location quotients of employment in business and professional services in metropolitan areas of one million or more persons.

Source: Ò hUallachàin and Reid 1991.

centers. This evidence implies two conclusions: first, a remarkably high degree of spatial continuity between Fordist and post-Fordist geographies; second, the enduring relevance of central-place theory—a theory devised, however, for firms that provision consumers rather than producers (Beyers 1996; Ó hUallahàin and Reid 1991).

A very different moral emerges from the pathbreaking, if often overlooked, analyses undertaken by Niles Hansen (1990, 1994). His is more nearly a story of regional variability and spatial fluidity than of continuity in the location of producer services. Hansen explores the regional differences in the association between metropolitan area incomes (in 1983), their densities of producer services and higher education, and the sizes of their population. His tricornered model of metropolitan income (the dependent variable) works best in the Pacific and Northeastern regions (all three coefficients are significant and the models are robust); moderately well in New England, Texas, and the North Central regions (two coefficients significant, models robust); and worst in the Central South and the South Atlantic regions (models are not robust). As one might expect, the effects of higher education and producer services are everywhere significant (and positive) excepting New England and the South Atlantic, respectively. Expectations are reversed, however, in the case of metropolitan population; contrary to the thesis of spatial continuity, the effects of city size are significant in only three of the seven regions: Pacific, New England, and Northeast. Moreover, even in these regions city size makes only marginal contributions to the models' explained variances. In the end, Hansen's findings pose a number of challenges for the thesis of continuity. First, they imply that the new producer services are not simply or proportionately absorbed into the older urban hierarchy; second, that the locational shuffling of producer services within the Fordist urban hierarchy is considerable, particularly in the southern and interior regions; third, that the locational theory of post-Fordist producer services should reserve a prominent place for higher education; and fourth, that the economies in some regions, most notably the prospering southeastern United States, are hardly enthralled to the growth of producer services. Insofar as generalizations on this motley mix of producer services are possible, Hansen's findings on regional and metropolitan variations might well serve as points of departure for a new locational theory of production.

Post-Fordist geographies thus present us with something old and something new. The *old* is represented by the Weberian theory of least-cost locations that applies as well today as in the past. Firms that seek out regions of cheaper labor or shift their costs by networking production systems are merely acknowledging the changes in cost conditions—changes that have been wrought by a half century of New Deal liberalism, trade unionism, and rising wages and a decade of stagflation and fierce foreign competition. The *new* is represented by the emerging geography of producer services. The evidence compiled thus far suggests that older locational theories, be they warmed-over versions of central-place theory or postmodern variants of Weber's "footloose firms," simply will not do in the case of these services. Herein lies the challenge for Weber's successor in the post-Fordist era of cost shifting and communications efficiency.

Three Consumer Revolutions

When "classical" liberal elites have been in the saddle of American history, they have ridden roughshod over the economic landscape. It is elites who gave us our first industrial revolution (the factory system, 1780–1840) as well as our second (mass production and massive corporations, or Fordism, 1880–1930) and our third (post-Fordist flexible specialization, 1980–date); who, in addition to restructuring the geography of production, fostered regional specialization, enlarged the nation's industrial core, and concentrated production therein. But the liberal ride eventually comes (or will come) to an end with periodic crisis and the seating of a new and more egalitarian regime. For these "classical" republican successors, the economy's problem is not supply but demand, not that the production system is inefficient (on the contrary) but that consumption is insufficient. Consumption lags behind for one reason above all others: the sizable and often gross inequalities in wealth and income that have arisen out of the profits generated by revolutionary production systems and their disproportionate accrual among the owners of the factors of production. In due course, egalitarian regimes make it their business to reduce wealth and income inequalities (for the reductions achieved during America's Second Democracy, see figure 5.6), to smooth off the highly specialized and concentrated geographies of elite regimes by dispersing economic opportunity across regions, and to broaden the geographical scope of consumption (i.e., to "nationalize" the markets for consumer

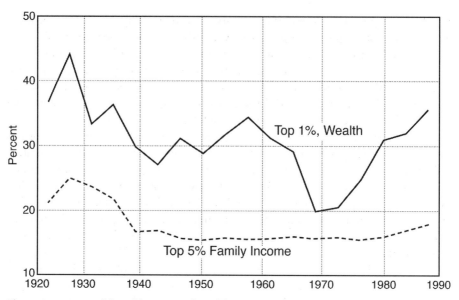

Figure 5.6.   Inequalities of income and wealth, 1922–1989.
Source: Wolff 1995.

goods). All of this presumes, of course, the republican installation of a proconsumer regulatory system.

We begin with the most recent, and perhaps best-known, of America's three consumer revolutions. The New Deal stopped short (unforgivably for some on the left) of a socialist revolution and settled instead for American capitalism's closest equivalent—a strategic "shift from production to consumption as the primary basis of political identity and focus of economic policy" (Sandel 1996: 267). This shift toward consumer-oriented policies was anything but rash, however. On the contrary,

> Roosevelt's turn to spending as an instrument of recovery marked a break with the assumptions that informed the early New Deal. For five years the New Deal had sought recovery under various programs designed to re-form the structure of the economy [read production system]. Now [in 1938], under the pressure of a new recession and with few practical alter-natives remaining, Roosevelt reluctantly adopted what amounted to Keynesian fiscal policy. By the end of World War II the central issues of economic policy had little to do with the debates that had preoccupied Americans from the Progressive era to the New Deal. The old debates about how to reform capitalism faded from the scene, and the macroeco-nomic issues familiar in our day came to the fore. (Sandel 1996: 260–61; see also Brinkley 1995: 65–77)

Securing full employment, enlarging aggregate demand, bettering the standard of living, and deploying fiscal and monetary policies toward these ends—these were the ways in which Roosevelt's New Deal would begin to remedy the insufficiencies of American consumption.

But New Dealers still had to choose among various regulatory actions. In this they were guided by egalitarian republican principles and, more precisely, by the pragmatic republicanism that we associate with Cromwell or the civic humanism of Machiavelli, with its emphasis on equality of opportunity, rather than by the leveling republicanism of the Commonwealthmen, the Old Whigs, and the populists, with its accent on equality of condition. Roosevelt's pragmatic republicanism thus had little truck with the radical populist critique of economic concentration, bigness, or oligopoly and monopoly. These things were not inherently bad; on the contrary, they were acceptable (and even welcomed) *insofar* and *in so long as* they provided American consumers with the highest quality products at the very lowest possible prices.

The New Deal's distinctive notions on consumer republicanism took shape in two cases during the 1930s: the administration's antitrust policy and the fate of anti–chain store legislation. Antitrust actions were relatively rare in the first third of the twentieth century. That situation changed abruptly with Roosevelt's appointment of Thurman Arnold to head the Antitrust Division of the Justice Department in 1937. Arnold quickly stepped up the pace of antitrust litigation, but in doing so he flatly declared that his policies were *not*

> designed to eliminate the *evil of bigness*. What ought to be emphasized is not the evils of size but the evils of industries which are not efficient or do not pass efficiency on to consumers. If the antitrust laws are simply an expression of a religion which condemns largeness as an economic sin they will be regarded as an anachronism in a machine age. If, however, they are directed at making distribution [i.e., consumption] more efficient, they will begin to make sense. (Arnold 1940: 3–4; see also Sandel 1996: 231–41)

Monopolists who could prove that they had provided consumers the best prices for value were unlikely candidates for antitrust action. In this case and in others, the consumerist vision of the New Deal served to reinforce rather than reject both the Fordist production system bequeathed by the second industrial revolution (1880–1930) and, as well, the Progressive era's commitments to the "gospel of efficiency." We had, it seemed, stepped across the threshold of a corporatist age of high-mass consumption.

The 1930s administered another blow to populist republicanism in the case of anti–chain store legislation. Chain stores of national retailers such as Sears Roebuck and Montgomery Ward had become commonplace by the 1920s in cities and bigger towns across the United States. In an attempt to protect and preserve local indepen-dent retailers from unfair competition, numerous state legislatures had passed anti–chain store legislation in the late 1920s and the early 1930s. During the latter decade, over half of the states had imposed chain store taxes of one sort or another. In parrying this attack, the national chains appealed to two of the New Deal's most important constituencies: consumers who "got good products at low prices" (thus maximizing consumer welfare) and labor unions who won favorable collective bargaining agreements from the chains (Sandel 1996: 227–31). The populist critique of bigness thus made little legislative headway during the New Deal, in large measure because that critique of the American system of production was out of step with the New Deal's commitments to corporatism and consumption. If Kresge offered lower prices than the corner store, so be it—the consumer was better off.

Herein were the optics for the New Deal's consumerist vision—the maximization of consumer welfare via Keynesian macroeconomic policies; the minimization of consumer prices via the corporate nationalization of consumer markets, and the efficient distribution of goods and services via a hierarchical geographical system of central places (hence the broad appeal of Christaller's demand-based theory of central-place locations), all abetted by innovations in consumer credit and installment buying (Calder 1999). But these policies were only the beginning for the New Deal and its legatees. Over the next three decades, they delivered more jobs and more consumer goods throughout the nation (on the convergence of consumption across the states, see Lebergott 1996: 22–28). Massive expenditures for defense (especially in the South) and highway construction expanded the labor force; the GI Bill vastly increased the consumption of housing (usually suburban home ownership; figure 5.7) and higher education; the Interstate Highway System along with national telephone and television networks laid the foundations for the nationalization of consumer markets; progressive tax cuts and welfare expenditures redistributed as they increased disposable incomes (Wolff 1995); and the civil rights movement and the "second reconstruction" of the South, painful though these were, opened up a vast consumer market for regional and national firms. The result was a marked convergence in state consumer expenditures over the course of the Second Democracy—their coefficients of variation falling from 3.92 in 1929 to 2.69 in 1970 and 1.49 in 1977. Conversely, in the republics, these coefficients diverged before 1929 (a coefficient of variation [c.v.] of 3.36 in 1900 to 3.92 in 1929) and held steady after 1977 (a c.v. of 1.49 in 1977 and 1.46 in 1982). Moreover, the convergence in consumer expenditures between 1929 and 1970 extended across a wide range of consumer goods—forty-eight of fifty-nine classes (81 percent) as compared to twenty-four of thirty-eight (63 percent) between 1900 and 1929 and twenty-five of fifty-nine (42 percent) between 1977 and 1982 (Lebergott 1996: 22–28). What is most impressive about American consumption between 1929 and 1970, then, is the breadth of its impact across industries and geographies.

These were flush times indeed. The economy grew at unprecedented rates, unemployment was effectively eliminated, the wild cycles in business activity had seemingly been tamed, and inflation had been brought to heel as the compact between business and labor coordinated the growth of wages with productivity (Rupert 1995). And with all the indicators pointing toward unending prosperity, Americans consumers went on an increasingly reckless shopping binge. By the end of the 1960s, even the Fordist system of production could not keep pace with the demand. In the 1970s, retail prices rocketed and stagflation jerked the American economy back to earth. The consumerist vision was unfortunately blinded to these

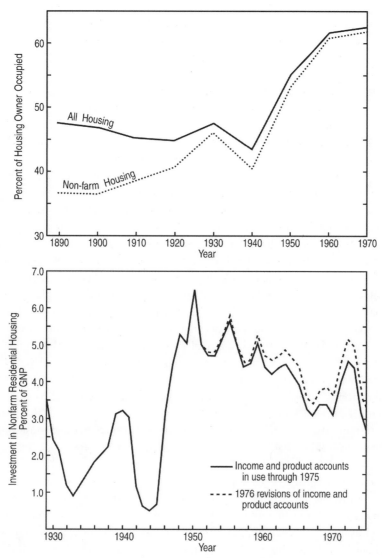

Figure 5.7.   Housing ownership and investment, 1890–1975.

Source: Berry 1981: 200–201.

new economic and geographical realities. The problem, as Ronald Reagan realized before all others, was lodged elsewhere in the American system of production.

Consumption was likewise the centerpiece of Jacksonian qua republican political economy a century before the New Deal. Of the various agencies of federal, state, and local government, the federal courts proved to be the most instrumental in unleashing the consumer revolution on the eve of the American Civil War. In a series of crucial decisions on commercial law and interstate commerce, the federal judiciary served as a nationalizing counterpoise to the parochializing tendencies of "state and local mercantilism"—tendencies that had made substantial headway in the early years of the republic. In the midst of the scramble to promote economic growth, mercantilist state legislatures and local governments had bestowed numerous advantages upon their private sectors. "State legislatures chartered hundreds of corporations and lavished them with land grants, lottery franchises, eminent-domain privileges, and tax exemptions" along with assorted bounties and subsidies for local products (McCurdy 1978: 246; Lively 1954–1955; Horwitz 1977). The widespread use of public inducements for the private sector, falling as they did within the jurisdiction of the states, invited little comment from the federal courts. But the justices took a dimmer view of punitive state actions that imposed fees and licensing regulations on products produced elsewhere and that, thereby, effectively raised the prices of products imported from other states. Over time, the federal courts came to regard these fees and regulations as tantamount to "hidden tariffs" on interstate commerce and on consumers generally. And Jacksonians (free traders that they were) had as little sympathy for these as for tariffs on imports from abroad. In 1839, the Supreme Court in the *Bank of Augusta v. Earle* chipped away at state mercantilism by declaring that while states could legislate against out-of-state corporations, they could not restrict the interstate business of the representatives of nonstate corporations. Three years hence, the Court's landmark decision in *Swift v. Tyson* struck an even more powerful blow for the nationalization of consumer markets. In this case, "Justice Story argued that there must be a general 'law merchant' in the United States. When the state laws [on commerce] conflicted with each other, the Supreme Court had the obligation to rule for all, so that the right rules could be found by the court in the 'general principles of commercial law.'" On economic matters thereafter, the Court sustained the liberal notion that a single national market must prevail— thereby ensuring the establishment of a free-trade area that for years ranked as the world's largest (Hughes 1987: 132).

In the small, *Swift v. Tyson* represented the Court's attempt to extend the province of commercial law from maritime trade abroad to the burgeoning internal trade at home. In the large, it represented the capstone of the Court's procommercial biases (Horwitz 1977: 252–54), but with this difference: Whereas earlier commercial jurisprudence had been biased in favor of producers, *Swift v. Tyson* tilted the balance toward consumer welfare—which is what one might expect of Jacksonian egalitarians. Story's opinion prepared the way for even bolder attacks on "state mercantilism." In *Cooley v. Board of Wardens* (1851), the Court—while admitting "that commerce embraced a great variety of subjects, some of such a nature as 'imperatively' to require a uniform, national rule whereas others admitted of local control until such time as Congress occupied the field"—also implied that "when Congress remained silent, the Court might supply its voice" (McCurdy 1978: 636). As cases allowed, the Court took up this "great variety of subjects." In *Watson v. Tarpley* (1857), the justices resolved a conflict between state and commercial law by reversing a Mississippi statute on the negotiability of bills of exchange (Horwitz 1977: 225). By the Civil War, the legal foundations for a commercial code and a nationalized market had been laid. These were reinforced when later Courts struck down licensing fees for out-of-state vendors (*Welton v. Missouri* in 1876 and *Webber v. Virginia* in 1880) and inspection fees (*Minnesota v. Barber* in 1890).

But if the verdict was by then clear—that commercial law had triumphed over state mercantilism—the Court had provided little guidance on the composition and codification of this body of law. These voids led to the formulation of a negotiable instruments law that was widely enacted by state legislatures by 1900 and that endured until suspended by work on a Uniform Commercial Code (UCC)—work that began in the 1920s and that was widely adopted by the 1950s and 1960s (Friedman 1973: 355). The UCC thus represented the legal culmination of the Court's landmark rulings on commercial law in the 1840s and 1850s. Like these earlier rulings, the code was the progeny of an age of consumption and egalitarian ideology. Also like these earlier decisions, it "was ruthless in its attitude toward regionalism. The notion that any state in the Union might conceivably have an economic or social interest requiring an exception to the code was considered heresy, and in fact not tolerated" (Friedman 1973: 582).

To understand this enduring streak of antiregionalism, one has to come to grips with the Jacksonian temperament of the Supreme Court in the middle third of the nineteenth century. To begin with, is it not paradoxical that Andrew Jackson, one of the most sectional presidents in American history, is simultaneously the source of a legal philosophy that, in the hands of justices such as Story and Field, served to weaken sections, states, and localities at the expense of national markets and cultural homogenization? Not if we recall that Jacksonian democracy constituted a new and distinctive ideological fusion of republican egalitarianism and liberal free trade (Meyers 1960; Benson 1961; Watson 1990). This fusion had several strategic ramifications for law, policy, and geography. First, the Jacksonian's egalitarian principles committed them to a political economy of consumption. Second, their free-trade principles provided them with the means for constructing a more egalitarian geography of consumption. In accordance with these principles, the Jacksonians lauded competition and free trade, at home and abroad, and they frowned upon (if not despised) federal monopolies such as the U.S. Bank and the various state restraints on the conduct of interstate trade.

In attacking these restraints on trade, the Jacksonians were also launching a sectional offensive against the East, against all those institutions that had sustained entrenched elites and established regions (mainly in the East) and that had, at the same time, thwarted economic and social opportunities in the newer regions emerging west of the Appalachians. They fought, in other words, for partisan ideas and institutions that would narrow regional differences in consumer prices (and economies more generally) and broaden the geographical base of economic opportunity and consumption. Free banking, internal improvements, opposition to tariffs, and the nationalization of the market were, in the Jacksonian mind, of one piece. From this perspective, one could argue that the Court's rulings on commercial law were more nearly proconsumer than procommercial in their biases. Over time, these rulings helped to nationalize the American market, to break the crust of state and local mercantilisms, to expand economic opportunities (and markets) in newer regions (especially the West), to promote the equality of regional opportunity, and, not least, to ignite the second of America's three consumer revolutions.

If most of the credit goes to the judiciary for our second consumer revolution and to the executive branch for our third, the honors for our premier consumer revolution should properly go to Parliament and its ministries in the middle third of the eighteenth century. It seems only fitting, given the American sport of Parliament bashing, to give credit where credit is long overdue. In the years immediately following the fall of Walpole's ministry (1742), the fiscal and monetary policies adopted by Parliament and Whitehall were unusually generous toward American consumers. A case in point is the discriminatory nature of British taxation at home and abroad. Americans shouldered surprisingly little of Britain's substantial fiscal burden, most of which Parliament loaded onto the backs of English consumers. As the costs of a republican empire mounted after 1745, taxes per head rose so sharply in Britain that by 1770 the average citizen paid over one pound sterling, mostly in the form of domestic excises and customs duties. This figure is all the more astonishing when we realize that it represented a doubling of the level of French taxes and a quintupling of the taxes levied on Americans in that same year (Mathias and O'Brien 1976). That Parliament was willing to risk resentment and dissent over high taxes at home is a telling indication of its considerable commitment to empire. Whatever the reason for Parliament's generosity toward American consumers, Britain's fiscal restraint was amply rewarded. Throughout the mainland colonies, the demand for imported goods shot upward. Between 1740 and the 1760s, as British taxes crept higher, American purchases of British imports increased by half or more in each of the several American regions.[1] One might say in this case that the pound Americans saved on taxes was a pound mostly spent on imported English goods.

Whereas British fiscal policy had the effect of leaving more cash in American pockets, the nation's monetary policies in due course presented colonial consumers with unusually favorable prices and long lines of consumer credit. The history of British monetary policy in the eighteenth century has a familiar and remarkably contemporary ring (Brewer 1990). In 1717, following a series of costly wars with the French, the Whigs found themselves saddled with a large and growing national debt. Their solution was two-pronged. In the first instance, the Whigs attempted to increase government revenues. Toward that end, they set about revamping the nation's fiscal policy by shifting the incidence of taxation from customs duties to excise taxes on domestic goods such as alcohol, leather, candles, and the like. The new excise taxes generated over £2.5 million in revenues (of which a million and a half represented entirely new revenues) within a decade and over £4.5 million by the 1760s—of which Americans, as we have seen, paid very little.

In the second instance, the Whigs launched an even bolder assault by way of revisions in national monetary policy. With interest payments on government securities running as high as 14 percent and on average about 5.5 percent, the nation was drowning in debt service. Walpole's administration unilaterally rescheduled the interest on all existing loans to 5 percent. Over the next several decades, the Whigs chipped away at the interest rate, but these adjustments paled in significance when compared to the 25 percent reduction in interest (from 4 to 3 percent) engineered by Henry Pelham between 1749 and 1757. The ramifications of these reschedulings, especially Pelham's, for America's first consumer revolution cannot be underestimated (Price 1980).

In a roundabout way, American consumers reaped the benefits of these reschedulings in the form of stable prices for imported goods and increasingly longer lines of credit for British goods. For American consumers, the "market price of finished goods [imported into the colonies] remained level or declined slightly" between 1720 and 1745 and "rose only slightly—about 10 percent"—in the ensuing thirty years (Egnal 1975: 215). Concurrently, American exports registered healthy increases in prices during the half century preceding the American Revolution. These very favorable terms of trade had two predictable consequences: First, the colonial economy grew at fairly high rates, most especially between 1745 and 1760 when incomes per capita rose at about 3 percent per annum; second, as incomes rose in the 1740s and 1750s, the demand for imports became more elastic to an extent that imports per capita in the various colonial regions rose by anywhere from 4 to 14 percent per annum (Egnal 1975). Such reckless consumption would hardly have been possible, however, in the absence of ample supplies of credit and an eager market for it. Indeed, "the increased liberality of credit between 1745 and 1760" (Egnal 1975: 215) was so widespread that the North American debt held by British merchants is said to have exceeded £1 million in 1757 and £5 million in 1766—an amount that equaled or surpassed Britain's total revenues from excise taxes (Price 1980: 8–9; Breen 1986, 1988; Main 1988).

America's first consumer revolution thus involves a connective tissue of generally stable consumer prices, a fivefold increase in credit, and a monetary policy that drove all three. To appreciate these revolutionary connections, I turn to Jacob Price's masterful account of the workings of capital and credit in the Scottish tobacco trade with the Chesapeake colonies of Virginia and Maryland. Price points out that interest rates on mortgages tended to follow

> interest rates on government securities with a margin of from 1/2 to 1 percent. When English mortgage rates reached 4 percent or thereabouts [i.e., when the interest on government securities stood at 3 percent], English investors looking for better returns were tempted to send money to Scotland where higher mortgage rates prevailed. This would have tended to bring down mortgage rates in Scotland too, forcing Scots who wanted the full 5 percent to leave the mortgage market and look for good bonds. Thus the rapid growth of the Virginia trade in Glasgow could have been facilitated by the influx of English money into the mortgage markets freeing Scottish funds for investment in the bonds of mercantile companies. (Price 1980: 19–20)

Something similar may have happened in England as investors shifted funds into industrial, mercantile, and banking enterprises, and the colonial trade was a primary beneficiary. We know, for example, that English wholesalers in the Chesapeake trade offered consumers twelve-months' credit or more on English goods (Price 1980: 28–30). But if America was awash in credit during the 1750s, these generous terms began to dry up in the 1760s. As the high costs of the Seven Years' War came due, Whitehall shifted its monetary policy into reverse, raising interest rates on government securities to 5 percent and setting in motion a chain reaction in capital and credit markets. As investors in merchant firms called in their bonds in order to switch them into governments securities, English merchants, industrialists, and bankers were put under great pressure. In short order, they turned the screws on American consumers, insisting that they pay down their current loans and pay off their "desperate" debts. To sum up, British monetary policies in the 1760s "crowded out" investors from the private sector, created a liquidity shortage therein, and slowed the pace of America's consumer revolution.

But if the effects of these policies on American consumption were quick and fairly substantial, they were far from devastating. American consumers continued acquiring imported goods, especially semidurables such as earthenware and assorted varieties of cloth. Indeed, American imports from England and Scotland actually rose slightly between 1760 and 1774. While it is also true that American imports in these years declined slightly on a per capita basis (by about 1 percent per annum), this retrenchment had more to do with a commensurate decline in colonial incomes per capita than with a flagging American interest in consumption. This interest Americans reaffirmed on their landscapes. A new geography of consumption had spread over the countryside in the course of the "age of empire." In America, retailing consumer goods became a way of life, in some cases as a part-time business, in others as full-time ventures, and in still others as the links in a series of "chain stores." In Massachusetts, perhaps the least commercialized of the larger colonies, consumers were well taken care of indeed. The colony's average retailer in 1771 served just 107 persons as compared to the U.S. average of 140 in 1967 and 150 in 1982 (Shammas 1990: 275). Retailers of goods and services were widespread elsewhere as well. In the middle colonies and the back country, retailers populated the burgeoning towns within an emerging hierarchy of central places (Lemon 1972; Mitchell 1977). And along the tobacco coast in the Chesapeake, in what was allegedly the most rural of colonial regions, decentralized retailers were sufficiently thick in numbers as to make up anywhere from a quarter to two-fifths of the heads of households. On the "southside" of the James River, we find Scottish firms and their American "factors" introducing the prototypical model for the chain store, in this case for wholesaling tobacco exports and retailing European imports (Price 1954; Earle and Hoffman 1976; O'Mara 1979; Farmer 1993). These new geographies of consumption were little deterred by what most regarded as a momentary pause in America's first consumer revolution.

Producer and Consumer Revolutions as Geographical Points and Counterpoints

Americans have experienced six revolutions in economic geography over the past three and a half centuries: the consumer revolutions in semidurables, household mechanization, and the electrification of home appliances in the middle thirds of the eighteenth, nineteenth, and twentieth centuries, respectively; and the producer revolutions associated with the factory system, Fordist mass production, and post-Fordist flexible accumulation on the thresholds of the nineteenth, twentieth, and twenty-first centuries, respectively. These revolutions had causes, mostly ideological, and consequences, mostly geographical. In the several consumer revolutions, egalitarian republicanism constituted the driving ideology. In accordance with its principles, Americans broadened the base of consumption, dispersed consumer opportunity, replicated a central-place geography in every region, and forged a common cultural bond among consumers in otherwise disparate regional societies. Consumer revolutions attempted to make one common market out of many; they were, in a word, nationalizing. In the colonial period, thanks to Parliament's fiscal generosity, the colonist's consumption of semidurable goods imported from Britain would serve as one of the few, though perhaps the most palpable, rallying points for an emerging American identity. And in our own century, thanks to the New Deal's applications of Keynesian theory, the nationalizing tendencies of consumption resurfaced; and something approaching an American cultural ideal (i.e., the nuclear family consisting of the breadwinning father, the homemaking mother, and their appreciative children) was widely disseminated via media and mobilities, both vicarious (radio, television, and the cinema) and real (the automobile) (for evidence of this regional convergence, see Lebergott 1996). These nationalizing tendencies were also at work in the 1840s and 1850s, thanks to the judicial branch, but in this case the regional diversification and involution of much of the antebellum South along with the Civil War momentarily obscured the effects of this consumer revolution (Earle and Cao 1993). These tendencies would resume with full force after the war, most especially in the small towns that provisioned the cotton South, as northern victors imposed their hegemony (Bensel 1990).

If one needs a reminder that consumer revolutions are at bottom ideological, the Civil War is it. Whenever these nationalizing tendencies have appeared, they have always been challenged, have always given rise to opposing tendencies (contentions) among those suspicious of metacultural national geographies and the homogenization of regional identities. For every nationalizing consumer revolution, there is, in consequence, an opposite if rarely equal counterrevolution, one that enlists regionalism as a means of preserving state and local autonomy and staving off the spatial onslaught of egalitarian consumerism. But in practice, the regional insurgents have failed in each and every case, beginning with the loyalists and the anti-Federalists in the 1770s and 1780s, continuing with the South's futile secession in the 1860s, and culminating with the southern rebellion against the movement for civil rights in the 1950s and 1960s. The irony is that these nationalizing egalitarians and their consumer revolutions, having thoroughly thrashed the sectional contenders for the crown of American identity, are themselves beaten down, first by economic crisis and ultimately by a new regime committed at once to an elitist ideology, a producer revolution, and a pronounced regional bias in the emergent geography of production.

The difference between these three consumer revolutions and the ensuing producer revolutions is the difference between classical republicanism's equality of opportunity and classical liberalism's "natural" inequality of condition, between nationalizing (i.e., diversified) geographies and parochializing (i.e., specialized) geographies. The liberal agenda has little room for egalitarian principles; it rather assumes that inequalities are inherent in human societies, that government's main task is to nurture the "natural" talent of American economic elites and bolster their efforts with timely interventions in the private sphere (what some have called corporate welfare)—everything from tariffs, subsidies, and bounties to governmental baleouts (e.g., the railroads in the 1880s and Chrysler a century hence), tax cuts and credits, and union busting. These dispensations to producers are themselves unequal; invariably they favor some industries and some regions over others. The Tariff of 1816, the very embodiment of Hamilton's economic policies for the promotion of infant industries, is a case in point. It clearly favored entrepreneurs who manufacture red inexpensive, low-count cotton textiles, and it just as clearly favored those regions that were endowed with cheap labor (i.e., in New England with its surplus of young women and in the Middle States with their abundance of seasonally unemployed farm workers; Harley 1992; Earle and Hoffman 1980; Goldin and Sokoloff 1982). These regions were the beneficiaries of this protective tariff, though some would argue that its benefits were national in scope. Indeed, it now seems likely that, in the absence of tariff protection, the American textile industry would have collapsed under stiff competition from the British and that the factory system and the industrial revolution itself would have been postponed (Bils 1984; Harley 1992).

Remarkably similar sorts of biases, regional and industrial, are evident in the Fordist and post-Fordist producer revolutions in the late nineteenth and twentieth centuries, respectively. During the Gilded Age, the resumption of high protective tariffs and the judiciary's support for a national system of railroads initiated a new geography of regional specialization and the agglomeration or concentration of mass-producing industries near the market (i.e., within the emerging American manufacturing belt in the northeastern United States and, more particularly, in metal-working districts therein). And more recently, in the 1980s, the probusiness (and antiunion) policies initiated by Ronald Reagan and carried forth under George Bush Sr. regularly favored entrepreneurs in the Sun Belt over those in the Rust Belt; of many examples, NAFTA represents perhaps the crowning achievement in the Republicans' southern strategy. The spoils of electoral victory have, in this case and others, been returned manyfold to the regions that delivered the victory for elite liberal ideologies—the Republican Sunbelt in the 1980s, the Republican Northeast and the Midwest in the 1880s and 1890s, and Federalist New England and the Middle States a century before.

Much of the theorizing about the American past pulls up short of a macrohistorical interpretation of these six revolutions, their associated geographical tendencies, and their inseparable alternations. In lieu of this, we are left with balkanized interpretations that are specific to one or another of the periods of American history. Geographers, for their part, have been largely innocent of the interplay between these revolutions and the long-run alternations in the American usage of space—the nationalizing and diversifying tendencies of egalitarian (republican) regimes and the regionalizing and specializing tendencies of elite (liberal) regimes. But if geographers may be faulted for insufficient awareness of these macrohistorical spatial trends, they deserve ample credit for their theoretical contributions on the geographies of specific periods and revolutions. In the case of producer revolutions, for example, "geographers," both here and abroad, have formulated a variety of enduring locational theories—from Hamilton's and Weber's on industry to Thunen's on agricultural land use, from Richard Hartshorne's (1939) on areal differentiation (the essence of regional specialization) to Harvey's (1990) on flexible accumulation.

These contributions to the location theory of production are all the more impressive when compared to the meager list of geographical contributions associated with consumer revolutions. Geographical theory simply does not fare very well during these revolutions. The exception, of course, is Walter Christaller's formulation of central-place theory and the broad appeal that this theory of retail location has enjoyed since its appearance in the 1930s—an appeal that makes eminent sense in the context of Keynesian economics and the consumer revolution that it entrained (Christaller 1966; Berry 1970). The pickings are leaner, however, when we turn to the consumer revolutions in the middle of the eighteenth and nineteenth centuries. There are no ready-made geographical theories of consumption, though one may discern in the writings of Tocqueville and Olmsted, and earlier still of Jefferson and Jedediah Morse, the rudiments of such a theory. It is in these consumer revolutions, in the shrouded sanctums of household domesticity, that we fully realize the inadequacies of a masculinized geographical theory for appreciating the extraordinary power of women in transforming economies at home and, in time, in the nation and its geographies at large (Boserup 1970; Jensen 1986). What is at stake here, in our several consumer revolutions, has little to do with feminist politics and everything to do with our standing as interpreters of an ample portion of the American past.

Theory falters as well when we come to explain the periodic alternations in the nation's six producer and consumer revolutions. We might begin the task with a proposition—namely, that these alternations constitute in themselves an inseparable, indeed indispensable, routine in the American repertoire of crisis and recovery. The sequential logic reduces to this: The elite excesses of producer revolutions are tempered by the egalitarian excesses of the next and so on *ad seriatim*. The reason that a producer revolution runs out of steam is because of its obsession with the welfare of economic elites, because the regime so maldistributes the great wealth generated by the producer revolution as to undermine its foundations: a prospering middle class, an expanding consumer market, and a cumulating aggregate demand.

As these economic problems come home to roost, the ensuing egalitarian regime eventually comes to see the economic crisis as one of too little consumption—of overproduction or, if one prefers, underconsumption—and it proposes to remedy the problem by broadening the base of consumer demand (the 1920s presents us with the classic case of overproduction; see Filene 1931; Beaudreau 1996).[2] The new egalitarian regime proceeds to tackle the problem of consumption: It introduces policies aimed at redistributing incomes, lowering the costs of money, freeing up credit, and generally cutting the costs of consumer goods (Sandel 1996; Calder 1999; on the ensuing urban and suburban landscapes, see Relph 1987: 96–97). But this nationalizing consumerist vision eventually loses sight of the mounting problems confronting American producers. With their patent protection exhausted, their aging plants wracked by wear and tear, their taxes on the rise, and their labor force demanding evermore, producers embark on the final stages of their product and process cycles. Competition is increasingly fierce, costs run too high, profits fall, and the once-generous lines of credit begin to dry up. A generation of reckless consumers want much more than the beleaguered producers are willing or able to deliver. Stagflation spreads across the land and engulfs the nation in a crisis of underproduction (overconsumption).

At this point, "what is needed . . . is a rethinking of old purposes, patterns, and priorities. . . . Traditional fixes . . . are not enough" (Smith 1995: xix; see also Drucker 1989). It is this rethinking, this experimentation by business and government with entirely new ways of making goods and services, that signals the onset of the latest in the series of recurrent revolutions in the mode of American production. Once again, in accordance with the principles of classical liberalism, the rewards of the producer's revolution are distributed unequally across classes, industries, and regions; its penalties are borne by the middle and lower classes; and its veiled contradictions are only unmasked when the producer revolution itself devolves into a crisis of underconsumption. And so, on the threshold of an egalitarian consumerist philosophy, the cycle of excess turns.

Notes

1. Americans paid customs taxes of £40,000 per year between 1768 and 1772. Imports to the northern colonies rose from £0.65 per person in 1743–1747 to £1.49 in 1758–1762; to the Lower South from £1.5 per white person in 1743–1747 to £2.2 in 1763–1767; and to the Upper South, from £1.3 per white person in 1733–1737 to £2.3 in 1758–1762 (Egnal 1975).

2. Very few Americans in the 1920s appreciated the impacts of electrification on industrial productivity and mass production and their impacts on labor and societal relations (Beaudreau 1996). Edward A. Filene (1931: 198–201) was an exception. "Under mass production," he wrote,

> the profit motive not only can be attached to the common welfare, but it cannot escape being so attached. . . . There can be no profit in mass production unless the masses are also profiting thereby. The time has come . . . when the greatest total profits can be secured only through supplying the masses with the best values. So there is no war now between selfishness and unselfishness; the only war is between the traditional notion of where self-interest lies and the newly discovered truths of profit-making.

CHAPTER 6

Spatial Enlargements in American Power

SECTIONAL, NATIONAL, AND TRANSNATIONAL STATES

The history of the United States after 1789 might be (and indeed has been) written in three parts, each with their own geopolitical leitmotif. Part I, between 1789 and the end of radical reconstruction (1877), would revolve around sections and sectional conflict; part II, between 1877 and 1980, around the ascension of federal power and the national state; and part III, between 1980 and the present, around the transnational extension of American power to the continental and global domains. Taken severally, these three histories emphasize one geographical unit over another; taken together, however, they tell a serial story of periodic enlargements in the domain of American power. In each case, Americans have enlarged the domain of national power, ratcheting it upward to the Sectional State in the 1780s, to the National State in the 1880s, and to the Transnational State and the continental trading bloc in the 1980s. In each case, Americans have embarked on these jurisdictional enlargements at amazingly regular intervals of a century more or less. Also in each case, these enlargements have arisen from similar causes—the imperative for egalitarian regimes to respond to the sectional stresses unleashed by their volatile geographies—and they have led to similar ends—the imperative for ensuing elite regimes to affirm the regional winners and losers, to govern within the enlarged jurisdiction of the new American state, to expand the range of opportunities, both economic and political, for newly ascendant sections (themselves the products of spatial volatility), and, thereby, to ensure, the long-run viability of American society. To present these scalar shifts in a coherent fashion, it is necessary to peel away some of the layerings of structure, dynamics, and spatial process noted earlier.[1]

This synopsis of these enlargements in American power makes five points. The first has to do with their century-long periodicity; the second with their origins in the sectional stresses resulting from the geographical reconstructions of policy regimes; the third with their sizable contributions to the viability of civil society (most notably to sustained economic growth and political opportunity); the fourth with the changing anatomy of state policies and American geopolitics; and the fifth with the geohistorical dynamics of state development.

The Periodicity of Three American States

I will make the case that American power has periodically ratcheted upward in scale—from provinces/states to sections to the state (federal government), and, perhaps at this moment, to the continental trading bloc. These scalar enlargements occur, moreover, at fairly fixed intervals of a century more or less—the 1780s (the section), the 1880s (the state), and again in the 1980s and 1990s (the continental bloc)—for reasons that have to do, in the most general sense, with regime dialectics and, more specifically, with republics and the expansionist strategies deployed by these elite protectionist (PE) regimes (e.g., strategies of frontier and urban expansion, demographic and economic concentration, and regional stability and specialization)—all, of course, with the interests of American elites in the forefront.

Once PE regimes have ratcheted power upward to a new scale (be it section, state, or continent), this domain remains in place for a century more or less. It then falls upon the succeeding regime of egalitarian free traders (the FTM democracies) to cultivate the use of power in this new domain, to refine and extend its applications within—but not beyond—that domain (and, we might add, to shoulder most of the blame when this scale no longer suffices, when its possibilities are exhausted). In other words, democracies (FTM regimes) consolidate power within this domain (albeit now in the interests of larger numbers, the masses), and they do so in ways that are perfectly consistent with their involutional strategies of spatial consolidation, dispersion, and diversified and volatile regional economic growth. My larger point is simply this: In the dialectical dance of expansion and consolidation that has paired regimes of radically different persuasion, it is the expansionist PE regimes that invariably take the lead in shifting outward the geographical scales of American political power. In this fashion, Americans have periodically created entirely new geographies (every century or so on the ascent of a new American republic)—geographies that have extended the terrain and the resources for regimes and their dialectical reconstructions of American space.

Causality

My second point has to do with causality. Attributing these periodic enlargements of power to the agency of expansionist republics (PE regimes), while technically correct, is not quite the heart of the matter. Of far greater consequence is the chain of events that leads up to these enlargements. The first link in this chain is the volatility of the spatial reconstructions in the preceding egalitarian regime; the second is the eruption of revolutionary conflict (revolution, as it were) over sectional definitions of civil rights; the third is the victor's enactment of a new and more sweeping body of civil rights law; and the fourth, coming with the transition from an egalitarian to an elite regime, is the jurisdictional extension of that body of law into a new and enlarged political domain.

The chain of events begins with mass or egalitarian regimes, and more precisely with their midterm accelerations of economic growth, regional disequilibration (volatility), and sectional stress. In these regimes (1740s–1780s, 1830s–1880, 1930s–1980), regional economies are unusually volatile—indeed, by one measure, anywhere from two to four times as volatile as those of elite regimes. While the hypervolatility of these regional economies serves useful egalitarian purposes—most notably, the spatial *dispersion* of prosperity into regions other than the older core (dispersion)—it also nurtures new sectional identities, inflames new sectional passions, and prompts new sectional alliances and coalitions, all of which is thoroughly upsetting for the existing balance of sectional power. These sectional strains invariably tear the ligaments of political union, ripping apart the tacit if uneasy consensus on the definition of citizenship and "the rights of man."

The first of these sectional tears is, of course, the American rebellion of 1775 over the Crown and Parliament's denial of the colonists' rights as Englishmen. One need not accept Jefferson's exaggeration that the British intended to reduce the colonies to slavery to appreciate the sectional struggle between Britain and the colonies, between a core burdened with the mounting debts of imperial administration, not to mention the French and Indian War, and a periphery burgeoning with people and wealth. The American provincials were catching up quickly. Their numbers, which were just one-thirtieth of the populations of England and Wales in 1700, increased tenfold (to two million) by 1770 and brought the Americans to within one-fourth of the population in the mother country. There was, of course, a good reason for this rapid peopling of America, and it was a booming economy. Some said of South Carolina, for example, that its rice planters were among the richest people in the world; and in every other region on the mainland, including New England after 1750, annual incomes equaled or surpassed those enjoyed in most parts of England (Jones 1980: 66–69). The Revolution—the second of our linked events—was thus very much a sectional conflict, a conflict between a mature core weary of warfare and a muscular periphery eager to assert the colonists' rights as Englishmen or, barring that, as independent Americans.

The Revolution decided that Americans would be independent. The Constitution—our third link—decided the nature of citizenship, the structure of compound governance, and the role of the section as the new domain of political power. In making this boldest of reconfigurations in American governance, the framers of the Constitution attempted to remedy the deficiencies that the 1780s had exposed in the Articles of Confederation. Buffeted by a depressed economy, farmer rebellions, and bickering over state tariffs on internal trade, the convention in Philadelphia created a republic that would resolve these sorts of problems. The new republic consisted of two concurrent and largely autonomous spheres or layers of governance. The topmost or federal layer was delegated jurisdiction over a restricted number of exclusively national matters (e.g., regulating interstate commerce, making peace and war, issuing currency, etc.). The bottommost layer, the sovereign states, was delegated jurisdiction over everything else. The separation in these layers of governance was strict indeed, applying even so far as the Amendments to the Constitution (e.g., the Bill of Rights), which, until 1868, had standing only in matters under federal jurisdiction.

The fourth and final link in our chain of events is forged in the crucible of practice, in the everyday testing of constitutional principles. Even before the ink had dried on the Constitution, some of its framers, not least James Madison, realized that the Constitution was not without its flaws, that the concurrent republic envisaged in this document had created a power vacuum that history would promptly fill with the "section" (Onuf 1996). Madison conceded as much in the *Federalist Papers*, acknowledging that the Constitution, with its separation of federal and state powers, invited sectional alliances as a means of shaping federal policy and legislation. Madison did not particularly like this result, but he was optimistic that the most baneful effects of sectionalism might be mitigated, in the short run, by transitional regions— the Middle States might side with the southern states on some issues and New England on others—and, in the long run, by the dynamics of spatial expansion—by continuously adding new regions and reshuffling the old ones, he trusted that expansion would soften the differences among regional "interests" and subvert enduring sectional alliances (McCoy 1987). It was his hope, not to mention the hope of Hamilton and their fellow nationalists, that one geographical process—expansion— would trump another—sectionalism. But Madison's harmonious vision of an "extended republic" was not to be; nationalist dreams of a benign sectionalism were soon dashed, crumpled under by the cotton belt's spectacular rise, slavery's remarkable resurgence, and the hardening of sectional interests along the visible line defined by slavery and freedom. What followed—the tendentious and often violent history of sectionalism from the Constitution through the Civil War—offers ample testimony that the framers of this concurrent republic had simultaneously ratcheted power to a new domain—from the provincial domain of the sovereign states to the sectional domain of slave states and free. If, in 1785, the sovereign states resembled thirteen clocks striking independently, the forces of sectionalism in 1860 had reduced the number of clocks to just two, one striking high noon for freedom, the other tolling midnight for slavery.

The expansionist polity cooked up by Madison and his fellow nationalists was, in the end, half-baked. Far from calming sectional passions, the implementation of an expansionist "extended republic" magnified the tensions and conflicts among sections that were already deeply divided over the utility and morality of slavery. To make matters worse, the rapid expansion of American settlement complicated the range and variety of divisive sectional issues. Instead of thirteen states, the nation in 1860 counted thirty-three—eighteen of them prohibiting slavery and fifteen of them depending on it for their economic survival. And instead of a territory of 865,000 square miles, there were nearly 3,000,000 by 1860. In less than a century, the new republic had entered into the ranks of world-class states, but without the power of the purse to back it up. One indicator of the paltriness of federal power is the ratio of federal to state government expenditures per capita. In 1840, the ratio was at par; twenty years later, the ratio was only slightly higher (1.14 or less) in every region east of the Mississippi, save one—the South Atlantic states (2.34) (Davis and Legler

1966). In the antebellum version of Madison's concurrent republic, the power over the purse resided in the states and their sectional coalitions.

The second of our enlargements in American power can be traced to a similar chain of events in the 1850s and 1860s—the nation's enormous prosperity and the volatility of its regional economies in the first of these decades (link 1), the eruption of sectional divisions over slavery in Civil War in 1861 (link 2), the northern triumph (link 3), and the radical restructuring of the Constitution and the sweeping expansion of federal jurisdiction in 1868 (link 4). With the secession of eleven slave states in 1861 following Lincoln's elections, Madison's worst fears over sectionalism were finally realized. In ways that are eerily reminiscent of the coming of the Revolution itself, the road to Civil War ran through one of the most affluent decades in American history, through mounting sectional division and strident and uncompromising rhetoric over slavery and the civil rights of American slaves. The impasse between two sections and two distinct and contradictory national agendas had arrived. While the Civil War would resolve this test of wills and resources, the northern victory did not of itself effect a fundamental revision in the law of the land. To be sure the War had ended slavery, but it left intact the concurrent republic enshrined in the Constitution. That would change in 1868, however, with the ratification of the Fourteenth Amendment to the Constitution.

The history of the Fourteenth Amendment borders on the bizarre. Here we have an amendment that proved more effective as an instrument of federal and corporate power than as a guarantor of the civil rights of those for whom it was intended—the ex-slaves and their descendants. Not until 1954 and *Brown v. Board of Education* would the courts right the scales of this injustice. In the interim, as Michael Sandel (1996: 39–42 *et seq.*) has pointed out, the Fourteenth Amendment provided the judicial pretext for a steady expansion of federal authority over affairs once reserved exclusively to the states—a pretext that was fully exploited by a new regime staffed largely by elite nationalists from the triumphant northeastern and midwestern states. The amendment declared, "No State shall make or enforce any law which should abridge the privileges or immunities of citizens of the United States; nor shall any State deprive any person of life, liberty, or property, without due process of law; nor deny to any person within its jurisdiction the equal protection of the laws." In these words were the legal foundations for the extension of the Bill of Rights to the states and the justification of a sweeping enlargement in the power of the federal government, corporations, and the Northeast and Midwest. This enlargement— what I have referred to as the ratcheting of power to the federal or nation-state domain—advanced under the banner of a "rights revolution" and under the direction of the "liberal" state.

Although the Supreme Court did not fully and finally affirm the collapse of the nation's concurrent republic until 1925, declension was well under way by the end of the nineteenth century. Corporations led the way, making a number of gains in a piecemeal series of judicial interpretations that reaffirmed their status as "persons," extended them federal protection (and even troops) under the Fourteenth Amendment, affirmed their right to avoid state attempts at regulatory intervention, and supported their claims that unions represented an abridgement of workers' civil rights (the infamous notion of "liberty of contract") (Roy 1997: 55, 108–9, 256–58; Friedman 1973: 446–59). As the courts expanded the powers of corporations and the state, the federal government grew steadily larger. In the sixty years after the Civil War, government spending in the United States rose from 2 to 3 percent of GNP to 10 percent or so, with the federal government accounting for 40 percent of all expenditures by the latter date (Niemi 1980: 356–57). The big change occurred between 1860 and 1880 with what Richard Bensel (1990, 2000) has called the rise of "Yankee Leviathan." In these two decades, federal funds poured into the triumphant northern states. In the core region consisting of New England, the Middle Atlantic States, and the East North Central States, the ratio of federal expenditures per capita in 1880 to those of 1860 exceeded nine; elsewhere, in the peripheral regions east of the Rockies, the ratio dropped to less than four in the East South Central States and to less than two in the three remaining census regions (Davis and Legler 1966). Federal expenditures would grow even faster after 1932, reaching 36 percent of GNP in 1975 during the height of the Cold War (Niemi 1980: 356–57). These figures thus represent something of a bottom line on American power and politics—on the declension of the concurrent republic, the rise of the corporatist state, the sectional triumph of the northeastern core, and the ratcheting of American power to the national domain.

The third and most recent of these enlargements of American power—to the continental and transnational domains—likewise has its origins in sectional debates over civil rights in the midterm of an egalitarian regime. Once again we begin with an affluent phase, the Second Democracy of the 1950s and early 1960s, and proceed through the linked chain of events—the social movement to ensure the civil rights of black Americans, the rebellious resistance in many parts of the Deep South (the so-called second civil war), the passage of the Civil Rights Act of 1964 (the "Gettysburg" of the civil rights struggle), and the "second reconstruction" of the South, and, lastly with the resurgence of an elite-protectionist-nationalist regime, the Civil Rights Act of 1991. I will not repeat this saga of events for Americans, most of whom have lived through these turbulent times or, at the least, with their memories fresh in mind. I will instead make two points, one obvious and the other obscured.

My first point, the obvious one, is that the civil rights movement represents an attempt to achieve closure, to conclude the unfinished business of racial equality. Just as the Civil War and the Fourteenth Amendment belatedly installed federal power into the constitutional vacuum that sectionalism had previously filled, the civil rights movement finally held Americans to account in fulfilling that Amendment's original intentions. In retrospect, it would appear that as a nation we have skillfully managed to snatch defeat from the jaws of victory or, perhaps more precisely, to defer republican concerns for due process and equal protection in favor of liberal commitments to the power politics of jurisdiction.

The second point about the Civil Rights Act of 1964, and the less obvious because buried within it, is Congress's intentional extension of the jurisdiction of American civil rights' law beyond the boundaries of the United States. The congressional presumption that American law has extraterritorial applications is a bold, even revolutionary, idea, and like all such ideas its aims have been and will be sharply contested. Insofar as this novel doctrine carries the day in the federal courts (and that remains an open question), it will project a sweeping extension of American sovereignty and, in the midst of and on the contrary to an era of globalization, a vast enlargement in the domain of American power (Maher 1993; Yamakawa 1992). We begin rather more uneventfully, however, by looking at the Civil Rights Act of 1964 and the minor provision that broached the problem of jurisdiction in the first place.

Title VII of that act implied that the civil rights of Americans employed by American companies overseas are protected under the terms of the act. The importance of this seemingly minor provision has been magnified with the passage of time and by the rapid growth in the numbers of American multinational corporations in the 1970s and 1980s and the equally rapid globalization of the world economy. Predictably, it was not long before Americans employed by American companies overseas were filing complaints with the Equal Employment Opportunity Office (EEOC; created by the 1964 act) claiming that their civil rights had been violated or before multinationals were challenging EEOC findings for the plaintiffs in the federal courts. In 1991, the Supreme Court finally took up the matter in the case of *EEOC v. Arabian American Oil Company (ARAMCO)*. In this case, the plaintiff, an American citizen employed in Saudi Arabia by the Delaware-based corporation ARAMCO, maintained that supervisory harassment over his race, origin (Lebanese), and religion had led to the termination of his employment with the company. The Court, however, ruled in favor of the corporate defendant. In the majority's view, the Civil Rights Act of 1964 did not extend so far as to cover American employees employed by American companies abroad; the majority held further that the extraterritorial application of civil rights was explicit in neither Congress's language nor its intentions. The matter was far from settled, however. Within months, Congress issued a rejoinder to the Court in the form of the Civil Rights Act of 1991. Section I of the bill, which President Bush signed into law, declared unequivocally that the "Protection of Extraterritorial Employment" was indeed the law of the land. In short order, Congress had issued a reproach to the Court and served it with the letter of the law.

The Civil Rights Act of 1991, like the Fourteenth Amendment to the Constitution, can be viewed on two levels. At one level, the act represents an important victory for the advocates of civil rights' protection; at the other, it represents the renewal of the periodic struggle over the jurisdictional limits of the American state. It is on this second level that the differences between the jurisdictional struggles of the nineteenth and twentieth centuries are most pronounced. Whereas the Fourteenth Amendment fostered a complementary expansion of federal and corporate power in the name of the "rights" revolution, the Civil Rights Acts of 1964 and 1991 are doing precisely the opposite. They are nudging, if not shoving, the American state and American multinational corporations in diametrically opposing directions. What we are seeing then are the opening volleys in the gathering conflict between Big Business and the Big American State, between the forces of globalization and nationalism, and between geoeconomics and geopolitics. As the forward salients of American nationalism's extension of regulatory intervention in the global economy, these acts constitute the first of many tests of the allegiance of the multinational corporation. Are they, in other words, the American wedge for the regulation of American multinational companies in the spheres of environmental protection, the terms and conditions of labor, antitrust, and, more radically perhaps, the extension of American jurisdiction to alien employees of overseas American firms? Some would hope so. One legal scholar (Westbrook 1990: 94) makes the case persuasively, arguing that the "sovereign regulation of multinational conduct" is a positive good, that it "serves international values . . . [because it] provides a measure of control over transnational economic activity pending international agreement, while simultaneously hastening the process of international negotiation." Moreover, Westbrook (1990: 94) is cautiously optimistic about the American prospects for this sort of regulation, noting that in litigation over antitrust, cartels, price fixing, and technology transfer, American judges have been fairly assertive in favoring sovereignty over laissez faire.

These juridical extensions of American sovereignty have been reinforced by recent legislative actions, most notably congressional approval of NAFTA (McConnell and MacPherson 1994). Congressional voting for and against NAFTA opens two windows: one on the geography of expansionist sentiment, the other on the sectional realignment that has taken place in the wake of the civil rights movement—a realignment that has fractured the nation into a growing and prosperous Sunbelt and a slowly growing or stagnating Rust or Frost Belt. The Sunbelt provided both the initiative and, in large measure, the authority for NAFTA. The impetus for extending a zone of free trade from Canada into Mexico (or, more alliteratively, "from the Yukon to the Yucatan") emerged in 1986 during the Reagan administration, was sustained by the Bush administration, and was signed into law under the Clinton administration—administrations headed in all cases by a Sunbelt resident. Meanwhile, in Congress, the legislative push for NAFTA's approval also came from the Sunbelt, from the delegations representing a sweeping arc of southern, southwestern, and far western states. Looking at the final vote in the House of Representatives, and only at those states with four or more delegates, states with a majority in favor of NAFTA included nine of the eleven former states of the Confederacy (the exceptions, South Carolina and Alabama); all three of the West Coast states along with Arizona; and six states elsewhere (Colorado, Oklahoma, Kansas, Iowa, Wisconsin, and Illinois). In other words, most of the Sunbelt states supported NAFTA, and most of the Rust Belt states did not (*U.S. Congressional Record* 1993: H 100048). Moreover, the most solid support for NAFTA's extension of American sovereignty came from the southern states. One might see in this the powerful ascent of a "Rebel Leviathan" were it not, of course, for the morally chastening and economically transformational impacts of the past four decades. What is clear is that in the years ahead it will be up to once-peripheral regions to effect the ratcheting of American power to a new territorial domain.

Although the debate over the extraterritorial application of American law is far from resolved, the forces in favor of it—of extending the jurisdiction of the American State—are formidable. Their hand has been strengthened, moreover, by the advent of multistate economic compacts such as NAFTA and the European Union (EU). At a stroke, the states in these two collectivities have greatly enlarged their jurisdictional domains as well as their power in bringing multinationals to the sovereign's heel. These ratchetings of power to the continental domain are easy to miss (or dismiss), of course, when we are caught up with what Ruggie (1993: 171) calls the "unbundling of territory" in an era of "postmodern globalization." No less impressive, I submit, are the territorial rebundlings now under way and their associated extensions of sovereignty via the law, the courts, and the principal continental trading blocs. The era of big government may be over, but the era of even bigger government may have only just begun. What we are seeing then is the recrudescence of nationalism, albeit at a new continental scale. That the American version of this new nationalism should flow most powerfully from the Civil Rights Acts of 1964 and 1991 may seem paradoxical, lest we recall that both of these doctrines—nationalism and equality, the power of the republic and the equality among its citizenry—spring from the same fount, from the classical republicanism of Harrington, Cromwell, and Machiavelli.

All this hammering has resulted in the fabrication of a chain of power—a series of crucial events linked into a process that has periodically enlarged the domains of American power. The first three of these links connect events in the middle and near the end of egalitarian regimes. The first link captures the sectional tensions over civil rights that arise in the midst of an unusually prosperous decade and sunder highly volatile regions; the second, the eruption of sectional civil war and rebellion; and the third, on the conclusion of this conflict, the revisions in the fundamental law of the land in ways that simultaneously redefine citizenship and enlarge the jurisdiction of the federal state. The fourth and final link connects these events with the rise of a new regime. Pursuant to its sectional, elite, and nationalist biases, this new regime is less interested in the extension of civil rights than in the aggrandizement of national power. It accordingly exploits the openings in the new law of the land and ratchets the power of the state to a new and enlarged domain. In this way, American history's greatest and most heroic events—the Revolution and the Constitution, the Civil War and Reconstruction, and the civil rights movement and the Civil Rights Acts of 1964 and 1991—are implicated—periodically, inextricably, and ironically—in our Machiavellian pursuit of republican nationalism and expansive power. It is only at this brief and transitional moment, on the razor's edge of republican equality and nationalist expansion, that the American polity embraces and then recoils from the purifications of republican ideology.

State Enlargement and the Viability of American Civil Society

My third point is that these periodic shifts of power bear directly on—indeed, are preconditions for—the viability of American civil society. At first glance, it may seem odd to juxtapose the notion of social viability with a geohistory dripping with dialectical contention, sectional jockeying, and wrenching shifts in the domains of power, but the fact remains that this notoriously contentious past has yielded a society that has managed to sustain economic growth; to mitigate, if not altogether preclude, class conflict; and to foster an incurable, if often charmingly naive, optimism even in the most nervous of times. The viability of American society, or perhaps more aptly its endurance, has several causes, not the least of which is the periodic structuring of the American past. Within this scaffolding, Americans have been able to veer between the liberal's faith in top-down entrepreneurialism (in the PE regimes of republics) and the republican's faith in bottom-up egalitarianism (in the FTM regimes of democracies) without ever fully capitulating to the excesses of either one. Thus, a republic's commitments to elites, a producer revolution, expansion, spatial concentration, and the specialization and stability of regional economies (the PE regime) are countered by a democracy's commitments to the masses, a consumer revolution, spatial consolidation, demographic dispersion, and the diversification and volatility of regional economies (FTM regimes). In the process, the dynamic dialectic that punctuates the short runs of the American past is transformed into the dynamic equilibrium that ensures the viability of American society over its long run.

That said, however, the dialectic of periodic structure is hardly a sufficient condition for long-run social viability. The latter hinges on two more fundamental considerations: first, an economy that continues to grow; second, a polity that ensures generally *pacific transfers of power* from one regime to another. These, of course, are two of the essential ingredients for civil society in a constitutional democracy.

Of these two prerequisites for a civil society, I will momentarily set to one side the economy, having dealt at some length with the dynamics of American economic growth and the reciprocal relations of producer and consumer revolutions, their progenitors (underconsumption/overproduction and overconsumption/underproduction, respectively), and their protagonists (elite and mass/egalitarian regimes), and focus instead on politics. In the study of politics, it is one thing to claim (rightly) that civil society rests on political institutions and quite another to push this idea to the extremes, as some of the "new institutionalists" tend to do, and maintain that political institutions owe their origins and their evolution to particular events more nearly than to generalized structures. In the American case, the listings of foundational or precedential events regularly include, among others, President Washington's insistence on a sharp separation between military and civil functions; Jefferson's thwarted attempt to suppress political opposition; the Constitution's balancing of power among government's several branches; as well as the Marshall Court's reaffirmations and extensions of constitutional authority and federal power. But before imputing too much explanatory power to these events, it may be wise to remember Madison's injunction that actions such as these are more nearly advisories on the application of power, and not power itself. The force of these advisories, and that of American power more generally, ultimately derives from "The People" as mediated through locales, provinces/states, and, most critical of all, sections. As Frederick Jackson Turner mostly understood, it is American sections that mobilize power, that deploy it for their own ends, that periodically ratchet it to larger domains (scales), and that check its monopolization by rival sections. These sectional dynamics, I hasten to add, precede most if not all of the political actions and events venerated by the "new institutionalists." These dynamics antedate the Constitution (as well as the precedential actions of Washington, Jefferson, and Marshall), and they postdate recent events such as NAFTA's ratcheting of power to the continental scale. Or, to put the point differently, events alone are not sufficient guarantors of social viability.

What Turner did not fully appreciate, given his morbid concerns over the ascent of federal power at the turn of this century, was that the very ratcheting of power that he so feared was, in fact, a logical outgrowth of his sectional thesis. The federal ratcheting that Turner observed throughout most of his adult life (circa 1890–1920) actually began with the sectional crisis of the Civil War (sparked in part by the hypervolatility of regional economies during an egalitarian regime), and it was carried through by an elite regime, a "Yankee Leviathan," predicated on a sectional alliance of the victors—of the elites of an industrialized Northeast and an agrarian Midwest. More to the point, this sectional shift of power to the federal scale, like those a century before (the Revolutionary era's ratcheting to the sectional scale) and a century after (the Sunbelt and Sagebrush ratcheting to the continental scale), served not to undermine the viability of American society but (contra Turner) to reinforce it. This they accomplished by expanding at once *the spaces for American economic advance* and the *billets for political actors, vanquished as well as victorious*. But precisely how did this happen? How did these enlargements in the domains of political power simultaneously enlarge the domains of economic and political opportunity?

After each of these enlargements in American power, political and economic opportunities have expanded in unison—and at an astonishing pace. Consider first the growth of political opportunities in federal employment in the century after the 1780s and its successor after the 1880s. In the "century of sectionalism," federal employment grew 10-fold between the 1790s (about 3,500) and 1861 (26,274) and 29-fold by 1880 (100,020). It would be reasonable, in turning the page to the ensuing "century of federal power," to anticipate even faster rates of expansion; but, in fact, the results are virtually identical. During this second enlargement of American power, the curve of federal employment again rose 10.4-fold between 1880 and 1940 (1,042,420) and some 30-fold by 1970 (2,981,524). What this meant, of course, was a vast and fairly rapid expansion in political opportunities—that is, in the number of billets available for those pursuing careers in politics and the federal service (*Historical Statistics* 1975, 2: 1102–3; Jensen 1950: 360–74). These figures are all the more impressive when compared to changes in the size of the American labor force. Federal employment in this century has doubled the annual rate of growth in total labor force (Meltzer and Richard 1978) and nearly tripled it in the nineteenth century (*Historical Statistics* 1975, 1: 139). At these rates, even the losers in American politics have usually been able to secure a place in or near the heart of the political action. Under such felicitous circumstances, the reigns of power are somewhat more readily relinquished. Some would argue, however, that the past is not prologue, that the transect of government has passed its zenith. They might point to NAFTA and the skeletal federal staff assigned to manage this vast enlargement in American power. True enough, but it is also worth recalling that slightly more than two hundred years ago the Department of War (the forerunner of the Department of Defense) consisted of a staff of five, Secretary Knox included, and an army of 679 officers and men!

A viable civil society also depends on its material achievements, on a growing economy. In this regard, the pace of American economic progress has been truly remarkable in the "century of sectionalism" as well as in the "century of federal power." In the former, from 1790 to 1880, the nation's gross national product (measured in constant [1910–1914] dollars) rose nearly 56-fold—from $0.188 billion in 1790 to $10.5 billion in 1880; and in the latter, from 1880 to 1970, by just under 20-fold—from $10.5 billion to $206.2 billion. This sequence—a big boom in GNP in the nineteenth century followed by a smaller boom in this century—is almost precisely the reverse of the trends in GNP per capita. In this case, the small boom precedes the larger one. Thus a 2.6-fold increase in GNP per capita during the nineteenth century (from $81 in 1790 to $209 in 1880) is followed by a nearly 5-fold increase between 1880 and 1970 ($1011) (Berry 1968; *Historical Statistics* 1975, 1: 8–9, 224). The larger points are these: American economic growth was extensive in the nineteenth century, in "the century of sectionalism"; in this era of rapid population growth and frontier expansion, the gains in total GNP more than doubled the gains in GNP per capita. Conversely, economic growth was much more intensive in the twentieth century, in "the century of federal power"; in this span, the gains in GNP per capita nearly doubled the gains in total GNP, thanks in large measure to productivity gains arising from technological innovations and improvements in human capital (e.g., education, health, etc.). Of course, all of this progress, intensive and extensive, could have gone straight downhill into class division and the immizeration of the proletariat (as Marx predicted) were it not for the timely and dialectical interventions of egalitarian regimes with their consumer revolutions and redistributional strategies in tow.

Civil society flourishes under these most favorable conditions. When economic and political opportunities are expanding, when they are underwritten by these periodic enlargements in American power, the good tends to outweigh the bad. Things that elsewhere are so exceptionally fragile—the pacific transfers of political power, sustained economic growth, and social viability itself—are here taken for granted precisely because they are so commonplace, because they are so much more the rule than the exception in the American past. But suppose that all these things were suddenly lost, that the American entitlements to peace and prosperity once again had to be earned. Would we be able to see bobbing hither and yon in the rising tides (scales) of power—tides that have periodically raised all ships (but not, by any means, all crews)—the bottled secret of the American Way?

> *The positive sum game of the American past* ← Social viability ← PE regime ([economic spaces ↑ + political places ↑] ← scalar ratcheting of power ↑) ← FTM regime (new sectional elites ↑ ← fundamental law ← sectional conflict ↑↑ ← regional volatility ↑↑)

Decrypting this message has some utility for the American past, for understanding where we have been—and not a little for the American future, for thinking (and perhaps rethinking) about where we seem to be headed. It should come as no surprise, by now, that my guess is that we will be headed up and out; that just as "the century of sectionalism" and the sectional state gave way to "the century of federal power" and the national state, it, too, shall pass on the road to "the century of continentalism" and the transnational state.

The Anatomy of American States: Politics and Policies

America's several successive states—the sectional, national, and transnational states—trace their origins back to two sources: first, the periodic enlargements in the jurisdictions of the federal government; second, the massive revisions in American politics—in both political organization and the politics of resource distribution—necessitated by these new and enlarged jurisdictions. The result was a series of distinctive American states—the first (1789–1880) was sectional in scope, intensely partisan in political organization, and distributive in the disposition of resources; the second (1880–1980), on these same dimensions, was national, postpartisan (interest groups), and regulatory and redistributive; and the third (1980–date) is transnational in scope and jurisdiction and, with respect to political organization and the politics of resource distribution, a mix of neoliberalism (in the classical sense of that term—e.g., the restrained state) and neoregulationism (in the form of federal bufferings of elite economic risk). Table 6.1 offers an anatomy of national-level policies and politics prevailing in each of the three American states.

THE SECTIONAL STATE: PARTY SYSTEMS, CONGRESS, AND POLITICAL STRATEGY IN THE "EXTENDED REPUBLIC"

The Sectional State prevailed from the 1780s to the 1870s. In this span, Americans were preoccupied by sectional tensions, by tensions over the appropriate balance between federal and state sovereignties (McDonald 2000: vii), and by the problems arising from the rapid pace of territorial expansion. The Sectional State addressed these issues by turning to political parties, to intense partisanship, and their crystallization into the nation's first and second party systems. With the aid of Congress and the courts, the Sectional State resolved these issues via strategies of sectional compromise and a distributive (and modestly coercive) polity—at least until 1861.

In the era of the Sectional State, political parties stood at the center of American politics. And there were many of them. Nineteenth-century Americans belonged to dozens of different political parties—Federalist, Democratic Republican, Democrat, Whig, Liberty, Free Soil, Know-Nothings, and so on. But all this variety, according to political historians, dissolves into just two fairly distinct party systems. The first party system, and the most rudimentary, was precipitated by a clash in the fundamental ideals held by the framers of the federal republic. This primordial division pitted Thomas Jefferson's preference for local authority against Alexander Hamilton's pre-

Table 6.1. An Anatomy of American States

State	Foundation	Scope	External Reference	Policies	Political Organization	Other
The Sectional State (1780s–1870s)	Constitution	Sections/nation	North America	Distributive	Parties/partisan "Courts and Congress	High voter turnout/ logrolling
The National State (1880–1970s)	14th Amendment	Nation/hemisphere	Western Hemisphere	Regulatory/ redistributive	Bureaucratic/interest groups; presidential power	Lobbying/risk management
The Transnational State (1980–)	Civil Rights Act	Hemisphere/globe	World	Restraint/ devolution	Multistrategic/client politics	Extraterritoriality

disposition for the "general authority." It poised Jefferson's distrust of a distant national state governed by an aristocratic elite against Hamilton's unbridled enthusiasm for the centralization of power—for a national bank, tariffs, excise taxes, the assumption of debts from the states and the continental congresses, and for a neomercantilist political economy (Burnham 1967: 291; Lowi 1967). However bitter the ensuing conflicts between Jeffersonian republicans and Hamiltonian federalists, the first party system managed to survive.

The party system's survival depended in large measure on the shared values of the political elite which, of course, rested on classical civic humanism and the leadership of a virtuous elite, and on the good health of an economy which afforded the federal government an ample budget capable of sustaining federal expenditures at two and a half times the level of state expenditures (Davis and Legler 1966; Berry 1968). When after 1800 factional divisions threatened to destroy the nation, moderate Federalists followed George Washington's example. Setting aside personal and partisan interests, they entered into a productive congressional coalition with Jeffersonian Republicans. The coalition swept the presidential elections of 1804, 1808, 1816, and 1820 with 70 percent or more of the electoral votes (figures 6.1A and 6.1B)—the only serious challenge coming after war began in 1812 when the fusion of antiwar Republicans and Federalists captured the electoral votes of New England (save Vermont), New York, New Jersey, and Delaware. This coalition, which would govern the nation until the contested election of John Quincy Adams in 1824, blurred the lines in the separation of powers, elevated the role of congressional elites, and, in the era before nominating conventions, lodged control over presidential succession in Congress and its caucuses (Lowi 1967).

The politics of the early republic thus rested on a spirit of cooperation and compromise among congressional political elites—all of which culminated in the geopolitical resolution of the slavery controversy with the Missouri Compromise of 1820. This was a spirit that looked at once to the past—to the precedents set by the delegates to the Constitutional Convention in 1787, to Hamilton and Madison's collaboration on the Federalist Papers, and to George Washington—and to the future—to the repeated search for solutions to the sectional problem of slavery in an "extended Republic." By 1820 the Sectional State had managed to stay the conflict over slavery by adding nine states to the thirteen original states, all the while retaining a balance between slave states and free. Although the first party system came to an end in the 1820s with the passing of the Revolutionary generation, the spirit of compromise endured for three decades in the alternating and orderly annexation of free and slave states between the Missouri Compromise of 1820 and the cumbersome and ill-fated Compromise of 1850. What did not endure, however, was the first generation of American nationalists and the mannered nature of this ruling coalition. The presidential election of 1824 introduced unusual rancor and confusion into American politics, not to mention four separate candidates, none with enough votes to prevent the election from an unseemly resolution in the House of Representatives.

The second party system arose out of the election of 1824 and the ensuing democratization of American politics and it lasted for nearly half a century, from the advent of Jacksonian democracy in 1828 to the end of radical reconstruction in the

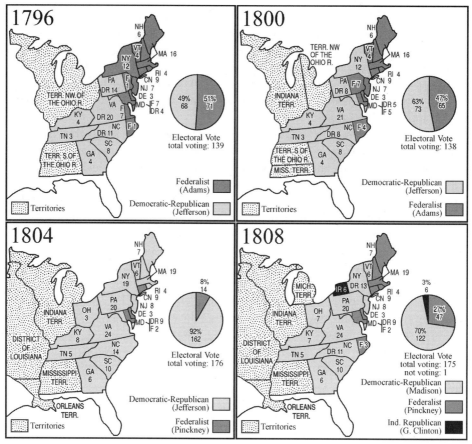

Figure 6.1A.   The geography of presidential elections, 1800–1808.

1870s. What distinguishes this party system from its predecessor is the intensely partisan nature of politics, the massive mobilizations of voters, and the predominance of two major parties—the Democrats and Whigs prior to 1854 and Democrats and Republicans thereafter—amid a sea of minor political parties. The Democratic Party had its origins with Andrew Jackson's presidential campaign and election in 1828. Under the tutelage of Martin Van Buren, the Democratic Party established a competitive party organization in all of the states. It mobilized voters by appealing to states' rights and the rights of the common man and by opposing tariffs, the national bank, and internal improvements. Six years of the Jacksonians were more than enough to drive the opposition into a party of its own. The newly organized American Whig Party offered stiff competition between 1834 and 1853, especially at the federal level. The Whigs demonstrated that theirs was a formidable national party capable of winning votes in all parts of the nation. Indeed, Whig candidates garnered support from nearly every section but especially from southern New England, the Mid-Atlantic states, the Lower Midwest, and the Upper South (save for Virginia) (figure 6.2). But it was the Jacksonians who dominated American politics (Burnham

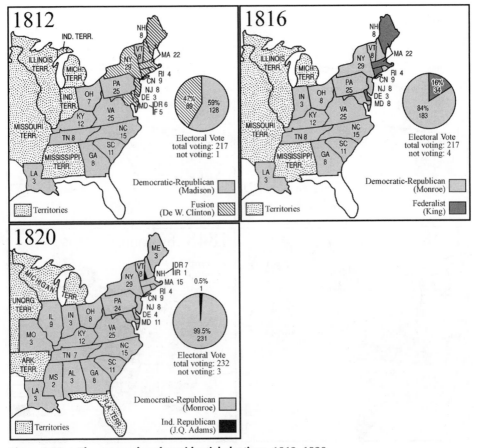

Figure 6.1B.   The geography of presidential elections, 1812–1820.

1967: 295). Democrats won the House of Representatives in eleven of the sixteen elections between 1828 and 1860 and the Senate in thirteen (table 6.2). And the Jacksonians won six of eight presidential elections in that same span—the Whigs winning only twice in thirty-two years with William Henry Harrison in 1841 and Zachary Taylor in 1849.

The Democratic and Whig holds on the national government began to weaken in the late 1840s and 1850s. The Whig Party collapse in 1854 and 1855 was as mercurial and as mysterious as its rise in the mid-1830s. And while the Jacksonians held on to the Senate between 1847 and 1861, they surrendered control over the House of Representatives in four of seven Congresses. And that was a sign of things to come. Over the next two decades, from Lincoln's election in 1860 through Civil War and Reconstruction, the Republican Party won every presidential election. The GOP also claimed the House of Representatives in six of nine Congresses and the Senate in eight (1861–1879) (Republicans lost the House in 1863, 1875, and 1877; and of the Senate in 1875; Martis 1989). The Jacksonian Democrats were rudely pushed aside. Between 1854 and 1873, they garnered just 29.4 percent of the vote

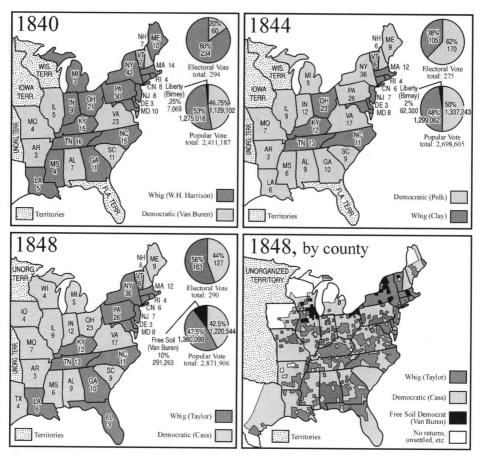

Figure 6.2.   The geography of presidential elections, 1840–1848.

Table 6.2.   Party Control of the U.S. House and Senate for the Congresses between 1827 and 1861

Number of Congresses, 1827–1861	16
Democratic control of the House	11
Non-Democratic control of the House	5
Whigs 1841–1843, 1847–1849	
Whigs and others 1849–1851	
Opposition parties 1855–1857	
Republicans 1859–1861	
Democratic control of the Senate	13
Non-Democratic control of the Senate	3
Anti-Jacksonians 1833–1835	
Whigs 1841–1843, 1843–1845	

Source: Martis 1989.

for presidential electors, 34.4 percent for U.S. representatives, 32.7 percent for U.S. senators, and 25.6 percent for state governors (Burnham 1967: 297, table 2).

While the Republican Party's dominance of national politics followed inexorably from its seminal role in prosecuting the Civil War and defining the nation's reconstruction, the outcome was not merely a morality play in which good triumphed over evil, in which the sacred party of antislavery smote the profane parties that had supported or condoned slavery. The Republicans prevailed for three very practical political reasons. First, the secession of the south tore a gaping hole in the Democratic Party's electoral base. Second, that hole was not repaired for a decade or more because of the slow pace of national reconciliation during Radical Reconstruction (all of which pared down Democratic support). Third, Republicans padded their congressional advantage by packing the House of Representatives and the Senate with party members representing newly created western states of dubious legitimacy (the so-called rotten boroughs of Kansas [1861], West Virginia [1863], Nevada [1864], Nebraska [1867], and Colorado [1876]; and six others that would follow in 1889 and 1890; figure 6.3).

The Republican Party's momentary good fortune is well illustrated by the changing composition of the House of Representatives. Before secession, in 1859, the number of House seats stood at 238; by 1863, that number had fallen to 184. In that time, the eleven seceding southern states surrendered fifty-nine seats (mostly Democratic), while the northern states added five. Republicans dominated the House as well as the Senate (which lost twenty-two seats with secession). After the war, Congress gradually readmitted southern states to the Union, and at first most of

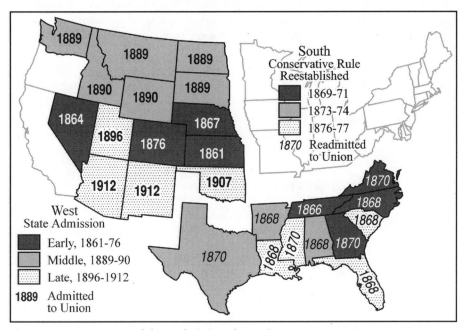

Figure 6.3.   New states and the readmission of secession states, 1860–1912.

these went to the Republicans. In 1867, during Radical Reconstruction, Republicans held thirty-seven of the forty-one seats regained by the South; Democrats held just two. Thereafter, however, southern Democrats made large inroads by winning twenty-nine of fifty-six seats in 1871 and sixty-four of seventy-one in 1877. Summing up the changes in the House as a whole, seats in that body rose from a low of 184 in the midst of the Civil War (1863) to 293 in 1877—a net gain of 109 seats. And three-fourths of these gains (71/109) came via the restoration of southern seats (90 percent of which were Democratic in 1877); the rest (38), from the free states (from new states and population growth). In providing over 20 percent of the House and 30 percent of the Senate, the southern Democrats henceforth constituted a formidable force in American politics (table 6.3). By 1876, as the United States prepared to celebrate its centennial, the Democratic Party was once again in a position to contest for control of the Congress and the presidency (Martis 1989). The party was increasingly competitive in the North, especially in the industrial cities, and its hold on the South was uncontested.

These changes in political parties and party systems resulted in significant shifts in the power of the states and the federal government in the life cycle of the Sectional State. These centripetal and centrifugal shifts in power are especially evident in the trend in federal and state expenditures between 1820 and 1880 (table 6.4). The first of these shifts occurred in the 1820s in the transition from the first to the second party system; the second, in the 1860s in conjunction with the Civil War and the Republican ascendancy. If we begin in 1820, before the Jacksonians, federal expenditures were fairly high. The per capita expenditure of $2.52 (in constant dollars of 1860) in the early national period was not exceeded until 1870; moreover, the ratio of federal-to-state expenditures was formidable (2.38). But with the rise of Jacksonian democracy after 1828, the federal role in American government was pared back sharply by 1840. With the reinvigoration of states' rights and the growing distrust of centralized power in Congress and the National Bank, the Jacksonians scaled back federal operations save for expenditures on internal improvements, the military, and patronage jobs in the expanding postal system. Federal expenditures fell from 2.6 percent of GNP in 1820 to 1.7 percent in 1840 and 1860. And per capita federal expenditures (again in real dollars) dropped from $2.52 in 1820 to $1.72 in 1840 before rising to $2.24 in 1860. Under the Jacksonians, it was the states that made the

Table 6.3.   Southern Seats in the House of Representatives, 1861–1877

Year	Southern Seats	Southern Democratic Seats	Total Seats in House
1859			238
1863	(−49)		184
1867	41	2	226
1871	56	29	243
1873	65	27	292
1875	71	56	293
1877	71	64	293

Source: Martis 1989.

Table 6.4.   Federal and State Expenditures, 1820–1900 (in real dollars of 1860)

Date	Federal Expenditure/ Capita	State Expenditure/ Capita	Federal Expenditures as % GNP
1820	2.52	1.06	2.6%
1840	1.72	1.73	1.7%
1860	2.24	1.56	1.7%
1870	13.12	4.36	4.3%
1880	11.24	2.24	4.3%
1900	8.75	2.84	3.2%

Sources: Davis and Legler 1966; Berry 1968.

most impressive fiscal gains. State expenditures rose from lows of $1.06 per person and a 42 percent share of federal expenditures in 1820 (near the end of the first party system) to $1.73 per person and parity with federal expenditures in 1840 before settling back to $1.56 and a 75 percent share in 1860. But while thrifty Jacksonians managed to cut back federal expenditures and to pay off the federal debt at the same time, they had the advantage of other resources at their command as we shall see.

The Jacksonian retrenchment in federal power came to an abrupt end during the Civil War and Reconstruction. The Republican Party's dominance of federal politics in the 1860s and 1870s resulted in a marked shift in power from the states to the federal government. Following the election of Abraham Lincoln in 1860, the Republican Party resurrected the Hamiltonian and the Federalist virtues of a powerful central government, a secure national currency, high tariffs, internal improvements, and the nationalization of banking and debt. These commitments to bigger government along with the fiscal exigencies of a civil war sharply boosted federal expenditures. Federal spending rose by over fivefold—from $2.24 per capita in 1860 to $13.12 in 1870 and $11.24 in 1880. And it was the victors that received most of the spoils. The geography of federal spending shifted sharply in favor of the victorious northern states—the American urban-industrial core. Before the Civil War, the core states in the Northeast and Midwest received slightly less than a third (32.2 percent) of federal expenditures. After the war, the shares claimed by these states jumped to 61.9 percent in 1870 and 72.5 percent in 1880—all of which reinforced the economic advantages of the urban-industrial core. Elsewhere, the southern states lost a great deal more than the war. Republican administrations slashed the South's share of federal spending from 58.4 percent in 1860 to 22 percent in 1880. They also pared back spending in the western states—from 13.4 percent in 1860 to 5.3 percent in 1880.

Nor could the states collectively keep up with the fast pace of federal spending. Despite a threefold increase in state spending between 1860 and 1870, the ratio of state to federal expenditures per person fell from 0.75 in 1860 to 0.35 in 1870 and just 0.20 in 1880. These massive realignments in state and federal expenditures (and power) heralded something entirely new—nothing less than the rise of big government and the highly centralized National State—but that gets us a bit ahead of our story.

Political parties roosted in all branches of the federal government, but nowhere was partisan politics more in evidence than in the halls of Congress. It was Congress that distributed the various resources that the Constitution permitted to the Sectional State; that repeatedly negotiated compromise of the sectional conflicts that the federal courts and the executive branch repeatedly managed to enflame; whose members were best known and whose leaders enjoyed the most prestige and esteem—men such as Henry Clay, Daniel Webster, and John Calhoun who were better known than most presidents; and it was Congress, and more precisely the congressional caucus, that until 1824 determined presidential succession. And despite fairly high rates of turnover in the House and Senate between 1789 and the 1870s (40–65 percent; Poole and Rosenthal 2000: 77), it was Congress that made politics fairly stable at the federal level. Indeed, it has been said that "the nation could have been governed by congressional committee and logrolling" (Lowi 1972: 301; 1967). Such minimalism was possible in a State that spent modestly, taxed hardly at all, gave away what resources it had rather too generously, and avoided the coercive policies (e.g., regulation and redistribution) that invited the disaffections of its citizens (leaving these issues to the several states; Novak 1996). This relaxed mode of governance is all the more remarkable for a state that in 1860 ranked as the world's third richest nation.

Congress and the Sectional State left the tougher tasks of governance to the states and the political parties therein. It was state politicians and state legislatures who had primary responsibility for building the party and making regulatory policy. It was party regulars in the states who did the "dirty work," who implemented the redistributional policies that taxed real property, financed patronage jobs, services and contracts, and channeled these to supporters of the party in power. Not surprisingly, this highly partisan system of resource redistribution mobilized statewide constituents. Voters turned out in record numbers during the second party system. Turnout in national presidential elections exceeded 50 percent after 1828 and hovered between 70 and 80 percent between 1840 and 1900—this despite fairly high rates of demographic turnover from one election to the next (Shelley et al. 1996: 115). Americans were preoccupied by state, local, and national politics and electioneering, they voted for candidates on the basis of their claims and those of their parties, and they held political parties responsible for their policies at state, local, and federal levels. As Michael Holt has pointed out, "there was a direct connection between electoral and legislative politics. . . . The more partisan governance was, the more voters seemed to like it." The American ideal, he suggests, "was a polity in which one major party or the other was clearly responsible for what government did or did not do, so that voters could reward or punish them as appropriate. Major parties did not shape all aspects of public life or civic participation . . . , but they seem to have been the primary engines driving political developments" during an era of sectional conflict (Holt 1999: 157). In this milieu, the "low" politics of state and local political organizations, patronage systems, and voter constituencies was inextricably linked with (and dependent on) the "high" politics at the federal level.

When it came to matters of "high" politics, it was sectional conflict and compromise that preoccupied Congress and American political parties from 1789 to

1877. Sectional tensions multiplied as the nation fractured into a mosaic of regions—new South and old; Upper South and Lower; Upper Midwest and Lower; New England and the Mid-Atlantic states. And in these tendentious times, political parties repeatedly clashed over issues that appealed or revulsed one section or another, issues such as the tariff, the national bank, internal improvements, and most of all slavery (Poole and Rosenthal 2000: 48–51); and they regularly fought over measures aimed at centralizing or peripheralizing governance (e.g., the national bank, loose vs. strict construction of the Constitution, cheap land vs. dear, state control over the votes of federal senators, etc.). Yet at the same time, the major parties exhibited an enormous capacity for compromise—at least until 1861 (Ellis 1971; Riker 1955; Holt 1992, 1999; Silbey 1991). This capacity owed much to the past—to the legacies of virtuous service demanded by civic humanism and organic republicanism passed on by the founding fathers—and something to the present—most notably, the large overlap in the political positions held by the members of the major parties in the House and the Senate (Poole and Rosenthal 2000: 81). These ingredients for cooperation came to the fore in a series of negotiated compromises on the geography of slavery in the United States. This series included the alternating admission of slave and free states between 1815 and 1850, the Missouri Compromise of 1820, the Compromise of 1850, and even Stephen Douglas's Kansas–Nebraska Act of 1854.

In addition to this preference for political compromise, the Congresses of the Sectional State had a penchant for distributive policies, for policies that were more generous than coercive. When they weren't dealing with sectional issues *sensu stricto*, political parties in Congress fashioned a low-coercion, low-cost distributive polity. No matter what their official positions on federal spending, political parties in Congress found constitutional authority for an array of resources suitable for distribution to their constituents. And in the first party system before 1828, they regularly and liberally distributed federal resources toward elites; and in the second party system beginning in the 1830s, they favored the masses of citizens (McCormick 1979, 1982; Lowi 1992). These distributions came in various forms including, among others, outright gifts, patent rights, tariff protection, and, less often, direct federal expenditures; the latter, as we have seen, were on the decline in the Sectional State (table 6.4). In the absence of vast fiscal resources, Congress distributed federal largesse in imaginative ways—sales of the public domain at less than market prices; outright land grants from the public domain; tariff-sheltering of infant industries from overseas competition; patent protection for inventions; and greater security of contract and property rights—along with direct expenditures for defense and internal improvements. The federal budget was not large, and much of it was consumed by direct federal spending on the army, navy, and veterans. Military spending, with all its contracts and multiplier effects, made up sizable and generally increasing shares of federal outlays between 1790 and 1850; the military's share exceeded 50 percent of federal outlays in 1800, 1830, and 1840 (proportions that were unmatched save for wartime; *Historical Statistics* 1975, 2: 1114–15). The Sectional State also provided compensation and pensions for military veterans; on occasion, these accounted for a fifth or so of federal outlays, particularly after wars (e.g., 18 percent in 1820 and 21 percent in 1880).

Having invested such large shares of federal outlays in national defense broadly defined, Congress had little money left for discretionary expenditure. But for an imaginative Congress, numerous resources remained to be defined and distributed by the Sectional State. And land was at the top of the list. Congress distributed land to hundreds of thousands of Americans. Land prices were fairly moderate and sales out of the public domain were ample, totaling over 150 million acres between 1800 and 1860. Because of lax surveillance of the public domain, as much or more acreage may have been occupied by squatters (judging from the discrepancies between the very large acreage of land settled and the smaller totals of public lands sold). Another 140 million acres of land was awarded in the form of federal land grants for aid in the construction of canals, roads, and railroads between 1823 and 1871—all of which totals to between 450,000 and 700,000 square miles or one-fifth to one-sixth the size of the United States. Equally generous were the homesteading provisions of the Morrill Act of 1862. By 1880, nearly 450,000 original entries for land had been recorded and homesteaders had registered final claims for over eighteen million acres (Lebergott 1985; *Historical Statistics* 1975, 1: 424, 428–30).

The Sectional State also provided indirect benefits for nearly all American producers. In most years, tariffs were levied on over 90 percent of imported goods, thus sheltering a wide range of American industries and jobs (Eckes 1995: 107). American inventors in the Sectional State likewise reaped the monopolistic benefits of a distributive polity in the form of a patent license. Although patents were not common—a few hundred per year—before 1828, the number of awards rose nearly fortyfold—to several thousand just before the Civil War and to twelve to sixteen thousand in the 1870s just as the Sectional State was coming to an end (population, meanwhile, rose only fourfold; *Historical Statistics* 1975, 2: 957–59).

Lastly, the Sectional State provided direct and indirect support for internal improvements. The sums were modest—some $54.9 million between 1800 and 1860 or an annual average of about $915,000 per year. The amounts are more impressive, however, when we realize that 45 percent of itemized expenditures came in just one decade—the 1830s—and 27 percent in another—the 1850s. Thus, contrary to received wisdom, it was the Jacksonian Democrats who were the big spenders on internal improvements. In the 1830s, the Jacksonians spent an average of $1.6 million per annum (this represented 5.7 percent of all federal expenditures in 1840). Received wisdom on the Jacksonians is further contradicted by the fact that it was not the frontier that benefited most from the Jacksonian's disbursements. When the Jacksonians were in power in the 1830s and 1850s, states west of the Appalachians received 56 percent or less of the federal outlays for internal improvements in the 1830s and 1850s; the western states' share jumped to 76 percent when the Whigs gained power in the 1840s (Malone 1998: 16–29; see also "Internal Improvements," 1852). Even more impressive is the distribution of some 140 million acres of federal land to aid in the construction of canals, roads, railroads, and the like; 94 million acres went into private hands and another 46.6 million acres flowed to the states (most of this went to railroads, and, in this case, 70 percent of the acreage was dispersed after the beginning of the Civil War—in 1863, 1865, and 1867; *Historical Statistics* 1975, 1: 424, 430). In this fashion, political parties at the federal level liberally defined and distributed the resources at their command. In so doing, they turned to the Constitution, which permitted the creation of a variety of property rights, and to Congress, which carried out these prerogatives with a modest expenditure of funds and effort. And concurrently, federal politicians deflected the more controversial, more costly, and more coercive sphere of regulatory and redistributive policy to the several states (Novak 1996).

Having exhausted themselves on domestic politics at state, local, and national levels, Americans had little energy left for international intrigue. Fortunately, external affairs and foreign policy issues were not of great moment in the Sectional State, save perhaps for matters of trade policy and conflicts arising from territorial expansion on the south and west. By and large, Americans in the Sectional State followed George Washington's advice and avoided entangling alliances. Americans kept their troops close to home; and for the most part, they minimized military interventions abroad. Over the eight decades of the Sectional State, the United States used forces abroad on just seventy-nine occasions, or about once a year (interventions averaged 0.8 per year between 1798 and 1828 and 1.1 between 1829 and 1879; calculated from Collier 1993). This level pales by comparison to the 2.4 interventions per year during the Second Republic—between 1880 and 1932. When Americans did engage in conflict overseas, they usually did not go far from home looking for a fight (figure 6.4). External conflicts usually involved geopolitical disagreements over territorial control or expansion into contiguous territorial regions. This was the case in large part with the various Indian wars, in large part with the War of 1812, and with the Mexican War (1846–1848), along with a host of treaties with the governments of France, Britain, Spain, and Mexico. The Tripolitan War of 1801–1805 and the purchase of Alaska are the exceptions proving the rule of geopolitical proxemics. The net result of continental American diplomacy and militance was a stunningly

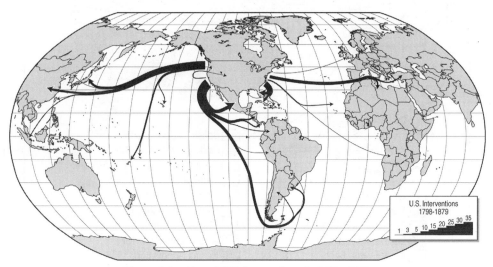

Figure 6.4.   Use of U.S. forces abroad, 1798–1879.
Source: Collier 1993.

rapid 3.4-fold expansion in U.S. territory during the course of the Sectional State—from 888,000 square miles in 1790 to 3 million square miles by 1853 (figure 6.5 and table 6.5). Some of this territory was added peacefully (the purchase of Louisiana and later Alaska); some came under the clouds of war (Florida, Texas, Oregon); and some via war itself (the southwestern United States and California)—and all of it was added so quickly and efficiently as to be deemed a reflection of the nation's "manifest destiny" (figure 6.5 and table 6.5).

As for the Monroe Doctrine, President James Monroe's 1823 warning against European interventions in the affairs of newly independent states in the Western Hemisphere, was more bark than bite—more an expression of American expectations and hope than a legitimate, enforceable threat—over the ensuing half century. Fortunately, these words were not put to the test by European powers that, at the midpoint of the nineteenth century, were greatly distracted by internal matters of their own—by the "hot air" of social unrest, civil strife, and suffrage; by prosperity and poverty; by utilitarianism and romanticism, communism and free trade. Thus, Monroe's Doctrine "did not become a 'doctrine' for at least twenty years, and was

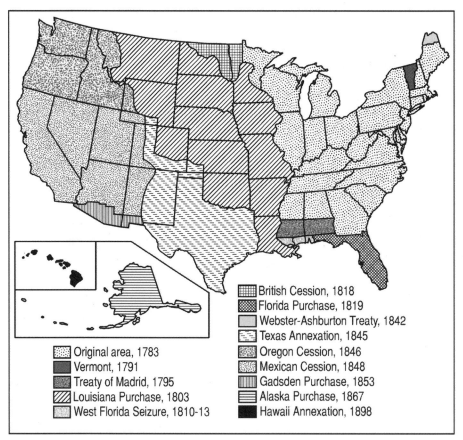

Figure 6.5.   U.S. territorial expansion, 1783–1898.

Table 6.5.   U.S. Territorial Expansion under the Sectional State, 1790–1867

Accession	Date	Area Added (sq. miles)	Cumulative Area
U.S. Territory	1790	888,685	
Louisiana Purchase	1803	827,192	1,715,877
Red River Basin	1818	46,253	1,834,183
Treaty with Spain	1819		
Florida, etc.		58,650	
Southern boundary, Louisiana			
Purchase		13,353	1,906,136
Texas	1845	390,143	2,296,279
Oregon	1846	285,580	2,581,859
Mexican Cession	1848	529,017	3,110,876
Gadsden Purchase	1853	29,640	3,140,516
Alaska	1867	586,412	3,726,928

Sources: Historical Statistics 1975, 1: 428; Morris 1970: 432, 441.

so apparently inconsequential that diplomatic historians took almost no notice of it until the closing years of the nineteenth century" (McDougall 1997: 58). One suspects that the little-used doctrine might have been forgotten altogether had it not been for its post-1880 revival by James Blaine, Theodore Roosevelt, and the expansionist-imperialist agenda of the emergent National State—to which we now turn.

THE NATIONAL STATE: THE COERCIVE HABIT AT HOME AND ABROAD

The National State (1880s–1970s) resolved once and for all the great debate over federalism—over "the nature of the Union and the line to be drawn between the authority of the general government and that of the several states" (McDonald 2000: viii). The powers of the several states receded swiftly after the Civil War even as the powers of the central government gained strength and were solidified—all of which undermined the Madisonian foundations of dual federalism. In short order, the National State tightened the loose structure of American governance, centralized political power in the federal branches, radically revised the content of domestic and foreign policies, and imbued all with nationalist aims, perspectives, and commitments. Henceforth, *e pluribus Unum* had become a reality—many states had, at last, become one. The plural definition of the Sectional State—"the United States are"— gave way to the singular definition of the National State—"the United States is."

This nationalizing transformation began with the North's victory over the South in the Civil War and was sustained by the passage of the Fourteenth Amendment. In guaranteeing all citizens the rights of due process and equal protection, that amendment extended the Bill of Rights and federal law to the states, and it vastly expanded the legal jurisdiction and the power of the federal government—albeit not ironically in the sphere of minority civil rights. In that sphere, the National State twice relinquished jurisdiction, first in the Compromise of 1877 and second in *Plessy v. Ferguson* (1896), thus enabling Jim Crow, the Bourbon ascendancy, and the rise of the solid Democratic South (Sandel 1996).

As racism and political realism combined to trump justice in the southern states, the rest of the nation witnessed the accumulation of power in the federal government and the northern quadrant of the National State. The war was exceedingly kind to this region; federal spending there rose from 32.2 percent of the U.S. total in 1860 to 62 percent in 1870 and 73 percent in 1880. Concurrently, the National State introduced policies and modes of governance more appropriate for the regulation of the complex urban-industrial society that had emerged after the Civil War. The Sectional State, with its lax mode of governance and generous dispensation of resources, gave way to the increasingly coercive policies of regulation after 1880 and redistribution after 1930. And as the policies of the National State took hold, the familiar informality of party politics, the political suspense associated with massive voter turnouts, and the superheated partisanship faded away into the dull-drab pluralism of postpartisan politics laden with interest groups, lobbyists, state bureaucrats, experts, commissions, campaign financing by special interests, falling voter turnouts, and, after 1932, corporatist voter coalitions sustained by the clientage of transfer payments and redistributive policies.

Two political parties shared in the formal governance of the National State; indeed, the leading roles of the Republican and Democratic Parties were contested on so very few occasions as to be memorable—most notably with the third-party challenges mounted by the Populist Party in the 1890s, the Progressive Party and the Socialist Party of America in 1912, the Dixiecrats in 1948, the segregationist campaign of George Wallace in 1968, and the independent bid of Ross Perot in 1992. While these challenges were ephemeral, the issues they raised often endured and were absorbed into the platforms of the mainstream parties.

The Republican Party prevailed during the Second Republic (1880–1930) and the first half of the National State. In the fifty-six years between the Compromise of 1877 and the election of FDR (1933), Republicans held the Senate for forty-four years, the presidency for forty years, and both the House and Senate for thirty years (fifteen of twenty-eight Congresses; table 6.6). For the most part, electoral politics had a distinctly sectional flavor (figure 6.6). Republican candidates regularly won election in the populous northeastern and midwestern states, Democrats regularly prevailed in the South, while both parties fought over the western states. In the northern states, Republicans had a sizable advantage on one key issue—namely, the matter of veterans' pensions. This issue loomed especially large toward the end of the century when more and more veterans claimed their pensions and when pension expenditures constituted one-third (34 percent) of total federal outlays (1890). But even with this electoral advantage, the road to Republican hegemony was not a smooth one. Indeed, Republicans were not assured control of the House even with the admission of five "Republican-friendly" states between 1860 and 1877—West Virginia, Kansas, Nebraska, Nevada, and Colorado. The Democratic Party remained competitive for several reasons—the readmission of the southern states that had se-

Table 6.6.   Party Control of the U.S. Presidency, House, and Senate, 1877–1980

The Second Republic (1877–1932)

Presidents elected:		
Republicans (10)		1877, 1881, 1889, 1897, 1901, 1905, 1909, 1921, 1925, 1929
Democrats (4)		1885, 1893, 1913, 1917

Congresses 28		
Republican Houses	16/28	
Republican Senates	22/28	
Republican House and Senate	15/28	(1889, 95, 97, 99, 1901, 03, 05, 09, 19, 21, 23, 25, 27, 29)
Democratic House and Senate	4/28	(1879, 93, 1913, 1915)
Divided House and Senate	9/28	(1877, 81, 83, 85, 87, 91, 1911, 17, 31)

The Second Democracy (1933–1980)

Presidents elected:		
Democrats (8)		1933, 37, 41, 45, 49, 61, 65, 77
Republicans (4)		1953, 57, 69, 73

Congresses 24		
Democratic Houses	23/24	
Democratic Senates	23/24	
Democratic House and Senate	23/24	(1933, 35, 37, 39, 41, 43, 45, 47, 49, 51, 55, 57, 59, 61, 63, 65, 67, 69, 71, 73, 75, 77, 79)
Republican House and Senate	1/24	(1953)
Divided House and Senate	0/24	

ceded, their installation of conservative Democratic regimes, and the independent streak displayed by western radicals and reformers. In the two decades after 1874, party politics "reflected the spirit of the age: reckless, competitive, blustering, and devoted to the nation's rapid material growth. Neither party dominated the federal government for any length of time. Although the Democrats won a majority of the presidential popular vote in four of the five elections and lost the election of 1880 by only 7,000 votes, they failed in 1876 and again in 1888 to secure a majority in the electoral college" (Hays 1957: 143). And although the Democrats managed to win five of six elections in the House between 1875 and 1887, they won the Senate and the presidency just once apiece. The resemblance of these times with today's "divided governance" is hard to overlook. Things might have been quite different, however, had Republicans failed to gain the admittance of the five "rotten boroughs" noted earlier. In that event, the Democrats would have won control over both the House and the Senate in five of the six elections and over the White House in two of three. But reality was little better for the Republicans. Having won the Civil War and packed the House and Senate, they had a hard time winning over the political nation a decade hence; two decades of stalemate was the best they could muster (Stewart and Weingast 1992).

The decisive turning point for the Republicans came in 1889 and 1890 with the admission of six more states—five reliably Republican (North and South Dakota,

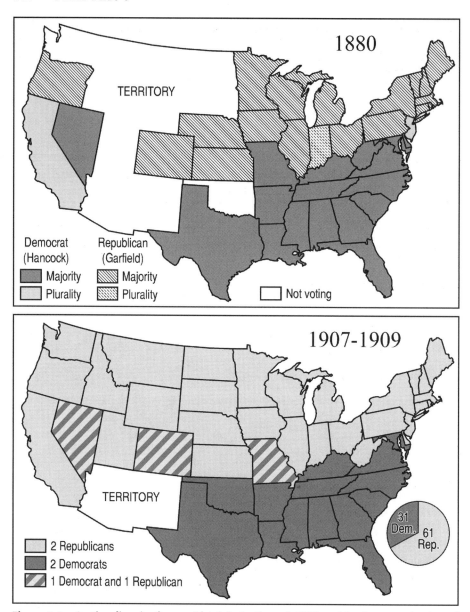

Figure 6.6. Sectionalism in the presidential election of 1880 and in Congress (top); and Democrats and Republicans in the Senate, 1907–1909 (bottom).

Montana, Idaho, Wyoming) and Washington (Stewart and Weingast 1992; figure 6.3). These states along with the five others admitted since 1860 accounted for fully one-fourth (twenty-two of eighty-eight) of the seats in the U.S. Senate. With the states now stacked in their favor, the Republicans reigned over both the House and Senate between 1895 and 1911 and again between 1919 and 1933. The Republican Party also enjoyed a long stay in the White House (1897–1913 and 1921–1933) interrupted only by the vexed elections of Woodrow Wilson in 1912 and 1916. The first defeat in 1912 followed a division within the Republican Party, the bolt of Theodore Roosevelt to the Progressives, and the third-party efforts of the Progressives and the Socialist Party that led to a split vote ensuring a narrow victory for Woodrow Wilson and the Democrats (Wilson won 82 percent of the electoral vote, but only 42 percent of the popular vote; the rest divided as follows: Republican Taft, 23 percent; Progressive Roosevelt, 27.5 percent; and Socialist Debs and other minor parties, 7.5 percent). The second defeat came four years hence; in this case, Wilson rode the clouds of war to victory, thus becoming the first incumbent Democrat to win reelection since Andrew Jackson.

The Republican hegemony over national politics came to an abrupt end with the onset of the Great Depression of the 1930s. The Democratic Party turned the tables—and decisively so—with Franklin Roosevelt's New Deal, the rise of the second American Democracy, and its commitments to equal opportunity, welfare, and income redistribution at home, and free trade, liberalism, and internationalism abroad. Roosevelt won an unprecedented four straight elections. And over the next half century (1933–1981), the Democratic Party virtually swept the electoral field holding the presidency for thirty-two of forty-eight years and winning both houses of Congress an astonishing forty-six of forty-eight years (table 6.6). Democrats accomplished this by building what seemed to be an unstable coalition of liberal and conservative geographies. This involved retaining white conservatives in the "solid democratic South" (while smoothing over the episodic boltings of the Deep South to the Dixiecrats in 1948, the Republican Goldwater in 1964 and Wallace in 1968) while winning over ethnic trade unionists, liberals, and African Americans in the industrial cities of the Northeast and Midwest.

The triumph of the two-party system and the predominance of one between 1880 and 1980 greatly facilitated the growth of federal power "from the Civil War to the Populists to the Progressives and the achievements of the New Deal, the Fair Deal, the Great Society, and the Nixon years" (Degler 1997: 8). This expansion unfolded in two distinct stages that were roughly equivalent to the Second Republic (1880–1932) and the Second Democracy (1932–1980). In the first stage from the Civil War to the onset of the Great Depression, Congress and the courts laid "the foundation for fundamental structural change which would lead to the disintegration of the Madisonian system [of limited government and the Sectional State]" and the rise of the bureaucratic state (North 1981: 193). Despite fairly modest levels of federal spending (3.2 percent of GNP in 1900 along with a cut in federal expenditures from $11.40 per capita in 1880 to $9.53 in 1913), the National State embarked on "the transformation toward greater government intervention . . . in the last quarter of the nineteenth century with the shift from state to federal regulation and from encouragement and promotion [i.e., the distributive policies in the partisan era of the Sectional State] to control [i.e., the coercion of regulatory and redistributive policies]" (North 1981: 191). In doing so, the federal government was in step with the growing scale and complexity of American society and with the organizational revolution that swept the nation after the Civil War. Everywhere one looked, formal organizations had sprouted up to voice the special interests and concerns of a wide array of groups. For workers, there were the Knights of Labor and the trade and industrial unions; for farmers, the Grange; for businesses, assorted trade associations and the National Association of Manufacturers; for the professions, professional associations; for municipalities, chambers of commerce; and so on.

The regulatory policies of the National State expanded rapidly after 1892, thanks in large measure to the federal courts and a loose interpretation of the commerce clause of the Constitution. In a series of decisions handed down between 1892 and 1911, the Supreme Court affirmed federal jurisdiction over interstate commerce. These decisions, along with the extension of federal jurisdiction and due process to corporations, opened the gates for a tidal wave of democratic reforms and regulatory restraints emanating from the American periphery (Sanders 2001)—from radical agrarians, populists, socialists, liberal progressives, and their representatives in the House and Senate. In short order, Congress regulated freight rates (initially in 1887 on railroads); trusts and monopolies (1890); meat packing (1891); food and drugs (1906); telephone, telegraph, and cable communications (1910); and money supply (1914). Regulation of other industries would follow in the 1930s. The number of federal regulatory agencies rose to ten between 1890 and 1929, fifteen by 1939, nineteen by 1959, twenty-six by 1969, and forty-four by 1979 (DuBoff 1996: 169). In the process, Congress ceded enormous power to the executive branch by granting commissions and agencies the power "to make rules within the broad policy objectives set out by Congress" (North 1981: 194–95). This broad delegation of regulatory authority initiated a fundamental restructuring of American politics. The new polity was tailor made for the array of associations and interest groups that had arisen during the organizational revolution after the Civil War. "The number and strength of . . . interest groups provided political alternatives to the parties in policy formulation, and by 1900 parties in Congress went into a decline in their capacity to discipline members, a decline from which they have never fully recovered" (Lowi 1972: 302). Interest groups and lobbyists mushroomed around regulatory agencies and commissions, influencing them in all cases and capturing them in some. Meanwhile, the major parties and the distributive polity that was their raison d'être, began their long decline; voter turnout in federal elections, having peaked at about 80 percent in the late nineteenth and early twentieth centuries, fell off to less than 50 percent.

The second stage of the National State dates from the crisis of the Great Depression and the policy response known as the New Deal. It begins with Franklin Roosevelt's grudging acceptance of the redistributive policies of wealth and income transfer and ends in the 1980s with Ronald Reagan's revolt against "the claimant era" (Campbell 1995: 4). Roosevelt's new policies further accelerated the decline of the major parties and hastened the erosion of legislative committee fiefdoms—voids that were filled by the instruments of political centralization: personalist presidential politics and the rise of the so-called plebiscitary presidency (based on the president's direct appeal to the people), the mobilization of public opinion via radio and later television, the flow of revenue to and from Washington, the continued expansion of regulatory authority within the executive branch, and the politicization of the upper echelons of the federal bureaucracy. In this fashion, the Democratic Party increasingly centralized power in the presidency, in the "administration" running the executive-branch agencies, and in the nation's capital itself. There it was applied "as a practical tool to remedy problems in society and reduce personal risk" (Campbell 1995: 4).

That power was ample, indeed—as were the resources that sustained that power. Drawing on the vast revenues generated by property taxes and customs duties before 1913 and income taxation thereafter, American governments spent freely, even lavishly. While federal, state, and local government spending rose threefold between 1927 and 1980 (12 percent of GNP to 36 percent), federal spending alone rose nearly sixfold—from less than 4 percent of GNP in 1929 to 23.4 percent in 1980 (see Niemi 1980: 358; Campbell 1995: 34, 113). All of this is reflected in the shift in fiscal and political power away from the several states where it had been lodged in the Sectional State and toward the federal government in Washington, D.C. If we go back to 1840, at the height of the Sectional State, we find that federal and state expenditures were identical and they were nearly so in 1860. But all of this changed after the Civil War; in the National State, the ratio in federal-state expenditures approached 3:1 in 1870 and thereafter ranged from 2:1 to 4:1 with spikes of 5.1:1 in 1880 and 13.3:1 in 1946 just after World War II (table 6.7). The growth of the National State is likewise reflected in gains in federal employment and in the population of the nation's capital between 1880 and 1980—the former rising thirty-fold to 2.98 million, the latter nearly twentyfold to 3.5 million.

Americans who lived through the Great Depression could not ignore the bleak realities of unemployment and economic uncertainty; nor could the federal government continue attributing these problems to individual shortcomings and consigning their solution to the private sector, philanthropists, social agencies, and state and local governments. Henceforth these concerns would become centerpieces of New Deal policy at the federal level. The first of these, unemployment and poverty, was addressed by increasing the level of welfare expenditures, the second, economic uncertainty, by the "socialization of risk."

As the New Deal kicked in, the Roosevelt administration and an overwhelmingly Democratic Congress initiated a series of redistributive policies and programs, levied increased taxes on American incomes, and then transferred these revenues to

Table 6.7.   Ratio of Federal to State Expenditures, 1820–1994

Year	Ratio	Year	Ratio
1820	2.35	1940	2.58
1840	0.99	1946	13.30
1860	1.44	1950	3.83
1870	3.01	1960	4.08
1880	5.02	1970	3.31
1900	3.08	1975	2.80
1913	3.24	1980	2.39
1922	3.35	1994	2.10

Sources: Davis and Legler 1966; Niemi 1980: 357; *Statistical Abstract 1997*: 299.

needy claimants. These transfers came in various forms—unemployment compensation, Social Security, subsidized housing, food assistance, and other welfare commitments. Federal expenditures on social welfare rose astronomically from just 0.6 percent of GNP on the eve of the Depression (1929) to 11.5 percent in 1980 (or nearly 50 percent of all federal expenditures) (Campbell 1995: 34, 113). For the special interests who lobbied for increased welfare spending, these were flush times. "As Congress became more decentralized, fragmented, policy-minded, and sensitive to constituent concerns, special interests found numerous niches in which to place and promote their favorite programs. Centralizing institutions were unable to prevent these programs from wending their way through the labyrinthine legislative process" or from securing repeated appropriations. Between 1962 and 1980, three-fourths of the growth in total federal spending could be chalked up to assorted special interests, including social welfare (Peterson 1990–1991: quotation on 550; also 547).

Welfare recipients were not the only claimants on federal funds. Another set of claimants arose among residents on the periphery and in the several regions that had been abused or ignored after the Civil War (table 6.8). For these claimants, the big changes took place between 1880 and 1930. In that span, the shares of federal dollars spent on the South and the northeastern core regions moved in opposing directions. Whereas the core's share of federal spending fell from 72 percent in 1880 to 51 percent in 1930, the South's share rose from the punitive level of 22 percent imposed after the Civil War to 34 percent. Elsewhere on the periphery, federal funds spent on the western states increased at a somewhat slower pace. The West's share rose in two stages: (1) the gain from 5 percent in 1880 to 16 percent in 1930 came at the expense of the core and (2) the gain to 22 percent in 1975 came at the expense of the core and the South.

But the "claimant era" was not merely concerned with equity and income redistribution from richer to poorer Americans or from prosperous to needy regions;

Table 6.8. Regional Shares of Federal Expenditures, 1880–1998 (in percentages)

Region	1880	1928–30	1933–39	1975	1989	1998
New England	18.5	5.9	5.4	6.1	6.4	5.4
Middle Atlantic	33.0	12.3	11.2	16.8	14.7	14.2
East North Central	14.4	6.0	18.2	14.8	14.1	13.5
West North Central	6.0	14.8	15.7	7.4	14.1	13.5
South Atlantic	16.2	16.6	11.3	16.8	19.6	21.4
East South Central	2.8	7.5	8.1	6.4	6.0	6.5
West South Central	3.1	9.9	13.6	9.3	9.7	10.0
Mountain	3.6	9.1	6.9	5.4	6.0	6.1
Pacific	1.7	7.2	11.5	17.0	16.0	15.2
Northern Core	71.9	49.0	50.6	45.1	42.8	40.1
South	22.1	34.0	31.0	32.5	35.3	37.9
West	5.3	16.3	18.4	22.4	22.0	21.3

Note: 1928–1930 equals federal aid to states.
Sources: Davis and Legler 1966; U.S. Seventy-sixth Congress 1939, *Federal Ownership*; Reading 1973; *State and Metropolitan Area Data Book 1991*: 299; Weinstein and Firestine 1978: 6–9, 31; *Statistical Abstract 1999*, 2000.

it was equally an era concerned with moderating economic uncertainty. Thus, with less and less hesitation, Americans of all classes turned to the federal government as the vehicle for reducing, if not eliminating altogether, personal and corporate risk. Indeed, the extension of federal guarantees on investments of all sorts was one of the chief contributors to the nation's spree in federal spending between 1930 and 1980. Federal guarantees for home mortgages (Federal Housing Administration [FHA] and Veterans Administration [VA]), farm mortgages and crop insurance, student loans, businesses and industries (e.g., Chrysler and Lockheed), and bank and savings-and-loan deposits, among many others, exceeded $368 billion in 1978, or approximately 15.8 percent of GNP (welfare expenditures, in contrast, totaled just 11.5 percent of GNP in 1980; Lowi 1979: 280–94). U.S. commitments to risk reduction are even more extensive today, if one adds in the implied federal guarantees for government-sponsored enterprises, most notably those that are operating in the multibillion dollar secondary mortgage markets. It is fair to say that the National State, having *regulated the reduction of risk* in its first half century (1880–1930), sought *to socialize financial risk* in the half century that began with the New Deal and ended with the Reagan Revolution. But beyond the protective cocoon spun by the National State, the world would remain a risky place.

As power ratcheted upward from the Sectional State to the National State, Americans at last began to speak of their collective "American interests" and to formulate a coherent foreign policy. And as the interests of the National State expanded from the Western Hemisphere to the world at large, defense and foreign affairs consumed increasingly larger shares of American time and resources. In less than a century, the United States embarked on five major wars—the Spanish American War, World War I, World War II, and the conflicts in Korea and Vietnam—orchestrated Panamanian independence and constructed and operated the Panama Canal; took possession of Hawaii, Puerto Rico, the Philippines (1899–1933), and the Virgin Islands (Zevin 1972); and, as an element of its post-1945 "Cold War" strategy for the "containment" of the Soviet Union, helped rebuild Western Europe and Japan; established various multilateral institutions ranging from the United Nations to the World Bank, International Monetary Fund, and General Agreement on Tariffs and Trade (GATT); invested ample amounts of foreign aid in anticommunist regimes and alliances abroad (e.g., NATO, Southeast Asia Treaty Organization [SEATO], Australia New Zealand United States Pact [ANZUS]); and intervened overtly and covertly in nations around the world, most especially in the Caribbean and Central America (McDougall 1997; May 1961; Pratt 1950; Williams 1969; Rosenberg 1982).

American interventions abroad rose steadily during the course of the nineteenth and twentieth centuries. These increases are evident in the uses of U.S. forces abroad, be they the sporadic eruption of high-magnitude conflicts such as the War of 1812, the Mexican War, the Spanish American War, World Wars I and II, the conflicts in Korea and Vietnam, and the Gulf War or the more frequent but lower-magnitude interventions. Table 6.9 records the rising trends in both the rates and durations of the usage of American forces abroad (these represent the actual usage of force as opposed to measures tabulating "interstate conflicts in which force was used or threatened." The latter measure, drawn from the Correlates of War Project, tends

Table 6.9.   Instances of Use of U.S. Forces Abroad

	Interventions	*Interventions/Year*	*Intervention Duration/Year*
1798–1828	24	0.77	1.65
1829–1879	55	1.08	1.12
Sectional State	79	0.96	1.32
1880–1932	80	1.51	3.40
1933–1980	35	0.73	1.71
National State	115	1.14	2.60
1981–1993	39	3.00	3.00
Transnational			
State	39	3.00	3.00

High-magnitude Events (with numbers of military personnel)

Sectional State:	War of 1812	(286,730)		
	Mexican War	(78,718)		
National State:	Spanish-American War	(307,000)	World War II	(16,354,000)
	World War I	(4,744,000)	Korean Conflict	(5,764,000)
	Vietnam War	(8,744,000)		

Note: Comparing these data on actual usages (U) of force with the Correlates of War (COW) data underscores the latter's inflationary trend:
   A. 43—1824–1871 (COW); 55—1829–1879 (U).
   B. 59—1872–1919 (COW); 80—1880–1932 (U).
   C. 102—1920–1967 (COW); 35—1933–1980 (U).
   D. 85—1968–1987 (COW); 39—1981–1993 (U).
Sources: Collier 1993; *Statistical Abstract 1999*: 377; *Historical Statistics* 1975, 2: 1135–40.

to exaggerate American belligerence, and the more so nearer the present as threat has become a primary instrument of diplomacy (for these data, see Pollins and Schweller 1999). As noted in table 6.9, the rate of U.S. military interventions doubles between the 1790s and 1992. The rate rises from less than one intervention per year (0.77) in the first half of the Sectional State (1798–1828; the First Republic) to 1.08 in the second half (the First Democracy, 1828–1880) to one and a half interventions per year (1.51) in the first half of the National State (1880–1932; the Second Republic). But after rising for a century and a third, American interventions decreased abruptly after the Great Depression (to 0.73) between 1932 and 1980 (in the second half of the National State). This exceptional interlude came to an end after 1980 when, with the onset of the Transnational State, the rate of intervention shot back up to three per year.

Associated with this upward trend in the rate at which Americans have used force abroad is a similar trend in geography—namely, the ever-widening deployment of American troops from the Western Hemisphere in the beginning to Asia and then the world at large. The broad outline of this geography is as follows:

1798–1828	Latin America	16 of 24 deployments
1829–1879	Latin America	26 of 55
	Asia	22 of 55

1880–1932	Latin America	37 of 80
	Asia	27 of 80
1933–1980	Asia	15 of 35
	Mediterranean	7 of 35
	Latin America	5 of 35
1981–1993	Mediterranean	12 of 29
	Middle East	12 of 39
	Latin America	8 of 39
	Africa	6 of 39

Latin American deployments lead the way in the first three policy regimes. Asian interventions nibbled into that lead after 1829, assumed the lead after 1933, and relinquished it to the Mediterranean and the Middle East after 1980 (figures 6.7 and 6.8). Put another way, the Sectional State was preoccupied with territorial and hemispheric concerns in two world regions; the National State was transitional in its preoccupation with Asia and the Mediterranean as well as Latin America and the exercise of bicoastal maritime power; and, lastly, the Transnational State has gone global in its preoccupation with all major world regions.

The 1930s thus represent a crucial turning point in American foreign policy. Henceforth we see a reversal in the long upward trend in the American usage of force abroad, and we also discern greater diversity in the geography of force deployments. As for the rate of American interventions, there are several reasons for the sharp fall (to 0.73 per year) during the second half of the National State (the Second Democracy, 1933–1980). First is the American preoccupation with three high-magnitude conflicts. Second is the wider usage of espionage and covert actions interlarded with development aid during the Cold War in lieu of the overt use of force.

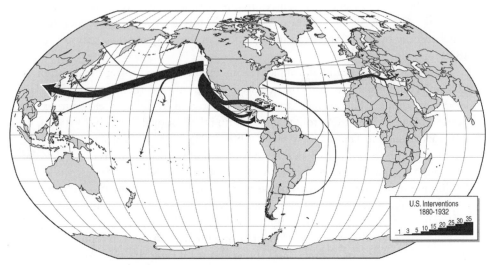

Figure 6.7A.   Use of U.S. forces abroad, 1880–1932.
Source: Collier 1993.

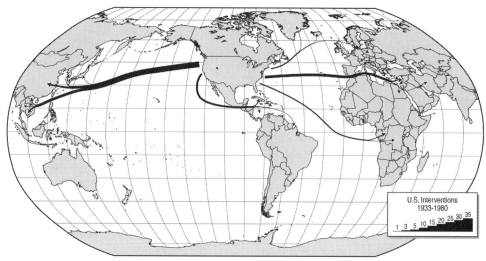

Figure 6.7B.   Use of U.S. forces abroad, 1933–1980.

Source: Collier 1993.

And third is the precipitous drop in American interventions in Latin America (from thirty-seven in 1880–1932 to five in 1933–1980)—a reduction arising from a profound shift in American foreign policy toward Latin America after 1933 from interventionism to "good neighbor."

Since 1980, however, the trend in the rate of U.S. interventions is once again on the rise (to 3.0 per year, 1981–1993). This time, however, the interventions are spread across four continental regions with each accounting for a sixth to a third of the total. The geostrategic accent falls on the Mediterranean and the Middle East with its abundance of energy resources (figure 6.8); these two regions together account for 60 percent of the uses of American forces—a level of predominance matched only by Latin American interventions in the early national period (1798–1828).

A similar though not identical picture emerges when we look at the duration of U.S. interventions. Here, too, the secular trend is upward (i.e., interventions last longer over time). The average duration has increased from 1.32 years during the Sectional State (1798–1879) to 2.60 years during the National State (1880–1980), to 3.0 years during the Transnational State (1981–1993). In the matter of secular trends, durations and rates of the uses of force both trend upward; the difference is that the big jump in durations occurs between the Sectional and National States, while the big jump in rates (tripling) comes between the National and Transnational States.

An equally noteworthy difference arises with respect to the shorter-term trend in durations across the five policy regimes of American history. The trend since 1789 is cyclical. Interventions last much longer during the three American republics (elite/protectionist-nationalist regimes) and much shorter during the two American democracies (mass/egalitarian regimes). And perhaps the most dramatic change in the cycle is associated with the tripling in the duration of U.S. interventions in the

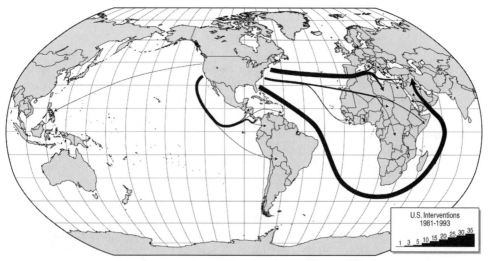

Figure 6.8.   Use of U.S. forces abroad, 1981–1993.

Source: Collier 1993.

half century after 1880—during the American foray into imperialism. In that span, American troops were deployed for long stays in Central America and the Caribbean—in Panama (1903–1914), Nicaragua (1912–1925, 1926–1933), Haiti (1915–1934), the Dominican Republic (1916–1924), and Cuba (1917–1922). The United States accomplished this by trebling military and naval personnel and sextupling their warship tonnage and, by 1920, deploying a well-disciplined force of 117,000 in a host of overseas territories, possessions, protectorates, and foreign nations. After 1930 to 1980, the long stays that were typical of American forces were cut in half.

To sum up, Americans have tended to be more aggressive in the use of force in the first halves of the Sectional, National, and Transnational States. Interventions tend to be higher in frequency and in duration during the First, Second, and Third Republics, but they also tend to be lower in magnitude. Republics have been responsible for only three of the nation's seven major international conflicts. And these three—the War of 1812, the Spanish American War, and World War I—ranked sixth to fourth, respectively. Interventions in democracies, by contrast, tend to be lower in frequency and duration but higher in magnitude. While democracies average less than one intervention per year and last for only 1.4 years (as compared to nearly two interventions lasting 2.8 years under American republics), they also account for the three largest high-magnitude conflicts (and four of the top seven).

The National State in particular paid a high price for this alternating patina of high-frequency and high-magnitude interventionism. No matter whether interventions were characterized by high frequency and duration (as in the Second Republic, 1880–1932) or by high magnitudes (as in the Second Democracy, 1933–1980), outlays for defense of the National State rolled in and out in symmetric swells of twenty to thirty years—rising from 20 percent of federal outlays in 1880 to crest at 45 percent in 1910, falling to 20 percent in 1940, and rising again to 47 percent in

1960. By the latter date—after four major international conflicts, over one hundred interventions abroad and at the peak of the Cold War with the Soviet Union—the military commitments of the National State loomed large. Defense expenditures accounted for about one half of all federal expenditures and 9.7 percent of U.S. gross national product. It was in the 1960s that Lyndon Johnson and a Democratic Congress discovered that the nation could not afford large expenditures on both "guns and butter" (i.e., on welfare, the socialization of risk, and national defense). In the retrenchment that followed the Vietnam War, defense and security expenditures declined precipitously from half of all federal expenditures in 1960 to about a quarter in 1980 (more precisely, defense amounted to 5.7 percent of GNP, while federal expenditures as a whole amounted to 23.4 percent; Campbell 1995: 113). These reductions were felt everywhere, but perhaps least of all in the periphery. As of 1980, some 55 to 60 percent of defense spending was directed toward the southern and western states—to what has been called the "defense perimeter" or the "gun belt" (Crump 1989; Markusen et al. 1991). Not surprisingly, it was these states that provided the strongest support for "Cold War internationalism" and its policy components—free trade, military preparedness, overseas investment, economic aid, arms sales, covert operations, defense spending, and anticommunism (these are examined more fully later in this chapter; Trubowitz 1992).

THE TRANSNATIONAL STATE: POLITICAL DIVISION, FISCAL RESTRAINT, AND FLEXIBLE GEOPOLITICS

A series of profound changes in world affairs in the 1980s helped to pave the way for the rise of the third American State. The end of the Cold War, the implosion of the Soviet Union, the globalization of the world economy, and the emergence of the United States as "the indispensable nation" all necessitated enlargements in the scope and jurisdiction of American sovereignty from the relatively crisp and well-defined boundaries of the National State to the fuzzier edges of the Transnational State. This new state has also necessitated an enlargement in the scholarly field of vision so as to encompass the fuzziness of transnationalism—with its multiperspectival agents and their multiscalar strategies ranging from multilateralism to regionalism to unilateralism (on multiple agents, see Ruggie 1992: especially 172; on multiple strategies, see Falke 1996; and Frankel 2001). The net result is a postmodern polity of extraterritoriality that is at once more flexible, more supple and nuanced, and better suited to the producer revolution of flexible specialization and globalization within transnational economies. And this polity, like the new economy, draws its inspiration from the imperatives of fiscal restraint and functional devolution. This most recent enlargement in the American state is apparent in the multifront advance of American interests and legal jurisdictions; this advance includes, among others, the free-trade agreements with Canada and Mexico (NAFTA); entry into the World Trade Organization (WTO); liberal usage of WTO's complaint procedures against violations of free trade by other nations juxtaposed with desultory compliance with adverse rulings against the United States; zealous litigation of trade disputes against foreign and American firms overseas over dumping, cartels, environmental protection, and civil rights; the extraterritorial extension of American jurisprudence for private plaintiffs in cases of terrorism and expropriation; coordinated monetary exchange-rate agreements; surgical military interventions in Grenada, Iraq, and Kosovo; and support for, but not obeisance to, the proposed court of international criminal justice (Ruggie 1993; Slaughter and Bosco 2000).

In this toned-down American version of lebensraum and manifest destiny, American administrations from Ronald Reagan to George Bush and Bill Clinton have extended American interests and sovereignty well beyond the boundaries of the United States. And lamentably so according to Jagdish Bhagwati (1994: 284–85), a long-standing critic of protectionist-nationalism and the kind of state enlargement embraced by the Third Republic. In his view, the United States has abandoned its post–World War II role as "altruistic" hegemon.

> Now the United States is in . . . "the diminished giant syndrome," where it . . . wants to look after its own interest. It seeks therefore to redefine the trading system to reflect its own needs and priorities, defined increasingly by its own lobbies: seeking excessive intellectual property protection, exploiting environmental and labor issues to reduce competitive pressures and so on. It then uses free trade areas as an incentive strategy and [section] 301 [of the 1974 and 1988 trade acts] as a punishment strategy to bargain to great advantage with individual countries . . . and then goes to the GATT [now the WTO], where these favorable bargains are codified by a divided, partially coopted and weakened opposition.

While the rest of the world routinely complains about the relentless expansion of American influence through movies, television, music, fast food, and other consumer products, our neighbors abroad may have more to fear in the long run from America's extraterritorial encroachments on their national sovereignties and legal jurisdictions.

But what appears to the French, Germans, and others abroad as a unified onslaught of the American way of life seems much less organized and less coherent to observers of the American political scene. Indeed, since the Nixon and Carter administrations in the 1970s, American domestic politics have been fettered by an era of governmental restraint and "divided government." While the Transnational State is vigorously expanding abroad, it is as vigorously contracting at home. The nation's "defining attributes are a hesitancy to expand government, the reduction of regulations, and opposition to spending and tax increases;" and its code words are *privatization, deregulation, devolution, tax cuts,* and *entitlement reform.* "These antistatist attributes" should not, however, be overexaggerated. In the first place, the federal public sector remains vibrant; it has "continued to perform all of the major functions that had become commonplace prior to 1975" (Campbell 1995: 5). The one slight exception may be defense. Because of the "peace dividend" made possible by the collapse of the Soviet Union and the end of the Cold War, the share spent on national defense was slashed from 27 percent of federal outlays during Reagan's administration to 17 percent in Clinton's second term in office (*Statistical Abstract* 1997: 332). This represented a sizable savings—but much of it was poured back into domestic programs. In one year alone, 1999, the "peace dividend" on post-1990 defense cuts amounted to $430 billion—a savings equivalent to federal expenditures on education, health, Medicare, and veterans benefits and services in 1999, or roughly 25 percent of all federal outlays in that year.[2] The federal government is far from shriveling away. In the second place, the Transnational State has gone beyond merely performing the "major functions . . . commonplace prior to 1975"; indeed, it has expanded the functions of the federal government. As later sections make clear, the United States since 1980 has steadily enlarged the sovereign jurisdiction of the Transnational American State—and it has done this in ways that constitute the omega of antistatism.

The current era of governmental restraint, of smaller government, tax cuts, and deregulation juxtaposed with extraterritorial activism and jurisdictional enlargement owes its origins to a polity of divided government and the popular desire for both welfare and patriotism (Kelly 1994). In this contrapuntal polity, the remnants of the two-party system have divvied up "the public consensus on social welfare provision" and the "historic values . . . that had long defined Americanism." The welfare consensus seeks "to protect against the harshness of life in the economic market-place," while the values consensus seeks to perpetuate the American ideals of "individualism, populism, personal autonomy, personal responsibility" not to mention patriotism and civic virtue (Shafer 1993: 472). In the absence of a classical republican party subscribing to these views, the mainstream political parties, like Solomon, sliced the popular consensus in two. "One party, the Democrats . . . [has espoused] the social welfare dimension, but showered contempt on . . . cultural-national values." The other party, the Republicans, has "refused to compromise . . . on social welfare, but offered a sharply drawn version of . . . the cultural-national dimension" (Shafer 1993: 472). In due course, the public discovered that its preferences for both sets of values—for welfare and Americanism—were best realized through the division of governance—that "the Presidency was more about fostering American values, at home and abroad, while Congress was more about insuring [social] benefits" (Shafer 1993: 472). The result of this trade-off is that Americans since 1980 have been the beneficiaries of a moderately generous (though not ample) system of social welfare and an increasingly powerful Transnational State able to maintain peace and prosperity in a globalizing economy—and largely on its own terms.

An era of divided government followed naturally and ineluctably, with Republicans "rightfully" controlling the Presidency and Democrats just as "rightfully" controlling the Congress—that is, until 1992–1994 to 2000 when the parties switched branches. All of this is reflected in the pneumatic balancing of centrist politics from 1981 to 2001 (table 6.10). In that span, the Republican Party won the White House four times, the Democrats twice. And they shared power in Congress—Democrats and Republicans controlling both houses for eight years each; Democrats holding the House in seven of eleven Congresses; and Republicans the Senate in seven of eleven. But within months of the 2000 election, the Senate once again reverted to the Democrats after one senator shifted allegiance from the Republican Party to

Table 6.10.   Party Control of the Presidency, House, and Senate in the Third Republic, 1981–2001

Presidents elected:		
	Republicans	1980, 1984, 1988, 2000
	Democrats	1992, 1996
Congresses under control of:		
House:	Republicans	4 (1995, 1997, 1999, 2001)
	Democrats	7 (1981, 1983, 1985, 1987, 1989, 1991, 1993)
Senate:	Republicans	7 (1981, 1983, 1985, 1995, 1997, 1999, 2001*)
	Democrats	5 (1987, 1989, 1991, 1993, 2001*)
Both Houses:	Republicans	4 (1995, 1997, 1999, 2001*)
	Democrats	4 (1987, 1989, 1991, 1993)

Note: *Although the seats were equally distributed after the election, a Republican vice president represented the tie-breaker. In May 2001, the Democratic Party regained control when one senator switched party allegiance.

Independent. This is about as neatly balanced as one can imagine, it is all the more so when we add in the centrist "New Democrat" policies of the Clinton administration, the compassionate conservatism of George W. Bush, and the even split in the party control of state legislatures (in state legislatures between 1995 and 1999, Republicans controlled eighteen states on average, Democrats eighteen, and they split or tied in twelve; on Clinton's centrism, see Burns and Taylor 2001).

The balance of parties throughout all levels of American politics reflects, above all, the Republican Party's resurgence in what was once the solid Democratic South. For over a century, from 1860 to 1960, white southerners demonized the Republican Party as the enemy of the southern way of life. But in the 1960s, Republicans made inroads into the southern electorate by capitalizing on the white backlash against the civil rights' policies of Lyndon Johnson. Barry Goldwater's stunning victories in the Deep South in the 1964 election broke the mould and prepared the way for the Republican "southern strategy" in the 1970s. This strategy, with its opposition to affirmative action in civil rights and to court-ordered school integration through busing, enabled the Republican Party to contest elections throughout the South after 1971 and to win five of eight presidential elections—losing only when the Democrats ran a southern candidate as in 1976, 1992, and 1996. Republicans also made inroads in the House of Representatives especially in the eleven states that had seceded from the union. In these states in 1950, the Republican Party held just two of 105 House seats; the party's share of these seats rose to 34 percent in 1990 and 57 percent in 2000. Once in power, southern Republicans in Congress have helped to divert federal resources into the region. This was the case in the early 1980s when relatively modest increases in southern congressional support for Reagan's military policies multiplied severalfold the growth of military-related spending and employment (Trubowitz 1992). And in recent rounds of pork-barrel politics, federal expenditures destined for the South (especially for defense-related purposes) rose from 32.5 percent to 38 percent, while the northern share fell from 45 to 40 percent.

Building "big government" took over a century, and it surely will not disappear overnight; the federal government will continue to perform many of its traditional roles. What will change is the size and salience of these roles, which will shrink because of deregulation, the devolution of governmental responsibilities, and the astonishingly high rates of growth in the private sector (Campbell 1995: 182). The reduction in the federal government began with the Reagan administration's assault on the mountain of rules and regulations compiled during the National State. Reagan's deregulation efforts trimmed thousands of pages of federal rules and regulations from the *Federal Register*. The *Register*, a surrogate for federal rule making, peaked at ninety thousand pages in 1979–1980; the number of pages fell to fifty thousand under Reagan, before rising to sixty to seventy thousand in the 1990s (Burns and Taylor 2001: 400–3). As existing regulations were cut back, legislation made it easier to identify and challenge new regulations, mandates, and preemptions. Meanwhile, federal expenditures grew at a slower pace. In the first decade of this new era (1980–1990), when state and local government expenditures grew by 33.7 percent, federal expenditures rose by 14.8 percent or just slightly faster than the 13.9 percent growth in U.S. GNP. The power of the federal purse diminished even further in the 1990s as a result of the "peace dividend" arising from the collapse of the Soviet Union, the devolution of federal governmental functions to state and local governments, and a decade of vigorous economic growth. The federal share of all government expenditures shrank from 64.4 percent in 1980 to 62.8 percent in 1990 to 55.0 percent in 1996 (*Statistical Abstract* 1999: 311, 324). Once again, as it was some two centuries ago, the air is filled with those time-honored questions on federalism and the proper balance between the states and the central government.

The devolution of functions and powers to state and local governments has been accelerated by two unrelated sets of events. The first of these involves a rash of peripheralizing decisions rendered by the Supreme Court under Chief Justice Rehnquist. These decisions, mostly decided by 5–4 margins of the justices, have shored up the rights reserved to the states under Article 10 of the Constitution. Most significant of these are the decisions that truncated the sphere of civil rights falling under federal jurisdiction (e.g., with respect to discriminations based on age or disability). The second set of events involves the proliferation of decentralized special districts and residential community associations within metropolitan areas (Stephens and Wikstrom 2000: 6–12). In a manner analogous to the new economy's accent on customized small-batch production, specialized districts serving specific needs have more than tripled in the past half century, rising from 9,300 in 1947 to 34,683 in 1997. Even more remarkable is the growth of residential community associations, or RCAs (including the "infamous" gated communities). These associations, with their promises of safety, security, and land use conformity, increased from fewer than 4,000 in 1960 to over 180,000 (mostly in the southern and western states) by the mid-1990s. In large measure, the rapid growth in these quasi-governmental RCAs has compensated civil society for the drastic reductions it has suffered in local governments, and most notably in the number of school districts, which has dropped from 128,548 in 1932, to 34,678 by 1962, to 13,726 by 1997. And while RCAs are rarely as powerful as school districts, they are probably our best bet as a venue, however parochial, for the discussion of local issues, for mobilizing for political action, and for political education. They will continue to provide a venue for civitas so long as most Americans reside in the burgeoning suburban counties beyond the reach of central-city governments (in 1996, metropolitan areas housed 211 million Americans, with 133.5 million of them residing in suburban and outlying areas).

As the devolution of governance continues, Americans will depend more and more on state and local governments. But the rub of decentralization is that some Americans will be better served than others. The range of services as well as the access to local government vary enormously from one state to another (figure 6.9). For example, access to governmental agencies and elected officials may be the greatest where it is needed the least, and vice versa. A case in point is the abundance of local government in the Upper Plains states. There, every ten thousand residents were served by over fifteen units of local government in 1997 and by fifty or more elected officials in 1992. Access diminishes as we move toward the coasts; local governments fall from over fifteen per ten thousand persons to under two in the coastal states of California, Louisiana, and all coastal states between Massachusetts and Florida save New Jersey (*Statistical Abstract* 2000: 23, 299; Shelley et al. 1996: 124).

These things being said on behalf of the devolution of American governance,

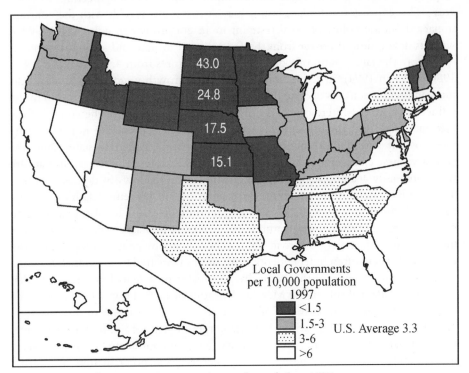

Figure 6.9.   Local governments per ten thousand population, 1997.

Source: Statistical Abstract 2000: 23, 299.

the fact remains that the federal government retains a great deal of political clout. State and local governments are more rather than less dependent on federal funds. In 1992, for example, local governments received 55 percent of their revenues from the federal government. This was up from 41 percent in 1972 and from just 26 percent in 1913 (Stephens and Wikstrom 2000: 14). Notwithstanding the many indicators of a pronounced shift toward deregulation since 1980 (e.g., the reductions in new regulatory legislation and in old rules and regulations; Burns and Taylor 2001), federal power continues to radiate to the states, first in the form of coercive legislative mandates (often unfunded) and preemptions on state policymaking authority over a wide range of policy spheres and federally imposed standards; second in the form of executive orders specifying new rules, regulations, and guidelines (Campbell 1995: 231).

The irony of contemporary scholarship on American political geography is that in placing the spotlight on antistatism, divided government, gridlock, and the devolution of the state, it has overlooked the larger story unfolding in the shadows—namely the sustained enlargement of the power and jurisdiction of the Transnational State. Administrations from Reagan to the second Bush have quietly formulated an expansionist foreign polity, one that aggressively extends the extraterritorial jurisdiction of the United States, that is as lean and as flexible as its adversaries abroad, and that consists of multiple strategies and multiple agents in venues ranging from the courts to major-power summits and from trade meetings to Congress. This expansionist foreign policy may at first seem at odds with the contractionary domestic policy of fiscal restraint in an era of divided governance—what with its devolution of power from the federal level to state and local governments (e.g., note the falling ratio of federal-state expenditures from 4.1 in 1960 to 2.4 in 1980 to 2.1 in 1994), its reductions in the rate of growth in government expenditures and regulations, its decline of political parties, and the incipient erosion in the influence of special-interest groups only recently so powerful in the course of the National State. But these restraints on federal power at home are not necessarily incompatible with the jurisdictional enlargements of the American state. Quite the contrary; these enlargements in the sovereign jurisdiction of the American state are the more easily accomplished without fanfare in the shadows of domestic policy. These enlargements thus are routinely carried out in piecemeal fashion and by agents within all branches of the federal government—by a legislature willing to craft and enact extraterritorial statutes, by an activist judiciary eager to stretch the limits of federal jurisdiction abroad if not at home, and by an increasingly powerful executive branch (often independently). All of this is abetted by a nationalist regime in the republican sense of that term; by personalist presidential politics (consider, e.g., the presidential role in the Mexican bale-out of 1995; Lowi 1995); and by the aggressive stances taken on behalf of American interests by agents of the executive branch—most notably by various U.S. trade representatives and by representatives of the Departments of Commerce, Treasury (e.g., on coordinated exchange agreements), and Justice (on dumping, cartels, mergers, and other matters of international litigation).

Americans are mostly unaware of these statist forays abroad (perhaps because they are so rarely reported in the news) or of the flexible polity of transnationalism that they represent. The advantage of too little knowledge is that Americans are able to invoke the nostalgia of their laissez-faire mythology, to turn back the clock and "see themselves as individualists, fearful of government intrusion and happy with a constitution in which checks and balance are embedded." And they are able to dismiss the expansion of big government between the 1870s and 1980 as an aberration that is being inundated by a new wave of indigenous American entrepreneurialism (Degler 1997: 23)—even as the agents of the Transnational State are expanding the limits of American sovereignty and jurisdiction into the furthest reaches of a globalizing economy. But while most Americans are oblivious of this stealthlike expansionism, the rest of the world is not. How long they will put up with American expansionism and the macroeconomic coordination on which it depends will hinge very much on how long the United States can endure in its role as the world's "indispensable nation" and, more important, as the indispensable market for the world's goods and services. Of one thing we can be sure—the nation's rivals are getting into line for the stretch run (see especially, Bergsten 2001).

The Dynamics of State Development

THE SECTIONAL STATE: ELECTORAL GEOGRAPHIES, SLAVERY, AND GEOPOLITICAL COMPROMISE

The first American State represented something of a compromise, a negotiated settlement between those who wanted a federal republic with a strong central government and others who wanted a federal republic that vested most of its powers in the hands of the constituent states. The compromise (effected by the Constitution) created a compound republic that achieved some of each, that reserved large powers to the constituent states while delegating power over purely national issues and concerns to the federal government. Under this arrangement, the states relinquished a great deal of their power over federal or national legislation in exchange for sovereignty over purely domestic matters.

Here the Constitution is fairly explicit. It granted the federal government the power

> to lay and collect Taxes, Duties, Imposts, and Excises, to pay the Debts and provide for the common Defence and general welfare of the United States. . . . To borrow money on the credit of the United States; To regulate Commerce with foreign Nations, and among the several States, and with the Indian Tribes; To establish an uniform Rule of Naturalization, and uniform Laws on the subject of Bankruptcies throughout the United States; To coin Money, regulate the Value thereof, and of foreign Coin, and fix the Standard of Weights and Measures; To Provide for the Punishment of counterfeiting the Securities and current Coin of the

United States; To establish Post Offices and post Roads; To promote the
Progress of Science and useful Arts by securing for limited Times to Au-
thors and Inventors the exclusive Right to their respective Writings and
Discoveries; To constitute Tribunals inferior to the supreme Court; To
define and punish Piracies and Felonies committed on the high Seas, and
Offenses against the Law of Nations; To declare War, grant letters of Mar-
que and Reprisal, and make Rules concerning Captures on Land and
Water; To raise and support Armies . . . ; To provide and maintain a Navy;
To make Rules for the Government and Regulation of the land and naval
Forces; To provide for calling forth the Militia to execute the Laws of the
Union, suppress insurrection, and repel invasions; To provide for organiz-
ing, arming, and disciplining the Militia, and for governing such part of
them as may be employed in the Service of the United States, reserving
to the States respectively, the Appointment of the Officers, and the Authority of training the Militia according to the discipline prescribed by
Congress; to exercise exclusive Legislation . . . over such District . . . as
may become the Seat of the Government of the United States . . . ; [and]
To make all Laws which shall be necessary and proper for carrying into
Execution the foregoing Powers, and all other Powers vested by this Constitution in the Government of the United States. (*Federalist Papers* 1961:
532–34)

Beyond this short list of federal powers, the Constitution left ample room for
debate over the limits in the powers of the states and the federal government. Some
shared the views of Jefferson and Madison who, in the Virginia and Kentucky Reso-
lutions, held that that the states and not the Supreme Court are the proper and
ultimate arbiters of the limits of federal power. John Calhoun concurred when,
three decades hence, he voiced his opposition to the Tariff of 1828. The states, he
proclaimed, reserve the right to determine the limits of federal power and, more
precisely, to nullify a federal statute. But these challenges to federal authority and
judicial review came up short. By the mid-1830s, following Andrew Jackson's stout
defense of the jurisdictional range of federal law, the debate was largely settled. The
Supreme Court henceforth was the supreme and indisputable authority for interpret-
ing the limits of federal power and the law of the land. When secession finally came
in 1861, the triggering issue for the South had nothing to do with constitutional
interpretation or the federal judiciary and everything to do with presidential politics.

The Constitution was much less ambiguous—and a great deal easier—when it
came to the creation of federal legislation. Unlike the Articles of Confederation,
which required a supermajority of state legislatures in order to ratify congressional
action, the Constitution customarily required a simple majority of votes in both
houses of Congress and the signature of the federal president. No further state approvals were required. In the event that a federal statute was challenged or a conflict
of laws arose in the jurisdictions of state and federal statutes, the Constitution ensured
that the case would be adjudicated in the federal courts (Ellis 1971; Lowi 1967).

Where did that leave the states who wished to oppose particular bills in the
House and Senate? They could not form multistate compacts since these were prohibited by the Constitution unless approved by Congress. And since no single state

or even a small group of states could block federal legislation, the states through their representatives in the House and their senators were compelled to form sectional and/or partisan coalitions or alliances in order to influence national legislation. These might consist of party coalitions cutting across state lines or sectional coalitions cutting across party lines. Partisan and sectional politics thus rushed into and filled the vacuum of governance that the compromise of 1789 had created. At first, electoral politics were fairly simple and unremarkable. During the first party system, each election involved a tussle between a major party that was nearly hegemonic (the "ins") and an embittered and largely sectional minor party ("the outs"). In the 1790s, the Federalists represented the "ins" and the Anti-Federalists gathered in the Back Country and on the frontiers of settlement, the "outs." Between 1800 and 1820, the Jeffersonian Democratic-Republicans in the southern and middle states had become the "ins" and the Federalists in New England were the "outs." There was little drama in these campaigns since there were no nominating conventions for president or vice president; nor were there formal debates between the candidates. Presidential succession was determined instead by the congressional caucuses of the major parties.

That would change with the election of 1824. In that election, party and section emerged as the mainsprings of American politics. Prior to 1824, presidential succession was largely determined by the congressional caucus's selection of the secretary of state, who ascended in his turn to the presidency. But in 1824, confusion reigned and outcomes were uncertain as various regions of the country put forth their favorite sons (figure 6.10). Andrew Jackson represented large swatches of the Old South and the southwestern frontier; Henry Clay, the middle border and the Midwest; John Quincy Adams, the remnants of Federalist New England; and William Crawford, a fourth candidate who died prior to the election, represented some of the Old South. Although Adams won the election in the House of Representatives, the real significance of 1824 is that it signals the turn toward the nation's second party system and toward its intensely partisan and fiercely competitive two-party politics—in this case, between the Democratic Party of Jackson and Martin Van Buren and the Whig Party of Clay and Daniel Webster.

In 1828, there was no logical successor to John Quincy Adams, nor was there a legitimate congressional caucus capable of anointing a successor. Victory in presidential politics would be based on merit, it would go to the best organized and the most innovative of the candidates. And it was on that basis that Andrew Jackson and the Jacksonian Democrats swept the field. Jackson's triumphs in 1828 and 1832 and his policy reforms were quite enough to consolidate one political party and to mobilize a coalition in opposition to "King Andrew"—a coalition of National Republicans, anti-Masons, and disaffected nullifiers and southern states righters—and to unite them under the banner of the American Whig Party in the winter of 1833–1834 (Holt 1999: 33–55). United by their opposition to executive tyranny and their support for banks, commerce and credit, property and hard money, and tariffs and internal improvements, the Whigs and their allies made an impressive showing in the state elections in 1834, 1835, and 1836. They won over 50 percent of the legislative seats in twelve of twenty-four states (as of 1836). These states were widely distrib-

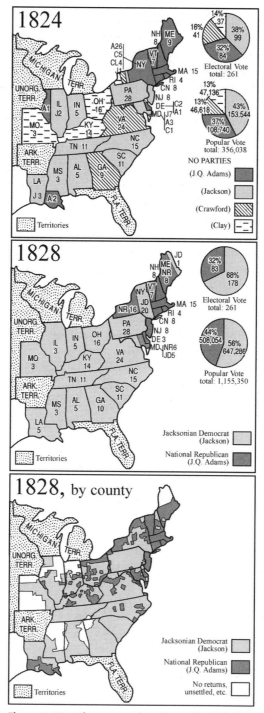

Figure 6.10.   The geography of presidential elections, 1824 and 1828.

uted—from four in New England on the north to Alabama in the South, and the rest in a bloc extending from Delmarva and Pennsylvania on the east through Kentucky, Ohio, and Indiana on the west. While the Whigs were not quite ready for the presidential election of 1836, their campaign against Martin Van Buren produced voter majorities in ten of twenty-five states. By 1836,

> a national pattern of two-party conflict had replaced the largely regional one of 1832 in the presidential vote. The Whigs had extended their voting base to the South and West, while competition between the two parties was also generally closer in the Middle Atlantic and New England States than it had been four years earlier. That the opposition's [the Whigs'] . . . share of the popular vote had increased from 45 to nearly 50 percent of the national total, and that it approached that average in every region of the country, testified to how far the Whigs had traveled in three short years. (Holt 1999: 47–48)

Over the next two decades, the Whigs and the Jacksonian Democrats provided the foundation for a genuine two-party system in most if not all of the states—a system characterized by intensely partisan politics, rising voter turnout, and repeated attempts to negotiate compromise on sectional issues, most especially on the matter of slavery (Shade 1965). But all of this came undone in the 1850s what with the failure of these attempts at compromise, the collapse of the Whig Party, and the ascent of a distinctly sectional party, the Republicans. Soon after, the second party system, with its commitment to sectional cooperation and compromise, was razed once and for all by the Civil War and radical Reconstruction.

Partisan politics and political compromise were the mother's milk of the Sectional State. In the matter of partisanship, Americans early set aside Madison and Adams's fears of factions and parties, and they followed their natural inclinations to organize formal parties and to reward their supporters. Not surprisingly, partisanship had its origins in the 1820s and 1830s in the midst of two decades of fiscal conservatism. In this span, federal spending fell from $2.52 per capita in 1820 to $1.85 and $1.70 in 1840. As if to signal the transition from the first party system to the second, political parties refined the practice of rewarding some regional constituencies and ignoring or punishing others (table 6.11). In the 1820s the budget axe wielded by

Table 6.11.   Regional Shares of Federal Expenditures, 1820–1880

Year	Mid-Atlantic	New England	South Atlantic	Other States
1820	29.0%	15.7%	46.6%	8.6%
1830	36.0%	13.5%	29.8%	20.7%
1840	15.1%	10.6%	53.6%	20.7%
1850	15.1%	10.6%	52.8%	21.5%
1860	11.3%	6.7%	42.3%	40.7%
1870	27.3%	15.0%	22.8%	32.9%
1880	33.7%	18.5%	16.2%	31.6%

Note: The other states include the states in the four Central regions and the Mountain and Pacific states.
Source: Davis and Legler 1966.

John Quincy Adams fell most heavily on the South Atlantic states. This region, which provided few votes for Adams in 1824 and 1828, saw its share of federal expenditures drop from 46.6 percent of all expenditures in 1820 to 29.8 percent in 1830. Voters in the mid-Atlantic were the winners; their region, which along with New England provided 85–90 percent of Adams's electoral votes in 1824 and 1828, saw its share of federal expenditures rise from 29 to 36 percent.

But what had been given in the second party system could just as easily be taken away. And in the 1830s, the Jacksonians boldly and just as crassly turned the tables. In repayment for the south Atlantic region's sustained support in the elections between 1828 and 1836, the Jacksonians boosted that region's share of federal spending from 30 to 53.6 percent (most of the change occurred on Van Buren's watch)—which more than offset the 8 percent cut in total federal spending. The Jacksonians also slashed the mid-Atlantic's share from 36 to 15.1 percent (in this case most of the cuts came before 1836 during Jackson's administrations). Not much changed during the 1840s and 1850s, perhaps because of the flip-flopping of parties and administrations in power. It was the late 1850s when the latter-day Jacksonians belatedly acknowledged the westward shift of people and political power by reallocating federal expenditures. They raised the federal share spent on states west of the Appalachians from 20 to 40 percent; the Old South accounted for another 42 percent with the rest going to New England and the mid-Atlantic states. But the Democrats missed the most important boat. Perhaps the most crucial regions from a demographic and geopolitical perspective lay between the Great Lakes and the Gulf. In 1860, two regions—the east north central states and the east south central states—accounted for 33.2 percent of the nation's population (20.1 percent and 13.1 percent, respectively) but received just 9 percent of total federal outlays. The Democrats might have been advised to spend a bit more on two regions having a third of the nation's population and domiciling all four of the leading presidential candidates.

Republicans learned their lesson well. Partisanship was ever more intrusive after the Civil War. In the two decades between 1860 and 1880, Republicans funneled federal spending toward the victorious regions. The shares going to the mid-Atlantic states and New England tripled—from 11.3 percent to 33.7 percent and 6.7 percent to 18.5 percent, respectively. And as if to compound southern defeat on the battlefield, the old South saw its share of federal spending cut by over half—from 42.3 percent to 16.2 percent. Americans in the Sectional State played hard at politics; they took their text in politics as in faith from the Old Testament; in both spheres, they reckoned "an eye for an eye, a tooth for a tooth."

Americans in the Sectional State were as deeply concerned with policy issues as they were with political parties, party-building resources, and voter constituencies. Parties and partisan politics constituted the vehicles for the expression of disagreement, division, and conflict. And in a young and growing nation, partisans disagreed over many vital issues. They disagreed about the location of power—was it to reside in the states as the Anti-Federalists, Jeffersonian Republicans, and later the Jacksonian contended or in the central government as averred by the Federalists and later the Whigs? And in the central government, then to whom—to Congress as the Whigs proposed or to the Executive as the Jacksonians wished? They also disagreed over the claimants—who were the proper recipients of the federal government's distributive largesse? Were resources best distributed to entrepreneurial elites (as assumed by the early nationalist coalition of Jeffersonian Republicans and moderate Federalists and later the Whig Party) or to the masses (as some Anti-Federalists and most Jacksonian Democrats presumed as an article of faith)? And to which regions—to the Mid-Atlantic states as did the National Republicans in the 1820s, to the Old South as did the Jacksonians in the 1830s, or to the rest of the nation as did the latter-day Jacksonians in the 1850s? Political parties crystallized around these partisan and regional divisions; they reduced issues to their simplest and most local terms and they refined biases and divisions into coherent policies, programs, and platforms, thus sharpening the debate; and they built responsive party organizations within all of the states (Silbey 1991; McCormick 1986; Holt 1999). Voters in turn took parties at their word, turned out in ever-increasing numbers, and held the parties to account for their policy actions.

Perhaps the greatest test of partisan politics—and its greatest achievement until 1861—was the resolution of the geopolitical debate over slavery, freedom, and the accessioning of new states to the union. If we go back to the beginning, to 1789, it is fair to say that most Americans, both northern and southern, believed that slavery was on the road to extinction—save perhaps in the rice districts in the low country of South Carolina and Georgia. Indeed, the Founders had written this into the Constitution when they agreed to abolish the overseas slave trade after 1807. By that date, most of the northern states had legally abolished slavery within their limits. Meanwhile in the Upper South, low tobacco prices had forced many planters (large and small) to turn to wheat and other grains and to manumit (privately emancipate) their slaves (Berlin 1980; Earle 1978). Slavery everywhere seemed in retreat with the exception of the confined ecological region known as the wet-rice low country of South Carolina and Georgia. In these extraordinarily wealthy districts, where slaves who operated the large rice plantations made up 80 to 90 percent or more of the residents, an agricultural economy in the absence of slavery was inconceivable. Most Americans, in the interest of harmony in the new nation, could wink at the endurance of an exotic slave economy in the lower South. But the impending devolution of slavery, which seemed so assured in the 1790s, was abruptly reversed in the ensuing decades. The invention of the cotton gin and the introduction of short-staple upland cotton opened up enormous possibilities for cotton cultivation—and for slave labor—in upland South Carolina and Georgia. The American slave population expanded rapidly, doubling between 1790 and 1820 and doubling again by 1850. Concurrently, calls for the abolition of slavery and/or the African colonization of emancipated slaves emanated from northern abolitionists.

Congress soon sought a legislative compromise. One of the most far-reaching and successful solutions involved the alternating admission of slave and free states (table 6.12 and figure 6.11). This geopolitical balancing act began in 1816 with the admission of the free state of Indiana and continued with Mississippi (1817 slave), Illinois (free 1818) and Alabama (slave 1819). In 1820, Congress institutionalized this geopolitical process in admitting Maine as a free state and passing the Missouri

Table 6.12.   Slave and Free States Admitted to the United States by 1860

	Slave States	Free States	Running Totals	
			Slave	Free
Prior to 1791	Maryland	New Hampshire		
	Delaware	Massachusetts		
	Virginia	Rhode Island		
	North Carolina	New Jersey		
	South Carolina	Connecticut		
	Georgia	New York		
		Pennsylvania	6	7
1791		Vermont		8
1792	Kentucky		7	
1796	Tennessee		8	
1803		Ohio		9
1812	Louisiana		9	
1816		Indiana		10
1817	Mississippi		10	
1818		Illinois		11
1819	Alabama		11	
1820		Maine		12
1821	Missouri		12	
1836	Arkansas		13	
1837		Michigan		13
1845	Texas		14	
	Florida		15	
1846		Iowa		14
1848		Wisconsin		15
1850		California		16
1858		Minnesota		17
1859		Oregon		18

Total Admissions: 1790s (3); 1800–21 (8); 1822–44 (2); 1845–60 (7)
Source: Historical Statistics 1975: 38.

Compromise. The compromise reciprocated by admitting Missouri as a slave state (1821), while prohibiting slavery in territories lying to the north of 36°30′ north latitude (the parallel of Missouri's southern boundary)—what many assumed to be slavery's approximate "natural limits."

Compromise was further facilitated by (1) a respite in the pace of annexation in the late 1820s and 1830s and (2) the rise of the second party system during this break in the action. After admitting six states into the union between 1816 and 1821, Congress admitted no states whatsoever until 1836 and only two for nearly a quarter of a century (1821–1845). In this hiatus from controversy, the second party system came to fruition. In 1827, the principal architect of that system pointed out the virtues of genuine political parties in a democratic society. Martin Van Buren observed that when party feelings "are suppressed, geographical divisions founded on local interests or, what is worse, prejudices between free and slaveholding states will inevitably take their place. Party attachment in former times furnished a complete antidote for sectional prejudices by producing counteracting feelings" (quoted in Caeser 1979: 138). Over the next decade, Van

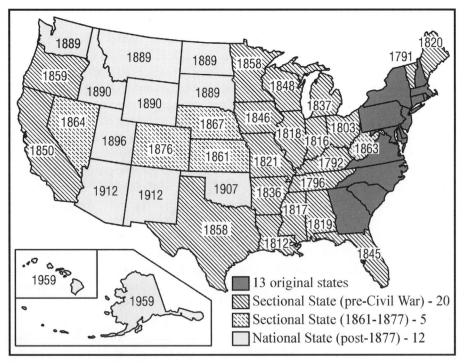

Figure 6.11.   State admissions to the Union, 1790–1959.

Buren and his adversaries set about creating a more free-wheeling democratic successor to the stiff and elitist party system established by the founding generation. And they succeeded beyond their wildest dreams in building two major national parties and displacing if not altogether stifling sectional tensions. Van Buren's Jacksonians and the Whigs thus rendered "oppositional coalitions [into] a nonsectional party system within a highly sectionalized country" (Archer and Taylor 1981: 61). The Whigs offered fairly stiff competition for the Jacksonians. Indeed, the most notable feature of the presidential politics in the era between Jackson and Lincoln (1836–1860) is opposition-party victories—in that span, the party out of office won four of five presidential elections (the exception being the sequential Democratic victories in 1852 and 1856), and no incumbent president managed to win reelection.

Americans were preoccupied by domestic economic problems during the 1830s. Not until the 1840s were they compelled to confront a second generation of sectional problems associated with lands previously belonging to Mexico. Congress waited until 1845, nearly ten years after Texas won independence from Mexico, before admitting the Lone Star Republic and Florida to statehood—doubtless because an equal number of free territories were close to satisfying the conditions for statehood (which Iowa and Wisconsin did in 1846 and 1848, respectively). The prospects for continuing this geopolitical minuet improved even more with the American victory in the Mexican War (1846–1848) and the Oregon settlement with

Britain (1846). These events paved the way for the full-scale occupation of the Southwest and the Northwest, and they provided ample room for the formation of new states, both slave and free. The Compromise of 1850 sought to partition these new lands while preserving the delicate sectional balance that, with the addition of Wisconsin in 1848, stood at fifteen free states and fifteen slave (figure 6.12). The compromise, which in reality consisted of five separate bills, had several geopolitical components. It admitted California as a free state; it established two territories—Utah and New Mexico; and it gave citizens of these territories the right to vote whether to permit or prohibit slavery in their state constitutions ("popular sovereignty"). At that point, the territorial score stood at sixteen free states, fifteen slave states, and two territories (along with the District of Columbia) open to slavery. While the compromise managed to maintain the sectional balance for the moment, it muddled the prospects for compromise in the long run. First, it erased the time-honored boundary drawn between slavery and freedom by the Missouri Compromise; that boundary was transgressed both in California (free) and in Utah (slave). The result was that the territorial process was rendered *de novo*. In the absence of a general rule, Congress was required to consider anew the issue of slavery or freedom in each territorial application. Second, southerners were hardly confident that New Mexico and Utah would have sufficient populations to justify statehood anytime soon or, in any event, that popular sentiment there would favor slavery. And then what? Where would the proponents of slavery look for additional states to balance off the free states anticipated to arise in the northern plains and in the northwest? (One indication of the seriousness of the South's geopolitical dilemma is that the region's best bets for new slave states in the 1850s entailed partitioning California into two states or carving new states out of the territories west of Missouri and Arkansas. In either case, the price was high. The former would provoke stiff opposition in Congress, while the latter would involve lands already occupied by native Americans who had been once removed. (See Fehrenbacher 2001: on California, 292–94; on slavery and geopolitics, 253–338.)

Enter Senator Stephen Douglas of Illinois—and what ranks as the most misbegotten compromise in the history of the Sectional State. In January 1854, Senator Douglas introduced a bill that called for the organization of the territories of Kansas and Nebraska, incorporated the principle of "popular sovereignty," and authorized their admission to the union with or without slavery in accordance with territorial referenda. The bill passed the Senate in March, scraped through the House in May, and almost immediately ignited a firestorm of controversy in the northern states (figure 6.12). In Massachusetts, the Emigrant Aid Society called for the migration of antislavery settlers to Kansas. In Wisconsin, a meeting of "anti-Nebraska" Whigs, Free Soilers, and Democrats called for the organization of a new party, the Republicans, dedicated to the opposition of slavery. The sectional controversy over slavery, so long contained by the assorted compromises of Whigs and Democrats and their predecessors, had at last been joined. Democrats by and large were taken by surprise since all the precedents for Kansas-Nebraska (popular sovereignty and the abrogation of the Missouri Compromise's free-slave boundary) had been established in the Compromise of 1850. The Whigs, meanwhile, bolted the party and enrolled in

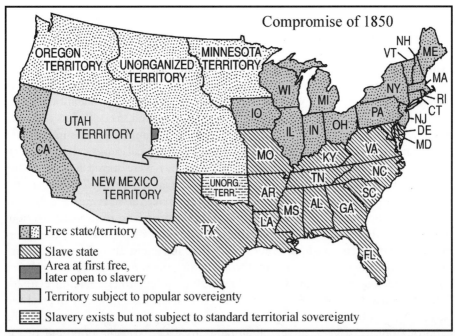

Figure 6.12.   The geography of states and territories after the Compromise of 1850 (top) and the Kansas–Nebraska Act (1854) (bottom).

antislavery and nativist political movements. Elsewhere, events careened out of control. Following the eruption of a violent civil war in "bloody Kansas" in May of 1856, pro- and antislavery forces in Kansas engaged in a period of intense political maneuvering to determine slavery's status in the territorial constitution.

In that same year, the newly created Republican Party drafted John Fremont as its nominee for president. While Fremont lost the election, he established a firm sectional foundation for the party by carrying New England, New York, Ohio, and the three states in the Upper Midwest and by running competitive races in northern Illinois and Indiana. Passions remained high with the installation of the Democrat James Buchanan as president in early 1857, and they were stirred further by the decision of the Taney Court in the *Dred Scott* case in March 1857 (ruling that a slave's temporary residence in free territory did not make the slave free and that the Missouri Compromise represented an unconstitutional taking of property without due process); the rejection of the proslavery Lecompton Constitution by the voters of Kansas and the continuation of territorial status in August 1858; by the Lincoln–Douglas debates between August and October 1858; the admission of two more free states (Minnesota in 1858 and Oregon in 1859); by John Brown's raid on Harper's Ferry Arsenal in October 1859, and the ensuing trial and executions; by the real and paranoid fears of unbridled extremisms—of the slave power's commitment to the nationalization of slavery, of the abolitionists to slavery's eradication; and of the southern mudsills to the most virulent forms of racism and "negro colonization" to Africa; by secession threats from the South; and, in the end, by the presidential election of 1860 replete with four major parties and their distinctive positions on the issue of slavery (figure 6.13A).

In a two-party political system, compromise over slavery was always possible, but it was well-nigh hopeless when there were four contending parties and points of view divided along geographical lines. In the Northeast and Midwest, antislavery Republicans (Lincoln) contended with states-rights Democrats (Douglas); in the South, a proslavery coalition of Democrats and Whigs (Breckenridge) prevailed in most places. And in the Border States, the compromise position of the Constitutional Unionists (Bell) forged a majority of the electorate. In the end, Lincoln and the new Republican Party just squeaked by, garnering just 39.8 percent of the popular vote and 180 of 303 electoral votes. The election barely missed being thrown into the House of Representatives as it had been in 1824. Indeed, that would have been the result had Douglas won slightly more than 18,000 strategically placed Lincoln votes (and 31 electoral votes)—nearly 6,000 in Illinois (11), nearly 12,000 in Indiana (13), nearly 400 in California (4), and 128 in Oregon (3).

It was this shattering of national politics as much as secession and Civil War that dashed the prospects of further compromise and signaled the impending collapse of the Sectional State. In December 1860, South Carolina seceded from the Union; the six states in the Deep South followed by February 1, as did Virginia in April and Tennessee, Arkansas, and North Carolina in May. Politics having failed, brute power resolved the conflict between slavery and freedom. Over the next four years, over three million Americans fought and a fifth of them died for their cause (figure 6.13B).

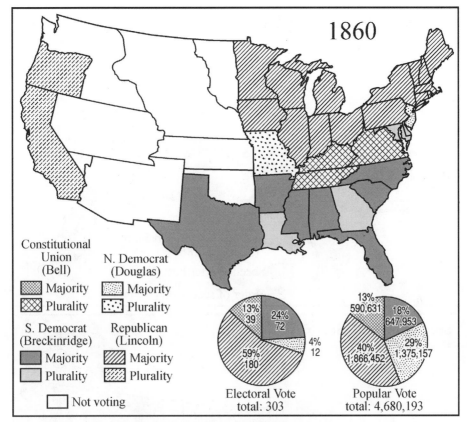

Figure 6.13A.   The geography of the presidential election of 1860.

THE NATIONAL STATE: GEOGRAPHIES OF CONFUSION, REFORM, AND ORDER—AND THEIR COSTS

Precisely when the first American state ended and the second began is a matter of some controversy. Some scholars date the origins of the National State in 1896 because it is then that voter turnout begins its sharp decline; others prefer the 1880s because it marks the origins of the Interstate Commerce Commission and the regulatory state; still others point backward toward the Civil War and the rise of a fiscally powerful federal government, the so-called Yankee Leviathan. There is truth, however partial, in each of these datings. My own preference is for 1877, first, because it splits the differences in the dating of a process that was far from instantaneous; second, because it coincides with the end of radical reconstruction (and hence the end of sectionalism) and with the historians' preferred division of American history; third, because 1877 marks the origins of the solid democratic South as a key element in the nation's political geography; and fourth, because by that date the ramifications of the Fourteenth Amendment's vast enlargement of federal power were reasonably

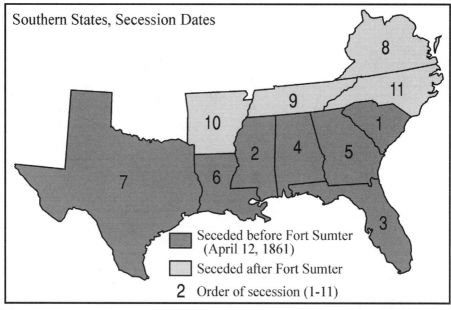

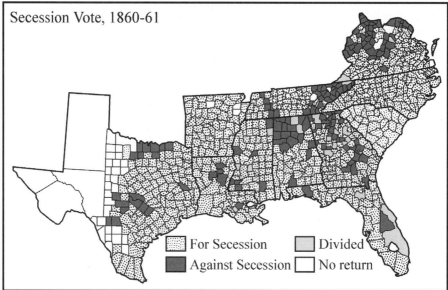

Figure 6.13B.   Southern secession: State chronology (top); and secession votes by county (bottom).

well understood as irreversible—short of constitutional amendment (for these dat-ings, see among others Bensel 1990; Degler 1997; North 1981; Anderson and Hill 1980; McCormick 1979, 1986; Lowi 1972; Campbell 1995).

Lastly, the ironies of using the Compromise of 1877 to mark the ending of a state that elevated political compromise to an art form are too precious to ignore.

Henceforth, it seems, the stakes of American domestic politics were not nearly as large, the issues not nearly as great or the compromises as vital as they had once been; the big action was increasingly located abroad. What the nation needed on its centennial was more bureaucratic experts and fewer political compromisers, more efficient uses of power and less time wasted in negotiation, more technique and less artifice, more interest groups and fewer partisans, more deals and fewer compromises. The kinds of men who made the Sectional State, men like Henry Clay, the Jacksonians, and Stephen Douglas, were making way for Teddy Roosevelt and the Wilsonians.

The National State was predicated on a constitutional revolution that extended the Bill of Rights and the due process and equal protection clauses of the Fourteenth Amendment to the states at large. These clauses fundamentally altered the constitutional balance in the power of the states and the federal government. By extending federal jurisdiction over the Bill of Rights into the daily affairs of the several states, the "Fourteenth Amendment empowered the Supreme Court to protect individual rights from state infringements as never before" (Sandel 1996: 39). The amendment nationalized the law, subordinated the rights of the states, and dismantled the Sectional State's concept of dual sovereignty and the balance between state and national authority. Although the Supreme Court hesitated in taking up its new authority, by the turn of the century the majority of justices shared the opinion of Justice Stephen J. Field that "the amendment was adopted . . . to place the common rights of American citizens [as expressed in the Bill of Rights] under the protection of the National government" (as quoted in Sandel 1996: 40). Armed with this more expansive interpretation of the amendment, the Court after 1900 invalidated nearly two hundred laws that abridged Field's notion of "the common rights of American citizens" (Sandel 1996: 39–43). The Court's interpretations of the Fourteenth Amendment steadily encroached on the jurisdictions of the states, eroded state sovereignties, and vastly enlarged the jurisdiction of the federal government within the second American state (Nelson 1988).

The timing of this enlargement in the National State could not have been better suited for American business, coming as it did as American entrepreneurs were embarking on the nation's second producer revolution. As they set about the process of economic restructuring that would transform an agrarian-mercantile economy of small and medium-sized firms serving local and regional markets into an increasingly complex urban-industrial economy of large, vertically integrated corporations serving national and international markets, American entrepreneurs were mindful of the federal judiciary's favorable rulings on behalf of nationwide railroad systems in the 1880s and the Court's bias for national over regional enterprises (Chandler 1977, 1990; Berk 1994). And national corporations were among the first to insist on their Fourteenth Amendment right to due process and the exercise of that right in the friendlier confines of the federal courts. Henceforth, big business and big government would advance in tandem, if occasionally at cross purposes.

To cope with the increasing scale of the economy and government, the complexity of policy issues, and the superheated clashes between "labor and capital" in the 1880s, governments at all levels were severely tested. Local governments, especially municipalities, sought to expand their autonomy and, short of that, their regulatory and fiscal powers over land use and infrastructure vis-à-vis state governments. Large cities annexed and consolidated built-up areas, constructed subways and streetcar lines, set aside park land, engineered water supply systems, and installed roads and gas and electric lines (Tarr 1985). Many of them also struggled to cope with massive numbers of immigrants from within the United States and from abroad. As of 1910, the share of Americans living in cities exceeded 70 percent in the Northeast and 50 percent in the Midwest and Far West as compared to 45 percent in the nation at large (Ward 1971: 40). Big-city machines and later "good government" commissioners struggled to maintain order and services in cities whose residents were usually newcomers and frequently foreign born. Nearly nine million immigrants, mostly southern and eastern Europeans, had entered the United States between 1880 and 1900; 14.5 million more followed in the next two decades. Most of these immigrants settled in American cities. In 1920, just before immigration restrictions were imposed, 75 percent of the foreign born in the United States resided in cities, mostly in the Northeast and Midwest (Ward 1971: 51–59). Added to these were the millions of African American sharecroppers who, after 1900, joined in the Great Migration to these same cities. As cities struggled to provide housing and jobs for these migrants and then to transport them from home to work, the surrounding suburban counties dealt with the influx of the professional and managerial classes in flight from the ghettoes emerging downtown, from labor unrest, and from associated urban pathologies. Work stoppages—which were on the rise from tens per year in the 1870s to thousands in the 1880s—were overwhelmingly concentrated in larger cities, and these threatened to bring urban economies to a halt (Gutman 1976). The administrations of large and middling cities had their hands full; and to make matters worse, the municipalities' range of response to these pressing urban problems was limited by the courts (and most especially Dillon's Rule) and their subordination of cities to state government. Cities, which had grown so vigorously since 1860, were put back in their (political) place by American jurisprudence (on cities as disempowered creatures of the state, see Frug 1980). The main hope for cities in response to their subordination was boosterism, economic development, and the building of a population base sufficient to challenge rural blocs in the state legislatures. Cities that pursued these emancipatory strategies—cities such as New York, Chicago, Boston, Philadelphia, Pittsburgh, Baltimore, and Cleveland, among others—became beacons for sustained immigration and, ironically, for the problems and pathologies associated with such growth.

State governments, meanwhile, addressed the full range of economic, social, and political problems arising from industrialization, immigration, labor unrest, and political corruption. States served as laboratories for the social experimentations that proliferated during the Gilded Age, the Age of Reform, and the Progressive Era. A few of the forty-five states in 1900 advanced the "interests" of business and capital while others promoted the interests of the people in the Commonwealth. In the first instance, probusiness states used their powers of incorporation in ways that conferred numerous advantages and imposed few restraints upon business. Of all the states, it was New Jersey that offered the most favorable conditions of incorporation for the largest of companies. Corporate lawyers and directors praised New Jersey "for its liberal laws on stock ownership and powers granted to boards of directors" as well as for "the moderation . . . of its laws on stockholder liability that made the state appealing for incorporations" (Roy 1997: 167). These advantages plus a location adjacent to the vast agglomeration of capital in New York City enabled New Jersey to become "the home of most of the giant corporations formed in the corporate revolution" (Roy 1997: 165). Even though New Jersey chartered only one-third as many corporations as Ohio between 1880 and 1913, Garden State incorporations amassed ten times the value of Ohio's corporate capital in the same period. More insulting still was the fact that Ohio's largest corporations, Standard Oil (Cleveland) and Procter and Gamble (Cincinnati), incorporated their operations in New Jersey (Roy 1997: 164–72).

In other states, politicians were more responsive to political reform, and their legislatures served as laboratories for popular, more democratic innovations. The most promising conditions for reform lay in the newer western states where politics was fluid, political parties were still weak, local economies were mixed, and political compromise remained a possibility. Reformers in these states sought to introduce more openness within the political system and to expand popular access to it; their goal was "to turn a system that pivoted on officeholding [and political parties] to one that pivoted on policy issues that were suppressed by the coalition structure of the national parties" (Sanders 1997: 78)—that is, to subvert the partisan infrastructure of the Sectional State while promoting the bureaucratic expertise so necessary in the National State. The achievements of the reformers circa 1913 are depicted in a map recording state adoptions of four distinct political reforms introduced during the Age of Reform and the Progressive Era (figure 6.14). These democratic reforms included some form of the Australian ballot, the mandatory direct primary, the initiative or referendum, and women's suffrage. As noted earlier, the western states proved to be the most supportive of these popular reforms; fifteen of nineteen western states supported three or four of these innovations. The eastern states, by contrast, expressed little interest in these reforms; just two of twenty-nine eastern states adopted three or four of these reforms (table 6.13). The West took the lead in these instances and in virtually all other political reform movements at the turn of the century; the eastern states, meanwhile, generally preferred the old politics rather than the politics of reform. Given this geopolitical division, the only chance for western reforms to become national was for them to win the support of state legislatures in the southeastern states—which, on occasion, they secured.

As the cities and states variously pursued reform or served the interests of corporations or the people or both, the federal government took steps designed to reform governance and to enlarge the power and jurisdiction of the National State. Toward these ends, Congress introduced two innovations that radically improved the efficiency and the scope of the federal government—albeit at the expense of decentralized governance and democratic politics in the long run. The first of these, signaled by the establishment of the Interstate Commerce Commission, was the creation of the bureaucratic state. From the 1880s onward, Congress increasingly depended on regulatory commissions and agencies that were staffed by "experts," delegated with

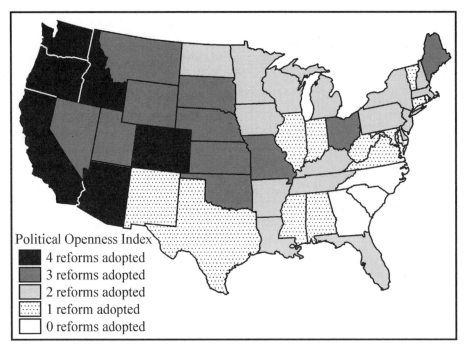

Figure 6.14.   Political reforms enacted in the states, circa 1913.

Note: The reforms are (1) some form of the Australian ballot, (2) the mandatory direct primary, (3) the initiative and/or referendum, and (4) woman suffrage.
Source: Adapted from Clemens 1997: 73–81.

broad legislative, executive, and juridical authority and, as it turned out, susceptible to the influence of special-interest groups. In a series of decisions between 1892 and 1911, the Supreme Court affirmed the power of the legislative branch to delegate discretionary power to executive branch agencies. "These decisions recognized the power of executive agencies to make rules within the broad policy objectives set out by Congress. In the *United States vs. Grimaud* (1911), the court decreed that administrative rulings had the rule of law" (North 1981: 195; Anderson and Hill 1980). In addition to this judicial victory, reformers and progressives (mostly from the South and Midwest) occasionally held the balance of power in Congress. In the 1909 session, for example, reformers made up 53.7 percent of the House of

Table 6.13.   Reform Innovations Adopted by 1913: Number of States and Location

Innovations Adopted	East of Mississippi River	West of Mississippi River
High (3–4)	2	15
Medium (2)	14	2
Low (0–1)	13	2
Totals	29	19

Note: See text for innovations.
Source: Clemens 1997: 73–81.

Representatives (Sanders 1999: 172). And when majorities were absent, reformers formed themselves into small but powerful voting blocs of fifteen to twenty (e.g., the "farm bloc" or "labor bloc"; Hays 1957: 154). These reformers steadily expanded the scope and the power of these unelected commissions and agencies into new spheres of American economic life—to trusts in 1890; food and drugs in 1906; telephone, telegraph, and cable in 1910; commerce and money supply in 1914; various factors of production in 1933; securities and exchange in 1933; markets in 1934; and continuing on to the "regulatory binge" of the 1970s (North 1981: 188–96; Lowi 1995: 51–59).

On the outset, the bureaucratic reform of capitalism seemed promising. The benefits of these regulatory commissions and agencies seemed to outweigh their costs. They were faster and more efficient than Congress; they assembled the foremost experts on any particular regulatory sphere; and, in the Progressive spirit, these experts and staffers provided regulatory advice that was detached, objective, scientific, and equitable. But the disadvantages of these regulatory structures soon became apparent. In the first place, as James Madison counseled, not all men—not even experts—are angels immunized from private interests or partisan causes. Second, because the members of these regulatory commissions and agencies are appointed not elected, their actions are relatively well insulated from oversight, public accountability, and the democratic process. Third, their charges from Congress are frequently broad, vague, and/or ambiguous (see especially Lowi's [1979] critique of legislative imprecision in language and guidance). Fourth, the decisions of even the most detached of regulatory agents are influenced by the biases of the officials who appointed them; the effectiveness of the special-interest groups lobbying them; the bargaining between these two; and the abstract values of detachment, objectivity, science, and equity. In this bargaining process, it is the abstract values of reform that have regularly suffered the most grievous overthrows. Fifth, regulation per se customarily favored big business serving national markets over small business serving regions. This was so for two reasons: larger firms could more readily bear the costs of incorporating regulations into their operations, and federal regulatory rules transcended state boundaries and thereby permitted economies of scale for firms serving national markets. Given the vested interests in the bureaucratic state, ridding American politics of entrenched reforms that have soured has proven to be extremely difficult.

The second innovation on behalf of federal efficiency—"Reed's rules"—had its origins in the House of Representatives in 1878, a few years in advance of the Interstate Commerce Commission (ICC). In that year, the speaker of the House, one Thomas Reed, formulated a new set of procedural rules that transformed the politics within that body. By centralizing power in the hands of the Speaker at the expense of committees and committee chairs, the new rules enabled the speaker to exercise greater control over the flow of legislation and to move bills forward at a much faster pace. Reed's specific revisions involved lowering the numbers required for a quorum, counting nonvoting members as part of a quorum, and permitting the Speaker to rule delaying motions out of order (Lowi 1967, 1972). Although the Speaker's power was checked somewhat after 1911, the core of Reed's procedural reforms managed to endure. The resulting "speed-up" of legislation made it even more difficult to block the sort of regulatory policies that, while well intentioned in most cases, threatened to subvert the republic—first by removing issues from popular control, second by bloating the federal bureaucracy, third by fostering the rise of special-interest groups and lobbyists, and fourth by the co-opting of federal regulatory commissions and agencies by the very "special interests" that they were supposed to regulate.

With these regulatory and legislative innovations in place by the 1890s and with the Congress increasingly populated by reformers from the periphery as well as by voting "blocs," the federal government embarked on an even bolder initiative: the transformation of the American state from one of generosity to one of coercion—from the distributive polity of the Sectional State to the regulatory and redistributive polity of the National State. One reasons for this transformation was the staggering rise in the costs of running an ever more centralized federal government and the need to finance the federal government on revenue streams other than tariffs and excises. The problem first became evident during the 1860s when the expenditures of the federal government reached new heights. Fueled by the massive expenditures of the Civil War, federal expenditures rose nearly eightfold between 1860 and 1870 and never looked back. The traditional retrenchment in postwar spending did not occur. And by 1900, the costs of big government had risen to over $6.3 billion (in 1860 dollars)—a tenfold increase from the $636 million spent in 1860. Some of this increase, though not all, can be explained by the rapid growth of population. When population is held constant, federal expenditures more than quadrupled between 1860 and 1900 (rising from $2.24 per capita in 1860 to $11.24 in 1880 to $8.75 in 1900; again in constant dollars of 1860) (Davis and Legler 1966; McCusker 1992).

Much of this expansion is explained by two factors. First is the American determination to become a world power. Toward that end, defense expenditures rose sevenfold between 1860 and 1900 (from $28 million to $191 million) and tripled in the 1890s alone. "Special emphasis was placed on a new navy and far-flung naval bases. . . . Congress authorized four steel ships in 1883; succeeding administrations continued the program until by 1909 the United States had moved from twelfth to second rank among the world's navies" (Hays 1957: 165). Second is the continuing expenditures for the pensions of military veterans, mostly from the Civil War. In 1900, these constituted $141 million, or 27 percent of federal outlays. Together, defense and pensions consumed 64 percent of federal outlays in 1900, and a historic high of 68 percent in 1910. The fact that these two components of the federal budget rose elevenfold between 1860 and 1900 goes a long way in explaining the rise of big government in the fin-de-siècle United States. Thus did Americans prepare themselves for becoming a world power and for repudiating their reputation as a free rider, for cheering on Great Britain while coming "to the rescue ourselves without a gun, nor a man, nor a ship with nothing but our 'moral support,'" for being viewed "as a nation of sympathizers and swaggerers—without purpose or power to turn our words into deeds and not above the sharp practice of accepting advantages for which we refuse to pay our share of the price" (Richard Olney, secretary of state, 1895–1897, quoted in Gardner 1966: 93–94).

Faced with these ever-increasing demands on the federal budget, Congress and the executive branch restructured fiscal operations. Henceforth the generous distributive polity of the Sectional State gave way to a more coercive redistributive polity of wealth transfer. This new polity hinged on the identification of new sources of federal revenues that were as ample, reliable, and constitutional as were tariffs on foreign imports. The most obvious of such sources was a tax on American incomes. A federal tax on income had its origins during the Civil War as an emergency measure for paying for the war. Forty years later, Congress

> enacted a modest tax on personal income in 1894, but it did not survive Supreme Court review (*Pollock v. Farmers' Loan and Trust Co.*, 1894). . . . But neither excises nor customs satisfied reformers' desire for a fairer apportionment of Federal taxes. They recommended a graduated rate structure that taxed individuals in accordance with their ability to pay. Theodore Roosevelt endorsed this idea during his second term. Prodded by advocates of income taxation from the South and West, Congress inched toward this objective in 1909 by approving the Sixteenth Amendment . . . which authorized Washington to levy taxes on earnings. (Campbell 1995: 177)

By 1913, thirty-six of forty-eight states—the required number—had ratified the Amendment; most of these were in the South and West. Of the twelve that did not ratify, seven were in New England and the Middle Atlantic States, one bordered these states (Delaware), and four were scattered Virginia, Florida, Utah, and Wyoming (the number of ratifiers rose to thirty-eight later in 1913 with the addition of Massachusetts and New Hampshire; Buenker 1985). Congress then wasted little time enacting a tax that fell on less than 1 percent of the workforce. This inaugural tax passed Congress in 1913 as part of the Underwood Tariff Act. In this act, Congress sought to achieve three goals; the first two of these "drastically reduced tariff levels and explicitly endorsed the goal of free trade within the international economy"—all for the purpose of export expansion (Lake 1988: 218)—and the third carried forth the Sixteenth Amendment by introducing a graduated income tax. The measure passed the House by a vote of 283–141. The map of that vote indicates that supporters of the tax came mainly from the periphery and that these proponents of reform surrounded the opposition which, by and large, resided in a tier of ten northern states stretching from Maine to the Dakotas (figures 6.15A and 6.15B). The Senate vote was a bit closer (44–37), but the geographies were similar; protax reformers garnered 60 percent of their support from the American periphery (Paullin and Wright 1932: 121–22, plate 120C; Sanders 1999: 229). It was not shocking to anyone that the more prosperous their states the more likely it was that their senatorial delegations would oppose income taxation. Henceforth, the graduated income tax provided the National State with a new and expandable source of revenue; government finance with a new arsenal of fiscal politics; and policy regimes with the means of taxing workers and regions with higher incomes, transferring these taxes to the public sector, and then redistributing them via public programs to poorer Americans or the public at large.

By and large, it was income taxes that funded the rapid expansion of the National State and its redistributive policies and programs. Between 1913 and 1980, it

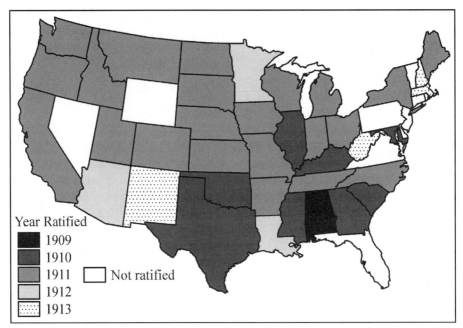

Figure 6.15A.   The income tax: Ratification of the Sixteenth Amendment.

Source: Paullin and Wright 1932: 121–22, plate 120C.

was these taxes that permitted a thirtyfold increase in federal expenditures (in real dollars) and a seventyfold gain in social welfare expenditures. Welfare outlays, which are at the heart of a redistributive polity, grew from about 15 percent of all federal expenditures in 1927 to over a third in 1940 to just under a half in 1980 (note the inversion with 1910 when defense and veterans received 68 percent of federal outlays) (Campbell 1995: 34, 182–83). Federal taxes on personal incomes, on corporations, and on wages for Social Security paid for the lion's share of these social programs. In the early years, income taxes on individuals contributed a very small share of federal revenues (just 13.7 percent). But by 1980, their contribution to federal revenues had more than tripled (to over 47 percent of federal receipts). Another 43 percent came from two revenue sources: taxes for social insurance (30.5 percent) and corporate taxes (12.5 percent) (*Historical Statistics* 1976, 2: 1121–22; *Statistical Abstract* 1997: 332). After 1913, the United States revamped the fiscal foundations of an increasingly bureaucratic National State. And from the Great Depression forward, taxes on incomes, wages, and social insurance provided the principal sources of revenue for the federal government. Tariffs and excise taxes, which had been the major sources of revenue for financing the Sectional State, contributed just 6 percent of federal receipts in 1980 (tariffs accounting for 1.4 percent, excise taxes 4.7 percent; *Historical Statistics* 1976, 2: 1121–22; *Statistical Abstract* 1997: 332).

　　In addition to the vast expansion of regulatory and redistributive policies made possible by income taxation, several other factors helped to sap the vitality of the nation's two principal political parties. In the first place, the Democrats who occu-

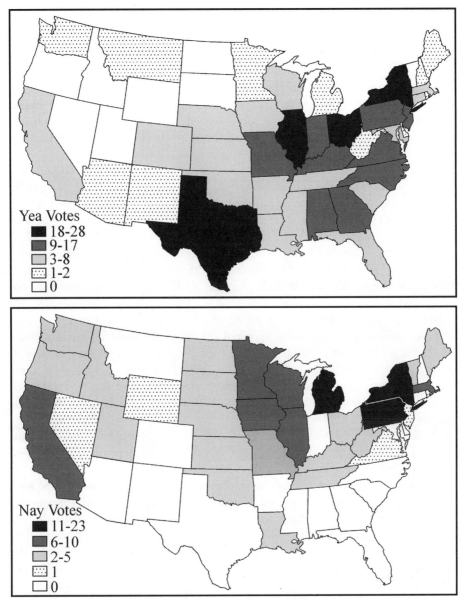

Figure 6.15B.   The income tax: Votes for and against the Underwood Tariff Act of 1913 in the House of Representatives.

Source: Paullin and Wright 1932: 121–22.

pied the White House for all but sixteen years between 1932 and 1980, and their lap-dog opposition, the Republicans, had become more and more alike. Americans sought consensus rather than conflict in domestic politics. And they confronted a series of common enemies—unemployment and insecurity in the 1930s, Hitler and the Japanese in the 1940s, and global communism in the next three decades. Political parties sought to smooth off the rough edges of partisanship on behalf of equity. Thus, when we turn to politics and patronage, we find that the vindictiveness of a partisan era had diminished. New Deal Democrats tended to distribute federal funds in ways that were more fair and equitable rather than crassly political.

To put the geopolitical equity of New Deal spending in context, consider the heavy-handed reallocations of federal spending that followed the Civil War. There was nothing resembling a "Marshall Plan" for the South after the war—quite the contrary (see table 6.8). The share of federal funds spent on the victors (the four northern regions) rose from 32.1 percent in 1860 to 62 percent in 1870 to a peak of 72.6 percent in 1880. With the rise of reform movements in the 1880s and 1890s and the emergence of the solid Democratic South, the distribution of federal funds became more equitable. By 1900, the northern share of federal funds had been cut back to 60 percent. Republicans did little to block these changes or those that followed. Three decades hence (1928–1930), the North's share had fallen to 49 percent. Just when one might have expected the North's downward trend to have continued (or even accelerated) with the New Deal, the new regime refused to redistribute the spoils of victory to their supporters in the periphery. Indeed, there was scarcely any change in the flow of federal spending before the New Deal and the flow of expenditures and loans between 1933 and 1939 (figure 6.16). There was not much evidence of bias in total expenditures; these were split fairly evenly between the northern states and the periphery. As for expenditures per capita, the most deprived states (the thirteen receiving less than the average expenditure of $300 to $500 per capita) were split between the Northeast and South Atlantic regions and in their support for FDR—the former having opposed FDR, the latter supporting him. Conversely, the eleven most favored states (those receiving more than the average) tended to be in the Great Plains and the Mountain West—regions that were not exactly Democratic hotbeds (Reading 1973; Wallis 1998; Shelley et al. 1996). The "old testament" politics thus had given away to the kinder, gentler politics of the National State. Amid all of this sweetness and light, partisanship and party politics receded in significance.

In the second place, political parties suffered because of the expansion of the bureaucratic state. In the course of the Second Democracy (1932–1980), Congress extended the regulatory state into virtually every sphere of the American economic system. Then, to make matters worse, Congress abdicated control over these spheres to regulatory boards, agencies, and commissions and granted them broad regulatory powers in lieu of precise guidelines (Lowi 1995). These regulatory bodies were in turn susceptible to the influence of industries in the spheres that they were supposed to regulate. In some cases, lobbyists and representatives from these industries assisted in making and implementing regulatory policy; in others, regulatory agencies were fully captured by the special interests. The results were not good in either case;

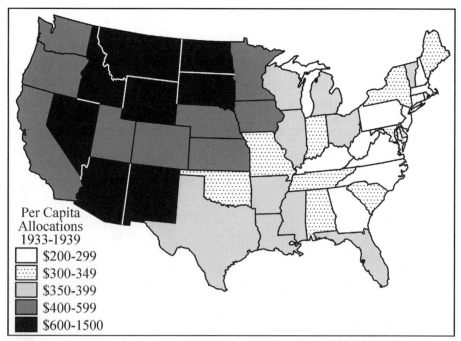

Figure 6.16.   New Deal expenditures, loans, and insurance per capita, 1933–1939.
Source: Reading 1973.

regulated industries were shielded from competition, economic inefficiency flourished, and representative democracy suffered. By the 1960s, the strategy of interest groups had been expanded from the narrowly economic sphere to encompass consumer, environmental and social advocacy (e.g., the Sierra Club, the American Association of Retired Persons, and various other environmental, minority, and "good government" groups). In this corporatist arrangement, the most important policy decisions were made behind the scenes in the meetings of the various regulatory agencies. The Federal Reserve, the National Labor Relations Board, the Securities and Exchange Commission, the Environmental Protection Agency, the Centers for Disease Control, and the Food and Drug Administration seemed to exercise more power and control over American life than the U.S. Senate and the House of Representatives.

While Congress and the political parties continued to provide much of the political bombast for the evening news, the reality was that both had been eclipsed by the executive branch and its vast array of regulatory agencies. Congress had gone downhill fast between the 1960s and 1980s; the difference in that body between the 1960s and 1980 was, according to one Washington insider, "the difference between chicken salad and chicken shit" (Robert Strauss quoted in Dahl 1994: 1). The glory days of the Sectional State, when the nation could be (and was) run by "Congress and the courts," when the Senate and House spawned national leaders, when voters turned out en masse for federal elections, were long gone. The nation had entered the "postpartisan" era of American politics. Voters no longer cared very much about federal elections, the Congress, or political parties, perhaps because so few rules and regulations actually were made in Congress and because parties had little control over the flows of federal funds to the states, which, in any event, were relatively equitable until the stagflation of the 1970s. Along the way, the National State had largely abandoned any pretense of a representative democracy of informed and mobilized voters; it had become instead a juridical democracy subject to the lobbying of special interests and predicated on rules and regulations and policies that, having been made and implemented in bureaucratic chambers one or several steps removed from Capitol Hill, are endlessly adjudicated in the federal courts.

Finally, the old politics of parties and citizen participation were being undermined by the sharp retrenchments in state and local governments. Tip O'Neil's adage that "all politics are local" ignored the bleak realities around him. Americans were literally deserted by the withdrawal of local governments in the 1930s and 1940s. Revenues available for local governments had fallen from 53 percent of all government revenues in 1902 to 32 percent by 1938. And expenditures on local government followed suit during World War II. The local share fell from 67 percent of all government expenditures in 1940 to 16 percent in 1950; the federal share, meanwhile, rose from 21 percent to 58 percent of all government spending (table 6.14). Inevitably local governments crashed, and one by one these local training grounds for American politics closed their doors. The numbers of local governments fell by over 100,000—from 182,602 in 1932 to 105,684 in 1952 to 79,862 in 1977. The losses of school districts alone exceeded seventy thousand between 1932 and 1952 and another forty thousand by 1972 (Stephens and Wikstrom 2000: 8). State governments fared somewhat better. The states' share of total government expenditures rose from 11 to 12 percent in 1902 and 1913 to 17.6 percent in 1927, fell back to 11 percent after the Depression, and then leveled off at between 19 and 22 percent between 1950 and 1970.

All of these trends—equity in the allocation of federal funds; the decline of Congress and the rise of the bureaucratic state; the collapse of local government— contributed to the steady drop in voter turnout and the growing apathy among Americans citizens during the twentieth century. The roles of political parties and

Table 6.14.   Share of Government Expenditures by Federal, State, and Local Governments, 1902–1970

Date	Local	State	Federal
1902	55.7%	10.9%	33.3%
1913	59.1%	11.7%	29.2%
1927	53.2%	17.1%	29.6%
1940	67.6%	11.0%	21.3%
1950	16.0%	19.6%	58.2%
1960	23.3%	18.8%	57.9%
1970	24.0%	22.0%	54.0%

Source: Historical Statistics 1975, 2: 1123–34.

partisanship diminished in importance. The old days when parties mattered, when a credible Congress made important laws on controversial issues, when the crude quid pro quo between sectional votes and federal expenditures had refueled partisan differences and filled party coffers, and when local government provided political opportunities, had come to an end with the rise of the National State. Federal expenditures to states and regions became much more equitable by the 1920s and 1930s, and as that trend continued, as "the geographical distribution of federal outlays has ever more closely matched the geographic distribution of the population in the USA," political parties had less and less to contest (Archer 1983: 388). In the matter of pork-barrel politics, "a geographically equal division of nonprivate goods is in the rational self-interests of territorially elected legislators. . . . Perhaps the Founding Fathers intuitively knew this when they opted for territorial representation" (Archer 1983: 396–97). But in opting for state and regional equity, political parties gave up one of their hottest issues for mobilizing voters. Parties also suffered because the National State's vast expansion of federal expenditures in the 1940s was channeled into an equally vast expansion in the federal bureaucracy—and was not reinvested in state and local government and thus in political parties. The decline of parties deepened voter apathy; so, too, did the erosion of local government which experienced drastic reductions in numbers and in its share of governmental expenditures. The result is an insular and apathetic politics. The next time that an American voices his or her frustration with our faceless bureaucracy, pause and ask when last they attended a party function, when last they spoke with their local council manic representative, and when last they participated in local government. The moral, of course, is that all are increasingly hard to find.

THE TRANSNATIONAL STATE: DIPLOMACY AND THE TRIPLE THREAT OF UNILATERALISM, REGIONALISM, AND MULTILATERALISM

Even as scholars and journalists lamented the shortcomings of the National State, the United States slipped quietly across the threshold of the Transnational State. And here history repeats itself. Just as the rise of big business, mass production, and urbanization in the late nineteenth century necessitated a "search for order" that culminated in the rise of the National State, big government, and a polity of regulation and redistribution, the globalization of the economy in our own times has invited a comparable search for order and control—for a geopolitical response that is as lean, as flexible, and as transnational (i.e., as extraterritorial) as the producer revolution that it seeks to sustain and control. And just as the Fourteenth Amendment provided the constitutional foundation for the enlargement of federal power and the rise of the National State after 1868, the Civil Rights Act of 1964 and its extensions provided the statutory basis for enlarging federal jurisdiction over American citizens and transnational corporations abroad. More generally, the thrust of international jurisprudence in American courts strongly suggests that much of the global economy lies within the reach of the long arm of American law, that when the United States is harmed by actions abroad—by cartels, price fixing, unfair labor practices, environmental pollution, or even terrorist atrocities—the nation is prepared to pursue remedies in the sphere of extraterritorial law (i.e., in transnational space) (Blumberg 1993: 168–201; the United States is less receptive to comparable infringements on American sovereignty).

The transnationalization of the American state is difficult to pin down. It is evident not so much in a single coherent strand of foreign policy as in a braided series of policies, not so much in a centrally coordinated plan as in multiple strategies deployed by various agents representing multiple perspectives on American interests overseas. These diplomatic strategies range from unilateralism to regionalism to multilateralism. Unilateral strategies involve Americans acting alone, as with the Helms–Burton Act on Cuba or cartel litigation. Regional strategies arise when Americans act in concert with their neighbors or functional allies, as with NAFTA or in the coordination of exchange agreements among the G-5 nations. And multilateral strategies unfold when Americans act in conjunction with most if not all of the world's states, as with GATT and the World Trade Organization. When all these are pursued simultaneously—albeit, one suspects, somewhat independently—the fuzzy, ill-defined, and often underestimated result is the Transnational American State (Ruggie 1993).

We begin at the strategic extreme that best suits the American inclination—American unilateralism. In the 1980s and 1990s the unilateral strategy of the United States shifted gears and venues. While the nation did not abandon the customary venues in the federal courts and the litigation of arcane economic issues (e.g., cartels, price fixing, dumping, etc.), it shifted the emphasis toward Congress and the executive branch and toward the sphere of geopolitics. In so doing, Americans visibly raised the stakes of an extraterritorial foreign policy. Setting aside partisan division, Congress approved and the president signed the Cuban Liberty and Democratic Solidarity (Libertad) Act of 1996, best known as the Helms–Burton Act, and then the Iran–Libya Sanctions Act of 1996, also known as the D'Amato–Kennedy Act. "Both laws were adopted to further U.S. foreign policy by isolating the targeted countries through the imposition of severe penalties upon certain persons and companies investing in these countries. . . . The laws [among other things] had extraterritorial effect, imposed secondary boycotts, violated the principle of sovereignty and non-intervention in domestic matters, and infringed rules" recognized by multilateral organizations such as the WTO and the UN (Smis and Van Der Borght 1999: 227).

These intrusive pieces of legislation were hardly quirky exotics on the fringe of American politics. Helms–Burton, for example, passed by large majorities in the House (336–86) and the Senate (74–22) in March 1996. President Clinton signed the bill on March 12, though he wisely deferred "the enforcement of Title III, using a loophole conveniently inserted in the text of the law" (Roy 2000: 28–31). The controversial aspect of Title III was that it aimed "at preventing anyone from 'trafficking' in U.S. property that was 'confiscated' (i.e., property whose owner was not given prompt, adequate, and effective compensation). To that end, any U.S. national who claims that his or her property was confiscated by the Cuban government after

January 1, 1959, may initiate an action in a U.S. court against a person engaged in such trafficking" (Smis and Van Der Borght 1999: 230). Title III constituted a direct assault on the jurisdiction of a sovereign state (Cuba) as well as an indirect extraterritorial intrusion on foreign investors in Cuba (e.g., most notably from Canada, the EU, and Mexico). Clinton's delaying action afforded an extended "cooling off" period. It provided time for the United States to assess European, Canadian, and Mexican objections to Helms–Burton and to negotiate an agreement with the European Union. Under terms of that agreement, the United States extended the period of nonenforcement through 2000 in exchange for EU efforts to promote democracy in Cuba and to defer the activation of a dispute procedure before the WTO (Roy 2000: 105–29; in July 2001, the Bush administration extended nonenforcement another six months).

Congress has likewise been supportive of punitive litigation aimed at foreign states that support or sponsor terrorism against American nationals. Under the Foreign Sovereign Immunities Act (1976) and its 1996 revisions, American citizens are able to sue foreign states designated by the U.S. State Department as supporting terrorism. The civil-suit damages thus far awarded by U.S. courts are sizable, amounting to multiple millions of dollars; and now, owing to the Clinton administration's decision to reverse its original position, these damages are now payable to terrorist victims out of the frozen assets of these foreign states (Slaughter and Bosco 2000: 112–15).

Congress and the executive branch have been less forthcoming with respect to the application of broad moral principles in foreign affairs. When Americans have nibbled at the edges of natural rights, it is usually the courts that have taken the lead. Consider the audacious and "almost forgotten Alien Tort Statute of 1789, which gives U.S. federal courts jurisdiction over violations 'of the law of nations or a treaty of the United States'" (Slaughter and Bosco 2000: 109; Rogers 1999). In a bold and sweeping ruling for the plaintiff in 1980, the Second Circuit's Court of Appeal held that under this law, "foreigners could be held liable for violations of international law, even if committed outside the United States and against non-Americans." It is hard to imagine a law that offers a more sweeping jurisdiction for both American jurisprudence and the principle of extraterritoriality. Although the courts and the prosovereigntist Reagan administration subsequently restricted the scope of the law (fearful perhaps of reprisals by foreign nations), it remains a powerful tool when employed against those without sovereign immunity.

The liberal interpretation of American law and the jurisdiction of U.S. courts is responsible for one other channel of transnational unilateralism (Slaughter and Bosco 2000; Vagts 1970; Blumberg 1993). In these cases, the federal courts have entertained a variety of civil suits brought by plaintiffs who now reside in the United States against overseas corporations for actions committed abroad and often long ago. Perhaps the best known are suits brought against Swiss banks for profiting from funds deposited by or stolen from Nazi victims during World War II. In the course of the trial, the Clinton administration and others intervened and helped to broker a $1.25 billion payment. In 1998, suits were brought against German corporations for using concentration camp prisoners as slave laborers; as in the case of the Swiss banks, the plaintiffs reached an out-of-court settlement (estimated at $5.1 billion). In these matters, American jurisdiction qua sovereignty has been extended across juridical space—the Atlantic—and over time—some six decades.

American courts are much clearer about the lines of jurisdiction in cases in which foreign citizens have filed civil suits against U.S. corporations for their conduct (or the conduct of their subsidiaries) abroad. Plaintiffs have sued American oil companies over alleged complicity in the violation of human rights in Burma; over the dumping of toxic wastes in Ecuador; over corporate complicity in the murder of political activists in Nigeria; and over the 1984 industrial disaster that killed almost two thousand and injured some three hundred thousand at Bhopal in India. These instances strongly suggest that American courts are likely to exercise their jurisdiction whenever an American citizen or corporation is involved in the litigation. American courts routinely assume jurisdiction when the plaintiffs are American citizens; they may also assert jurisdiction when the United States has an interest "in applying its legal resources and in monitoring the legal activity of the multinationals" (Shew 1986: 660; Slaughter and Bosco 2000; Vagts 1970). A note on toxic torts in the *Vanderbilt Journal of Transnational Law* (1986) puts the matter succinctly: "United States-Based Multinational Corporations Should be Tried in the United States for their Extraterritorial Toxic Torts." That—and more—the federal courts have done.

These courtly adventures in extraterritoriality reinforce the American propensity for unilateralism. Americans, by and large, are an insular bunch; they prefer to act alone and are usually reluctant to enter into multilateral arrangements that may encroach on the nation's sovereignty. The international sphere of criminal law underscores this reluctance. In recent years, the United States has been actively involved in discussions on the establishment of an international criminal court (the ICC). American representatives have been supportive of the goals of the ICC and have expressed American willingness to assist in the court's formation. But that's as far as it goes, given the United States' unique global role as well as its abiding commitments to autonomy and independence. Americans simply will not concede sovereign jurisdiction over criminal matters to a multilateral agency. In the words of David J. Scheffer, the U.S. ambassador-at-large for War Crimes Issues (1999: 18):

> It is simply and logically untenable to expose the largest deployed military force in the world, stationed across the globe to help maintain international peace and security and to defend U.S. allies and friends, to the jurisdiction of a criminal court the U.S. government has not yet joined and whose authority over U.S. citizens the United States does not yet recognize. . . . The theory that an individual U.S. soldier acting on foreign territory should be exposed to ICC jurisdiction if his alleged crime occurs on that territory, even if the United States is not party to the ICC treaty and even if that foreign state is also not a party to the treaty and consents ad hoc to ICC jurisdiction, may appeal to those who believe in the blind application of territorial jurisdiction. But [these terms] could render nonsensical the actual functioning of the ICC.

For these reasons, among others, "the United States will not sign the treaty in its present form." While France, the U.K., Russia, and seventeen other states voted in favor of the treaty in Rome in 1998, the United States joined with five others (including some branded as terrorists by the United States) in opposing the treaty. In some quarters this was regarded as hypocritical—but surely not in a Transnational American State long suspicious of entangling alliances and infringements on American sovereignty.

The upshot of American unilateralism is an uneasy shuffling back and forth between the aims of the federal judiciary and the executive branch. In juxtaposing the aggressive expansion of the federal courts in foreign affairs with the executive branch's "continued . . . refusal to participate in bodies like the International Criminal Court," the United States conveys "the image of a country happy to haul foreign defendants into its own courts while stubbornly resisting even the remote possibility that its own citizens might be called to account" (Slaughter and Bosco 2000: 115). But then, of course, the preservation of American autonomy is no less the primary aim of the Constitution's separation of powers than the pursuit of self-interest is the primary aim of unilateralism. Since Washington's farewell address in 1796, working in groups—that is to say multilateralism and Wilsonian interdependence—has not come easily to the United States; nor, for that matter, has the quest for altruism.

At the opposite extreme from the unilateralism of Helms–Burton, toxic waste torts, and suits in juridical space/time is multilateralism. This strategy engages large numbers of states in the formulation and implementation of global policies and is exemplified by the ICC, the United Nations, and the World Bank and the International Monetary Fund (see, among others, Roberts 1995). Perhaps the best-known case of American multilateralism involves the GATT founded in 1948 and its successor, the WTO founded in 1995 and supplanting GATT in 1996. The aims of GATT and its successor, the WTO, are fairly straightforward: the establishment of a global trade regime predicated on neoliberal economic principles. Toward that end, the WTO seeks to foster the globalization of free trade, to reduce tariffs and nontariff barriers, promote free trade in services as well as in merchandise trade, facilitate investment across borders, ensure transparency and accountability in securities and capital markets, establish effective procedures for dispute settlement and resolution, and extend these principles to all of the states in the world (as of 2000, roughly three-fourths of all states belong to the WTO). But as the WTO meeting in Seattle in 2000 clearly revealed, the opposition to trade liberalization is deep-seated, if not fully unified. The opponents, an odd coalition of Greens (environmentalists), nationalists, and trade unionists, are energized by a broad base of concerns ranging from the erosion of national sovereignty to the inability to enforce environmental regulations, protect wages, or prevent plant closures, from the loss of flexibility in economic development planning to the lowering of environmental, technical, and labor standards—their harmonization—across nations (i.e., the notorious "race to the bottom" in exchange for profits and shareholder return; Dunkley 2000).

The WTO's current problems are traceable, in large measure, to its origins in an older world order—in GATT, Bretton Woods, and the international political economy envisioned during the New Deal. One of the central premises of the New Deal's program of economic recovery was a foreign policy predicated on the vigorous extension of free trade (or, to be more faithful to its proponents, "fair trade").

Under the energetic leadership of Secretary of State Cordell Hull, the United States negotiated scores of bilateral reciprocal trade agreements and conferred "most-favored nation" trading status on these signatories. At Bretton Woods, New Hampshire, in 1944 and after World War II, Hull's vision of "fair trade" for Americans was extended to the world at large first in the form of the International Trade Organization (ITO) and later—after the United States failed to ratify the ITO—its successor, the 1948 GATT (Diebold 1952; Eckes 1995). For nearly half a century, trade negotiations proceeded in what became an endless series of GATT "rounds." By the mid-1990s, the prospects for global trade had improved markedly what with the post-1978 economic reforms in China and the collapse of the Soviet Union in the late 1980s and early 1990s—and the proposal for the ITO was reincarnated in the WTO.

While the prospects for WTO are good, the politics of trade at the dawn of the twenty-first century are vastly more complicated than they were in the 1940s and 1950s. The consensus on free trade that had held up through the 1980s is now vigorously contested by various political and social movements. Negotiators are no longer able to focus exclusively on the economic benefits of trade or to conduct their negotiations behind closed doors. Forces of democratization insist on public disclosure, a vastly enlarged agenda, and a host of interests and agents representing new social movements, trade unions, and numerous nongovernmental organizations (NGOs). Thus, the debate must go beyond the narrow parameters of trade and economic growth and come to grips with issues of economic equity and welfare within states (e.g., minimum wages) and across states (e.g. uneven economic development), human rights, environment and sustainability, product safety and liability, as well as the socialization of risk and uncertainty (i.e., the notion of social "safety nets") (Dunkley 2000 and the sources cited therein).

The irony of the WTO is that freeing up world trade has resulted in an extensive body of rules, regulations, and procedures in order to ensure compliance and to resolve disputes. Institutional issues complicate matters. In a large body in which each state has one vote and the levels of economic development across states are so varied, the prospects for agreement on controversial issues are not good. As Richard H. Steinberg (1997: 233) observes, sheer numbers are a problem with respect to environmental issues:

> The relative power of richer, greener states [to effect environmental policy] varies [with the composition of multilateral] . . . trade organizations. The more poor nations in trade organizations [as for example in the WTO], the less power richer, greener countries have to solve trade-environment problems, *ceteris paribus*; this is because the currency of rich-country power in trade negotiations—access to rich country markets—has to be spread more thinly across more poor countries. Thus while U.S. power to solve trade-environment problems in the NAFTA (where the U.S. market is a source of great power over Mexico) may be roughly equivalent to the power of various European countries . . . to solve trade-environment problems in the European Union . . . [the] combined [power of] the U.S. and the European Union . . . is less effective on the

WTO because the market power must be used to solve trade-environment problems with scores of developing countries.

While richer nations such as the United States may set the agenda for multilateral organizations such as the WTO (or the UN) (Krasner 1983: 1–21), their capacity to determine the direction of policy is disproportionately constrained by the number and variety of participants (on the special position that GATT afforded less developed countries, see Finlayson and Zacher 1983: 293–96). The disadvantages of multilateralism thus are many—be it the surrender of sovereign jurisdiction as required by the ICC or the thinning of American power within the multitude of poorer nations in the WTO; indeed, its virtues may be restricted to the kind of forum-provisioning offered by the UN (and even then, contingent on access to the trump of veto power).

All of the prior points bring us to a more promising set of strategies that lie between the bullying posture of unilateralism and the wimpish accommodation of multilateralism. Regional strategies are predicated on cooperation among a small number of states organized into one of two distinct types of regions. The first of these types is the formal region in which the several states are united on the basis of spatial proximity (e.g., NAFTA). The second is the functional region in which several states are united by high levels of interaction and exchange across space (e.g., the G-5 to G-7 summit nations united by trade and by shared policies such as "managed trade" and exchange-rate coordination).

The American turn toward the region and a regional strategy came during the 1980s amid a decade of momentous changes in American society and economy. Americans worried over a host of problems: hyperinflation and spiraling unemployment; the reorganization of production via flexible specialization, downsizing, and outsourcing; the restructuring of regional geographies as firms gravitated toward the Sunbelt, selective metropolitan areas, and locations overseas (Smith 1988: 143). But the larger problem for American policymakers was the European Community's astonishing decision to create a single and unified Europe. In light of the European decision, the Reagan administration was compelled to rethink this nation's long-standing commitment to multilateralism, internationalism, and the strategic troika of the IMF, the World Bank, and GATT (i.e., to revisit the foundational premises of New Deal foreign policy).

The proposal for the formation of a multistate European Union constituted a shot across the bow of the second American state. The proposal envisioned the creation of a free-trade area in Western Europe that would exceed the scope and power of the U.S. market; the passage of the Single European Act of 1985 put flesh on these bones by promising completion of the Single European Market by 1992. The act aimed "to remove all the remaining internal barriers [to trade]: physical, technical, and fiscal. . . . After 1992, therefore, there will be a single unified market of approximately 330 million people" (Dicken 1992: 166). Europe's bold break with the old world order of Bretton Woods posed two challenges for the United States: first was the sheer size of this competing European market; second, and more immediately, was the reduction in European support for American multilateral initiatives such as GATT and the WTO (Bhagwati 1994: 284–85).

Americans wasted little time in parrying the plan for a European Union; the U.S. proposal called for the creation of a regional trade bloc of its own—what came to be known as the North American Free Trade Union—and within the same time frame. "In March 1985 President Reagan, during a visit to Quebec, proposed a free-trade agreement to Canadian Prime Minister Brian Mulroney that would eliminate all tariffs and non-tariff trade barriers (NTBs) between the two countries. What became the U.S.–Canada Free Trade Agreement (FTB) was the precursor to the North American Free Trade Agreement (NAFTA)" (Kaplan 1996: 137). The negotiations for the U.S.–Canada Agreement were completed in 1987 and 1988—as the European Community moved toward a single Europe. Formal approvals followed; the Agreement passed the U.S. House and Senate by September 1988, the Canadian House of Commons in December, and went into effect in January 1989. In the ensuing four years, with the support of Canada and Republican president Bush and Democrat Clinton, the regional bloc was expanded to include Mexico. On January 1, 1994, NAFTA went into effect. Here was the institutional foundation for a suitable rival to the European Union and a platform for the hemispheric expansion of free trade—on American terms (Cameron and Tomlin 2000: 51–80).

Support for NAFTA in the United States was not universal, however. A sizable opposition mobilized among trade unionists and politicians (mostly Democrats) in the northeastern manufacturing belt who were fearful of losing industries and jobs to lower-cost labor in Mexico. The 1993 vote for NAFTA in the U.S. House of Representatives underscored the geographical realignment in American politics, the decline and relocation of manufacturing in the northeastern core region, and the southward and westward shifts in population underway since the 1970s (figure 6.17). NAFTA narrowly passed the House of Representatives by a vote of 234 to 200 (53.9 percent of the total vote), with Republicans providing 132 of the yea votes (56.4 percent) and Democrats the remaining 102. Most of the support for NAFTA (some two-thirds) came from the increasingly prosperous thirty-state periphery. And most of the opposition (59 percent) clustered in the twenty core states in the northeastern quadrant (from Maine to Minnesota to Maryland to Missouri)—states that had lost large numbers of manufacturing jobs since 1970 (Clark 1994; *Congressional Quarterly* 1993; *Congressional Record* 1993; Doran 1994).

The geography of the NAFTA vote in the House of Representatives was somewhat more complicated than this simple core-periphery division (table 6.15). In the five regions of the United States listed in the bottom half of table 6.15, the vote for NAFTA tends to rise as one moves away from the North and East and toward the South and West. In the two core regions in the North (New England and the Mid-Atlantic states) and Midwest, the vote tended to split along partisan lines with Democrats opposing NAFTA and Republicans favoring it. And given the strength of the Democratic Party in these heavily unionized regions, support for NAFTA was modest. In the northeastern states, only one in three Representatives (34 percent) voted for NAFTA. The legislation did much better in the Midwest, where it registered a respectable 46.5 percent of the House vote and won over the delegations in Iowa, Wisconsin, and Illinois. Support rose again in the South, where NAFTA won the support of many in both parties, registered nearly 60 percent in favor of the legisla-

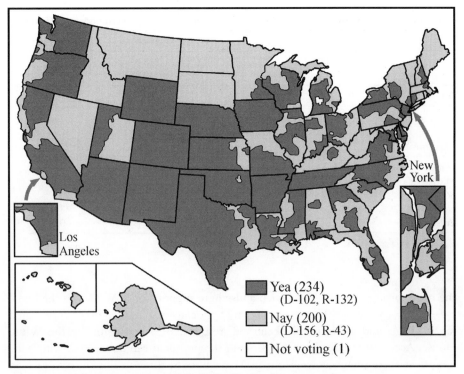

Figure 6.17.   The 1993 vote on NAFTA in the House of Representatives.

Source: Congressional Quarterly Weekly Report 1993: 3494–95.
Note: The abstention comes from northern Michigan.

tion, and scored victories in nine of eleven states formerly belonging to the Confederacy (save Alabama and South Carolina). Lastly, representatives in the West and Near West (the Mountain states) provided the most resounding levels of support for NAFTA (60.9 percent and 77 percent, respectively)—including a clean sweep of the Pacific Coast (for a region that tends to oppose most Republican initiatives, the NAFTA vote is telling). These high levels of support reflect two considerations, above others: first, the concentration of Republican representatives in the western United States; second, the tendency for Democrats in these regions to cross party lines in the House and vote with the President and with regional interests (Shelley et al. 1996: 222–27).

It is worth noting that while NAFTA originated as a Republican initiative, first of Ronald Reagan and then of George Bush, final passage came on the watch of a centrist Democrat, Bill Clinton. And while the majority of House Democrats voted against NAFTA, 102 Democrats backed the president, and their support was crucial for the bill's passage. Why did these 102 Democrats break ranks with their leadership in the House? Just over half of them (fifty-five) were predictable given their ideology and eight other variables characterizing his or her district (Livingston and Wink 1997). Of the forty-seven who could not be predicted based on ideology and constituency, the majority (thirty-two) resided in peripheral states which stood to gain

Table 6.15.   The NAFTA Vote in the House of Representatives: Core/Periphery and Regions

		For	Against	Total
Core	(20 states)	78	118	196
Periphery	(30 states)	156	82	238
Totals		234	200	434

Source: *Congressional Quarterly Weekly Report* 1993: 3494–95.

Regions	For	Against	Percent for in region
North	31	60	34.1%
Midwest	46	53	46.5%
South	65	45	59.1%
Near West	50	15	77.0%
West	42	27	60.9%

Source: Clark 1994.

the most through trade with Mexico and where support for NAFTA was the highest—and reasonably so. That leaves fifteen Democrats who resided in the core, voted for NAFTA, and were, in all likelihood, responsive to persuasion by the White House. According to this line of argument, the president can be credited with winning over these fifteen votes—four in Massachusetts, three in Illinois, two each in New York, Ohio, and Maryland, and three others elsewhere in the core (Livingston and Wink 1997). NAFTA would have passed without these votes, but the margin of victory would have been shaved from 234–200 to 219–215.

In the Senate, NAFTA passed with more room to spare—sixty-one to thirty-eight or 61.4 percent of the vote (Clark 1994). And contrary to the logics of economic geography and self-interest, the Senate bill did even better in the core (28–15) than in the periphery (33–23). Yet neither vote in the House nor the Senate was veto-proof—both fell well below the two-thirds vote required to override a presidential veto. But that was unnecessary given the sustained support for NAFTA from presidents Reagan, Bush, and Clinton. Nor would the Senate vote have been sufficient if NAFTA had been defined as a treaty rather than as an agreement—in which case a two-thirds vote of the Senate would have been required. In the absence of a constitutional ruling by the courts clarifying NAFTA's status as a treaty or an agreement, the statutory basis for NAFTA seems reasonably secure (on the questionable constitutionality of NAFTA, see Ackerman and Globe 1995).

In the afterglow of NAFTA's passage, diplomatic hyperbole flowed freely. From the president on down, there were visions of an even larger free-trade area that would, in due course, encompass the Caribbean and then Central and South America. But these plans were dashed when in 1994 Congress refused to renew fast-track authorization for trade negotiations to the president. (Note: "Fast-track enables the president to negotiate an international trade agreement but requires him to notify and receive approval to negotiate from Congress and to consult with Congress during negotiations. In return, the Congress will move the agreement through Committee on an accelerated timetable, prohibit amendments, and limit floor debate, thereby ensuring that the agreement will be voted up or down without amendment within a fixed period of time" [Cameron and Tomlin 2000].) In the absence of fast-track authority, nations negotiating with the United States could not be assured that the agreements made would be honored and unamended by the U.S. Congress. This action effectively stalled further negotiations to enlarge NAFTA membership and the regional trade bloc—at least for the moment.

But these restraints on NAFTA's enlargement have had certain advantages. Time has provided the opportunity to negotiate and refine side agreements on the environment, labor, and transportation safety (Aceves 1999; Steinberg 1997). Time has also revealed problems with NAFTA's liberal protections for investors, most notably in Chapter 11. To protect "investors from arbitrary or underhanded treatment by governments, [this Chapter] allows companies to sue governments directly" (Walker 2001: 1). Nationalists regard this as an infringement on sovereignty, and revisions in this provision along with the dispute procedure itself are likely if and when NAFTA is expanded to the hemisphere at large. The passage of time and events has also added depth to the economic integration of the principals. In response to Mexico's "peso crisis" in 1994 and 1995, the United States put together a package of financial assistance that was both risky and generous. The loans from the United States (which were made without Congress's approval) amounted to $20 billion; the IMF provided $18.5 billion; and another $10 billion came from various central banks (Weintraub 1995). It seems unlikely that this would have happened in the absence of NAFTA.

NAFTA's impacts on trade have also been profound. In the case of merchandise exports, U.S. trade within NAFTA rose by 109.4 percent between 1990 and 1998 as compared to a gain of 59.2 percent in exports to the rest of the world (table 6.16; WTO 1999, 2: 29). In this same period, Canada's intra-NAFTA trade rose by 92.1 percent and Mexico's by 217.8 percent. Intra-NAFTA trade as a whole increased by 117.3 percent as compared to a 53.1 percent gain in extra-NAFTA trade. When we examine the ratios of intra- and extra-NAFTA trade in 1990 and 1998 (table 6.16), we find that the ratios for the three countries and NAFTA all increased. It is worth noting that while trade strengthened the bonds among NAFTA countries, it failed to do so in western Europe. The ratio of intra- and extra-EU trade in the 1990s fell by 10 percent as compared to NAFTA's gain of 40 percent. Thus, despite the creation of the EU, the EU's trade with the rest of the world rose even more than internal trade.

Table 6.16.   Ratios of Intrabloc and Extrabloc Exports, NAFTA and EU

	NAFTA	EU
1990	0.75	1.85
1993	0.85	1.67
1996	0.91	1.65
1997	0.95	1.59
1998	1.05	1.68

Source: World Trade Organization Annual Report 1999, 2: 7.

However promising NAFTA's early returns, the Clinton administration temporarily shelved its plans for enlarging the bloc to a Free Trade Area of the Americas (FTAA). The closeness of the vote for NAFTA was an early warning, and the ensuing defeat of fast-track authorization were forceful reminders of the fate of overly ambitious policies in an era of "divided governance." Conversely, prospects are brightened by cooperative efforts elsewhere in the hemisphere; these have been somewhat more constructive. As of 1997, nine other regional trade arrangements were in effect; and six more were in the planning stage (El-Agraa 1997: 24–25). These involved thirty-one nations, most of which were principals in two or more hemispheric trade arrangements. These achievements brighten the prospects for more extensive regional integrations such as President Bush's plan for a Free Trade Area of the Americas or Representative Henry Hyde's call for a Commonwealth of the Americas.

Insofar as the prospects for a hemispheric trade bloc in the twenty-first century are contingent on the United States, the key for success is to eliminate the geographical division and polarization of American foreign policy that swept the nation in the 1970s and 1980s and to restore a consensus on America's role in the new world order. Once upon a time, between the end of World War II and the humiliation of Vietnam, there was a consensus on foreign policy. Americans were united by an ideology of "cold-war internationalism" and its corollary commitments to national defense, free trade, and anticommunism. But that consensus collapsed during the 1970s. While one part of the nation sought to stay the course, to preserve that ideology through continued investments in defense and the promotion of free trade, the other part insisted on new priorities with much less spent on defense and much more on trade protection, subsidies for troubled industries, and a comprehensive socioeconomic safety net. The geographies of polarization that unfolded between swatches of the Truman years (1945–1952) and the Reagan years (1981–1988) are clearly revealed in Trubowitz's (1992) study of the roll-call votes of state congressional delegations on key foreign policies.

Consider the graph of roll-call votes in the Truman years of consensus (figure 6.18). It reveals a sizable amount of regional overlap, few sharp divisions between the northeastern and southern states, and a slight tendency (if one exists) for the consensus to be stronger in the coastal states and the "isolationist" opposition to prevail in the interior states of the Midwest and the Great Plains. But the main theme is the widespread predominance of Cold War internationalism, particularly on the three coasts. Much had changed by the 1980s. State delegations had become more sharply divided (even polarized) between an "old America" and a "new." On one side was an "old America" consisting of twenty states—fifteen in the Sunbelt, three in the Great Plains (Kansas, Nebraska, and Wyoming), and two in the Rocky Mountains (Idaho and Utah). These peripheral states continued to support the main tenets of Cold War internationalism along with the newer commitments to regional trade blocs (NAFTA) and free trade ("fast track"). On the other side is a "new America" worried by an unrestrained economy and by economic uncertainty and consisting of twenty-seven states in all—twenty in the manufacturing belt of the Northeast and Midwest, three each on the West Coast and in the northern plains and Nevada.

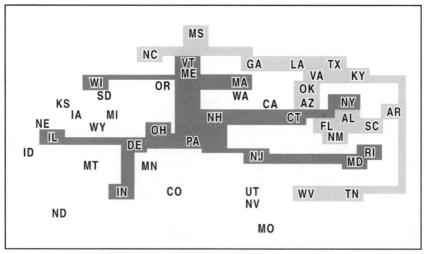

a) Truman Years 1945-1952

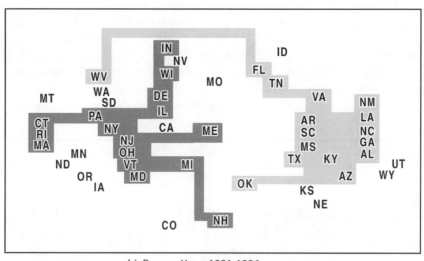

b) Reagan Years 1981-1986

Sunbelt States   Manufacturing Belt States

Figure 6.18.   Similarities in the votes of state delegations in the House of Representatives on key foreign policy legislation in times of ideological consensus (the Truman administration, top) and division (the Reagan administration, bottom).

Source: Trubowitz 1997.

Note: The Truman-era graph shows ideological mixing across regions while the Reagan-era graph shows ideological homogeneity within regions.

These two Americas were evident in the support for Ronald Reagan's military policies in the House of Representatives in 1983 and 1984. Of the twenty-five state delegations supporting Reagan's intensified high-tech version of Cold War internationalism, only three came from the core—New Hampshire, Illinois, and Indiana. The rest came from the periphery with Kentucky and the secession states providing twelve; the mountain states minus Colorado seven; and the central plains states three (Kansas, Nebraska, and Oklahoma) (figure 6.19). These two Americas were also on call during the presidential election of 2000, with George W. Bush winning most of the South, the Plains, and the Mountain states (i.e., most of "old America") and the Democratic Party winning most of the manufacturing belt and the West Coast. These are also the relevant geographies for the future of American foreign policy. If the Bush administration is to succeed in enlarging NAFTA to the hemisphere at large, it will surely need to reconstruct the older consensus of Cold War internationalism, albeit along new and more parochial lines, and to expand the reach of the consensus from the Sunbelt, the Plains, and the Rocky Mountains to the Pacific Coast, the Midwest and the northeastern core as a whole.

NAFTA (and FTAA) represent(s) the first, and most visible, of two regional strategies that have been pursued by American policymakers and entrepreneurs in a transnational state. In this case, NAFTA represents the formal region, its unity is predicated on hemispheric proximity, and its viability is contingent on publicly contested democratic processes. The second regional strategy (the functional region) involves a union of a handful of powerful states—the so-called summit nations variously constituted as the G-5 (the United States, Japan, France, Germany, and the

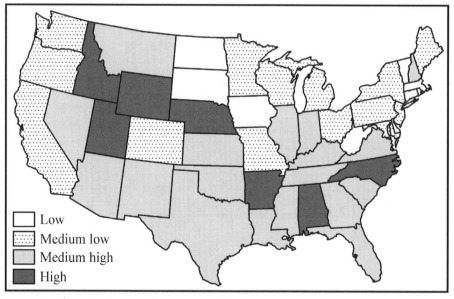

Figure 6.19.   Levels of support for Reagan's military policies by state delegations in the House of Representatives, 1983–1984.

Source: Trubowitz and Roberts 1992.

U.K.), the G-6 (add Canada), and G-7 (add Italy). In these cases, regional unity is predicated on the functional interactions of the world's most powerful nations. Their interactions serve to unite the global system of trade and commerce by cutting across hemispheric trade blocs. But the power of these nations extends far beyond the flows of trade and commerce between them. It is these nations that have been responsible for setting the global rules of the game, for guiding and coordinating the macroeconomy and polity of a neoliberal international regime. Operating beneath the radar of normal constitutional debate, as it were, their coordinated actions extend across a wide range of crucial policy spheres ranging from targeting (and realizing) exchange rates; advising on trade and tariff levels; formulating domestic monetary (interest rates) and fiscal (taxation) policies; improving safety nets, working conditions, and wages; and military-strategic coordination (see especially Feldstein 1988; Dobson 1991; Keohane 1984). That so wide and potent a range of foreign policy actions is subject to so few checks and balances is one of the great mysteries as well as great advantages of this regional strategy for American administrations. These administrations confront many more political obstacles when, in attempting to build trade blocs based on regional trade agreements, Congress becomes involved. In such situations, a strategy that complements the free-wheeling aspects of regional "summitry" with the more cautious and conventional democratic strategy of regional trade agreements may be the wisest path for American geopolitics.

The geopolitical significance of summit regionalism is underscored by the privileged status of these larger and more powerful nations in the Central Intelligence Agency's *Handbook of International Economic Statistics* (1999). Their inclusion is not surprising given that power is the CIA's business; what is remarkable is their neglect almost everywhere else. Whereas other sources—whether published by scholars or by NGOs—aggregate international data by geographical regions (e.g., western Europe), level of development (more or less), or trade blocs (e.g., the EU), only the CIA aggregates data for the G-7 summit powers. And thus while others talk about global geoeconomic and geopolitical power, only the CIA attempts to capture it in charts, graphs, and maps.

Trade statistics once again are revealing. Merchandise exports from the summit powers are enormous. The G-7 accounted for about half of the world's exports in 1986 (51.5 percent) and slightly less in 1997 (48.4 percent) (the proportions are about the same when commercial services are added in; table 6.17). Of the 1997 amount, the G-6 accounted for 44.1 percent; the G-5, 40.1 percent; Germany, France, the U.K., and Italy, 24.2 percent; the United States and Canada, 16.5 percent; and Japan, 7.7 percent.

What emerges from these data is a panregional hierarchy of global trade, one that enmeshes the Transnational American State in a network of formal (trade bloc) and functional (summit) regions. It begins with the summit powers and extends through their trade links via NAFTA and the EU. *Level 1* of the hierarchy consists of trade among the summit powers alone. In 1997, this amounted to 11.5 percent of world trade for the G-5 nations, 17.3 percent for the G-6, and 20.5 percent for the G-7 (table 6.18, especially note). *Level 2* adds in G-7 trade with all other nations. In this case, the proportion of world trade (merchandise exports) rises to 48.4 per-

Table 6.17.   Total Exports of G-5, G-6, and G-7 Nations to All Trading Partners, 1986 and 1997 (in billions of dollars)

Merchandise Exports

	1986	*Percent World Exports*	*1997*	*Percentage World Exports*
U.S.	227.2		688.7	
U.K.	107.1		281.6	
Germany	243.3		511.7	
Japan	210.8		421.0	
France	125.0		289.6	
G-5	**913.4**	**42.7%**	**2,192.6**	**40.1%**
Canada	90.3		214.4	
G-6	**1,003.7**	**47.0%**	**2407.0**	**44.1%**
Italy	97.2		238.2	
G-7	**1,100.9**	**51.5%**	**2,645.2**	**48.4%**
World Exports	2,137.0		5,464.0	

Exports of merchandise and commercial services

	1986			*1987*		
	Mer-chandise	*Commercial Services*	*Total*	*Mer-chandise*	*Commercial Services*	*Total*
G-5	913.4	204.7	118.1 (43.2%)	2,192.6	551.8	2,744.4 (40.5%)
G-6	1,003.7	214.6	1,241.2 (48.0%)	2,407.0	581.6	3,051.6 (45.0%)
G-7	1,100.9	237.5	1,338.4 (51.7%)	2,645.2	648.0	3,293.2 (48.5%)
World	2,137.0	449.6	2,586.6	5,464.0	1,320.9	6,784.9

Sources: World Trade Organization Annual Report 1997, 2; World Trade Organization Annual Report 1998, 2; World Trade Organization Annual Report 1999, 3.

cent. Note that intra–EU and intra–NAFTA trade together already account for just under a fifth (19.3 percent) of world merchandise trade (table 6.19). Lastly, *level 3* adds in EU and NAFTA exports over and above G-7 flows (e.g., Mexico's exports to non-NAFTA nations). This increment boosts the 1997 exports from the panregional hierarchy to 51.6 percent of the world's trade.

Panregionalism has room for expansion within *level 3* of the hierarchy. Some likely possibilities are as follows: the establishment of the Free Trade Area of the Americas in the Western Hemisphere (building on NAFTA, Mercosur, and other trade agreements already in place; El-Agraa 1997: 24–25); the extension of the EU to Eastern Europe and, less likely, to Russia; and the formalization of an ASEAN trade bloc within east and southeast Asia. Regional trade agreements offer several advantages over the WTO or macroeconomic summitry. First, they more fully preserve sovereignty; second, they permit larger states such as the United States to exercise more power within the arrangement (thus increasing viability); and third, they afford greater play for the operation of contentious democratic processes at home as opposed to the empowerment of remote bureaucracies or delphic proclamations. Thus are prospects improved for the betterment of the environment and working conditions.

Table 6.18. Merchandise Trade Exports among the Summit Powers (G-5, G-6, G-7) in 1996 (United States) and 1997

Merchandise	Exports to							
Exports From	U.S.	U.K.	Germany	Japan	France	Canada	Italy	Total
U.S. (1996)	0	28.7	22.2	63.6	13.5	119.1	8.3	255.4
U.K.	32.0	0	29.7	6.7	22.8	3.2	11.3	105.7
Germany	42.4	41.6	0	11.1	52.1	3.8	36.4	187.4
Japan	117.1	13.7	18.0	0	5.6	6.1	3.8	169.3
France	18.5	28.7	45.0	4.9	0	2.4	26.3	125.8
G-5	**210.0**	**112.7**	**114.9**	**86.3**	**94.0**			**617.9**
Canada	165.5	2.6	1.9	8.0	1.2	0	1.1	180.3
G-6	**375.5**	**115.3**	**116.8**	**94.3**	**95.2**	**135.6**		**932.7**
Italy	18.9	16.9	38.9	4.7	29.0	1.9	0	110.3
G-7	**394.4**	**132.2**	**155.7**	**99.0**	**124.2**	**137.5**	**87.2**	**1,103.2**

Note: The summit-power shares of 1997 world merchandise exports are as follows: G-5, 11.5 percent; G-6, 17.3 percent; and G-7, 20.5 percent.
Source: Statistical Abstract of the United States 1999: 863.

In the hierarchy of globalization, the United States stands out as the world's most powerful economy. But the fact that it accounts for just 12.6 percent of the world's merchandise exports is humbling, as is the slightly larger (17.8 percent) share of commercial services and the 16 percent share of all imports (1997). These figures make it clear that the United States is merely the first among four or five contenders. Indeed, three of these contenders—Germany, France, and the U.K., as partners in the EU—report combined totals that exceed the United States in merchandise exports (19.9 percent to 17.5 percent), commercial services exports (18.3 percent to 17.5 percent), and merchandise imports (18.1 percent to 16.0 percent). While such data underscore the relative decline of the United States since World War II, they also obscure the remarkable resurgence of the American economy since the Plaza Agreement in 1985. American merchandise exports more than tripled between 1986 and 1997. None of the other G-7 powers comes close to matching the U.S. pace of 203 percent (Germany 163 percent; the other five in the G-7, between 110 percent and 145 percent). Moreover, the United States doubled merchandise exports by 1992 as compared to by 1995 for the rest of the G-5. The pace of U.S. exports of commercial services was even faster as these tripled between 1986 and 1997; but in this case Japan and Canada matched the U.S. performance, and the U.K. and Italy were close behind (see sources cited in table 6.17).

These trade statistics paint a portrait of an emerging world order of dispersed hegemony, one in which power is distributed among three formal regions (the hemispheric trade blocs), six or seven functional regions (the summit nations), and their promise of an interdependent panregionalism. This is assuredly not the neoliberal's vision of the world. In this portrait, three sets of summit powers—Japan; the United States and Canada; and Germany, France, the U.K., and Italy—are busily engaged

Table 6.19. Merchandise Exports of Summit Powers and Their Trade Bloc Partners (NAFTA and EU), 1997 (in billions)

European Union		
Intra EU trade	$559.4	
Extra EU trade	$825.6	
Total		$1385.0
NAFTA		
Intra NAFTA trade	$495.7	
Extra NAFTA trade	$517.8	
Total		$1,013.5
Japan	$421.0	$421.0
Total export trade of G-7 nations and their trade blocs		$2,819.5
As percentage of world trade	($2,819.5/$5,460)	51.6%

Source: World Trade Organization Annual Report 1998, 1: 4, 29, 41.

in carving out hemispheric trade blocs (most notably NAFTA, the FTAA, and the EU) and cross-linking them via coordinated agreements among the several powers on macroeconomic and macrostrategic policy. Toward these ends, the several summit nations behave in rather different ways, tending to seek dominance (i.e., hegemony) nearer to home in their hemispheric blocs while promoting cooperation across the oceans.

Agnew and Corbridge (1995) have captured the central components of the new dispersed hegemony with its mix of money, power, and space.

> [It] is both polycentric and expansionist. . . . It is polycentric because power in the modern geopolitical economy is no longer . . . monopolized by nation-states. Economic, cultural and geopolitical power is now embedded in a network of dominant but internally divided countries (including the USA, Germany and Japan), regional groupings like the European Community (European Union), city regions in the so-called Second and Third Worlds, international institutions including the World Bank, the IMF, GATT, [the WTO,] and the United Nations, and the main circuits and institutions of international production and finance capital [not to mention some portion of the international non-governmental organizations (NGOs) which have grown from about 6,000 in 1990 to more than 26,000 in 1999 ("The Non-governmental Order" 1999: 20–21)]. What binds these diverse regions and actors together is a shared commitment to an ideology of market economics and a recognition that territory alone is not a secure basis for economic or geopolitical power. . . . The new hegemony threatens to be almost as diffuse [as the market], with economic and political power being shared unevenly between an overlapping network of discrete geographical power centers and space-spanning "sovereign bodies." (Agnew and Corbridge 1995: 205, 207)

What are the prospects for stabilizing this inherently diffuse and fluid regime of dispersed hegemony? "The new stability might," according to Agnew and Corbridge, "take the form of a further internationalization of state activities to part-regulate the global market-place (as through the G-3 and G-7 summits), and by more piecemeal attempts to diffuse risks within particular markets [recall Lowi's brief for the socialization of risk during the Second Democracy]." Stability might also emerge out of the relations among the great powers where "the balance . . . has shifted from conflict toward cooperation," from multipolarity toward pluralism and the diffusion of power, and from selfishness toward accommodation if not altruism (Agnew and Corbridge 1995: 135).

Others are not as sanguine on the prospects for panregional cooperation in an international regime that is as dispersed, as polycentric, and as susceptible to disruption by the clashing of civilizations on the edges of this neoliberal regime. The first and most obvious obstacle is external—terrorism's threat to the *pax Americana*, to the peace and security on which the trade of a neoliberal regime depends. The second and more challenging obstacle is internal—the vulnerability of the several states that make up this protoregime (and especially the United States) to the neuroses of multiple personalities in foreign policy. This is so because so many voices are involved in policy formulation within constitutional democracies; it is the product of too many agents with too many perspectives operating over too many scales and venues of action. The Transnational State, with its several branches and its elaborate array of checks and balances, is the perfect case in point. Rarely does it speak with one voice, notwithstanding the claims of unanimity emanating from a centralized executive and the sanctions often imposed on "leakers." But polyvocality is not merely a curse; the interplay of voices, perspectives, and strategies has certain advantages in foreign policy, not the least being their ambiguity and ultimate deniability (on the blurring of strategies, see Yarbrough and Yarbrough 1994). By and large, American policymakers seem untroubled by the mixing of agencies and strategies—by the fact that multilateral support for GATT and the WTO has proceeded side by side with the regional strategy of NAFTA (and the FTAA) and the unilateralism embedded in the Trade Act of 1988 (and Super 301), the Helms–Burton Act, and the Trading with the Enemies Act. Nor are they troubled when one strategy trumps another—when, for example, the unilateralism of American jurisprudence aggressively and repeatedly extends American jurisdiction (and sovereignty) well beyond the limits of the United States, even as the United States refuses elsewhere to concede jurisdiction as a signatory to the multilateral commitments and global jurisdiction of the International Criminal Court (or to the Kyoto agreement on atmospheric emissions).

Criticisms of American foreign policy are almost invariably guilty of reductionism, of singling out one perspective or one strategy from among many and reifiying that concern into an indictment of American foreign policy as a whole. But one brick does not make a house. Consider the response to the withdrawal of American support for the Kyoto agreement on atmospheric emissions, in general, and the critique of Alex Lennon, editor of the Center for Strategic and International Studies' journal *Washington Quarterly*, in particular: "'A number of countries are concerned that this [the G. W. Bush] administration, while not isolationist, is unilateralist'" (Grier and Kiefer 2001: 1, 8). In a sentence, Lennon obscures the complexity and the sophistication of the conduct of American foreign policy since 1980. More astute and insightful is Jeffrey Frankel's (2001: 159) appreciation of the international economic policies of the Reagan, Bush, and Clinton administrations.

> While pursuing regional liberalization, each of these administrations [and the George W. Bush administration as well] also pursued multilateral liberalization. The Uruguay Round of negotiations, which eventually established the WTO, was started by the Reagan administration, continued by the first Bush administration, and concluded successfully by the Clinton administration. The strategy all along has been to pursue liberalization at both regional and global levels simultaneously, seeking progress on the regional front when the multilateral path is politically infeasible.

And when neither of these sufficed, as in the case of cartels, dumping, Cuba, and Libya, Americans have unhesitatingly taken the path of unilateralism.

These multiscalar strategies have provided Americans with a wide range of options, not to mention ample room for political maneuver. By having unilateralist, regional, and multilateralist strategies at their command, American citizens and policymakers have been able to pick and choose among them and to mix and match them as needed. They have been able (1) to play off one strategic level against another (e.g., when in the mid-1980s the viability of GATT was threatened by the founding of the European Union, the United States responded by negotiating NAFTA with Canada); (2) to ignore, circumvent, or override multilateral rulings on the basis of decisions in the U.S. federal courts (e.g., dumping litigation that overrides rulings of GATT or the WTO; Lowe 1993: 143); (3) to respond to domestic political problems (e.g., when in 1984 and 1985 sentiments in favor of unilateral protectionism welled up in Congress, the Reagan administration responded with the G-5 regional strategy of exchange-rate coordination and dollar devaluation); and (4) to defuse criticism by spreading responsibility (and blame) among various agents and agencies (e.g., when the president defends the administration's commitment to the regional strategy of NAFTA as a logical step toward globalization, free trade, and the multilateralism of the WTO or, when addressing a different and more nationalist audience, as a logical step toward hemispheric free trade).

The prospects for harmony and cooperation in an international regime of dispersed hegemony are diminished when the most powerful of these nations speaks with several tongues—when, owing more to the Constitution's separation of powers than to any duplicity, the foreign policy of the United States is fractured among multiple agents and agencies, multiple perspectives, and a variety of multiscalar strategies. The virtues of polyvocality thus are decisively and one-sidedly in favor of American diplomacy. At home, polyvocality gives voice to the antisystemic forces of opposition. It means that Americans who oppose the nation's dominant strategy (e.g., the multilateralism of WTO because it sacrifices American sovereignty, workers' welfare, and/or global environments) always have other options, other avenues of strategic subversion (e.g., unilateralism or regionalism). And sooner or later, by osmosis, co-optation, and transference, some portion of the opposition's thoughts and ideas are insinuated into mainstream politics. But polyvocality also serves the prevailing policy regime in foreign affairs. It provides that regime with a variety of geopolitical options for parrying the strategies of other powers (as, e.g., when, in response to the founding of the EU, the United States resorted to a regional strategy that led to NAFTA) or for pursuing remediation in other venues (as, e.g., when the United States initiates antidumping litigation in the federal courts following unsuccessful resolution of disputes over import pricing before the WTO). When seen from abroad, however, polyvocality is less a source of "homespun" democratic virtue and more nearly a sign of the American imperium—of the "perfidiousness," the "selfishness," and the unreliability of the Transnational American State. For many of these observers, "today's hegemonic U.S. presence represents a distinctively American national undertaking, one broadly acknowledged by the citizenry of the dominant 'hyperpower.'" But the truth of the matter, as polyvocality signifies, is that there is not one American transnational project but many. And thus while the "U.S. has global power . . . it [simultaneously] lacks a conception of what such power means, and what to do with it" (Judt 2001: 19).

Notes

1. The successive scheme of Sectional, National, and Transnational States bears some resemblance to the stages of constitutional history formulated by Ackerman (1991) and Hardt and Negri (2000). Ackerman (1991: 158) proposes "a three-solution narrative—in which both Reconstruction Republicans and New Deal Democrats appear as the equals of the Founding Federalists in creating higher lawmaking process and substantive solutions in the name of We the People of the United States." The criteria for partitioning these phases are quite explicitly biased, namely "to show how the crises and transformations of the past can best be understood as a popular struggle . . . for egalitarian democracy" (Ackerman 1991: 130). In other words, higher law is inextricably bound up with the popular struggle for egalitarian democracy. My three phases, by contrast, are defined by clearly specified enlargements in the territorial jurisdiction of the courts—namely, in the 1780s, the 1860s and 1870s, and the 1960s and 1970s. Lastly, Hardt and Negri (2000: 168) define four stages or "material regimes of juridical interpretation and practice that is exercised not only by jurists and judges but also by subjects throughout the society." These include (1) the "open space" regime from the Constitution to the Civil War and Reconstruction; (2) the "closed space" of the Progressive era, from 1880 to the 1920s; (3) "American imperialism" in a bipolar regime; and (4) the indispensable nation in a post–Cold War world (Hardt and Negri 2000: 160–82).

2. The dividend represents the difference between defense outlays in constant dollars in 1990 and 1999 ($354 and $263 billion, respectively) augmented by the hypothetical outlays had it grown at the rate of nondefense outlays (21.3 percent); *Statistical Abstract* 2000: 342–43.

PART II

COLONIAL FOUNDATIONS

CHAPTER 7

Backing into Empire

It has been said that the English backed into empire, and the evidence from North America is fairly persuasive on that score. To begin with, the English were late entrants into the scramble for American territory. Roanoke, their first and ill-fated colony, was founded nearly a century after Columbus's landfall in the New World and some six decades after Cortez's conquest of the Aztec empire. Not until the 1570s did the English give much thought to the Americas, and only then because of English privateers and their string of remarkable successes in American waters. Privateering—legalized piracy, as it were—represented something of a desperate gamble for Queen Elizabeth I and the English nation. But the stakes were large indeed for an economy besotted by reckless consumption, by the excessive importation of exotics from the Levant (silks especially) and the Mediterranean (mainly citrus, sugar, currants, and wine), and by the deficits that these were creating.

Born of Piracy—and of Private Enterprise

As huge quantities of American silver and gold began to flow back from New Spain in the 1560s, English disinterest in the New World suddenly gave way to the promise of enormous profits from privateering (as it was known in polite circles). The greatest of the English privateers, and rightly so, was Francis Drake. On his return to England in 1580 following nearly three years of plundering the Spanish in the New World, the English were astonished by the value of his prizes—variously estimated at $25 million or more by today's standards (Andrews 1964). His achievement at once galvanized an industry into action and a country into a nationalist frenzy (Cawley 1966: 285–86). In the two decades after Drake's return, Englishmen by the thousands followed suit, entering into this new industry as privateers proper or investors who assumed the considerable risks of a "venture" (Andrews 1964).

The English turn toward privateering and toward America was not an easy one for the Crown. Although Queen Elizabeth had occupied the throne for nearly two decades by the time of Drake's voyage, her political position was hardly secure either at home or abroad. She could ill afford a frontal challenge to Catholic Spain abroad while she was dousing the flames of sectarian hatreds among Puritans, Catholics, and

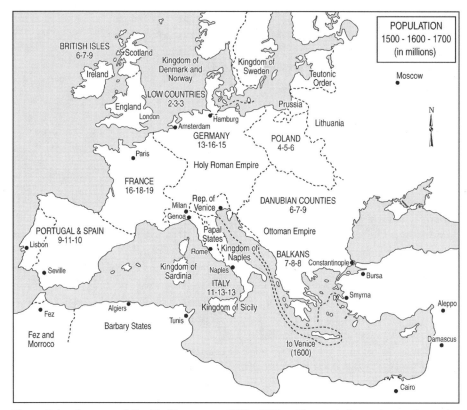

Figure 7.1.   Europe and the Mediterranean, 1500–1700, with population estimates for major regions/nations/empires.

Anglicans at home, unless, of course, the rewards were high. And as it turns out, they were high indeed.

To understand Elizabeth's willingness to risk everything in her support for Drake and for the privateering industry is to come to grips with the perilous state of the English economy, circa 1575. Population had grown at a spectacular pace; prices had risen to unprecedented levels; English grain prices, for example, increased by as much as 500 percent during the century, and raw wool commanded exceptionally high prices from Flemish weavers (Phelps-Brown and Hopkins 1957: 298), all of which "loosed" the strings of English society. For some, these changes translated into astounding prosperity; for others, a miserable poverty. In a time when "sheep ate men," to use Marx's apt expression, enclosing landlords evicted the unfortunate peasants and cottagers whose tenures were insecure. For these poor families, the new economy dictated a term of unemployment (seasonal or year-round) that they served out as squatters in the country forests or adrift among London's teeming masses (the city approached 120,000 by 1575; Coleman 1955–56; Stone 1966). Conversely, those blessed with secure tenures in land, that is, owners or even tenants with long leases at fixed rates, soon acquired greater wealth and hurriedly spent it in a gluttony of conspicuous consumption. The rising yeomen and gentry rebuilt their homes

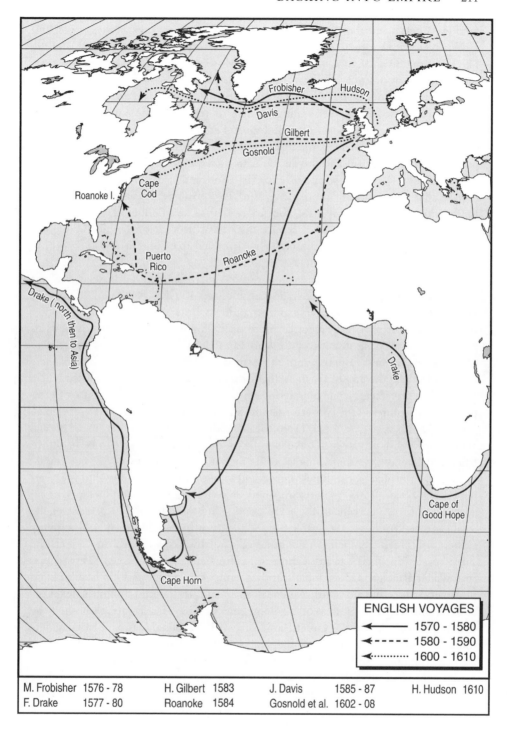

Figure 7.2A.   English voyages to North America, 1576–1610.

(and the English landscape), decorated them with the finest silks and tapestries, and tabled them with exotic foods, including fine wines and spices, citrus, sugar, and the like, imported from Venice, the Levant, and Morocco and which, by 1590, constituted 65 percent of English imports (Stone 1949–50).

This was not the worst of it, however. The impact of unrestrained consumption was soon reflected in a deteriorating balance of trade. By the last quarter of the sixteenth century, the value of English imports fast approached the value of exports. On the eve of Drake's voyage, the spectacular growth of English population, agrarian prices, and consumption had driven the nation to the brink of a fiscal crisis. Elizabeth's options were few (e.g., currency deflation and taxation), and all but one, privateering, was politically unpalatable. With two provisos, privateering constituted the quickest and least painful fix; the first was that the plundering was discretely distanced from the Crown, the second, that Elizabeth's charms could subdue the anger of Phillip II of Spain. Elizabeth thus gambled that English privateers would balance the nation's trade while she preoccupied the Spanish with her dalliances. The strategy, in retrospect, proved an enormous success. English privateers lived up to their end of the bargain, generating an income of £100,000 to £200,000 per year—nearly a fifth of all English exports (Andrews 1964: 128–29; Stone 1949–50). Inspired by returns of 60 percent or more on their initial investment, investors in privateering operations sustained the boom. Elizabeth held up her side as well, deferring a hostile Spanish response until the Armada of 1588 and the war for Holland's independence in the 1590s. By then, the fiscal crisis had been met and passed.

English privateers, while plundering on a global scale, secured the bulk of their prizes from captures in the western Atlantic, and this geography initiated a reorientation in English strategy abroad. From the start, the American theater held a special appeal for English privateers. Drake had shown the profits that were to be had from Spanish gold and silver, but in addition the Iberian fleets carried valuable commodities such as Brazilian sugar, hides, spices, and logwood (for cloth dyes). In the years between 1585 and 1603, captures in American waters were the most lucrative of all, accounting for 70 percent of the prize-good value though only 30 percent of the total captures (Andrews 1964: 132–33). While "northern men" such as Humphrey Gilbert continued trumpeting the virtues of a northwest passage to the Orient, the smart money inclined toward a more southern venue (figure 7.2A). Thus it was that Walter Raleigh, Gilbert's half-brother, embarked on the task of establishing a privateering base on the North American mainland. In the mid-1580s, Raleigh secured a charter for a New World colony, and in 1585, his agents established the colony of Roanoke on the Outer Banks of North Carolina. It is hard to imagine a more ideal location for privateering operations. Perched on the western edge of the sea lanes running from Mexico back to Spain, Roanoke offered easy and direct access to the gold- and silver-laden caravels; moreover, the base afforded a secure refuge for privateers, protected as it was from Spanish pursuers by the treacherous currents around Cape Hatteras and the shoals and shifting channels inside the island barrier. Such a site, Raleigh declared, would make them "the lords of navigation" ([figure 7.2B]; Taylor 1935, II: 329–30, 334).

Raleigh's initial expedition arrived in 1585, and after a couple of false starts,

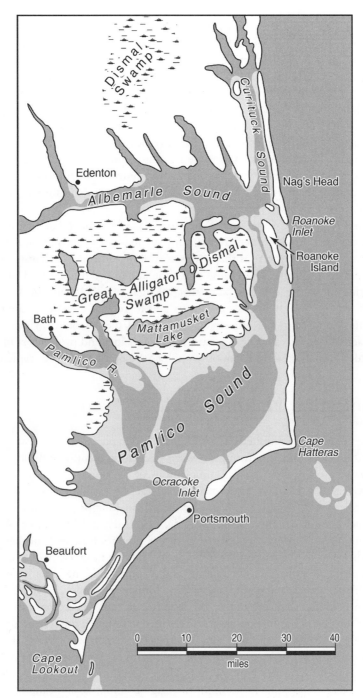

Figure 7.2B.   Roanoke Island and the North Carolina coast.

John White established a fort and surveyed the peoples and resources in the vicinity of Roanoke. In 1587, White set sail for England, leaving an armed contingent to secure the base and await resupply from England—much as Columbus did in Navidad, Hispaniola, in January 1493 (and with the same sad results). The plan for a return expedition in 1588 was disrupted, however, by the general mobilization for repulsing the Spanish Armada, and relief was delayed until 1591. When the expedition finally arrived at Roanoke, they discovered that the colonists—sixty-eight men, seventeen women, and nine children—had disappeared without a trace. After a futile search for the "lost colonists" and some reconnoitering in the surrounding region (including the Chesapeake Bay), the expedition returned to England, thus closing the first abortive chapter in the history of English overseas colonization (Quinn 1955; Andrews 1964; DeVorsey 1987).

Several storylines emerge out of the Roanoke experience. The first is the salacious theme that Anglo-America was born of piracy; the second, and the more important over the long run, is that it was as well the offspring of private enterprise and the pursuit of profit. The House of Tudor simply could not afford the costs of privateering or of the colonial bases that it might entail. While the Crown was prepared to commission English privateers and to receive a share of their profits, neither the Tudors nor the Stuarts who succeeded them would finance or direct English activities overseas. These were left to companies and proprietors in the private sector within the English economy—which is a precedent worth remembering.

Colonization Hakluyt Style

Even as Roanoke languished, two English geographers—the cousins Richard Hakluyt the Elder and the Younger—were circulating a more ambitious colonial plan. Drawing on their extensive compilations of overseas voyages of exploration and discovery, the Hakluyts promoted a plan for the establishment of permanent English colonies in America. Their plan rested on four propositions. Permanent English colonies in America would provide, first, a dependable source of colonial staple commodities in exchange for settlers and supplies from the mother country (one of the roots of mercantilism, I suspect); second, the production of exotic staples that complemented the English economy and eliminated the need for costly importations of silk, spices, wine, and sugar from foreign powers—provided that these American colonies were located in the latitudes of the "Mediterranean;" third, a "vent for the glut of population" that had resulted in so much misery and unemployment in England, most especially among skilled craftsmen who were "devouring" one another through fierce competition; and fourth, a challenge, albeit oblique, to Catholic hegemony in the New World. These propositions and a little deduction inexorably targeted a single location for the English colonization of the New World: on the Atlantic Seaboard of North America, and, more precisely, in the "Mediterranean latitudes" of what is today Virginia and North Carolina (Taylor 1935, II; Parks 1928).

What the Hakluyts did not say, however, is equally important. On the matter of bullion, they were unusually restrained, noting merely that gold and silver might eventually be found in the interior mountains. Similarly, their plan pretty much ignored a role for the "native inhabitants," perhaps because previous expeditions had confirmed the low densities and modest technology of the sedentary peoples along the Atlantic Seaboard of North America. These silences are pregnant reminders of the Hakluyts' radical departure from the Spanish model of colonization. They had little time for bullion chasing or native conversion; their ruthlessly singular intent was the establishment of enduring English settlements and economies in North America. In seeking after the nation's glory rather than American gold, after permanence rather than ephemerality, these geographers brought a distinctively modern cast to their colonial plan (Taylor 1935, II).

The virtues of their motives notwithstanding, the Hakluyts' plan did not win immediate acceptance. The Crown, preoccupied by the continuing flow of privateering profits and the Anglo-Dutch alliance against the Spanish during the 1590s, temporarily shelved plans for American colonization. But matters had changed substantially by 1604. The profits from privateering had dried up, and an Anglo-Spanish treaty had been concluded by James I, shortly after his ascendance to the throne following the death of Elizabeth in 1603. In this context, English merchants and gentry seeking new investment opportunities dusted off the Hakluyts' plan. Their opportunity arrived in 1606 when the Crown chartered the Virginia Company of London, a joint stock company modeled after the English trading companies working the Mediterranean, the Levant, and the Baltic. But this was not a company in the usual sense; the Virginia venture symbolized all of the hopes and aspirations of a restless nation. It would also, in short order, serve as England's template for New World colonization in the ensuing century (Rouse 1955; Rabb 1967; Brenner 1972). In this distinctively English scheme, private investors would provide the capital and the labor; the state, the land (via the chartering or franchising of colonial territories of highly insecure title), and the public their enthusiasms, variously nationalist and parochial.

Virginia: Grand Plan, Gruesome Reality

In the marketplace of ideas, there is a kind of Gresham's law of geographical theory by which bad theory drives out good. The consequences of this unsettling depreciation are hardly trivial in the realm of human affairs. One example of the widespread appeal of bad theory is environmental determinism in the late nineteenth century; another is the expansionary imperative of German *geopolitics* in the 1930s; yet another is the climatic theory that informed English colonization in the seventeenth century.

Francis Bacon and the origins of English empiricism notwithstanding, the conventional wisdom in seventeenth-century England oversubscribed to environmental theories that had been handed down from the ancient Greeks. One of these theories assumed that climate was overwhelmingly controlled by latitude, and most contemporaries, including the Hakluyts, believed it. And from this the Hakluyts and their readers inferred that the climates along the Atlantic Seaboard of North America would be identical to the climates at similar latitudes in Europe. The climate of the Chesapeake region thus would replicate the Mediterranean climate of southern France or Spain, while northward the climate would more nearly resemble that of England. It is this reasoning that led the Virginia Company to target the Chesapeake Bay for its colony and to issue instructions that called for the production of the most desirable of Mediterranean commodities—silk from silkworms fed on native mulberry trees and wine from native and imported grapevines. The problem with all this theorizing, as Carl Sauer once observed, was that the climates of North America were more robust and more vigorous. The continental climates of North America were, by comparison to the temperate climates of Western Europe, far more extreme: temperatures were hotter in summer and colder in winter; precipitation was more variable; seasons were more sharply delineated; storms were more violent (figure 7.3).

While the crop failures that resulted from this fallacious climatic theory were costly for the Virginia Company, the demographic consequences would prove to be far more grievous. The melancholy story properly begins in the spring of 1607 with the dispatch of the first Virginia expedition. Following their instructions to the letter, the colonists entered the Chesapeake Bay, chose one of its largest arms, reconnoitered upstream forty or fifty miles, and, having encountered sizable numbers of "clean, well-made naturals," dropped downstream to the security of an island site that they named Jamestown, in honor of their king. All went well at first, as the expedition of highly skilled artisans and soldiers set about building a fort and a town on the island and laying the groundwork for an exotic economy based on silviculture, viticulture, and citrus. The weather was pleasant, freshwater was readily available directly from the river, and the Indians busied themselves planting crops. But as summer approached, the vision turned nightmarish. By mid-July, most of the 104 settlers were racked with diseases bearing the ghoulish names of the "bloudie fluxe" and the "burning fever" (most likely, dysentery and typhoid). Deaths mounted steadily, and by summer's end, the toll stood at nearly half of the original 104. Autumn brought an end to the carnage, but after a respite of eight months, the nightmare resumed. Disease and mortality returned in the summer of 1608 and every summer thereafter (save for 1613–16) until 1624 when the Crown, in exasperation, dissolved the company into a royal colony and thus began the process of backing into empire (Earle 1979).

This tragicomic scene has its root causes in pigheadedness and bad geographical theory, in the company's pigheaded insistence on remaining in Jamestown and its reliance on a temperate climatic model that obscured Jamestown's location in one of the world's most dynamic and deadly ecological niches—in the fresh-salt transition (the oligohaline zone) of the James River estuary. In this zone, wrote colonist George Percy (1907: 21–22), "our drink [in summer] was cold water taken out of the River, which was at floud [tide] very salt, at low tide full of slime and filth [including *Salmonella typhi* and *Endameoba histolytica*], which was the destruction of many of our men." The combination of a riverine water supply, a sharp reduction of freshwater runoff owing to high summer temperatures and high rates of evapotranspiration, the entrapment of pollutants by the landward summer migration of

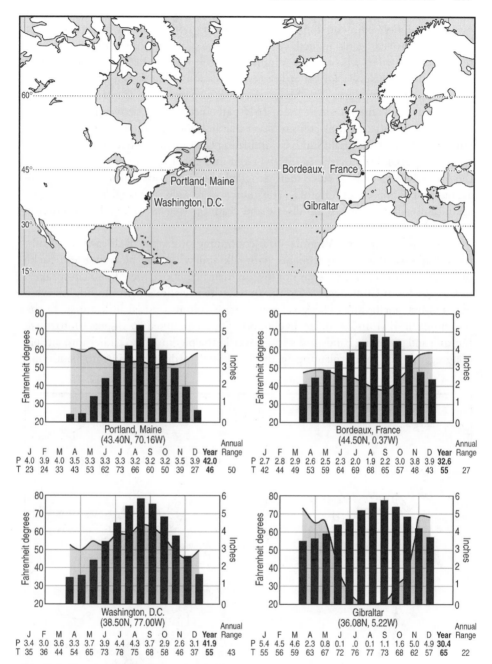

Figure 7.3. Climatic comparisons along similar latitudes.

Note: The large range in temperatures and the relative uniformity of precipitation in the continental climate of Washington, D.C., and the converse in the Mediterranean climate of Gibraltar.

estuarine salinity/sediment traps, and the ongoing concentration of settlement at Jamestown proved deadly indeed, costing the lives of perhaps three thousand of the five thousand settlers who came to Virginia between 1607 and 1624. Ironically, most of them died needlessly, for on at least two occasions some Virginians understood the nexus between climate, the Jamestown site, and mortality. Captain John Smith in 1608 and Sir Thomas Dale in 1613–1616 perceived the link between water supply and mortality, and they took steps to sever that link through the preventative medicine of settlement dispersal (Smith by emulating the Indian practice of seasonal population dispersal, Dale by relocating the chief settlement upriver in the "freshes" of the James River), only to have their geographical insights overturned by company agents freshly arrived in Virginia. The results were sadly predictable: theory once again displaced experience, and disease and death once again stalked the land (figure 7.4).

The disarray in early Virginia—the continuing onslaught of disease and death, the collapse of fanciful experiments with silk and wine, the bickering and backbiting among the colonists—was not lost on their neighbors, the Algonkian speakers of the Powhatan Confederacy. On the outset, their relations with the English were guarded but not hostile. The small numbers of colonists posed little threat to the seminomadic rhythm of Indian livelihood. They continued to disperse into small hunting and gathering bands and winter over in the piedmont, to gather into a tribal congregation for spring planting in the tidewater, to divide again into bands and

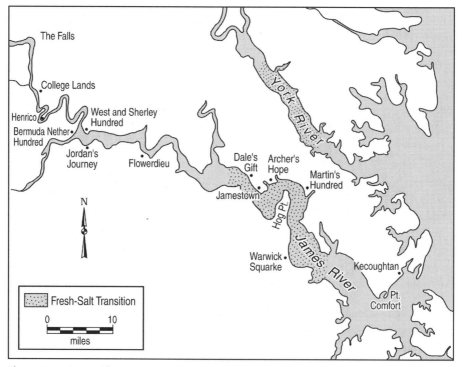

Figure 7.4.   James River, 1607–1624.

forage in the low country during the deadly summer, and to reassemble the tribe for the fall harvest. Cultural exchanges were not uncommon—the English acquiring practical knowledge of maize or Indian corn, tobacco, and other useful indigenous plants; the Indians acquiring a gun or two as well as an assortment of trade goods. Were it not for the generosity of the Indians, many colonists in their sickened state would have starved to death.

But this phase of equanimity would not last. The new leadership of the Virginia Company after 1616 moved aggressively to enlarge the colony. Migrants rose from a few score per year to several hundreds; and while settlement remained concentrated in Jamestown, the excess spilled upriver into the "freshes." The English invasion increasingly encroached upon ecological zones that were vital elements in the seminomadic system of Powhatan's Confederacy. To make matters worse, there is some evidence that Siouan groups were encroaching on the confederacy's hunting grounds in the piedmont. Trapped between the English on the east and the Sioux on the west, the Indians of the confederacy bided their time. The period of watchful waiting came to an abrupt end on Good Friday morning, March 22, 1622. In the early morning hours, the Indians launched their attack, killing over 350 of the 1,200 colonists in Virginia. Although the colony managed to survive, almost everything else would change. Henceforth, the colonists regarded Indians as barbarians fit for extermination rather than accommodation; henceforth, the ineptitude of the company's leaders became painfully obvious, and in short order the Crown was compelled to dissolve the company in favor of a colony under royal authority.

Virginia officially became a royal colony in 1624, and the initial English experiment in private sector colonization had come to a dismal end. The Crown reluctantly and lightly assumed its colonial responsibility. Operating under royal regulations that were exceedingly loose, the colony at last flourished. Within a decade, Virginia's population had recovered from the losses of the massacre of 1622, tobacco planting had displaced silk and wine production, settlement had spread from the James to the York and Rappahannock estuaries, and mortality levels had declined sharply.

The Template of English Colonization

The Virginia Company never quite lived up to the nation's expectations, yet certain key elements in that experience would serve as a template for subsequent English colonization. The template delineated a series of distinct policies on matters of location, agent, geographical extent, resource evaluation and allocation, and political dissolution. A word on each is in order. The template first targeted locations at the hem rather than the center of Iberian spheres of influence; second, in acknowledgment of the sharp constraints on royal finances, shifted the risks of colonial ventures from the Crown to the monopoly colonization of private franchises—companies in Virginia and Massachusetts Bay and proprietors in Maryland, Carolina, and Pennsylvania; third, restricted the extent of territorial grants (Virginia after all was initially bounded in a square with a side of just one hundred miles), thus affording ample opportunities for future royal benefices; fourth, placed a premium on colonial grants located in the Mediterranean latitudes on the assumption that these would produce staples that complemented the English economy; fifth, allocated the best lands to friends of the Crown and lesser lands to religious dissenters; and sixth, when colonies failed, defined a mechanism for dissolving their franchises and incorporating them as royal colonies (figure 7.5; Earle 1977).

This template for English colonization, replete with all of the constraints imposed by practical geopolitics, royal finance, climatic theory, and hard reality, defined the critical parameters of the Anglo-American encounter with the New World. The result was a geographical process predicated on *geopolitical decentralization* via the franchising of several colonies of modest size and relative autonomy; on *ethnocultural pluralism* through the allocation of the best lands to royal friends and coreligionists and the worst lands (those that replicated England—i.e., "New England") to religious dissenters such as the Puritans and later the Quakers; and lastly, on a *reluctant imperium* via the inexorable absorption of failed franchises into the royal domain. In this fashion, the English colonized the Atlantic Seaboard of North America, ensuring as they went a variegated strand of decentralized colonial administrations, a multiplicity of Judeo-Christian religious faiths and Caucasian ethnicities, and an empire endlessly in need of royal salve.

Beyond Virginia

With Virginia on the way to recovery, the Crown was besieged by other colonial suitors. Soon after assuming the throne in 1625, Charles II issued a series of colonial

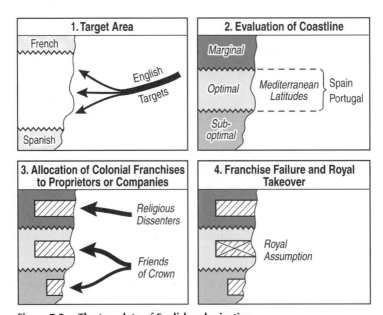

Figure 7.5. The template of English colonization.

charters—one to the Massachusetts Bay Company and two others to Robert Heath and Cecilius Calvert, Lord Baltimore, now proprietors of Carolina and Maryland, respectively. Here was a distribution that would have warmed the heart of even the most ardent of multiculturalists. Heath and Calvert were extremely well connected, Calvert was also a Roman Catholic, and the Massachusetts Bay Company was generally acknowledged as a front for East Anglian Puritans seeking both a refuge from religious persecution and a millennial "city upon a hill" (figure 7.6).

ON THE MARGINS IN PURITAN NEW ENGLAND

The Massachusetts Bay Company was awarded a colony in the marginal environs of "New England." The ostensible goal of the colony was the harvesting of fish, furs, and timber; the true goal, however, was the harvesting of puritan souls. The company thus provided a loose cover for the "great migration" of some twenty thousand Puritans mostly from the flatlands of East Anglia between 1630 and 1650 (figure 7.7A). These were the friends and neighbors and coreligionists of Oliver Cromwell, men and women who dissented from the Anglican faith and its elaborate clerical hierarchy and who instead vested authority in local congregations of believers eagerly anticipating the Second Coming of Christ. For the migrants, Massachusetts provided a place to begin anew, a pristine place for perfecting their lives and their spirits on the eve of the millennium (Innes 1995).

Even as England was rent by civil war between king and Parliament in the 1640s, puritan migrants continued coming to Massachusetts, most of them stopping in Boston for provisions, livestock, implements, and the like, and then on to establish agrarian villages like those at home. The result was a wildly divided geography of Yankee merchants in port towns such as Boston and Salem surrounded by a hinterland of the devout. By 1650, Boston had mushroomed into a port town of several thousand people, most of whom earned their living by servicing the migrants that flowed through the town. But the immigrant boom was fast coming to an end. With the puritan triumph in the English Civil War and the ascension of Oliver Cromwell as Lord Protector of the English commonwealth, East Anglian puritans had little reason to venture into the wilds of America, especially when the millennium at home seemed so close at hand.

This turn of events did not deter Boston merchants. They responded by introducing one of the most remarkable economic innovations in American history—the "coastwise trade." Capitalizing on their initial advantage as an immigrant way station, they quickly shifted their resources from catering to immigrants to providing transport and mercantile services for the other English colonies on the mainland as well as in the West Indies. Merchants from Boston and Salem organized this complicated trade. Their vessels transported fish and timber from New England and corn and pork from the Chesapeake to the sugar islands of the West Indies, initially to English islands and eventually and in contravention of the Navigation Acts to French, Spanish, and Dutch islands. In return, the backhaul conveyed molasses for the rum distilleries popping up in Boston and, on occasion and most especially after 1680,

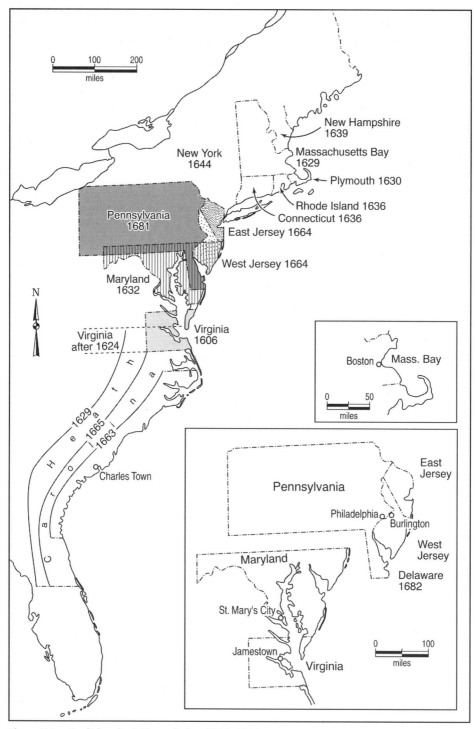

Figure 7.6.   English colonial boundaries, 1600–1682.

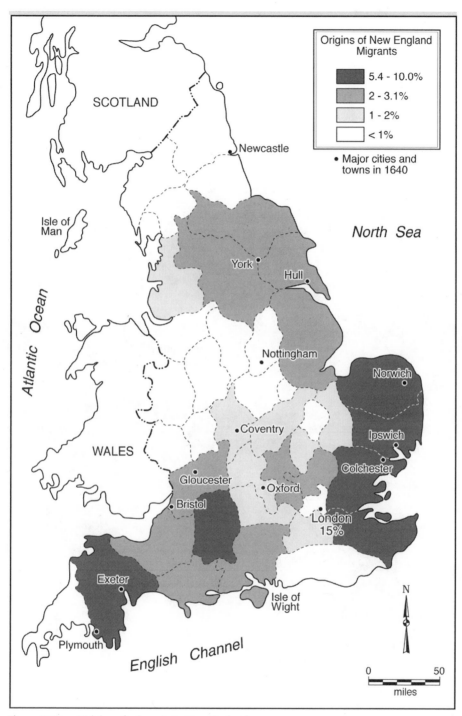

Figure 7.7A.   Origins of migrants to New England.

Source: Paullin and Wright 1932: 46–47, plates 70C and 70D.

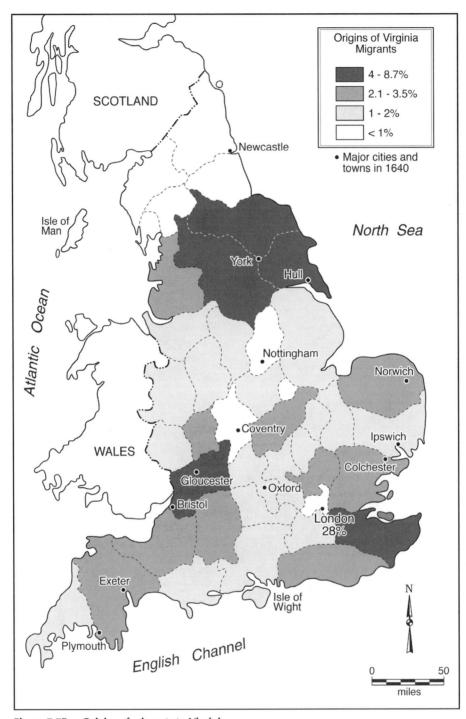

Figure 7.7B.   Origins of migrants to Virginia.

Source: Paullin and Wright 1932: 46–47, plates 70C and 70D.

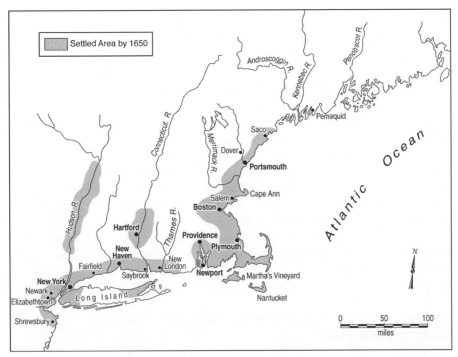

Figure 7.8. Early settlements in New England.

slaves for sale in the Chesapeake. All of this activity deepened the geographical divisions within New England, between the sharp-dealing Yankee traders in the coastal ports and the disputatious sectaries within the congregational subsistence communities nestled in the interior of Greater New England (figure 7.8). Aside from certain superficial similarities in faith and origin, the singular common bond between these divergent geographies was the ferocity of competition that they nurtured within their respective societies. But whereas competition in the marketplace served to weld together Yankee New England into a cohesive and powerful economy, the competition over faith, doctrine, and true belief served to fracture the theocratic society of the puritan interior into a mosaic of disputatious religious communities and, in the cases of Connecticut and Rhode Island, entire colonies.

CAROLINA DREAMING

Colonization was proving to be a baffling process. The Crown expected little from New England, yet in the course of the century its population came to exceed Virginia's. Conversely, the Crown expected much of Carolina, and it came to naught. The patent to Sir Robert Heath in 1629 for a large colony to the south of Virginia may have been a victim of bad timing. The colony seems to have been designed, at least in part, as a buffer zone between the Spanish in Florida and English colonists in the mid-Atlantic region. Royal commitments for this purpose may have wavered with the cessation of Anglo-Spanish hostilities in that year (Craven 1970). The patent thereafter would lapse until reissued in 1663 to a new set of well-to-do proprietors, men who had remained loyal to the Stuart monarchy throughout the Civil War and the Interregnum. But even they made little headway. Not until 1680 would their efforts begin to produce results, thanks in large measure to the unexpected influx of families with extraordinary wealth. Carolina may be the great exception to the old adage that "dukes don't migrate." One group consisted of wealthy sugar planters who abandoned Barbados in the midst of the economic depression that began in the late 1670s; the other was composed of prosperous French protestants, the Huguenots, who fled from France following the revocation of the Act of Nantes in 1685. These migrants fueled the rapid growth both of Charles Town—the chief port and administrative center located very nearly at the center of Carolina's coastal boundary—and of a domestic economy based initially on the Indian trade (mainly deerskins) and provisioning the West Indies and later on low-country irrigated rice for the European markets.

ON THE DEFENSIVE: CATHOLICS ON MARYLAND'S FEUDAL FRONTIER

While religious toleration was not the long suit of the Stuart dynasty in England, the reverse was the case in England's colonies overseas. In America, Stuart policies wittingly or not afforded numerous havens for the expression of European religious beliefs. And when Charles I issued a colonial patent to Cecilius Calvert, second Lord Baltimore, in 1632, he added Roman Catholics into the mix. Maryland's charter reveals a great deal about Stuart perspectives on religion and colonization. First, the granting of a colony in the most valued region of the Atlantic Seaboard—in the Mediterranean latitudes—to a Roman Catholic, albeit one whose father had served as secretary of state—is indicative both of the high Anglianism of Charles II and of his affinities for and close relations with Catholic monarchs on the continent. To do so was a fairly bold move given English fears of a "popish plot" to restore England to Roman Catholicism. Second, the granting of a colony that was literally carved out of Anglian Virginia and the assignation of extraordinary feudal powers to the Maryland proprietor are indicative of the absolutist tendencies that would eventually cost Charles his neck. To be sure, there were extenuating circumstances, most notably the desire to blunt Dutch colonial efforts along the Delaware River and near the head of the Chesapeake Bay; that said, the broad powers and the valuable territory awarded to Calvert seem disproportionate to the dangers at hand.

Calvert's vision of a feudal landscape of lords, manors, and manorial courts is usually dismissed as an anachronism, a throwback to a world that had been lost. But the merits of his vision depend on the strategic geographies at play. In areas where chaos reigns, where the dangers of hostile attackers are commonplace, and where one is outnumbered, feudalism or its variants have flourished. The hacienda and encomienda system of Spanish America are cases in point. But these conditions did not exist on the frontiers of the upper Chesapeake; the Dutch outposts were small, and the Indians in the region were scattered, ethnically diverse, and less well organized than those in Virginia. In the absence of genuine danger, the military society envisioned for Maryland was badly misspecified.

The colony had a hard time attracting immigrants, despite the generous terms that Calvert provided for prospective lords of the manor. The entire plan hinged on attracting wealthy men, preferably Catholics, who would in turn cover the costs of transporting and outfitting themselves, their families, and their manorial tenants. When such men failed to materialize, Calvert was forced to cut and trim his feudal system and to offer smaller, but still generous, parcels of land for those who paid for their transportation into the colony. Precisely why Maryland failed to receive a large influx of English Catholics in the 1630s remains a mystery. Perhaps they were scared away by the militant imagery that was implicit in Calvert's feudal model; perhaps they believed that the lot of English Catholics had greatly improved in the reign of Charles I; perhaps it was both. Equally important may have been the sharp depression in the price of Chesapeake tobacco, which, as Calvert would soon observe, "is our life and our all."

On Balance

By midcentury, the English had begun to catch up to the Iberians in the scramble for territory in the New World. The Stuarts had granted large chunks of the Atlantic Seaboard of North America, from Maine to Florida, to two companies and two proprietors. In that space, English colonists had established three permanent colonies: one in the marginal north, two in the "Mediterranean" center, and none as yet in the south. Paradoxically, these efforts enjoyed their greatest successes where they were least expected—in New England. Elsewhere, the results were not especially promising. Virginia had failed to live up to the grandiose dreams of company leaders, and the colony had lapsed into royal receivership. Maryland had struggled to attract settlers so long as the proprietor persisted in his commitment to frontier feudalism. And Carolina was little more than a "paper colony," a territorial claim unsubstantiated through either exploration or occupation. On a more positive note, the English strategy of franchise colonization could lay claim to certain achievements by midcentury. A good part of the seaboard had been occupied at relatively little expense to the Crown; the several colonies had grown to just over fifty thousand colonists; the tobacco trade and the coastwise trade were well started; a variety of religious faiths—congregational puritans, Anglians, and Catholics—had taken root; the Crown had demonstrated its willingness to rescue a colony in danger of total collapse; the Spanish had largely ignored English colonial activities; and the native inhabitants had generally receded into the interior in the face of the English invasion (figure 7.9).

The English advance was not, however, unfettered. Intruding on their space was their former ally, the Dutch. Dutch farmers and fur traders occupied the Hudson Valley in New Amsterdam, and plans for a comparable occupation of the Delaware

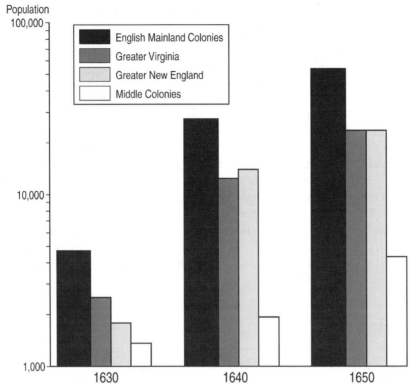

Figure 7.9.   Population distribution in the English Colonies of North America, 1630–1650.

Source: Historical Statistics 2: 1975.

Valley were under way. Dutch merchants and traders also sought to secure a foothold in the growing tobacco trade of the English Chesapeake as well as in the northern fur trade along the southern coast of New England. But that would soon change. England was through with backing into empire; the time had come for battering down the front door—and the Dutch just happened to be in the way.

CHAPTER 8

"We are all English. That is one good fact."

CROMWELL'S MODEL REPUBLICAN GEOGRAPHIES, 1630s–1680s

The idea of empire would prove to be far less elusive after 1630, once the hard times in that decade had set in motion the chain of events that would culminate in the English Civil War, regicide, and the ascent of Oliver Cromwell, Lord Protector of the Commonwealth. In just two explosive decades, the English would find them-selves emboldened—or victimized, depending on one's point of view—by a grand imperial vision. But the story of Cromwellian republicanism and its egalitarian and expansionist ideology begins somewhat earlier and in rather more insular and myopic times.

The Road to Civil War

The Anglo-American geographies created between the 1570s and 1640 were twice removed from empire—once because of the absence of an overarching vision or coordinating plan, twice because of the absence of agents and institutions committed to and capable of managing colonial affairs in the interests of the state. Visions of an American empire were far from the minds of the early Stuart monarchs who, having awarded colonial charters without much forethought, were content to turn over the direction of these franchises to their proprietors and corporate directors. In colonial matters, colonial drift rather than imperial mastery was the royal order of the day.

But events at home were conspiring against the Stuarts for precisely the opposite reasons. In domestic affairs, the Crown's posture was both bolder and more aggres-sively authoritarian. Royal assertions of the divine right of the monarchy and the hegemony of high Anglicanism in matters of faith and morals, when tossed into the crucible of English sectarianism, inevitably kindled resentments that burst into flames during the economic crash of the 1630s and consumed the nation and the colonies in civil war during the 1640s. Dissatisfaction with the absolutist religious and political policies of the Stuarts was expressed in various ways. Some, like the Puritan émigrés from East Anglia, voiced their dissent by migrating to the new world; others joined ranks and their coalitions attacked the corruption that oozed from the royal court. The political crisis deepened when these coalitions rose in unison—when merchants in the city of London had grown "exasperated by the [royal] manipulation of patents, monopolies, charters, and impositions"; when the rural gentry and the peasantry "had been alienated by the cynical or ignorant tactics that awarded stretches of countryside to the fortune-hunters who infested the Court"; when the aristocracy and gentry had borne enough of the "burdens of an imprudent and absurd revival of feudal dues in a desperate campaign to stop up the leaks in the Crown's financial boat" (Wilson 1965: 105); when, in short, "the rot had set in" (Wilson 1965: 106).

Things came to a head in the late 1630s when Charles I and Archbishop Laud ignored the storm clouds of protest and launched an ambitious and ill-advised attempt to extend the royal prerogative. The tumult began in Scotland, the Stuarts' ancestral home, with Laud's attempts to revise the prayer book and to assume control of church lands held by the aristocracy. Laud's actions ignited "a national explosion with which the English government was totally unable to cope" (Hill 1970: 33). As the Presbyterian Scottish army marched southward, Charles I desperately summoned Parliament into session in 1640 to secure funds for an English army to repel the invasion, only to dissolve that body when it refused to authorize funds. Having fended off the invasion and reached terms of peace with the Scots in October 1640, Charles once again summoned Parliament and sought funds for carrying out the terms of the truce. The tenure of the Long Parliament had begun. In short order, the parliamentary opposition to the Crown took command, impeaching Laud, executing Charles's lord deputy of Ireland, and enacting legislation that ensured Parliament's independence of the king (most notably the Triennial Act, which guaranteed the calling of Parliament at least one year in three). Armed confrontation between the king and Parliament was now unavoidable.

By the end of 1641, the civil war had gotten under way. In the long and bloody conflict that followed, the lines of battle were seldom precise. By and large, the hostilities pitted royalists loyal to Charles I against parliamentarians opposed to Stuart absolutism, high Anglicans against Puritans and religious independents, and supporters of a territorial-administrative society against the partisans of a commercial republic. The geographical divisions between the adversaries were even more telling. Parliamentarians, by and large, were concentrated in the enclaves of commerce—in the cities, outports, and along the coast and up the navigable waterways. Royalists mostly resided inland and to the north and west of London (figure 8.1A). The English Civil War thus represented a clash between England's two distinct societies—the one territorial, the other maritime; the one committed to tradition, land, and royal authority, the other to commerce, negotiation, and constitutional democracy (Hochberg 1984).

The Civil War waged between 1641 and 1648 was a long and costly affair. Hostilities consumed the better part of the 1640s. Not less than one hundred thousand men gave their lives (roughly 5 percent of the adult male population) in a series of bloody battles; the economic costs for both sides were equally large (figure 8.1B; Wilson 1965: 108). The end came in 1648 when the royalists conceded defeat and,

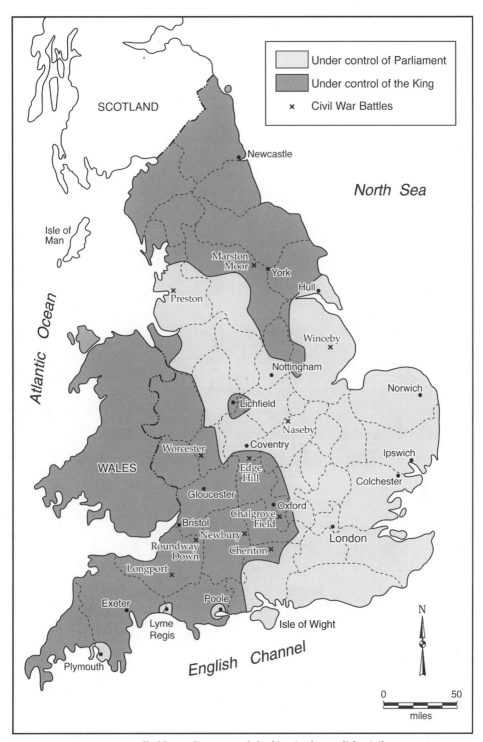

Figure 8.1A.   Areas controlled by Parliament and the king in the English Civil War.

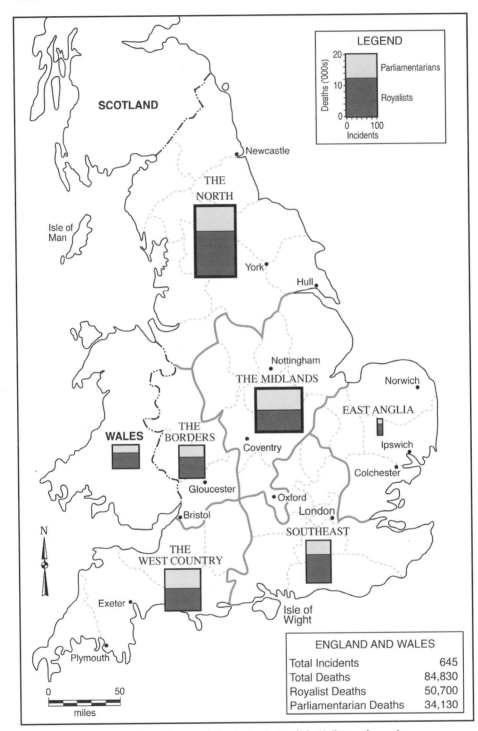

Figure 8.1B.   War-related incidents and deaths in the English Civil War, by region.

Source: Carlton 1992.

with somewhat more finality, on January 30, 1649, when King Charles I lost his head. For the republican theorist James Harrington, the explanation of the civil war was simple: We (the parliamentarians) blew up the king before the king blew up us. Doing so, however, required nine years and all of the military prowess and fiscal efficiency of Oliver Cromwell and the parliamentary forces under his command. With victory secured on the battlefield, the parliamentary representatives of a commercial society turned their attention to the English nation and the task of refashioning a monarchical system into a powerful commercial republic. And the more lyrical among them envisioned nothing less than a commonwealth blessed with the commercial vibrancy of Venice and the imperial grandeur of Rome. The progress of this parliamentarian project was soon apparent to the Venetian ambassador to England who, in 1651, observed that "merchants and trade are making great strides, as government and trade are ruled by the same persons" (quoted in Hill 1969: 155). But if trade and republican government advanced together, they were hardly equals in the republican mind. In the emerging English polity, commerce was, and would remain, the means to the larger end of a republican Commonwealth.

England's *Prince*: Cromwell and the Rise of Republican Ideology

Regicide created a vacuum in English politics that was soon filled by the looming presence of Oliver Cromwell. An East Anglian by birth, a Puritan by faith, and a republican nationalist by political inclination, Cromwell had risen from fairly modest social origins to a parliamentary backbencher and then to generalship of the parliamentary army. With his neighbors, he sought to perfect the world in preparation for the millennium and, toward that end, and in what might seem an odd alliance of puritanism and civic humanism, placed his abiding faith in the virtues of a commonwealth predicated on opportunity, talent, property, and Parliament.

It was the Civil War that provided Cromwell with his opportunity. In the heat and confusion of warfare, he quickly demonstrated his considerable logistical and organizational abilities. Not only did he manage to ensure a steady flow of funds to his troops, but he also built his "model army" in accordance with egalitarian principles. Paying little attention to the social origins or status of his troops, Cromwell sought out troops and officers who were capable of delivering results. In an age in which the nobility and the gentry regularly demanded obeisance, Cromwell's "equal opportunity" army, in which a carpenter or a fish seller might rise to the rank of colonel, represented a radical departure from military convention.

Cromwell's egalitarian commitments were tempered, however, by his equally fervent commitment to the sacredness of property. He was no "leveler"; nor even would he go so far as James Harrington and redistribute society's wealth on a more equal basis. For Cromwell, property fairly earned was the foundation of citizenry and citizenship was the foundation of the sovereign republic or, as he termed it, the Commonwealth. Cromwell's republic rested in turn on an elaborate kinetic philosophy that was at once organic, systematic, millennialist, and nationalist. As an organicist, he believed that the survival of the English Commonwealth depended on growth and power; as a systematist, he believed that power depended on a clear and decisive plan; as a millennialist, he believed that the English plan would, God willing, be divinely inspired; and as a nationalist, he believed that the Commonwealth would be defined by the enmity of its external foes as much as by its internal aims and achievements. Armed with this apocalyptic, realist, and ethnocentric perspective on the world, it was a short step to Cromwell's declaration "We are all English. That is one good fact." One suspects that Machiavelli himself could not have created a more apt model of the republican prince—one who was selflessly committed to the equality of opportunity among the citizenry at home and ruthlessly committed to the expansion of England's empire overseas.

Republican Organics: Nationalism and Empire

Having risen through the ranks by virtue of his logistical talent, Cromwell turned that talent to good use on his elevation by Parliament as lord protector of the Commonwealth. In 1649 and 1650, he prepared and then launched an ambitious plan of organic imperial expansion. The first desideratum was, as one might expect, logistical. On the fiscalist premise that every action, imperial or otherwise, entailed financial costs, Cromwell insisted that the costs of expansion had to be recouped in the operations that followed. Second, Cromwell proposed to resolve the "Irish problem" once and for all. The native unrest that had festered since the Irish revolt of 1641 was to be eliminated through the brutal reduction of the Gaelic opposition; Irish lands were to be transferred to English control; and, in accordance with Cromwell's "cash and carry" imperialism, the costs of these actions were to be underwritten by the sale of confiscated Irish lands to English buyers. Third was the "Western Design," Cromwell's plan for imposing a semblance of order and organization upon England's disparate American colonies.

Cromwell's "Western Design" had two aims: the first, to expand and strengthen England's New World empire; the second, to put the several American colonies in their proper and subordinate place within the Commonwealth (figure 8.2). Breaking sharply with the opportunism that had prevailed under the Stuarts, Cromwell proposed the creation of an interdependent colonial system in which trade and commerce between England and the colonies served the interests of the republic. The result was the Navigation Act of 1651. The act specified that the trade of the colonies was to be conveyed in English vessels and destined for ports in England or its colonies—that is, within England's "empire." Henceforth, mercantilism was placed in the service of the Commonwealth. Henceforth, foreign interlopers, mainly the Dutch, were prohibited from doing business in the lucrative sugar trade of Barbados and the tobacco trade of the Chesapeake colonies. And henceforth, shipments of sugar, tobacco, and certain other high-value colonial commodities would flow ex-

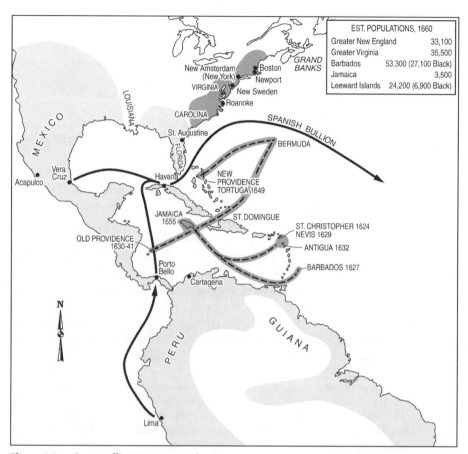

Figure 8.2.   Cromwell's "Western Design."

Note: Dashed lines indicate English expansion in the 1650s; gray shades indicate settled areas of various nations.

clusively through English ports. There, of course, they were subject to the customs duties that, in the Cromwellian fiscal system, provided the resources for underwriting the costs of an expanding empire.

Cromwell's "Western Design" was as provocative as it was ambitious. It constituted an unambiguous challenge to the Dutch republic, England's chief commercial rival and arguably the richest if not the most powerful nation in the world of the mid–seventeenth century. The Dutch, who had enjoyed pretty much a free hand in trading with England's colonies during the reign of the Stuart kings, were not disposed to abandon the gains they had made in the Anglo-American trades. The first of several Anglo-Dutch wars erupted in 1652 and concluded somewhat inconclusively in 1654. Over the next two decades, and after Cromwell's death in 1658, two other wars would follow before the Dutch were driven from the American mainland, and the lord protector's goals were fully and finally achieved.

Cromwell's achievements were breathtaking. "What needs most of all to be stressed," writes Cromwell's biographer Christopher Hill (1970: 165–66), is the fantastic scope of Cromwell's foreign policy. It is taken for granted because it set the pattern for the future. But we must see it as contemporaries saw it. In the 1620s and 1630s England had been powerless to take any action while the fate of Europe was being decided in the Thirty Year's War. . . . The transformation a mere fifteen years later is astonishing. The governments of the 1650s were the first in English history to have a world strategy.

And for the first time, the American colonies were at the center rather than the hem of English policy.

Cromwell's protectorate likewise furnished England with its first and most coherent union of political ideology and policy regime. Cromwell's was an ideology of unvarnished Machiavellian republicanism—egalitarian (though not leveling) in its commitment to a republic and a citizenry of equals, nationalist in its ruthless commitment to organic and systematic expansion on behalf of the republic, and puritanical in its perfectionist commitment to an apocalyptic and millennialist interpretation of the immanence of the second coming of Christ and the urgency that entailed.

With the ascension of Cromwell to the lord protector of the Commonwealth, England's days of backing into empire were over. Even after Cromwell's death in 1658 and the restoration of the Stuart monarchy in 1660, his imperial policies and republican ideology continued to guide the course of England and its American colonies. "In trade, colonial and foreign policy," in particular,

> the end of the Middle Ages in England came in 1650–51, when the republican government was free to turn its attention outward. The Navigation Act of 1651, "perhaps the wisest of all the commercial regulations of England," as Adam Smith called it, laid down that the colonies, chartered or proprietary, should be subordinated to Parliament, thus making a coherent imperial policy possible, and that trade to the colonies should be monopolized by English shipping. As modified in 1660, the act laid the basis for England's policy over the next century. (Hill 1969: 155)

The terms of the monarchy's restoration in 1660 prevented the wholesale reversal of this imperial policy by the Stuart kings, Charles II and James II (Trevor-Roper 1992: 213–29). In the words of James Harrington and intonations straight out of Machiavelli, England was and would remain "a commonwealth for expansion"; it "was both island and agrarian territory, [a nation] capable of breeding an armed people who should be democrats at home and conquerors abroad" (Pocock 1975: 391–92). The zeal for imperial expansion persisted after 1660. Two more wars with the Dutch resulted in the conquest of New Amsterdam, henceforth the royal colony of New York, in 1664 and the complete elimination of Dutch interlopers from the Chesapeake tobacco trade by 1675. By the latter date, England could lay reasonable claim to all of the territory along the Atlantic Seaboard of North America stretching from Maine to the Savannah River.

But to what end was England's imperial expansion aimed? Charles Wilson, who is rarely wrong, has perhaps overstated the state's case in arguing that "with the Navigation Act [of 1651] we have arrived at a fully fashioned conception of economic policy in an essentially national form. Its dynamic was no longer Christian ethics working against private greed or exploitation. It was the welfare of Leviathan" (Wilson 1965: 63). The benefits to the state were sizable, to be sure, not least being a tenfold gain in England's customs revenues over the remainder of the seventeenth century (Hill 1969: 157). But Cromwell's "Western Design" served equally well the egalitarian aims of republican ideology. For land-hungry English freemen, the English "plantations" overseas offered the opportunity to acquire land and all of the perquisites of citizenship that this entailed. In Ireland and in the Americas, Harrington and most other republicans envisioned both an enlarged and Greater England and an open frontier "where every citizen will in time have his villa," both empire and egalitarian opportunity (quoted in Pocock 1975: 392).

America as Opportunity

English freemen were reasonably well aware of the opportunities for betterment in the Americas (figure 8.3A). Stories had filtered back from Virginia, where in the 1620s the fortunate survivors had gone from rags to riches when tobacco sold at three shillings per pound and an ordinary laborer producing five hundred pounds of tobacco boosted his annual income from the £10 typical in England to over £70. Likewise, tales from New England told of English Puritans who had acquired sufficient acreage for the arable and pasture lands so essential for the mixed husbandry of subsistence farming. With these felicitous examples and repeated promises of cheap land, some 378,000 people—nearly 70 percent of England's natural increase—departed the British Isles for the Americas between 1630 and 1699 (figure 8.3B; Clay 1984, I: 25–26; Bailyn 1986: 40, citing Wrigley and Scofield 1981: 1750). Of these migrants, roughly two-thirds emigrated to the English colonies on the mainland, with the rest going to the English West Indies. Even larger proportions went to the mainland after 1640 once the West Indian economy had shifted from the staple crop of tobacco to sugarcane and from a labor force predominated by white indentured servants to one predominated by African slaves. On the mainland, meanwhile, indentured servants from the British Isles continued to be the principal source of immigrant labor until the turn of the century.

At least half and perhaps as many as two-thirds of the British emigrants to the mainland English colonies came as servants—men and women who agreed to serve their masters for periods ranging from four to seven years in exchange for their transportation to the colonies. Of the 180,000 servants who arrived on the mainland prior to 1690, roughly one-third (68,000) went to the Chesapeake tobacco colonies, one-third to the English West Indies (65,000 to the islands of Antigua, Barbados, Jamaica, St. Kitts, Nevis, and Montserrat), and one-third to the other mainland colonies (57,000) (Smith 1947: 336; Galenson 1981: 216–18). The brisk flow of servants as well as other emigrants—some 5,400 per year on average—was a boon to English shipping. At £5 per passenger, emigrants proved to be an especially lucrative cargo capable of generating over £27,000 per annum. In addition to producing shipping earnings that rivaled or surpassed the earnings from transporting the entire Chesa-

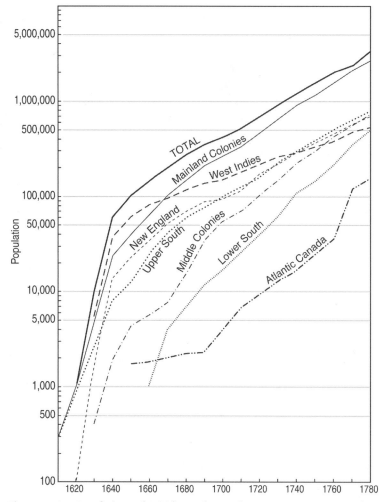

Figure 8.3A. Populations of British North America, 1610–1700.

Source: Historical Statistics 1975, 2.

peake tobacco trade, this passenger business filled the holds of vessels that would otherwise have been largely empty on their backhaul voyages to the American colonies.

A Republican Hothouse: Equality and Expansion in Greater Virginia

The conventional characterization of Virginia and the Chesapeake colonies more generally as the domain of elites and royalist cavaliers is scarcely appropriate for the third quarter of the seventeenth century. It would be more accurate to characterize

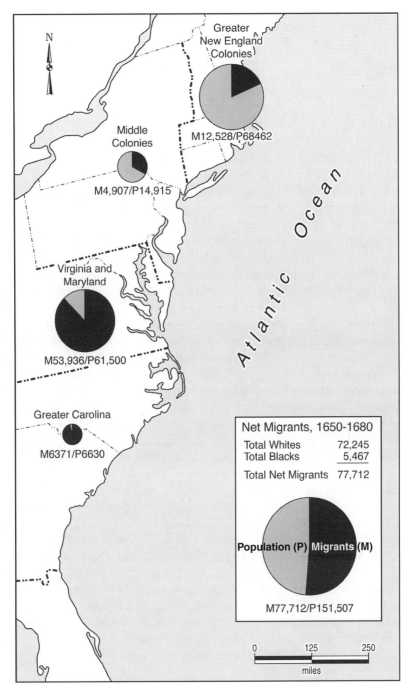

Figure 8.3B.   Net migrants, 1650–1680, as a proportion of population in 1680.

Source: Galenson 1981: 212–18.

Greater Virginia as something of a hothouse of imperial and egalitarian republican-ism. While this was probably not the intention of Virginia's governors nor of Mary-land's proprietor, it was in fact the improbable consequence of an economy built on tobacco and servant labor.

EQUALITY OF OPPORTUNITY

Tobacco "is our life and our all," or so proclaimed Maryland's proprietor in 1634. Tobacco's grip on the Chesapeake economy remained firm, but much else had changed. The spectacular boom in tobacco prices in the 1620s and early 1630s had collapsed before making a modest recovery in the 1640s (figure 8.4). When prices fell from thirty-six pence per pound in the boom to one to two pence in the 1630s, planters desperately considered alternatives to the tobacco staple. But instead of abandoning tobacco as did the planters in the West Indies, Chesapeake planters sought to salvage their staple crop by raising productivity. Sometime between 1630 and 1650, they introduced two obscure but crucial innovations: tobacco topping and tobacco house curing. Prior to these innovations, a typical planter was lucky to raise five hundred pounds of tobacco with his own labor. And once harvested, the leaves were cured by stacking them in piles on the ground. At prices of three shillings per pound, planters did not worry very much about yield or quality. All that changed when prices collapsed. In an effort to increase yields, planters introduced the practice of topping the tobacco plants just before they flowered and went to seed. With plant nutrients now diverted to the leaves rather than to seeds, output rose from 500 to 1,500 to 2,000 pounds per worker—an increase of three- to fourfold. And in a concurrent effort to improve the quality and price of leaf, tobacco planters intro-duced the practice of air curing leaves hung from the rafters of specially designed tobacco houses. As the reputation of Chesapeake tobacco improved, an industry that was nearly moribund made a stunning recovery.

Demography attests to the important role of servants in the Chesapeake econ-omy. The two colonies of Virginia and Maryland, which numbered just under ninety thousand residents in 1690, had received over sixty-eight thousand servants since 1640. From the standpoint of tobacco planters, servants had several advantages. Fore-most among these, servants offered a relatively cheap and dependable source of labor for a region cursed by high mortality and an acute scarcity of workers. In return for paying the costs of the servant's transportation, the planter enjoyed the services of a laborer or artisan bound for four to seven years. Most servants worked in tobacco, clearing fields, planting, tilling, harvesting, and curing tobacco, and constructing tobacco houses. In a time when tobacco fields were cultivated perennially, servants were doubly important because their improvements represented a permanent addi-tion to the plantation's capital stock. Servants also raised corn, tended livestock, and performed a host of miscellaneous chores. In addition, planters who imported ser-vants were entitled to receive fifty acres of land from the land offices of the colonial governments.

From the standpoint of the servant, servitude afforded opportunities for socio-

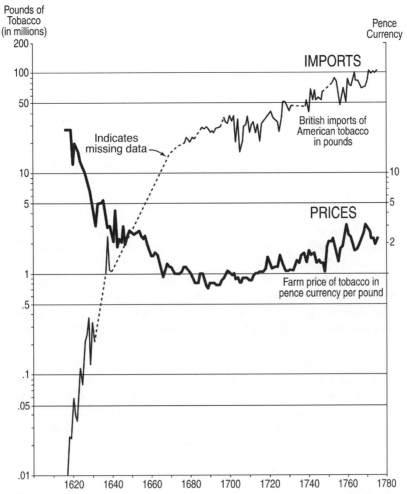

Figure 8.4.   Farm prices of Chesapeake tobacco and British imports of Chesapeake tobacco.

Source: McCusker and Menard 1985: 121.

economic mobility to poorer English men and women in exchange for binding them to labor during a fixed duration. And it was this promise of opportunities for mobility that mattered most for republican ideology. Consider the situation of servants in the Chesapeake colonies at the conclusion of their temporary bondage. Once their contracts expired, servants became "freemen." In addition, they received a suit of clothes, rude tools, and some corn from their masters and a warrant for fifty acres of land from the colonial land offices—a munificence to which most could not have aspired and of which most would not have dreamed back in England. While some servants sold their warrants, others accumulated a bit of capital, exercised their warrants, and crossed the magical threshold from freeman to citizen freeholder. The upward draft from servant to freeholder seems to have been most vigorous just after midcentury. One scholar's tracking of servant progress in Maryland has shown that 40 to 50 percent of the servants arriving in the colony between 1662 and 1672 and residing their ten years hence had acquired land and that 60 to 64 percent of these new freeholders exercised their citizenship through participating, in one fashion or another, in local or provincial government (e.g., petty jurors, witnesses, etc.) (McCusker and Menard 1985: 138; Menard 1973: 63). A similar outcome has been documented for the 1660s in Middlesex County, Virginia, where former servants first accumulated capital as tenants or croppers and then acquired small parcels of land. Here, in Cromwell's wake, was a protean society, one that afforded ordinary men and women the opportunity to rise through the ranks of Chesapeake civil society, much as Cromwell's parliamentary troops had risen through the ranks of his model army. While not every freeman in Greater Virginia would "in time have his villa," the majority of immigrants, servant and free, between 1650 and 1680 seem to have succeeded in this hothouse of republican opportunity.

There was, of course, a price to be exacted for all of the advantages that life in Maryland and Virginia afforded. In the first place, life was harrowingly short. The risks of disease and death in the tidewater lowlands were unusually high, especially for newcomers susceptible to the deadly waterborne diseases of dysentery and typhoid and debilitating malarial infections. Under such conditions, men who were alive at twenty years of age did not expect to live much beyond forty. Widows and orphans were commonplace. Second, families were hard to establish in an immigrant society where males made up two-thirds of all newcomers, and they were harder to maintain given the high rates of mortality. Unmarried women were, accordingly, in great demand, and most widows were soon remarried. Third, as a consequence of high male mortality, the imbalance among the sexes, and the fragility of the family unit, the growth in the native or Creole population through 1700 was regularly outpaced by the population gains attributable to immigration.

EXPANSION

The Chesapeake's immigrant society was sustained as much by the generous inducements for colonization as by the region's arduous demographic regime. In both Virginia and Maryland, (figures 8.5A and 8.5B) royal and proprietary officials pursued an expansionist policy in which immigration was inextricably tied and in direct relation to the Chesapeake land market. Under the "head rights" system, planters were entitled to receive fifty acres of land for every person, servant or free, that they brought into the colonies (Harris 1953: 204, 206, 217–18). Thus the post-1650 boom in the servant trade and immigration immediately triggered a land rush in the Chesapeake. In Virginia between 1663 and 1674, head rights were claimed for 25,872 immigrants and over 1.3 million acres, with the average grant (patent) running between 671 and 890 acres (Craven 1971: 15; Harris 1953: 207). In just a dozen years, Virginia's planters, their families, and servants occupied an area the size of the state of Delaware, filling in the empty spaces in "necks" of land in the tidewater coastal plain and pushing inland up the navigable rivers and onto the undulating surface of the piedmont. The pace of frontier expansion rapidly accelerated. In the third quarter of the seventeenth century, Greater Virginians expanded their settled area at a rate of 3.9 percent per annum—a third again the colonial rate of 2.96 percent and the highest rate of American frontier expansion ever recorded over a period of comparable length (Earle 2000: tables 1 and 2; Friis 1940).

At this furious pace, the advancing frontier of Anglo-American settlement inexorably encroached upon the retreating frontier of native Americans. In May 1676, following a quarter century of breakneck expansion, hostilities, both real and imagined, erupted. Settlers in Virginia's "backcountry" called for military assistance, and when these appeals were ignored by the governor in Jamestown, a frontier rebellion ensued. In the summer of 1676, rebels led by Nathaniel Bacon drove the governor from the capital, sacked the town, and assumed effective control over the colony. The conflict continued into the fall when on October 26, 1676, Bacon died suddenly of the "Bloody flux"; within three months, the rebel remnant was brought to heel (Washburn 1957: 40–91).

The controversy over the meaning of the events of 1676 has subsequently focused on Bacon rather than his rebellion. Was he a hero, a democratizing "torchbearer" of the American Revolution, or an opportunistic scoundrel trumping up false charges against beleaguered native Americans? But whatever biography reveals of Bacon's motivations, his rebellion underscored certain larger issues, most notably its exposure of the contradictions that were (and are) inherent in a republican ideol-

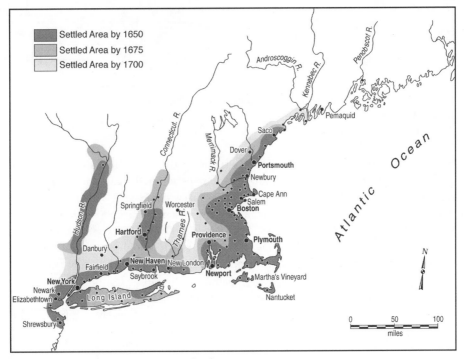

Figure 8.5A.   Settlements in New England, 1650–1700.

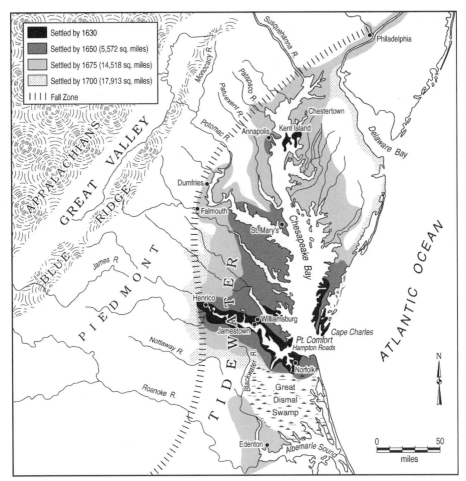

Figure 8.5B. Settled areas of Greater Virginia, 1650, 1675, and 1700.
Source: Earle 2000.

ogy of egalitarian expansion. Alongside its stature as the first of many challenges that frontier expansion would present for older, more established areas, Bacon's rebellion offered an object lesson on the social volatility that could arise when fast-moving frontiers were coupled with a rampant equality that fast-tracked the lower orders into the ranks of citizen-freeholders. For those who preferred a more orderly and less volatile society, the prescriptions were fairly obvious: tighter controls over the behavior of former servants, greater restrictions on their opportunities for land ownership, and firmer restraints on frontier expansion (Morgan 1975). In practical terms, this meant the dismantling of the head rights system and the abandonment of servant labor in favor of a permanently bound and more manageable labor force. And it was this agenda—antirepublican, antiexpansionist, and antiegalitarian—that liberal reformers would soon pursue.

These challenges to republican ideology would come eventually, but there was little momentum in that direction back in England. Thanks in large part to the vast outmigration to the American colonies after 1650, economic opportunities in England had become fairly widespread. Labor markets were tight, upward economic mobility was commonplace, and the successful were being accorded a greater voice in politics through enfranchisement. In that effort, the upwardly mobile were assisted by the country gentry whose "persistent policy [was] to enlarge their political base by enlarging the electorates in the boroughs where they exercised influence so that by the reign of Anne [1702–1714] a larger proportion of the male population voted than was the case even after the Reform Bill of 1832. . . . The era of large electorates, even after the Restoration, coincided with and helped cause an era of intense political competitiveness" (Pocock 1980: 12–13). While the gentry may not have shared the egalitarian ideology that had been set loose by Cromwell, Harrington, and their republican allies, the practical effects were the same. The roots of this optimistic Commonwealth vision of opportunity in a citizen-republic thus ran deep in the English countryside as well as in several of England's colonies abroad.

Barren Ground: Greater New England and the Trials of Republicanism

New England stood apart as the great paradox in England's "Western Design"—a puritan region unenamored of "the revolution of the saints" and the republican ideology it brought to fruition. Of all the colonies in place by 1680, it was among the least republican, the least expansionist, and the least egalitarian of England's American plantations. Whereas republicanism presumed a mobile, land-hungry immigrant society modeled along the lines of the Chesapeake colonies, New England represented the theoretical antithesis of such an expansionist and egalitarian society.

Following the "great migration" of the 1630s and 1640s, immigration to New England had slowed to a trickle as puritans in England ascended into positions of influence and power. Henceforth, with the spigot of immigration nearly closed, New England's population growth was propelled almost exclusively by exceedingly high rates of natural increase (i.e., by the large excess of births over deaths). The facts are not in dispute. "New England settlers, especially in the rural areas . . . , enjoyed low mortality, a high percentage of married women, and a vigorous birth rate that, for most of the seventeenth century, produced completed families averaging in excess of seven children" (Greene 1988: 56). New Englanders thus lived much longer than their counterparts in the Chesapeake and West Indian colonies; and their prospects for marriage and family formation were much better given the balanced distribution of males and females (owing, in large part, to the pattern set by the pre-1650 migration of families rather than servants). In the healthier environs of New England, couples who married regularly watched their children grow to maturity, marry, and form families of their own—all of which gives credence to the claim that it was New Englanders who invented the terms *grandparents* and *grandchildren* (figures 8.6 and 8.7).

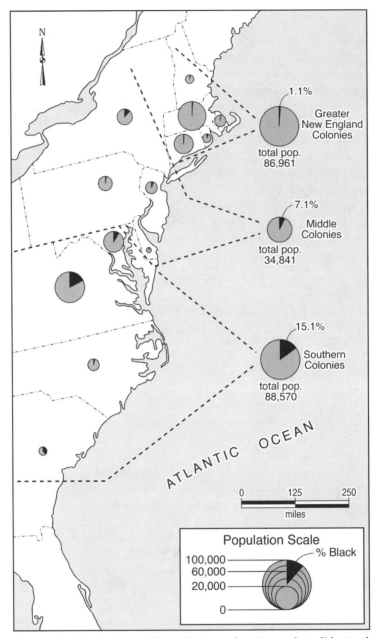

Figure 8.6. Population of the colonies and regions of English North America, 1690.

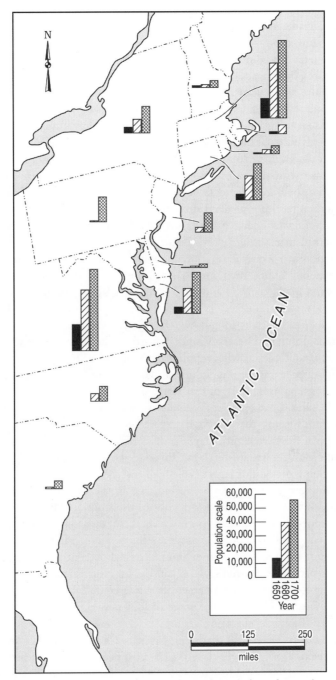

Figure 8.7.   Population of the English colonies of North America, 1650, 1680, and 1700.

But the advantages of a healthier environment, a subsistence economy, and a high-fertility, low-mortality society were, at times, a mixed blessing. As two and then three generations commingled within New England's rural "towns," domestic difficulties reared their head. Only later did these problems affect the first generation of settlers; on the outset, they had been too busy with other problems—carving their settlements out of the wilderness, clearing land for their subsistence economy of hardy grains, vegetables, and livestock, erecting the congregational churches around which life revolved, establishing the institutions of rural township governance, and distributing town lands in rough proportion to the settlers' roles and statuses. The difficulties arose with the second generation, with the native-born children who discovered that their long-lived fathers were reluctant or unwilling to relinquish control over their patrimony—land and farms—and instead used it to keep their sons in a state of paternal dependence. And thus did many a young man grow old working on father's farm and awaiting father's death. By and large, this second generation of New Englanders acted obediently, staying at home, fulfilling their familial obligations, and patiently biding their time. As a consequence, the frontiers of New England settlement between 1650 and 1675 came to almost a complete stall. In a span when Greater Virginia doubled its settled area every eighteen years, Greater New England took four times as long (seventy-two years). It is hard to imagine two more different frontiers. Greater Virginia's, with its hell-for-leather expansion and its ample opportunities, was what republican theorists had in mind. New England's, with its sluggish pace and demographic inertia, seemed to these same theorists as an anachronism in the purest sense of that term.

Glimpsing ahead, we see that the tables were reversed between 1675 and 1700. It was in Greater Virginia that westward expansion was brought to its knees, battered by the depths of the transatlantic depression of the 1680s and 1690s and the liberal reforms that followed. In greater New England, by contrast, the third generation broke with their elders and sharply accelerated the pace of frontier expansion. Faced with dwindling prospects of ever acquiring land in the towns of their parents and grandparents, this generation struck out toward the frontier. There they established new communities closely modeled on the ones that they had left. Thus as the southern frontier collapsed in the last quarter of the seventeenth century (the rate of expansion falling from 3.9 percent per annum to 0.84 percent), the northern frontier picked up the pace. In this same span, expansion on New England's frontier jumped by fifty percent—rising from 1.05 percent to 1.52 percent. As a result, New England added 209 new townships and an average of four new ones in every year between 1660 and 1710 (Bailyn 1986: 93).

Kenneth Lockridge (1970) was close to the mark in describing rural New England as a collection of relatively closed corporatist peasant communities. Unlike the Chesapeake, where life was attuned to the fanciful transatlantic rhythms of tobacco prices and the market, affairs in rural New England adhered to the flatter local rhythms of demography, family, faith, land, and subsistence. Circumscribed by the boundaries of the rural townships, life in New England revolved around the institutions of mixed farming, the rural village, and the congregational church. So long as there was sufficient land for families in the town, this involutional way of life might persist. But as demographic pressures mounted and land grew scarce, the unlanded members of the third- and fourth-generation settlers were compelled to seek land elsewhere. Because these new settlements were so often hived off of older ones, the familiar institutions of a closed corporatist community reappeared, and, in time, the involutionary process initiated in the older settlements was regularly repeated in the newer ones two generations hence.

In the process, cracks began to develop in the puritan faith that had cemented the millennial aims of the first settlers. It was increasingly obvious that their "errand into the wilderness" was jeopardized by corrupt and wayward behaviors in city and countryside. In a curious geographical reversal of the situation in Greater Virginia, it was the merchants in the coastal ports of Boston, Salem, and Newport rather than the frontier rebels (as in Virginia) who were most feared by rural New Englanders. Albeit for different reasons, inland Puritans worried as much about mercantile prosperity in the coastal trade as did the president of the Lords of Trade who, in 1672, feared that in twenty years, these merchants were "likely to be mighty and powerfull and not at all careful of theire dependence upon Old England" (quoted in Barrow 1967: 8–9). Worse, it was these cities that served as the conduit for the "new knowledge" of science and skepticism that too readily mocked faith and providence.

These harbingers of Mammon's triumph, when combined with the mounting local pressures on rural land and the exodus of a younger generation, sustained a broodish pessimism, a vain search for prodigious signs, and deep fears of declension among New England's puritan communities. Countless jeremiads from the pulpits of New England condemned the loss of a sense of millennial mission and the corrosion in the congregational bonds of community. Perhaps, as some scholars have suggested, reality was not so bleak, and perhaps as late as 1700 the "peaceable kingdoms" of rural New England and their "traditional institutions of community, family, and church continued to display a vitality . . . and the corporate impulse probably remained strong" (Greene 1988: 65; Innes 1995). However, the stack of sermons proclaiming otherwise provided credible evidence, at least in some eyes, of a society in disorder and a faith in decay. Were not these sermons, when taken in tandem with the collateral evidence of the profiteering, usurious charges, and sharp dealing of New England's merchants, Bacon's rebels in Virginia, and the enlargement of the electorate in England itself, premonitory indicators of a republican ideology run amok? By 1680, the need for reform, for a restoration of social order, for social consolidation were increasingly apparent to the sectarian conservatives of rural New England as well as to their philosophical adversaries, the secular liberals in the cosmopolitan centers of old England.

Prospect: Republicanism under Duress

The republicanism of the Commonwealth, as refracted in the policies of the Restoration, was by the 1680s, increasingly tainted, discredited, and in disarray. The Western design for egalitarian expansion had arrived at an impasse with the collapse of Greater Virginia's frontier. Although New England's frontier showed signs of life, the pace of expansion would remain modest and the opportunities it offered paled by comparison to the hypermobility of Cromwell's officer corps or Greater Virginia's frontier in the 1660s and 1670s.

Elsewhere along the seaboard, English gains were modest. This, too, was in agreement with republican theory, which by analogy with Harvey's organic theory of the heart's role in circulation, favored the systematic and concentrated expansion of empire. Although New York was added by conquest in 1664 and Carolina and the Jerseys were patented to royalist proprietors in 1660, the figures cut by their populations were small indeed. Of the 250,000 mainland colonists as of 1690, nearly 70 percent resided in Greater Virginia and Greater New England. But that also would change following the glorious revolution of 1689 and the eclipse of Commonwealth ideology by Lockean liberalism, salutary neglect, and the Whig oligarchy.

Retrospective

The republican experiment initiated by the English Civil War and, with significant modification, extended by Restoration policies encountered mounting opposition as the century wore on, but not before recording several notable successes. With regard to empire and expansion, Charles II and his ministries carried Cromwell's aggressive nationalism to its logical conclusion, prosecuting hostilities against the Dutch in two successful wars, shoring up the Navigation Act of 1651 in a series of enactments in the 1660s and 1670s, chartering proprietary colonies in Carolina and the Jerseys, and assuming royal control over the colonies of Connecticut and Rhode Island. In the process, the Dutch were forced to surrender New Amsterdam (thereafter New York) and they were effectively excluded from the Chesapeake tobacco trade after 1675. New England merchants were less compliant. They regularly flouted the law by trading with Dutch and Spanish islands in the West Indies, to the point that English officials noted that these illegalities "dayly grow more destructive to the trade of this Kingdome" wherefore it may be necessary "to hinder theire growth as much as can be" (remarks of 1672 quoted in Barrow 1967: 8–9).

Concurrently, the Navigation Acts prepared the foundations for the rapid expansion of settlement in Greater Virginia. In the first place, since tobacco had to be hauled in English vessels, shipping interests discovered that passengers, both free and servants, provided a remunerative back-haul cargo for the annual tobacco fleet. The rapid growth of servant populations after 1650 attests to these impacts. In the second place, because immigrants brought to the Chesapeake were entitled to fifty acres of land, the immigration boom simultaneously initiated a land rush. In the quarter century after the initial Navigation Act, the southern frontier expanded at the phenomenal rate of almost 4 percent per annum. In New England, by contrast, the expansionist ideology made little headway, blocked as it was by the corporatist impulses of congregationalism and subsistence.

Republicanism's other triumph had to do with its commitment to egalitarian opportunity. The fires of Cromwell's egalitarianism were banked but not extinguished by Restoration policies. In England, the English electorate expanded rapidly during this period, and there is some evidence that

> while it may be conceded that the most obvious beneficiaries of the new [economic] policies were the "producers" . . . , it can hardly be doubted that a rising volume of employment followed in the wake of their enterprise. Standards of living for the people at large might not yet show any spectacular or measurable rise, but certainly a larger population was living at standards that were not falling and were in some respects tending to improve. (Wilson 1965: 237–38)

Partly, if not largely, this was so because of the massive emigration to America that had siphoned off two-thirds of England's natural increase between 1630 and 1699. As for those who went to mainland colonies, the overwhelming numbers eventually acquired land. Many ordinary men and women, arriving in the temporary bondage of servitude, had the opportunity to acquire land, rise to the status of citizen-freeholder, and then participate in the affairs of local government. In the end, this was all that Cromwell asked—the opportunity for Englishmen of all ranks to prove their mettle in war and in peace and to be rewarded accordingly. To the good fortune of many of them, neither the Stuart kings nor their court ministers would have much success in drowning out Cromwell's republican overture.

CHAPTER 9

Lockean Geographies

LIBERALISM AND ITS GEOGRAPHICAL CONSEQUENCES, 1680s–1730s

The geographies along the Atlantic Seaboard of North America circa 1680 and circa 1740 were as two sides of an imperial coin. The one side, bearing the date 1680, was Anglo-American in origins, republican in design, and expansionist, concentrative, egalitarian and volatile in geographical motif. The other side, bearing the date 1740, was more nearly American, decidedly more liberal, and entirely contrary in geographical motif—which is to imply geographies that were more consolidated, more dispersed, more specialized, and, in their stability, more attuned to the interests of the American Creole elite then emerging. While the politics of this transformation are reasonably well understood, particularly among historians who have examined the rise of Lockean liberalism or the British colonial policy of "salutary neglect," the same cannot be said for the concurrent transformation in American geographies. Nor, given the insular histories of politics and geography, should we be surprised that the origins of these new geographies are regarded as the scholarly equivalent of spontaneous combustion. One could, of course, go to the opposite extreme and portray these geographies as springing verily from the brow of John Locke.

Neither vitalism nor idealism, however, is an altogether satisfactory remedy for the maleficiencies of disciplinary boundaries. More appropriate in the case of these liberal geographies is an amalgam that is one part policy, one part political philosophy, and one part geography. Of these ingredients, the first deals with the origins of negligence as a colonial policy; the second, with "salutary neglect" as a corollary of the emergent philosophy of liberalism; and the third, with the newly minted American geographies as fabrications of high-liberal ideology and low-Whig politics. But before turning to the adventures of Locke and the Whigs, it may be useful to ask why these liberal transformations were necessary in the first place. The answers, in this case, are to be found not in the crisp beginnings of English liberalism but rather in the forlorn and untidy endings of a discredited republican regime that liberals would soon displace.

The Draining of Commonwealth Republicanism

Republicanism did not die with Cromwell; indeed, the thrust of this nationalist, egalitarian ideology, having staggered through the 1660s and 1670s, lingered on until the 1680s before fading into the gloomy mist that had settled over England. The wonder is that it survived so effectively and for so long in the face of the restoration of the Stuart monarchy in 1660 and the widespread disdain for Cromwell's authoritarian and at times brutal administration. But Cromwell, it should be noted, never traded in the stock of charisma—a historical force of political legitimacy which is much overrated in any case; Cromwell's gift was more nearly artisanal. Above all, he demonstrated the capacity for molding, casting, and finishing—molding the abstract ideals of republicanism into concrete policies, casting into these molds the superheated and liquefied raw materials of society, and hardening them into social forms that were neither easily broken or soon displaced, not even by restoration courtiers who hated them all dearly.

While king and court despised republicanism beyond measure, they never quite managed to wriggle free from the expansionist and egalitarian ethos of the Commonwealth. With regard to expansion, Cromwell's so-called Western Design was not only retained during the Restoration but amplified and extended by the Navigation Acts of 1660 and 1673. Similarly, Cromwell's assault on Dutch commercial dominance in the 1650s was sustained through the prosecution of two more Anglo-Dutch wars under Charles II—albeit in these cases, the king's actions seem to have been prompted as much by politics and his sympathies for French interests as by his desire for English commercial supremacy over the Hollanders. Restoration politics, it seems, did little to blunt republican commitments to the expansion of a commercial empire (Trevor-Roper 1992: 213–30; Pincus 1996).

The later Stuarts had even less success in damming up the egalitarian raceway cut by Commonwealthmen. In fact, during the course of the Restoration, standards of living improved modestly in England (a rare feat in itself) and expansively in the mainland American colonies; opportunities for social and economic advancement improved markedly, and upward mobility was fairly common in both places; the ranks of the citizenry and the electorate grew at unprecedented rates; the institutions of social deference were eroded; and, amid these volatile atmospherics, rebelliousness was lighter than air (Stone 1980; Pocock 1980).

Republican ideology, albeit watered down by Charles II and his courtiers, exerted influence on restoration policy and society well into the 1670s; but at that point, the residuum of republicanism was confronted by a crisis of two dimensions. One was economic—the long depression that lasted for the better part of the next two decades; the other, political—the recrudescence of Stuart absolutism, rebellion, and the advent of republicanism's newest adversary, liberalism. To the liberal mind, the complicity of republican policy and Stuart absolutism, however ungainly, implicated them both as enemies of freedom and property. By the time the dust had settled, England had embarked on a new course with profound implications for its peoples and its colonies.

Troubling Times

The 1680s were trying times in England and the colonies. The economic problems commenced in 1678 and persisted for a dozen years. The crisis began with a sharp fall in the prices of English commodities as well as of West Indian sugar and Chesapeake tobacco. The reverberations were felt throughout England's transatlantic empire (figures 9.1A and 9.1B). One ripple triggered rising levels of unemployment in England; another, a spate of bankruptcies in the lucrative West Indies trade, and yet another, a hasty retrenchment toward self-sufficiency by Chesapeake tobacco planters. Nor were New England merchants unaffected by these shocks, since their prosperity hinged on the good fortune of their West Indian and Chesapeake partners in the coastal trade. With hard money (specie) exceedingly scarce, desperate measures were in order (Bailyn 1955: 182–92). On top of all of this, while England's population had ceased to grow between the 1640s and 1700 (figure 9.2A), the nation's imports from abroad (excluding reexports) had increased by 75 percent in the aggregate and by 80 percent when measured on a per capita basis (Clay 1984, II: 155–58, 181; I: 37–52; Wrigley and Schofield 1981). This sort of reckless consumption had

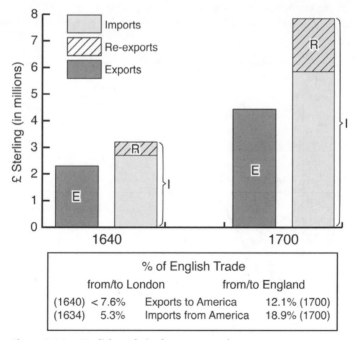

Figure 9.1A.   English trade in the seventeenth century.

Source: Adapted from Clay 1984, II: 181.

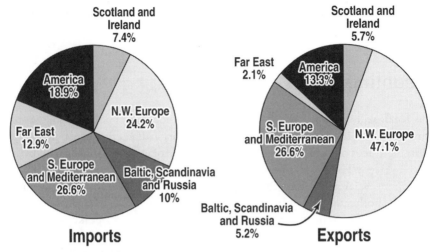

Figure 9.1B.   English imports and exports, proportion by value, averages for the years 1699–1701.

Source: Adapted from Clay 1984, II: 142, 160.

not been seen in England since Elizabethan times, almost precisely a century earlier, and some were quick to fix the blame where it lay—on the egalitarian achievements inaugurated by a republican regime.

As if these economic conditions were not problem enough, the 1680s added political turmoil into the equation. In the colonies, frontier expansion seems to have

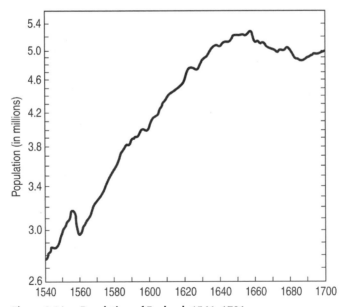

Figure 9.2A.   Population of England, 1541–1701.

Source: Clay 1984, I: 4.

spun out of control. With the memories of Bacon's Rebellion and King Philip's War fresh in mind, the lords of trade sought to impose greater control over the seaboard colonies. Their timing was not propitious; nor was it wise.

> In a running contest with Massachusetts . . . [the Lords] converted New Hampshire into a royal colony by 1679. . . . In 1684 they won in the courts an annulment of the charters of Massachusetts and of the Bermuda Company. And after New York has passed automatically to the crown with the Duke of York's accession to the throne as James II in 1685, the Lords of Trade undertook their most ambitious experiment—a short-lived attempt to consolidate all of the New England colonies and New York under a single royal government [the Dominion of New England],

as well as make revisions in the governance of the royal colony of Virginia (Craven 1970: 395–96). Having earlier revoked the charters of Connecticut (1662) and Rhode Island (1663), the Stuarts seemed well on their way to exercising firm control over 90 percent of the peoples in the mainland colonies. This was imperial over-stretch with a vengeance that went far beyond the loose-fitting governance envisioned in Cromwell's "Western Design" or in Harrington's utopian republic.

These actions appeared even more draconian when combined with Charles II's purge of Parliament (1679–1681) aimed at eliminating certain members of that body who had voted to exclude a Catholic heir (the king's son, James, duke of York) to the throne. Following the purge, the fears of absolutism again took wing in England and the colonies (Hill 1980: 200) and remained aloft until 1688 when, in accordance with Harrington's doctrine of preemptive strike, a curious coalition of old Whigs (commonwealth republicans), Tory gentry, moderate Whigs, and radicals launched the "Glorious Revolution." In short order, their conspiracy won the day, driving James II and the Stuarts from England; installing a Dutch monarch, William, on the English throne; and, in the longer term, bestowing enormous autonomy and power (if not yet supremacy) on Parliament (Trevor-Roper 1992: 231–48).

But as the motley coalition of conspirators implies, this was as yet a revolution without ideological portfolio. Unlike the republican ideology that had emerged organically and with such seeming effortlessness out of the English Civil War, the revolutionaries of 1688 were united mainly by their opposition to unbridled royal authority. The intellectual untidiness of their revolt was especially distressing to John Locke who deplored the compromises that diverted attention from constitutional reforms that would secure "'the civil rights and the liberty and property of all the subjects of the nation'" (quoted in Trevor-Roper 1992: 246). Afterward, having defeated James II, the victorious conspirators were compelled to invent an ideology that would, at once, help preserve their political triumph and serve their material interests. So it came to pass that a version of Locke's liberalism was rescued from the dustbin of philosophy and placed in the service of ideology.

Liberalism: From Philosophy to Ideology

The foundations of liberalism were laid by John Locke and, somewhat more obliquely, by Isaac Newton and the proponents of the new science. It was Locke who maintained that governments rested exclusively on a social contract with the English people, a contract that guaranteed liberty, the rights to property, and a spirit of toleration for assorted English ideas and creeds. Governments were far from passive, however, in Locke's scheme; they served as guarantors of liberty and social stability, without which all would come to naught. In the first instance, governments ensured that the terms of the social contract were carried out, that the rights of Englishmen (here Locke's sonorous rhetoric unwittingly opened the door to a more ample definition of citizenship) were honored and appropriately amplified. In the second instance, they ensured the sanctity of property, the preservation of economic stability, and the maintenance of social equilibrium (Ashcraft 1986, 1987; Huyler 1995).

To speak of contracts and their enforcement is to speak of law, and, not surprisingly, the new liberals venerated the common law above other variants—it was, after all, the closest thing that they had to a paper trail running back to their fictive social contract. But beyond the precedents of common law, liberals had little patience with history and the past. They rejected most of the history that had preceded liberalism—including the "overwrought" republicanism of Cromwell and the Old Whigs—in favor of epistemologies of stability and, most especially, of social analogies with Newtonian equilibria. Liberalism looked to the present and the future, not the past; it was designed to unleash the ingenuity and creativity of propertied elites, not to laden them down with the dead weight of egalitarian opportunities, imperial dreams, authoritarian restraints, or the past itself.

A Tawdry Scene: The Fine Line between Liberty and License

The transit from the Lockean theory of liberalism to hegemonic ideology was not unimpeded. In the quarter century after 1688, the English and French were at war in twenty-one of those years, and this unsettled state of affairs meant that liberalism would not reach full flower until the hostilities ended and Robert Walpole and the Whig oligarchy came to power. It was during Walpole's watch between 1714 and 1742 that liberalism flourished. The principal beneficiaries were English elites, the proponents of a freer system of trade, and, above all others, members of Parliament who, in accordance with liberal principles, first helped themselves. Without shame and in the Lockean spirit of positive government, they provided "English political elites with real distributional benefits through private enclosure acts, grain bounties, and patents for overseas trading companies in which elites held a share [not to mention protective tariffs for industrial elites]. However, these benefits did not come at the costs of general political stability because they were restricted [as in France] to numerous networks of ministerial cronies" (Root 1991: 369). Everyone in these networks fed at the trough of corruption (figure 9.2B); the masses, meanwhile, bore the brunt of the growing expense of this largesse in the form of evictions, higher prices, escalating excise taxes on consumption, and a falling standard of living (Bailyn 1986; Murrin 1980).

Corruption was the one corollary of liberalism that a philosopher more cynical of human nature than Locke might not have overlooked (a lesson that was not lost on James Madison). We may presume, judging from Locke's very distinguished career as a civil servant, that he placed too much stock in virtue—a quaint republican notion indeed—as a constraint on self-interest in political affairs. We may also assume that he would have been sadly disappointed by the crude ways in which wealth was redistributed by and to those in power. Liberal self-interest did not stop, it seems, at Parliament's edge.

Liberty of Trade and Property

Locke's liberalism, co-opted and perverted as it was by Whig politicians, fared somewhat better with respect to one of liberty's corollaries—the commitment to greater freedom in overseas trade (figure 9.3). As Christopher Hill has written, "the Revolution of 1688 was a turning point in economic as well as political and constitutional history. . . . 1688 saw the end of old-style commercial monopoly [which] . . . was now felt to be a fetter on [economic] expansion" (Hill 1980: 227). That said, the emergence of free trade as a full-fledged doctrine was constrained by financial exigencies in England in ways that it was not in the colonies. At home, national finances had been shredded by over two decades of war. To sustain English troops and sailors, Parliament had been forced to raise revenues quickly and in large quantities, and the only practical way of doing this was by increasing customs duties and land taxes— neither of which served the interests of Parliament's clientele—the nation's trading, agrarian, and industrial elites—nor of freer trade abroad (Davis 1966).

All that would change in 1713 following the conclusion of the War of Spanish Succession. Parliament moved swiftly in setting the English house in order by initiating a radical restructuring of government finances. The restructuring steadily shifted

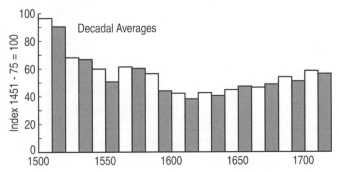

Figure 9.2B.   Purchasing power of the wages of building craftsmen in England, 1500–1719.

Source: Clay 1984, II: 30.

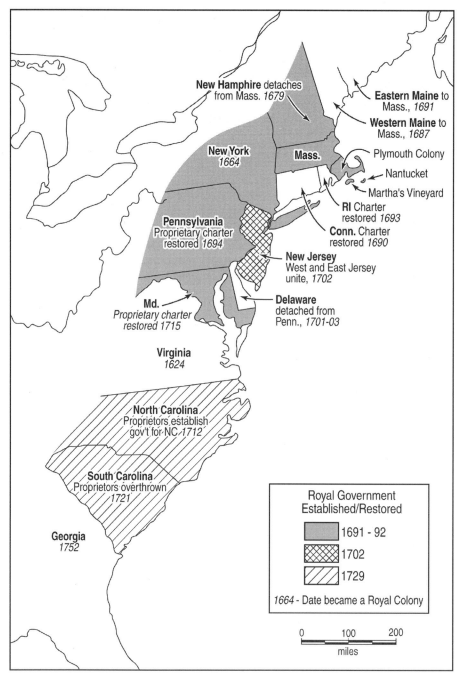

Figure 9.3. Aftermath of the Glorious Revolution: American political geography, 1690–1730.

the tax burden from English elites to the English masses and thereby effected a regressive redistribution of the nation's income. Over the next two decades, excise taxes on consumption rose from 30 percent of net government revenues to 55 percent. Simultaneously, land taxes fell from 40 percent of national revenues to 16 percent while customs duties fluctuated between 20 and 25 percent (Brewer 1990: 97–99). Walpole's reforms of 1722 further diminished the effects of tariff barriers on trade. Over the next two decades, the intake from customs duties dropped precipitously, falling from £1 million to half a million in the 1740s. Freed at last from the constraints of wartime finance, liberal Whigs set England on the path toward freer trade abroad and class power at home (on tariffs generally, see Wilson 1965: 238–64).

In theory, liberalism offers lofty sentiments on behalf of liberty, freedom, and government restraint; in practice, however, it served the grubbier interests of English elites, freer trade, social stability, and political corruption. These were as much a part of Locke's legacy as his vaunted social contract and his paean to individualism, and they could not help but have an impact on England's colonial policy after 1688. But just as the graduate student typically exaggerates the style and manners of his or her major professor—occasionally to the latter's advantage—the colonies would come to represent a rather less tawdry caricature of English liberalism.

Liberal Geographies and the Colonies

"In America, as in England," Craven (1968: 247) has written, "the full meaning of the great revolution [of 1688] . . . , whether for the development of imperial policy or for the institutional life of the colonies, waited on time for clarification." With Crown and Parliament preoccupied almost continuously until 1713 by war with Louis XIV of France, colonial affairs were handed off to the newly established Board of Trade. Subordinate to the king and Privy Council, the board consisted of eight appointed members, John Locke being the most famous of them. One of the first tasks undertaken by the board involved sharpening the lines of governance. Henceforth, while the territorial integrity of the various colonies would be maintained, all colonial governors were to be appointed by the Crown or, in the case of the proprietary colonies of Pennsylvania, Carolina, and New Jersey, were subject to royal approval (Craven 1968: 255–61).

THE GREAT COMPACTION: CONSOLIDATING SETTLEMENT, DISPERSING PEOPLES

The new governors tended, on the whole, to be energetic and activist (a reflection, no doubt, of the board's preferences). They busied themselves by relocating the capitals in some of the colonies, approving the layouts of the new capital or other new towns, and generally promoting commerce and trade. These interventions, when combined with similar initiatives by proprietors and lower houses of the colonial assemblies, soon resulted in even more profound changes in American life and landscape. First, their actions severally and together greatly slowed the pace of frontier expansion. With westward expansion stalled after 1680, colonial settlement intensified and populations and economies were consolidated in areas already settled. In less than two generations, population density in the colonies more than tripled, rising from just three persons per square mile of settled area in 1675 to over ten by 1720. Meanwhile, the pace of frontier expansion plummeted, falling from nearly 3 percent per annum before 1675 to less than 1.4 percent between 1675 and 1720. Slow-moving frontiers were the rule between 1700 and 1720, save in Pennsylvania and the lightly settled backcountry (figure 9.4).

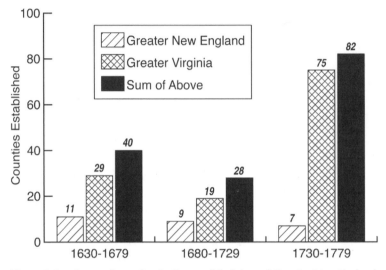

Figure 9.4.   County formation in Greater Virginia and Greater New England.

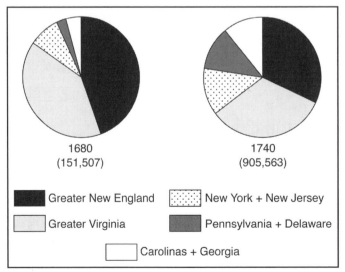

Figure 9.5.   The dispersion of population in the mainland colonies, 1680 and 1740.

The ascension of liberalism was also confirmed by the continuing dispersion of populations among the mainland colonies (figure 9.5). The demographic dominance of greater Virginia and greater New England was soon contested by the colonization of Pennsylvania and Carolina, by rapid growth there and in New York, and by their preferential treatment by the Board of Trade. The older colonies' share of the mainland population fell precipitously, dropping from 90 percent of all mainland colonists in the late seventeenth century to about 66 percent by 1740. With liberalism in the saddle, geographies were redesigned so as to reflect new commitments to production and commerce. In short order, organic republican geographies were set aside. The republican imperative of spatial expansion was appreciably weakened, and, to expedite the flow of commerce, regional economies were intensified and consolidated. Concurrently, the republican principle of demographic concentration was abandoned and, on behalf of a greater range and variety of staple commodities, colonial populations were dispersed into the more recently established middle colonies and the Carolinas.

THE INSTRUMENTS OF LIBERALISM: THE ENDEARMENT OF LAND

The liberal (or protoliberal) reconstruction of Anglo-American economic space hinged largely, though not exclusively, on the restructuring of land and labor markets. With respect to American markets in land, the liberal artifice contrived to impose land scarcity upon older regions that were otherwise endowed with an overabundance of land. The logic was impeccable and perhaps too clever by half. The intention was to boost the price of land, however artificially, in greater Virginia and greater New England but not elsewhere on the mainland; the regional differentials in land prices were then permitted to work their magic, by slowing the pace of expansion in these older regions while diverting the flow of new settlers toward cheaper lands in newer regions.

In the Chesapeake, this artificial and discriminatory strategy was implemented by abolishing the head rights system and regularizing the collection of annual quitrents on real property. The first victim in the Chesapeake land system was the generous practice that gave away land to immigrants in the form of head rights. This system of land distribution was repealed or allowed to lapse by 1700. Henceforth, land had to be acquired either from the government at the rate of five shillings per fifty acres in Virginia and fifty to one hundred pounds of tobacco per fifty acres in Maryland (the sterling equivalent of four shillings, two pence to eight shillings, four pence) or on the private market at prices that were several times higher (Harris 1953: 245–46, 248–49). Having demolished the head rights system, the authorities in Virginia and Maryland turned to quitrents on real property. These rents, which were payable annually to the governor or proprietor, were collected with more regularity and efficiency after 1696. In Virginia, the establishment of rent rolls and regular collection resulted in a quadrupling of quitrent revenues between 1684 and 1715; concurrently, Maryland increased the quitrent on fifty acres by 60 percent (Bond 1919: 234–35; Harris 1953: 218). Yet even as the Chesapeake colonies tightened their land systems and boosted land prices and quitrents, the remaining colonies outside New England continued to award head rights to immigrants and to levy lower quitrents—all of which had the discriminatory effects of diverting immigrants to and dispersing colonial populations among these younger colonies (Harris 1953: 218; Bond 1919: 255). Such were the geographical consequences of a dear-land policy in one region and a cheap-land policy in all of the rest save, of course, for New England, which presented unique sorts of problems for an emergent liberal regime.

In New England, where the head rights system was never employed, liberals deployed a rather different spatial strategy to moderate the pace of population growth and frontier expansion. Recall that New England was the only region on the mainland in which the rate of frontier expansion increased between 1675 and 1700. That rate was cut in half, however, during the succeeding two decades. The post-1700 collapse of the frontier cannot be explained by population pressure and land scarcity for the simple reason that not even a third of the area settled by 1790 was occupied as of 1720. Nor could the blame be placed on Indian hostilities or a remarkable recovery of patriarchal authority. The key to the deceleration of New England's frontier, as in the Chesapeake, is to be found in a restructuring of the land system.

Throughout most of the seventeenth century, the New England colonies granted land to proprietors who were willing and able to establish a town. While towns varied in size, anywhere from five square miles to over one hundred; the proprietors typically distributed the land among the initial inhabitants with a measure of rough equality. Some towns admitted new inhabitants, though the proprietors generally restricted their access to common lands and waste (Harris 1953: 273–88). In others, the children and grandchildren of the founders were forced to move out and to establish new towns on the frontier. As population grew and the pace of town founding accelerated, the newer towns tended to be smaller in size. In Connecticut, for example, the area of the average new town established after 1675 fell by nearly 40 percent—from 106 square miles for towns founded before that date to 65 square miles for those established between 1686 and 1734 (Lemon 1984: 108).

While the shrinking size of Connecticut's new towns served as a brake on settlement expansion, even more powerful changes were at work. As Richard Bushman (1967) has shown, Connecticut's land system was radically revised between 1685 and 1705. Under the new rules, older towns were no longer required as of 1685 to provide land to newcomers or to the sons of town inhabitants; nor were the towns established thereafter. Moreover, the new rules conferred the title of new town lands upon the proprietors named in the town's patent, and they were free to sell or lease it at market prices (Bushman 1967: 46–103). Connecticut's imposition of land scarcity had several immediate consequences: land was concentrated in the hands of town elites, land speculation became rampant, land prices spiraled upward; tenancy increased, and the bubble of settlement expansion burst. Worse, in the two decades after 1690, emigrants leaving New England exceeded immigrants arriving by at least twenty thousand, and probably more. In a few strokes, the application of a liberal policy of land scarcity in New England had managed to curtail the region's expansion and to redistribute its peoples among the colonies to the south.

All this liberal tinkering with colonial land systems produced the desired effects in greater Virginia and greater New England. In these regions, liberal policies created a vast private market in landed property, raised sharply the prices for land, constricted opportunities for social mobility, slowed the pace of frontier expansion, and, in the name of dispersion, fostered outmigration from these regions into other colonies where land was available on more generous terms. For the old Commonwealthmen who were still alive in 1700, these outcomes were painful reminders of the more virtuous world that had been lost.

THE INSTRUMENTS OF LIBERALISM: REFORMING COLONIAL MARKETING SYSTEMS

The reformers were not finished, however. Having liberalized the land systems in the Chesapeake and New England, they turned their attention to reforms in colonial marketing systems that would promote greater efficiencies in the flows of colonial trade and commerce. The tobacco trade of the Chesapeake was the object of their most vigorous and far-reaching reforms. In the 1690s, orders were given to abandon the old ramshackle capitals of Jamestown in Virginia and St. Mary's City in Maryland and replace them with the new cities of Williamsburg and Annapolis, replete with their ordered plan and symmetrical streets and buildings. Soon after, the members of England's newly formed Board of Trade insisted on the creation of new towns where few had existed before. These declarations were followed by a series of acts of the provincial assemblies authorizing the creation of scores of new towns throughout the tidewater region (figure 9.6). These came not a moment to soon for English travelers who never tired of pointing out how scattered—and barbaric—the lives of Chesapeake planters were. To be sure, these new towns would help to remedy some of the perceived "deficiencies" in Chesapeake cultural geography, but liberal planners had other goals in mind. Above all, they envisioned a network of urban places which would serve as an instrument for effecting improvements in the conduct of the trade and commerce in tobacco (Rainbolt 1969; Earle 1992: 88–106).

The principal problem with settlements as thinly dispersed as those of the Chesapeake was the costly inefficiencies of the region's marketing system. In the absence of central places for assembling tobacco in advance of the arrival of the tobacco fleet in late autumn, captains were forced to spend months in the Chesapeake, plying their vessels up and down the estuaries, gathering tobacco here and selling goods until they had emptied their holds of the one and filled them with the other—all the while bearing the high costs of operating their vessels. The new towns, with their gaggle of merchants, eliminated these costly maneuvers and greatly expedited the turnaround of the tobacco fleet. By assembling the local tobacco crop in advance of the fleet, a town with eight to ten merchants could collect most of the tobacco produced in a typical estuary—on the order of two thousand hogsheads of tobacco at four hundred pounds each—and that amount (roughly equal to five hundred shipping tons) would fill the better portion of a vessel in the tobacco fleet and speed it on its way. While many of these towns never materialized, others managed to

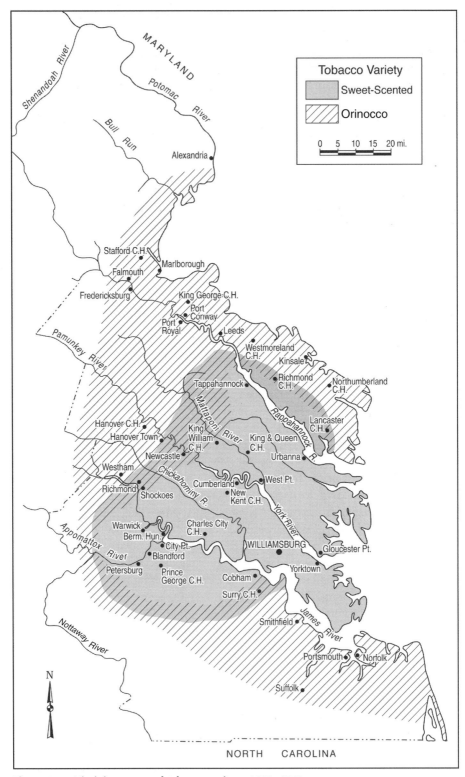

Figure 9.6.   Virginia towns and tobacco regions, 1680–1740.

prosper by attracting a couple hundred residents, accelerating turnaround time, reducing the freight rates for tobacco, and increasing the productivity of the Chesapeake marketing system.

The liberalization of the Chesapeake trade also advanced on other fronts. Of greatest moment was the official union of Scotland with England in 1707. The Act of Union opened up important new markets for tobacco planters and initiated a major restructuring in the regional trading system. Once in the empire, Glasgow merchants quickly capitalized on the lively French demand for snuff (powdered and perfumed tobacco)—a taste acquired, ironically enough, because of war with the English and the French success in capturing English vessels laden with tobacco. With the return of peace in 1713, Scottish merchants emerged as the principal middlemen between Chesapeake tobacco planters and French consumers (Price 1973). Factors or agents of Scottish trading houses were dispatched to the Chesapeake and instructed to purchase large supplies of orinocco tobacco (the lesser and cheaper of the two main varieties of tobacco) from the planters of southern Maryland, the Northern Neck, and the Southside of the James. The Scottish trade expanded rapidly; between 1708 and 1722, Scottish imports of Chesapeake tobacco increased sixfold (from about one million to six million pounds) (figure 9.7; Price 1954: 180). As this new market expanded, the tobacco coast subdivided into two main producing regions: in the center, the sweet-scented region of the Virginia tidewater, which supplied high-quality leaf for pipe smoking; and on the edges, the orinocco region, which supplied the raw leaf for snuff and cheaper blends. On the outskirts of these two regions was a third consisting mainly of marginal producers who resided nearer the head of the bay, on the Eastern Shore, and in the ill-drained areas around Norfolk. This roughly concentric zonation of regional specialization was something new in the Chesapeake, as, indeed, were the Scottish factors, the French market, and the policies of trade liberalization that had prompted this partitioning of economic space.

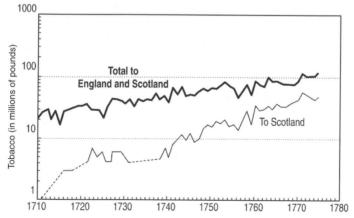

Figure 9.7.   Tobacco exports from the Chesapeake to England and Scotland, 1710–1775.

NO POLICY IS ALSO A POLICY: "SALUTARY NEGLECT" AND THE FREEDOM OF TRADE

The fetters on colonial commerce were greatly relaxed after the Glorious Revolution. Unlike the English, Americans were not burdened with high tariffs that were necessary to finance the French wars. Americans were allowed to trade with fewer restrictions and to drift ever closer to the Lockean ideal of free trade. This drift can be explained by three factors: the nonchalant and lax application of the Navigation Acts by English authorities; the reluctance or outright refusal of colonial traders to adhere to these acts, and, somewhat later, to the Whigs' indifference toward colonial behavior so long as tranquility prevailed.

Even when a conscientious administrator such as Maurice Birchfield sought to apply the Navigation Acts in America, he "encountered one of the basic truths of the customs officers situation: obstruction, not cooperation, was usually to be expected from the local colonial authorities, while in particular the provincial courts and legal apparatus would be employed to the full to delay and frustrate the enforcement of undesirable regulations" (stonewalling, it seems, is an ancient American art; quoted in Barrow 1967: 87). Unable to trust the provincial courts, denied in most cases access to Admiralty Court, and owing to the impracticality of shifting cases to English jurisdiction, colonial customs officials merely nipped at the heels of the increasing freedoms of colonial trade and the willful violations of mercantilist statutes. Nor were laments such as Birchfield's of much interest to the Whig oligarchy back in England. When, for example, the need to ensure admiralty jurisdiction in the colonies came before the Privy Council in 1719, it referred the request to a legal expert who suggested an act of Parliament, "but the whole matter thereafter was put aside and forgotten for forty or more years" (Barrow 1967: 89).

Sir Robert and the Whigs were committed to two principles: peace and commerce.

> To these aims the colonies could best contribute by creating no new problems and by cooperating voluntarily in the advancement of the motherland. To keep the colonies content required a policy of appeasement, not of coercion. . . . The Whig leaders were quite impartial in their adherence to the creed that well enough should be left alone. Colonial administrative details were only erratically of concern to them, so little was accomplished in that area. *"Salutary neglect" was not an accident but a precise policy.* (Barrow 1967: 116; italics added)

For all practical purpose, Whig colonial policy was the next best thing to laissez-faire and free trade. With Whig MPs busying themselves in corruption and affairs of state, colonial merchants were left to pursue certain illegalities of their own. They violated the spirit if not always the letter of the Navigation Acts of 1651, 1660, and 1672 by exploiting certain loopholes in these statutes. While these protectionist acts had attempted to rope off colonial commerce for the purpose of channeling trade through English ports, these laws hardly touched on the American trade with foreign colonies. Americans could export with impunity to Spanish, French, and Dutch possessions in the West Indies. But imports from these islands were more problematic. Aside from surplus slaves, the islands' only saleable commodities consisted of sugar and molasses and these were dutiable goods under the Navigation Acts. While it is clear that many American merchants circumvented these legal niceties by dealing in foreign sugar and molasses smuggled into the mainland, the magnitude of American smuggling will never be known with any precision. Thus far, much of the attention of historians on the underground economy has focused on the smuggling of molasses into Massachusetts following the Molasses Act of 1733. Yet even greater opportunities for smuggling may have been present in the provisions trade from the mainland colonies to the West Indies (McCusker and Menard 1985).

THE WEST INDIAN TRADE: LAW OR ORDERS?

The West Indian trade expanded rapidly with the recovery of the sugar economy in the Caribbean after the depression of the 1680s and 1690s. In the course of their recovery, sugar producers of every nationality had become so specialized and so large in scale that they were compelled to rely on provisions from the British colonies on the mainland in order to feed their slaves and to provide the materials for making barrels and kegs for sugar and molasses. American merchants who delivered these commodities to Spanish and French islands as well as to English ones stood to make substantial profits, and the response was proportionate (figure 9.8A and 9.8B). They dispatched corn from South Carolina; corn, pork, beef, some flour, staves, hoops, and shingles from the margins of the Chesapeake, mainly via the youthful port of Norfolk; corn and flour from Philadelphia's hinterland inland and in the lower Delaware Valley and upper Chesapeake; the same from New York City's hinterland up the Hudson River; and salted fish and all manner of imported goods from Boston, America's wholesaling center. In return, the American traders acquired sugar, molasses (for colonial rum distilleries), and, more rarely after 1700, surplus slaves (among others, Earle 1992: 88–152; Pares 1956).

The West Indian trade was large. The legal trade alone amounted to 28 percent of total annual exports from the mainland in the early decades of the eighteenth century. But if the West Indian trade was large, the typical lading in the trade was quite small—a consideration that held certain advantages for smuggling interests. The bulk of the trade was conducted on small vessels capable of carrying perhaps a month's worth of provisions and supplies. Anything more would have rotted in the tropical sun and humidity. The cargo of a typical vessel, in this case from Virginia, might consist of one thousand bushels of corn, one hundred barrels of flour, six to eight barrels of beeswax, forty to forty-five barrels of pork, white oak staves, pine boards, and tar. With mixed cargoes such as these, sloops and schooners departed from the mainland ports of Boston, New York, Philadelphia, Norfolk, and Charles Town and sailed toward targets of opportunity identified by the latest intelligence. But the risks were large. A captain who arrived at an island recently supplied by another vessel soon discovered that the market was completely glutted; he was then forced to sail to another island where he could unload his cargo before the weather

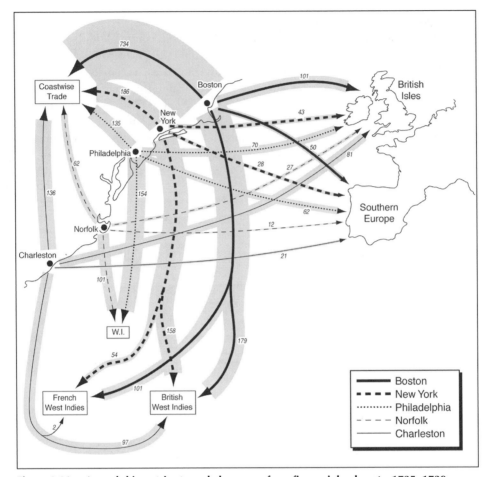

Figure 9.8A.   Annual ship entries to and clearances from five mainland ports, 1735–1739.

Notes: The Philadelphia figures represent an annual average for the period 1735–1739; the other ports use data for the old-style year of 1737–1738, beginning on March 25. Four trade regions (the British Isles, Southern Europe, the West Indies, and the Coastwise trade) account for most of the entries and clearances from these port regions: for Boston, 1,165 of 1,237 (94.2 percent); for New York, 469 of 482 (97.3 percent); for Philadelphia, 421 of 421 (100 percent); for Charles Town, 346 of 367 (94.3 percent); and for Hampton, 200 of 200 (100 percent).
Sources: Steele 1986: 288, 294, 298, 301; *Historical Statistics* 1975, 2: 1181.

spoiled his profits. With the entire venture at risk at this point, it was the wise captain who set aside law and sold his cargo for whatever he could get (even foreign sugar and molasses) and to whomever would buy—English preferably, but French, Spanish, or Dutch would do in the pinch.

THE WEST INDIAN TRADE: INTERDEPENDENCE AND THE PATH TOWARD REGIONAL SPECIALIZATION

Setting aside the loopholes and illegalities of the West Indian trade, one would be hard-pressed to find a better working model of the liberal paradigm of free trade,

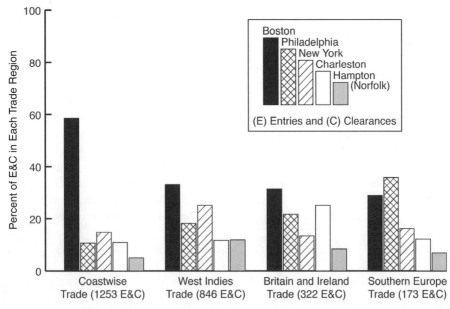

Figure 9.8B.   Annual shipping flows between five mainland ports and their principal trading regions, 1735–1739.

Sources: See figure 9.8A.

economic interdependence, and regional specialization. The results were stunning indeed. According to James Henretta's accounting, the lawful portion of the West Indies' trade yielded the mainland colonies a surplus of £2 million sterling over the period from 1698 to 1717 (table 9.1). In earlier times, the mainland exports to the islands were modest in volume, and most of the trade was conducted in New England vessels. By 1717, however, West Indian exports had risen to 28 percent of the

Table 9.1.   Imperial Balance of Payments (in millions of constant pounds sterling, 1700–1702)

Region	Commodity Exports	Imports from England	Shipping and Marketing Fees	Capital Costs Slaves	Bullion or Credit: Flow	(Must be zero)
West Indies	12.7	− 5.9	− 2.0	− 2.4	− 1.2	0
Southern mainland colonies	4.4	− 2.8	0	− 1.3	0	0
Northern mainland colonies	2.7	− 2.4	0	0	0	0
England and Wales	11.1	—	− 17.8	2.8	1.2	0

Sources: These estimates by James Henretta are based on the work of Curtis Nettels, *The Money Supply of the American Colonies before 1720* (1934: 49–85).
Notes: As Henretta (1973) admits, these are rough estimates of the balance of payments. They are deficient in two respects: their neglect of invisible earnings (mainly shipping services) in the mainland colonies, especially New England; their oversight of the coastwise trade. These deficiencies introduce a downward bias in the estimates of colonial earnings.

mainland's total exports (the rest going to England and Scotland) (Henretta 1973: 245–49). In Barbados, perhaps the most productive of the sugar islands and the jewel in England's American crown, four of every ten ships arriving in 1700 originated in mainland ports. Nearly four decades later (1737–1738), the ratio had risen to five of every ten. In 1700, Massachusetts led the way in the Barbadian trade with 112 entries and 60 percent of the North American arrivals. The advantages of Massachusetts in the coastal trade were considerable, thanks in large measure to a half-century head start, but its position was not impregnable. By 1737–1738, the entries from Massachusetts had slipped into a tie with the combined entries from Virginia and Pennsylvania (Steele 1986: 284–85). New York and South Carolina lagged behind somewhat, perhaps because the former was more engaged in an illicit trade with the Dutch colonies in Curaçao and Surinam, while the latter was rapidly converting its economy from provisions to the production of rice for European markets (figures 9.9A and 9.9B).

The geographical impacts of the West Indian and coastwise trades were most apparent in the seats of transmission—the entrepôts of Boston, Newport, New York, Philadelphia, Norfolk, and Charles Town (figure 9.10). The populations of Boston and Philadelphia quadrupled in size between the 1680s and 1741; New York, Newport, and Charles Town tripled their numbers; and Norfolk rose from obscurity to several thousand persons by midcentury (Steele 1986: 294).

For the merchants and shippers in these ports, there was as much to do at home as in their maritime forelands in the West Indies. Their principal task involved nurturing and then serving nearby hinterlands of primary production or, in their absence (as was the case in Boston and Newport), forging maritime linkages with farmers and merchants in other colonies and connecting them with coastwise and West Indian markets. With regard to the foreland trade, Bostonians had long enjoyed a reputation for turning adversity to good account. Stuck in a place where fertility was measured in terms of children and piety rather than soil quality, Bostonians gathered what they could from sea (mostly cod) and forest (timber), built ships, and offered their mercantile services and ships to all takers. They were legendary for sending their vessels where others would not go—into the smaller estuaries of the Chesapeake or the shifting shoals and channels inside the Outer Banks—selling imported European goods in exchange for local produce, hauling it to markets in the West Indies, and returning home laden with molasses (a trade that brought £5,500 of legal imports into New England in the 1730s) for the city's distilleries to turn into rum (Barrow 1967: 134–37).

But while Yankee traders were legendary for their ingenuity, they were not universally loved by their customers—a point made unambiguously in 1739 by the Virginian William Byrd in his advisory to Norfolk merchants. Buying Maryland wheat, he warned, will leave much Virginia wheat unsold; worse, it will "bring in the New England Men again amongst us, who will send a great many West Indize Commoditys . . . and furnish us with Wine for our Wheat. . . . These must be the Effects of our wheat being left on our Hands . . . [better] to truck it for what we want and have those Commoditys from Forreigners" ("Letters" 1928: 359).

Bostonians might have worried over such slights had they not been so busy

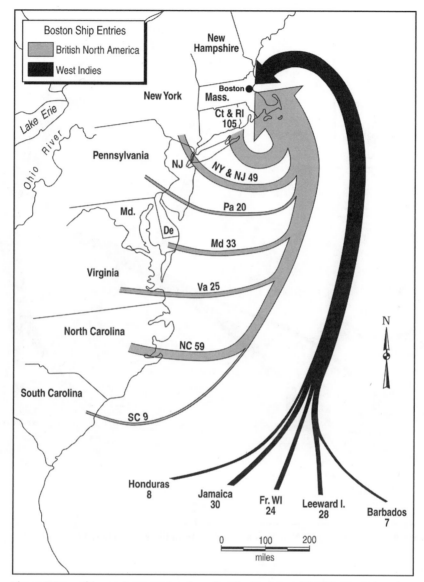

Figure 9.9A.   Ship entries to Boston from the West Indies and British North America, 1737–1738.

Sources: See figure 9.8A.

making money. Using their profits from the West Indian and coastal trades, the city's merchants financed a spectacular expansion in shipbuilding between 1698 and 1714; in that short span, the Massachusetts fleet increased by over sixfold, from 171 vessels to over 1,100 (Bailyn and Bailyn 1959). And this does not count the additional tonnage constructed for merchants and shippers in the other colonies. Thanks to liberalism and a bit of illegality, business was good indeed.

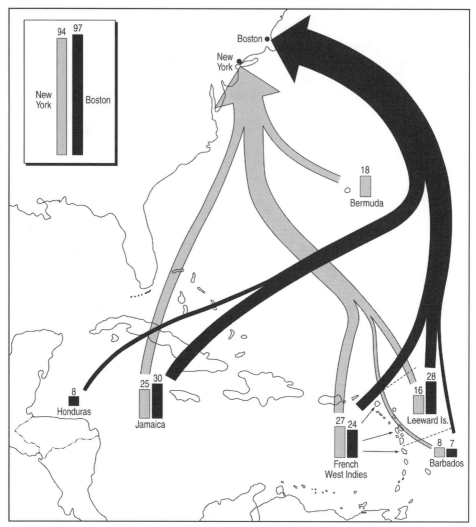

Figure 9.9B.   Ship entries to New York and Boston from the West Indies, 1737–1738.

Sources: See figure 9.8A.

Boston's maritime foreland was an unconventional way to build a regional economy; but so, too, were the Chesapeake's paltry little towns and their miniscule
hinterlands or Puritan New England's involuted agrarian villages and their subsistence production. Other cities along the seaboard followed the more conventional
path of carving out hinterlands from the agricultural areas surrounding them. In
Philadelphia, merchants assembled corn and flour from the small farms in southeastern Pennsylvania, the lower Delaware, and the upper Chesapeake. The merchants
of Norfolk served an even more eclectic hinterland; they gathered corn, pork, and
beef from planters on the Southside of the James; staves, hoops, shingles, and tar

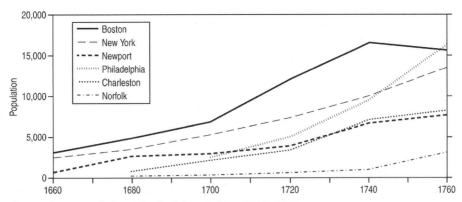

Figure 9.10.   Populations of colonial port cities, 1660–1760.

Sources: Steele 1986: 294; Earle 1992: 118–20.

from residents in and near the Great Dismal Swamp to the south of the city; and wheat and corn from the eastern shore and upper bay. New York's hinterland centered mainly on the Hudson Valley and the wheat, corn and livestock that flowed from the valley's productive estates; elsewhere the city's hinterland was squeezed by Boston and Philadelphia, the former encroaching on the trade of eastern Jersey and Long Island Sound, the latter on western Jersey (Steele 1986: 66–77). As for Charles Town, the city's merchants extended the provisions trade into the inner coastal plain and piedmont, but the real action lay elsewhere—in the production and marketing of wet rice on and from the large slave plantations that had arisen in the wetlands of the Low Country. It was rice that made rich men even richer.

When economists tire of using Robinson Crusoe's island as their model of a laissez-faire economy, the American colonies, circa 1680–1740, offer an abundance of fresh material—not to mention empirical evidence for the splendors (and the horrors)—of an unfettered market economy. One of the splendors of this liberalized economy was surely the speed at which such a vast space was reconstituted into a functioning system of highly specialized and interdependent regional economies. In this regard, the Whig policy of negligence exerted truly salutary effects on colonial economies and geographies. In just six decades, the Atlantic Seaboard of North American was transformed from just two main regions (Greater Virginia and Greater New England) in the 1670s to a mosaic consisting of six or seven specialized regions as of 1740 (figure 9.11). If there was an epicenter for the fracturings of this mosaic, it was surely located somewhere within the Chesapeake region. Here in 1680 stood a region that was largely undifferentiated; nearly everyone planted tobacco, raised corn, and tended hogs. By 1740, after nearly a half century of economic liberty, this same area housed at least five distinctive economic regions. At the center was the tobacco coast with its two distinctive regions—a core specializing in the production of high-quality sweet-scented tobacco and marketing by planter-merchants; and a periphery specializing in the production of lower-quality Orinocco tobacco and marketing mainly by Scottish factors (Rutman and Rutman 1984b: 18–22). Three other regions had arisen as well on the hem of the Chesapeake—the first, which was located on the Southside of the James and served by Norfolk, specialized in diversified provisions and wood products; the second, which occupied the upper eastern shore of Maryland and fell within Philadelphia's orbit, specialized in wheat and corn; and the third, which took up most of the lower eastern shore, got what it could out of the wetland soil, mostly corn, and sold a portion of it to merchants from Norfolk or New England. One might easily add to this list a sixth region centered on the wheat and flax economy then emerging in the "back parts" of Virginia and Maryland. The scope of regional specialization within the Chesapeake invariably transformed the aggregate economy as well as landscapes. While tobacco continued to dominate the exports from Greater Virginia as a whole, the chief staple received stiff competition from grains, iron, livestock products, wood products, and so on. By 1733, these lesser commodities accounted for nearly a quarter of the exports of the increasingly misnomered "tobacco coast" (McCusker and Menard 1985: 132). Tobacco was no longer "our life and our all."

Specialized economic regions appeared elsewhere as well. Along the fertile stretches of the Connecticut and Hudson Valleys, farmers produced grain and cattle for local markets as well as the West Indian trade. Mixed farming for the market also made headway in the Jerseys and in southeastern Pennsylvania. While most of this farm output was retained at home for subsistence, as much as a quarter to a third of farm output in these more specialized regions seems to have entered into local and long-distance trade (Lemon 1972).

To the south of greater Virginia there were fewer enclaves of specialized commodity production by 1740. The most notable exception was, of course, the rice-producing districts nestled within the Low Country of South Carolina. Although this region shared with many others an emphasis on grain production, it was unlike these American counterparts in virtually every other respect. What set the Low Country apart was that it was, first and foremost, a hydraulic society. In their shaping of this unique society, planters and slaves introduced a series of sophisticated techniques for managing and regulating water flows for the production of wet rice in the wetland marshes and swamps of coastal Carolina. The system entailed vast amounts of capital for land and for slave labor. One had to be rich to begin with in order to ante up the funds for the five hundred acres and fifty slaves that were the prerequisites for entry into this expensive agrarian system. The risks of venturing such large sums of capital were likewise substantial, and rice planters who took the plunge fully expected certain assurances. Most critical was the prospect of an expanding market. This assurance was provided by the lively demands for Carolina's high-quality, long-grain rice emanating from consumers in England as well as on the continent. Indeed the markets in southern Europe proved to be so good that in 1730 Parliament relaxed the Navigation Acts and permitted direct shipments of rice and other grains from the American colonies to Portugal, Spain, and the Mediterranean. Although Carolinians were the first to take advantage of these new trade provisions, they would not be the last; but that is a story for a later time.

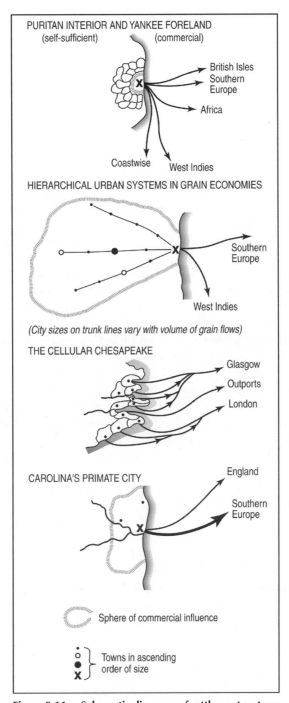

Figure 9.11.   Schematic diagrams of settlement systems in the British colonies of North America.

The Horrors of Liberalism: Labor and Inequality

Liberalism is at base an ideology of production; production, in turn, is premised on the resources of land, labor, and capital. And in land-rich America in the seventeenth century, the greatest of these was labor. For those of liberal persuasion, it was only natural that they would seek ways of economizing on this most scarce American resource.

Labor scarcity was always a problem in colonial America. For most of the seventeenth century, the American solution consisted of three elements: immigration, the institution of indentured servitude, and a generous land system that awarded land in exchange for the transportation of new colonists. This solution fell out of favor, however, as the century progressed. The climacteric for American labor arrived with the crisis of the 1680s and 1690s when, with incredible speed, the massive importation of slaves transformed the labor forces in the Chesapeake and the Carolinas. This transformation of American labor was not confined, however, to the so-called plantation economies producing tobacco or rice. Simultaneously in the incipient regions of commercial grain and livestock production, farmers tapped the labor of a growing pool of wage laborers—men who hired themselves out for the day, the season, or the year—and, in so doing, converted their family farms from subsistence to commercial operations.

The ramifications of slavery and the rise of rural wage labor cannot be underestimated since these extended far beyond the economics of production and shook at the very foundations of colonial society. In all of these commercial agrarian regions, opportunity and status henceforth came to depend on access to labor. While some families rose on the backs of slaves or wage laborers, the majority fell behind. For planters and farmers with land and labor, these were the best of times; for the rest, the growing numbers of slaves, laborers, and tenants, prospects were not nearly so good. For most Americans, the halcyon days of egalitarian opportunity was by the 1730s but a distant memory. In this harsher world, liberalism and the propertied elites that it sustained were firmly in command.

THE SOUTHERN SOLUTION: SLAVERY

The introduction of slavery on a massive scale was a mistake of massive proportions for Americans then as well as now. For the participants in the process, life would never be quite the same. It was in addition, however bloodstained the outcome, one of the principal components for liberalism's producer revolution.

Although slaves were first introduced in Virginia in 1619, the peculiar institution made surprisingly little headway over the next six decades, not even during the 1630s when tobacco prices collapsed or the 1640s when Caribbean sugar planters adopted slavery en masse. In the interim, Chesapeake tobacco planters continued to rely on indentured servants well into the 1670s when slaves constituted just 5 or 6 percent of the region's population. But beginning in the 1680s and continuing over the next two decades, slaves were imported in record numbers. In Virginia, slave numbers probably doubled between 1698 and 1708 (Craven 1968: 290). By the end of Walpole's administration (1742), the proportion of black slaves in the Chesapeake had risen to over 28 percent of the population (figure 9.12).

While slaves were increasing in number and proportion, the trade in indentured servants made an about-face. Fewer servants arrived in the Chesapeake after 1690, and the ones that did tended to be skilled artisans and craftsmen, and not the raw field laborers so typical of the seventeenth century. The transformation was swift indeed. In the 1680s servants outnumbered slaves by three to one in an Orinocco-producing parish of central Maryland; but in the very next decade, slaves outnumbered servants by five to one. By the 1730s the ratio had risen to twenty-one to one; by the 1740s to twenty-nine to one. While the timing of the switch from servant to slave labor varied from place to place, the process was largely completed by 1720 within the principal tobacco regions; at that point, slaves probably outnumbered servants by ten to one (Earle 1975: 49; Main 1982: 26).

Any explanation of this stunning transformation in the Chesapeake labor force must acknowledge several factors. First, the surge in slave imports began in the midst of the depression of the 1680s and continued amidst the slack economy that prevailed through 1715 or so. Net slave imports per decade increased from less than two thousand before 1680 to over seven thousand during the next three decades;

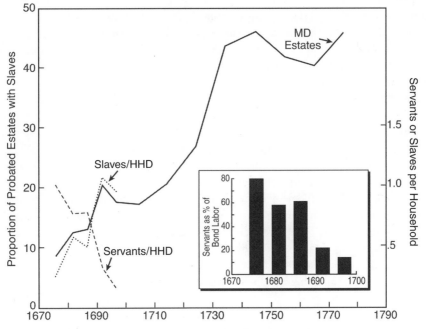

Figure 9.12.   Slaves and servants in Maryland probate inventories, 1670–1775.

Note: The scale for bond labor per household is on the right vertical axis.
Sources: Payne 1968; Sharer 1968.

the aggregate of net imports for the three decades before and after 1680 rose from nearly 4,800 to 25,700 (Galenson 1981: 216–17). Second, many though by no means all of these slaves were imported from the sugar islands that had suffered so acutely during the depression of the late seventeenth century. Third, the rising price of servants and the falling price of slaves worked in favor of slave acquisitions. The former probably reflects a shrinkage in the supply of servants owing to the decline of fertility and improved opportunities for upward mobility in England after 1650; the latter, an increase in slave supply attributable in part to the troubles in the West Indies and the liberalization of competition in the African slave trade in 1698 when the Royal African Company's monopoly on the African trade ran out (Menard 1977).

While the price differentials of servants and slaves go a long way in accounting for slavery's advantages on the supply side, they fall short with respect to the demand side. Aside from price, what advantages accrued to the Chesapeake planter who shifted from British servants to African and African American slaves? The first advantage had to do with social control. Servants had become a problem for the authorities and well-to-do planters. For them, the increasingly unruly and rebellious behavior of former servants—Bacon's Rebellion being the prime case in point—represented a serious and continuing threat to social order (Morgan 1975). The second and more prosaic advantage had to do with agrarian innovation in the midst of the crisis of the 1680s and 1690s. Confronted by falling tobacco prices and profits, planters scurried about in search of ways to salvage their economy. Of the countless experimentations in agricultural reform conducted at the end of the seventeenth century, one—the innovation of recyclical shifting cultivation—proved to be more promising than the others. There was, however, one difficulty with this agrarian innovation. The economic advantages of this mobile agrarian system hinged almost entirely on the availability of a more permanent and reliable source of labor for the unending process of land clearance. But this was a difficulty that massive slave imports swiftly surmounted (Earle 1992: 258–99).

The innovative union of shifting cultivation and a permanent slave labor force was, in large measure, a response to the cumulating deficiencies in the prevailing methods of tobacco production in the Chesapeake colonies. These deficiencies, though increasingly obvious in the 1680s, had been obscured earlier by the fairly high price of tobacco. In these times nonetheless, tobacco planters were repeatedly confronted by the problem of soil exhaustion. When, after three or four years in tobacco, the fertility and productivity of soil began to decline, planters resorted to one of two solutions. The first of these relocated tobacco production to a new parcel of land as yields and soil fertility declined; land was used, exhausted, and then abandoned for fresher lands on the expanding frontier. The problem with this solution was that it entailed high and recurring costs for land clearance. The second and more common solution sought to restore the fertility of exhausted lands through crop rotations of tobacco, corn, and small grains and manuring with horse and cattle dung; in this case, arable lands were used again and again. Neither solution was entirely satisfactory, however: the first increased the costs of land clearance and contributed to overly rapid frontier expansion, the second resulted in declining yields and, in the case of manuring, a foul taste that lowered the quality and price of the tobacco leaf.

These problems were magnified in the 1680s when tobacco prices, having fallen well below a penny a pound, hit bottom. It was in these desperate times that tobacco planters devised and then diffused a third and more durable solution to the problem of soil exhaustion. Under the new system of land rotation, planters set aside the old solutions of crop rotation, manuring, or abandonment and instead recycled land once it was exhausted. When soil fertility began to decline on the three acres of tobacco land typically tended by each worker (usually after three or four years), the planter temporarily abandoned the "old field" and shifted tobacco onto a new parcel. The sequence of use and abandonment was repeated seven or eight times; in that interval of twenty to thirty years, a succession of grasses, shrubs, and trees colonized the old fields and restored the fertility of their soil. At this juncture, the planter revisited the eldest old field, deadened the trees, and planted tobacco once again. Three or four years hence, depending on the strength of the soil, operations were rotated onto the next eldest old field and so on *ad seriatim*. In this fashion, old, "worn-out" land was recycled; soil fertility, productivity, and profits were maintained; and the needs for manure, crop rotations, or frontier expansion were largely eliminated.

This sustainable agroecological system was not, however, without its problems. The first, and the more trivial, was that it enjoyed a bad press. The transient and untidy landscape that it produced invited the scorn and relentless criticism of English visitors who never quite understood the ecological functions of land rotation. Seeing the worst in disheveled old fields and dilapidated tobacco houses in motion, they tarred the reputations of planters and slaves alike with the brush of laziness and slovenliness unbecoming of Englishmen. Second, and far more serious, was the heavy demands that land rotation placed upon labor. Unlike the older system of continuous cultivation that could make due without servant labor once tobacco and corn lands had been cleared, the newer system of land rotation required a more reliable and continuous stream of labor because capital improvements in land were ephemeral. Under land rotation, tobacco land was repeatedly created (land clearing) and then destroyed (by the reversion to old fields). In an agrarian system of perpetual land clearance, a perpetual labor force had a decided advantage. Whereas an adult male slave was able to clear land eight times or more in a lifetime (even a short one), a servant was able to do so just twice during his term; slaves were, in other words, more than four times as productive as servants, all else being equal, under the new system of land rotation.

Slavery changed everything along the tobacco coast. Henceforth, fortune and fame depended on having the capital with which to buy slaves. Those with capital and a bit of luck could aspire to the ranks of the middling planters and, before the 1730s, perhaps even the region's elite; those without capital found themselves boxed into the status of tenants or pushed out to new regions. Tenancy, which had been a temporary status for most of the seventeenth century, was more nearly a permanent status after 1700. In the orinocco belt, as many as a third of the households were tenants as early as 1707; by the 1740s, the fraction had risen to nearly half (Earle 1975; Clemens 1980; Stiverson 1977; Papenfuse 1972).

These unhappy changes in Chesapeake society were promptly reflected in rising levels of inequality in income and wealth. Inequalities were firmly established in Virginia's sweet-scented core as early as 1720. In Middlesex County, for example, 61.5 percent of the county's inventoried wealth was in the hands of just 6 percent of the decedents (Rutman and Rutman 1984b: 120, 129–30). Similar levels of inequality prevailed among orinocco producers. In five Maryland counties, the richest 10 percent of the decedents between 1713 and 1719 garnered 64 percent of the inventoried wealth—up from 43 percent for the pre-1683 inventories (Main 1982: 55). The inventories of one central Maryland parish offer a hint as to how remarkably unrelieved immizeration was in these liberal years. Over the long haul in All Hallows, there was one exception to the rule of compensating equality. The singular exception to this rule of rising inequality during hard economic times and diminishing inequality during good times came in the span between 1705 and 1733. In that period, through good times and bad, inequality steadfastly increased and the rich became even richer. At the end of these three decades, with almost 60 percent of the wealth in the hands of the Chesapeake's richest 10 percent, the transit of inequality had reached its apogee.

And with wealth came power. The stunning concentration of wealth between 1680 and 1740 provided the foundation for a political elite that would span several generations. Thus it was that in "the decades preceding the war for independence no less than 70 percent of the 110 leaders of the Virginia House of Burgesses were drawn from families resident in Virginia before 1690" (Henretta 1973: 91). It was these ancestral families who, in the embrace of liberalism and its sometimes Faustian bargains, made their fortunes on slavery, amassed political power, crystallized social hierarchy, and, in due course, assured themselves and their descendants both place and fortune.

The introduction of slavery on a massive scale thoroughly altered life and landscape along the tobacco coast. In the course of a half a century, slaves accounted for a third of the region's population. In many locales, tenants constituted a third or more of the white households in many locales; landowners without slaves, another third; and slaveholding landowners, the remainder. In this increasingly stratified society, a tiny elite, no more than a tenth of all households, commanded enormous influence as well as over 60 percent of the region's wealth. Most of what was left was in the possession of another minority—the 20 percent who, as middling planters, owned land and a small number of slaves.

It was the large planters with their scores of slaves and thousands of acres who were increasingly responsible for running the society, for constructing the impressive Georgian mansions that adorned their plantations, for providing the political leaders who stood for election to the assemblies of Virginia and Maryland, and, owing to their access to English and Scottish capital, for supplying the tissue of credit that connected local, provincial, and Atlantic economies (Isaac 1982; on the contribution of the broader electorate, see Kolp 1998). These men were hardly rustic agrarians; while much of their initial success can be attributed to the profits of an agrarian slave economy, their continuing prosperity hinged on finance and, more precisely, on the access to capital that slave collateral afforded. The crystallization of the Chesapeake elite by 1730 meant that the prospects of entering into the upper tier of wealth and society were slight indeed—even for middling planters who owned land and a handful of slaves. As for the lesser freeholders who did not own slaves, their best hope was for a rude sufficiency and luck enough to avert a downward slide into the oozing mass of the tenantry.

Slavery had equally potent impacts further south in the Carolina Low Country (figure 9.13). Settled in the 1680s around the nucleus of Charles Town, the colony of Carolina early on attracted men of capital, most notably Barbadian sugar planters and French Huguenots. Initially, they invested their funds in the Indian trade in deerskins and in the production and marketing of provisions for the West Indies. In the 1690s, however, more and more of their investment found its way into the production of wet rice using slave labor. Between 1700 and 1740, rice exports rose tenfold in the aggregate and by twelvefold on a per capita basis—from sixty-nine pounds per capita to nine hundred pounds (McCusker and Menard 1985: 176–77, 181). Slave imports kept pace. Net slave imports rose from 1,575 in the 1690s to 7,902 in the following decade. By the 1730s, gross imports were running at over two thousand per year. "As early as 1708, blacks outnumbered whites . . . ; by 1730 the ratio of blacks to whites stood at 2 to 1, by 1740 at 2.6 to 1" (McCusker and Menard 1985: 181). In some parts of the Low Country, the black majority made up

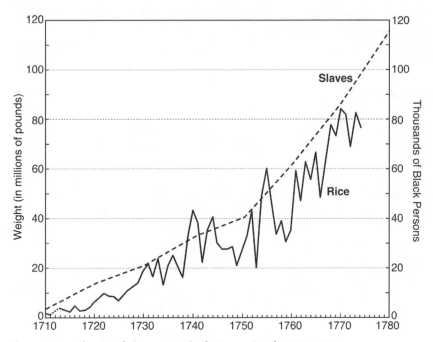

Figure 9.13. Slaves and rice exports in the Lower South, 1710–1780.
Source: Egnal 1998: 102.

90 percent of the population; the only whites in these districts were the families of the masters—who regularly left the fetid and deadly swamps in summer—and the plantation overseers (on South Carolina generally, see Chaplin 1993; Clowse 1971; Coclanis 1989; Wood 1974).

In the production of wet rice, slaves were indispensable (figure 9.14). Their labor was required for the endless round of tasks demanded by a hydraulic society. Slaves cleared the land; graded the surfaces for the paddy fields; and constructed the embankments, canals, freshwater ponds, sluices, and gates that channeled the flow of freshwater through the rice fields. Having constructed this artificial landscape, slaves then did the work of regulating the flow of water on the fields; doing the seeding, transplanting, weeding, harvesting, threshing, and barreling; and, in the off-season, maintaining this fragile complex and protecting it from the depredations of a subtropical environment.

Rice planting was big business. Entry was restricted to the very few who could afford, for starters, to join the ranks of the "five-hundred-acre planters" as well as the added costs of buying and maintaining fifty or more slaves. The costs were high, but so, too, were the rewards. When the economic historian Alice Hanson Jones (1980) finished compiling her list of the wealthiest men in the mainland colonies as of 1774, she found that nine of ten resided in the Carolina Low Country. Their wealth, which ranged from £6,891 to £32,700, made them among the wealthiest in the world and vastly wealthier (by sixtyfold or more) than the average American in 1774. South Carolinians were not unaccustomed, of course, to such opulence. Their hyperelite society, with its overwhelming black majority and its vast riches, had been firmly in place long before Walpole relinquished his post as prime minister and liberalism beat its first retreat.

THE NORTHERN SOLUTIONS: WAGE LABOR AND SUBSISTENCE

Liberalism had looked kindly on the elites of Greater Virginia and the Carolina Low Country, and it would be nearly as generous elsewhere. In the middle colonies, where the seasonality of agriculture rendered slavery unprofitable, the impacts of liberalization on regional labor markets and wealth distribution were equally significant, if less hyperbolic. The changes in the labor market in southeastern Pennsylvania are evident in the distribution of wealth between 1690 and 1760. While the inequalities of rural wealth were never so extreme as in the southern colonies, they were on the increase. The share of wealth held by the top 10 percent of all wealth holders rose from 23.8 percent in 1693 to 28.6 percent by 1730—and then hovered there until the 1780s and 1790s when it rose to 33 to 38 percent (Lemon and Nash 1968). These data put the best face on the deteriorating situation prior to 1750. Had the pre-1750 estimates included freemen as well as freeholders in the denominator, the results would have been even more unfavorable for equality.

The upward creep of inequality among rural Pennsylvanians was one of the inexorables that attended the growth of the West Indian trade, the commercialization

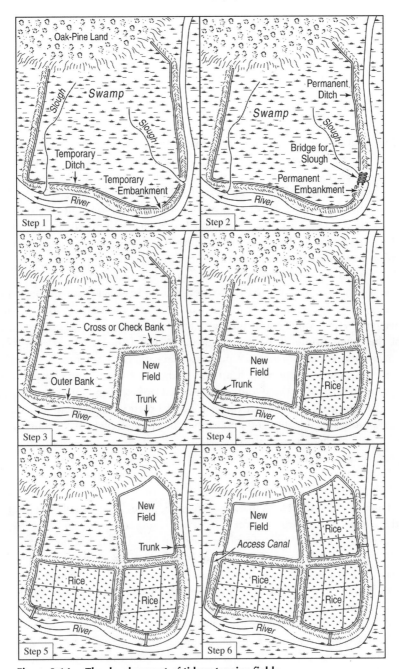

Figure 9.14.   The development of tidewater rice fields.

Source: Hilliard 1978: 106.

of mixed farming, and the reconfiguration of wage labor markets in rural Pennsylvania as well as in the mixed-farming economies of New Jersey and the Hudson Valley. As wheat and corn production expanded in response to the export market, farmers in these regions required seasonal supplies of labor. Wheat farmers needed additional labor in a single burst during the frantic two-week harvest in early summer. Corn farmers needed supplemental labor for planting and tillage from March through June. These needs were supplied by several sources: the growing numbers of rural laborers who hired out by the day or the month; the artisans and craftsmen who earned extra cash during the peak seasons; the sons who worked for their fathers. By midcentury, farmers in Chester County, Pennsylvania, were able to draw upon a substantial reservoir of rural labor. Most important were the "inmates" who lodged in the households of others. As early as 1715, inmates constituted 11 percent of the males in Chester County; by 1740, the proportion had risen to 13.5 percent. Farmers also mobilized the seasonal labor of their sons as well as local artisans, craftsmen, tenants, and croppers who set aside their normal duties in return for the very high wages that could be earned during the wheat harvest (Simler n.d.: table 1; Simler 1990).

Rural society soon reflected the critical role of seasonal labor in these mixed-farming regions. By the late 1750s, landowning farmers in rural Lancaster County in southeastern Pennsylvania constituted a minority (42 to 46 percent) of the taxpayers. As for the others, some 20 percent of taxpayers listed themselves as craftsmen, 15 percent as laborers, and 18 to 19 percent as tenant farmers or croppers (Lemon 1972: 94–96). Here, in the very heartland of the American "family farm," farmers understood that access to these sources of seasonal labor was the surest path to expansion and prosperity. They likewise understood that their interests were served neither by the promotion of equality and opportunity nor by too vigorous upward mobility. Better for them that their sources of labor were stable, reliable, abundant, and as cheap as could be expected.

The liberalization of rural markets and rural labor forces made lesser headway in rural New England. What is clear is that population continued to grow through natural increase; that local land markets tightened, prices rose, speculation flourished; that the expansionary surge between 1675 and 1700 collapsed; and that New England became a net exporter of population. In this turbid setting, opportunities dwindled and inequalities were magnified. In Hingham, Massachusetts, for example, the share of town wealth owned by the richest 10 percent of townsmen rose from less than 30 percent in 1700 to nearly 40 percent a half century later (Henretta 1973: 105). Although these proportions resemble those in the mixed-farming communities of rural Pennsylvania, the causes are quite different.

The emerging consensus among economic historians of New England is that commercial activity before 1750 was largely confined to the coastal cities and to areas endowed with fertile soil and good transportation (e.g., the Connecticut River Valley) or with valuable timber resources for the shipbuilding industry (e.g., New Hampshire watersheds). Elsewhere, in the rural towns in the interior of New England, most farmers clung to a subsistence economy which accommodated local exchanges of modest farm surpluses. Not until the 1750s and 1760s, in a society revitalized by the Great Awakening and the spirit of individual salvation, did the farmers in these "peaceable kingdoms" begin to integrate their farming operations into the commercial orbits of the coastal ports (Rothenberg 1981; Greene 1988: 74–77).

Liberalism, Toleration, and Colonial Diversity

The last, though not the least, of liberalism's initiatives was ethnoreligious toleration. Soon after liberals had risen to power, they sought to put out the fires of intolerance that had long threatened to consume England in a conflagration of sectarian division at home and English nationalism abroad. Led by Locke, the liberal reformers of the 1680s and 1690s were eager to temper the disputes then raging among protestant sectaries and, no less, to dampen the residual impulses of Cromwellian anglocentrism. The Toleration Act of 1689 served as the centerpiece of ethnoreligious reform. For all of its weaknesses, and despite its failure to embrace Roman Catholics and to eliminate sacramental tests and tithes for dissenters, the act "perhaps . . . achieved as much toleration, in that century, as was continuously practical" (Trevor-Roper 1992: 267–85).

The effects of this new spirit of toleration, however pinched and restrained, were most apparent in the migratory streams destined for the mainland colonies of British North America (figure 9.15A). Before 1680, these colonies were, with the exceptions of the Dutch in New York and a handful of Swedes in the Delaware Valley, mainly composed of British stock—mostly English with a smattering of Irish and Scots. Over the next two decades, the mainstream of British migrants was joined by tributary flows of African and African American slaves into the Chesapeake, Quakers and Welsh into Pennsylvania, and slaves and French protestants into South Carolina. But it was after 1700 that the floodgates of ethnic and religious diversity were thrown wide open. In Pennsylvania, the proprietor William Penn sought to attract new immigrants from the continent. Using promotional literature which promised emigrants land and religious freedom and enlisting the services of Benjamin Furley—a friend and correspondent of the English liberals Sidney and Locke—Penn's effort set in motion the migration of tens of thousands German protestants—Mennonites, Lutherans, and Calvinist Reformed—through Rotterdam on their way from their homes in the Rhine Valley. A bit later, Pennsylvania added Scots-Irish Presbyterians (after 1718) and German Dunkards (1725) to the ethnocultural mix. By 1725, Pennsylvania's diverse German community exceeded twenty thousand and constituted perhaps half of the population in the colony. While the governor's 1747 estimate that German speakers made up 60 percent of Pennsylvania's population is surely too large, the German population in some areas may have equaled or surpassed 60 percent (a fraction of one-third may be more accurate; Lemon 1972: 13–23; Bailyn 1986: 147, n. 40; Meinig 1986: 138–40).

The advantages of the "new immigration" soon dawned on Pennsylvania's southern neighbors. In the 1720s, Maryland officials also began to offer land on very

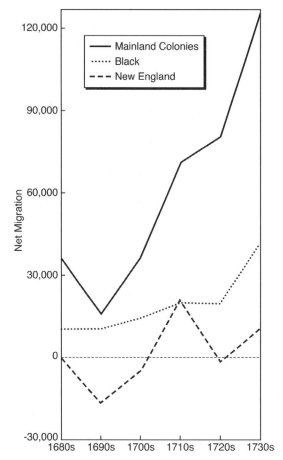

Figure 9.15A.   Net migration in British North America, 1680–1740.

Notes: New England was a net exporter in three of five decades—the exceptions, the 1710s and the 1730s. The black share of net migrants peaked in 1700 and dwindled steadily thereafter.

Source: Galenson 1981.

favorable terms for groups of settlers from Pennsylvania and Europe; these officials were less forthcoming, however, when it came to the expanding tenantry established on Maryland's tobacco coast. Immigrants also filtered south into the piedmont and Great Valley of Virginia, abetted in this case by the land speculations of wealthy Virginians anxious to realize a profit from settlement in the back country.

The "new" immigration and liberalism went hand in hand. As the liberal solvent of toleration ate away at the crumbling pillars of ethnocentric republican nationalism, England was reinvented. With Parliament and, later, the Whig oligarchy firmly in command of England's domestic polity, the nation opened its doors for Scottish union, for foreign immigration from the continent, and for a massive expansion of non-English peoples in the American colonies. The liberal principle of imperial diversity had at last trumped the republican principle of imperial homogeneity. The Commonwealth dream of an empire built and populated by "God's Englishmen" was, as they say, "history."

Following the leads of Pennsylvania and South Carolina, several other colonies adopted a promotional strategy of unrestricted immigration, and the impacts were swift and dramatic. In the first four decades of the eighteenth century, the mainland attracted not less than 310,000 immigrants of whom roughly 217,000 were white and mostly freemen and 94,000 were slaves from Africa or the West Indies (Galenson 1981: 212–218). Although immigrants represented a dwindling share of colonial population after the 1680s, the sheer numbers of immigrants arriving between 1700 and 1740 far exceeded those before or after 1780. The largest slew of white immigrants (some 196,000) entered the colonies between 1710 and 1740 in conjunction with the economic recovery that followed the War of the Spanish Succession. The cessation of hostilities on the continent and the promotional promises of cheap American land encouraged German immigrants to journey down the Rhine and across the Atlantic to British North America. In Pennsylvania alone, Germans numbered over twenty thousand in 1725, and not less than twenty thousand others arrived over the next fifteen years (Lemon 1972: 13–23, 236). And after 1718, Scots-Irish Presbyterians were added to the mix of English Quakers and German Mennonites, Lutherans, and Reformed Calvinists. Doubtless many of these immigrants into Pennsylvania eventually continued their journey southward into Maryland, Virginia, and North Carolina. Indeed, the overwhelming majority (some 83 percent) of the 196,000 white immigrants between 1710 and 1740 ended up in the middle colonies (51,974) and the Upper South (110,792 with the inclusion of North Carolina; 89,531 without) and, more precisely, on the back-country frontiers of these colonies.

Slave imports followed a somewhat different trajectory (figure 9.15B). Unlike white migration, which largely collapsed in the 1690s and did not fully recover its vigor for another decade, net slave imports quadrupled in the 1680s, doubled in the 1710s and 1720s, and doubled again in the 1730s and 1740s (table 9.2).

One estimate of net slave migration over this six-decade span points to the arrival of over 114,000 slaves with the majority (more than 80 percent) destined for Virginia and Maryland (68,000) and South Carolina (26,000). This rapid pace of net slave imports notwithstanding, white immigrants outnumbered slaves in most decades; the exceptions to white predominance arose in the depressions of the 1690s and 1740s when white migration collapsed under the weight of these recurrent crises in the transatlantic economy. The reciprocation of slave imports and white migration contributed mightily to the growth of population. Together with natural increase slave imports and white migration helped boost the population of the colonies from 210,000 in 1680 to 906,000 in 1740—a number that would have been smaller by one-third in the absence of white migration and slave imports (Galenson 1981: 212–18).

The Legacies of Liberalism, Whig Style

By the 1730s, the mainland colonies of British North America had been reconstructed in accordance with the principles of an emergent liberalism. It was liberalism

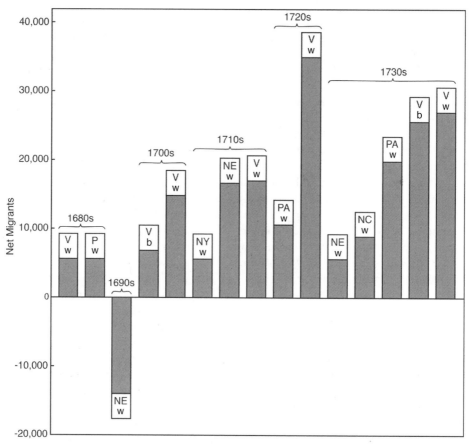

Figure 9.15B. Leading regions and races among net migrants in British North America, 1680–1740.

Notes: The uppercase abbreviations refer to general regions: *V,* Virginia; *P,* Pennsylvania; *NE,* New England; *NY,* New York; and *NC,* North Carolina. The lowercase abbreviations refer to race: *w,* white; *b,* black.
Source: Galenson 1981.

that was responsible for the policies of *"salutary neglect"* that had freed up trade and fostered regional specialization; for the principle of *toleration* that had opened the doors of the empire to ethnic and sectarian minorities; for the commitments to *spatial consolidation* that had promoted more efficient systems for marketing staple crops and to *demographic dispersion* that, owing to the liberal engineering of land scarcity in older colonies, had diverted migration flows into the middle colonies and the Lower South; and for the machinations of a *producer revolution* that liberalized American labor markets (through massive slave importations into the South and the pooling of rural wage labor in the middle colonies), expanded the export of colonial staple commodities, and, not least, concentrated income, wealth, and power in the hands of a small American elite. In this fashion, English liberalism implanted the seed that would, in due course, germinate into a new and distinctively American society, blossom into rebellion, and bear the fruit of a new nation.

Table 9.2.   Decennial Estimates of Net Slave Migration in the Mainland Colonies

Decade	New England	Middle Colonies	Chesapeake	North Carolina	Lower South	Net Total
1650–1660	63	−29	1,322			1,366
1660–1670	−306	−20	1,832	146		1,652
1670–1680	−12	401	1,707	73	186	2,355
1680–1690	300	491	7,259	95	1,368	9,512
1690–1700	397	412	7,738	103	892	9,542
1700–1710	382	1,344	10,747	477	1,575	14,525
1710–1720	568	2,514	6,616	2,110	7,902	19,710
1720–1730	925	1,142	6,376	2,927	7,599	18,969
1730–1740	623	1,322	29,109	4,015	6,854	41,923
1740–1750	44	293	47,262	7,001	5,385	59,985
1750–1760	−1,175	2,199	3,785	7,581	8,968	21,358
1760–1770	−799	−1,977	8,096	24,608	7,235	37,163
1770–1780	−4,599	−2,056	−19,136	1,765	7,390	−16,636
1650–1680	−255	351	4,871	314	186	5,467
1680–1740	3,195	7,225	67,845	9,632	26,190	114,087
1740–1780	−6,529	2,127	40,007	40,415	28,618	104,638

Note: Galenson's (1981) estimates of net slave migration are residuals remaining after estimates of the decennial natural increase in the population are deducted from total population at the end of a decade.
Source: Galenson 1981: 212–18.

CHAPTER 10

Imperial Geographies
THE REPUBLICAN RESTORATION, 1740s–1780s

Great Britain's Age of Empire dates from the fall of Walpole in 1742 to the Treaty of Paris in 1783. In this span, the nation set aside the liberal policies of the Whig oligarchy and lurched in a new, though not entirely unfamiliar, direction. In fast succession, ministers and parliaments demoted liberalism and salutary neglect; implanted a more contemporary version of nationalist republican ideology; added some neomercantile wrinkles to the Cromwellian imperial model; fought a long and expensive war with the French; displayed an insensitivity to American geographies that would eventually prove fatal; and endured the humiliation of colonial rebellion, military defeat, and the conferral of independence on two and a half million American subjects, not to mention the loss of a million square miles of Britain's North American empire.

Events and geographies unfolded quickly in the four decades of the Age of Empire. In the North American colonies, population nearly tripled from just over 900,000 in 1740 to nearly 2.8 million in 1780. Most of this growth (perhaps 86 to 87 percent) was attributable to high rates of natural increase among the Creole population; net immigration (245,811) probably contributed no more than 13 or 14 percent to the population increase as compared to nearly half (48 percent) between 1680 and 1740. While both periods enjoyed similar rates of population growth (3.0 percent and 2.8 percent per annum, respectively), the sources of growth were quite different.

Liberal geographies were revised as well. In accordance with the organic geographical model of a neorepublican regime, frontier expansion resumed and demographic dispersion largely ceased. Once the dust of the French and Indian War had settled (1763), the pace of frontier expansion accelerated as Creoles and immigrants rushed westward, flooded the back countries of the middle and southern colonies, and alleviated population pressures along the coast. Simultaneously, the authorities put an end to the sprawling dispersion of colonial population that was so typical between 1680 and 1740 (table 10.1). For the descendants of Yankees, puritans, and cavaliers, this was good news. Greater Virginia and Greater New England, having seen their share of colonial population wither from 90 percent in 1680 to 73 percent in 1740, managed to hold on to most of their lead between 1740 and 1780.

These new geographies had sizable consequences. Frontier expansion greatly

Table 10.1. Population and Population Growth in the Mainland Colonies, 1630–1780

Date	Population	Dates	Population Growth (per annum)
1630	4,640		
1650	50,368	1630–1680	7.0%
1680	151,507	1650–1680	3.7%
1720	466,185	1680–1720	2.8%
1740	905,563	1680–1740	3.0%
1780	2,780,369	1740–1780	2.8%

advanced the egalitarian as well as the nationalist aspirations of the new age. Spatial expansion opened up new lands and afforded economic opportunities for immigrants and for the growing mass of tenants and hired hands. It also underlined regional differences and engendered levels of regional volatility that helped to spark the French and Indian War, exacerbate sectional tensions and conflicts between older and newer regions, and, eventually, ignite a revolution. Equally fateful was the geographical preservation of a demographic majority in the oldest colonies. By retaining their hold on the demographic balance of power among the mainland colonies, the colonies of Greater Virginia and Greater New England assured themselves of a decisive role in imperial, intercolonial, and, later, interstate politics. While the egalitarian frontier regularly stirred the political pot, it was the ancestral colonies that, in the end, wielded the club.

The rest of the agenda of the Age of Empire was as ambitious as its geographies. In addition to the promotion of spatial expansion, demographic concentration, and regional volatility, the neorepublican agenda called for tightening *neomercantilist* controls on colonial commerce, anglicizing and subordinating the empire through *parliamentary law*, and stimulating *mass consumption* and regional diversification both at home and in Britain's colonies overseas.

The Eclipse of Liberalism

Lockean liberalism was the best thing that ever happened to English Whigs and the American elites who had risen to power between 1680 and 1740. Rarely has a public ideology been so perfectly matched with private interests, nor have so few enjoyed so much at the expense of so many. But the free ride could not last forever, nor could the sleight of hand on which elite advantage depended. While the masses at home and in the colonies might be deceived by Whig duplicity, the liberal rhetoric of liberty, peace, and freedom of commerce could not forever veil the regressive taxes which the Whigs had imposed nor fumigate the smelly stench of cronyism and corruption which the Whigs had sustained. By the 1730s, the oligarchy's blatant pursuit of interests was fast becoming an embarrassment, and nobler minds called for an end to "the robinarchy" and the restoration of virtue in political affairs. In 1742, after nearly three decades of Whig rule, Sir Robert Walpole obliged. In the housecleaning that followed his resignation as prime minister, liberalism and the private geographies that had long sustained elites on both sides of the Atlantic were given the boot.

But even before the Whig's eviction from power, the political opposition in Britain had been preparing the path for a new regime (on the emerging ideology of empire, see Armitage 2000: 171–97). In the 1730s, the quaint republican ideals of nationalism and empire, opportunity and consumption, circulated once again in the chambers of British politics. In the midst of so much cronyism and corruption, talk of political virtue, public interests, and, public geographies was a welcome tonic for the cynicism that permeated English political discourse. This turn of moral events was not, however, pleasing to everyone, least of all to the British and American elites who continued to be the prime beneficiaries of Whig corruption and liberalism.

The unraveling of Walpole's regime began in earnest in the early 1730s. In 1732 and 1733, his bold attempt to advance the cause of free trade ended in failure when his proposal to eliminate most of the duties on colonial tobacco (and thus undermine one of the crucial bulwarks of mercantilism) and replace them with an excise tax on consumption (i.e., a regressive tax on the masses) was soundly beaten back in Parliament—much to the chagrin of the larger tobacco planters in the Chesapeake and tobacco trading interests in London (Hemphill 1964: 190–286). Having repulsed Walpole's assault on the Navigation Acts, the parliamentary opposition took the offensive, reinforcing mercantilist principles with the Molasses Act of 1733 and the imposition of high duties on molasses exported from the West Indies to the mainland colonies. "[F]or a brief moment in 1735 it seemed that the policy of 'salutary neglect' was to be abandoned," but the Whigs were not yet powerless. Lax enforcement by Whig appointees in the customs office made the Molasses Act a dead letter by the early 1740s (Barrow 1967: 134–37, 143–44).

Egalitarian ideas were also in the air in the 1730s. Neorepublicans voiced a renewed compassion for the plight of England's "worthy poor." These were the innocent victims of the structural malignancies in Britain's transatlantic economy—of the collapse of the American market for indentured servants and the incapacity of an overproducing economy to absorb a rapidly expanding population. As economic opportunities dried up in the 1720s and early 1730s, several English philanthropists pledged their fortunes on behalf of an ambitious experiment in social engineering (figure 10.1). Constituted as the Trustees for Establishing the Colony of Georgia in America, these benefactors set out to establish a new American colony that would provide land and opportunity for a handful of England's "worthy poor." King George II awarded the trustees a colonial charter for territory to the south of the Savannah River; Parliament authorized supplementary funds for this egalitarian, philanthropic enterprise; and the icon of republicanism, James Harrington, provided the utopian inspiration. Georgia's experiment in "agrarian law provided the 'unfortunate poor' with equal quantities of land on which they could labor and improve themselves. The citizen-farmer-soldier who would emerge . . . would be the backbone of the colony, the embodiment of the Trustee's philanthropic goals" (Stewart 1996: 45, 31–33). Of such a citizenry, Oliver Cromwell would have heartily approved.

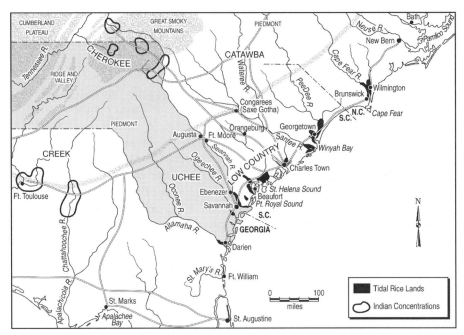

Figure 10.1. A neorepublican sign: The establishment of Georgia in the context of Lower South geographies, 1732.

Source: Harris 1953: 138–40.

The Whig oligarchs rightly understood that these interventions were antiliberal. They understood as well that the neomercantilist appeals for restraints on the freedom of colonial trade and the egalitarian overtures to England's "worthy poor" represented the first in a series of counterattacks by a resurgent republican ideology. But the rumblings of neorepublicanism that were distant and muffled in the 1730s would explode with concussive force in the decade following the fall of Walpole in 1742. The anti-Walpolean ideology of the 1730s and early 1740s served to define an emergent "conception of empire . . . derived from Britain's historic achievements as a maritime power, as a commercial economy, . . . a parliamentary democracy with a common-law tradition," and a protestant heritage (Armitage 2000: 196–97). In the transitional ministries of Carteret and the Pelhams, Whigs and Tories wasted little time in attacking the common-law foundations of Lockean liberalism and introducing a radically revised interpretation of empire, parliament, and the role of parliamentary law. Neorepublican MPs and jurists celebrated the supremacy of Parliament and the virtues of law as an instrument of science and a therapeutics for social change. The social reformer James Oglethorpe certainly believed as much in 1732 when, armed with the agrarian law of social reform, he had set sail for the Georgia colony. And fifteen years hence, in the aftermath of Scottish rebellion, Parliament concurred when, in retaliation via statute, it tried to anglicize the culture of rebel Highlanders out of existence. Henceforth, statutory law and social reform went hand in hand; henceforth in the Age of Empire, ministers and members of Parliament routinely acted on the assumption that parliamentary statutes were the surest means of effecting the compliance of an empire that was increasingly unruly and non-English—as it seemed to be in Ireland, Scotland, French Canada after 1763, India, and even Anglo-America where English descendants were often outnumbered by slaves and émigrés from the continent. Toward that end, Parliament embarked on a long and increasingly aggressive campaign of legislative intervention in colonial affairs. In due course, the jurisdiction of parliamentary law (not to mention parliamentary supremacy) was extended to the empire at large and, as importantly, Parliament's will was enforced both at home and in Britain's colonies overseas.

This new faith in parliamentary activism and the therapeutic power of statutory law was confirmed by pronounced shifts in the volume and composition of parliamentary business. In the first instance, the sheer number of laws increased dramatically, rising from just 13 per session of Parliament between 1689 and 1727 to 33.2 between 1727 and 1760 and 60 between 1760 and 1820 (table 10.2). In the second instance, the compositional ratio of public to private laws increased as well, rising from 0.7 between 1689 and 1727 to 1.8 between 1727 and 1820 (Root 1991: 356). But if members of Parliament were much busier and more appropriately committed to the public's business as liberalism fell by the wayside, Parliament's collective judgment was rarely infallible, especially when doling out legislative prescriptions for unfamiliar colonies and colonists far from home. There, in colonies accustomed to neglect, parliamentary activism and ill-informed interventions were not always well received.

Parliamentary activism was especially distressing to American elites who, having risen to power before 1740, had grown accustomed to British indifference. In the old days, when Americans did not get their way, they relied on London lobbyists to represent their interests before the Whiggish Board of Trade. But as the focal point of imperial relations shifted from the fairly relaxed proceedings of the board to the hurly-burly of Parliament, American elites encountered new obstacles in exercising influence over British colonial policies. The cozy lobbying tactics that had worked so well with the Board of Trade were much less effective in Parliament where power was widely dispersed and the costs of maneuvering legislation through that body were quite high (Root 1991: 354–61; Olson 1980). The futility of the old politics was increasingly evident after 1742, and painfully so after 1763. Faced with an onslaught of neomercantile regulations from Parliament following the British victory

Table 10.2. Parliamentary Laws, 1689–1820 (laws per session reported in parentheses)

Period	Public Laws		Private Laws		Total		Number of Sessions
William III (1689–1702)	343	(5.9)	466	(8.0)	809	(13.9)	58
Anne (1702–1714)	338	(4.3)	605	(7.8)	943	(12.1)	78
George I (1714–1727)	377	(6.5)	381	(6.6)	758	(13.1)	58
George II (1727–1760)	1,447	(17.9)	1,244	(15.4)	2,691	(33.2)	81
George III (1760–1820)	9,980	(39.3)	5,257	(20.7)	15,237	(60.0)	254
Pre-1727	1,058	(5.5)	1,452	(7.5)	2,510	(12.9)	194
Post-1727	11,427	(34.1)	6,501	(19.4)	17,928	(53.5)	335

in the French and Indian War, American elites were ill prepared for Parliament's repeated interventions in colonial affairs. Over the next two decades, Americans would regroup and reconceptualize the imperial relationship between the mother country and her colonies. With liberal Creole elites on the mainland seeking one thing—the conservation of the liberties and property that Americans had so recently earned—and British neorepublicans in parliament seeking another—the expansion of power, order, equity, and uncontested parliamentary supremacy—a collision of interests and ideologies seemed increasingly inevitable.

"A Dark Place of Persecution"

But parliamentary activism and the jurisprudence of statutory law were hardly the only threats to the hegemony of American elites who had risen to power after 1690. From within, an equally formidable challenge was stirring on the backcountry frontier. A "great awakening" of evangelical protestantism in the 1740s roused frontier settlers from the slumber induced by a half century of liberalism, enlightenment rationality, and the hypocrisy of religious toleration with all of its high Anglican biases (Isaac 1982). "When widespread social dislocations [associated with migration into the interior] led to deep-seated personal stress and cultural distortion, the common people became eager to hear the words of invading itinerant revivalists from the Middle Colonies and New England. The spiritual message of these men of God brought extensive emotional responses from the poorer sort, but it also aroused the antagonism of those in authority" (McLoughlin 1978: 89). In addition, local preachers and circuit riders electrified the spiritual world of the interior settlements with high-voltage appeals to chiliastic evangelicalism, millennialism, and the imperative of salvation. With the reenchantment of American religious life, Puritanism at last reaped its revenge (figures 10.2A and 10.2B).

As "new light" Presbyterians and Baptists made inroads in New England and throughout the backcountry, a curious thing happened. The enormous sectarian diversity that was so characteristic of America's Christian believers was quickly boiled down to us and them—to "two groups with fundamentally different orientations: the nationalists [or, to be more precise, the cosmopolitan Anglican elites], who preached reason as a means to social order [the liberal program], and the evangelicals, who promoted disordered holiness in the expectation of renewed brotherhood [in ways reminiscent of commonwealth ideology]" (Appleby 1984b: 299). While there were exceptions, the two camps were typically divided by social class and geography. The evangelicals enjoyed their greatest successes among the lower and middling orders of Americans, among the multitudes who, for an infinite variety of reasons, had not fared well under liberalism and who had found refuge and opportunity in the "back parts" of the several colonies (for the view that frontier gentry played a larger role in the Awakening, see Payne 1995).

The conflictions between evangelicals and rationalists in the 1740s culminated in "a profound cultural crisis involving the convergence of political, social, economic, and ideological forces" (Appleby 1984b: 300). The rationalists, whose num-

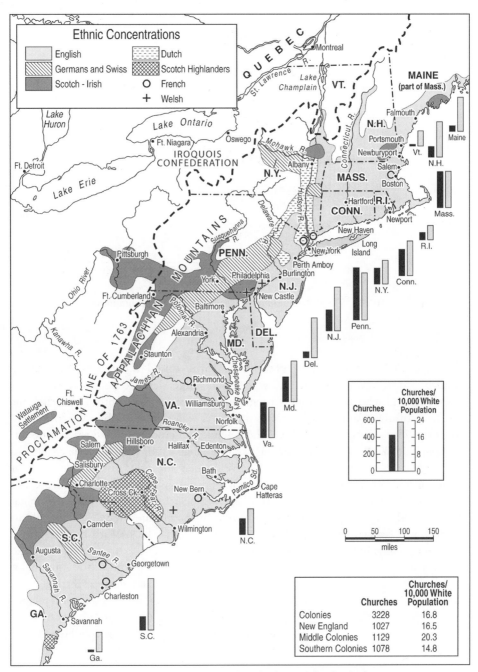

Figure 10.2A. Churches and ethnic concentrations in the mainland colonies, 1775–1776.

Sources: Paullin and Wright 1932: 49–50, plates 82A–M; Cappon 1976: 37–39.

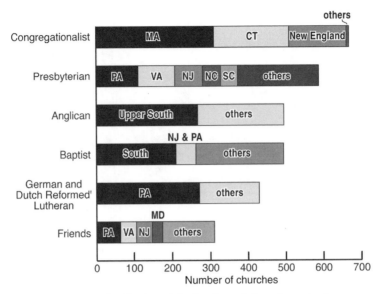

Figure 10.2B.   The distribution of the leading religious denominations.

Sources: See figure 10.2A.

bers included Anglicans and most liberal elites, found themselves increasingly surrounded by frontier evangelicals who, by and large, despised deference and social hierarchy and who saw nothing wrong with social leveling or with harsh criticisms of the antifrontier policies of elites in the lower houses of assembly. When matters of faith elided so easily into politics, the defenders of rationalism had reason enough to conclude that the Great Awakening was more than a little tinged by the egalitarian ideology of their republican adversaries. With their authority under attack, coastal elites proceeded cautiously, nimbly making concessions when necessary to prevent the gathering forces of evangelism from spilling over from the frontier into coastal regions and placing their power in jeopardy. In the ensuing decades, a republican veneer was slapped over the liberalism of the eastern elites. With remarkable, if grudging, ingenuity they opened up the electoral process, extended the franchise more widely, and, with voter participation on the rise, pandered to the interests of voters by wooing them with treats and liquor as election day neared (Brown 1955; Brown and Brown 1964; Sydnor 1952; for electoral variations by county and region, see Kolp 1998). For the truly righteous, however, these machinations merely confirmed that the colonies had become "a dark place of persecution, enlightened only by the divinely inspired witnesses of evangelists and martyrs" (Isaac 1982: 300).

Hard Times and the Road to Recovery

The 1740s were not kind to liberals, elites, protestant rationalists, or the Anglo-American economy. In ways that were reminiscent of earlier economic crises, the

Atlantic economy had once again become mired in a deep slump. Not since the crisis of the 1680s and 1690s had tobacco exports been so stagnant nor the cuts in the rate of frontier expansion so sharp—the latter being pared by half in the 1740s as compared to 64 percent at the end of the seventeenth century. The affinity of these two economic crises is also suggested by their departure from immigration trends. Only twice in the decades spanning 1650 and 1780 did net slave imports exceed net white immigration—the first, with a ratio of 1.47, came in the 1690s; the second, with a much higher ratio of 3.27, in the 1740s. In times of crisis, white immigration seems to have collapsed while slave imports either held steady, as they did in the 1690s, or rose quite sharply, as in the 1740s.

The 1740s dealt another heavy blow to the merchandise trade between England and the mainland colonies (figure 10.3). After peaking at £1,800,000 in 1741, the bottom fell out of this trade in the mid-1740s (£1,089,000 in 1745) before recovering by the end of the decade (*Historical Statistics* 1975, 2: 1176, 1190–91). Prices that had risen so briskly during the first quarter of the eighteenth century reversed their course and fell through the 1730s and into the 1740s. Beginning in 1737 and lasting through 1755, the British and American economies contracted in more years than they expanded (McCusker and Menard 1985: 62–64). Economic growth in the mainland colonies stagnated. Marc Egnal has suggested that American per capita income may actually have declined by about 1 percent per annum in the colonies as a whole and by as much as 2 to 4 percent in the northern colonies and in the lower south. The Chesapeake colonies posted the only positive performance (+1 percent) in these hard times, but even there tobacco prices sank to their lowest levels since the 1680s (Egnal 1975: 192–93).

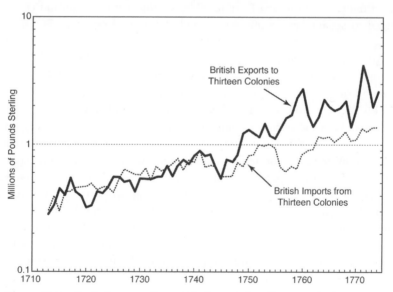

Figure 10.3.   Trade between Great Britain and the thirteen colonies, 1713–1774.

Source: Adapted from Mitchell and Deane 1967: 309–11.

The crisis in the Anglo-American economy in the 1740s had several causes, not the least of which was the Whigs' overweening emphasis on the forces of British production. By the 1730s, overproduction in Britain's economy had resulted in lower prices, lower incomes, and lower demand for American commodities; in short, "all of the forces of growth seemed weak" (Wilson 1965: 359). In Britain,

> the level of consumer demand depended [in large part] on conditions in the countryside. [And these were not good.] Between 1720 and 1745 Britain's farm economy was depressed because of overproduction. Various techniques [not to mention the Whigs' scaling down of land taxes and their support for private enclosures] had increased output, while at the same time population grew slowly. . . . As a result, agricultural prices fell, and the disposable income of individual farmers decreased. (Egnal 1975: 203)

In this glutted market, the output of both British manufactures and American staples went wanting.

The overproduction crisis of the 1740s was, in retrospect, a fairly predictable consequence of a liberal regime. In serving so adroitly the private interests of men of property, the Whig oligarchy bore responsibility for overloading the system with goods and deepening the crisis. More ironically, the oligarchy also bore responsibility for the breadth of a crisis that was so rapidly transmitted throughout the empire by the very geographies that the Whigs had promoted. Dense populations, consolidated and efficient marketing systems, and regional interdependence expedited the flow of bad news in the guise of falling prices for colonial commodity exports, deteriorating terms of trade, and shrinking incomes. The surplus that the mainland colonies had managed to accumulate in the British trade between 1698 and 1717 (more than £0.76 per capita per annum) had largely evaporated by 1740 (having fallen to less than £0.13 in constant prices of 1700). Not even a doubling in the mainland's consumption of British goods in this span was sufficient to siphon off Britain's surplus production. In the end, Walpole and the Whigs had created the economic crisis of the 1740s, and it would cost them their place in English politics.

After 1742, a succession of ministries took up the problem of overproduction, redefined it as one of underconsumption, and introduced monetary and fiscal policies that stimulated mass consumption and launched a consumer revolution at home and abroad. The crucial policy, as noted earlier, involved lowering the interest rates on government securities thereby inducing leading investors to shift their capital from public finance to the private sector and, more specifically, to mortgage and credit markets. The flow of funds toward higher returns in the private sector soon enabled British manufacturers and wholesalers as well as American merchants to offer long lines of credit to retailers and consumers (Price 1980). By the 1750s, Americans were awash in credit and consumer goods. Consumption expanded dramatically. American imports from England and Scotland nearly doubled between 1740 and 1770 and the small trade surplus of 1740 had turned into a deficit by 1770 (-£0.3 per capita). Only the invisible earnings from shipping, mercantile services, and British expenditures in the colonies rescued the mainland colonies from indebtedness (Mc-Cusker and Menard 1985: 80–83).

Neorepublican Geographies

Like the great depression of the 1930s, the recovery from the crisis of the 1740s took time, and victory was not finally sealed until a world war (in this case, the French and Indian War between 1755 and 1763) had been brought to a triumphant conclusion. At that point, Britain's Age of Empire was firmly in place, and the goals of the neorepublican regime were reasonably clear. These included, among other things, steadfastly aggrandizing the power of Parliament and the republic; throwing the harness of parliamentary law over Britain's vastly enlarged empire; regulating colonial trade in the interests of the mother country; promoting orderly spatial expansion within the empire; expediting the Anglicization of the colonies abroad; and sustaining the consumer revolution in ways that would eliminate the glut of overproduction inherited from the Whigs, benefit the masses of consumers (even at the risk of disturbing the interests of British and American elites), and pay down the enormous debt rung up during the French and Indian War.

FRONTIER EXPANSION AND DEMOGRAPHIC CONCENTRATION

Not even the stoutest of colonial America's liberal geographies could survive unscathed in the face of neorepublican determination. By midcentury, these geographies seemed increasingly anachronistic and, in some cases, in flat contradiction to the policies of an ascendant neorepublicanism. The old and tottering geographies of consolidation and dispersion were bulldozed aside by the organic geographies of expansion and concentration. Signals that the liberal era of spatial consolidation was coming to an end were evident as early as the 1720s and 1730s when the lethargic pace of frontier expansion between 1675 and 1720 shifted gears and picked up speed, especially on the fast frontiers of the southern backcountry (table 10.3). Over the six decades after 1720, the frontiers of settlement advanced quite rapidly, moving westward at the rate of 2.4 percent per annum—a pace that was 50 percent faster than

Table 10.3. Settled Areas and Rates of Frontier Expansion, 1650–1780

Dates	Settled Area (in square miles)	Dates	Rates of Frontier Expansion (per annum)
1675	30,220	1675–1720	1.2%
1720	52,068	1675–1740	1.8%
1740	99,014	1720–1780	2.4%
1780	223,211	1740–1780	2.0%

the rate between 1675 and 1720 (1.2 percent) but some 17 percent slower than the rate between 1650 and 1675 (2.9 percent) (figure 10.4). Moreover, expansion on the frontier began to catch up with the pace of population growth. The ratio of their growth rates (population growth: frontier expansion) narrowed from 1.7 under a liberal regime (1675–1740) to 1.4 under the neorepublican regime of 1740–1780 (not coincidentally, the 1740–1780 ratio compares favorably with the ratio of 1.3 under the first republican regime between 1650 and 1680).

Although the pace of settlement expansion slowed dramatically during the 1740s and the ensuing French and Indian War, it regained momentum after 1763 in spite

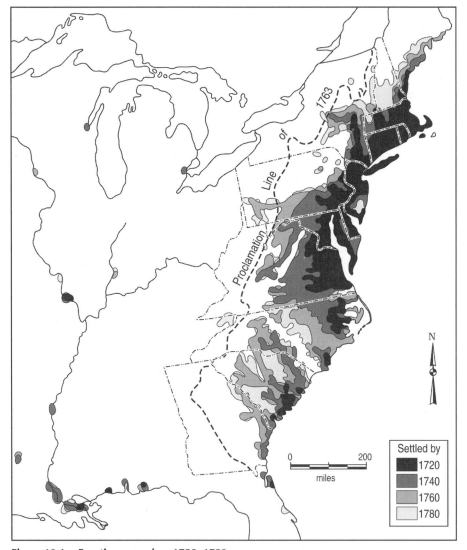

Figure 10.4.   Frontier expansion, 1720–1780.

Source: Earle 2000.

of British attempts to prohibit settlement beyond the crest of the Appalachians. In the 1760s, for example, South Carolina's frontier expanded at nearly 3.5 percent per annum; and in the following decade, the settled area in Greater Virginia's backcountry increased by over 11 percent per year. Doubtless the British restrictions on far western settlement slowed the frontier's pace; but far from being inconsistent with expansionist republican principles, these restrictions were designed to promote *orderly*—as opposed to unsystematic and chaotic—expansion within the vast unsettled spaces that lay between the de jure and de facto boundaries of colonial settlement. That goal seems to have been achieved under the Proclamation of 1763 with two crucial exceptions—the frontiers of New York and in the backcountry in the western parts of Pennsylvania, Maryland, and Virginia. Frontier expansion in these two regions in the 1760s virtually collapsed under the weight of British restrictions on settlement.

From the standpoint of classical republicanism, a healthy empire depended on two organic geographical processes: growth at the extremities and concentration in the heart and vital organs. Neorepublicans in the Age of Empire satisfied the first of these imperatives, as we have seen, by promoting orderly frontier expansion; the second, by amassing of peoples and economic power in London—the heart of the empire—and in the ancestral colonial regions of Greater New England and Greater Virginia—the vital organs of the mainland colonies. While London was the undisputed heart of the matter, vital colonial geographies were not ignored. Colonial policies after 1742 gradually undermined the liberal bias toward demographic dispersion among the mainland colonies and thereby preserved the vital functions of older core regions. Recall that Greater New England and Greater Virginia had not fared well under a liberal regime. In the six decades between 1680 and 1740, their share of the mainland population had plummeted from 90 percent to 72 percent. But matters improved greatly in the Age of Empire. Discriminatory biases in intercolonial land markets were largely eliminated; immigration dwindled as industrialization took hold in Western Europe; and natural increase became the primary source of colonial population growth. All of these processes worked in favor of the older colonies and enabled Greater New England and Greater Virginia to hold their own from the 1740s through the 1770s. In that span, their combined share of the mainland population fell very slightly dropping from 72.7 percent to 65.1 percent, mainly owing to a decline in New England's share from 32 percent in 1740 to 25.6 percent in 1780. Indeed, these two regions would not finally relinquish their vital roles in the American polity until 1828 and the election of the first outlander, Andrew Jackson, to the presidency of the United States.

REGIONAL VOLATILITY, EQUALITY, AND SECTIONAL CONFLICT

Neorepublican ideology was simultaneously nationalist and egalitarian. The former stimulated the organic processes of growth, expansion, and concentration; the latter, the fluidity and volatility of structural relations within and between regional societies. And nowhere, after 1742, was volatility more pronounced than in New England with its sharp division between a Yankee mercantile coast and a puritan-subsistence interior. Over the next three and a half decades, thanks in part to neorepublican policies, the lines of regional division would begin to blur. The rapid economic advances made by Boston and the coastal regions prior to 1740 swiftly ground to a halt thereafter as the locus of economic growth shifted toward the "peacable kingdoms" in the interior. Boston's population, which had risen steadily to sixteen thousand and first rank among American cities by 1740, went into a deep stall for the next thirty years. The tonnage of new ships built in the city fell from 6,300 in 1738 to under 2,700 in 1749 and again in 1769 (Usher 1928, 2: 400). In this same span, the city fell from first to third rank as its numbers were surpassed by Philadelphia and then by New York City; worse, Charles Town and Newport, Rhode Island were hot on Boston's heels (table 10.4).

Boston confronted another challenge in the interior as New England farmers broke with their past and began producing for the market, both local and overseas. From 1750 onward, "Massachusetts' agriculture, the preindustrial economy which rested upon it, and (apparently) the farm family it rested upon were transformed by and under the subtle domination of emerging regional and interregional markets for labor, farm commodities, and capital" (Rothenberg 1988: 561). To interpret this transformation as the inevitable triumph of an emergent Lockean paradigm is, however, to do a grave injustice to what was essentially a victory for secular republicanism and religious revitalization. In the late 1730s and 1740s, rural New Englanders were preoccupied by the quest for salvation: the religious salvation of redemption as "new light Baptists" and the economic salvation of cheap money and paper currency underwritten by a land bank. Their faith in cheap money was not shared by the hard-money interests in the coastal entrepôts, and most especially Boston, which saw the land bank as an inflationary plot. When the land bank scheme sailed through the General Assembly, coastal merchants "began, in the fall of 1740, to turn towards parliament for relief, and steps were taken to secure action in that behalf in England" (Davis 1970, II: 146). Their lobbying of the lords commissioners of trades and plantations in London paid swift dividends. Scarcely had the land bank begun its operations when Parliament enacted legislation prohibiting all currency emissions, past and future, and calling for the orderly retirement of the land bank. When the new

Table 10.4.   The Populations of Boston and Its Mainland Competitors

Date	Boston	Newport	New York	Philadelphia	Charles Town	New Haven	Norwich
1690	7,000	2,600	3,900	4,000	1,100		
1720	12,000	3,800	7,000	10,000	3,500		
1742	16,382	6,200	11,000	13,000	6,800		
1760	15,631	7,500	18,000	23,750	8,000		
1775	16,000	11,000	25,000	40,000	12,000	8,300	7,000

Notes: The populations for the Connecticut towns of New Haven and Norwich are for 1771 and 1774, respectively. Norfolk (6,250) and Baltimore (5,934) were the next largest cities in 1775.
Sources: Bridenbaugh 1955a: 6, 303; 1955b: 5, 216–17.

governor of Massachusetts, William Shirley, delivered the bad news, he was greeted with an angry chorus of opposition from the countryside. While Shirley had little choice but to begin the liquidation of the land bank, in doing so he concocted a monetary strategy so favorable to cheap money interests as to restore his political credit in rural Massachusetts. In 1744, emboldened perhaps by the resignation of Walpole and the outbreak of war with the French, he persuaded his superiors of the urgent need for occasional currency emissions in order to counter French initiatives in Acadia (Nova Scotia today). In just five years (1744–1748), Shirley's nineteen "occasional" emissions pumped over £600,000 sterling into the Massachusetts' economy, fueled inflation, sent exchange rates into a tizzy, slashed the profits of creditors, and toned down the interior's outrage over the abolition of the land bank (Davis 1970, I– 152–71).

Governor Shirley's actions are worth noting for two reasons. First, that Shirley's inflationary policy was allowed to proceed at all is a testimonial to the transition in British political regimes following Walpole's resignation—from the Whig oligarchy with its cronyism and its elite liberal biases toward the neorepublican Age of Empire and its inclinations toward economic equity for the masses of the citizenry. Second, the fact that the proponents of hard money had won the battle over the land bank only to lose the war when routed by Shirley's inflationary counteroffensive makes sensible Boston's deepening antipathy toward the egalitarian proclivities of the new political regime and kindred spirits among the brethren in the rural fasts of New England (Davis 1970, I: 152–71I; II: 130–255).

The commercialization of rural New England thus unfolded in a milieu more suited for and in a manner more suited to republican than liberal ends. Energized by the expansion of the money supply, by inflation, and by credit and consumption as much as by advances in production, market institutions diffused rapidly throughout rural Massachusetts between the mid-1740s and the early 1770s. Drawing upon the long lines of credit that became available in the 1740s and 1750s, merchants seized the opportunity of opening up the vast and largely untapped interior market—and with some success. In Connecticut and Massachusetts on the eve of the Revolution, the share of consumer goods in the typical estate was substantially larger in the interior regions of subsistence farming than in their coastal and commercial counterparts. In Connecticut, the ratio in these regional shares of consumption goods favored the interior at 1.5; and likewise in Hampshire County, Massachusetts at 1.3. The consumer demands of the interior led, in turn, to a thickening of retail establishments and their associated entrepreneurial opportunities. Economic growth soon followed. Between 1735–1754 and 1765–1774, the wealth held in the average estate increased at a much faster pace in the interior than in the older commercial regions such as Boston, the towns along the Connecticut Sound, and in the Connecticut Valley. Wealth increased by just 30 to 35 percent in the older commercial regions as compared to 42 to 109 percent in six of seven interior regions (the exception was in the upland area of Hampshire County, where wealth fell by 24 percent). The commercialization of interior New England increased regional volatility as it narrowed the distance between the interior and the coast. While Boston remained the largest and perhaps the richest place in New England as of 1776, the city ranked near the bottom in its rate of economic growth (Main and Main 1988: 38).

The egalitarian thrust of the Age of Empire penetrated as well into the middle and southern colonies. In older regions in Pennsylvania and the Chesapeake, the downward trend in the distribution of personal wealth and income between 1680 and 1740 was arrested by outmigration to the frontier. In long-settled Chester County, Pennsylvania, for example, the distribution of wealth did not become more unequal in the Age of Empire in the way that it did before 1740, nor would it do so again after 1780. Similarly modest victories occurred in an older parish along the tobacco coast where the wealth concentrated in the hands of the richest ten percent of the household heads actually declined—from 50 to 60 percent before 1740 to 40 to 50 percent from 1740 to 1766—and tenancy, having reached its peak of roughly 50 percent of all households in the 1740s, managed to remain at that level through 1783 (Lemon and Nash 1968; Earle 1975: 115–17)

Merely holding the line against inequality in the older regions was no mean achievement. Indeed, the results might have been even more depressing in the absence of massive outmigrations from these regions to the rapidly expanding frontiers in the backcountry of Pennsylvania, Maryland, and Virginia between 1740 and 1760 and, after 1760, in South Carolina. "Moving out and moving on" was becoming a familiar feature of American life. "Although southerners were more mobile than New Englanders, no region had a persistence rate much above 60 percent [per decade] during the third quarter of the eighteenth century, and farmers everywhere showed an especially strong propensity to move. Residents from New York north tended to move longer distances north into upper New York and New England; those from Pennsylvania south tended to move west and south into the broad upland areas between the seacoast and the Appalachian mountains" (Greene 1988: 181).

The churning of American populations had taken on new dimensions. Persistence rates in older regions, which had begun to fall as early as the 1710s, hit their colonial low points between 1740 and 1770. It was not uncommon for 40 to 50 percent of the residents in an area to disappear in a single decade—mostly to the frontier. In Virginia between 1750 and 1755, eighteen tidewater counties lost nearly 1,000 white residents (–1.7 percent) and gained 2,756 blacks (+6.6 percent); simultaneously, ten piedmont frontier counties grew by 10,000—just over 6,000 whites and some 5,400 blacks (Brown and Brown 1964: 72–73). Such massive relocations tended to reduce inequality by stripping older regions of many of their smaller farmers, planters, and tenants (the "lower orders") who, having departed for the frontier, left behind a residuum of middling and wealthy households (figure 10.5).

Not all was pure gain, however. As the dynamics of outmigration sharpened the divisions between older regions and new, between the suppliers of population in the coastal regions and the recipient regions in the rapidly expanding backcountry, sectional conflicts came to the surface in a number of colonies. Colonial legislatures, long accustomed to being under the thumb of coastal representatives, were reluctant to share power, and they regularly dissembled on matters of concern to backcountry residents. Despite the rapid growth of settlement on the frontier, coastal politicians resisted attempts to establish institutions of local governance or to provide military

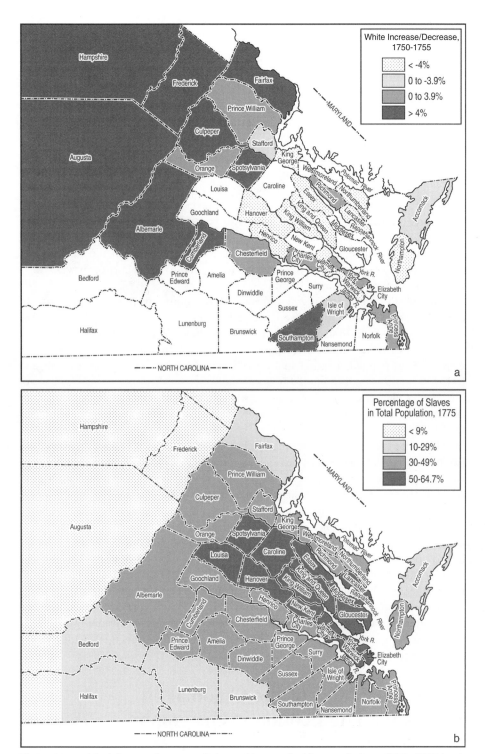

Figure 10.5. Virginians on the move: Gains and losses of white populations, 1750–1755 (top); and the geography of slavery in Virginia, 1775 (bottom).

Source: Adapted from Brown and Brown 1964.

assistance to settlers besieged by Indian attacks. As the ferocity of these attacks mounted during the French and Indian War, frontier settlers in the western parts of Pennsylvania, Maryland, and Virginia fled from the Appalachian valleys to the safer piedmont uplands of Virginia and the Carolinas. The forward salients of the frontier in New York and New England were also put into retreat. This backflood of refugees soon inundated the small towns and way stations that had popped up to serve their needs as well as the institutions of local government that had not.

The situation was volatile, and tensions finally erupted in the backcountry of South Carolina in 1767. In the following year, rebellious frontier farmers issued a "'Plan of Regulation' which elevated local tribunals and denied the 'jurisdiction of the courts holden in Charlestown' over the western reaches" (Egnal 1988: 236). Convinced of the dangers of an aroused backcountry and mindful of Nathaniel Bacon's successes a century earlier, the South Carolina assembly made a concession of modest power to the rebels in exchange for an end to the regulator movement— but not, however, to sectional enmities.

But what of the situation where frontier opportunities were not as abundant? In these cases, the tensions arising from inequality were occasionally manifested as class conflict. That seems to have been the case in New York's "Great Rebellion of 1766." The growing numbers of tenants on the large estates along the Hudson River were literally trapped. Penned in by the brutal hostilities during the French and Indian War between 1755 and 1763 and thereafter by the tapering seaward arc of the Appalachian crest, they could not easily escape the oppressive practices of their landlords by moving to the frontier. They instead were forced to resort to agrarian revolt.

As Frederick Jackson Turner made plain more than a century ago, the American frontier was a safety valve for releasing the pressures of inequality and class conflict. But the valve only worked when and where it was open. And it was not open, generally speaking, during the liberal reign between 1680 and 1740. It was open, however, in most places and at most times during the expansionist and egalitarian decades of the Age of Empire—save, of course, where peculiar conditions intervened as in upstate New York and the Hudson Valley. But solving one problem invariably led to another. Even as the fast pace of expansion afforded opportunities on the frontier and subverted class conflict, the inertial forces of power within older regions fostered sectional tensions and conflict. Occasionally between 1742 and 1776, these erupted in sectional violence; more generally, however, the pressures of sectionalism were vented through the ultimate safety valve—the diffusion of a stunning economic recovery, the spread of a consumer revolution, and the convergence of regional economic performance.

The Golden Age of the Colonial Economy: The Economic Geography of Recovery

The recovery of the Anglo-American economy from the hard times of the 1730s and 1740s was fairly vigorous. Beginning in the late 1740s and lasting until the

Revolution, prices for colonial commodities shot upward, albeit in ever shorter and more volatile cycles, as new demands for American goods rolled across the Atlantic. The resumption of population growth in Europe as well as the diffusion of industrial production created an expanding market for food, initially for wheat and rice in southern Europe and, by the 1760s in England and Ireland. In Britain and on the continent, European consumers demanded more tobacco for snuff and pipe and whale oil for illumination; textile manufacturers demanded indigo (for dye) and flaxseed for linseed oil; and shipping firms demanded pitch, tar, and turpentine for their seagoing vessels. Concurrently, West Indian planters, hard-pressed to supply all of the sugar wanted by their European consumers, stepped up their demands for provisions (corn, fish, flour) and cooperage materials (hoops and staves) from mainland suppliers. In the British Caribbean alone, populations that had stagnated between 1690 and 1740 increased by 29 percent between 1740 and 1780.

Credit provided most, if not all, of the fuel for this economic recovery. Thanks to the long lines of credit that had become available from private investors following the British decision to lower interest rates on government securities, British merchants, manufacturers, and wholesalers were able to boost prices, offer generous terms for repayment, and advance funds to American producers and consumers.

The volume of credit coursing through the bulging veins of the American economy was truly staggering. Alice Hanson Jones has suggested that American financial liabilities in 1774 may have amounted to £6.35 million sterling. Of this amount, Americans owed roughly £3.47 million abroad (and mostly to British creditors) and another £2.88 million to creditors in the middle colonies (mostly, one suspects, for food purchases from New England). This first round of credit enabled borrowers to advance credit in a series of supplemental rounds to the tune of £12.41 million (deducting for intercolonial financial liabilities). On balance, the volume of credit in the mainland colonies stood at nearly £19 million, or roughly 64 percent of American income (generously estimated at £29.42 million). With this much credit on the loose, a consumer revolution was perhaps inevitable. But so, too, was massive indebtedness. Some sense of the dangers may be gained by looking at the American economy in 1998 and the alarms that are raised when the proportion of after-tax income spent on interest and principal rises into the midteens—barely a quarter of what it was on the eve of the Revolution (the preceding estimates are based on reworkings of the income and wealth estimates in Jones 1980: especially 128, 135).

Credit was in bountiful supply throughout the colonies. New England and the southern colonies owed £3.16 million and £3.54 million, respectively, to creditors overseas and in the middle colonies. On top of this, the volume of intraregional credit was massive, amounting to 53 percent of regional income in New England, 62 percent in the middle colonies, and 24 percent in the southern colonies. All this suggests, first, that New England was swamped with easy credit—which helps to explain the rapid commercialization of New England's interior; second, that the credit markets in the southern colonies were equally supplied by overseas (mainly British) and internal sources; and, third, that the sources of credit in the middle colonies were largely, though not exclusively, home grown.

In the long term, British policies of mass consumption would breed resentment from Americans entangled in a thickening web of debt; but in the short term, these policies infused energy into capital and credit markets and fueled a stunning recovery of the Anglo-American economy. In the colonies, trade expanded briskly in the 1750s and imported consumer goods were readily available. The resumption of growth in the merchandise trade with England was accompanied by sudden shift in favor of imports. Before 1746, the value of imports from England exceeded exports to it in just eight of the thirty preceding years; after 1746, imports exceeded exports in twenty-nine successive years. In this case, trade seems to have followed the flow of consumer credit. Colonial exports shot upward as well. During the middle third of the eighteenth century, tobacco exports more than doubled, rice exports rose by fivefold, and by 1770 the wheat, corn, pork, and beef exports (£734,000) ranked just behind the value of tobacco exports (£756,000).

The fruits of economic recovery were widely and evenly distributed among the colonies in this republican Age of Empire. Although the southern colonies held a commanding lead in the export commodity trade—together they accounted for £1,559,000 of annual merchandise exports from the mainland colonies of £2,565,000 circa 1768–1772—the differentials in regional income per capita were much narrower once allowance is made for the inclusion of "invisible earnings" from shipping, insurance, and mercantile services. According to estimates for 1774 prepared by Alice Hanson Jones, incomes per capita comes ranged from 11.2 in New England and in the South to 12.4 in the middle colonies (Jones 1980: 63). While comparative data are lacking for earlier times, it seems unlikely that the regional differential of just 10 percent in 1774 was any less in 1740 and very likely that it was much more given the subsistence economy then prevailing in rural New England and the late start in the colonization of Pennsylvania.

Coinciding with the convergence of regional incomes after 1740 was a trend toward the diversification of regional economic activity. By 1768–1772, the leading staple commodities accounted for smaller shares of regional merchandise exports (figure 10.6). By this measure, New England was the most diversified region (fish at 35 percent) followed by the Lower South (rice at 56 percent), and the middle colonies (grain at 72 percent) and the Upper South (tobacco at 72 percent). In the colonies as a whole, 28 percent of merchandise exports were divided amongst a wide variety of commodities ranging from whale oil and meat to indigo, potash, and deerskins. The market destinations for these commodities were diversified as well, with 77 percent of the trade of the middle colonies going to the West Indies and southern Europe, 63 percent of New England's going to the West Indies, and 71 and 74 percent, respectively, of the Lower and Upper south's going to the British Isles. On the eve of the American Revolution, no region remained utterly dependent on a single staple or on a single market. The changes in Virginia's exports between 1733 and 1773 nicely illustrate the magnitude of economic diversification. While the value of tobacco exports nearly tripled in rising from £121,078 to £337,391, the value of grain exports rose by over fifteenfold from £9,447 to £145,360 (McCusker and Menard 1985: 108, 130, 174, 196, 199).

With export markets booming and prices on the rise in the 1760s, frontier expansion received a sharp boost. Higher prices for wheat, corn, livestock, and flax-

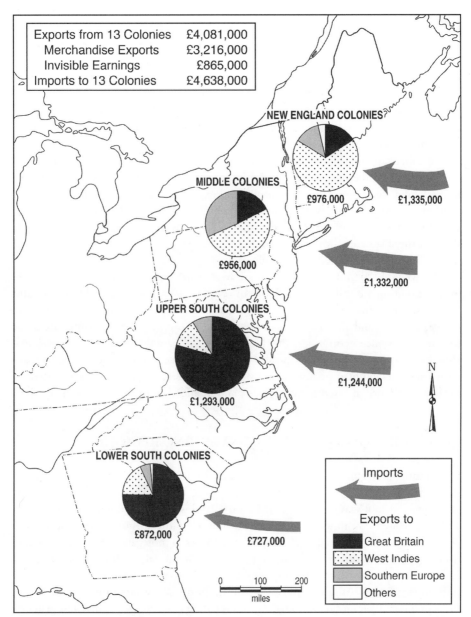

Exports from 13 Colonies	£4,081,000
Merchandise Exports	£3,216,000
Invisible Earnings	£865,000
Imports to 13 Colonies	£4,638,000

NEW ENGLAND COLONIES

£976,000

£1,335,000

MIDDLE COLONIES

£956,000

£1,332,000

UPPER SOUTH COLONIES

£1,293,000

£1,244,000

N

LOWER SOUTH COLONIES

£872,000

£727,000

Imports

Exports to

Great Britain

West Indies

Southern Europe

Others

0   100   200
miles

Figure 10.6.   Regional trade: Imports, exports, and invisible earnings of the mainland colonies, 1772.

Source: *Historical Statistics* 1975, 2: 1182.

seed pushed the frontiers of profitable production deep into the interior. The limits of commercial farming and planting that in the 1730s had been confined to a zone little more than thirty miles from the coast had been pushed eighty to ninety miles into the interior by the 1770s. In the Chesapeake, the escalating prices of grain enabled farmers far inland to produce wheat and transport it by wagon through a string of way station towns and onto coastal ports such as Baltimore, Georgetown, Alexandria, Richmond, and Fredericksburg for export. Similarly, in Pennsylvania, the zone of commercial production was extended west of the Susquehanna River, where some farmers shipped their commodities back to Philadelphia while others directed them to the upstart port of Baltimore to take advantage of that city's proximity, longer shipping season, flour mills, and excellent connections with markets in southern Europe and the West Indies. The influence of the market also extended up the Hudson and Connecticut River valleys as well as into the Carolina piedmont. Beyond these spheres, however, commercial farming gave way to subsistence and sectional tensions mounted accordingly.

Between 1720 and 1770, the settled area of the colonies more than tripled—from 52,000 square miles to 167,500—in response to rising commodity prices and the interior penetration of commercial agriculture. But beyond these zones of commerce, distance and the high costs of overland transport reserved ample areas for frontier subsistence economies. Precluded from the benefits of the market and excluded from the perquisites of power and governance, subsistence farmers in the egalitarian backcountry (many having fled from coastal inequalities) constituted an explosive mixture of resentment, distrust, and disaffection from the powers that be.

CONSUMING GEOGRAPHIES, CONVERGING REGIONS

Commitments to widespread economic opportunities for the citizenry, mass consumption, and consumer geographies are among the inexorables of a republican ideology, and so it was in the Age of Empire. In this case, consumerist policies after 1742 stimulated consumption by lowering interest rates on government securities; chasing private funds into private sector investments in mortgages, mercantile operations, and manufacturing; and running up the national debt—all of which resulted in a vast expansion of credit. In fairly rapid succession, credit lubricated consumption in both Britain and America; and mass consumption necessitated fundamental revisions in the geographies of wholesaling and retailing marketing systems. These geographies, in turn, fostered a convergence among American regional economies and nurtured a sense of identity among Americans. This was so for two reasons: first, because colonials from a series of highly specialized economic regions were now united by common consumer interests and the consumption of similar consumer goods (mostly English); and second, because American regions increasingly resembled one another (i.e., their economies were more diversified) as geographies of retailing, with their tiered hierarchies of central places, were replicated in one colony after another.

As credit worked its way across the Atlantic, the American consumer revolution got under way. Imports into the mainland colonies expanded rapidly in the middle of the eighteenth century. As we have seen, imports from England consistently outpaced exports to England between 1740 and 1770. On a per capita basis, imports from Britain had risen by 25 percent between the 1720s and 1740s and would rise by another 20 percent by 1770. By the latter date, the middle colonies had become the largest consumers of English goods at £1.50 per capita (they also had the highest per capita incomes) followed by the Chesapeake (£1.30), the Carolinas (£1.10), and New England (£1.00) (McCusker and Menard 1985: 280). Americans in 1770 were spending freely, lavishing roughly 10 percent of their annual incomes on British goods alone—and for good reason. As Timothy Breen has pointed out, American consumers participated in a colonial market place that since midcentury was distinguished by "an exceptionally rapid expansion of consumer *choice*, an increasing *standardization* of consumer behavior, and a pervasive *Anglicization* of the American market"—not to mention a rising tide of easy credit (Breen 1988: 79). By the 1770s, the consumer revolution had smudged the lines that had separated one American region from another to the extent that one could speak with confidence of "an American market."

These forces of geographical convergence were further reinforced by the thickening of retailing networks and central-place systems in every American region (figure 10.7). These networks were anchored by evermore numerous retailing establishments and staffed, in ascending order of status, by peddlers, traders, shopkeepers, and merchants (Main 1965: 83–91). Massachusetts in 1771 reported one retail establishment for every 106 persons; the ratio rises above 200, however, when the eastern counties of Suffolk (Boston) and Essex (Salem) are excluded. To the south, the retailing establishments in the Chesapeake were, if more scattered, nearly as frequent. In one Maryland parish in the 1740s, a typical merchant served the retailing needs of 218 persons; a bit later, his counterpart in a nearby county between 1760 and 1765 served 234 persons. The achievements of colonial retailing are all the more impressive once we realize that the colonial ratios are not so very far apart from the U.S. ratio of 150.4 persons per retail establishment recorded in 1982—over two centuries later. Conversely, these American ratios pale by comparison to England's in 1759 when, in the midst of Britain's consumer revolution, that "nation of shopkeepers" registered one retail establishment for every forty-two persons (Shammas 1990; Earle 1975; Kulikoff 1986)!

As the numbers of American retailing establishments grew, so too did they cluster together in central places in order to serve larger markets. In Virginia, for example, the number of towns rose from fourteen in 1730 to thirty-one in 1770; adding in the forty-eight local trade centers that emerged in that span yields an increase of over sixfold in the number of urban places. To the north, Pennsylvanians also founded new towns at a furious pace. In the forward rush of the consumer revolution between 1741 and 1770, they founded forty-nine new towns as compared to just eleven between 1680 and 1740 and a score or so between 1771 and 1800. Towns also proliferated in Massachusetts; in the average year between 1740 and 1765, the colony added 2.24 new towns as compared to just 1.28 new towns per year in the preceding half century (O'Mara 1983: 223, 227–29; Lemon 1972: 123; Sly 1928:

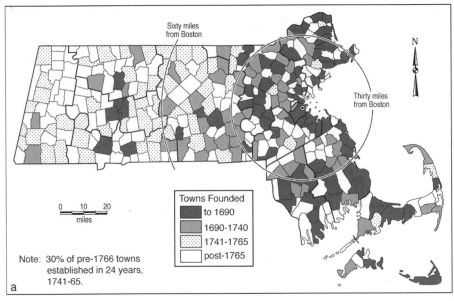

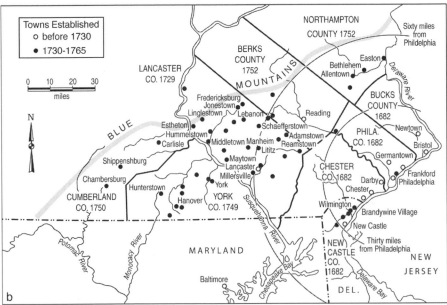

Figure 10.7.   The development of towns in Massachusetts, 1630–1776 (top), and Pennsylvania, 1680–1765 (bottom).

Sources: Adapted from Sly 1928; Lemon 1972.

96–115). With so many new towns and hamlets and so many retailers serving large communities and small, we should not be surprised by Englishman William Eddis's observation that most Americans in the 1770s were supplied with the finest of English goods as readily as were English consumers outside of the major cities.

The consumer revolution in the mid–eighteenth century effected several changes in American lives and landscapes. First, and most obviously, the revolution in consumption provided nearly all Americans with easy credit and ready access to the output of British manufactures, to what Ben Franklin called the "necessaries, mere conveniences, or superfluities" (Breen 1986, 1998). Second, the Revolution fostered a boom in retailing and wholesaling establishments and occupations. Third, it lasted long enough to allow American retailing to congeal in a spatial array of small and large towns and to harden into spatial networks and hierarchies that radiated into virtually every community within the perimeter of the market. Fourth, in creating this extensive retailing system, it increased the efficiency and the velocity of information flows within and between the colonies. Fifth, it served, however unwittingly, to promote regional convergence and to unify American regions which otherwise shared little in common. Lastly, it offered the means by which Britain would surmount the liberal crisis of overproduction and by which Americans, after 1775, would make one new nation out of many. Republican ideology was, as it turned out, revolutionary in more ways than one.

Neomercantilism and the Gathering Storm

The tide of economic nationalism that was rising in Britain in the 1740s, and most evidently in Lord Halifax's view of colonial affairs after 1748, took a while to reach the shores of North America owing in large measure to the preoccupation with the French and Indian War (1755–1763) (Olson 1980; Speck 1984). But with the defeat of the French in 1763 and the acquisition of most of their North American empire, Americans found themselves inundated by a floodtide of old and new imperial rules and regulations. Suddenly, or so it seemed, the freedoms they had long enjoyed— freedoms that enabled some Americans to accumulate great wealth during the era of "salutary neglect"—were being taken away. And when their right to political representation was denied, some Americans proclaimed that Parliament's actions were tantamount to the imposition of slavery. Here, then, were the volatile premises for sectional and ideological conflict between a staunch neorepublican regime in the mother country and a thoroughly liberal elite on the mainland of North America.

The British had a point, however. Victory over the French in 1763 presented the empire with three immediate problems. First, someone had to pay for the enormous war debt rung up by William Pitt's vigorous prosecution of the war effort. Second, someone also had to pay for the costs of peace, most notably the expenses for garrisoning British troops west of the Appalachians and in French Canada and for quelling the residual hostilities from the war in these areas. Third, the mother country's continued supremacy over the colonies had to be ensured. For the architects of empire, it was the last of these that ranked highest on their list of imperial

imperatives. The great fear of British policymakers, according to one American ob-
server, was that they might grow too large. "His Majesties possessions in North
America are so many times more extensive than the island of Great Britain, that if
they were equally well inhabited, Great Britain could no longer maintain her dominion over them. It is therefore evidently her Policy to set bounds to the Increment of
People, and to the extent of the settlement in that Country" (quoted in Barrow
1967: 176). Toward that end, the British Proclamation of 1763 declared that the
western expansion of the North American colonies should be confined "to such a
distance from the seacoast, as that those settlements should lie *within the reach of the
trade and commerce of the kingdom* . . . and also of the exercise of that authority and
jurisdiction, which was conceived to be so necessary for the preservation of the
colonies in due subordination to, and dependence upon, the mother country"
(quoted in Barrow 1967: 176). The line of settlement as delimited was actually quite
generous to the Americans stretching as it did for the most part to the headwaters of
Atlantic drainage. In fact, the boundary lay far beyond "the reach of colonial trade
and commerce" at that date; it fell short, however, of the boundary envisioned by
wealthy Americans eager to speculate in western lands. It was these sorts of overzealous speculators whose operations in western Pennsylvania had helped to trigger the
recent war in the first place and whose activities the Crown and Parliament sought
to restrain after 1763 (figure 10.8).

Once the colonies were properly bounded in a way that might guarantee their
subordination and dependence, Parliament turned to the costs of war and peace, and
these were enormous. The war had cost Britain £137,000,000, an amount that was
seventeen times larger than the government's annual budget of £8,000,000. The
annual interest on this debt alone amounted to £5,000,000. On top of this, the costs
of garrisoning troops in America required expenditures of an additional £225,000
each year (Barrow 1967: 177). To pay down Britain's sizable debt, sacrifices had to
be made both at home and abroad. It was clear that the colonies would be compelled
to pay their fair share, and a bit more perhaps owing to their earlier evasions of the
Navigation and Molasses acts as well as to their part in precipitating the recent war.

But what seemed a prudent and equitable fiscal solution for the British was
worrisome to Americans, at least some of whom suspected along with John Adams
that a larger and more malevolent plan was afoot—one in which "the king, ministry,
parliament, and nation of Great Britain . . . [were] determined to new-model the
colonies from the foundation, to annul all their charters, to constitute them all royal
governments, to raise a revenue in America by parliamentary taxation, to apply that
revenue to pay the salaries of governors, judges, and all other crown officers" and
thereby free them from the fiscal control of colonial assemblies (Adams 1856: 286).
If the Proclamation line of 1763 was the first step in this plan of subordination, the
Sugar Act of 1764 was the second. This lengthy, multipurpose statute sought, among
other things, to eliminate the smuggling of contraband between the mainland colonies and the non-British West Indies and to use the American customs revenues to
pay for the colonies' defense (Barrow 1967: 174–85). To achieve these goals, the
treasury and the Privy Council moved swiftly to reorganize the colonial customs

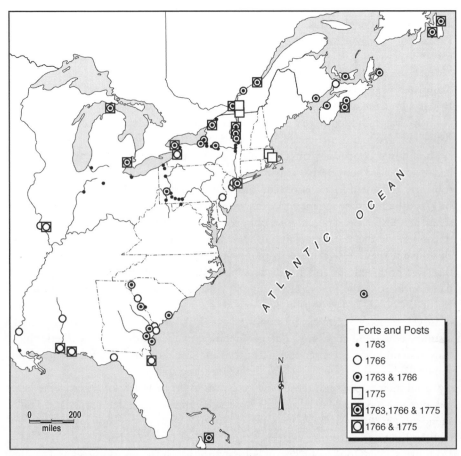

Figure 10.8.   British Army posts and forts in North America, 1763–1775.

Source: Adapted from Cappon 1976: 41.

offices and to reinforce the authority and jurisdiction of the Admiralty Court over litigation on colonial trade.

As the machinery of regulation was being put into place, Parliament enacted the Currency Act of 1764 and then the Stamp Act of 1765. The former prohibited issues of colonial currency; the latter imposed taxes on selected American items (e.g., newspapers, legal documents, insurance policies, ship's papers) in a fashion that was comparable to the excise taxes that had long burdened citizens in England. Had these statutes been enacted a quarter century earlier, Americans would have attempted to scuttle them by calling on their agents in London to play off (and pay) Whig ministers and factions; but by 1765, colonials had far less influence on members of Parliament and were resigned to voice their outrage through an assorted repertoire consisting of protest, mob violence, the calling of the Stamp Act Congress, petitioning the king and Parliament, and bans on the importation of British goods. To the surprise of many, these more confrontational tactics worked exceedingly well.

In the following year, in the first of what would become a continuing round of action, reaction, and counterreaction, Parliament repealed the Stamp Act. But what Parliament gave with one hand, it took away with the other by passing the Declaratory Act reasserting Parliament's authority to make laws for the American colonies "in all cases whatsoever." While Parliament's intentions were clear, the repeal of the Stamp Act was sufficient cause for Americans to harbor the suspicion that while Britain's imperial spirit was willing, the imperial muscle was weak.

It was at this juncture that British neomercantilists made a fatal miscalculation of American geographies (figure 10.9). Inadvertently, the impacts of their policies crashed down upon one American place above all others—a place whose growth had been stalled for the past quarter century and whose misfortunes its denizens routinely attributed to a quarter century of unfriendly if not hostile British policies. In 1767, the British made matters even worse for Bostonians. In that year, the Townshend acts levied taxes on colonial imports, established an American Board of Commissioners of the Customs, and located that board in the port of Boston. For Bostonians, these new duties on imports presented a threat to the city's economy that was both unique and far more serious than the Stamp Act. For a city that had flourished as the preeminent colonial wholesaler, as the entrepôt that imported European goods and redistributed them to American markets via the city's active coastwise trade, a British tax on imported goods struck at the very heart of Boston's distinctive foreland economy. The geographical incidence of the Townshend duties thus was unduly concentrated on Boston and the city's merchants, insurers, and shippers who made their livings by the wholesaling trade.

And their response to these new taxes was swift. In a circular letter to the other colonies in 1768, the Massachusetts House of Representatives denounced the Townshend Acts as "taxation without representation." Matters spun quickly out of control. In June, after customs officers seized a vessel of John Hancock's, a crowd of Bostonians assaulted the officers; in September, British troops were ordered to quell the Boston "mob." Calls for nonimportation, though variously heeded in the other colonies, contributed to Parliament's repeal of these duties (except for the one on tea) in 1771. The calm was broken by the Boston Massacre in 1770 and once again in the summer of 1772 when Governor Hutchinson of Massachusetts announced two changes in policy: first, that his salary and the salary of the colony's judges would be paid by the Crown and not by the colony; second, and even worse for Bostonians, his intention to transfer the jurisdiction of smuggling cases from American courts, which rarely convicted, to friendlier English courts. Bostonians, of course, were well aware of the consequences: that English justice would cost much more than American justice and that the probabilities of verdicts favorable to American defendants were now substantially lower.

In October of 1772, beleaguered Bostonians took another step toward rebellion. They established a standing committee of correspondence to communicate the city's position "to the world." In the ensuing fifteen months, seven other colonies established similar committees. The latest news of Boston's troubles flashed through this communications network: toward the end of 1773, the news that Boston's Sons of Liberty had dumped duted tea from a vessel in the city's harbor; in 1774, that Parliament had responded with the Coercive Act closing the port of Boston and

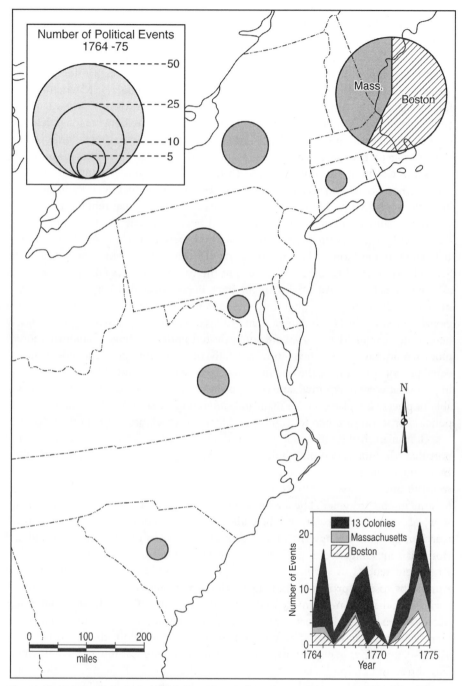

Figure 10.9.   The historical geography of key political events prior to the American Revolution, 1764–1775.

Sources: Morris 1970; Earle 1992.

restructuring the governance of Massachusetts. The stakes were now very high, and in that same year, the network of colonial committees issued a call for a "continental congress" to be held in Philadelphia in September. The delegates, who represented all of the colonies save Georgia, endorsed the Suffolk Resolves (Boston's county) declaring the Coercive Acts unconstitutional, urging the people of Massachusetts to form their own government, encouraging the residents to form their own militia, and recommending economic sanctions against Britain. The congressional delegates entertained an even more radical idea—the notion that the mainland colonies, severally and together, were as separate realms, beyond the pale of Parliament's authority and subject only to the power of the British Crown. Thus, when push came to shove, when liberal American elites were forced to choose between Parliament and king, they sided with Hobbesian absolutism over Harringtonian republicanism.

Bostonians, meanwhile, had moved well beyond arcane points of philosophy. Rebellion began in April 1775 with the skirmish between rebels and British troops at Lexington and Concord on the outskirts of Boston. Less than a month later, the Second Continental Congress voted to put the twelve colonies (all but Georgia) in a "state of defense." All of this might have been avoided, I suspect, had British strategists been a bit more attentive to geography—to the enormous variety of regional economies in North America, and to taxation policies that were geographically neutral in their incidence. A more sophisticated understanding of colonial geographies would have saved them from the folly of apportioning tax stamps in nearly equal proportions among the colonies, of levying what amounted to a double tax on imports that were reexported, and of imposing the heaviest taxes on the most vulnerable of places. No place on the mainland suffered quite so much from these myopic policies, or stood so much to gain by an American rebellion, as the port of Boston.

Bostonians had good reason to be in the vanguard of revolution. For a foreland port that had long relied on wholesaling, reexports, shipping services, and the West Indies trade, the costs of British neomercantile policies were large and the grievances real. But one city does not make a revolution. What led the other mainland colonies to join in the struggle? The precipitating factors have to do with parliamentary supremacy, Boston's dissent, and the endless rounds of action, reaction, and counter-reaction, all spiraling upward in a hyperbolic trajectory of parliamentary will and Bostonian intransigence. Equally important was the timing of events. In the 1760s, Parliament tended to vacillate; it enacted measures only to withdraw them when Americans rose in protest against them. But Americans took too much credit for vacillations that had much more to do with the unsettled state of British politics in a decade when prime ministers came and went with astounding regularity. "The times were extremely unsettled. The government was in confusion; there had been [by 1768] six ministries in eight years; trade was bad; and there was much unemployment and distress in London" (Harris 1963: 183). But then, in 1770, George III discovered a prime minister who shared his vision of the monarchy, who would remain in that position until 1782, and who would pursue a policy that "ended in utter disaster . . . [as] humiliation after humiliation was inflicted on the nation and its institutions brought into grave disrespect" (Plumb 1956: 122). Lord North was determined, inflexible, and a pure blessing for his American adversaries.

But neither Boston's grievances nor Lord North's incompetence were sufficient for a widespread rebellion. What prompted Americans outside of Boston to join the rebellion? Certainly one conditioning factor was American anger at British attempts to restrict the liberties that American elites had won prior to 1742. Having prospered under liberalism, American elites bridled at the imposition of British controls on colonial trade and commerce. Second, Americans anxious to speculate in western lands were irate at British prohibitions on settlement beyond the crests of the Appalachians. For the expansionist factions throughout the colonies, the British policy of orderly expansion was a restraint on profits and property. Third, for colonists who had recklessly overextended their credit at home and abroad and spent too lavishly on consumer goods, rebellion may have seemed a way out from under a mountain of debt. Rebellion shifts the advantage to the debtor because the collection of debts becomes more difficult and because creditors are compelled to carry unpaid loans on their books or write them off altogether. Fourth, American revolutionaries appealed to the egalitarian sympathies of an Age of Empire in ringing proclamations of political equality and their right to enjoy it. Their appeal, however genuine, resonated among sufficient numbers of Americans in the "middling and lower orders" of society to make a revolution.

The American Revolution thus falls into a fixed pattern of political revolution in the midst of egalitarian times—a pattern that begins with the English Civil War in the 1640s, the Revolution itself, the American Civil War in the 1860s, and the civil rights revolution of the 1960s. The first secured the civil rights of English citizens; the second, the civil rights of American freeholders, the third, the rights of slaves to freedom; and the fourth, the civil rights of African Americans. Moreover, colonists in the 1770s were more unified then ever. Most of them had been born in the colonies and thought of themselves as Americans. Most of them consumed similar kinds of goods and more than they could afford. And most of them were more aware of distant events thanks to the cities, towns, and hamlets that had arisen to serve their needs. While these shreds of unity worked to the advantage of American revolutionaries, most Americans were not fully convinced that liberal elites could be trusted. Even as the question of public virtue was being debated, some Americans, momentarily suspending disbelief, marched off into war.

Geographies of Rebellion

In the six years that separated Lexington and Concord from the climactic battle of Yorktown (1781), Americans conducted an improbable war to an improbable conclusion. In these years, an ill-financed and ill-equipped American army and navy managed to defeat the most powerful nation in the world and to ensure, when victory was finally sealed in the Treaty of Paris in 1783, that this newly independent nation would exercise sovereignty over nearly a million square miles of Britain's empire and nearly three millions of its former subjects.

The military geography of the Revolution unfolded in two nearly equal phases: the inconclusive northern campaign between 1775 and 1778 and the triumphant

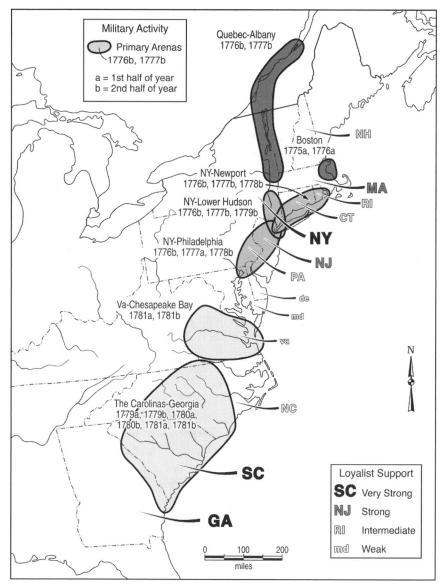

Figure 10.10.   Loyalism and the primary arenas of military activity, 1775–1781.

Sources: Adapted from Brown 1969; Cappon 1976: 44–49.

southern campaign between 1778 and 1781. By the usual rules of European warfare, Britain should have declared victory by 1778. British armies had won nearly all of their battles and had captured the two largest cities—Philadelphia and New York— and the British navy had isolated the third—Boston. American moral was at a low ebb among both the troops and the citizenry. In the face of so much adversity, massive support for the patriot cause had not materialized (figure 10.10). Many Americans, perhaps a third, were disaffected, caring little for either of the combatants; another 10 to 20 percent proclaimed their loyalty to the Crown (eventually, eighty thousand to one hundred thousand loyalists—some 5 to 6 percent of the white population in the mainland colonies—emigrated from the United States); and similar proportions shifted their allegiances with the tides of battle (the so-called sunshine patriots). It was left to a minority, variously estimated at a third to two-fifths of the population, to supply the troops, the matériel, and the revenue for an effort that produced few victories and much retreat.

In an attempt to isolate rebellious New England and to take advantage of the chief stronghold of loyalism, the British focused their military operations on New York City. It was there in 1777 that they launched a campaign that would prove to be the turning point of the Revolution. The goal was to drive a land wedge between New England and the rest of the colonies. The mission consisted of a coordinated three-pronged advance. British troops in New York City, the Mohawk Valley, and in Canada were to advance northward up the Hudson River, eastward down the Mohawk Valley, and southward up the Richilieu Valley, respectively, and converge on the city of Albany on the Hudson. The Mohawk advance stalled in August 1777 when it met fierce colonial resistance. And in October, American rebels crushed the southward advance from Canada at the Battle of Saratoga—less than fifty miles short of the British objective. When news of General Burgoyne's defeat at Saratoga and his surrender of 5,700 men reached Europe, France took its revenge and, in February 1778, entered into an alliance with the rebels before the British could put forth a plan for reconciliation.

France's entry into the fray effectively closed the northern theater of warfare and announced the opening of a southern theater. The key to both was in the hands of the French navy. Following the Franco-American alliance, the British navy was compelled to reposition most of its American operations so as to ward off French threats to the British West Indies. And as the fleet went, so went the British army. The British evacuated Philadelphia in the spring of 1778; captured the port of Savannah, Georgia in December of that year; burned Norfolk and Portsmouth in Virginia in May 1779; evacuated Newport, Rhode Island in October of that year; and captured Charles Town in May 1780. At this point, the southern campaign was in full swing, and the northern campaign had come to an end. New York City was practically the only northern place remaining in the British fold.

From their bases of supply in Savannah and Charles Town, British General Cornwallis and his troops marched into the interior, hoping to win the support of the disaffected settlers in the backcountry of the Carolinas. This was not an unreasonable strategy given the history of acrimonious relations, and sectional tensions between the wealthy coastal planters and the small farmers in the piedmont. Cornwallis's strategy might have succeeded were it not for the enormous size of the region, its distance from his supply bases along the coast, and the wily tactics of his American adversary, General Nathanael Greene. After taking command in 1780, General Greene used hit-and-run guerilla tactics to lead Cornwallis's army ever deeper into the Carolina backcountry, stretching thin his supply line to Charles Town, compelling the British to commandeer supplies from the local inhabitants, and, in the process, driving droves of disaffected colonials straight into the patriot camp. When

Cornwallis retreated to Wilmington on the North Carolina coast, Greene stepped up his campaign in South Carolina and confined the British to Charles Town and its environs.

In May 1781, Cornwallis launched his final ill-fated campaign, pushing northward from Wilmington into the Virginia piedmont. Following a string of minor victories and in need of supplies, he cut back toward the coast, marching down the peninsula between the James and York Rivers toward a rendezvous with the British fleet at Yorktown. Meanwhile, an army of Americans led by Lafayette trailed behind him; another led by Washington barged down the Chesapeake Bay toward Yorktown; and the French navy at the mouth of the Bay denied entry to the British navy. The trap had been sprung, and after a siege of a month and a half, on October 19, 1781, Cornwallis surrendered his army. The end was now near. Peace negotiations began in April 1782 and concluded with British ratification in January of 1783 and congressional ratification in April of that year.

Hard Times and Hard Choices: The Perils of Capitalist Independence

Winning the war was one thing; winning the peace was another kettle of fish. A series of problems bedeviled the loose confederation of sovereign American states. Perhaps the least of these was the matter of loyalist property. The several states and the courts quickly assumed jurisdiction, confiscating loyalist holdings worth in excess of £15,000,000. These takings, the equivalent of 13.7 percent or more of the colonies' aggregate wealth in 1774, constituted an enormous windfall for the states.

The vast area of land acquired under the Treaty of Paris posed a second problem, and in this case the states did not fare as well as the new nation. The terms of the treaty were quite generous. In a few strokes of the pen, the United States acquired 370,000 square miles of land, increased the territory of the thirteen colonies by 43 percent (to 865,000 square miles), and boosted the American stock of unsettled land to 642,000 square miles. With the addition of virtually the entire area west of the crests of the Appalachians to the Mississippi River and south from the Great Lakes to just north of the Gulf of Mexico, states scrambled to make their claims for territorial jurisdiction (figure 10.11). As Hilliard (1987: 152–54) points out, all of the new land

> was claimed by one or more of the original 13 colonies. Altogether, seven states had western claims. . . . Virginia claimed the largest area—all the new western lands from the mountains to the Mississippi River that lay north of 36–1/2 degrees north latitude. It was overlapped by several other claims. Connecticut claimed an intermittent strip that extended to the Mississippi River, a part lying in western Pennsylvania. Massachusetts argued for a part of western New York and a strip that extended to the Mississippi across what later became Michigan and Wisconsin; and New York had a nebulous claim based on Indian negotiations that included most of the Old Northwest and south to the Tennessee River. North Carolina's claim extended westward to the Mississippi. . . . [as did] Geor-

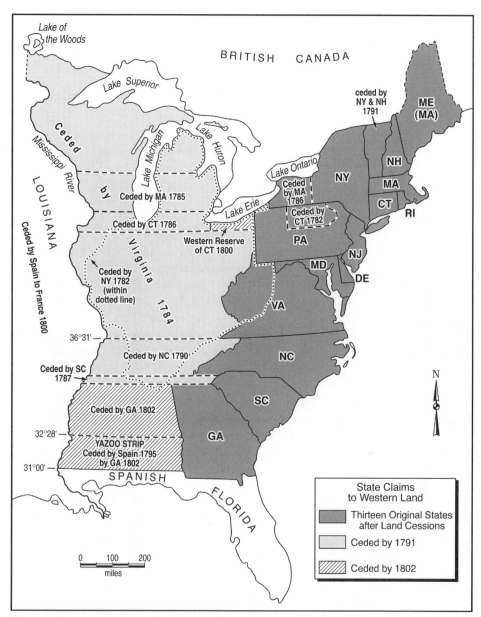

Figure 10.11.   State claims on western lands.

Source: Hilliard 1987: 153.

gia's . . . [which conflicted] in the north with a narrow strip also claimed
by South Carolina . . . and in the south with Spain (the Yazoo Strip).

The squabbling over land became so unseemly that Maryland flatly refused to sign
the Articles of Confederation. Taking the high road, New York ceded its western
claims to the national government and one after another of the state claimants, save
for Georgia, followed suit between 1784 and 1790 (Onuf 1983).

With the central government now in possession of over 90 percent of all western
lands, Congress turned its attention to the administration and distribution of the
public domain (Onuf 1983: 3–45). The Ordinance of 1784 and the Northwest
Ordinance of 1787 established the procedures for an orderly transition of the public
domain from territorial status to statehood. Congress began the process by defining
the boundaries of a territory. In the transitional territorial phase, "government was
effected through a governor, secretary, and three judges, all congressionally appointed" and, as population increased, by an elected assembly. When the territorial
population exceeded sixty thousand, the residents were permitted to "frame a constitution and apply for admission to the Union on equal terms with the original states"
(Hilliard 1987: 154–55).

The whole process was premised on two imperatives: first, the settlement of
western lands; and second, the orderly and efficient distribution of the public domain. Toward that end, Congress established the American rectangular land survey
system. The survey departed from the conventional practices of "metes and bounds"
surveying with all of its inaccuracies arising from ephemeral boundary markers, idio-
syncratic surveyors, and the "jigsaw puzzle" arrangement of landholdings. The new
survey was systematic; it created a hierarchy of rectangular units in which thirty-six
sections a mile on each side were nested in a township measuring six miles on a side.
Land was then sold by the section of one square mile or 640 acres. The ideals of
the rectangular survey were occasionally compromised, however. Concessions were
sometimes made to nature or when an area was too small to accommodate the thirty-
six-square-mile townships. Nor, of course, was the system employed on lands outside
the public domain as, for example, in the Virginia Military Reserve in southwestern
Ohio.

While the rectangular survey facilitated the orderly and efficient distribution of
land, it was far less successful in promoting the settlement of western lands. For most
Americans, the idea of purchasing 640 acres at a price in excess of $1 an acre was so
far beyond their means as to be unthinkable. The result, at least initially, was that
land companies filled the void by snapping up Ohio land for speculation. But when
Congress put a halt to this practice in the old Northwest, the settlement of the region
tended to languish. For Americans moving west, far better bargains on land were to
be had in Kentucky, Tennessee, Alabama, and Mississippi beyond the reach of the
public domain. To make matters worse, the federal government raised the price of a
section to $2 in 1796. The results of this elitist "dear-land" policy were predictable.
By 1800, the federal government had disposed of just over 1,500 square miles of the
public domain—an amount equal to less than a half a percent of the 370,000 square
miles ceded to the United States by 1802. In the meantime between 1789 and 1795,

Georgia had sold off over thirty-nine thousand square miles of present-day Alabama and Mississippi. The old Northwest seemed truly vacant by comparison to the South, where there was little land left that was not already spoken for or under Indian control (Hilliard 1987: 150–65; Lebergott 1984: 78).

The United States had won the land lottery in the 1780s and frittered away the opportunities it presented in the 1790s. To have behaved in this way seems foolhardy for a nation saddled with a war debt that has been estimated at $65 million, of which $40 million was owed by the central government and the rest by the states. By 1787, the United States had managed against all odds to liquidate $27.4 million. Land sales provided some of these funds, but most derived from state contributions, both direct and indirect. Direct contributions mainly served to keep the central government afloat, but these varied erratically, falling as low as $478,000 in 1786 and rising to triple that amount in 1788 (Jensen 1950: 382–83, 387). Indirect contributions, principally in the form of state assumptions of the nation's military debt, played a more crucial role in debt liquidation. The middle states alone assumed over $9 million of the national debt incurred during the Revolution (Jensen 1950: 388–98).

Paying off the American debt would have been difficult in the best of circumstances; it was doubly difficult when the nation's economy stood on the brink of crisis. Contrary to the sanguine views of the Confederation economy popularized by progressive historians from Charles Beard to Merrill Jensen, scholarly reassessments of the 1780s have painted a darker portrait of American economic life. Although Americans managed to increase exports (in constant £) by 34.5 percent between 1770 and 1790, population grew at a much faster clip (by 83 percent); exports per capita plummeted over 26 percent, falling from £1.30 to £0.96 (table 10.5). The southern states, which relied most heavily on British markets for tobacco and rice, suffered most as per capita exports fell by 39.1 percent in the Upper South and by 49.7 percent in the Lower South. As for the northern regions, New England held steady, while the middle states registered a 9 percent gain in exports per capita. From the standpoint of the several states, only five recorded an increase on this measure. All were in the north, with three in New England (Massachusetts, Rhode Island, and Connecticut) and two in the middle states (New York and New Jersey).

The negative growth of American exports (on a per capita basis) reflects the diversion of the American trade from Great Britain and the empire. Americans diverted over £750,000 of their annual exports away from the empire between 1770 and 1790 (figure 10.12). Great Britain's share of American exports fell from 58 percent to 31 percent, while the share of the British West Indies dropped from 27 percent to 10 percent. Americans partially compensated for these losses by expanding its exports to northern Europe and the foreign West Indies; these accounted for 16 percent and 24 percent, respectively, of American exports in 1791–1792. But the earnings from these new markets merely replaced the British earnings that were lost (Walton and Shepherd 1979: 190). The southern staples of tobacco and rice took a beating in these decades, falling from 38.4 percent of American exports in 1770 to 33.2 percent in 1790. Meanwhile, the exports of wheat, corn, flour, and bread—the staples of the middle states economy—rose from 21.7 percent to 29.1 percent of American exports.

Table 10.5.   Exports from the Mainland Colonies, 1768–1772, and the United States, 1791–1792

American Exports (annual average exports in constant prices, 1768–1772)

Region	1768–72			1791–92		
	Total exports ('000s £)	% of Colonial exports	Per capita exports (£)	Total exports ('000s £)	% of U.S. exports	Per capita exports (£)
New England	477	17	0.82	842	22	0.83
Middle Atlantic	559	20	1.01	1,127	30	1.11
Upper South	1,162	41	1.79	1,160	31	1.09
Lower South	603	22	1.75	637	17	0.88
Colonies/states	2,801		1.30	3,766		0.96
States with rising exports per capita:						
New Jersey			0.02			0.03
New York			1.15			1.51
Connecticut			0.50			0.62
Rhode Island			1.39			1.72
Massachusetts			0.97			1.14

Source: Walton and Shepherd 1979: 190–97.

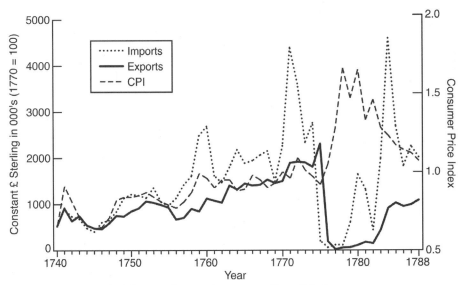

Figure 10.12.   American imports from and exports to Great Britain.

Source: Historical Statistics 1975, 2: 1182–83.

The sharp dip in American export growth in the 1780s seems not to have frightened American consumers who eagerly resumed their reckless ways soon after the Revolution. Imports regularly exceeded exports, and by a substantial margin. Before the Revolution (1768–1772), Americans spent about 43 percent more on imported goods than they earned on merchandise exports; by the early 1790s (1791–1792), the surplus of imports had pushed above 50 percent (*Historical Statistics* 1975, 2: 886, 1182–83). Consumer demand remained high, through the thin of hyperinflation between 1779 and 1781 and the thick of an economic depression in which, by one estimate, "the level of performance of the economy of the United States . . . [between 1774 and 1790] fell by 46 percent"—a figure that bears comparison to the 48 percent fall during the nation's worst economic crisis, the Great Depression of the 1930s (McCusker and Menard 1985: 373–74).

But unlike the Great Depression, prices did not collapse in the 1780s. Following the interlude of hyperinflation during the war, prices (in constant currencies) settled in at a level some 10 to 15 percent higher than the level in the early 1770s (*Historical Statistics* 1975, 1: 202; 2: 1196–97). The new price level was propped up by the postwar demand for imports and the credit to buy them. Americans had grown accustomed to living with debt long before the 1780s, and so long as the new nation and the several states attempted in good faith to pay off their debts and so long as they and their citizens could put up land and slaves as collateral, the lines of credit and consumer goods from abroad (mainly Britain) would continue to flow in—especially in light of the turbulence of continental markets in the "Age of Revolution."

PART III

NATIONAL GEOGRAPHIES

CHAPTER 11

Out with the Old, in with the New

THE RECONSTITUTION OF THE AMERICAN STATE AND ITS GEOGRAPHICAL PARAMETERS

The point of this chapter is straightforward. The United States Constitution is as much a geographical document as a political one; it is as much the product of the geosophical perspectives of the Founders and their adversaries as of their political philosophies. Toward this end, we begin with a glimpse of the rush of events that led up to ratification in the late 1780s.

Narrative

The 1780s were not the best of times for the American Confederation. Besieged by economic adversity, piled under by a mountain of debt, and unable to extract sufficient revenues from the sovereign states, the Confederation's "financial string simply ran out" (Lebergott 1984: 53–54). As criticisms mounted, Americans in larger numbers voiced doubts about the Articles of Confederation. Was a government conceived in war and revolution suited for managing the peace? The principal opposing faction, the nationalists, feared that in trying to hold together the revolutionary coalition the Confederation government had delegated too much power to the states. Lamenting the weaknesses inherent in a loose confederacy, the nationalists extolled the compensating virtues of a federal republic with exclusive jurisdiction over purely national matters. They dreamt of a stronger central government, one that would preserve the nation's security through the making of war and treaties with other nations; promote unfettered commerce among the states as well as a degree of uniformity in American commercial policies abroad; and coordinate the distribution of the public domain, the regulation and taxation of overseas trade, and the establishment of a national currency.

The drumbeat for change thumped even louder in 1786 at a commercial convention in Annapolis, Maryland. Concluding that stronger measures were imperative, the delegates at Annapolis issued a call for a constitutional convention to be

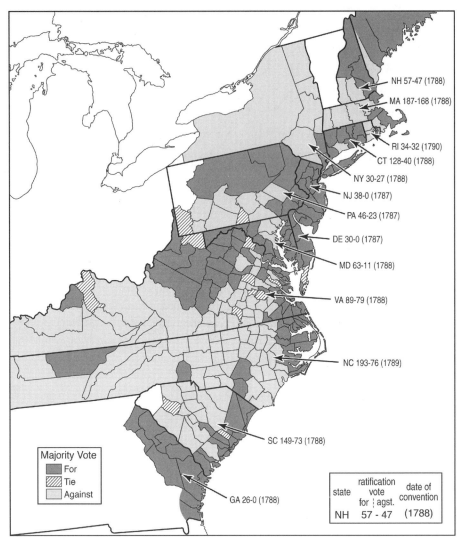

NH 57-47 (1788)

MA 187-168 (1788)

RI 34-32 (1790)

CT 128-40 (1788)

NY 30-27 (1788)

NJ 38-0 (1787)

PA 46-23 (1787)

DE 30-0 (1787)

MD 63-11 (1788)

VA 89-79 (1788)

NC 193-76 (1789)

SC 149-73 (1788)

Majority Vote
- For
- Tie
- Against

GA 26-0 (1788)

state	ratification vote for : agst.	date of convention
NH	57 - 47	(1788)

Figure 11.1.   The geography of the ratification of the Constitution.
Source: Adapted from Cappon 1976.

held in Philadelphia in the following year. As that convention got under way, it quickly became apparent that the nationalist faction was in command. Under the leadership of James Madison and Alexander Hamilton, the proponents of "federalism" drafted and secured the convention's approval of a constitution that greatly strengthened the powers of the central government. Over the next two years, the nationalist faction and their allies in the several states waged a fierce and narrowly successful campaign to secure the Constitution's ratification by legislative assemblies in the majority of states (nine). With the ratification of New Hampshire, the ninth state to do so, on June 21, 1788, the adoption of the U.S. Constitution was assured.

By 1791, ratification had been secured in the four remaining states and Congress and the states approved ten in a series of proposed amendments (the "Bill of Rights") to the Constitution (figure 11.1).

Constitutional Geographies

There is more geography in the U.S. Constitution than meets the eye. While "geography" per se does not appear in the Constitution, geographical concepts and ideas are shot through the seven articles in the foundational document of the American state. It is to the Constitution that we must go to understand the peculiar nature of American sectionalism, or to fathom the creation of the largest free-trade area among the nations of the world, or (to recall Clement Atlee's biting assessment of the Constitution as a document designed for an isolationist state) to account for the nation's enigmatic and reflexive insularity from world affairs, or, yet again, to decipher the geographical foundations of American political representation.

New Geographies

These constitutional geographies flowed, in turn, from the geosophical biases and perspectives that were implicit in the competing ideologies held by the framers of the Constitution and their adversaries. In their ongoing geosophical debate, Federalist and Anti-Federalist factions argued over geographical issues that were simultaneously old and spanking new, simultaneously familiar and refreshingly novel, simultaneously derivative and *sui generis*. Much of the debate was very new indeed. A case in point is the factional dispute over the relative power of federal and state governments. On this issue, neither experience nor ideology offered much in the way of guidance. In the absence of clear British or imperial precedents, the interpretation of federal-state relations stimulated a continuing series of highly original and uniquely American debates over such tendentious and enduring issues as states rights, concurrent majorities, sectionalism, and decentralism. While the Constitution may have enshrined Federalist biases in favor of a stronger federal government, the Constitution did not, by any means, resolve the interpretive debate over federal-state power relations. Indeed, by compelling states to form coalitions in order to exercise power, the constitutional compromise of 1787 seems to have agitated sectional tensions and heightened the prospects for sectional conflict.

Old Geosophies, Sliced and Spliced

Our reverence for the Founding Fathers at times obscures the reality that the Constitution did not spring out of nothing. The actions of Federalists and Anti-Federalists alike were rooted in ideologies and geosophies that had been planted long before by

Cromwell and Harrington and Walpole and Locke. The genius of the Federalists and Anti-Fedederalists notwithstanding, both factions borrowed heavily and unashamedly from the geosophical formulations of English liberalism and republicanism. Both factions reconsidered these venerable formulations in the 1780s and 1790s; both factions reformulated them into new and distinctively American ideologies and geosophies.

The essentials of this subtle and often mysterious process are as follows. First, Americans sliced liberal and republican ideologies into two parts—domestic and foreign policy. Second, the Federalists spliced the nationalist biases of republican foreign policy with the elitist biases of liberal domestic policy. In doing so, Hamiltonian Federalism inherited all of the geographical tendencies of republican nationalism—spatial expansion and demographic concentration—on the one hand, and elitist liberalism—expanded production, regional specialization, and regional stability—on the other. Third, the Anti-Federalists did exactly the reverse. In ways that were congenial to Thomas Jefferson and, even more so at a later date, to Andrew Jackson, they spliced egalitarian republican domestic policy—with its geographical tendencies of expanded consumption, regional diversification, and the volatility incumbent upon regional convergence—with the internationalism (free trade) of liberal foreign policy—with its geographical tendencies of spatial consolidation and demographic dispersion. The result was not one eclectic and inchoate American biformity, as Michael Kammen (1972) has suggested, but two geosophical biformities spliced in a polity of paradox.

In this fashion, Americans in the late eighteenth century rewired the circuitry of American politics. They sloughed off the doctrinal orthodoxies of liberalism, republicanism, and their geosophical tendencies and slithered toward the freedoms and opportunities promised, and variously delivered, by nationalist elites and egalitarian free traders. Henceforth, few Americans have taken a stand for liberalism or republicanism in the classical senses of these terms. And the folks who have—republicans such as Henry Carey and Patrick Buchanan or liberals such as Milton Friedman—are usually regarded as a tributary short of the mainstream. Most Americans are, it seems, both and neither. All of this helps to explain why interpretations of post-1790 Americans as unalloyed liberals or pure republicans are invariably doomed to failure and why we have such a hard time speaking about American politics without dreadfully mixing the geographical metaphors of a mechanistic liberalism and an organic republicanism.

The body of literature devoted to the geographical significance of the Constitution and the debate over its meanings is as pathetically small as it is painfully embarrassing. While I have neither the space nor the competence to remedy this imbalance or to capture all of the subtleties and nuances of constitutional history, the gravity of the geographical issues justifies, at the very least, a sketch of the peculiar conditions, agents, and geosophical ideologies that shaped the Constitution as well as the geographies of the early nationalist regime. I take these topics up in that order.

Conditions

1. The Treaty of Paris acknowledged the arrival of a nation of substance, if not yet of the first rank. The United States was one of the largest nations in the world,

encompassing over nine hundred thousand square miles—though less than half had been effectively occupied—and a population pushing three million. The nation was well endowed with ample rainfall, numerous navigable waterways, generally fertile soils, moderate to long growing seasons, terrain that was mostly flat to undulating (save for the Appalachians), and a variety of vegetation which, in combination, sustained an abundance of staple commodities and a mosaic of specialized economic regions (figure 11.2).

2. The American polity consisted of thirteen sovereign states loosely linked in a confederacy and governed under a document, the Articles of Confederation, that conferred modest powers on the central government.

3. The United States and the several states were deeply indebted both at home and abroad. At the worst, the collective debt of the United States may have amounted to 38 percent of the nation's gross national product—not as high as the

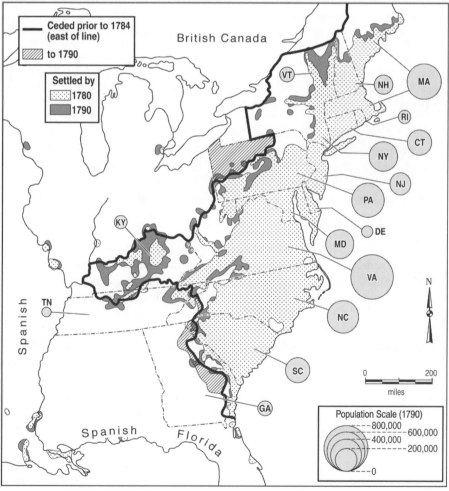

Figure 11.2.   The United States after the Revolution: Settled areas, Indian land cessions, and territorial boundaries.

69 percent registered by the United States in 1996, but dangerously large nonetheless for a new nation (Jensen 1950; Berry 1968: 32; McCusker and Menard 1985: 363).

4. The economy of the newly independent American nation was in bad shape, caught as it was in the double bind of a slashing depression that had cut the level of economic performance by nearly half since 1774 and had initiated a frantic search for new markets that might replace those that had been lost during the Revolution.

5. The financial string of the Confederation government was running out. The central government was largely at the whim of the states with respect to operating revenues and debt finance. While a large portion of the war debts were off-loaded to the states, the states were less forthcoming with other revenues. The Confederation's only other source of revenue was the public domain, but this was largely limited to land sales in portions of the Northwest Territory. South of the Ohio River, western lands were tied up by the extensive claims of Georgia, by treaty allotments to Indian populations, and by prior sales in Kentucky and Tennessee. The odds on the central government paying off its debts were rising fast. In 1786, when certificates issued by Congress were worth just twelve cents on the dollar, the odds had risen to eight to one. "Better odds were actually offered for Confederate bonds [in 1865] a week before Lee surrendered" (Lebergott 1984: 55–56).

Agents

1. John Adams had no difficulty identifying the ringleaders of reform in the 1780s. "The Federal Constitution was," in his opinion, "the work of the commercial people in the seaport towns, of the slaveholding states, and the property holders everywhere" (quoted in Bogart 1937: 244). While the thrust of Adams's assessment is in the right direction, it misses the mark by a generous margin. More precisely, the Constitution was the work of a truncated commercial and landed elite, shorn of "Tory" loyalists. Somewhere between eighty thousand and a hundred thousand loyalists had fled the colonies, and their departure represented some 5 percent of the population and 15 percent of American wealth. The impacts on the structure of the American political elite were even greater. Consider the situation in Massachusetts where over a third of the barristers in 1774 (seventeen of forty-seven) had fled the province by 1783 and just under a third (fourteen) of the rest wore the labels of "tory symapthizer or reluctant patriot" (Henretta 1973: 167). What this means, insofar as the barristers of Massachusetts are in anyway representative, is that the small American elite in 1774—some 10 percent of the population—had been reduced by half to two-thirds. In the absence of such an informed and influential conservative opposition—one that would have muddied the political waters in the 1780s—the Federalist task of making the Constitution was a much easier business.

2. The elite that remained or had not been discredited divided into two factions: the nationalists or Federalists who advocated a stronger federal government and the Anti-Federalists who preferred that power devolve mainly on the sovereign states. By and large, the nationalists tended to have "forged their identity in service to the war and the national cause in dealing with the individual states' reluctance to

assist that continental effort" (Kramnick 1988: 25; Cornell 1999). Within these two coarse factions, opinions varied greatly over the peculiar rights and obligations of the national government. While the Federalists might agree on the need for a stronger central government, individuals such as Hamilton and Madison would differ sharply over a range of specific issues related to the liquidation of the national debt, the government's role in the economy, or the relative importance of agriculture, commerce, and industrial development for the new nation—all of which would spill over in the political debates of the 1790s. But in the late 1780s, these differences were temporarily put on hold as nationalist elites embarked on their reconstitution of the United States of America.

3. The Federalists were deprived, however, of a free hand to do as they wished. Their political goals and ambitions were constrained by the democratic impulses inherent in British republicanism and the Revolution itself. These impulses had enfranchised and mobilized larger numbers of colonial voters before 1776 and provided greater access to political office after 1776. Neither Federalists nor Anti-Federalists could afford to ignore the impacts of political democratization. Whereas in the third quarter of the eighteenth century, "less than one in five of the delegates to the colonial assemblies . . . had been artisans or yeoman farmers, . . . in the aftermath of war and reapportionment these social groups now constituted a majority in some of the northern legislatures and a powerful minority in the southern assemblies" (Henretta 1973: 168). Factional elites rightly understood that concessions to the "popular forces" were a necessity if their democratizing impulses were to be contained. Moreover, since the Constitution required ratification by at least nine of the thirteen states, both Federalists and Anti-Federalists made their cases to these popular constituencies and to the delegates who represented their interests in the state legislatures in the form of a running campaign in the press (most famously, in what are now called the Federalist Papers).

Ideologies

1. In the fierce campaign for and against the Constitution, ideologies were mixed and matched, split and spliced, and abused and misused in the interests of partisan advantage. This partisan jumbling of fairly distinct ideological positions was, as we shall see, the indispensable preamble for the eventual consolidation of two uniquely American ideologies: elite nationalism and egalitarian internationalism. But clarity awaited confusion.

> In the "great national discussion" of the Constitution Federalists and Antifederalists . . . tapped several languages of politics in 1787–1788. None dominated the field, and the use of one was compatible with the use of another by the very same writer or speaker. There was a profusion and confusion of political tongues among the founders. They lived easily with that clatter. . . . Reading the framers and the critics of the Constitution, one discerns the languages of republicanism, of Lockean liberalism, of

work-ethic Protestantism, and of state-centered theories of power and sovereignty. (Kramnick 1988: 4)

Confusing indeed!

2. In the cacophony of this "great national discussion," Federalists and Anti-Federalists mixed and matched these languages in ways that emancipated political programs and policies from the chains of doctrinal (and doctrinaire) ideologies. The big issues, as always, were liberty and/or equality; nationalism and/or internationalism. The Federalists took up the cause of liberty. They endorsed liberalism's commitment to the transcendent moral order of justice and "the rule of law" as the bulwarks of personal rights and property rights. And, as if to ensure themselves against the charges that their Mandevillian pursuit of private interests would redound not to the public good but to deepening inequality, the Federalists simultaneously invested in the protestant ethic and its presumptions that work and frugality were virtuous and rewarding endeavors. But as Alexander Hamilton was wont to observe, liberty and equality were rarely compatible. "It was certainly true: that nothing like an equality of property existed that an inequality would exist as long as liberty existed, and that an inequality would exist as long as liberty existed, and that it would unavoidably result from that very liberty itself" (Hamilton as quoted in Huston 1998: 5). While other Federalists were somewhat more optimistic than Hamilton, by and large they shared his view that liberty and the unequal distribution of talents ultimately mitigated against widespread equality of condition. In opposition to these liberal Federalist sentiments, Anti-Federalists emphasized the need for a republican moral order of civic virtue based on widespread land ownership and the relatively homogeneous and egalitarian communities that they associated with the citizenry of a freeholding agrarian society (Cornell 1999:174–87). Also, in a sharp departure from Cromwellian political economy, commerce came under suspicion as one of the vices that, along with luxury and avarice, "had destroyed all republics in the past" (Huston 1998: 13). While agrarianism had a great deal of appeal in the 1780s and 1790s, the course of events would soon diminish the prospects of this physiocratic detour from the path of a mixed economy advocated by English republicans.

3. At home, Federalists embraced Lockean liberalism; but abroad, they defined the nation's position in the world of nations in terms that were unabashedly republican. For Federalists such as Hamilton and Washington, the republican notion that the security of the republic depended on power and sovereignty was axiomatic. They "intended a victory for power, for the 'principle of strength and stability in the organization of our government and vigor in its operations'" (Kramnick 1988: 23). They likewise shared Hamilton's sentiments that only a strong nation-state could avert the "feudal anarchy" of medieval Europe (not to mention the current anarchy of sovereign states) and enable the United States to guarantee its freedom and independence. "Let Americans disdain to be the instruments of European greatness! Let the thirteen States, bound together in a strict and indissoluble Union, concur in erecting one great American system superior to the control of all transatlantic force or influence, and able to dictate the terms of the connection between the old and the new world!" (*Federalist* No. 11, 1961: 91).

The temperament of that other erstwhile Federalist, James Madison, was some-what more cautious. But despite his reservations on the overly energetic exercise of national power, Madison was hardly timid in his assertions on behalf of national sovereignty. It was Madison who urged (unsuccessfully) convention delegates to confer on the national government the authority to veto noxious state legislation (Wood 1987: 71–77). And it was Madison who emerged as the most eloquent pro-ponent of expansionism and the sharpest critic of the naysayers who claimed that the institutions of republican government could only thrive in small and relatively homogeneous nation-states. He pointed out that expansion was perfectly compatible with his notion of an "extended republic," with its provisions for the continuing incorporation of diverse environs, economies, and people into the American polity, first as territories and then as states (McCoy 1987: 226–58; Onuf 1995: 50–80). In the Madisonian view, the coupling of expansion with the orderly addition of new states to the nation promoted the formation of new sectional coalitions, which, in turn, fostered political equilibrium through the mechanistic workings of sectional checks and balances on the excesses of one region or another. Expansion thus meant different things to the two wings of Federalism. For the Madisonian wing, frontier expansion constituted new sources of national diversity and political equilibrium that were crucial for the viability of an "extended republic"; for the Hamiltonian wing, preoccupied as it was by power, prestige, and imperial hegemony, frontier expansion added imperial appendages that were peripheral and subordinate to and dependent on the commercial and industrial core regions within the original thirteen states (figure 11.3; Banning 1995).

Federalists shared a commitment to national strength and stability, but the Ham-iltonian and Madisonian factions differed sharply over how to achieve these goals. "Since early in the decade [of the 1780s], Hamilton had taken Britain as an archetype of national success . . . he saw the Constitution as an instrument that would permit a vigorous administration to construct the economic and financial props of national greatness. For Madison, by contrast, the Constitution was the means by which the new world would avoid the European curses of professional armed forces, persistent public debts, powerful executives, and other instruments or policies [e.g., protective tariffs, industrial bounties and subsidies, a national bank] that Hamilton associated with effective statehood" (Banning 1995: 39). Fortunately, the notion of an "ex-tended republic" and the vastness of the public domain afforded ample room for the rivalry of these competing nationalist visions—Hamilton's playing out in the commercial and industrializing economies in the Northeast; Madison's in the fee-simple empire of frontier expansion and sectional parity that was arising west of the Appalachians (Pocock 1975: 506–52). In these expansive playing fields, Federalists pursued the dual geographies that were inherent in nationalist republicanism: the expansion of settlement in the West and the spatial concentration of economic and political power in the Northeast. But in each of these fields of republican nationalism the Federalists also provided a common set of ground rules—namely, the liberal presumption that economic growth and development, in the East or the West, hinged on the leadership and the investment of American propertied elites.

In the end, the genius of the Federalist framers of the Constitution lay in their

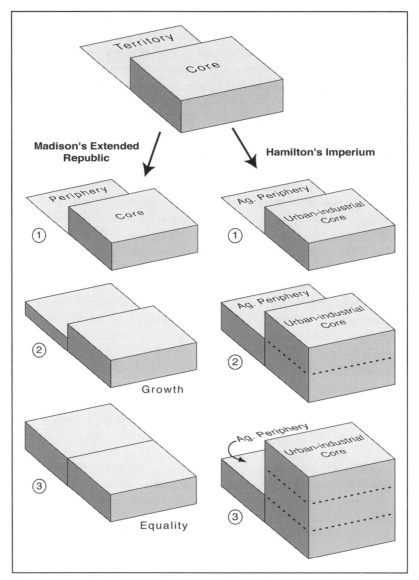

Figure 11.3.   Federalist perspectives on spatial expansion.

Note: Ag. is the abbreviation for agrarian.

atavistic fusings of the republican nationalism of Machiavelli and Cromwell, the liberal individualism and property rights of Locke, and the complementary refrains of American protestantism. In this compound ideology, "the language of Protestantism [and its emphasis on the virtues of work and individual salvation] was complementary to and supportive of liberalism" just as "the state-centered language of power was closer to and more easily compatible with the discourse of republicanism" (Kramnick 1988: 24; also Kammen 1972; Mason 1971).

Federalists thus laid the foundations for a liberal economy, a distributive elite polity, and a protestant work ethic at home; an expansive republican empire and a neomercantile economy on the periphery and abroad; and their geographical corollaries of westward expansion, spatial concentration at the heart of the republic (the core), regional specialization, and, above all, stability within the American space economy.

There is little doubt that this was the Hamiltonian view of American policy, but to what extent was it shared by Jefferson and by Madison? While much of what they wrote in the 1770s and 1780s seems at odds with Hamilton's elitist nationalism, their actions tended to be relatively consistent with the Hamiltonian vision. As for their streak of egalitarianism, "their own violations of the bill of rights dwarfed Federalist repression. Committed to minimalist government they did nothing to effect the redistribution of wealth from rich to poor. And any sympathy for 'a little rebellion now and then' disappeared the moment the people rose against the repressive measures of the Jeffersonian administration" (Ben-Atar 1996: 13). And recall that it was President Jefferson who engineered the largest, boldest, and most discretionary expansion in the history of the American empire (the Louisiana Purchase) and President Madison who in 1812 took the nation into a risky war that few wanted. In short, neither of these luminaries lived "up to the glorious ideals they expressed in the 1770s and 1780s" (Ben-Atar 1996: 13). They were at heart as elitist and as nationalist as Hamilton himself—which of course is why we speak of their era as "the early nationalist period" of American history and of their policies as cut from the same cloth. As for those Americans who dreamt of democracy, equality, opportunity, and the freedom of trade, patience was a virtue. They would be forced to wait until the "Age of Jackson" before forceful measures were taken to reverse the policies and geographies of this elitist-nationalist regime.

CHAPTER 12

Space/Time

FOUR SPATIAL VARIABLES ACROSS TWO CENTURIES AND FIVE POLICY REGIMES: THE NATIONAL ERA, 1780s–2000

This chapter offers an overview of the long-term trends of certain spatial variables across the past two centuries and the past five policy regimes of the American past. The chapter begins with a highly compressed history of American policy regimes and their continuing alternation between republics and democracies; and it ends with a chronicle of the congruent cyclical paths of four prominent spatial variables— settlement expansion/consolidation, demographic concentration/dispersion, regional stability/volatility, and regional specialization/diversification—at multiple scales (nation, region, and locale) across two centuries and five policy regimes. These longitudinal surveys leave little room for doubt that the two—policy regimes and geographies—are intimately and causally related. But to understand why, we must go back to their first embrace in the early national period and the American formulation of two novel and rival ideological positions: the federalist synthesis of republican nationalism and liberal elitism and the Jacksonian antithesis of liberal internationalism and republican egalitarianism. These ideological consummations would lead, in the case of the former, to the First, Second, and Third American Republics and, in the case of the latter, to the nation's First and Second Democracies.

The Revolutionary Road to Republics, Democracies, and the American Way

Was the American Revolution revolutionary? From the vantage point of geography, the answer is both yes and no. The Revolution was emphatically *not* revolutionary in terms of the structuring of geographical processes before and after 1776. Indeed, the Revolution caused scarcely a ripple in the processual continuities that now, on the outset of the twenty-first century, extend across three and a half centuries, two national sovereignties, and eight successive policy regimes. In fact, the processes responsible for shaping American geographies before and after 1776 have a great deal in common. These structuring processes are, among other things, similarly cyclical, similarly initiated in times of severe and protracted economic hardship, similarly rooted in the half century or so alternations of two hegemonic ideologies and policy regimes, and similarly transformational of life and landscape. In matters of process, the American Way of geographical change since 1776 is virtually indistinguishable from the Anglo-American Way prior to that date. But beyond these commonalities, the geographical similarities come to an end.

The Revolution was far more revolutionary when we look at the geographical substance of American policy regimes. Geographies changed, and quite radically and irreversibly, after 1776. The Revolution set this process in motion by smashing apart both the organic geographical model of English republicanism and the mechanical geographical model of English liberalism. To borrow a metaphor from Michael Zuckert's account of ideological transformation in seventeenth-century England, the Revolution "served as a cyclotron, barraging . . . [liberal and republican ideologies and geosophies] with high-energy particles that split . . . [these] into their constituent parts" (Zuckert 1994: xvii).

On the eve of this revolutionary bombardment, liberalism and republicanism had seemed impregnable and irreducible, their geographies, little more than electrons, in mindless orbit about their respective ideological nuclei (in the manner suggested in table 12.1). The constituents of England's two ideological atoms were, for all practical purposes, inseparable. Thus, one could not easily conceive of republicanism apart from its nationalist geographies of organic expansion and demographic concentration or its egalitarian regional geographies of volatility and diversification; nor could one imagine liberalism shorn of its internationalist geographies of spatial consolidation and demographic dispersion or its elitist regional geographies of stability and specialization.

The Revolution changed all that. Once they had split the atoms of English liberalism and republicanism, Americans groped for successors to these doctrinal ideologies during the 1780s. Some attempted, with little success, to reassemble the classical syntheses of ideology and geography. Jefferson came as close as anyone to recreating the classical republican ideology of nationalism and equal opportunity, but his efforts ultimately foundered on the rocks of an overly strident anticommercialism that was out of touch with the main strand of English republican thought—not to

Table 12.1.   Anglo-American Ideologies, Policies, and Geographies

Republicanism		Liberalism	
Foreign Policy	*Geographies*	*Foreign policy*	*Geographies*
Nationalist	*Spatial expansion *Demographic concentration	Free(r) Trade	*Spatial consolidation *Demographic dispersion
Domestic Policy	*Geographies*	*Domestic Policy*	*Geographies*
Egalitarian	*Regional diversification *Regional volatility	Elitist (property rights)	*Regional specialization *Regional stability

mention with English individualism. Whiggish liberalism enjoyed even less support in the dangerous days of an "Age of Revolution." The few Americans who appealed for greater freedoms in the conduct of overseas trade were repeatedly drowned out by practical political concerns over peace and security, the sources of public finance (the most reliable of which was tariffs), and the political jurisdiction over these matters (i.e., the sovereign states or the nation at large). In any event, more creative solutions were at hand.

Of all the ideological doctrines that surfaced in the 1780s, the most successful was the Federalist synthesis of republican nationalism and liberal elitism. Quite apart from federalism's widespread appeal among the nation's political elites, the Federalist synthesis of elite nationalism had the advantage of addressing two urgent political concerns: peace and liberty. For the proponents of federalism, republican nationalism afforded a means of securing American peace and security through the provision of a strong central government; and, simultaneously, liberal elitism provided a means of ensuring American liberty through the preservation of existing property rights—of which the Federalists had more than their share. It was these elite nationalists—men such as James Madison, Alexander Hamilton, John Randolph, and John Dickenson—who formulated the Federalist synthesis of elite nationalism, who constituted the powerful faction of "strong" Federalists, who framed the Constitution, and who implemented the policies and geographies of the "early nationalist" regime. But they were not unopposed (Lenner 2001).

The Anti-Federalists represented the antithesis of federalism. Their philosophical position, if we may call it that, was more diffused than unified, more negative than positive, and more in the way of an oppositional critique of federalism than an autonomous, polar ideological synthesis. Anti-Federalists strenuously opposed a strong central government, but most of them stopped well short of liberalism's logical alternative—internationalism and the freedom of overseas trade. The problem from the Anti-Federalist point of view was not mercantilism but rather who—the states or the federal government—should exercise it. And when they combined their vision of thirteen independent mercantilisms with egalitarian rhetoric, as many of them did, Anti-Federalists came awfully close to embracing the warmed-over tenets of classical English republicanism—albeit in the sovereign states one step removed from the nation at large (Main 1961; Kruman 1997; Wood 1969).

The Federalist synthesis of elite nationalism inevitably brought geographies in its tow. Over the first four decades of American history, the agents of American nationalism followed republican precedent in foreign policy and promoted rapid spatial expansion at the extremities of the republic as well as demographic and economic concentration in the heart of an incipient megalopolis. Similarly, their elitist domestic agenda adhered to liberal precedent in domestic policy and maintained stability among American regions and promoted economic specialization within them. But beyond these immediate impacts on the geographies of the new nation, these early nationalists fixed a course for the future. Their policies and geographies implemented between 1790 and 1828 established the permissible and narrow range of ideological and geographical parameters—and thus the ideological and geographical alternatives—available to subsequent policy regimes. Also, when, in the depths of future economic crises, the political "outs" sought to discredit the policies of the political "ins," they had little choice but to turn the "inside out"—that is, to invert the substance of antecedent ideologies, policies, and geographies. And 1828 afforded the first opportunity to do so. But unlike the Anti-Federalists, who shied away from the liberal notions of freer trade in favor of a nation of mercantilist sovereign states, their successors did not blink. Thus did Andrew Jackson's blunt rejection of elite nationalism and his enthusiastic endorsement of egalitarian free trade after 1828 set the tone and affix the extremes for the pendular alternation of American polities and geographies in the 1880s, 1930s, and 1980s.

Tables 12.2 and 12.3 summarize the mixed ideologies, regimes, and geographies that constitute the resynthesis of American politics. The first of these tables characterizes American regimes according to their prevailing policy commitments. This characterization yields two regimes—the one more or less elitist and protectionist-nationalist (or PE) and the other more or less egalitarian (mass) and internationalist (free trade) (or FTM). The second table (12.3) streamlines these clumsily labeled policy regimes in accordance with their primary ideological commitments. The choices of the terms *republic* and *democracy* serve, in the case of the former, to underscore the *nationalist* (and republican) thrust of elite nationalist regimes (PE) and, in the latter, to highlight the mass-egalitarian commitments (likewise rooted in classical republicanism) of mass free-trading regimes (FTM). These terms, in addition to their utility as a shorthand for purposes of exposition, resonate with the popular characterizations of the first period of American history as "the early nationalist period" (nationalism being a *republic*an concept) and the second as "Jacksonian Democracy." What is curious about these labels, insofar as they are fitting characterizations of the first two periods of American history, is that in both of our cases republicanism provides the major motif and liberalism the minor. The implications are not, at least in my opinion, that liberalism matters any less for Americans, but rather that it strikes too uncomfortably closely to our baser self-interested natures—natures that Madison, above all others, acknowledged and sought to constrain through his intricate system of constitutional checks and balances. Americans and their historians thus have been inclined to offer a more upbeat republican interpreta-

Table 12.2.   American Ideologies, Policy Regimes, and Geographies

Republics		Democracies	
Foreign Policy	*Geographies*	*Foreign Policy*	*Geographies*
Nationalist/protectionist	*Spatial expansion *Demographic concentration	Free trade	*Spatial consolidation *Demographic dispersion
Domestic Policy	*Geographies*	*Domestic Policy*	*Geographies*
Elitist/property rights	*Regional specialization *Regional stability	Equality of opportunity	*Regional diversification *Regional volatility

Table 12.3.   Republics and Democracies in the American Past

The Sectional State (1780s–1870s)—partisan and distributive polities
The First Republic (PE) (1780s–1828)	[The Early National Period]
The First Democracy (FTM) (1828–1877)	[The Middle Period/Jacksonian Democracy]

The National State (1880s–1980)—interest groups, regulatory and redistributive polities
The Second Republic (PE) (1880s–1932)	[Gilded Age and Progressive Era]
The Second Democracy (FTM) (1932–1970s)	[The New Deal Era]

The Transnational State (1980s–?)—"neoliberalism," neoregulationist at global scale
The Third Republic (PE) (1980–?)	[Reagan's America]

tion of the values enshrined in the nation's first two regimes and in their successor Republics and Democracies. The chronology of these regimes is roughly as presented in table 12.3.

With every swing in the pendulum of American policy regimes, American geographies have hung in the balance. And with every swing in the alternating succession of republics and democracies, the nation's geographies have been subjected to a thorough reconstruction—and not merely at the national scale. If we are to make sense of these geographical reconstructions, we can proceed in one of two distinct ways. The first approach is synchronic. It takes the several regimes one by one and then explores the complex relations between ideology, policies, and geographies in each of their swings. The second approach, and the one that will be used in the remainder of this chapter, is diachronic. It takes all regimes together and offers a longitudinal survey of geographical change at multiple scales—nation, region, and locale—and across two centuries and five policy regimes.

On the outset, we must disabuse ourselves of the notions that American geographies are flat and unleavened by comparison to the yeasty mix of American politics, that geographies are inert, glacial, and largely uncontroversial by comparison to the activism, dynamism, and tendentiousness of politics. To make these distinctions is to obscure the inseparable relations between national geographies and American foreign policies and between regional geographies and the domestic policies of American regimes. Worse, it is to erase from view their most substantial achievements on the American scene.

Pendular Geographies at the National Scale

Since the 1780s, geographies at the *national* scale have alternated with the rhythms of American policy regimes and, more precisely, with the rhythms of their foreign policies on overseas trade. Republics, given their commitment to nationalist-protectionist foreign policies, have regularly sought to expand the limits of American settlement and to concentrate populations in core regions. Republics concentrate their peoples even as they extend the limits of their effectively occupied territory. Democracies, given their biases in favor of internationalist/free-trade foreign policies, have sought to consolidate the American settlement system and to disperse population within its limits. Democracies consolidate their geographies even as their citizens disperse within them. Figure 12.1 graphs the long-run trends in these two variables of *expansion/non-expansion* and of *concentration/dispersion*.

FRONTIER EXPANSION AND SETTLEMENT INVOLUTION

The expansion of American settlement is here measured as the annualized and compounded rate of growth in the settled area of the United States. The "settled area" is defined as the area of the United States that is settled at population densities of greater than two persons per square mile. High rates of expansion mean what they say; low rates of expansion are indicative not only of slow or nonexpansion but also of the affirmative policies of spatial consolidation or involution. For the two hundred years between 1790 and 1990, national rates of settlement expansion exhibit certain general trends. By and large, expansion rates rose during the tenure of the nation's three republics and fell during the tenures of the two democracies (figure 12.2). The settled area of the United States expanded very rapidly in the First Republic, slowed sharply during the First Democracy, and accelerated modestly during the Second Republic before collapsing once and for all by 1920. If we take the long-run view of frontier expansion and look at the period between 1650 and World War I, a persuasive case can be made that the centrifugal momentum of the American frontier had largely been spent by the 1840s. At no point thereafter did expansion rates exceed two percent per annum nor did they approach the rates achieved at the high-

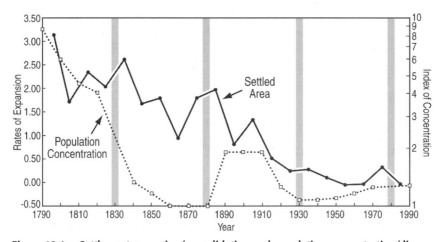

Figure 12.1. Settlement expansion/consolidation and population concentration/dispersion.

Sources: Adapted from Otterstrom 1997; Earle 2000.

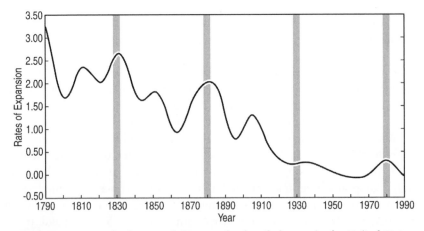

Figure 12.2.   Smoothed curve of the growth of settled areas in the United States, 1790–1990.

Source: Otterstrom 1997: 68.

water marks of expansion in 1650–1675, 1740–1780, and 1780–1840—all of which came during republican or nationalist regimes. If, however, one takes the shorter-run view since 1790, a case can be made for two short and final bursts of expansion, one in the 1880s and another in the 1910s—during the early and middle decades of the expansionist Second Republic. But whatever the temporal perspective, the pendular trend is fairly clear: faster frontiers are most closely associated with the foreign policies of nationalist/protectionist/neomercantile regimes; slower frontiers and the consolidation of settlement, with the foreign policies of internationalist/free-trading regimes in the periods 1680–1740 and 1830–1880. This is by now a familiar story of fast- and slow-moving frontiers in periodic alternation; what is not so familiar, and therefore deserving of at least brief consideration, is the weakening state of these settlement cycles during the course of the nineteenth century.

Over thirty years ago, the geographer William Warntz reported that the rate of American frontier expansion decelerated in three successively higher geometric progressions. "From 1790 to 1840 the [effectively occupied] area [of the United States] grew as the square root of the demographic energy [i.e., Warntz's measure of the amassing of American peoples]. From 1840 to 1890 it grew as the cube root, and from 1890 to the present as the one-fifth root." Warntz goes on to argue that "this [staged deceleration] is apparently related to the changing nature of the physical environment into which the frontier moved and suggests that additional . . . reduction in the unsettled area could be achieved only through increasingly large increments of demographic energy" (Warntz 1967: 207). Few would disagree that the semiarid environments in the western United States posed serious obstacles to settlement, but these alone fail to account for Warntz's periodizations of frontier deceleration. Why did Americans run the frontier at full throttle until the 1830s, step on the brakes after 1840, and jam on the brakes after 1910?

The post-1840 deceleration had as much to do with Jacksonian policies as with environmental obstacles. In truth, the edges of American settlement in 1840 had a considerable way to go before they ran up against the obstacles of a semiarid grassland environment. Nor were Americans in any particular hurry to occupy an environment so widely characterized as the "great American desert." But nor were they encouraged to do so by the Jacksonians. In the 1830s, Andrew Jackson himself set the stage for the deceleration of frontier expansion and the involution of the American space economy by lowering protective tariffs and advancing the cause of free trade. When economic conditions improved in the 1840s, most Americans kept closer to home. In lieu of migrating to the western frontier, they availed themselves of the ample economic opportunities within already-settled areas. And they prospered by doing so as freer trade opened up new markets, prices for American staple commodities soared, and spatial involution took root. In the buoyant regions behind the frontier, population densities rose sharply, small towns proliferated as distribution points for the unfolding consumer revolution, post offices were established in ever smaller villages and hamlets (an indication, perhaps, of the Jacksonians' egalitarian inclinations as well as their liberal usage of patronage), and postal routes grew so numerous and so dense as to be virtually unmappable at the national scale. In sum, the positive contributions of Jacksonian policies to American spatial involution in the middle third of the nineteenth century rivaled or surpassed the negative contributions west of the one-hundredth meridian.

However compelling the evidence for spatial involution during the First Democracy (1830–1880), the thesis of nonexpansion would seem to be in direct conflict with the period's designation as the apogee of manifest destiny and territorial expansion (and most especially during Polk's administration). In fact, the two processes of territorial and settlement expansion operated independently and indeed they often moved in different directions. Consider that while the United States vastly expanded its territory during the Mexican War, American settlement did not follow suit—and for several good reasons. First, the economic gains accruing from free trade blunted the expansionary impulse, and this was especially true after 1846 with the repeal of Britain's corn [grain] laws and the opening up of Britain's vast market for American wheat produced in the Midwest. Second, American farmers and planters likewise stalled frontier expansion by introducing innovations (e.g., the reaper in the Midwest and the crop rotation of cotton, corn, and cowpeas in the cotton South) that increased productivity within existing regions, and most notably along the entire length of the Mississippi Valley. The productivity gains from innovations such as the reaper for wheat, riding cultivators for corn, and crop rotations for cotton were augmented by nature's benevolence. Warmer and drier weather throughout the Mississippi Valley enabled row-crop producers to reduce the rounds of tillage; expand the acreages per laborer of cotton and corn; and nudge northward the limits of corn, cotton, wheat, and sugar production. With high prices and rising output in the countryside increasing the demand for slaves and wage labor in these established regions and blunting outmigration to the frontier, involution settled in on the American landscape.

The frontier's diminishing impact on American life was increasingly evident after 1840 and painfully obvious after 1890. Not even the rise of the expansionary

Second Republic in the 1880s was sufficient to reinvigorate the domestic expansion of settlement—save for the small burst associated with World War I. It was much easier, as the expansionist policies of the presidents from Rutherford Hays to Teddy Roosevelt would soon affirm, for Americans to march their frontiers southward straight into central America and the Caribbean. Henceforth, the Second and Third Republics sublimated the process of American frontier expansion in one of two directions: the one aggressively promoted trade-and-investment expansion abroad, and most especially in the Caribbean and Central America and, more recently Mexico via NAFTA (a theme pursued earlier in chapter 6); the other quietly promoted demographic concentration at home. In between the aggressive posture of these republics, the Second Democracy attempted to undo these processes—to shrink American imperial expansionism overseas and to disperse Americans from the northeastern core region into the peripheries at home (see sources cited in chapter 6 and Pletcher 1998).

SPATIAL CONCENTRATION/DISPERSION

For three and a half centuries, the English and later the Americans have fought over the geographies that were best suited for their respective nations and empires. They have clashed repeatedly over their geographical models of republican nationalism and liberal internationalism, over the desirability of spatial expansion or consolidation, and, as vitally, over the imperative of spatial concentration or dispersion of the peoples and economic activities in their nations and empires. From the time of Cromwell, the organic republican state has advanced its nationalist aims through the simultaneous implementation of two geographical processes—spatial expansion at the extremities and demographic concentration at the heart of the republic. Conversely, since Locke and the Whigs, the mechanical liberal state has furthered its internationalist aims through the spatial dispersion of populations within an involutional system of specialized and interdependent regions arising out of a competitive free-trade economy. The American Revolution did nothing to blunt these tendentious geographies of Cromwellian concentration and Lockean dispersion, and, in due course, they were indelibly imprinted on the successive landscapes of America's republics and democracies.

The trends in the American geographies of concentration and dispersion are shown in the cyclical curvings plotted in figure 12.1. This charting of the demographic concentration of American population density for the decades since 1820 uses a measure known as Moran's I. The Moran index ranges from $+1$ when population is fully concentrated in one areal unit to -1 when population is uniformly dispersed over all areal units.

The graph of these data underline two points: that American populations have been more rather than less concentrated and that the long-term trend tends to be cyclical (a trend overlooked in the provocative economic geographies of Krugman 1991a and 1991b). On the first point, the geographies of American population densities are more or less concentrated; that is, they vary from modestly concentrated to highly concentrated. The indices for U.S. counties between 1820 and 1990 are all positive (i.e., concentrated); they range from a low of 0.216 (modestly concentrated) in 1880 to a high in excess of 0.8 in 1820. The actual range of spatial concentration in the United States thus is just 30 percent of the theoretical range of Moran's I—which is to say that in the United States demographic concentration is invariably the rule and dispersion is always relative to it.

The second point of interest is that the curve of American demographic concentration/dispersion is cyclical; and, not coincidentally, these cycles are closely aligned with the alternations of American policy regimes. In the first American state (1780–1880), concentration reaches its highest levels at the end of the First Republic (to 1830) and then, after a half century of demographic dispersion during the First Democracy, falls to its lowest level in 1880. The cycle is repeated in the second American state (1880–1980); spatial concentration rises sharply in the 1880s with the installation of the Second Republic and the rise of mass production. The level of concentration doubles in that decade and then remains highly concentrated through the 1920s. That trend is reversed during the 1930s with the advent of the Second Democracy and the consumer durables revolution. Over the next three decades, New Deal policies dispersed the American population and lowered Moran's I in the direction of the historic lows registered during the First Democracy of the Jacksonians.

Is this cycle continuing as the nation careens forward into the Third Republic? The answer, based on the early returns from the 1970s and 1980s, is "probably yes." Concentration levels between 1970 and 1990 rose sharply, running roughly 12 percent above those of the 1960s. But this is still a far cry from the volatile changes in earlier times—for example, between 1830 and 1880 when the First Democracy reduced demographic concentration by 80 percent or between 1880 and 1930 when the Second Republic boosted the level of concentration by 100 percent.

These periodic reshufflings of American population were just the beginning. American policy regimes simultaneously reshuffled the locations of economic activity—and in a similarly systematic fashion. The reconfiguration of the geographies of American manufactures since 1860 offers a case in point. Thanks to Sukkoo Kim (1995, 1998, 1999), we have a long-run record of the locational concentration of regional manufactures based on Hoover's coefficient of localization. In Hoover's index, a value of $+1$ indicates that industry is completely localized [concentrated] in one [census] region and a value of 0 indicates that industry is completed dispersed across regions. Kim provides Hoover coefficients of manufacturing localization for ten dates between 1860 and 1987 (graphed in figure 12.3); the plot forms an inverted U with values ranging from a concentration high of 0.327 in 1927 to a low of 0.197 in 1987.

The trends in the concentration of manufactures differ from the demographic trends in two respects. First, manufactures are more or less dispersed over time while populations are more or less concentrated. Second, while the concentration trends in regional manufactures and populations are cyclical, the manufacturing cycle lags behind the demographic cycles by a decade or more. Thus, the dispersion of manufacturing initiated during the First Democracy (1860) continues through 1900—two

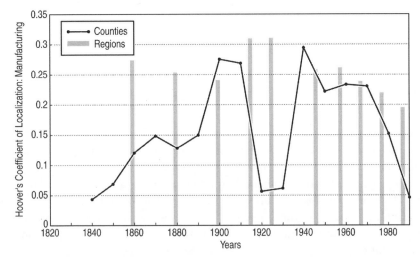

Figure 12.3. **The concentration of manufacturing employment using the Hoover Index calculated for counties and regions.**

Sources: Adapted from Otterstrom 1997 and Kim 1998.

decades after the end of that policy regime. In this span, dispersion across regions prevails in eleven of nineteen industries, led by tobacco; lumber and wood; stone, clay, and glass; petroleum and coal; and machinery. Thereafter, industrial concentration rises sharply over the last three decades (1900–1930) of the Second Republic. Concentration increases in fifteen of twenty industries, led in this instance by four of the "most dispersing" industries between 1860 and 1900 (tobacco; lumber and wood; petroleum and coal; and machinery) along with instruments. A second lag appears in the 1930s and 1940s. The decentralizing policies of the New Deal are slow to take hold, and manufacturing dispersion does not fully get under way until after World War II. Once begun, however, the dispersionary turnaround is dramatic. Over the ensuing forty years, concentration levels are slashed by 38 percent from their historic highpoint in 1927. Dispersion prevails in nearly three-fourths of all manufacturing industries (fourteen of twenty, to be precise), though in this case, a very different cluster of industries leads the way—namely, food; lumber and wood; rubber and plastics; machinery; electrical machinery; transportation; instruments; and miscellaneous firms.

What next? If the lag in manufacturing locations holds true to form, we should momentarily expect to see a renewal of manufacturing concentration as the policies of the Third Republic take root. But the increase in manufacturing concentration is unlikely to be as pronounced as in the past given the serious erosion of employment in this sector. Indeed, our best evidence of a resumption of spatial concentration in the American economy is likely to come from faster-growing sectors such as producer services. And, as we noted in chapter 5, that sector already offers provisional indications of locational concentration. But whether the sectoral shift from manufacturing to producer services will sustain the two-century cycling in the concentration and dispersion of American economic activity through a fifth cycle remains to be seen.

THE SUM OF NATIONAL-SCALE PROCESSES

Three conclusions emerge out of this longitudinal overview of national-scale geographies. The first is that the geographies of expansion/consolidation and concentration/dispersion are cyclical. The second is that these geographical cycles are inextricably related to the pendular alternations in American republics and democracies. Third, and perhaps most important, is the declension in the amplitude of these geographical cycles over time. The first two of these conclusions are fairly obvious from the evidence; the third is a bit more puzzling and thus is deserving of somewhat more attention.

American economic historians have made a persuasive case that the American economy in the twentieth century was quite different than its nineteenth-century predecessor (Abramovitz 1993). The case for a comparable divide in American geographies seems to be emerging from the evidence of national-scale spatial changes. Consider first the declensionary secular trends in the cycles of both spatial expansion/consolidation and demographic concentration/dispersion. Over the course of two centuries, the secular trends are steadfastly downward—toward lower rates of settlement expansion, lower concentration levels, lower amplitudes in both cycles, and a narrowing in the range of spatial differences between successive American republics and democracies. In the case of the frontier, the cycle largely ceases after 1910 as expansion rates move toward zero. Even before that date, however, the Second Republic had sublimated its expansionary impulses, shifting its energies from expansion at home to expansion overseas in Central America and the Caribbean. In this case, the arena had changed, but not the process. By the 1920s, American troops had variously enforced American interests in Panama, Honduras, Nicaragua, Cuba, the Dominican Republic, Mexico, and Puerto Rico. It was left to the Second Democracy to untangle this web of intervention and to reweave these strands into the web of internationalism known ever since as the "Good Neighbor" policy. While this "neighborly" policy was occasionally contradicted by American support for authoritarian regimes and covert operations in the region, it generally succeeded in cutting back on American interventions and on the overt exercise of imperial control over nations within the region (save, of course, in the Canal Zone, Puerto Rico, the Virgin Islands, and the naval base at Guantanamo Bay, Cuba). More recently, the Third Republic has demonstrated a willingness to be somewhat more aggressive. The military's insertion into Grenada during the Reagan administration is a clear example of the new interventionism; and the creation of the North American Free Trade Area is arguably an illustration of the expansionary extraterritorial impulse of American Republics since 1880. The larger point is that while the domestic cycle of settlement expansion/consolidation had largely ended by the turn of the century, the cycling of American expansion abroad has continued long after the closure of the

American frontier. All of these points reinforce the argument on behalf of the 1880s and 1890s as a geographical divide in American history.

Declension is also apparent in cycles of demographic concentration and dispersion which are considerably less dramatic than they once were. The vast differences between the mountains of concentration and the vales of dispersion in the First American State (1780s–1880) have been leveled off in the course of the second and third American states. The convergence is evident across both peaks and troughs. Across the peaks, concentration levels in the several republics fell from over 0.8 in 1820 to 0.43 in 1900 to 0.28 in 1970–1990; conversely in the troughs, dispersion levels in the two democracies rose slightly from 0.22 in 1880 to 0.24 under the New Deal. What we see here then is a rapid decline in the levels of demographic concentration and a striking convergence in these levels across policy regimes. The old saying that there is not a dime's worth of difference in American politics is an exaggeration—but only a slight one—when applied to the recent geography of American population. The difference in recent years is more nearly about seventeen cents (i.e., seventeen represents the percentage difference between the concentration levels of the post-1970 Third Republic, twenty-eight, and the trough of New Deal liberalism, twenty-four). When the geographical differences in concentration/dispersion are so small, there is little reason for fervent partisan politics. But in the past, when the configuration of domestic geographies was at stake, when American space was roiled and then rearranged, and when landscapes were uprooted and then replanted, and when concentration levels were cut by 73 percent—as they were in the nineteenth century—there was every reason for partisanship. Thus, the Jacksonian assault on the American core in the northeastern United States was deadly serious business. It is a measure of the Jacksonians' success that they managed to reduce demographic concentration (and increase dispersion) by over 70 percent. In the ensuing counterattack, the Second Republic was far less successful as it reclaimed only about a third of what had been lost between 1830 and 1880. On the basis of this evidence, one might argue that the geographical cycles of domestic spatial expansion/consolidation and demographic concentration/dispersion have been tempered, if not altogether eliminated, by the postpartisan politics and the regulatory policies of the twentieth-century National State.

The Regional Geographies of Elite and Egalitarian Regimes

America's national geographies of expansion/consolidation and concentration/dispersion have been greatly moderated in conjunction with the convergence of foreign policies on free trade and the military obligations of a superpower. Not so with regional geographies. These have remained remarkably robust because the cleavages in elite and egalitarian domestic policy have deepened during the twentieth century. In consequence, American regional geographies have alternated periodically on two principal dimensions—stability/volatility and specialization/diversification—and these alternations are largely a function of the domestic policies of elite or egalitarian American policy regimes. Regional economies invariably exhibit more stability and relatively greater specialization under elitist republics and, in contrast, more volatility and diversification under egalitarian democracies. More important, the swings in these regional variables continue to be vigorous. As of the 1990s, there are no signs of the declensionary trends in cyclical amplitude that have characterized the national geographies of expansion/consolidation and concentration/dispersion in the twentieth century.

THE SWING AND SWAY OF REGIONS: STABILITY AND VOLATILITY IN AMERICAN REGIONAL ECONOMIES

Policy regimes play an important role in shaping American geographies at both national and regional scales. Whereas national geographies hinge largely on a regime's foreign policies on overseas trade (either nationalist protectionism or internationalist free trade), regional geographies largely turn upon a regime's ideological commitments to liberty or equality (i.e., elitism/egalitarianism) and their corollary domestic policies. Thus, regimes that assign liberty and property a higher value tend to do the same with respect to regional stability and economic specialization, while regimes that place a higher value on equality of opportunity do likewise with respect to regional volatility and regional economic diversification.

We begin with the regional geographies of stability or volatility. In the venerable debate over liberty and equality, America's three republics have invariably come down on the side of liberty and property rights. Taking their text from Locke and, to a lesser extent Newton, these advocates of liberty place a premium on the prosperity of a propertied producer elite and the stability of regional economies and societies. American democracies, by contrast, come down on the side of equality of opportunity and its geographical consort, regional volatility. To deliver the socioeconomic mobility promised by equal opportunity, the agents of democracies set about reshuffling the nation's regional economies so that the privileges which accrue to the favored few are withdrawn and redistributed among the many (the masses). Regional volatility is thus an inextricable component of this egalitarian process.

One of the most informative and most useful measures of regional stability/volatility focuses on the trends in the regional shares of aggregate national income and the sizable swings that these reveal. Table 12.4 presents these regional income shares at six dates strategically posted near the end of one policy regime and the beginning of the next. The estimate for 1774 comes from Alice Hanson Jones (1980); the estimates for 1840, 1880, and 1930 are from Richard Easterlin (1961); and the 1980 and 1994 figures are from the U.S. Bureau of the Census 1975, 1991, 1997, 2000. Regional units are the regions as defined by the Census Bureau, save for the 1774 estimate that divides the colonies into three regions: northern, middle, and southern and a comparable grouping of Easterlin's 1840 estimates.

Recall that regional stability/volatility is measured by the sum of the percentage unit changes in regional income shares between the beginning and the ending of a

Table 12.4.   Regional Stability/Volatility: Regional Shares of Personal Income in the United States, 1840–1994, and the Net Changes in Regional Shares

Census Region	1774	1840	1880	1930	1970	1980	1994
New England		17%	11%	9%	6%	6%	6%
Mid-Atlantic		41%	33%	32%	24%	18%	17%
East North Central		12%	23%	23%	21%	19%	17%
West North Central		2%	11%	9%	8%	7%	7%
South Atlantic		14%	6%	6%	11%	15%	17%
East South Central		11%	6%	4%	5%	5%	5%
West South Central		4%	4%	6%	8%	10%	10%
Mountain		—	2%	2%	4%	5%	5%
Pacific		—	4%	9%	14%	16%	16%
New England	25%	21%					
Middle colonies/states	38%	49%					
Southern colonies/states	37%	44%					

Net change in regional shares	1774–1840 (22*)	1840–80 (45*)	1880–1930 (14)	1930–70 (29)	1930–80 (47)	1980–94 (5)

Notes: *The tabulation of changes in regional shares 1840–1880 excludes regions not present in 1840; were these two included, volatility would rise from forty-five units to fifty-one units. The comparison of incomes in 1774 and 1840 matches Easterlin's (1961) states with Jones's (1980) colonial regions. The comparison excludes new regions added to the United States between 1774 and 1840; income shares in 1840 are adjusted accordingly. If we include new regions, regional shares in 1840 equal New England, 17 percent; Mid-Atlantic, 41 percent; South Atlantic, 25 percent; and New Regions, 17 percent. Regional shares do not always sum up to 100 percent owing to rounding.
Sources: Jones 1980; Easterlin 1961; *Historical Statistics* 1975, 1: 242.

policy regime. Low scores are indicative of modest changes in regional income shares and of regional stability; high scores, conversely, of substantial shifts in regional income and regional volatility. As predicted, regional stability prevails in the First, Second, and Third American Republics with scores of 22, 14, and 5, respectively (the score for the Third Republic is of course partial, covering just the first fourteen years of this regime). By contrast, regional volatility peaks during the First and Second American Democracies when scores rise to 45 and 47, respectively. Regional economies under democracies thus are two to three times as volatile as their counterparts under republics. Moreover, and contrary to national-scale cycles of expansion and concentration, time has not dampened the amplitude of these cycles in regional stability/volatility. Regional volatility increased by 104 percent in the First Democracy, decreased by 69 percent in the Second Republic, and increased by 235 percent in the Second Democracy. This alternating trend seems to have continued since 1980. In the first decade and a half of the Third Republic, stability reigns. In that span, U.S. regions have registered a 5-unit percentage shift or the equivalent of an annual rate of 0.3 units of volatility. This stands in sharp contrast to the highly volatile 1970s when regional shares recorded an 18-unit change and an annual rate of 1.8 units. Put another way, the level of regional volatility has declined by 83 percent since the Reagan Revolution. And put a third way, the reduction of volatility in the early years of the Reagan era already surpasses the 74 percent decline in volatility engineered by the Second Republic between 1880 and 1930. It is to John Agnew's (1987) credit that his study of American regions encapsulates three of these geographical swings as successive epochs. These are the epochs of regional competition (pre-1870), regional dominance (to 1930), and regional volatility (to roughly 1980). These, by another name, are nothing less than the regional economic geographies prevailing under the nation's volatile First Democracy, its stable Second Republic, and its volatile Second Democracy. Agnew misses only the first and last of the nation's regimes—the First and Third Republics before 1830 and after 1980, respectively.

It is also clear that these alternations in regional stability and volatility had important spatial consequences; most notably, they resulted in regional winners and losers. Suffice to say that elite regimes (republics) tended to reinforce the status quo in the American space economy generally and the core in particular; regional stability was thus the inexorable concomitant of a republic's pursuit of life, liberty, and property. By contrast, egalitarian regimes (democracies) tended to promote vigorous and occasionally radical redistributions of the nation's income into peripheral regions; regional volatility thus was the concomitant of a democracy's pursuit of equal opportunity. Like a couple of veteran card players, American democracies shuffled and reshuffled the regional cards in hopes of drawing an inside straight; republics, meanwhile, played with the regional cards that they were dealt.

There is an important message in the fact that the high amplitude of these swings in regional volatility and stability has not diminished over five regimes and two centuries even as frontier expansion has ceased entirely and the swings of demographic concentration and dispersion are greatly reduced. The message is that the domestic policies of regimes, with their predispositions to liberty or equality and their biases toward the elites or the masses, have retained their edge in shaping American regional geographies (and most notably, their volatility or stability), while the foreign policies of regimes, with their nationalist or internationalist biases, have lost much of their purchase on national-scale geographies. Indeed, the large swings in settlement expansion and demographic concentration/dispersion during the nineteenth century were sharply attenuated with the closure of the frontier in the 1890s and the ensuing displacement of tariffs as the principal source of finance for the U.S. government. The emergence of the graduated income tax as the primary source of federal revenue had the effect of discounting the foreign policy debate over protectionism or free trade while elevating the domestic policy debate over income distribution (and liberty versus equality) to the forefront of the policy arena.

Before taking up other trends and changes in American regional economies, a caveat on the stability or volatility of regional incomes is in order. My notion of regional stability/volatility is a narrow one; it applies to, *and only to*, the distribution of incomes among regions. One should not confuse the regional shares of aggregate income with measures of regional inequality/equality that are based on regional distributions of per capita incomes. While there is good reason to believe, on philosophical grounds, that regional volatility, regional equality, and egalitarian Democracies go hand in hand, the empirical evidence presents a problem or two. Using Jeffrey Williamson's (1965; see also Drennan et al. 1996) measure of regional inequality, we find that the curve of inequality describes an inverted U with a squiggle at the end (table 12.5). The index rises (by 42 percent) between 1840 and reaches its

Table 12.5.   U.S. Regional Inequality across Policy Regimes: 1840–1996

Date	Index of Regional Inequality
1840	0.279
1880	0.355
1930	0.395
1961	0.192
1980	0.125
1990	0.148
1996	0.128

Sources: For 1961 and prior dates, Williamson 1965; thereafter, *Statistical Abstract of the United States* 1997.

historic high in 1930, falls (by 68 percent) between 1930 and its historic low in 1980, and then wobbles upward (by 9 percent) in the 1980s (under the Reagan–Bush administrations) and then back down (by 13.5 percent) in the 1990s (under the Clinton administration).

According to these data (table 12.5), the trends in American regional inequality since 1880 have behaved in accordance with our model of alternating regimes: regional inequality rose during the Second Republic (by 11.3 percent 1880 to 1930) and fell even more during the Second Democracy (by 68.4 percent 1930 to 1980). But if the trend since 1880 is predictable, what is not predictable was the steady rise in regional inequality during the First Democracy (1840–1880)—a time when the Jacksonian policies of an egalitarian regime should have lowered the levels of regional inequality. The most obvious explanation of this perverse trend toward inequality is that Jacksonian policies were swept aside by the destructive impacts of the Civil War and Reconstruction on the southern economy and by the postwar redistribution of American income toward the Midwest (most notably toward the North Central states; see table 12.4). Thus, when we focus on the years between 1860 and 1880, we find that per capita incomes were falling by anywhere from 25 to 48 percent in three southern regions as they were rising by between 36 and 48 percent in the Midwest (Easterlin 1961: 528; *Historical Statistics* 1975, 1: 242). The upshot is that the high volatility and growing inequality of regional incomes between 1840 and 1880 is less a reflection of Jacksonian egalitarian policies and more a reflection of the disruptions of the Civil War, the punitive policies of Radical Reconstruction, and the erasure of two decades (1828–1860) of regional income convergence by the political concentration of resources within the "Yankee Leviathan" emerging in the Northeast and the Midwest (Bensel 1990, 2000). In their blunting of Jacksonian policies of regional equity and their delivery of the spoils of war to the victors, radical Republicans laid the foundations for a dominant core region and a dependent periphery, and they deepened the trench of inequality among American regions. The Civil War thus stands alone among the nation's three revolutions—the others being the American Revolution in the 1770s and the civil rights movement in the 1960s—as the only one in which Americans decisively and, for a time, ruthlessly meted out punishment to the losing side. And southern Americans, like Germans after World War I, would not soon forget their "lost cause."

REGIONAL SPECIALIZATION/DIVERSIFICATION

Adam Smith long ago emphasized the productivity gains associated with the division of labor and economic specialization. David Ricardo went further, noting the superior efficiency of regions that specialized in the production of commodities in which they enjoyed a comparative economic advantage. But in truth, the horse was already out of the barn. The insights of Smith and Ricardo merely added a theoretical gloss to liberal economic strategies that had been put in place between the Glorious Revolution and the 1740s. From the time of Locke and the Whigs, elite liberal regimes had come to regard regional specialization as an integral component of liberal domestic policy (Appleby 1978). In fixing their sights on a producer revolution, the Whigs and their elite successors have consistently looked upon regional specialization as a means toward the larger ends of restructuring production systems and increasing the efficiency and productivity of the economy as a whole. In every one of their restructurings, from the financial revolution engineered by English Whigs (1689–1742) (Brewer 1990), to the industrial revolution of the early nationalists in the First Republic (1780–1830), to mass production and the rise of Fordist production systems (1880s–1930), down to flexible accumulation in the 1980s and 1990s, liberal domestic policies have encouraged regional entrepreneurs to exploit their comparative economic advantages and, in due course, to increase their levels of regional economic specialization.

But one man's virtue is another man's vice. Even as Adam Smith and Alexander Hamilton extolled the advantages of economic specialization, Thomas Jefferson lamented its corrosive effects on individual autonomy and self-reliance. Drawing upon a reservoir of republican egalitarian ideas from Cincinnatus to Harrington and the old Whigs, Jefferson extolled the advantages of economic diversification and an independent, self-reliant yeomen-citizenry. In his mind, as in theirs, economic diversification was nothing more or less than the indispensable condition for independence and equality. While Jefferson's views were too anticommercial to prevail, his advocacies of equality of opportunity and economic diversification were widely endorsed and, with the election of Andrew Jackson, elevated to the level of national policy. But Jackson, unlike Jefferson, eagerly embraced commerce—insofar as it broadened the base of consumption and raised the standard of living—and toward these ends he and his followers actively encouraged vigorous expansions in the supply of consumer goods, service occupations, and market centers, all of which ratcheted upward Jeffersonian notions of diversification and independence from the scale of the household to the scale of involutional regions. As the Jacksonian consumer revolution took hold, regions as well as households became more diversified, market centers proliferated, urban hierarchies fleshed out, and consumer durables spread across the American landscape. These Jacksonian regions were not autarchic by any means, but they were becoming more insulated from one another. And for the nation at large in 1860, involution would proved to be far less a blessing than a curse.

Egalitarian regimes thus see the world quite differently. Dismissing liberal claims for regional specialization, interdependence, and trade as a veil over the narrow interests of producer elites, egalitarian democracies advance instead the ideal of diversified economies—economies that are more conducive to the equitable distribution of incomes and consumer goods among the mass of citizens and less vulnerable to external shocks. It was in the eighteenth century that "'affluent, articulate and ambitious' Londoners, along with their provincial imitators, bent their minds to considering ways to make the world safe for egoism. Because the English had dealt with political tyranny in a previous century, they could address the more fundamental modern problem . . . of how individuals could pursue life, liberty, wealth, and happiness"—that is, pursue consumption (Appleby 1993: 167). Since these times and toward these ends, English republicans and American democracies have repeatedly promoted monetary and fiscal policies designed to stimulate both consumption and regional diversification. This was as true of the neomercantilists' expansion of consumer credit through the reduction of interest rates on government securities in the 1740s and 1750s as it was of the Jacksonians' elimination of the federal debt and the redistribution of federal deposits from the Bank of the United States to state banks as it was of the redistributive fiscal policies of the New Deal in the 1930s. In each of these regimes, egalitarian monetary and fiscal policies, consumer revolutions, and the diversification of regional economies invariably ensued.

The evidence of alternating trends toward regional specialization and diversification is largely impressionistic before 1860 but fairly precise thereafter. The impression of diversification during the Age of Empire (1740–1780s) is verified by the rapid dissemination of consumer goods, the emergence of an increasingly elaborate hierarchy of central places, and the widespread demonstration of the American capacity to reduce their reliance on imports in support of nonimportation protests in the late 1760s (see chapter 10).

One gains a quite different impression after the Revolution. Over the next five decades, the elites of the First Republic shifted the American space economy toward the kinds of specialized and interdependent regions so fully described by Nobel laureate Douglass C. North (1966). Jettisoning the processes of regional convergence along with the national identity that these processes had fostered in the 1760s and 1770s, the early nationalists placed their bets on interdependence and the divergent (and often divisive) processes of regional specialization. It is in these times, between the 1780s and 1828, that we first speak of a tripartite economy of Northeast, West, and South engaged in the specialized production of manufactures, foodstuffs, and plantation staples, respectively, and bound together by interregional and transatlantic trading and transport systems. American economic growth between the 1780s and the 1830s thus hinged on regional specialization, trade complementarities among regions, regional exchange and interdependence, and, ultimately, the healthy state of the British market for cotton.

The evidence of regional specialization and diversification improves substantially after 1860 thanks in large measure to Kim's pathbreaking studies (1995, 1998) of regional specialization in American manufactures between 1860 and 1987. The growing significance of manufacturing production and employment in this span invites the use of this sector as a surrogate for regional specialization across all economic sectors. While Kim has attempted to broaden his study from manufactures to primary and tertiary sectors of the economy, the fragmentary nature of the data afford only very crude estimates of specialization/diversification trends. Figure 12.4 reports regional specialization indices for twenty two-digit SIC manufacturing industries in a series of years between 1860 and 1947 and in most years thereafter.[1] Kim's index ranges from a score of zero for manufactures that are completely diversified across all census regions to a score of two for manufactures that are fully specialized within each region. The first point worth noting is that the geography of regional manufactures in the United States invariably tilts in favor of diversification. Kim's index of specialization never exceeds 1 (the midpoint in the continuum) and has a range that varies from a high of 0.89 in 1914 (weakly diversified) to a low of 0.43 in 1987 (moderately diversified). In other words, regional specialization in manufactures peaks at 45 percent of the theoretical maximum and troughs at just under 22 percent. While the range is fairly narrow in theory, the practical differences are not trivial given that regional manufactures in 1914 were twice as specialized as their counterparts in 1987.

A second point of interest is that the indices are cyclical, diversifying under egalitarian regimes and becoming more specialized under elite regimes. As expected, diversification increases in the final decades of the First Democracy (i.e., the index falls from 0.69 in 1860 to 0.59 in 1880); specialization then increases sharply during the Second Republic (peaking at 0.89 in 1914); and diversification is resurgent in the Second Democracy (the index falling to 0.43 in 1987). A closer look at these

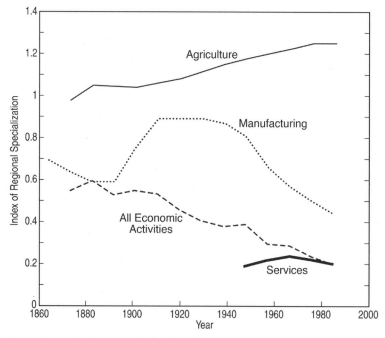

Figure 12.4. Regional specialization of American economic activity, 1860–1987.

Source: Adapted from Kim 1998.

cycles of diversification/specialization reveals that their amplitude seems to be on the increase. The differentials in the peak-to-trough indices rise from 29 percent between the First Democracy and the Second Republic to 52 percent between the latter and the Second Democracy. A third point worth noting is the tendency for the index of specialization/diversification to lag some two or three decades behind the installation of policy regimes. The regional lag is particularly evident between the advent of the New Deal in the 1930s and the trend toward regional diversification which did not begin in earnest until the 1950s. If such lags between policy regimes and geographies are typical—and our earlier data on concentration/dispersion suggest that they probably are—then the predictable manifestations of regional specialization in the Third Republic are unlikely to be evident until after the turn of the century.

A fourth point is that when we look beneath the national trends in regional specialization—when we disaggregate—we find that the trends in most American regions are remarkably similar. Indeed, over the spans of the Second Republic (1880–1930) and the Second Democracy (1930–1980), every region followed the national trend. In the former (and using Kim's data for 1880 and 1939), specialization across all regions increased by 47.5 percent, and specialization within regions exceeded the national average in five of six regions in the periphery of the American space economy (the exception in the periphery being the West South Central Region at 41.5 percent) and one of three regions in the core (the East North Central Region at 78.8 percent). The growth of specialization was least vigorous in New England (0.6 percent) and the Middle Atlantic States (21.9 percent), the oldest of the three regions in the urban-industrial core of the northeastern United States. What we are seeing in the Second Republic is the diffusion of regional specialization from an already-specialized core region into a periphery that is becoming increasingly more specialized between 1880 and 1930 (note, however, that most regions made their greatest strides toward specialization by 1914)—all set within the context of relative stability in regional income shares and of deepening regional inequality in incomes per person.

The Second Republic's headlong drive toward specialization in regional manufactures stalled after World War I and was thrown into reverse by the Great Depression, the rise of the Second American Democracy, and, in the wake of World War II, strategic initiatives aimed at decentralizing American productive capacity during the Cold War. Over the next five decades (1939–1987), the mean level of regional specialization fell by 51 percent—or slightly more than the 48 percent gain that it had recorded between 1880 and 1939. No region was spared. Indeed, manufacturing diversification registered substantial gains in all nine census regions; and six of these, led by New England (65 percent) and the West North Central states (66 percent), exceeded the mean increase for all regions (50.6 percent).

Are we in for another seismic shift with the turn toward the Third Republic and the resumption of regional specialization? Judging from the lags experienced during the two preceding regimes, it is probably too soon to tell. Consider that it took two decades (1880–1900) of the Second Republic before regional specialization began to increase; and similarly in the case of the Second Democracy (here the lag was between 1927 and 1947). Given this twenty-year lag between new policies and geographies, we should not expect to see definitive evidence of a resurgence in regional specialization much before the turn of the century. At this point, the evidence on behalf of an impending turnaround is mixed. On the negative side, the level of regional specialization in manufacturing decreased between 1977 and 1987 when it should have held steady. On the positive side in that same decade, two of the fastest-growing regions—the Pacific Coast and the East South Central states—halted or largely eliminated the decline in regional specialization. And two other regions—the Mid-Atlantic states and West South Central states—substantially slowed the pace of decline. It is worth noting that these four regions, in addition to their key role in the contemporary restructuring of the American economy, include three of the five regions in the so-called Sun Belt, arguably the most dynamic region in the traditional core region of the United States, and a tricoastal presence stretching from New York City to Houston to Seattle. If regional specialization is to rear its head once again, these are precisely the kinds of regions where we would expect the process to begin. Lastly, as manufacturers and producer services play lesser and larger roles, respectively, in the U.S. economy, we should expect some evidence of regional specialization in the service sector. On that score, Kim (1998) reports that specialization in that sector has held relatively steady in the 1970s and 1980s after peaking in 1967.

Geographies at the Local Scale: Cities and City Systems

The geographical effects of policy regimes are not confined to national and regional scales. These effects have also trickled downward into American localities, and the geographies of American cities and towns offer cases in point. If our trickle-down proposition is correct, we should expect to find evidence of the following sort: (1) that American urban geographies are cyclical rather than linear in their evolution; (2) that they alternate in conjunction with national policy regimes; and (3) that they tend to expand, concentrate, stabilize, and specialize when republics are in command and, conversely, to consolidate, disperse, fluctuate, and diversify when democracies are in the ascendant. Evidence for or against this proposition can be pieced together from previous inquiries on urban geography's two principal dimensions—the first of these deals with cities as members of a collective system of cities (e.g., their frequencies, sizes, and rank orderings); the second, with the internal structuring of land use within cities.

With respect to cities as systems, Borchert (1967; but see also Gordon 1978) has documented four stages in the evolution of American metropolitan systems and American transport technologies. The first of these stages or "epochs" he labels the Sail-Wagon epoch, 1790–1830; the second, the "Iron-Horse" epoch, 1830–1870; the third, the Steel Rail epoch, 1870–1920; and the fourth and most recent, the Auto-Air-Amenity epoch, 1920–late 1960s (and perhaps beyond). It is no accident, *en passant*, that the timing and duration of Borchert's epochs of urbanization and transport innovation happen to coincide—and almost precisely so—with the tenures of American policy regimes. The association makes even more sense when we consider the periodic changes in the size and frequency of cities in American urban systems. Following Borchert's lead, we find that the urban system in the first of these epochs (the First Republic, 1790–1830) is characterized by extraordinary stability; in the second (the First Democracy, 1830–1870), by revolutionary change; in the third (the Second Republic, 1880 to 1920–1930), by the "knitting together" of the national urban system; and in the fourth (the Second Democracy, 1930–1980) by the addition of new "amenity" cities and the dispersion of cities within the system as a whole. Borchert's story, desperately compressed, is a tale of periodic alternation between stable and volatile urban systems—which, of course, is precisely what we would expect of American republics and democracies, in that order.

These regime swings between stable and volatile urban geographies are faithfully registered in the hierarchical structuring of these systems. Table 12.6 summarizes the changes in the hierarchy between 1790 and 1994 using Christaller's k-value—a measure of the grand mean of the ratios of the frequencies of urban places at successively lower ranks in the urban system. In urban systems dominated by commerce, marketing, and transportation, as was the United States, k-values range from 2 to 4 on average. Within that range, rising k-values indicate increases in the frequency of lower-order centers—a result that is at once more egalitarian, more volatile, and more in accordance with the aims of American democracies (a caveat is in order, however, for exceedingly high k-values of the sort usually associated with hypersurveillant urban systems—i.e., Christaller's "administrative principle"). Conversely, falling values of k are indicative of urban systems dominated by large cities (elitist), greater stability, and the policies associated with the first, second, and third Republics. As table 12.6 affirms, the k-values of the American urban system invariably fall, albeit at a diminishing pace, during elitist republics—by 34 percent in Republic I;

Table 12.6. The Changing Urban Hierarchy of the American Urban System as Measured by k-Values, 1790–1994

Rank Ratios	2/1	3/2	4/3	5/4	6/5	7/6	Grand Mean
Date
1790	1.50	6.33					3.91
1830	3.00	1.00	5.30	1.03			2.58
1870	2.50	1.40	1.57	2.45	4.30	4.27	2.75
1930	1.60	3.00	2.33	1.75	1.89	3.28	2.31
1970	3.33	1.50	3.33	2.40	2.17	2.66	2.57
1980	2.67	2.10	3.50	2.20	2.10	2.40	2.50
1994	2.00	2.60	3.50	2.40	1.70	2.30	2.42

Notes: Population classes for rankings within the urban system are as follows: + 1 million (1880 on); 500,000–999,999 (1850 on); 100,000–249,999 (1820 on); 50,000–99,999 (1800 on); 25,000–49,999 (1790 on); 10,000–24,999 (1790 on); and 2,500–9,999 (1790 on).
Sources: Statistical Abstract 1997: 44; *Historical Statistics 1975*, 1:11.

by 16 percent in Republic II; and by 3.2 percent in Republic III (the decline rises to 5.8 percent if we measure change between 1970 and 1994 rather than from 1980). And k-values just as invariably rise during our two democracies—by 6.6 percent in Democracy I and by 11.3 percent in Democracy II. Generally speaking, American republics promoted economic growth that concentrated development within the larger centers within the existing urban system (i.e., reinforcing urban dominance). American democracies, in contrast, thickened the ranks of lower-order regional and local urban places. The Jacksonians, for example, pursued a strategy of egalitarian patronage which, in addition to creating a "spoils system," resulted in the profusion of smaller urban places (2,500–10,000) and tens of thousands of post offices—the lowest rung on the urban hierarchy. New Dealers took a different tack; they beefed up the ranks of metropolitan areas (greater than fifty thousand persons) and especially of cities of the second and fourth ranks (0.5 to 1 million persons and 0.1 to 0.25 million persons, respectively).

Urban geography tells a similar story about the internal structure of American cities. The plot in this case revolves around the periodic dynamics of spatial expansion and consolidation. And this is as it should be in light of the venerable, if now neglected, scholarly debate over the role of centrifugal and centripetal forces in the structuring of large American cities. It is fair to say that urban geography suffered a setback when this once-lively debate was cut short when the two sides settled on a compromise, when they agreed to agree that both forces were important and to disagree over which carried the most weight. Had they instead considered the historical evidence, the controversy might have been resolved fairly quickly. By and large, the historical evidence suggests that centrifugal forces of expansion are much more powerful during the tenures of the three American republics. In these times, in conjunction with the producer revolutions set in motion by these elite nationalist regimes, bits and pieces of the city were flung far into the surrounding countryside and plopped down in an archipelago of suburban islands amid a rural sea. Such was the case with the suburban industrial centers that arose several miles from Boston, Philadelphia, and Baltimore between 1790 and 1830; or again with the industrial and residential suburbs that grew up ten to thirty miles from the centers of the nation's largest cities between 1880 and 1930; or yet a third time with the explosive growth of edge cities and nonmetropolitan areas on metropolitan rims during the 1980s and 1990s. In each of these epochs, large American cities vastly expanded the scope (as measured by their radii) and scale of their operations.

But with the rise of American democracies, all this changed. In the late 1820s through the 1830s and once again in the 1930s, the forces of centrifugal expansion gave way to the centripetal forces of spatial consolidation and involution. As political priorities shifted, the new regimes installed proconsumer policies aimed at stimulating aggregate demand. Henceforth, two issues—the accessibility of the masses within the city and the provision of adequate housing—took precedence over the promotion of laissez-faire suburban expansion (both residential and industrial).

Toward these egalitarian ends, American democracies wasted little time in revamping urban transportation systems. In the First American Democracy, the introduction of the horse-drawn omnibus and the addition of new radial routes led to the establishment of peninsular urban corridors which connected insular industrial sub-urbs established before 1830 to the urban mainland. And soon after, real estate developers and city dwellers began to fill in the interstitial areas with middle-income housing. A century hence, this extend-and-fill process was repeated on the outset of the Second Democracy with the construction of a dense urban road network (not to mention the creation of a federally guaranteed mortgage market) during the New Deal. But even greater improvements in metropolitan accessibility and consolidation were in store with the post-1956 construction of the Interstate Highway System and, most especially, of its high-speed, limited-access circumferential highways or "beltways" (figure 12.5). Within two decades, the driving forces of urban circulation were more nearly lateral than centripetal—much to the detriment of the nation's "downtowns" and "inner cities."

With these preliminaries out of the way, the time is right for a closer look at the periodic and coaxial changes in American cities and city systems, transport technologies, and policy regimes.

THE SAIL-WAGON EPOCH OF THE FIRST AMERICAN REPUBLIC (1790–1830)

Stability is the key word in describing the American urban system in the early national period. In the words of Borchert (1967: 314), "the absence of any major change in the technology of land transport permitted most Atlantic ports to retain essentially the same functions through most of the epoch and to register neither

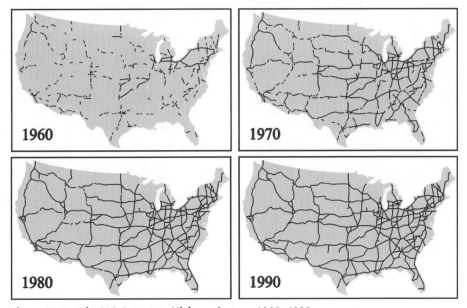

Figure 12.5.   The U.S. Interstate Highway System, 1960–1990.

relative increase nor decrease in the size order [i.e., city rankings] up to 1830"; the boom cities "were mainly along the inland waterways that penetrated the new western lands." Indeed, nine of the ten largest cities lined the Atlantic coast in 1790 and seven of ten did so in 1830 (table 12.7). Urbanization increased modestly from 5 to 9 percent, and though the number of cities and towns rose fourfold, that gain pales in comparison to the tenfold gain between 1830 and 1880 (Lampard 1968: 107).

But while stability prevailed in the system of cities, great changes were underway in the economy and the mercantile-pedestrian cities carried forward from the colonial period. The new nation made a heady start (figure 12.6). In just four decades, the economy grew nearly sixfold, population trebled, and GNP per capita nearly doubled. Trade continued to be the key to prosperity, with the internal coastwise trade taking up some of the slack that appeared in the overseas trade. The majority of both trades centered on the linkages within an incipient megalopolis—linkages that involved the exchange of Boston's boots, shoes, and textiles; Philadelphia and Baltimore's textiles and flour; and New York City's finance capital (Pred 1973). In this emerging corridor, industrialization and urbanization proceeded in tandem, and much the most important of these changes tended to occur in factories on the outskirts of the mercantile cities.

These suburban transformations were easy to miss for students of the city whose attentions were focused on the compact older city. Economic life there continued to revolve around trade and commerce; urban interactions were circumscribed by walking distances of a few miles; and population densities, though on the rise, remained well below the levels that they would achieve later in the century. The really big changes—and the ones overlooked in most sociogeographical models (Baerwald 1984; Pred 1966)—were taking place a few miles away in conjunction with the rise of industrial "suburbs" replete with factories, machinery, and inexpensive supplies of unskilled labor (figure 12.7). In these suburbs located well beyond the edge of the built-up city and three to six miles from the centers of Boston (Waltham), Philadelphia (Manayunk), and Baltimore (Hampden), entrepreneurs from these northeastern cities invested large sums in the establishment of cotton-textile mills (Earle 1992;

Table 12.7.   The Ten Largest Cities in the United States, 1790 and 1830 (in thousands of persons)

	1790		*1830*
New York	33.1	New York	202.6
Philadelphia	28.6	Baltimore	80.6
Boston	18.3	Philadelphia	80.5
Charleston	16.4	Boston	62.4
Baltimore	13.5	New Orleans	46.1
Salem	7.9	Charleston	30.3
Newport	6.7	Cincinnati	24.8
Providence	6.4	Albany	24.2
New Haven	4.5	Washington	18.8
Albany	3.5	Providence	16.8

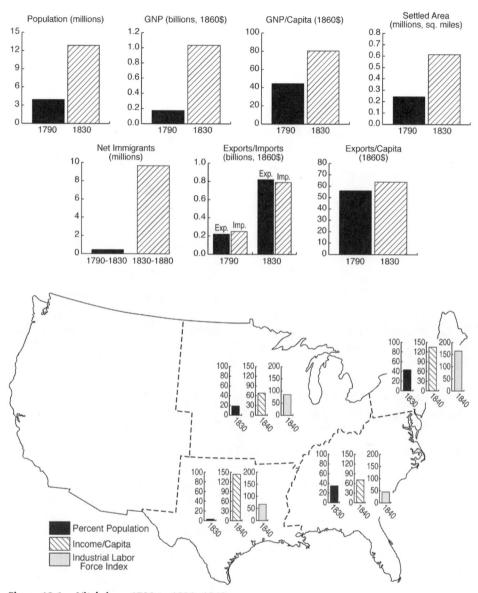

Figure 12.6.   Vital signs, 1790 to 1830–1840.

Wallace 1978; Dublin 1979; Gitelman 1967; Shelton 1986). The new sites afforded several economic advantages: access to cheaper unskilled labor (women, children, and seasonally unemployed rural laborers); separation from unions and labor organizers in the city proper; the availability of water power along the "fall zone"; and reasonable proximity to ports of entry for raw cotton. Sheltered from foreign competition by the wartime disruptions of trade before 1816 and by protectionist tariffs thereafter, these "greenfield" mill towns flourished and came to represent an inte-

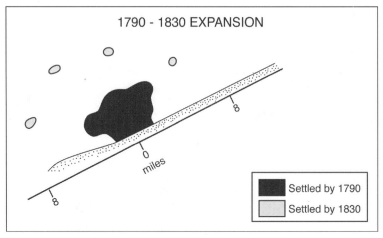

Figure 12.7.   The evolution of urban structure, 1790 to 1830.

gral, if spatially disjunct, component of the American cityscape and, when combined with the collieries, furnaces, and rolling mills of iron manufactures in the rural Mid-Atlantic states and the metal workers in the Connecticut Valley, they served as the landscape signature of the early nationalist regime qua the First Republic.

THE IRON-HORSE EPOCH OF THE FIRST DEMOCRACY (1830–1880)

The advent of the railroad and Jacksonian Democracy signaled the beginnings of far-reaching changes in the American urban system and in the internal geographies of the nation's leading cities (figures 12.8A and 12.8B). Indeed, "the urban pattern of the United States was revolutionized by the development of a national system of transportation, albeit a crude one." By 1850, railway lines criss-crossed the midwestern states on their way to regional termini; by 1856, interregional rail connections linked that region with the northeastern states. This epoch "saw not only the emergence of a first-order center [New York City] but also the greatest increase, both relative and absolute, in the number of second- and third-order centers in the nation's history" (Borchert 1967: 315–19; Pred 1980). In addition, five of the ten largest cities in 1880 were new since 1830 (table 12.8). But what was truly revolutionary was that a system (or more properly, systems) of American cities that numbered just ninety cities and towns in 1830 had grown over tenfold (to 939) by 1880. Simultaneously, the ranks of the largest cities were bolstered by the addition of thirty-nine new cities, mostly between the Appalachians and the Mississippi River—a region that also accounted for six of the nation's ten largest cities in 1880. The Jacksonians were not yet done, however. Concurrently, post offices in the United States (a function that embraces the lowest as well as the highest levels of the central-place system) increased nearly fivefold—from 8,450 in 1830 to 42,989 in

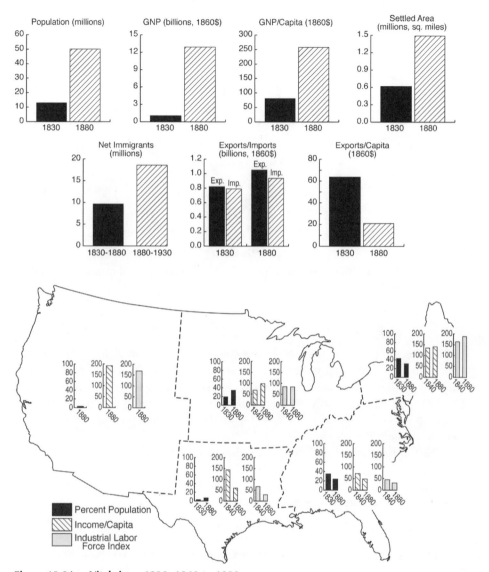

Figure 12.8A.   Vital signs, 1830–1840 to 1880.

1880 (U.S. Department of Commerce 1930: 351). Aided by the explosive pace of economic growth (a tripling of incomes per capita) and a comparable expansion in American exports, the democratization of the American urban system made substantial headway.

In the South, neither of these revolutions was imperative. By and large, these revolutions in city systems and rail transportation skirted the region. Steamboats supplemented by short-line railroads served adequately for transporting the cotton staple; meanwhile, the growth of cities and towns was attenuated by a staple that was neither as bulky nor as perishable as midwestern grains and livestock, that generated

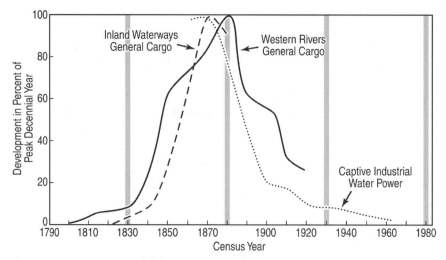

Figure 12.8B.   Innovation diffusion: Captive water power and general cargoes on inland waters and western rivers.

Source: Historical Statistics 1975.

miniscule earnings for middlemen in the commodity trade, and that handicapped industrialization with high wages for both skilled and unskilled labor (Earle 1992). But none of these is to blame for the poverty that enshrouded the region by 1880. The blame in that case falls on the Civil War and the political bungling of the region's fortunes by outsiders and natives alike (i.e., by radical reconstructionists and then by southern Bourbons).

The southern experience notwithstanding, the half century between 1830 and 1880 may well rank as the most volatile, the most revolutionary, and the most egalitarian epoch in the history of American urban systems. The share of Americans living in cities had risen from 9 to 29 percent of the nation's population and even more in

Table 12.8.   The Ten Largest Cities in the United States, 1830 and 1880 (in thousands of persons)

	1830		*1880*
New York	202.6	New York	1,206.3
Baltimore	80.6	Philadelphia	847.2
Philadelphia	80.5	Chicago	503.2
Boston	62.4	Boston	362.8
New Orleans	46.1	St. Louis	350.5
Charleston	30.3	Baltimore	332.3
Cincinnati	24.8	Cincinnati	255.1
Albany	24.2	Pittsburgh	235.1
Washington	18.8	New Orleans	216.0
Providence	16.8	Cleveland	160.2

the northeastern states (51 percent), which, with the midwestern states, accounted
for 68 percent of the population. Much of this urban growth was attributable to the
urban goals of Jacksonian Democrats. On the one hand, they encouraged the creation of hundreds of new cities and towns (i.e., of a raucous volatility within the
American urban system). On the other, they sought to consolidate and to unify the
mercantile-pedestrian city and its outlying industrial suburbs. The proper Jacksonian
solution was cheap mass transit, and toward that end the emerging interurban rail
system afforded one link and the intraurban horse-drawn omnibus yet another (figure 12.9). As residential and commercial development clustered along these key
radials in the 1830s and 1840s, the contiguous built-up area connected cities and
industrial suburbs and the form of this consolidating city took on a starlike configuration by the 1850s (Hershberg 1980). Over the next thirty years, the democratizing
push for spatial consolidation was extended to the problem of public facility provision. These decades witnessed a continuous shift "from piecemeal and fragmented
provision of infrastructure to an increased emphasis on centralized and networked
systems." These consolidations included the addition of streetcar systems powered by
horse and cable, steam-powered elevated railroads; the extension of gas distribution

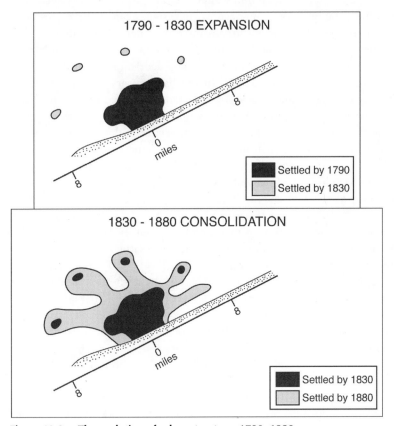

Figure 12.9.   The evolution of urban structure, 1790–1880.

systems; improved methods of lighting; and innovations in sewer and water systems (Tarr 1985: 72).

On the whole, cities in this epoch made sizable advances in the provision of the essential facilities of public accommodation. But the geographical results were not always as egalitarian as the Jacksonians intended. Even as the consolidated city permitted a greater range of movement, the gains in accessibility crystallized into new and decidedly less democratic social geographies. Even as cheap transport improved accessibility and enabled workers to lengthen the average journey to work (and to home), the greater elasticity of daily travel sundered the bond between workplace and residence and reinforced residential differentiation and segregation along class, ethnic, and racial lines. Mass transit, paradoxically, planted the seeds of an urban mosaic of homogeneous and segregated social areas.

THE STEEL-RAIL EPOCH OF THE SECOND REPUBLIC (1880–1930)

American urban geographies turned back the clock with the rise of a new policy regime in the 1880s. In ways reminiscent of the First Republic, the Second Republic restored the stability of the American urban system even as the forces of suburban expansion enlarged the scale and transformed the internal structures of the nation's larger cities (figure 12.10A and 12.10B). The renewed stability of urban systems is evident in two sorts of changes. First is the sharp deceleration in the system's addition of new cities and towns after 1880. In the half century preceding that date, the numbers of U.S. cities and town rose over tenfold; in the half century after 1880, the numbers increased by just 3.4-fold—a figure that is more nearly in line with the 3.75-fold increase during the First Republic. Second is the increased stability in the population rankings of the nation's one hundred largest cities. When urban-system volatility/stability is measured as the sum of all rank shifts by decile per decade, our index registers a drop of 34 percent between the high-water mark of volatility in the middle third of the nineteenth century (when the index exceeds 1,100) and the restoration of stability in the 1870s and 1880s (when the index falls below 730). The trend toward the stabilization of urban ranks is even more impressive (43 percent) when measurements are run between the precise volatility peak in the 1840s and its precise trough in the 1870s (Lukermann 1966: 31). Third is the stability evident at the upper end of the urban hierarchy where eight of the ten largest cities in 1880 retained that status for the duration of the Second Republic (table 12.9).

In this more stable context, Americans could set about the task of "knitting together" a distended and insular collection of cities into a national urban system—a system on the way to housing 69 million urban Americans (56.2 percent of the nation's population) by 1930 (as compared to 14.1 million in 1880) along with the majority of the 18.6 million immigrants arriving in the United States between 1880 and 1930. By the end of the century, an integrated, interdependent, and hierarchical system had been put into place. In this system, "New York retained national influence at the primary level and considerable influence at other levels as other major

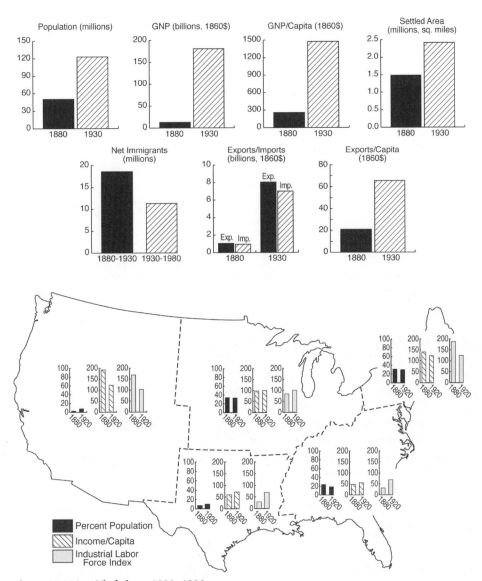

Figure 12.10A.   Vital signs, 1880–1930.

[regional] cities took over responsibility for regional subsystems" and for facilitating regional interdependence with "New York or Chicago but also to each other" (Conzen 1977: 108). This was a remarkably sleek urban system, one that consisted more nearly of a continuum than a hierarchy of cities by rank and size; streamlined the flow of goods and services necessary for mass production in the heavy industries of iron, steel, coal, metals, and petroleum, among others; facilitated unprecedented gains in economic growth (a nearly sixfold increase between 1880 and 1930) and a comparable gain in overseas trade; and enabled the urban population to surpass the rural by 1920 (54.2 to 51.6 million, respectively).

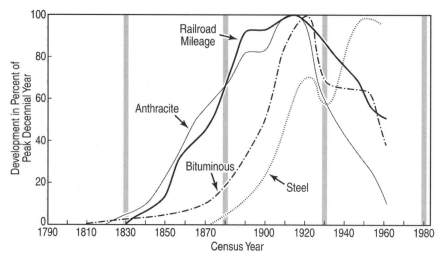

Figure 12.10B.   Innovation diffusion: Railroad mileage, coal and steel production.

Source: Historical Statistics 1975.

In this nationalizing process, the advent of steel rails counted for far less than raw power and elitist politics. One of the rawest of all of these new politics was the judiciary's unseemly rescue of national railroads that were nearly defunct and their resuscitation under the exceedingly friendly receiverships imposed by the courts. Under these cozy arrangements, national roads were able to slash their operating costs to the point that regional railroads were placed at a competitive disadvantage. Not far behind on the scale of raw politics was a series of regulatory rulings (most notably on long-haul and carload freight rates) that consistently favored national railroads over regional carriers (Berk 1994). By 1900, the decisions of the judiciary and the Interstate Commerce Commission had laid the foundations for a thorough restructuring of American railroading. A small group of northeastern financiers, with J. P. Morgan at the head, had managed to gain control over the principal national

Table 12.9.   The Ten Largest Cities in the United States, 1880 and 1930 (in thousands of persons)

	1880		*1930*
New York	1,206.3	New York	6,980
Philadelphia	847.2	Chicago	3,380
Chicago	503.2	Philadelphia	1,960
Boston	362.8	Detroit	1,570
St. Louis	350.5	Los Angeles	1,230
Baltimore	332.3	Cleveland	900
Cincinnati	255.1	St. Louis	820
Pittsburgh	235.1	Baltimore	810
New Orleans	216.0	Boston	790
Cleveland	160.2	Pittsburgh	670

railroads and, as important, over the economic futures of cities within the American urban system. It was these powerful men who, in the course of constructing a national railway system, would impose order, integration, hierarchy, and stability on a distinctively American urban system. The system they created enabled unprecedented economic growth even as it constrained radical changes in the spatial structures of regional economy and population distribution. It ensured that the northeastern core would continue to dominate the American economy at the expense of the regions in the southern and western periphery (note, on that score, that the level of regional inequality hit its historic peak of 0.395 in 1930 before falling by 68 percent over the next half century). By 1930, this core region provided nine of the nation's ten largest cities, and these constituted 15 percent of the nation's population (the top three alone accounting for 10 percent; table 12.9).

But if the systemic relations among American cities had grown more stable after 1880, the cities themselves were caught up in the tumultuous processes of suburbanization (or, as it was known in some academic circles, urban decentralization), industrialization, and immigration. Suburbanization greatly increased the range and expanded the scale of the nation's largest urban–industrial cities after 1880; industrial entrepreneurs and residential developers transformed the city by establishing suburban enclaves within the rural–urban fringe of these cities (figure 12.11). By and large, expansion was most vigorous along sectors that were defined by railroad lines leading into and out from the central city. Many of the new suburbs had their origins as centers of manufacturing. Indeed urban population grew most rapidly in cities that specialized in manufactures. According to a 1905 survey of thirteen of the nation's largest cities, suburban "industrial districts" accounted for 28.6 percent of the manufacturing employment and 29.9 percent of the value of manufacturing products in these cities. Equally impressive from a geographical perspective, the suburban portions of these industrial districts nearly quadrupled the area within the orbit of these industrial cities (from 1,083 square miles in central cities alone to 3,919 square miles in these cities and their industrial suburbs [U.S. Department of Commerce and Labor 1909]). Industrial entrepreneurs and corporations typically established suburban factories along rail-line sites located ten, twenty, or more miles from the center of the larger American cities. A few of the largest firms and corporations went a step further and established factory towns or, more presumptuously, "satellite cities" such as Pullman outside Chicago, Norwood in the Mill Valley north of Cincinnati, and the U.S. Steel towns of Gary, Indiana, east of Chicago and Vandergrift in the Pittsburgh metropolitan region (Taylor 1915; Mosher 1995).

The advantages of industrial suburbanization were fairly obvious. Sites on the rural-urban fringe offered entrepreneurs (1) ample land at prices that were much lower than in the city itself—an important consideration given the emphasis on horizontal, one-story facilities for assembly-line production; (2) ready accessibility to the city center and to the American urban transport system via the railroad; and (3) thanks to the distance from older city centers, the opportunity to create a new, more malleable, and more docile nonunion suburban labor force.

As members of the working class rented or bought housing in areas located near these suburban factories and "satellite cities," prospering members of the professional

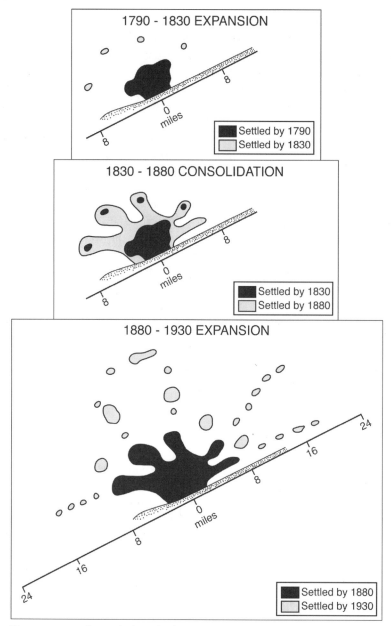

Figure 12.11.   The evolution of urban structure, 1790–1930.

and business classes were beginning to buy lots and homes in the tonier "commuter suburbs" then under development. For the developers of these residential enclaves no less than their occupants, a fashionable location was imperative; that meant a site that was conveniently located along interurban railroad or trolley lines emanating from the city, that was located astride the more scenic portions of these radial routes, and that was at some considerable distance from the noxious social and environmental attributes of the central city as well as from the new sites of suburban manufacturing. Residential sorting, by social class, income, race, and ethnicity, when reinforced by progressive zoning laws and restrictive covenants partitioned these expanding cities into a mosaic of increasingly segregated and homogeneous compartments (a city of multiple nuclei, as it were). Segregation of blacks and whites in seventeen northern cities increased by 41 percent between 1890 and 1930—and by 25 percent in just the last two decades (Lieberson 1980: 71). At the latter date, whites were also segregated by nativity. Foreign-born whites in ten cities in the northeastern United States were as segregated from native whites in 1930 as were blacks from all whites in 1890 (Lieberson 1963: 46). In both cases, 40 to 50 percent of these populations would have had to relocate in order to have eliminated segregation (the figure jumps to 62 percent for blacks in 1930). With the addition of these new industrial and residential suburbs, most large American cities doubled or trebled the effective radius of urban activity and functions. The urban population densities that in 1880 had declined precipitously at distances of four to six miles from city centers had by the 1920s been pushed some ten to twenty-five miles out into the countryside—into the "rural-urban fringe" (Berry and Horton 1970; Anderson 1977: 52–65).

The residential and industrial sprawl within large American cities would not have been possible in the absence of an unusually rapid diffusion of "suburban infrastructure" between 1890 and 1910 (figure 12.12). In this case, diffusion entailed massive investments in capital improvements such as the construction of water and

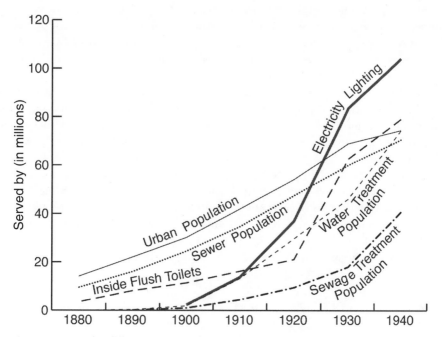

Figure 12.12. The diffusion of urban infrastructure, 1880–1940.

Sources: Tarr 1988; Lebergott 1993.

sewage lines; water filtration and sewage treatment plants; streetcars, electric traction subways, and elevated lines; electrical lines for the distribution of power to both commercial and residential customers; and telephone networks. When "contrasted with earlier developments [in the provision of urban infrastructure], these innovations and extensions were larger in scale . . . and often utilized new materials such as concrete and steel as well as electricity as a power source" (Tarr 1985: 72; 1988; figure 12.12). They were also costlier; and much of the financial burden would fall upon American municipalities, which, between 1880 and 1932, registered a sixfold increase in their levels of municipal debt (from an average of $20 per capita in 1880 to $120 in 1932). Put more positively, the nation's cities by 1930 accounted for some 24 percent of the nation's net capital formation (Tarr 1985: 63; Anderson 1977: 11).

THE AUTO-AIR-AMENITY EPOCH (1920s–1970s) AND THE SECOND AMERICAN DEMOCRACY

The last of Borchert's urban epochs coincides more or less with the hegemony of the nation's Second Democracy, i.e., the egalitarian free-trade policy regime commonly known as "New Deal Liberalism." The trends in the geographies of cities and city systems are predictable: City systems are characterized by increases in the volatility and dispersion of cities and towns; and intraurban structures, by the reconstruction ("renewal") of inner cities and the metropolitan consolidation of urban cores and suburban spatial enclaves. In the case of urban systems, "regional and metropolitan dispersal, inherent in the shift to auto and truck and in the development of a dense highway network, is reflected . . . [in] the entry into the metropolitan ranks of numerous 'satellite' cities on the fringes of the historic Manufacturing Belt and within 100 to 150 miles of great metropolitan industrial centers" and of "amenity boom centers" located in the warmer climes of Florida, the desert Southwest, and southern California—regions that were the joint recipients of 11.4 million migrants from other regions between 1920 and 1960 (Borchert 1967: 321). "Utilizing and improving on a virtually fully developed transportation system since World War I," Americans embarked on the nationalization of regional economies and urban systems (Borchert 1967: 307). In these times of unparalleled affluence, anything seemed possible. With prices rising by 500 percent, per capita incomes exploding upward from $1,473 in 1930 to over $121,000 in 1980, and American trade pushing over $5.5 trillion and penetrating markets around the globe, American consumers flush with cash and credit flooded into the new shopping centers and malls that were popping up in the suburbs (figures 12.13A and 12.13B).

More impressive, even astonishing, was the sheer quantity of new entrants into the American urban system—the addition of 3,270 cities and towns of 2,500 people or more between 1930 and 1970 more than doubled (103.3 percent) the number of urban places in the system. A very few like Columbia, Maryland, or Reston, Virginia, were entirely new, while the others sprouted out of small towns, hamlets, and villages. And, as befitted an egalitarian regime, most of the additions accrued on the

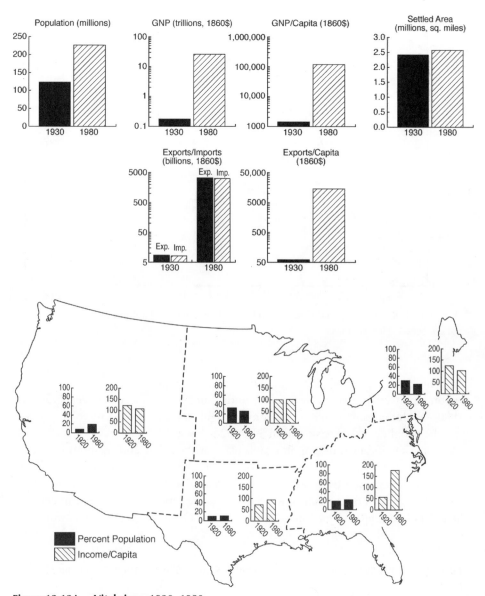

Figure 12.13A. Vital signs, 1930–1980.

lower limbs of the urban hierarchy. When we restrict attention to those urban places with 10,000 persons or more, 84.5 percent of the 1,319 new entrants were smaller cities and towns with populations between 10,000 and 49,999. These were precisely the kinds of places that registered disproportionate gains in manufacturing production workers between 1947 and 1982—and most especially in smaller cities and towns located outside of the traditional Manufacturing Belt—with the dispersion of American demographic and economic activity (Moriarty 1991). All of these devel-

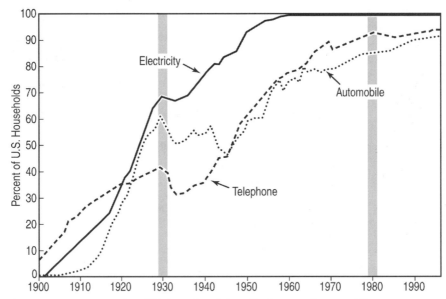

Figure 12.13B.   Innovation diffusion: Electricity, telephone, and automobile.

Source: Historical Statistics 1975.

opments hastened the redistribution of the American population from the northeastern and midwestern manufacturing belt to the Sunbelt periphery between 1930 and 1980—with the core's share of the nation's population falling from 66 to 48 percent and the periphery's share rising from 34 to 52 percent.

Some significant shuffling also took place at the other end of the urban scale (table 12.10). In 1930, on the outset of the Second Democracy, nine of the ten largest cities occupied the northeastern industrial core bounded by Boston, Baltimore, St. Louis, and Chicago. Los Angeles was the lone exception. A half century hence, Los Angeles was joined by San Francisco, Washington, D.C., Houston, and

Table 12.10.   The Ten Largest Cities in the United States, 1930 and 1980 (in millions of persons)

	1930		*1980*
New York	6.98	New York	18.90
Chicago	3.38	Los Angeles	11.50
Philadelphia	1.96	Chicago	8.12
Detroit	1.57	Washington	5.79
Los Angeles	1.23	Philadelphia	5.65
Cleveland	0.90	San Francisco	5.37
St. Louis	0.82	Detroit	5.29
Baltimore	0.81	Boston	5.12
Boston	0.79	Houston	3.12
Pittsburgh	0.67	Dallas	3.05

Dallas. Moreover, the largest metropolitan areas stood out boldly by 1980. New York and its four-state metropolitan area nudged 19 million persons followed by Los Angeles with 11.5 million and Chicago with just over 8 million. The top ten metropolitan areas alone housed 72 million people—or nearly a third (31.9 percent) of all Americans, a level not surpassed by the nation until the 1890s.

This was not the most volatile period for the American urban system—indeed, the 103.3 percent increase in urban places between 1930 and 1970 paled in comparison to the 237.1 percent and 943.3 percent gains in 1870–1930 and 1830–1870, respectively. Yet in other respects it seemed the most volatile. Spontaneous growth centers (SGCs), mostly in peripheral amenity locations, increased from 42.7 per decade between 1900 and 1930 to 67 per decade between 1930 and 1970. SGCs, which grow at twice or more the mean growth rate of SMSA populations, constituted 31.6 percent of all Standard Metropolitan Statistical Areas (SMSAs) between 1930 and 1970 and were responsible for nearly half (49 percent) of total SMSA population growth (Alonzo and Medrich 1972). Even more notably, the urban system seemed more volatile because of the widening differentials in the rates of urban and rural population growth. In the half century after 1930, the American rural population ceased growing and the numbers stagnated at about 53.8 million; meanwhile, the American urban population more than doubled, rising by 116.4 percent (from 69 million to 149 million). Americans were on the move—one in every ten between 1935 and 1940 and one of every six in the 1970s, many of them moving to metropolitan areas (43 percent) in the 1930s and most of them (69 percent) doing so in the 1970s (Wilson 1987: 217). A bare majority (56 percent) in 1930, urban dwellers had become the overwhelmingly dominant population (74 percent) by the 1970s. Whereas American cities had had to share the stage with rural America before 1930, that changed after 1930. Thanks in large part to the prourban sympathies of New Dealers and postwar "liberal" Democrats, cities took center stage. Rural America, meanwhile, was increasingly limited to bit parts in the ongoing American saga—a saga that, in its metropolitan version, pitted one part of the city (the downtown and the inner city) against another (the suburbs).

The addition of eighty million urbanites between 1930 and 1980 transformed the internal geographies of cities within the American urban system. Many of these new cityfolk—over 54.5 million in 1970—resided not in the central city proper but in the burgeoning suburbs. More precisely, these suburbanites filled in the interstitial slivers and chunks that nestled between the radial routes and the residential and industrial suburbs that had been laid out by developers and entrepreneurs during the Second American Republic (1870–1930). Post-1930 suburbanization thus was not a mindless sprawling across new landscapes as it was a fairly systematic "infilling" of the rural areas between the city's principal radial routes and their streetcar suburbs. This infilling was, of course, a peculiar geographical product of an egalitarian democracy, American style. The key, as usual, was the privatization of egalitarian incentives—in this case pertaining to the matter of housing provision for the masses of American consumers (Jackson 1981; figures 12.14A and 12.14B).

During the 1930s, with a quarter of the American labor force out of work and foreclosures and evictions mounting daily, New Dealers experimented with a variety

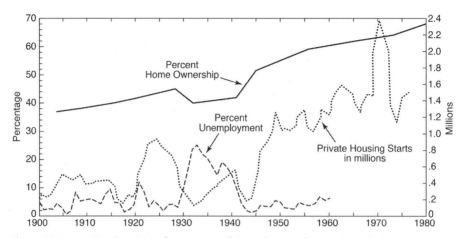

Figure 12.14A.   Housing starts, home ownership, and unemployment, 1900–1980.

Sources: Borne 1981: 42–44; Doan 1997.

of housing policies and programs. One set of experiments, modeled partly on European housing policies and partly on the ideas of American reformers like Jane Addams and Catherine Bauer, involved the federal provision of rental public housing (Radford 1996; Rodgers 1998: 160–208, 461–84; Marcuse 1980). Another set of experiments involved creating federal incentives for the private sector through the federal underwriting of mortgage risk in the otherwise private housing market. After World War II, both Democrats and Republicans veered away from direct state involvement in the provision of public housing; they instead encouraged federal policies that promoted homeownership, the private real estate market, and the construction industry (most notably the building trades) through federal guarantees of long-term, low-interest loans via the Federal Housing Administration (FHA) or the Veterans Administration (VA) (as part of the so-called GI Bill) (Jackson 1985).

With these mechanisms in place, the suburban "land rush" hit its stride. In the decade after World War II (1946–1956), with FHA and VA loans underwriting 30 percent of all nonfarm housing starts and 42 percent of the nation's outstanding nonfarm mortgage debt (Doan 1997: 189), suburban developers built more houses—two million in 1950 alone—than Americans could use. In this decade, the postwar housing boom became an overbuilding frenzy. A nation that added some 12,590,000 new households added some 17,215,000 units to the national stock of new housing (figures 12.14A and 12.14B). As housing supply outran demand, the pace of housing construction slowed dramatically. Housing starts fell to 1.5 million by 1960 and the ratio of new housing units to new households fell from 1.37 in 1946–1956 to 1.04 and 1.03 in 1957–1965 and 1966–1973, respectively (Doan 1997: 188; Borne 1981). With the restoration of some semblance of equilibrium between the growth of households and new housing, new housing starts rose once again in the 1960s and peaked at nearly three million (including mobile homes) in 1972 on the eve of the energy crisis and the perverse stagflation that throttled back the housing market in that decade.

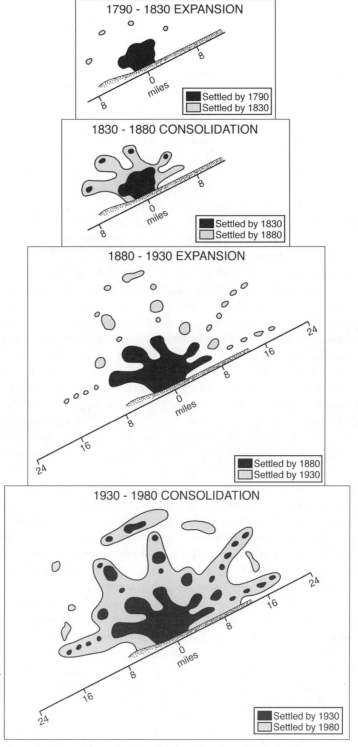

Figure 12.14B. The evolution of urban structure, 1790–1980.

Federal underwriting of a sizable chunk of the mortgage market helps to explain the timing of postwar suburbanization, but not the geography. It explains neither the suburban locational bias of housing starts nor the preference for "filling in" the interstitial wedges in the suburbs over entirely uncontrolled and uncoordinated sprawl. The advantages of these wedge locations were obvious enough to realtors and bankers in the 1950s. First, these wedges offered ample areas of low-cost farmland for the construction of "tracts" of new single-family housing units. Second, wedge tracts near older residential and commercial suburbs rather readily tapped in to existing water, sewer, drainage, electrical, and telephone lines. Third, wedge sites required a private automobile for work and shopping trips, yet most sites were within walking distance or a short drive of mass transit lines and commercial ribbons on the main radials. In the wedge suburbs of the 1950s, cars ruled. Thus between 1947 and 1956, the proportion of American families owning a car rose from just over half (54 percent) to 72 percent. By 1970, 82 percent of all families owned a car and 28 percent owned two or more (*Historical Statistics* 1975, 2: 717).

Postwar suburbanization transformed the geometry of older American cities, papering over the stellate or starlike configuration of the "steel-rail" city with the circular shape characteristic of the "auto epoch." This "rounding off" of urbanized areas involved two processes: the interstitial infilling just noted and the construction of circumferential highway loops or beltways. Initially, the concept of beltways bypassing cities had nothing to do with suburbanization. The beltway idea arose after the war in connection with federal plans for the construction of a limited-access interstate highway system capable of moving military troops and matériel swiftly and efficiently in the case of national emergencies. No one fully expected the powerful impact that this defense highway system would have on civilian urban life.

Soon after the beltways came on line in the late 1950s and early 1960s, regional shopping centers followed at the prime intersections of radials and beltways (Cohen 1996). It soon became obvious that two lanes on each side were not enough to handle the lateral suburban traffic flows to the retail malls, strip shopping areas, and light industrial parks that had arisen at the intersections of the beltways and the older radial routes. By the late 1960s, with lateral traffic flows from one suburb to another rivaling the traditional "hub and spoke" flows from suburbs to downtown, central cities confronted a host of problems: the decay of downtown shopping districts, the loss of jobs to suburban malls and industrial parks, and the suburban "flight" of the white middle class that left cities increasingly black and poor.

The suburbanization of American cities between the 1930s and the 1970s was a process almost exclusively confined to white Americans. African Americans were not so eager to abandon the cities that, since the turn of the century, had served them as refuges of freedom several steps removed from Jim Crow rules and regulations, lynchings, the Klan, and the assorted threats and assaults that more easily escaped detection and prosecution in rural America. As early as 1910, just over seven of every ten African Americans who resided in the northeastern quadrant of the United States lived in cities; by 1940, just under nine of ten did so. Why should they leave the city for the suburbs? Why should they endure the discriminatory practices of realtors, bankers, suburban governments, restrictive deed covenants, and land-use zoning, not to mention the enmity of white neighbors? The only reasonable racial alternative to discriminatory suburbanization, and all of its subtle reminders of Jim Crow days, was the involutional process of black ghettoization.

But this solution was not without its risks as the liberal attack on slums and the policies of public housing and urban renewal in the 1950s and 1960s soon demonstrated through their destructive impacts on the physical and social fabric of uprooted African American communities (Flanagan 1997). Out of this adversity, however, emerged a new source of solidarity. By 1970, black Americans outnumbered whites in the nation's capital (74 percent) and Atlanta (51 percent), and they exceeded four of every ten in Baltimore, St. Louis, and Detroit and the southern cities of New Orleans, Birmingham, Richmond, Jackson (Miss.), Savannah, Charleston (S.C.), and Augusta, Georgia (Morrill and Donaldson 1972: 2, 15). Proportions such as these soon translated into votes and municipal political power, especially after the Voting Rights Act of 1965.

While the Second American Democracy deserves credit and praise for its intellectual assaults on racial discrimination and segregation, the practical results of these integrationist efforts were far less impressive. Indications of racial integration are scarcely evident on the urban landscapes constructed between 1930 and 1980. Indeed, one can find more evidence in these landscapes of the starker images associated with deepening racial apartheid, ghettoization, and suburbanization (Massey and Denton 1993; Hirsch 1983). These are the images of a morality play too long suspended, one which juxtaposes the urban grittiness of deteriorating inner cities—black, impoverished, overcrowded, and crime laden—against the well-manicured suburban scenes of "happy days" prosperity—white, secure single-family homes with good roads and good schools. But what really made these racial tensions explosive was their geographical proximity, by the sheer fact that suburb and ghetto were bottled up within the looping confines of circumferential beltways. When, in the mid-1960s, these tensions erupted in a series of major racial disturbances ("riots"), suburbanites in Detroit, Chicago, and Baltimore fully realized just how very close they were to the black ghetto.

For most Americans, however, the problems associated with the "inner cities"—the white euphemism for black urban America—were several steps removed. Consider that between 1965 and August 1, 1968, no major racial disturbance was reported in over 80 percent of all midwestern cities. Or, to put it another way, 100 percent of the region's disturbances and 35.5 percent of the nation's took place in just 17.5 percent (one in six) of the region's cities (Adams 1972; Warren 1969). American apartheid was, it seems, an unusually concentrated sociospatial process; it was as well an involutional process in several ways comparable to the sectional involutions of the North and the South circa the 1840s and 1850s in the First American Democracy, and not least in their inexorable progressions toward protest and rebellion in the Dissent phase of these egalitarian policy regimes.

The racial divisions and the urban riots of the 1960s called into question the legitimacy of the nation's Second Democracy. Defenders of the regime feared that their dream of equality of opportunity was foundering on the rock of racism; opponents of the regime feared that social order, authority, and control was collapsing in wild and unruly "inner cities." What is clear is that racial tensions were intensified within the increasingly segregated metropolitan hothouses that had been created between the New Deal and the presidencies of Carter and Reagan. In the usual metropolitan geographies, city and suburb were jammed up against one another, confined within the encircling boundary (eight to twelve miles in radius) of a circumferential beltway (or, more grimly, "the urban noose"). White suburbanites fled the city and its "problems," but most did not go very far out into the rural-urban fringe, preferring instead to settle within the interstitial wedges. That postwar suburbanization was nearly a process of spatial infilling than of randomized sprawl is apparent in, inter alia, the 35 percent flattening of metropolitan population density gradients and the clustering of urban populations in radial bands three to fifteen miles from city centers during the 1950s (Glickman and White 1979). For most suburbanites, the urban troika of "downtown," the central business district (CBD), and the inner city continued to serve as the most important source of local and regional identity, not to mention the most important center for metropolitan employment. Moreover, these were the places where they had grown up. And it was these mixed feelings toward the city that helped to check rampant suburban expansion—of the sort that prevailed between 1880 and 1930 and has appeared again since 1980—and, by ensuring that suburbs and ghetto remained in close juxtaposition, exacerbated the racial tensions that erupted in the urban riots of the mid-1960s.

But expansion was also checked by the consolidationist policies of the Second Democracy (on the attitudes of planners, see Brownell 1980). The "liberal" prourban strategy of cobbling together the metropolis would have made more sense if it had been reinforced by resolute efforts to promote racial integration in the society at large. The regime's failure in eliminating discrimination from real estate and mortgage markets (something that could have been achieved given the importance of federal mortgage guarantees) combined with the regime's prourban ideology virtually guaranteed the worst possible geographical case—the case of American apartheid or, more precisely, the case of the spatial polarization of suburbanized whites and ghettoized blacks in the consolidated confines of the metropolis. In such situations, the processes of spatial involution, "regionalism," and revolutionary sectional conflict (in this case, between ghetto and suburb) are all too predictable.

THE TELECOMMUNICATIONS EPOCH (1980–?) AND
THE THIRD REPUBLIC

If the cyclical rhythms in American policy and geosophy hold true to form, then our urban forecast for the Third Republic is for urban systems that are more stable and intraurban geographies that are more expansionary than their predecessors during the nation's Second Democracy (1930–1980). The evidence for these forecasts, while preliminary and provisional, is generally supportive.

These forecasts should not be surprising given the history of urban-system stability and urban sprawl in urban systems during the nation's two previous producer revolutions. The contemporary revolution in telecommunications and information

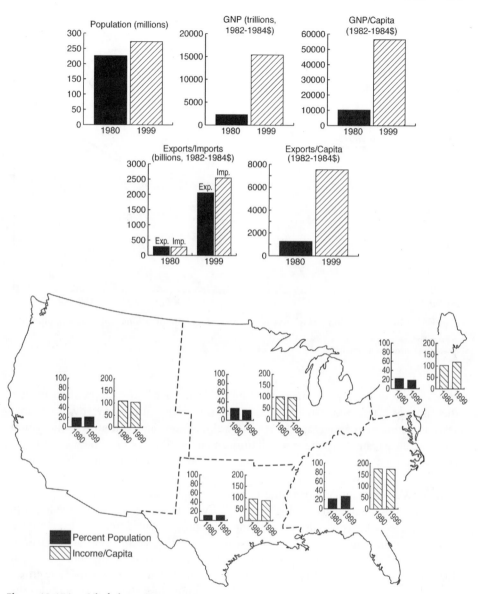

Figure 12.15A.   Vital signs, 1980–1999.

technology under way since the 1980s promises more of the same. These earlier revolutions, be it the rise of machines and the factory system between 1780 and 1830 or the triumph of vertically integrated mass production between 1880 and 1930, yielded remarkably similar urban geographies—geographies that simultaneously reinforced the existing urban system, streamlined the existing urban hierarchy, heaped the cumulative advantage of increasing returns on the nation's leading cities, and thrust the new production sites into suburbs on the outskirts of the leading

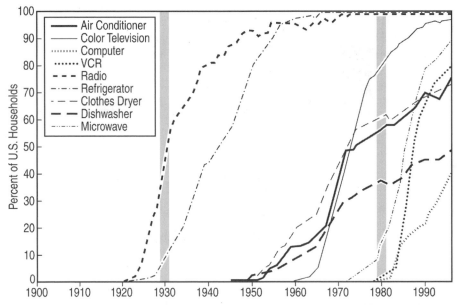

Figure 12.15B.   Innovation diffusion: Computers, telecommunications, and home appliances.

Source: *Fortune*, June 8, 1998, 64.
Note: Gray shaded columns depict "crisis" turning points.

cities. In these times, as in our own, "them that has gets" as entrepreneurs exploit the forces of inertia and initial advantage and trigger the cumulative advantages that serve to define the winners and losers in the emerging space economy. As the nation embarks on its latest producer revolution, often heralded as "the new economy," Americans seem inclined to reaffirm these steadfast tendencies in our urban geographies. But the "new economy," like its predecessors, is also earth-shakingly revolutionary. We are not merely running in place. In these times, "rapidity of change is [fast becoming] a new technology cliché." Everything seems to be speeding up. While Moore's law proclaims that computing power will double every eighteen months, the Internet is expanding access to information at an even faster pace. In 2000, "the World Wide Web consisted of about twenty-one terabytes (a terabyte is 1,000 gigabytes) of static HTML (hypertext markup language) pages and was growing at a rate of 100 percent annually." With some allowance for hyperbole, the Commerce Department advised that "the Internet's pace of adoption eclipses all other technologies that preceded it. Radio was in existence thirty-eight years before fifty million people tuned in; TV took thirteen years to reach that benchmark. . . . Once it was opened to the general public, the Internet crossed that line in four years." Meanwhile, online users have tripled from 14 to 44 percent between 1995 and 2000, and web sites rose fivefold to over seven million in October 2000 (U.S. Department of Commerce 1998; Rosenzweig 2001: 550–51; Madrick 1999; figures 12.15A and 12.15B).

The baubles of modern telecommunications are now so widespread in the United States that they have catapulted the nation ahead of all others in the race for the digital economy. A recent assessment of telecommunications technology demonstrates that the United States is far and away the global leader when it comes to the proportion of persons online, the number of Internet hosts per capita, and the number of secure servers per capita ("Measuring Globalization" 2001). Moreover, the United States leads the world with 5.6 radios for every household, not to mention 2.1 color television sets, and 1.1 computers. While the United States ranks only ninth with one mobile phone for every two households, cellular phone subscriptions have skyrocketed, rising from 5.6 million in 1990 to 69 million in 1998 (*Statistical Abstract* 2000: 584, 846; "Economic Indicators" 1999). Throughout the nation, city streets are being torn up in order to lay the high-speed fiber optic cable that serves as the backbone of the digital economy.

The supply side of the telecommunications revolution is vastly more concentrated than the virtually ubiquitous users of the new technologies. The economic gains arising from information technologies tend to be highly localized within familiar metropolitan regions such as New York, Los Angeles, Chicago, San Francisco, and Houston and their peers in the upper ranks of the American urban hierarchy. In these cities and throughout the nation the producer revolution is predicated on innovations in telecommunications—in hardware, software, and communications services—and more precisely on the marriage of information technology manufactures (IT) and the producer services that use this hardware and software in the provision of services for finance, insurance, real estate (the so-called FIRE sector), business, and so on. Collectively, these information-handling industries have been on a long climb upward since the advent of secretarial pools and middle-level management in the 1920s when they garnered 30 percent of the labor force to their 48.3 percent share in 1991. Perhaps the most potent of these industries is one of the smallest. While IT manufactures accounted for just 2.4 percent of the civilian labor force in 1997 and just 8 percent of GDP (1995–1998), these firms also contributed an astonishing 35 percent of the net growth in U.S. GDP in the 1990s—all of which reflects their gains in income of 81 percent between 1990 and 1997 and 121 percent between 1990 and 1999 (Castells 2000: 148–49, 318). The users of IT also flourished in the 1990s. The FIRE sector, one of the major users, grew by 41.4 percent to $1.5 trillion between 1990 and 1996—as compared to the 64.7 percent gain in IT manufactures. Together in 1996, these two sectors (IT and FIRE) constituted 26 percent of U.S. total GDP of $7.7 trillion.

In tandem, IT manufactures and their users have tended to reinforce rather than reconfigure the American urban system. The ranks of our leading cities have scarcely changed since 1980, all of which reflects the ongoing concentration of IT production and information flows—often within the edge cities of our largest metropolitan regions. Consider these trends (table 12.11): first, the concentration of U.S. FedEx flows in the 1980s among ten cities ranked in the twelve most populous cities as of 1996; second, in these same upper-echelon cities in the mid-1990s, the nearly perfect correlation between a city's share of metropolitan population and its share of FIRE employment; and third, the internal shuffling of producer services from central cities to suburbs (as in New York City's 7 to 12 percent losses in advertising, legal services, computerized data processing, engineering and management services, and FIRE be-

Table 12.11.   Metropolitan Area Populations, FIRE Employment, Information Flows, Producer Services, and Online Users

	Share of Metrop. Population 1996		Share of U.S. FIRE emplymt. 1994		Nodal links (a) & Info flow (b) 1982–90				Producer Services earnings share of all city earnings		Online users (millions) 1998	
					(ranks in parentheses)							
					(a)	(b)						
New York	9.4%	(1)	12.5%	(1)	12	6,766	(4)	48.4%	(1)	3.48	(1)
Los Angeles	7.3%	(2)	6.4%	(2)	5	5,056	(7)	21.8%		2.31	(2)
Chicago	4.1%	(3)	4.4%	(3)	1	7,663	(2)	25.9%	(5)	1.53	(5)
Washington	3.4%	(4)	1.9%	(8)	2	7,826	(1)	25.9%	(5)	1.86	(3)
San Francisco	3.1%	(5)	3.1%	(4)	2	7,506	(3)	40.5%	(2)	1.71	(4)
Philadelphia	2.8%	(6)	2.9%	(5)	2	1,565–1,890	(11)	24.2%	(9)	1.03	(7)
Boston	2.6%	(7)	2.4%	(6)	2	783–1,565	(12)	37.0%	(3)	1.14	(6)
Detroit	2.5%	(8)	1.7%	(9)	—	—		13.5%		0.78	(8)
Dallas	2.2%	(9)	2.3%	(7)	1	5,646	(5)	25.9%		0.77	(9)
Houston	2.0%	(10)	1.6%	(11)	0	1,890	(10)	22.4%			
Atlanta	1.7%	(11)	1.6%	(12)	2	5,196	(6)	27.6%	(4)		
Miami	1.7%	(12)	1.7%	(10)	1	1,565–1,890	(11)	22.9%			

Note: Seattle ranks ninth in information flows (1972) and tenth in online users (750,000); Denver ranks eighth in information flows (2,901).
Sources: See sources cited in the text; also Wheeler and Greene 1999; Mitchelson and Wheeler 1994; Greenman 1998; Drennan et al. 1996: 81.

tween 1984 and 1996) (Mitchelson and Wheeler 1994; Wheeler and Greene 1999; and Muller 1997).

On the heels of the Reagan Revolution and the post-1980 revolution in telecommunications, the American urban system has entered into a new epoch of metropolitan evolution. These newer Third Republic urban geographies are triply distinguishable from the geographies of the Second Democracy that they are replacing. First is the greater stability evident within the system of cities as a whole. Second is the explosive suburban expansion under way in three dozen or so of the nation's largest metropolitan centers—expansions that have given rise to the prosperous office-and-retail complexes known as "edge cities" and the urban sprawl associated with the residential dormitory communities that have spilled over the countryside as far as forty to fifty miles from the centers of metropolitan areas such as Atlanta, Washington, D.C., Houston, and Los Angeles (Garreau 1991). Third is the deterioration and collapse of social geographies in the metropolitan core—most apparent in the declension of inner-city neighborhoods from the economic heterogeneity and the vibrancy of the "classic ghetto" to the impoverished homogeneity and the hopelessness of the "outcast ghetto" (Marcuse 1997). These trends have magnified the spatial inequalities in the geographies of our largest cities. While the suburbs of these cities have been enriched by the post-Fordist prosperity of producer services and telecommunications firms, which have tended to cluster within edge cities, the ghettoes in these cities have been impoverished first by the flight of manufacturing and services employment from the inner cities and second by the flight of middle-class minorities who, having reaped the benefits of a generation of affirmative action and economic opportunity policies, have moved to the suburbs (Wilson 1996). Urban geographies are being transformed by these centrifugal processes, albeit within a context of relative stability in the nation's regional economies and, as we'll now see, and in its system of cities.

Is the urban system becoming more stable? Yes, judging from the fact that the annual increment of cities and towns of ten thousand or more persons has been cut by 31 percent—from 33 towns per year between 1930 and 1970 to 21.9 new towns between 1980 and 1994 (note: the number drops to 24.5 per year for the period 1930–1980). Yes, too, judging from the growing dominance of larger centers implied by the 5.8 percent reduction in the system's k-values in the twenty-five years since 1970 (a reduction that compares favorably with the 9.5 percent fall in k-values in the sixty years of the Second Republic, i.e., 1870–1930). What little volatility there is in the urban system is concentrated mainly in "middling cities" ranging from fifty thousand to half a million persons. Smaller cities and towns (10,000–49,999 populations) have not fared well. These sorts of places, which provided 84.5 percent of the new entrants to the urban system in the egalitarian Second Democracy (1930–1970), account for just 26.1 percent of the new entrants since 1980. The contrast in the geographical consequences of egalitarian and libertarian policy regimes could hardly be any sharper than these.

But what is the prospect for systemic urban stability over the remaining decades (three) of the Third Republic? One set of projections of the North American urban system through 2060 envisions "a revolution inside stability" (Tellier 1995). These projections, which are as utterly dependent on past demographic and spatial trends as they are innocent of policy regime swings, forecast a fair amount of rank shifting in the upper end of the North American urban hierarchy. Here presumably is the "revolution," what with New York dropping from first to third rank by 2035 (on its way to twelfth rank by 2060); Chicago from third to sixth; Philadelphia from fourth to fourteenth; Detroit from fifth to fifteenth; Boston from eighth to seventeenth. Taking their places are Los Angeles (1), Dallas–Forth Worth (2), Toronto (4), Houston (5), Riverside (7), and San Diego (8).

Perhaps, but my guess is that the more volatile shifts in urban rankings will await the 2030s and the arrival of America's Third Democracy. Evidence on that point comes from the stability among the top-ranking cities at century's end. The ten largest cities in 1980 remain unchanged in 1996 (table 12.12). Some have changed ranks, but not by more than one unit in any case. Moreover, while the populations of the largest cities have converged somewhat since 1980 (judging from the ratios of the largest city's population to those of smaller cities), the degree of convergence is nowhere near Tellier's predicted levels for 2035. As for "stability," these projections argue on behalf of modest and gradual changes in the locational distribution of an

Table 12.12.   The Ten Largest Cities in the United States, 1980, 1996, and 2035 (projected) with Ratios to the Population of the Largest City in Each Period (in parentheses)

1980			1996			2035	
New York	18.9	(1.00)	New York	19.9	(1.00)	Los Angeles	(1.00)
Los Angeles	11.5	(1.64)	Los Angeles	15.5	(1.28)	Dallas	(1.68)
Chicago	8.1	(2.33)	Chicago	8.6	(2.31)	New York	(1.85)
Washington	5.7	(3.26)	Washington	7.2	(2.76)	Houston	(1.97)
Philadelphia	5.6	(3.34)	San Francisco	6.6	(3.02)	Chicago	(2.00)
San Francisco	5.3	(3.52)	Philadelphia	6.0	(3.32)	Riverside	(2.03)
Detroit	5.3	(3.57)	Boston	5.6	(3.55)	San Diego	(2.26)
Boston	5.1	(3.69)	Detroit	5.3	(3.75)	Washington	(2.33)
Houston	3.1	(6.06)	Dallas	4.6	(4.33)	Atlanta	(2.52)
Dallas	3.1	(6.20)	Houston	4.3	(4.62)	Phoenix	(2.56)

Note: Projection ratios for 2035 are based on Tellier 1995.

increasing North American urban population (from 184 million in 1990 to 300 million by 2035). Over the course of the half century between 1980 and 2035, the redistributive processes that held in the past are expected to sustain regional economic stability and, in due course, to nudge the geographies of American population and economy from the northeastern United States to the Sunbelt and the Pacific Coast—and in doing so confer modest comparative advantages upon cities within these regions (but without extensive shuffling in the urban hierarchy).

The general stability prevailing within the American urban system since 1980 contrasts sharply with the vigorous resumption of centrifugal forces on the outskirts of the nation's largest cities (Stanback 1991). Most obvious is the emergence of a new species of suburbanization, the edge city, which typically arises in suburban sites located at the intersection of major freeways (table 12.13; Garreau 1991). In these suburban centers, high-rise towers and buildings have arisen to provide over five million square feet of leasable office space and over six hundred thousand square feet of retail space. These attributes point to the edge city's primary function as a work or employment center; to its secondary function as a mixed-use center for jobs, shopping, and entertainment; and to this paradox of spatial concentration in an age of telecommuting, video conferencing, and similar space-annihilating functions of modern telecommunications. As of 1991, 118 suburban centers qualified as edge cities, and another seventy-three were in waiting (the so-called near-edge cities; table 12.13; figure 12.16). All of these 191 centers were packed into just thirty-five cities, and nearly half (49 percent) of the full-blown edge cities (58/118) were jammed into just four metropolitan areas—New York, seventeen; Los Angeles, sixteen; Washington, sixteen; and Houston, nine—and over two-thirds in just eight (San Francisco, seven; Boston, five; Detroit, five; and Atlanta, four (Garreau 1991: 425–39). These represented seven of the nation's ten largest metropolitan areas in 1996.

In several of our largest cities, edge cities offer more office space for tertiary and quaternary services than their respective CBDs. In 1991, the edge-city advantage

Table 12.13. Edge Cities and Near-edge Cities circa 1990 and Their "Wired Index" Rank

City	(Pop. Rank)	Edge Cities	Near-edge Cities	Total	Wired Index Rank
Group 1:					
New York	(1)	17	4	21	8
Los Angeles	(2)	16	8	24	16
Washington	(4)	16	7	23	3
Houston	(10)	9	2	11	17
Group 2:					
San Francisco	(5)	7	5	12	1
Boston	(7)	5	5	10	7
Detroit	(8)	5	3	8	28
Atlanta	(11)	4	3	7	2
Phoenix	(15)	3	4	7	26
San Diego	(17)	3	2	5	12
		118	73	191	
% in Group 1		49% (58/118)	29% (21/73)	41%	
% in Groups 1 & 2		72% (85/118)	59% (43/73)	67%	
% others		28% (33/118)	41% (30/73)	33%	

Sources: Garreau 1991: 425–39; Greenman 1998.

exceeded 70 percent in five cities (Tampa, Dallas, Houston, Boston, and San Diego, 70.2–75.7 percent) and 58 percent in five others (Denver, Miami, Kansas City, Baltimore, and St. Louis). It is worth noting that only three of these (Boston, Baltimore, and St. Louis) ranked among the top ten in the numbers of edge cities and near-edge cities (with five or more). Clearly having lots of edge cities was not a prerequisite for the suburbanization of office space within large metropolitan areas (on Houston, see Mesyanshinov 1997). In any event, edge cities and other "suburban locations have increasingly enjoyed the benefits of agglomeration, making them attractive not only for economic sectors traditionally located there (for example, retailing and other consumer services) but also for a wide range of business services—from finance, insurance, and real estate (FIRE) to research laboratories and often including hotel complexes, theaters, and convention sites—that make these suburban complexes direct competitors to CBDs" (Gordon and Richardson 1996b: 1739; Stanback 1991: xii). In cities such as Los Angeles, which may prove to be the model for the future, these suburban centers have become so frequent and are so widespread that they are more nearly dispersed than polycentric (on Los Angeles, see Gordon and Richardson 1996a).

The edge cities plopped down in metropolitan areas quickly generated ripples in the land uses of surrounding suburbs and well out into the nonmetropolitan periphery. These new employment centers at first stimulated demands for a well-educated white- and pink-collar labor force, and these workers in turn stimulated a further round of demands for residential expansion. An edge city on the north side of Atlanta, some twenty miles from the CBD, has triggered residential and retail construction some forty miles or more from Atlanta's center. And Atlanta is far from

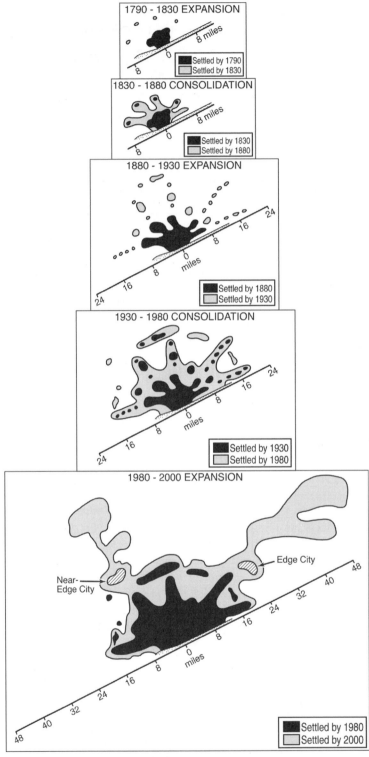

Figure 12.16.   The evolution of urban structure, 1790–2000.

alone. Washingtonians are now homesteading at similar distances in the once-bucolic Frederick and Washington Counties of western Maryland and in their counterparts in the Virginia piedmont.

Peripheral expansion represents not a rejection of the city as posited by the 1980s proponents of the counterurbanization thesis but rather a fairly sustained if multistaged suburban expansion. In this process, American population growth has been more rapid at the hem than at the center of the metropolitan region. Since the 1970s, the geography of population growth has been concentrated in "crossover counties"—that is, in counties that have switched from nonmetropolitan to metropolitan status (Morrill 1995). The rates of growth in crossover counties, which accounted for 15.2 percent of U.S. population growth in 1994, have invariably surpassed the rates of growth in metropolitan and nonmetropolitan counties—and usually by large margins. The foundations of the "new suburbanization" seem to have been laid in the 1970s when the growth rate on the crossover periphery exceeded 2 percent per annum—and when, ironically, this growth was misinterpreted as evidence of antiurban counterurbanization. To be sure, some of the peripheral expansion reflected a rejection of the city—of urban flight and an escape to rural exurbia (especially the peaking in nonmetropolitan growth in the 1970s)—but it was suburbanization that led the way. The headiest growth in the 1970s took place not outside the metropolis but rather among the suburban crossovers. In these new suburbs, growth peaked at 2.33 percent per annum, and, perhaps more decisively, it was sustained at fairly high rates (1.7 percent) in the 1980s and 1990s. As table 12.14 affirms, growth was invariably fastest in these new suburbs (the crossovers), and the geographic differential in their growth rates ranged from sizable (1.3) to astounding (10.3).

Suburban expansion is likely to continue, albeit more vigorously in some metropolitan areas and regions than in others. Morrill (1995) offers this by way of prediction: Suburbanization is most likely in counties already on the threshold of crossing over from nonmetropolitan to metropolitan status. These incipient suburbanites range from just 6 percent of the population in the Northeast to 12.8 percent in the Midwest (and to round out, 8.6 percent in the South and 10.1 percent in the West).

Table 12.14.   Annual Growth Rates in Metropolitan, Nonmetropolitan, and Crossover Counties in the United States, 1960–1994 (differentials with crossover counties in parentheses)

	U.S.	Continuously Metropolitan		Continuously Nonmetropolitan		Crossover Counties
1960–70	1.26	1.52	(1.3)	0.19	(10.3)	1.96
1970–80	1.08	0.79	(1.5)	1.22	(1.9)	2.33
1980–90	0.93	0.99	(1.7)	0.25	(6.8)	1.70
1990–94	1.08	0.97	(1.8)	0.89	(1.9)	1.70

Note: The differentials in parentheses are the ratios of the growth rates for crossover counties with those of metropolitan and nonmetropolitan counties.
Source: Morrill 1995.

When we look at the suburban prospects of particular metropolitan areas, Seattle and Minneapolis (22 percent each) lead the way, followed by St. Louis (19.4 percent) and Denver (19.1 percent). Next, with 8 to 13 percent of the population available, come Chicago, Atlanta, Dallas, Cleveland, Boston, Cincinnati, and Houston.

The new suburbanization is not without its problems and paradoxes. Consider the prospects of the edge city. Having been drawn to certain suburban locations by their high accessibility, their antecedent residential geographies, and their ample supplies of educated workers, edge cities and their office-retail complexes invariably invite externalities. Traffic becomes increasingly congested and the associated air pollution worsens. Housing is in short supply, thus driving up housing costs, forcing workers to move ever farther out into the suburban and nonmetropolitan periphery, and speeding up the conversion of farms and woodlands to suburban land uses. As diseconomies of scale impose the pathologies of congestion, overcrowding, and even crime on edge city neighborhoods, residents increasingly voice antigrowth sentiments, insist on tighter regulation of urban sprawl, and appeal for new planning solutions. These appeals range from the neotraditional concepts of "the new urbanism" to the libertarian notions of assessing developers with the full costs of suburban infrastructure and services to the "liberal" solution of imposing taxes on jobs created within local jurisdictions. (On governance in these "anonymous giants," see Teaford 1997. One estimate for the 1990s places the conversion of rural to urban land at one thousand square miles—or double the rate between 1982 and 1992; "Urban Sprawl" 1999; Lardner 2000; Platt 1985.)

There is, regrettably, a flip side to the unbounded opportunities for the high flyers in the gleaming edge cities, and it arises from the entrapment of the poorest Americans in the "outcast ghettos" within the nation's inner cities. "Over the past three decades [since 1970], urban poverty has grown distinctly worse and the number of people living in ghettos where 40 percent of the population is below the poverty line has doubled. This is the corollary of the evacuation of city centers by the middle classes, who take jobs and revenues with them" ("Urban Sprawl" 1999: 25). The poorest of the poor, "the outcasts" among the minority communities, remained in the inner cities, while those who escaped the bonds of poverty joined in the rush toward employment centers in the suburbs.

And the escapees have been growing since the early 1980s, at least among the African American population. The proportion of African Americans entrapped in poverty has fallen sharply, from nearly 36 percent in 1982 and 1983 to 31.5 percent in 1990 to 26.5 percent in 1997 and 22.1 percent in 2000 (*Statistical Abstract 2000*: 483–84; *Poverty in the United States* 2001). In this same period, African Americans made impressive gains in homeownership and income, even while the gap in wealth remains large (Wolff 1995: 70–72). Moreover, some of the worst cases of segregation were mended (figure 12.17). In the 1980s, for example, the metropolitan areas with the most egregious racial residential segregation (i.e., those classed as highly segregated and hypersegregated cities) decreased from twenty-eight cities to twenty-two. In this decade, nine cities (six in the South) were removed from this ignominious list, nine others (seven in the Northeast and Midwest) made improvement, and six remained unchanged. Of the eighteen cities that reduced levels of segregation, sev-

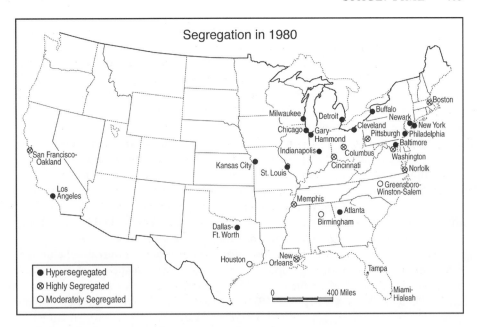

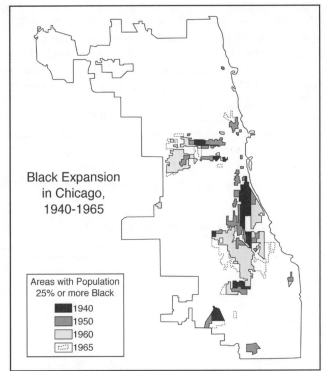

Figure 12.17.   American apartheid: Segregation in American cities, 1980 (top); and expansion of the Chicago ghetto, 1940–1965 (bottom).

Sources: Adapted from Massey and Denton 1993; Hirsch 1983.

enteen were located in the eastern half of the nation—ten in the Northeast and Midwest and seven in the South. Conversely, segregation worsened in just seven cities—three that were newcomers and four persisters (of these, five were located in the South; table 12.15). As for the geography of racial segregation, the data divide into two broad regions: the northern improvers and the southern backsliders. In the Northeast and Midwest, the racial problems that came home to roost in the 1970s seem to have improved substantially in these regions by the 1990s; segregation was reduced (ten) or did not worsen in sixteen of seventeen cities in the region. The same cannot be said for the South where the results are mixed; although residential segregation improved in seven cities, the situation worsened in five of twelve southern cities. One might say that efforts on behalf of racial integration in the North were not adversely affected by the region's ongoing economic problems; conversely, the general prosperity enjoyed by the southern states was not matched by unambiguous gains in the residential integration of American minority groups.

These advances at one scale are illusory at another. Consider the case of Chicago, where improvements at the metropolitan-wide scale largely disappear when we look at the neighborhood scale. Chicago's 825 census tracts reveal a steady expansion in underclass neighborhoods between 1970 and 1990. These communities of extreme poverty were, on average, poor (43.3 percent), black (90.1 percent), sustained by public assistance (41.4 percent), riven by unemployment (24.6 percent), with families (about half) guided by women. These neighborhoods mushroomed in the 1970s, rising from 2.6 percent to 22.7 percent of all neighborhoods, and again in the 1980s, rising from 22.7 percent to 31.0 percent. Most of this trend resulted from the downward mobility of working-class neighborhoods (these provided 151 of the underclass net gain of 165 in the 1970s and all of the net gain in the 1980s (Morenoff and Tienda 1997: 69).

Areas of extreme poverty were on the increase elsewhere, especially in the nation's largest metropolitan centers. In the fifty-one largest centers, the share of poor African Americans residing within neighborhoods of extreme poverty (greater than 40 percent poverty) rose from 20.6 percent in 1970 to 28.5 percent by 1990. That share rose even faster in the seventy-one metropolitan areas of the Middle Atlantic

Table 12.15.   Changes in Hypersegregated and Highly Segregated Cities, by Region

	Number of cities	Northeast	Midwest	South	West
Highly segregated and hypersegregated cities					
1980	28				
1990	22				
Dropouts 1980 to 1990	9	1	2	6	
Persisters 1980 to 1990	19				
Reduced segregation	9	3	4	1	1
Segregation unchanged	6	2	4		
Increased segregation	4			3	1
Newcomers	3		1	2	0
Segregation reduced or same	24	6	8	7	1
Segregation increased	7	1	1	5	1

Sources: Massey and Denton 1993; Denton 1994.

and East North Central regions—from just 7.7 percent in 1970 to 17.5 percent in 1980 to 27.9 percent in 1990 (Strait 2001: table 1).

For the city dwellers who remained behind, the outcast ghetto represented a sink of urban pathologies. In an empowerment zone in Harlem and the Bronx in New York City, 42 percent lived below poverty levels, 18 percent were unemployed, others had given up looking for work so that just 51 percent constituted the labor force, and 27 percent of all households were headed by a single woman (Marcuse 1997: 236). And for these households, perhaps six in ten lived in poverty (Kodras 1997: 47). Or consider Philadelphia's outcast ghetto circa 1980 wherein 47.5 percent were on public assistance, 44.3 percent of the black families had single-parent heads, and a third had dropped out of the labor force. The figures are grim. In 1990 poverty was the fate of one of every three black Americans who resided in central cities; the rates jumped to four in ten in the Midwest, and to six to seven in ten for urban black families with female heads (Kodras 1997: 45–47).

Entrapment was compounded by failing schools (so bad as to prompt state take-over in the case of Philadelphia schools) and the inaccessibility of employment centers increasingly located in the suburbs. Minority students and minority schools generally lagged behind white students and schools in the usage of computers and the Internet. While the vast gap that existed in the 1980s has largely been eliminated, many inner-city schools remain outside the telecommunications circle. In 1996, personal computers were not readily available in 23 percent of minority schools, and they were not regularly used in half of all minority schools (*Statistical Abstract 2000:* 184). Internet usage was even less frequent. Three of every four minority schools lacked Internet access, and 96 percent did not make regular use of this form of communications. And poor students who lacked computer access in school were unlikely to secure it through private resources at home given that (1) black usage of home computers stood at 14.7 percent (1997) and of the Internet at 20.1 percent (as compared to white usage of 35.5 percent and 33.8 percent, respectively; *Statistical Abstract 2000:* 581–82); and (2) among the poorest Americans, those earning less than $25,000 per year, only one in seven owned a personal computer (*Statistical Abstract 2000:* 735).

Compounding these constraints on minority access to telecommunications are the similarly severe constraints on the movements of residents of the outcast ghetto. Automobiles are relatively scarce, and over 35 percent of low-income black households (less than $20,000 per annum) did not own a vehicle in 1990; and in any event, some 20 percent of black men and 30 percent of black women were not licensed to drive an automobile (these nationwide figures doubtless run even higher in inner cities). Daily travel is further attenuated by race and income to the extent that urban black men average twenty-four passenger-miles per day as compared to thirty-nine miles for urban white men. The attenuation is even greater for residents of outcast ghettos—for black women (twenty miles), the poor (sixteen miles), and nondrivers (eleven miles) (U.S. Department of Transportation 1997: 267).

These constraints on the mobility of poor black Americans have become even more pressing as jobs have vacated the central city and moved to the suburbs. This is especially a problem for urban black teenagers who typically found work in unskilled jobs in retailing. Jobs in that sector are increasingly scarce in the central cities.

These jobs have grown very modestly from 2.5 million in 1977 to just over 3 million in 1992; suburban retailing, meanwhile, has exploded, rising from 2.25 million to 3.75 million jobs in that same period. This deterioration in inner-city labor markets was soon reflected in the dramatic decline in the employment probabilities for urban black teenagers in the 1980s (Holloway 1996).

Opportunities and hope have largely disappeared from the outcast ghettos in America's central cities. So, too, have black men, jobs, and any semblance of the middle class. The men have been incarcerated for crimes or they have died in the streets. Jobs have left the city for the suburbs as have black families who could afford to make the move. What remain are the female-headed households, the children, and the dealers and the runners in the drug trade. Life is attuned to the rhythms of the monthly welfare check and to the lyrics that lament "the lack of social potency . . . low organizational density . . . the massive inferiority of its residents and institutions . . . de-solidarizing effects . . . an impossible community, perpetually divided against [itself]" (Wacquant 1993: 372, n. 15).

The modern metropolis consists of much more than the outcast ghetto and the edge city. To focus exclusively on these extremes of poverty and plenty is to obscure the enormous range and variety that currently constitute the modern American metropolis. The prosperity associated with the telecommunications revolution, information technology, and producer services has spilled over from the edge cities, raising incomes, reducing the ranks of the impoverished, improving opportunities for many minority group members, and transforming the expanding metropolis into a more diverse set of communities. In this process, the stereotypical metropolitan geography of New Deal liberalism—with its prosperous white suburbs set against the "poorer but not destitute" black ghettos of the inner city—has been fractured into a mosaic of social geographies. Consider the geographies of the twelve largest metropolitan areas in the 1990s and the 162 counties and cities that comprised them. Some of these 162 subunits are characterized by sizable racial concentrations of African Americans (in table 12.16's notation, B [black]; greater than 20 percent); others by poverty (P [poverty]; greater than 10 percent); others by slow growth in residential building (H [housing]; less than 15 percent of the housing stock added between 1990 and 1996); by some combination of the three; and still others, by none of these. Dichotomizing these variables yields eight classes of community within metropolitan areas (table 12.16).

Most frequent are the slow-growth (H) counties. These forty-eight counties, with their aging housing stock, constitute 30 percent of the 162 metropolitan units, and most of these occur in older cities located east of the Mississippi River. Second in frequency are the forty-five counties (27.6 percent) characterized by both poverty and housing lags (P and H). Members of this class appear in all twelve metropolitan areas, but they are the main mode in cities with sizable Hispanic populations (e.g., Los Angeles, Dallas, Houston). Further down the list, third and fourth in frequency, are the classical residential communities—the thirty-three (20.3 percent) prosperous white suburbs (nonblack, nonpoor, and fast-growth) and the twenty-five (15.3 percent) poor, black ghettos (P and H). These four classes combined account for nearly 93 percent of all metropolitan counties. But it is the remaining classes that may be

Table 12.16. Metropolitan Communities in the Twelve Largest Cities, 2000

City	None	Black (B)	Poverty (P)	Housing	PH	BH	BP	BPH	Total
New York				17	5	1		6	29
Los Angeles					5				5
Chicago	7		1	2	1			2	13
Washington	12	2	2	8	3	1	1	4	33
San Francisco				5	5				10
Philadelphia				6	3			2	11
Boston				6	3			1	10
Detroit	1			4	3			2	10
Dallas	3				8			1	12
Houston					5			3	8
Atlanta	10				3	1	3	3	20
Miami					1			1	2
	33	2	3	48	45	3	4	25	163
	(20.9%)	(1.2%)	(1.8%)	(29.5%)	(27.6%)	(1.8%)	(2.5%)	(15.3%)	

Note: Black (B) refer to counties or cities with black populations equal to or greater than 20 percent. Poverty (P) refer to counties or cities in which 10 percent or more of the population is below the poverty level. Housing (H) refers to counties and cities in which 15 percent or more of the private residential housing units were built between 1990 and 1996.
Source: State and Metropolitan Area Data Book 2001: 138–53.

the most interesting for the future. Eight counties shatter the once-inexorable association of poverty and African Americans. Five of these counties capture the suburbanization of the black middle class in Washington, D.C. (the booming suburbs of Charles County, Maryland, and King George, Virginia, and the slower-paced Prince Georges in Maryland), Atlanta (Clayton), and New York (Trenton, New Jersey).

If these examples of black suburbanization offer clues to the future, then metropolitan residential diversification is more nearly the rule of the day. In Washington, D.C., for example, the classical black inner city (four) and the white suburb (twelve) have been surpassed by a mottled mix of racial, income, and residential communities (seventeen in all). It is these sorts of mottled communities that have displaced the classic white suburb in seven of the nation's twelve largest metropolitan areas. The same cannot be said for the classic inner city. These poor, black, aging communities persist in ten of the twelve metropolitan areas (the exceptions being the California cities of Los Angeles and San Francisco. The dynamic stability that Wyly (1999) observes in the urban landscape of Minneapolis–St. Paul represents, I believe, an apt characterization of the sociogeographic changes under way in American metropolitan areas more generally. While "technological change and industrial restructuring intersect with the continued spatial expansion of metropolitan regions to inscribe more polycentric urban forms and [perhaps] widen the social and economic disparities between affluent neighborhoods, inner-city ghettos, and deteriorating inner-ring suburbs," the opportunities afforded by the telecommunications revolution and abetted by ongoing affirmative actions in these dynamic economic sectors have steadily blurred the sharp lines of American apartheid—the lines that had separated white suburbs and black inner cities. So too have the social geographies of Hispanic populations in Sunbelt cities, Asian immigrants in West Coast cities, and the assortment of ethnic immigrants in other metropolitan centers such as New York, Detroit, Washington, and Atlanta. In the process, the classical juxtaposition of white suburb and black inner city persists alongside suburbs that are aging or shiny and new; predominantly black or Hispanic or ethnic immigrant or white or some of each, and occasionally poor, but more often on the way up. To be sure, underclass communities had grown very fast in a city such as Chicago in the 1970s and 1980s. But that city's 256 underclass communities were vastly outnumbered by the 569 others arrayed among the working class, the yuppies, and the middle class; not to mention the hundreds of similar communities in the suburbs surrounding the city.

In sum, "the American city [in the Third Republic] has lost its neat social patches of the 1950s and . . . witnessed a resorting that is reminiscent of the period of ecological competition [in the Second Republic] in the first decades of" the twentieth century (Kirby 1989: 16). Blessed by economic prosperity and ample opportunity, urban Americans have created a mosaic of social geographies within their metropolitan areas and then blurred the lines between these geographies. They have mixed and matched the variables of race and ethnicity, income, and built environment in ways that are both new and refreshingly diverse. These achievements, and they are not inconsiderable, have created a whole new set of problems.

Consider one of the problems that has arisen from desegregation and affirmative action. While these heroic efforts greatly reduced the size and extent of the black ghetto, they also contributed to the creation of the outcast ghetto—this bleak residual, this extraordinarily resistant crucible of social pathology and one of the most perversely fertile incubators of crime and violence known to humanity. Similarly, the economic prosperity and opportunity dripping from American cities in the mid- to late 1980s and 1990s resulted in a shortfall of labor that was eventually satisfied by indiscriminate immigration flows—flows that proceeded so swiftly as to mock assimilation and to multiply the legions of identity politics. The hideous events of September 11, 2001, remind us that the pace of immigration before that date may have been too fast for assimilation by American cities or, for that matter, by the American republic. The fortunes of a republic, after all is said and done, hinges on the citizenry and the depth and passion of its allegiances. Cromwell understood this all too well in asserting that "we are all English. That is one good fact." This is especially true in a world beset by terrorism. In these times, identity politics seem by contrast provincial, divisive, riskier, and less beguiling. Better perhaps "that we are all Americans"—which is, I believe, precisely the lesson that is discernible in the evolving social geographies of contemporary American metropolitan regions in the Third Republic.

Note

1. SIC refers to the standard industrial classification of manufactures devised by the U.S. Bureau of the Census. The two-digit classification is the broadest categorization of manufactures.

References

Abramovitz, Moses. 1993. "The Search for the Sources of Growth: Areas of Ignorance, Old and New." *Journal of Economic History* 53: 217–43.

Aceves, William J. 1999. "NAFTA–North American Agreement on Labor Cooperation—Freedom of Association." *American Journal of International Law* 93: 224–26.

Ackerman, Bruce. 1991. *We the People I: Foundations.* Cambridge, Mass.: Harvard University Press.

Ackerman, Bruce, and David Globe. 1995. *Is NAFTA Constitutional?* Cambridge, Mass.: Harvard University Press.

Adams, Charles Francis, ed. 1856. "John Adams to Hezekiah Niles, February 13, 1818." In *The Works of John Adams*, 10 vols., 10: 286. Boston: n.p.

Adams, John S. 1972. "The Geography of Riots and Civil Disorders in the 1960s." *Economic Geography* 48: 24–42.

Agnew, Jean-Christophe. 1993. "Coming Up for Air: Consumer Culture in Historical Perspective." In *Consumption and the World of Goods*, ed. John Brewer and Roy Porter, 19–39. London: Routledge.

Agnew, John. 1987. *The United States in the World-Economy: A Regional Geography.* Cambridge: Cambridge University Press.

Agnew, John, and Stuart Corbridge. 1995. *Mastering Space: Hegemony, Territory and International Political Economy.* London: Routledge.

Albion, Robert G. 1939. *The Rise of New York Port, 1815–1860.* New York: Scribner's.

Alonzo, William, and Elliott Medrich. 1972. "Spontaneous Growth Centers in Twentieth-Century American Urbanization." In *Growth Centers in Regional Economic Development*, ed. N. H. Hansen, 349–61. New York: Free Press.

Amin, Ash, ed. 1994. *Post-Fordism: A Reader.* Oxford: Blackwell.

Anderson, Alan D. 1977. *The Origin and Resolution of an Urban Crisis: Baltimore, 1890–1930.* Baltimore: Johns Hopkins University Press.

Andrews, Kenneth R. 1964. *Elizabethan Privateering: English Privateering during the Spanish War, 1585–1603.* Cambridge: Cambridge University Press.

Anselin, Luc. 1995. "Local Indicators of Spatial Association—LISA." *Geographical Analysis* 27: 93–115.

Appleby, Joyce O. 1978. *Economic Thought and Ideology in Seventeenth-Century England.* Princeton, N.J.: Princeton University Press.

———. 1984a. *Capitalism and a New Social Order: The Republican Vision of the 1790s.* New York: New York University Press.

———. 1984b. "Value and Society." In *Colonial British America: Essays in the New History of the Early Modern Era*, ed. Jack P. Greene and J. R. Pole, 290–316. Baltimore: Johns Hopkins University Press.

———. 1992. *Liberalism and Republicanism in the Historical Imagination.* Cambridge, Mass.: Harvard University Press.

————. 1993. "Consumption in Early Modern Social Thought." In *Consumption and the World of Goods*, ed. John Brewer and Roy Porter, 162–73. London: Routledge.

Archer, J. Clark, and Peter J. Taylor. 1981. *Section and Party: A Political Geography of American Presidential Elections from Andrew Jackson to Ronald Reagan*. Chichester, U.K.: Research Studies Press.

Armitage, David. 2000. *The Ideological Origins of the British Empire*. Cambridge: Cambridge University Press.

Arneil, Barbara. 1996. *John Locke and America: The Defence of English Colonialism*. Oxford: Oxford University Press.

Arnold, Thurman. 1940. *The Bottlenecks of Business*. New York: Reynal & Hitchcock.

Ashcraft, Richard. 1986. *Revolutionary Politics and Locke's "Two Treatises of Government."* Princeton, N.J.: Princeton University Press.

————. 1987. *Locke's Two Treatises of Government*. London: Allen & Unwin.

Baerwald, Thomas. 1984. "The Geographic Structure of Modern North American Metropolises." Paper presented to the Twenty-fifth International Geographical Congress, Paris.

Bailyn, Bernard. 1955. *The New England Merchants in the Seventeenth Century*. New York: Harper & Row.

————. 1959. "Politics and Social Structure in Virginia." In *Seventeenth-Century America: Essays in Colonial History*, ed. James Morton Smith, 90–115. Chapel Hill: University of North Carolina Press.

————. 1967a. *The Ideological Origins of the American Revolution*. Cambridge, Mass.: Harvard University Press.

————. 1967b. *The Origins of American Politics*. New York: Vintage.

————. 1986. *The Peopling of British North America: An Introduction*. New York: Vintage.

Bailyn, Bernard, and Lotte Bailyn. 1959. *Massachusetts Shipping 1697–1714: A Statistical Study*. Cambridge, Mass.: Harvard University Press.

Baker, Alan R. H. 1982. "On Ideology and Historical Geography." In *Period and Place: Research Methods in Historical Geography*, ed. Alan R. H. Baker and Mark Billinge, 233–43. Cambridge: Cambridge University Press.

Banning, Lance. 1987. "The Practicable Sphere of a Republic: James Madison, the Constitutional Convention, and the Emergence of Revolutionary Federalism." In *Beyond Confederation: Origins of the Constitution and American National Identity*, ed. Richard Beeman, Stephen Botein, and Edward C. Carter II, 162–87. Chapel Hill: University of North Carolina Press.

————. 1995. "Political Economy and the Creation of the Federal Republic." In *Devising Liberty: Preserving and Creating Freedom in the New American Republic*, ed. David Thomas Konig, 11–49. Stanford, Calif.: Stanford University Press.

Barrow, Thomas C. 1967. *Trade and Empire: The British Customs Service in Colonial America, 1660–1775*. Cambridge, Mass.: Harvard University Press.

Bartelt, David W. 1993. "Housing the Underclass." In *The Underclass Debate: Views from History*, ed. Michael B. Katz, 118–57. Princeton, N.J.: Princeton University Press.

Beard, Charles A. 1913. *An Economic Interpretation of the Constitution of the United States*. New York: Macmillan.

————. 1923. *The History of the American People*. New York: Macmillan.

Beaudreau, Bernard C. 1996. *Mass Production, the Stock Market Crash, and the Great Depression: The Macroeconomics of Electrification*. Westport, Conn.: Greenwood.

Becker, William H. 1982. *The Dynamics of Business-Government Relations: Industry and Exports, 1893–1921*. Chicago: University of Chicago Press.

Beer, Samuel H. 1993. *To Make a Nation: The Rediscovery of American Federalism*. Cambridge, Mass.: Harvard University Press.

Ben-Atar, Doran. 1995. "Alexander Hamilton's Alternative: Technology Piracy and the Report on Manufactures." *William and Mary Quarterly* 3d ser., 52: 389–414.

———. 1996. "Private Friendship and Political Harmony." *Reviews in American History* 24: 8–14.

Bengsten, C. Fred. 2001. "America's Two-Front Economic Conflict." *Foreign Affairs* 80: 16–27.

Bensel, Richard F. 1984. *Sectionalism and American Political Development, 1880–1980*. Madison: University of Wisconsin Press.

———. 1990. *Yankee Leviathan: The Origins of Central State Authority in America, 1859–1877*. Cambridge: Cambridge University Press.

———. 2000. *The Political Economy of American Industrialization, 1877–1900*. Cambridge: Cambridge University Press.

Berk, Gerald. 1994. *Alternative Tracks: The Constitution of American Industrial Order 1865–1917*. Baltimore: Johns Hopkins University Press.

Berlin, Ira. 1980. "Time, Space, and the Evolution of Afro-American Society on British Mainland North America." *American Historical Review* 85: 44–78.

Berman, William C. 1994. *America's Right Turn: From Nixon to Bush*. Baltimore: Johns Hopkins University Press.

Bernstein, Michael A., and David E. Adler, eds. 1994. *Understanding American Economic Decline*. Cambridge: Cambridge University Press.

Berry, Brian J. L. 1970. *Geography of Market Centers and Retail Distribution*. Englewood Cliffs, N.J.: Prentice Hall.

———. 1981. "Inner-City Futures: An American Dilemma Revisited." In *Modern Industrial Cities: History, Policy, and Survival*, ed. Bruce M. Stave, 187–219. Beverly Hills, Calif.: Sage.

———. 1991. *Long-Wave Rhythms in Economic Development and Political Behavior*. Baltimore: Johns Hopkins University Press.

———. 1992. *America's Utopian Experiments: Communal Havens from Long-Wave Crises*. Hanover, N.H.: Dartmouth College and University Press of New England.

Berry, Brian J. L., and Frank E. Horton 1970. *Geographic Perspectives on Urban Systems with Integrated Readings*. Englewood Cliffs, N.J.: Prentice Hall.

Berry, Thomas S. 1968. *Estimated Annual Variations in Gross National Product, 1789–1909*. Bostwick Paper No. 1. Richmond, Va.: Bostwick.

Beyers, William B. 1996. "Trends in Producer Services Growth in the Rural Heartland." In *Economic Forces Shaping the Rural Heartland*, 39–60. Kansas City: Federal Reserve Bank of Kansas City.

Beyers, William B., and David P. Lindahl. 1996. "Explaining the Demand for Producer Services: Is Cost-Driven Externalization the Major Factor?" *Papers in Regional Science* 75: 351–74.

Bhagwati, Jagdish. 1994. "The World Trading System." *Journal of International Affairs* 48: 279–93.

Billings, Warren M. 1996. "Sir William Berkeley and the Diversification of the Virginia Economy." *Virginia Magazine of History and Biography* 104: 433–54.

Bils, Mark. 1984. "Tariff Protection and Production in the Early U.S. Cotton Textile Industry." *Journal of Economic History* 44: 1033–48.

Blackstone, William. 1871. *Commentaries on the Laws of England*. American ed. Chicago: n.p.

Blumberg, Phillip I. 1993. *The Multinational Challenge to Corporation Law: The Search for a New Corporate Personality*. New York: Oxford University Press.

Bogart, E. 1937. *Economic History of the American People*. 2d ed. New York: Longmans, Green.

Bond, Beverley W., Jr. 1919. *The Quit-Rent System in the American Colonies*. New Haven, Conn.: Yale University Press.

Borchert, John R. 1967. "American Metropolitan Evolution." *Geographical Review* 57: 301–32.

———. 1983. "Instability in American Metropolitan Growth." *Geographical Review* 73: 127–49.

Bordo, Michael, and Anna J. Schwartz. 1991. "What Has Foreign Exchange Market Intervention since the Plaza Agreement Accomplished?" *Open Economies Review* 2: 39–64.

Borne, Larry S. 1981. *The Geography of Housing*. New York: Wiley.

Boserup, Ester. 1970. *Women's Role in Economic Development*. London: St. Martin's.

Bowles, Samuel, David M. Gordon, and Thomas E. Weisskopf. 1987. *Beyond the Waste Land: A Democratic Alternative to Economic Decline*. Garden City, N.Y.: Anchor.

Brady, Dorothy S. 1964. "Relative Prices in the Nineteenth Century." *Journal of Economic History* 24: 175–88.

Braudel, Fernand. 1979–1984. *The Structures of Everyday Life: Civilization and Capitalism, 15th–18th Century*, trans. Sian Reynolds. 3 vols. Vol. 1, *The Structures of Everyday Life*; vol. 2, *The Wheels of Commerce*; vol. 3, *The Perspective of the World*. New York: Harper & Row.

Breen, Timothy. 1986. "An Empire of Goods: The Anglicization of Colonial America, 1690–1776." *Journal of British Studies* 25: 467–99.

———. 1988. "'Baubles of Britain': The American and Consumer Revolutions of the Eighteenth Century." *Past and Present* 119: 73–104.

Brenner, Robert. 1972. "The Social Basis of English Commercial Expansion, 1550–1650." *Journal of Economic History* 32: 364–65.

Brenner, Robert, and Mark Glick. 1991. "The Regulation Approach: Theory and History." *New Left Review* (July/August): 45–119.

Brewer, John. 1980. "English Radicalism in the Age of George III." In *Three British Revolutions: 1641, 1688, 1776*, ed. J. G. A. Pocock, 323–67. Princeton, N.J.: Princeton University Press.

———. 1990. *The Sinews of Power: War, Money and the English State, 1688–1783*. Cambridge, Mass.: Harvard University Press.

Bridenbaugh, Carl. 1955a. *Cities in the Wilderness: The First Century of Urban Life in America 1625–1742*. New York: Capricorn.

———. 1955b. *Cities in Revolt: Urban Life in America 1743–1776*. New York: Capricorn.

Brinkley, Alan. 1995. *The End of Reform: New Deal Liberalism in Recession and War*. New York: Knopf.

Brown, Robert F. 1955. *Middle Class Democracy and the Revolution in Massachusetts, 1691–1780*. Ithaca, N.Y.: Cornell University Press.

Brown, Robert F., and B. Katherine Brown. 1964. *Virginia, 1705–1786: Democracy or Aristocracy?* East Lansing: Michigan State University Press.

Brown, Wallace. 1969. *The Good Americans: The Loyalists in the American Revolution*. New York: Morrow.

Brownell, Blaine A. 1980. "Urban Planning, the Planning Profession, and the Motor Vehicle in Early Twentieth Century America." In *Shaping an Urban World*, ed. Gordon E. Cherry, 59–78. New York: St. Martin's

Buenker, John. 1985. *The Income Tax and the Progressive Era*. New York: Garland.

Burnham, Walter Dean. 1967. "Party Systems and the Political Process." In *The American Party Systems: Stages of Political Development*, ed. William Nisbet Chambers and Walter Dean Burnham, 277–307. New York: Oxford University Press.

———. 1970. *Critical Elections and the Mainsprings of American Politics*. New York: Norton.

Burns, James MacGregor. 1956. *Roosevelt: The Lion and the Fox*. New York: Harcourt, Brace.

Burns, John W., and Andrew J. Taylor. 2001. "A New Democrat? The Economic Performance of the Clinton Presidency." *Independent Review* 5: 387–408.

Bushman, Richard L. 1967. *From Puritan to Yankee: Character and the Social Order in Connecticut, 1690–1765.* New York: Norton.

Caeser, J. W. 1979. *Presidential Selection: Theory and Development.* Princeton, N.J.: Princeton University Press.

Calder, Lendol. 1999. *Financing the American Dream: A Cultural History of Consumer Credit.* Princeton, N.J.: Princeton University Press.

Cameron, Maxwell A., and Brian W. Tomlin. 2000. *The Making of NAFTA: How the Deal Was Done.* Ithaca, N.Y.: Cornell University Press.

Cappon, Lester J., ed. in chief. 1976. *Atlas of Early American History: The Revolutionary Era, 1760–1790.* Princeton, N.J.: Princeton University Press.

Carlton, Charles. 1992. *Going to the Wars: The Experience of the British Civil Wars, 1638–1651.* London: Routledge.

Carr, Lois G., Russell R. Menard, and Lorena S. Walsh. 1991. *Robert Cole's World: Agriculture and Society in Early Maryland.* Chapel Hill: University of North Carolina Press.

Castells, Manuel. 2000. *The Information Age: Economy, Society and Culture: Vol. I. The Rise of the Network Society.* 2d ed. Oxford: Blackwell.

Cawley, Robert Ralston 1966. *The Voyagers and Elizabethan Drama,* The Modern Language Association of America, Monograph Series, VIII. 1938. Reprint, New York: Kraus Reprint Corporation.

Central Intelligence Agency. 1999. *Handbook of International Economic Statistics 1998.* Washington, D.C.: Author.

Chandler, Alfred D., Jr. 1977. *The Visible Hand: Managerial Revolution in American Business.* Cambridge, Mass.: Harvard University Press.

———. 1990. *Scale and Scope: The Dynamics of Industrial Capitalism.* Cambridge, Mass.: Harvard University Press.

Chaplin, Joyce E. 1993. *An Anxious Pursuit: Agricultural Innovation and Modernity in the Lower South, 1730–1815.* Chapel Hill: University of North Carolina Press.

Christaller, Walter. 1966. *Central Places in Southern Germany,* trans. Carlisle W. Baskin. Englewood Cliffs, N.J.: Prentice Hall.

Clark, David. 1985. *Post-industrial America: A Geographical Perspective.* New York: Methuen.

Clark, Gordon L. 1994. "NAFTA: Clinton's Victory, Organized Labor's Loss." *Political Geography Quarterly* 13: 377–84.

Clark, J. C. D. 1986. *Revolution and Rebellion: State and Society in England in the Seventeenth and Eighteenth Centuries.* Cambridge: Cambridge University Press.

Clay, C. G. A. 1984. *Economic Expansion and Social Change in England, 1500–1700.* 2 vols. Cambridge: Cambridge University Press.

Clemens, Elisabeth S. 1997. *The People's Lobby: Organizational Innovation and the Rise of Interest Group Politics in the United States, 1890–1925.* Chicago: University of Chicago Press.

Clemens, Paul G. E. 1980. *The Atlantic Economy and Colonial Maryland's Eastern Shore: From Tobacco to Grain.* Ithaca, N.Y.: Cornell University Press.

Clowse, Converse D. 1971. *Economic Beginnings in Colonial South Carolina, 1670–1730.* Columbia: University of South Carolina Press.

Coclanis, Peter A. 1989. *The Shadow of a Dream: Economic Life and Death in the South Carolina Low Country, 1670–1920.* New York: Oxford University Press.

Cohen, I. Bernard. 1994. "Harrington and Harvey: A Theory of the State Based on the New Physiology." *Journal of the History of Ideas* 55: 187–210.

Cohen, Lizbeth. 1996. "From Town Center to Shopping Center: The Reconfiguration of Community Market Places in Postwar America." *American Historical Review* 101: 1050–81.

Coleman, D. C. 1955–56. "Labour in the English Economy of the Seventeenth Century." *Economic History Review,* 2d ser., 8.

Collier, Ellen C. 1993. *Instances of Use of United States Forces Abroad, 1798–1993.* Washington, D.C.: U.S. Department of the Navy, Naval Historical Center.

Congressional Quarterly Weekly Report. 1993. 3494–3495. Washington, D.C.: CQ Press.

Conzen, Michael P. 1977. "The Maturing Urban System in the United States, 1840–1910." *Annals of the Association of American Geographers* 67: 88–108.

———. 1981. "The American Urban System in the Nineteenth Century." In *Geography and the Urban Environment: Progress in Research and Applications,* ed. D. T. Herbert and R. J. Johnston, 295–347. Chichester, U.K.: Wiley.

Conzen, Michael P., Thomas A. Rumney, and Graeme Wynn, eds. 1993. *A Scholar's Guide to Geographical Writing on the American and Canadian Past.* Chicago: University of Chicago Press.

Cooke, Jacob E. 1975. "Tench Coxe, Alexander Hamilton, and the Encouragement of American Manufactures." *William and Mary Quarterly,* 3d ser., 32: 369–92.

Cornell, Saul. 1999. *The Other Founders: Anti-Federalism and the Dissenting Tradition in America, 1788–1828.* Chapel Hill: University of North Carolina Press.

Craven, Wesley Frank. 1968. *The Colonies in Transition, 1660–1713.* New York: Harper & Row.

———. 1970. *The Southern Colonies in the Seventeenth Century, 1607–1789.* Baton Rouge: Louisiana State University Press.

———. 1971. *White, Red, and Black: The Seventeenth-Century Virginian.* Charlottesville: University Press of Virginia.

Crump, Jeff R. 1989. "The Spatial Distribution of Military Spending in the United States, 1941–1985." *Growth and Change* 12: 38–63.

Dahl, Robert A. 1994. *The New American Political (Dis)Order.* Berkeley: Institute of Government Studies Press, University of California.

David, Paul A., and Peter Solar. 1977. "A Bicentenary Contribution to the History of the Cost of Living in America." *Research in Economic History* 2: 1–80.

Davis, Andrew McFarland. 1970. *Currency and Banking in the Province of the Massachusetts Bay.* 2 vols. New York: Augustus M. Kelley; reprint of editions of 1900 (vol. 1) and 1901.

Davis, Lance E., and John Legler. 1966. "The Government in the American Economy, 1815–1902: A Quantitative Study." *Journal of Economic History* 26: 514–55.

Davis, Ralph. 1961. "England and the Mediterranean." In *Essays in the Economic and Social History of Tudor and Stuart England,* ed. F. J. Fisher, 117–37. Cambridge: Cambridge University Press.

———. 1962. "English Foreign Trade, 1700–1774." *Economic History Review* 15: 285–303.

———. 1966. "The Rise of Protectionism in England, 1689–1786." *Economic History Review* 19: 306–17.

DeGeer, Sten. 1927. "The American Manufacturing Belt." *Geografiska Annaler* 9: 233–359.

Degler, Carl N. 1997. "History Counts: The Burden of American Politics." In *American Political History: Essays on the State of the Discipline,* ed. John F. Marzaek and Wilson D. Miscamble, 7–24. Notre Dame, Ind.: University of Notre Dame Press.

Dennis, Richard. 1994. "At the Intersection of Time and Space." In *Engaging the Past: The Uses of History across the Social Sciences,* ed. Eric H. Monkkonen, 154–88. Durham, N.C.: Duke University Press.

Denton, N. A. 1994. "Are African Americans Still Hypersegregated?" In *Residential Apartheid: The American Legacy,* ed. R. D. Bullard, J. E. Grigsby III, and C. Lee, 49–81. Los Angeles: Center for Afro-American Studies, University of California.

Destler, I. M., and C. Randall Henning. 1989. *Dollar Politics: Exchange Rate Policymaking in the United States.* Washington, D.C.: Institute for International Economics.

De Vorsey, Louis. 1987. "The New Land: The Discovery and Exploration of Eastern North America." In *North America: The Historical Geography of a Changing Continent,* ed. Robert D. Mitchell and Paul Groves, 25–47. Totowa, N.J.: Rowman & Littlefield.

deVries, Jan. 1993. "Between Purchasing Power and the World of Goods: Understanding the Household Economy in Early Modern Europe." In *Consumption and the World of Goods*, ed. John Brewer and Roy Porter, 85–132. London: Routledge.

Diamond, Martin. 1992. *As Far as Republican Principles Will Admit: Essays by Martin Diamond*, ed. William A. Schambra. Washington, D.C.: AEI Press.

Dicken, Peter. 1992. *Global Shift: The Internationalization of Economic Activity*. 2d ed. New York: Guilford.

Diebold, William. 1952. *The End of the ITO*. Essays in International Finance No. 16. Princeton, N.J.: Princeton University Press.

Doan, Mason C. 1997. *American Housing Production 1880–2000*. Lanham, Md.: University Press of America.

Dobson, Wendy. 1991. *Economic Policy Coordination: Requiem or Prologue?* Washington, D.C.: Institute for International Economics.

Dockès, Pierre. 1969. *L'espace dans la pensée economique du xvie au xviiie siècle*. Paris: Flammarion.

Doran, Charles F. 1994. "The NAFTA Vote and Political Party: A Partial Test." In *The NAFTA Puzzle: Political Parties and Trade in North America*, ed. C. Doran and G. Marchildon, 247–62. Boulder, Colo.: Westview.

Drennan, Matthew P. 1991. "Gateway Cities: The Metropolitan Sources of U.S. Producer Services Exports." *Urban Studies* 29: 217–35.

Drennan, Matthew P., Emanuel Tobier, and Jonathan Lewis. 1996. "The Interruption of Income Convergence and Income Growth in Large Cities in the 1980s." *Urban Studies* 33: 63–82.

Drucker, Peter F. 1989. *The New Realities in Government and Politics/in Economics and Business/in Society and World View*. New York: Harper & Row.

Dublin, Thomas. 1979. *Women at Work: The Transformation of Work and Community in Lowell, Massachusetts, 1826–1860*. New York: Columbia University Press.

DuBoff, Richard B. 1996. "The Growth of the Federal Regulatory Sector in the United States: A Brief Economic History." *Research in Economic History* 16: 157–84.

Dunkley, Graham. 2000. *The Free Trade Adventure: WTO, The Uruguay Round and Globalism: A Critique*. London: Zed.

Earle, Carville. 1975. *The Evolution of a Tidewater Settlement System: All Hallow's Parish, Maryland, 1650–1783*. Department of Geography Research Paper No. 170. Chicago: University of Chicago Press.

———. 1977. "The First English Towns of North America." *Geographical Review* 67: 34–50.

———. 1979. "Environment, Disease, and Mortality in Early Virginia." *Journal of Historical Geography* 5: 365–90.

———. 1987. "Regional Economic Development West of the Appalachians, 1815–1860." In *North America: The Historical Geography of a Changing Continent*, ed. Robert D. Mitchell and Paul A. Groves, 172–97. Totowa, N.J.: Rowman & Littlefield.

———. 1992. *Geographical Inquiry and American Historical Problems*. Stanford, Calif.: Stanford University Press.

———. 1993. "Divisions of Labor: The Splintered Geography of Labor Markets and Movements in Industrializing America, 1790–1830." *International Review of Social History* 38: 5–37.

———. 2000. "Place Your Bets: Rates of Frontier Expansion in American History, 1650–1890." In *Encounters with the Environment: Enduring and Evolving Geographic Themes*, ed. Alexander B. Murphy and Douglas L. Johnson, 79–105. Lanham, Md.: Rowman & Littlefield.

Earle, Carville, and Changyong Cao. 1993. "Frontier Closure and the Involution of American Society, 1840–1890." *Journal of the Early Republic* 13: 163–79.

Earle, Carville, and Ronald Hoffman. 1976. "Staple Crops and Urban Development in the Eighteenth-Century South." *Perspectives in American History* 10: 5–78.

————. 1980. "The Foundations of the Modern Economy: Agriculture and the Costs of Labor in the United States and England, 1800–1860." *American Historical Review* 85: 1055–94.

Easterlin, Richard A. 1961. "Regional Income Trends, 1840–1950." In *American Economic History*, ed. Seymour Harris, 525–47. New York: McGraw-Hill.

Eckes, Alfred E., Jr. 1995. *Opening America's Market: U.S. Foreign Trade Policy since 1776.* Chapel Hill: University of North Carolina Press.

"Economic Indicators." 1999. *The Economist,* September 18: 114.

Egnal, Marc. 1975. "The Economic Development of the Thirteen Continental Colonies, 1720–1775." *William and Mary Quarterly*, 3d ser., 32: 191–222.

————. 1988. *A Mighty Empire: The Origins of the American Revolution.* Ithaca: N.Y.: Cornell University Press.

————. 1998. *New World Economies: The Growth of the Thirteen Colonies and Early Canada.* New York: Oxford University Press.

Eisenach, Eldon J. 1990. "Reconstituting the Study of American Political Thought in a Regime-change Perspective." *Studies in American Political Development* 4: 169–228.

El-Agraa, Ali M. 1997. "Regional Trade Arrangements Worldwide." In *Economic Integration Worldwide*, ed. Ali M. El-Agraa, 12–33. New York: St. Martin's.

Elazar, Daniel J. 1994. *The American Mosaic: The Impact of Space, Time, and Culture on American Politics.* Boulder, Colo.: Westview.

Ellis, Richard E. 1971. *The Jeffersonian Crisis: Courts and Politics in the Young Republic.* New York: Oxford University Press.

Ethington, Philip, and Eileen McDonagh. 1995. "The Eclectic Center of the New Institutionalism: Axes of Analysis in Comparative Perspective." *Journal of Social History* 19: 467–77.

Ettlinger, Nancy, and Wendy Patton. 1996. "Shared Performance: The Proactive Diffusion of Competitiveness and Industrial and Local Development." *Annals of the Association of American Geographers* 86: 286–305.

Falke, Andreas. 1996. "American Trade Policy after the End of the Cold War." In *The American Impasse: U.S. Diplomatic and Foreign Policy after the Cold War*, ed. Michael Minkenberg and Herbert Dittgen, 264–97. Pittsburgh: University of Pittsburgh Press.

Farmer, Charles. 1993. *In the Absence of Towns: Settlement and Country Trade in Southside Virginia, 1730–1800.* Lanham, Md.: Rowman & Littlefield.

Farrand, Max, ed. 1911. *The Records of the Federal Convention of 1787.* 4 vols. New Haven, Conn.: Yale University Press.

The Federalist Papers: Alexander Hamilton, James Madison, John Jay. 1961. Ed. Clinton Rossiter. New York: New American Library.

Fehrenbacher, Don E. 2001. *The Slaveholding Republic: An Account of the United States Government's Relation to Slavery.* Completed and ed. by Ward M. McAfee. Oxford: Oxford University Press.

Feldstein, Martin. 1988. *International Economic Cooperation.* Chicago: University of Chicago Press.

Filene, Edward A. 1931. *Successful Living in this Machine Age.* New York: Simon & Schuster.

Finlayson, Jock A., and Mark W. Zacher. 1983. "The GATT and the Regulation of Trade Barriers: Regime Dynamics and Functions." In *International Regimes*, ed. Stephen D. Krasner, 1–21. Ithaca, N.Y.: Cornell University Press.

Fischer, David Hackett. 1996. *The Great Wave: Price Revolutions and the Rhythm of History.* New York: Oxford University Press.

Fisher, James S., and Ronald L. Mitchelson. 1981. "Forces of Change in the American Settlement Pattern." *Geographical Review* 71: 298–310.

Flanagan, Richard. 1997. "The Housing Act of 1954: The Sea Change in National Urban Policy." *Urban Affairs Review* 33: 265–86.

Flippin, Percy Scott. 1925. "William Gooch: Successful Royal Governor of Virginia." *William and Mary Quarterly* 2d ser., 5: 225–58.

Fortune. 1998. June 8: 64.

Fox, Edward. 1971. *History in Geographic Perspective: The Other France.* New York: Norton.

Frankel, Jeffrey. 2001. "The Crusade for Free Trade: Evaluating Clinton's International Economic Policy." *Foreign Affairs* 80: 155–61.

Freudenthal, Gideon. 1986. *Atom and Individual in the Age of Newton: On the Genesis of the Mechanistic World View.* Boston Studies in the Philosophy of Science, vol. 88. Dordrecht: Reidel.

Freyer, Tony A. 1979. *Forums of Order: The Federal Courts and Business in American History.* Greenwich, Conn.: JAI.

Friedman, Lawrence M. 1973. *A History of American Law.* New York: Simon & Schuster.

Friis, Herman R. 1940. "A Series of Population Maps of the Colonies and the United States, 1625–1790." American Geographical Society, Mimeographed Publication No. 3. New York: American Geographical Society.

Frug, Gerald E. 1980. "The City as a Legal Concept." *Harvard Law Review* 93: 1059–1154.

Funbashi, Yoichi. 1988. *Managing the Dollar: From the Plaza to the Louvre.* Washington, D.C.: Institute for International Economics.

Galenson, David W. 1981. *White Servitude in Colonial America: An Economic Analysis.* Cambridge: Cambridge University Press.

Gardner, Lloyd, ed. 1966. *A Different Frontier: Selected Readings in the Foundation of American Economic Expansion.* Chicago: Quadrangle.

Garreau, Joel. 1991. *Edge City: Life on the New Frontier.* New York: Doubleday.

Getis, A., and J. K. Ord. 1992. "The Analysis of Spatial Association by Use of Distance Statistics." *Geographical Analysis* 24: 189–206.

Gipson, Lawrence H. 1936–1970. *The British Empire before the American Revolution.* 15 vols. Caldwell, Idaho, and New York: Caxton Printers and Knopf.

Gitelman, Howard. 1967. "The Waltham System and the Coming of the Irish." *Labor History* 8: 227–53.

Glickman, N. J., and Michelle J. White. 1979. "Urban Land-Use Patterns: An International Comparison." *Environment and Planning A* 11: 35–49.

Goe, W. Richard. 1991. "The Growth of Producer Services Industries: Sorting through the Externalization Debate." *Growth and Change* 22: 118–41.

Goldin, Claudia, and Kenneth Sokoloff. 1982. "Women, Children, and Industrialization in the Early Republic: Evidence from the Manufacturing Censuses." *Journal of Economic History* 42: 741–74.

Goldstein, Joshua S. 1988. *Long Cycles: Prosperity and War in the Modern Age.* New Haven, Conn.: Yale University Press.

Gomes, Leonard. 1987. *Foreign Trade and the National Economy: Mercantilist and Classical Perspectives.* New York: St. Martin's.

Goodwyn, Lawrence. 1976. *Democratic Promise: The Populist Moment in America.* New York: Oxford University Press.

Gordon, David M. 1978. "Capitalist Development and the History of American Cities." In *Marxism and the Metropolis,* ed. William K. Tabb and Larry Sawers, 21–53. New York: Oxford University Press.

Gordon, Peter, and Harry W. Richardson. 1996a. "Beyond Polycentricity: The Dispersed Metropolis, Los Angeles, 1970–1990." *Journal of the American Planning Association* 62: 289–95.

———. 1996b. "Employment Decentralization in U.S. Metropolitan Areas: Is Los Angeles an Outlier or the Norm?" *Environment and Planning A* 28: 1727–43.

Gottmann, Jean. 1969. *The Renewal of the Geographic Environment: An Inaugural Lecture Delivered before the University of Oxford on 11th February 1969*. Oxford: Clarendon.

———. 1973. *The Significance of Territory*. Charlottesville: University Press of Virginia.

———. 1975. "The Evolution of the Concept of Territory." *Social Science Information* 14: 29–47.

———. 1980a. "Organizing and Reorganizing Space." In *Centre and Periphery: Spatial Variation in Politics*, ed. Jean Gottmann, 217–24. Beverly Hills, Calif.: Sage.

———. 1980b. "Spatial Partitioning and the Politician's Wisdom." *International Political Science Review* 1: 432–55.

Gowing, Marilyn K., John J. Kraft, and James C. Quick, eds. 1998. *The New Organizational Reality: Downsizing, Restructuring, and Revitalization*. Washington, D.C.: American Psychological Association.

Greene, Jack P. 1988. *Pursuits of Happiness: The Social Development of Early Modern British Colonies and the Formation of American Culture*. Chapel Hill: University of North Carolina Press.

———. 1998. "Empire and Identity from the Glorious Revolution to the American Revolution." In *The Oxford History of the British Empire: The Eighteenth Century*, ed. P. J. Marshall II, 208–30. Oxford: Oxford University Press.

Greenman, Ben. 1998. "America's 100 Most Wired Cities & Towns." *Yahoo!* March: 74–81.

Grier, Peter, and Francine Kiefer. 2001. "Nations Resist Bush's Harder Line." *Christian Science Monitor*. April 5: 1, 8.

Groves, Paul A. 1987. "The Northeast and Regional Integration, 1800–1860." In *North America: The Historical Geography of a Changing Continent*, ed. Robert D. Mitchell and Paul Groves, 198–217. Totowa, N.J.: Rowman & Littlefield.

Gutman, Herbert G. 1976. *Work, Culture and Society in Industrializing America*. New York: Knopf.

Haig, R. M. 1927. *Major Economic Factors in Metropolitan Growth and Arrangement*. New York: Regional Plan of New York and Its Environs.

Hansen, Niles. 1990. "Do Producer Services Induce Regional Economic Development?" *Journal of Regional Science* 30: 465–76.

———. 1993. "Producer Services, Productivity, and Metropolitan Income." *Review of Regional Studies* 23: 255–64.

———. 1994. "The Strategic Role of Producer Services in Regional Development." *International Regional Studies Review* 16: 187–95.

Hardt, Michael, and Antonio Negri. 2000. *Empire*. Cambridge, Mass.: Harvard University Press.

Harley, C. Knick. 1992. "International Competitiveness of the Antebellum American Cotton Textile Industry." *Journal of Economic History* 52: 559–84.

Harrington, John W., and Barney Warf. 1995. *Industrial Location: Principles, Practice, and Policy*. London: Routledge.

Harris, Chauncy D. 1943. "Suburbs." *American Journal of Sociology* 49: 1–13.

Harris, Chauncy D., and Edward L. Ullman. 1945. "The Nature of Cities." *Annals of the American Academy of Political Science* 242: 7–17.

Harris, Marshall. 1953. *Origin of the Land Tenure System in the United States*. Ames: Iowa State University Press.

Harris, P. M. G. 1996. "Inflation and Deflation in Early America, 1634–1860: Patterns of Change in the British American Economy." *Social Science History* 20: 469–505.

Harris, R. W. 1963. *England in the Eighteenth Century: A Balanced Constitution and New Horizons*. London: Blandford.

Harris, Richard. 1988. "American Suburbs: A Sketch of a New Interpretation." *Journal of Urban History* 15: 98–103.

Harrison, Bennett. 1994. *Lean and Mean: The Changing Landscape of Corporate Power.* New York: Basic Books.

Hart, John Fraser. 1988. "Small Towns and Manufacturing." *Geographical Review* 78: 272–87.

Hartshorne, Richard. 1939. *The Nature of Geography: A Critical Survey of Current Thought in Light of the Past.* Lancaster, Pa.: Association of American Geographers.

Hartz, Louis. 1955. *The Liberal Tradition in America: An Interpretation of American Political Thought since the Revolution.* New York: Harcourt, Brace & World.

Harvey, David. 1990. *The Condition of Postmodernity.* Oxford: Blackwell.

Hatch, Nathan O. 1995. "The Second Great Awakening and the Market Revolution." In *Devising Liberty: Preserving and Creating Freedom in the New American Republic,* ed. David Thomas Konig, 243–64. Stanford, Calif.: Stanford University Press.

Hays, Samuel P. 1957. *The Response to Industrialism, 1885–1914.* Chicago: University of Chicago Press.

Hemphill, John M., II. 1964. "Virginia and the English Commercial System, 1689–1733: Studies in the Development and Fluctuations of a Colonial Economy under Imperial Control." Ph.D. diss., Princeton University.

Henretta, James A. 1973. *The Evolution of American Society, 1700–1815: An Interdisciplinary Analysis.* Lexington, Mass.: Heath.

Hershberg, Theodore, ed. 1980. *Philadelphia: Work, Space, Family, and Group Experience: The Nineteenth Century.* New York: Oxford University Press.

Higgs, Robert. 1987. *Crisis and Leviathan: Critical Episodes in the Growth of American Government.* New York: Oxford University Press.

Hill, Christopher. 1969. *Reformation to Revolution, 1530–1780.* Harmondsworth, U.K.: Penguin.

———. 1970. *God's Englishman: Oliver Cromwell and the English Revolution.* New York: Harper & Row.

———. 1980. *The Century of Revolution: 1603–1714.* New York: Norton.

Hilliard, Sam B. 1978. "Antebellum Tidewater Rice Culture in South Carolina and Georgia." In *European Settlement and Development in North America: Essays on Geographical Change in Honour and Memory of Andrew Hill Clark,* 91–115. Toronto: University of Toronto Press.

———. 1987. "A Robust New Nation, 1783–1820." In *North America: The Historical Geography of a Changing Continent,* ed. Robert D. Mitchell and Paul Groves, 149–71. Totowa, N.J.: Rowman & Littlefield.

Hirsch, A. R. 1983. *Making the Second Ghetto: Race and Housing in Chicago, 1940–1960.* Cambridge: Cambridge University Press.

Hirschman, Albert O. 1958. *The Strategy of Economic Development.* Yale Studies in Economics, No. 10. New Haven, Conn.: Yale University Press.

Historical Statistics (see U.S. Bureau of the Census 1975).

Hochberg, Leonard. 1984. "The English Civil War in Geographical Perspective." *Journal of Interdisciplinary History* 15: 729–50.

Hofstadter, Richard. 1955. *The Age of Reform: From Bryan to FDR.* New York: Vintage.

Hogan, Joseph J. 1990. "Reaganomics and Economic Policy." In *The Reagan Presidency: An Incomplete Revolution,* ed. Dilys M. Hill, Raymond A. Moore, and Phil Williams, 35–60. New York: St. Martin's.

Holloway, S. R. 1996. "Job Accessibility and Male Teenage Employment, 1980–1990: The Declining Significance of Space?" *Professional Geographer* 48: 445–48.

Holt, Michael F. 1992. *Political Parties and American Political Development: From the Age of Jackson to the Age of Lincoln.* Baton Rouge: Louisiana State University Press.

———. 1999. "The Primacy of Party Reasserted." *Journal of American History* 86: 151–57.

Horn, James. 1998. "British Diaspora." In *The Oxford History of the British Empire: Vol. II. The Eighteenth Century,* ed. P. J. Marshall, 28–52. Oxford: Oxford University Press.

Horwitz, Morton J. 1977. *The Transformation of American Law, 1780–1860.* Cambridge, Mass.: Harvard University Press.

———. 1992. *The Transformation of American Law, 1870–1960: The Crisis of Legal Orthodoxy.* New York: Oxford University Press.

Howes, Candace, and Ann R. Markusen. 1993. "Trade, Industry, and Economic Development." In *Trading Industries, Trading Regions: International Trade, American Industry, and Regional Economic Development,* ed. Helzi Noponen, Julie Graham, and Ann R. Markusen, 1–44. New York: Guilford.

Hudson, Alan. 1999. "Beyond the Borders: Globalization, Sovereignty and Extra-Territoriality." In *Boundaries, Territory, and Modernity,* ed. David Newman, 89–105. London: Cass.

Hughes, Jonathan. 1987. *American Economic History.* 2d ed. Glenview, Ill.: Scott, Foresman.

Huston, James L. 1998. *Securing the Fruits of Labor: The American Concept of Wealth Distribution, 1765–1900.* Baton Rouge: Louisiana State University Press.

Huyler, Jerome. 1995. *Locke in America: The Moral Philosophy of the Founding Era.* Lawrence: University Press of Kansas.

Innes, Stephen. 1995. *Creating the Commonwealth: The Economic Culture of Puritan New England.* New York: Norton.

"Internal Improvements by Government—Pacific Railroad." 1852. *DeBow's Review* 12: 402–3.

Isaac, Rhys. 1982. *The Transformation of Virginia, 1740–1790.* Chapel Hill: University of North Carolina Press.

Jackson, John B. 1972. *American Space: The Centennial Years, 1865–1876.* New York: Norton.

Jackson, Kenneth T. 1981. "The Spatial Dimensions of Social Control: Race, Ethnicity, and Government Housing Policy in the United States, 1918–1968." In *Modern Industrial Cities: History, Policy, and Survival,* ed. Bruce M. Stave, 79–128. Beverly Hills, Calif.: Sage.

———. 1985. *The Crabgrass Frontier: The Suburbanization of the United States.* New York: Oxford University Press.

Jensen, Joan. 1986. *Loosening the Bonds: Mid-Atlantic Farm Women, 1750–1850.* New Haven, Conn.: Yale University Press.

Jensen, Merrill. 1950. *The New Nation: A History of the United States during the Confederation, 1781–1789.* New York: Vintage.

Jones, Alice Hanson. 1980. *The Wealth of a Nation to Be: The American Colonies on the Eve of the Revolution.* New York: Columbia University Press.

Jones, Charles O., ed. 1988. *The Reagan Legacy: Promise and Performance.* Chatham, N.J.: Chatham House.

Jones, J. R. 1979. "Parties and Parliament." In *The Restored Monarchy, 1660–1688,* ed. J. R. Jones, 48–70. Totowa, N.J.: Rowman & Littlefield.

Judt, Tony. 2001. "The French Difference." *New York Review of Books.* April 12: 18–22.

Kammen, Michael. 1972. *People of Paradox: An Inquiry Concerning the Origins of American Civilization.* New York: Knopf.

Kaplan, Edward S. 1996. *American Trade Policy, 1923–1995.* Westport, Conn.: Greenwood.

Kates, Robert W. 1995. "Lab Notes from the Jeremiah Experiment: Hope for a Sustainable Transition." *Annals of the Association of American Geographers* 85: 623–40.

Kellerman, Aharon. 1993. *Telecommunications and Geography.* London: Belhaven.

Kelly, Sean Q. 1994. "Punctuated Change and the Era of Divided Government." In *New Perspectives on American Politics,* ed. Lawrence C. Dodd and Calvin Jillison, 162–90. Washington, D.C.: CQ Press.

Keohane, Robert O. 1984. *After Hegemony: Cooperation and Discord in the World Political Economy.* Princeton, N.J.: Princeton University Press.

Kerridge, Eric. 1953. "The Movement of Rent, 1540–1640." *Economic History Review* 6: 16–34.

Key, Newton E. 1998. "Whig Interpretation of History." In *A Global Encyclopedia of Historical Writing,* ed. D. R. Woolf, II: 941–42. New York: Garland.

Kim, Sukkoo. 1995. "Expansion of Markets and the Geographic Distribution of Economic Activities: The Trends in U.S. Regional Manufacturing Structure, 1860–1987." *Quarterly Journal of Economics* 110: 881–908.

———. 1998. "Economic Integration and Convergence: U.S. Regions, 1840–1987." *Journal of Economic History* 58: 659–83.

———. 1999. "Regions, Resources, and Economic Geography: Sources of U.S. Regional Comparative Advantage, 1880–1987." *Regional Science and Urban Economics* 29: 1–32.

Kirby, A. 1989. *Time, Space, and Collective Action: Political Space/Political Geography.* Discussion Paper No. 89–1. Tucson: Department of Geography and Regional Development, University of Arizona.

Kissinger, Henry A. 1961. *The Necessity for Choice: Prospects of American Foreign Policy.* New York: Harper.

Klein, Michael, Bruce Mizrach, and Robert G. Murphy. 1991. "Managing the Dollar: Has the Plaza Agreement Mattered?" *Journal of Money, Credit, and Banking* 23: 742–51.

Kodras, Janet E. 1997. "Restructuring the State: Devolution, Privatization, and the Geographic Redistribution of Power and Capacity in Governance." In *State Devolution in America: Implications for a Diverse Society,* ed. Lynn A. Staeheli, Janet E. Kodras, and Colin Flint. Urban Affairs Annual Reviews 48, 79–96. Thousand Oaks, Calif.: Sage.

Kolp, John Gilman. 1998. *Gentlemen and Freeholders: Electoral Politics in Colonial Virginia.* Baltimore: Johns Hopkins University Press.

Kondratieff, Nicolai. 1935. "The Long Wave in Economic Life." *Review of Economic Statistics* 17: 105–15.

Konig, David Thomas. 1995. "Jurisprudence and Social Policy in the New Republic." In *Devising Liberty: Preserving and Creating Freedom in the New American Republic,* ed. David Thomas Konig, 178–216. Stanford, Calif.: Stanford University Press.

———. 2001. "Legal Fictions and the Rule(s) of Law: The Jeffersonian Critique of Common-Law Adjudication." In *The Many Legalities of Early America,* ed. Christopher L. Tomlins and Bruce H. Mann, 97–121. Chapel Hill: University of North Carolina Press.

Kramnick, Isaac. 1988. "'The Great National Discussion': The Discourse of Politics in 1787." *William and Mary Quarterly,* 3d ser., 45: 3–32.

———. 1992. "The Discourse of Politics in 1787: The Constitution and Its Critics on Individualism, Community, and the State." In *To Form a More Perfect Union: The Critical Ideas of the Constitution,* ed. Herman Belz, Ronald Hoffman, and Peter J. Albert, 166–216. Charlottesville: U.S. Capitol Historical Society by the University Press of Virginia.

Krasner, Stephen D. 1983. "Structural Cause and Regime Consequences: Regimes as Intervening Variables." In *International Regimes,* ed. Stephen D. Krasner, 1–21. Ithaca, N.Y.: Cornell University Press.

Krugman, Paul. 1991a. *Geography and Trade.* Cambridge, Mass.: MIT Press.

———. 1991b. "Increasing Returns and Economic Geography." *Journal of Political Economy* 99: 183–99.

Kruman, Marc W. 1997. *Between Authority and Liberty: State Constitution Making in Revolutionary America.* Chapel Hill: University of North Carolina Press.

Kukikoff, Allan. 1986. *Tobacco and Slaves: The Development of Southern Cultures in the Chesapeake, 1680–1800.* Chapel Hill: University of North Carolina Press.

Kuznets, Simon. 1930. *Secular Movements in Production and Prices: Their Nature and Their Bearing upon Cyclical Fluctuations.* Boston: Houghton Mifflin.

Ladurie, Emmanuel LeRoy. 1977. "Motionless History." *Social Science History* 1: 115–36.

Lake, David A. 1988. *Power, Protection, and Free Trade: International Sources of U.S. Commercial Strategy, 1887–1939.* Ithaca, N.Y.: Cornell University Press.

Lampard, Eric E. 1968. "The Evolving System of Cities in the United States: Urbanization and Economic Development." In *Issues in Urban Economics*, ed. Harvey S. Perloff and London Wingo Jr., 81–139. Baltimore: Johns Hopkins University Press.

Lardner, George, Jr. 2000. "Home Prices Go Through the Roof." *Washington Post National Weekly Edition*, June 19: 20.

Lebergott, Stanley. 1984. *The Americans: An Economic Record*. New York: Norton.

———. 1985. "The Demand for Land: The United States, 1820–1860." *Journal of Economic History* 45: 181–212.

———. 1993. *Pursuing Happiness: American Consumers in the Twentieth Century*. Princeton, N.J.: Princeton University Press.

———. 1996. *Consumer Expenditures: New Measures & Old Motives*. Princeton, N.J.: Princeton University Press.

Lemon, James T. 1972. *The Best Poor Man's Country: A Geographical Study of Early Southeastern Pennsylvania*. Baltimore: Johns Hopkins University Press.

———. 1984. "Spatial Order: Households in Local Communities and Regions." In *Colonial British America: Essays in the New History of the Early Modern Era*, ed. Jack P. Greene and J. R. Pole, 86–122. Baltimore: Johns Hopkins University Press.

Lemon, James T., and Gary B. Nash. 1968. "The Distribution of Wealth in Eighteenth-Century America: A Century of Change in Chester County, Pennsylvania, 1693–1802." *Journal of Social History* 2: 1–24.

Lenner, Andrew C. 2001. *The Federal Principle in American Politics, 1790–1833*. Lanham, Md.: Rowman & Littlefield.

Lerner, Ralph. 1987. "The Constitution of the Thinking Revolutionary." In *Beyond Confederation: Origins of the Constitution and American National Identity*, ed. Richard Beeman, Stephen Botein, and Edward C. Carter II, 38–68. Chapel Hill: University of North Carolina Press.

"Letters of the Byrd Family." 1928. "William Byrd II to Mr. Campbell of Norfolk, November 3, 1739." *Virginia Magazine of History and Biography* 36: 353–62.

Lewis, Jan. 1995. "The Problem of Slavery in Southern Political Discourse." In *Devising Liberty: Preserving and Creating Freedom in the New American Republic*, ed. David Thomas Konig, 265–97. Stanford, Calif.: Stanford University Press.

Lieberson, Stanley. 1963. *Ethnic Patterns in American Cities*. New York: Free Press.

———. 1980. *A Piece of the Pie: Black and White Immigrants since 1880*. Berkeley: University of California Press.

———. 1981. "An Asymmetrical Approach to Segregation." In *Ethnic Segregation in Cities*, ed. C. Peach, V. Robinson, and S. Smith, 61–82. London: Croom Helm.

Lively, Robert. 1954–1955. "The American System: A Review Article." *Business History Review* 28–29: 81–96.

Livingston, C. Don, and Kenneth Wink. 1997. "The Passage of the North American Free Trade Agreement in the U.S. House of Representatives: Presidential Leadership or Presidential Luck?" *Presidential Studies Quarterly* 27: 52–70.

Locke, John. 1970. *Two Treatises of Government: A Critical Edition*, ed. Peter Laslett. 2d ed. Cambridge: Cambridge University Press.

Lockridge, Kenneth. 1970. *A New England Town, the First Hundred Years: Dedham, Massachusetts, 1636–1736*. New York: Norton.

Lovejoy, David 1980. "Two American Revolutions, 1689 and 1776." In *Three British Revolutions: 1641, 1688, 1776*, ed. J. G. A. Pocock, 244–62. Princeton, N.J.: Princeton University Press.

Low, Patrick. 1993. *Trading Free: The GATT and U.S. Trade Policy*. New York: Twentieth Century Fund Press.

Lowi, Theodore J. 1964. "American Business, Public Policy, Case Studies, and Political Theory." *World Politics* 16: 677–715.

———. 1967. "Party, Policy and Constitution in America." In *The American Party Systems:*

Stages of Political Development, ed. William Nisbet Chambers and Walter Dean Burnham, 238–276. New York: Oxford University Press.

———. 1972. "Four Systems of Policy, Politics and Choice." *Public Administration Review* July/August: 298–310.

———. 1979. *The End of Liberalism: The Second Republic of the United States.* 2d ed. New York: Norton.

———. 1995. *The End of the Republican Era.* Norman: University of Oklahoma Press.

Lukermann, Fred. 1966. "Empirical Expressions of Nodality and Hierarchy in a Circulation Manifold." *East Lakes Geographer* 2: 17–44.

Madrick, Jeffrey. 1995. *The End of Affluence: The Causes and Consequences of America's Economic Dilemma.* New York: Random House.

———. 1997. "The Cost of Living: A New Myth." *New York Review of Books* 44, no. 4 (March 6): 19–24.

———. 1999. "How New Is the New Economy?" *New York Review of Books*, September 23: 42–50.

Maher, Linda. 1993. "Drawing Circles in the Sand: Extraterritoriality in Civil Rights Legislation after ARAMCO and the Civil Rights Act of 1991." *Connecticut Journal of International Law* 9: 1–50.

Main, Gloria L. 1982. *Tobacco Colony: Life in Early Maryland, 1650–1720.* Princeton, N.J.: Princeton University Press.

———. 1988. "The Standard of Living in Southern New England, 1640–1773." *William and Mary Quarterly*, 3d ser., 45: 124–34.

Main, Gloria L., and Jackson T. Main. 1988. "Economic Growth and the Standard of Living in Southern New England, 1640–1774." *Journal of Economic History* 48: 27–46.

Main, Jackson Turner. 1961. *The Antifederalists: Critics of the Constitution, 1781–1787.* Chapel Hill: University of North Carolina Press.

———. 1965. *The Social Structure of Revolutionary America.* Princeton, N.J.: Princeton University Press.

Malcolm, Joyce Lee. 1999. *The Struggle for Sovereignty: Seventeenth-Century English Political Tracts.* 2 vols. Indianapolis: Liberty Fund.

Malone, Laurence J. 1998. *Opening the West: Federal Internal Improvements Before 1860.* Westport, Conn.: Greenwood.

Mancall, Peter C., and Thomas Weiss. 1999. "Was Economic Growth Likely in Colonial British America?" *Journal of Economic History* 59: 17–40.

Marcuse, Peter. 1980. "Housing Policy and City Planning in the United States, 1893–1931." In *Shaping an Urban World*, ed. Gordon E. Cherry, 23–58. New York: St. Martin's.

———. 1997. "The Enclave, the Citadel, and the Ghetto: What has Changed in the Post-Fordist U.S. City." *Urban Affairs Review* 33: 228–64.

Markusen, Anne R., et al. 1991. *The Rise of the Gunbelt.* New York: Oxford University Press.

Martis, Kenneth C. 1989. *The Historical Atlas of Political Parties in the U.S. Congress, 1789–1989.* New York: Macmillan.

Marx, Karl. 1936. *Capital, a Critique of Political Economy.* New York: Modern Library.

Mason, Alpheus Thomas. 1971. "The Federalist—A Split Personality." In *The Contrapuntal Civilization: Essays toward a New Understanding of the American Experience*, ed. Michael Kammen, 181–205. New York: Crowell.

Massey, Douglas S., and Nancy A. Denton. 1993. *American Apartheid: Segregation and the Making of the Underclass.* Cambridge, Mass.: Harvard University Press.

Mathias, Peter, and Patrick O'Brien. 1976. "Taxation in Britain and France, 1715–1810: A Comparison of the Social and Economic Incidence of Taxes Collected for the Central Governments." *Journal of European History* 5: 601–50.

May, Ernest R. 1961. *Imperial Democracy: The Emergence of America as a Great Power.* New York: Harcourt, Brace & World.

McConnell, James, and Alan MacPherson. 1994. "The North American Free Trade Area: An Overview of Issues and Prospects." In *Continental Trading Blocs: The Growth of Regionalism in the World Economy,* ed. R. Gibb and W. Michalak, 163–87. New York: Wiley.

McCormick, Richard L. 1979. "The Party Period and Public Policy: An Explanatory Hypothesis." *Journal of American History* 66: 279–98.

———. 1982. "The Realignment Synthesis in American History." *Journal of Interdisciplinary History* 13: 85–105.

McCoy, Drew R. 1987. "James Madison and Visions of American Nationality in the Confederation Period: A Regional Perspective." In *Beyond Confederation: Origins of the Constitution and American National Identity,* ed. Richard Beeman, Stephen Botein, and Edward C. Carter II, 226–58. Chapel Hill: University of North Carolina Press.

McCurdy, Charles W. 1975. "Justice Field and the Jurisprudence of Government–Business Relations: Some Parameters of Laissez Faire Constitutionalism, 1863–1897." *Journal of American History* 61: 970–1005.

———. 1978. "American Law and the Marketing Structure of the Large Corporation, 1875–1890." *Journal of Economic History* 38: 631–49.

McCusker, John J. 1992. "How Much Is That in Real Money? A Historical Price Index for Use as a Deflator of Money Values in the Economy of the United States." *Proceedings of the American Antiquarian Society* 101, pt. 2: 297–373.

McCusker, John J., and Russell R. Menard. 1985. *The Economy of British America, 1607–1789.* Chapel Hill: University of North Carolina Press.

McDonald, Forrest. 2000. *States' Rights and the Union: Imperium in Imperio, 1776–1876.* Lawrence: University Press of Kansas.

McDonald, J. F., and D. P. McMillen. 1990. "Employment Subcenters and Land Values in a Polycentric Urban Area: The Case of Chicago." *Environment and Planning A* 22: 1561–74.

McDougall, Walter A. 1997. *Promised Land, Crusader State: The American Encounter with the World since 1776.* Boston: Houghton Mifflin.

McLoughlin, William G. 1978. *Revivals, Awakenings, and Reform: An Essay on Religion and Social Change in America, 1607–1977.* Chicago: University of Chicago Press.

"Measuring Globalization." 2001. *Foreign Policy* 122: 56–65.

Meinig, Donald W. 1986. *The Shaping of America: A Geographical Perspective on 500 Years of History: Vol. 1. Atlantic America, 1492–1800.* New Haven, Conn.: Yale University Press.

———. 1993. *The Shaping of America: A Geographical Perspective on 500 Years of History: Vol. 2. Continental America, 1800–1867.* New Haven, Conn.: Yale University Press.

———. 1998. *The Shaping of America: A Geographical Perspective on 500 Years of History: Vol. 3. Transcontinental America, 1850–1915.* New Haven, Conn.: Yale University Press.

Meltzer, Allan H., and Scott F. Richard. "Why Government Grows (and Grows) in a Democracy." *Public Interest* 52: 111–18.

Menard, Russell R. 1973. "From Servant to Freeholder: Servant Mobility and Property Accumulation in Seventeenth-Century Maryland." *William and Mary Quarterly* 3d ser., 30: 37–64.

———. 1977. "From Servants to Slaves: The Transformation of the Chesapeake Labor System." *Southern Studies* 16: 355–90.

Merrens, H. Roy. 1964. *Colonial North Carolina: A Study in Historical Geography.* Chapel Hill: University of North Carolina Press.

Mesyanshinov, Dmitry. 1997. "Suburbanization of Office Space: A Case Study of Houston, Texas." Ph.D. diss., Louisiana State University.

Meyer, David R. 1983. "Emergence of the American Manufacturing Belt: An Interpretation." *Journal of Historical Geography* 9: 145–74.

———. 1989. "Midwestern Industrialization and the American Manufacturing Belt in the Nineteenth Century." *Journal of Economic History* 49: 921–37.

Meyers, Marvin. 1960. *The Jacksonian Persuasion.* Stanford, Calif.: Stanford University Press.

Mitchell, B. R., and Phyllis Deane. 1967. *Abstract of British Historical Statistics.* 2d ed. Cambridge: Cambridge University Press.

Mitchell, Robert D. 1977. *Commercialism and Frontier: Perspectives on the Early Shenandoah Valley.* Charlottesville: University Press of Virginia.

Mitchelson, R. L., and J. O. Wheeler. 1994. "The Flow of Information in a Global Economy: The Role of the American Urban System in 1990." *Annals of the Association of American Geographers* 84: 87–101.

Morenoff, Jeffrey D. 1997. "Underclass Neighborhoods in Temporal and Ecological Perspective." *Annals, American Academy of Political and Social Science,* 59–72.

Morgan, Edmund S. 1963. *Virginians at Home: Family Life in the Eighteenth Century.* Charlottesville: University Press of Virginia.

———. 1975. *American Slavery, American Freedom: The Ordeal of Colonial Virginia.* New York: Norton.

Moriarty, B. M. 1991. "Urban Systems, Industrial Restructuring, and the Spatial-temporal Diffusion of Manufacturing Employment." *Environment and Planning A* 23: 1571–88.

Morrill, Richard L. 1995. "Metropolitan Concepts and Statistics Reports." In *Metropolitan and Nonmetropolitan Areas: New Approaches to Geographical Definition,* ed. Donald C. Dahmann and James D. Fitzsimmons, 191–250. Population Division, U.S. Bureau of the Census, Working Paper No. 12. Washington, D.C.: U.S. Government Printing Office.

Morrill, Richard L., and O. Fred Donaldson. 1972. "Geographical Perspectives on the History of Black America." *Economic Geography* 48: 1–23.

Morris, Richard, ed. 1970. *Encyclopedia of American History: Enlarged and Updated.* New York: Harper & Row.

Mosher, Anne E. 1995. " 'Something Better than the Best?' Industrial Restructuring, George McMurtry and the Creation of the Model Industrial Town of Vandergrift, Pennsylvania, 1883–1901." *Annals of the Association of American Geographers* 85: 84–107.

Muller, Peter. 1997. "The Suburban Transformation of the Globalizing American City." *Annals of the American Academy of Political and Social Science* 551: 44–58.

Murrin, John. 1980. "The Great Inversion, or Court versus Country: A Comparison of the Revolution Settlements in England (1688–1721) and America (1776–1816)." In *Three British Revolutions: 1641, 1688, 1776,* ed. J. G. A. Pocock, 368–453. Princeton, N.J.: Princeton University Press.

———. 1987. "A Roof without Walls: The Dilemma of American National Identity." In *Beyond Confederation: Origins of the Constitution and American National Identity,* ed. Richard Beeman, Stephen Botein, and Edward C. Carter II, 333–48. Chapel Hill: University of North Carolina Press.

Myrdal, Gunnar. 1957. *Rich Lands and Poor.* New York: Harper.

Nelson, John R., Jr. 1979. "Alexander Hamilton and American Manufacturing: A Reexamination." *Journal of American History* 65: 971–95.

Nelson, William. 1988. *The Fourteenth Amendment: From Political Principle to Judicial Doctrine.* Cambridge, Mass.: Harvard University Press.

Nettels, Curtis. 1934. *The Money Supply in the American Colonies before 1720.* University of Wisconsin Studies in the Social Sciences and History, no. 20. Madison: University of Wisconsin Press.

Niemi, Albert W., Jr. 1980. *U.S. Economic History.* 2d ed. Chicago: Rand McNally.

Niskanen, William A. 1988. *Reaganomics: An Insider's Account of the Policies and the People.* New York: Oxford University Press.

"The Non-Governmental Order." 1999. *The Economist,* December 11: 20–21.

Noponen, Helzi, Julie Graham, and Ann R. Markusen, eds. 1993. *Trading Industries, Trading Regions: International Trade, American Industry, and Regional Economic Development.* New York: Guilford.

North, Douglass C. 1955. "Location Theory and Regional Economic Growth." *Journal of Political Economy* 63: 243–58.

———. 1966. *The Economic Growth of the United States, 1790–1860*. New York: Norton.

———. 1981. *Structure and Change in Economic History*. New York: Norton.

North, Douglass C., and Barry Weingast. 1989. "Constitutions and Commitment: The Evolution of Institutions Governing Public Choice in Seventeenth-Century England." *Journal of Economic History* 49: 803–32.

Novak, William J. 1996. *The People's Welfare: Law and Regulation in Nineteenth-Century America*. Chapel Hill: University of North Carolina Press.

Ò hUallachàin, Breandàn, and Neil Reid. 1991. "The Location and Growth of Business and Professional Services in American Metropolitan Areas, 1976–1986." *Annals of the Association of American Geographers* 81: 254–70.

Olney, Martha L. 1987. "Advertising, Consumer Credit, and the Consumer Durables Revolution of the 1920s." *Journal of Economic History* 47: 489–91.

———. 1990. "Demand for Consumer Durable Goods in 20th Century America." *Explorations in Economic History* 27: 322–49.

Olson, Alison Gilbert 1980. "Parliament, Empire, and Parliamentary Law, 1776." In *Three British Revolutions: 1641, 1688, 1776.*, ed. J. G. A. Pocock, 289–322. Princeton, N.J.: Princeton University Press.

O'Mara, James J. 1979. "Urbanization in Tidewater Virginia during the Eighteenth Century: A Study in Historical Geography." Ph.D. diss., York University.

———. 1983. *An Historical Geography of Urban System Development: Tidewater Virginia in the Eighteenth Century*. Geographical Monographs No. 13. York University, Atkinson College, Department of Geography. York, U.K.: York University.

Onuf, Peter S. 1983. *Origins of the Federal Republic: Jurisdictional Controversies in the United States, 1775–1787*. Philadelphia: University of Pennsylvania Press.

———. 1995. "The Expanding Union." In *Devising Liberty: Preserving and Creating Freedom in the New American Republic*, ed. David Thomas Konig, 50–80. Stanford, Calif.: Stanford University Press.

———. 1996. "Federalism, Republicanism, and the Origins of American Sectionalism." In *All Over the Map: Rethinking American Regions*, ed. Edward L. Ayers, et al., 1–37. Baltimore: Johns Hopkins University Press.

Ord, J. K., and A. Getis. 1995. "Local Spatial Autocorrelation Statistics: Distributional Issues and an Application." *Geographical Analysis* 27: 286–306.

Osterman, Paul. 1994. *Securing Prosperity: The American Labor Market: How It Has Changed and All Over the Map: Rethinking American Regions*, ed. Edward L. Ayers, et al,Otterstrom, Samuel M. 1997. "An Analysis of Population Dispersal and Concentration in the United States, 1790–1990: The Frontier, Long Waves, and the Manufacturing Connection." Ph.D. diss., Louisiana State University.

Paolino, Ernest N. 1973. *The Foundations of the American Empire: William Henry Seward and U.S. Foreign Policy*. Ithaca, N.Y.: Cornell University Press.

Papenfuse, Edward C., Jr. 1972. "Planter Behavior and Economic Opportunity in a Staple Economy." *Agricultural History* 46: 297–311.

Pares, Richard. 1956. *Yankees and Creoles: The Trade between North America and the West Indies before the American Revolution*. Cambridge, U.K.: Cambridge University Press.

Parks, George Bruner. 1928. *Richard Hakluyt and the English Voyages*, American Geographical Society Serial Publications No. 10. New York: American Geographical Society.

Patterson, James T. 1996. *Great Expectations: The United States, 1945–1974*. New York: Oxford University Press.

Paul, Arnold M. 1959. "Legal Progressivism, the Courts, and the Crisis of the 1890s." *Business History Review* 83: 497–509.

Paullin, Charles O., and John K. Wright. 1932. *Atlas of the Historical Geography of the United States*. Washington, D.C.: Carnegie Institution of Washington and the American Geographical Society.

Payne, Philip M. 1968. "Slaveholding and Indentured Servitude in Seventeenth-Century Maryland, 1674–1699." Master's thesis, University of Maryland.

Payne, Rodger M. 1995. "New Light in Hanover County: Evangelical Dissent in Piedmont Virginia, 1740–1755." *Journal of Southern History* 61: 665–94.

Percy, George. 1907. "Observations of Master George Percy." In *Narratives of Early Virginia, 1606–1625.* New York: Scribner's.

Perloff, Harvey S., Edgar S. Dunn, and Richard F. Muth. 1960. *Regions, Resources and Economic Growth.* Baltimore: Johns Hopkins University Press.

Phelps-Brown, E. H., and Sheila V. Hopkins. 1957. "Wage Rates and Prices: Evidence for Population Pressure in the Sixteenth Century." *Economica,* 2d ser., 24: 289–306.

Phillips, Kevin. 1999. *The Cousin's War: Religion, Politics, and the Triumph of Anglo-America.* New York: Basic Books.

Pincus, Steven C. A. 1996. *Protestantism and Patriotism: Ideologies and the Making of English Foreign Policy, 1650–1668.* Cambridge: Cambridge University Press.

Platt, Rutherford H. 1985. "Farmland Conversion Debate: NALS and Beyond." *Professional Geographer* 37: 433–42.

Pletcher, David M. 1998. *The Diplomacy of Trade and Investment: American Economic Expansion in the Hemisphere.* Columbia: University of Missouri Press.

Plumb, J. H. 1956. *The First Four Georges: England and her German Kings.* Boston: Little, Brown.

Pocock, J. G. A. 1975. *The Machiavellian Moment: Florentine Political Thought and the Atlantic Republican Tradition.* Princeton, N.J.: Princeton University Press.

———. 1980. "1776: The Revolution against Parliament." In *Three British Revolutions: 1641, 1688, 1776.,* ed. J. G. A. Pocock, 265–88. Princeton, N.J.: Princeton University Press.

———. 1985. "The Varieties of Whiggism from Exclusion to Reform: A History of Ideology and Discourse." In *Virtue, Commerce, and History: Essays on Political Thought and History, Chiefly in the Eighteenth Century,* ed. J. G. A. Pocock, 215–310. Cambridge: Cambridge University Press.

Pole, J. R. 1978. *The Pursuit of Equality in American History.* Berkeley: University of California Press.

———. 1992. "The Individualist Foundations of American Constitutionalism." In *To Form a More Perfect Union: The Critical Ideas of the Constitution,* ed. Herman Belz, Ronald Hoffman, and Peter J. Albert, 73–106. Charlottesville: United States Capitol Historical Society by the University Press of Virginia.

Pollins, Brian M., and Randall L. Schweller. 1999. "Linking the Levels: The Long Wave and Shifts in U.S. Foreign Policy, 1790–1993." *American Journal of Political Science* 43: 431–64.

Poverty in the United States: 2000. 2001. U.S. Census Bureau: Current Population Reports: Consumer Income. Washington, D.C.: Government Printing Office.

Pratt, Julius W. 1950. *America's Colonial Experiment: How the United States Gained, Governed, and in Part Gave Away a Colonial Empire.* New York: Prentice Hall.

Pred, Allan R. 1966. *The Spatial Dynamics of U.S. Urban-Industrial Growth, 1800–1914: Interpretative and Theoretical Essays.* Cambridge, Mass.: MIT Press.

———. 1973. *Urban Growth and the Circulation of Information: The United States System of Cities, 1790–1840.* Cambridge, Mass.: Harvard University Press.

———. 1980. *Urban Growth and City-Systems in the United States, 1840–1860.* Cambridge, Mass.: Harvard University Press.

Price, Jacob M. 1954. "The Rise of Glasgow in the Chesapeake Tobacco Trade, 1707–1775." *William and Mary Quarterly,* 3d ser., 11: 179–99.

———. 1973. *France and the Chesapeake: A History of the French Tobacco Monopoly, 1674–1791, and of Its Relationship to the British and American Tobacco Trades.* 2 vols. Ann Arbor: University of Michigan Press.

————. 1980. *Capital and Credit in British Overseas Trade: The View from the Chesapeake, 1700–1776*. Cambridge, Mass.: Harvard University Press.

Price, Jacob M., and Paul G. E. Clemens. 1987. "A Revolution of Scale in Overseas Trade: British Firms in the Chesapeake Trade, 1675–1775." *Journal of Economic History* 47: 1–43.

Quinn, David. 1955. *The Roanoke Voyages, 1584–1590*. 2 vols. London: The Hakluyt Society.

Rabb, Theodore K. 1967. *Enterprise and Empire: Merchant and Gentry Investment in the Expansion of England, 1575–1630*. Cambridge, Mass.: Harvard University Press.

Radford, Gail. 1996. *Modern Housing for America: Policy Struggles in the New Deal Era*. Chicago: University of Chicago Press.

Radford, John. 1981. "The Social Geography of the Nineteenth-Century U.S. City." In *Geography and the Urban Environment: Progress in Research and Applications*, ed. D. T. Herbert and R. J. Johnston, 257–93. Chichester, U.K.: Wiley.

Rainbolt, John C. 1969. "The Absence of Towns in Seventeenth Century Virginia." *Journal of Southern History* 35: 343–60.

Rakove, Jack N. 1996. *Original Meanings: Politics and Ideas in the Making of the Constitution*. New York: Vintage.

Reading, D. C. 1973. "New Deal Activity and the States, 1933 to 1939." *Journal of Economic History* 33: 792–810.

Records (see Farrand, Max, ed. 1911).

Relph, Edward. 1987. *The Modern Urban Landscape*. Baltimore: Johns Hopkins University Press.

Riefler, Roger F. 1979. "Nineteenth-Century Urbanization Patterns in the United States." *Journal of Economic History* 39: 961–74.

Riker, William H. 1955. "The Senate and American Federalism." *American Political Science Review* 49: 452–69.

Roberts, Susan M. 1995. "Global Regulation and Trans-State Organization." In *Geographies of Global Change: Remapping the World in the Late Twentieth Century*, ed. R. J. Johnston, Peter J. Taylor, and Michael Watts, 111–26. Oxford: Blackwell.

Roche, John P. 1963. "Entrepreneurial Liberty and the Fourteenth Amendment." *Labor History* 4: 3–31.

Rodgers, Daniel T. 1992. "Republicanism: The Career of a Concept." *Journal of American History* 79: 11–38.

————. 1998. *Atlantic Crossings: Social Politics in a Progressive Age*. Cambridge, Mass.: Harvard University Press.

Rogers, John M. 1999. *International Law and United States Law*. Brookfield, Vt.: Aldershot.

Rohrbough, Malcolm J. 1968. *The Land Office Business: The Settlement and Administration of American Public Lands, 1789–1837*. New York: Oxford University Press.

Roncaglia, Alessandro. 1985. *Petty: The Origins of Political Economy*. Armonk, N.Y.: Sharpe.

Root, Hilton L. 1991. "The Redistributive Role of Government: Economic Regulation in Old Regime France and England." *Comparative Studies in Society and History* 33: 338–69.

Rosenberg, Emily S. 1982. *Spreading the American Dream: American Economic and Cultural Expansion, 1890–1945*. New York: Hill & Wang.

Rosenzweig, Roy. 2001. "The Road to Xanadu: Public and Private Pathways on the History Web." *Journal of American History* 88: 548–79.

Rothenberg, Winifred B. 1981. "The Market and Massachusetts' Farmers, 1750–1855." *Journal of Economic History* 41: 283–314.

————. 1988. "The Emergence of Farm Labor Markets and the Transformation of the Rural Economy: Massachusetts, 1750–1855." *Journal of Economic History* 48: 537–66.

Rouse, A. L. 1955. *The Expansion of Elizabethan England*. New York: St. Martin's.

Roy, Joaquin. 2000. *Cuba, the United States, and the Helms–Burton Doctrine: International Reactions*. Gainesville: University of Florida Press.

Roy, William G. 1997. *Socializing Capital: The Rise of the Large Industrial Corporation in America*. Princeton, N.J.: Princeton University Press.

Ruggie, John Gerard. 1993. "Territoriality and Beyond: Problematizing Modernity in International Relations." *International Organization* 47: 139–74.

Rupert, Mark. 1995. *Producing Hegemony: The Politics of Mass Production and American Global Power*. Cambridge: Cambridge University Press.

Rutman, Darrett B., and Anita H. Rutman 1984a. *A Place in Time: Middlesex County, Virginia, 1650–1750*. New York: Norton.

Rutman, Darrett B., and Anita H. Rutman 1984b. *A Place in Time: Middlesex County, Virginia, 1650–1750: Explicatus*. New York: Norton.

Sabel, Charles. 1994. "Flexible Specialization and the Re-emergence of Regional Economies." In *Post-Fordism: A Reader*, ed. Ash Amin, 101–56. Oxford: Blackwell.

Sandel, Michael. 1996. *Democracy's Discontent: America in Search of a Public Philosophy*. Cambridge, Mass.: Harvard University Press.

Sanders, Elizabeth. 1999. *Roots of Reform: Farmers, Workers, and the American State, 1877–1917*. Chicago: University of Chicago Press.

Sargent, Charles W. 1964. "Virginia and the West Indies Trade, 1740–1765." Ph.D. diss., University of New Mexico.

Scheffer, David J. 1999. "The United States and the International Criminal Court." *American Journal of International Law* 93: 12–22.

Scheiber, Harry N. 1975. "Federalism and the American Economic Order, 1789–1910." *Law and Society Review* 10: 57–118.

Schlesinger, Arthur, Jr. 1986. *The Cycles of American History*. Boston: Houghton Mifflin.

Schumpeter, Joseph. 1939. *Business Cycles*. 2 vols. New York: McGraw-Hill.

Shade, William G. 1981. "Political Pluralism and Party Development: The Creation of a Modern Party System: 1815–1852." In *The Evolution of American Electoral Systems*, ed. Paul Kleppner, et al., 77–112. Westport, Conn.: Greenwood.

Shafer, Byron E. 1993. "Political Eras in Political History." *Journal of Policy History* 5: 461–74.

Shammas, Carol. 1990. *The Pre-industrial Consumer in England and America*. Oxford: Clarendon.

———. 1993. "Changes in English and Anglo-American Consumption from 1550 to 1800." In *Consumption and the World of Goods*, ed. John Brewer and Roy Porter, 177–205. London: Routledge.

Sharer, George Terry. 1968. "Slaveholding in Maryland 1695–1775." Master's thesis, University of Maryland.

Shelley, Fred M., et al. 1996. *The Political Geography of the United States*. New York: Guilford.

Shelton, Cynthia J. 1986. *The Mills of Manayunk: Industrialization and Social Conflict in the Philadelphia Region, 1787–1837*. Baltimore: Johns Hopkins University Press.

Shepherd, James F., and Gary M. Walton. 1976. "Economic Change after the American Revolution: Pre- and Post-war Comparisons of Maritime Shipping and Trade." *Explorations in Economic History* 13: 397–422.

Sheridan, Richard B. 1984. "The Domestic Economy." In *Colonial British America: Essays in the New History of the Early Modern Era*, ed. Jack P. Greene and J. R. Pole, 43–85. Baltimore: Johns Hopkins University Press.

Shew, Dianna Baker. 1986. "United States–Based Multinational Corporations Should Be Tried in the United States for Their Extraterritorial Toxic Torts." *Vanderbilt Journal of Transnational Law* 19: 651–70.

Shy, John. 1965. *Toward Lexington: The Role of the British Army in the Coming of the American Revolution*. Princeton, N.J.: Princeton University Press.

Silbey, Joel H. 1991. *The American Political Nation, 1838–1893*. Stanford, Calif.: Stanford University Press.

Simler, Lucy. 1986. "Tenancy in Colonial Pennsylvania: The Case of Chester County, Pennsylvania." *William and Mary Quarterly* 43: 542–69.

————. 1990. "The Landless Worker: An Index of Economic and Social Change in Chester County, Pennsylvania, 1250–1820." *Pennsylvania Magazine of History and Biography* 114: 163–200.

————. N.d. "The Union of Manufacturing and Agriculture in Colonial Pennsylvania, 1683–1776." Unpublished manuscript.

Skowronek, Stephen. 1982. *Building a New American State: The Expansion of National Administrative Capacities, 1877–1920.* New York: Cambridge University Press.

————. 1993. *The Politics Presidents Make: Leadership from John Adams to Bill Clinton.* Cambridge, Mass.: Harvard University Press.

Slaughter, Anne-Marie, and David Bosco. 2000. "Plaintiff's Democracy." *Foreign Affairs* 79: 102–16.

Sly, John F. 1928. "Geographical Expansion and Town System." In *Commonwealth History of Massachusetts,* ed. Albert B. Hart, 2: 96–115. New York: States History Company.

Smis, Stefaan, and Kim Van Der Borght. 1999. "The EU–US Compromise on the Helms–Burton and D'Amato Acts." *American Journal of International Law* 93: 227–36.

Smith, Abbot Emerson. 1947. *Colonists in Bondage: White Servitude and Convict Labor in America, 1607–1776.* Chapel Hill: University of North Carolina Press.

Smith, Adam. 1976. *An Inquiry into the Nature and Causes of the Wealth of Nations,* ed. R. H. Campbell, A. S. Skinner, and W. B. Todd. 2 vols. Oxford: Clarendon.

Smith, Hedrick. 1995. *Rethinking America: Innovative Strategies and Partnerships in Business and Education.* New York: Avon.

Smith, Neil. 1988. "The Region Is Dead! Long Live the Region!" *Political Geography Quarterly* 7: 141–52.

Smithies, Arthur. 1946. "The American Economy in the Thirties." *American Economic Review* 36: 11–27.

Sokoloff, Kenneth. 1986. "Productivity Growth in Manufacturing during Early Industrialization: Evidence from the American Northeast, 1820–1860." In *Long-Term Factors in American Economic Growth,* ed. Stanley L. Engerman and Robert E. Gallman, 679–736. Chicago: University of Chicago Press.

Speck, W.A. 1984. "The International and Imperial Context." In *Colonial British America: Essays on the New History of the Early Modern Era,* ed. Jack P. Greene and J. R. Pole, 384–407. Baltimore: Johns Hopkins University Press.

Spulber, Nicolas. 1995. *The American Economy: The Struggle for Supremacy in the 21st Century.* Cambridge: Cambridge University Press.

Stanback, Thomas M. 1991. *The New Suburbanization: Challenge to the Central City.* Boulder, Colo.: Westview.

Statistical Abstract (see U.S. Bureau of the Census and the appropriate year).

Steele, Ian K. 1986. *The English Atlantic, 1675–1740: An Exploration of Communication and Community.* New York: Oxford University Press.

————. 1994. *Warpaths: Indians of North America.* New York: Oxford University Press.

Steinberg, Richard H. 1997. "Trade–Environment Negotiations in the EU, NAFTA, and WTO: Regional Trajectories of Rule Development." *American Journal of International Law* 91: 231–67.

Stephens, G. Ross, and Nelson Wikstrom. 2000. *Metropolitan Government and Governance: Theoretical Perspectives, Empirical Analysis, and the Future.* New York: Oxford University Press.

Stewart, Charles, III, and Barry R. Weingast. 1992. "Stacking the Senate, Changing the Nation: Republican Rotten Boroughs, Statehood Politics, and American Political Development." *Studies in American Political Development* 6: 223–71.

Stewart, John Q. 1947. "Empirical Mathematical Rules Concerning the Distribution and Equilibrium of Population." *Geographical Review* 37: 461–85.

Stewart, Mart A. 1996. *"What Nature Suffers to Growe": Life, Labor, and Landscape on the Georgia Coast, 1680–1920.* Athens: University of Georgia Press.

Stiverson, Gregory A. 1977. *Poverty in a Land of Plenty: Tenancy in Eighteenth-Century Maryland.* Baltimore: Johns Hopkins University Press.

Stone, Lawrence. 1949–50. "Elizabethan Overseas Trade." *Economic History Review* 2d ser., 2: 30–57.

———. 1966. "Social Mobility in England, 1500–1700." *Past and Present,* no. 33: 16–55.

———. 1972. *The Causes of the English Revolution 1529–1642.* London: Routledge & Kegan Paul.

———. 1980. "The Results of the English Revolutions of the Seventeenth Century." In *Three British Revolutions: 1641, 1688, 1776.*, ed. J. G. A. Pocock, 23–108. Princeton, N.J.: Princeton University Press.

Storper, Michael, and Richard Walker. 1989. *The Capitalist Imperative: Territory, Technology, and Industrial Growth.* Oxford: Blackwell.

Strait, John B. 2001. "The Disparate Impact of Metropolitan Economic Change: The Growth of Extreme Poverty Neighborhoods, 1970–1990." *Economic Geography* 77: 272–305.

Striner, Richard. 1995. "Political Newtonianism: The Cosmic Model of Politics in Europe and America." *William and Mary Quarterly,* 3d ser. 52: 583–608.

Sugrue, Thomas J. 1993. "The Structures of Urban Poverty: The Reorganization of Space and Work in Three Periods of American History." In *The Underclass Debate: Views from History,* ed. Michael B. Katz, 85–117. Princeton, N.J.: Princeton University Press.

Sydnor, Charles. 1952. *Gentlemen Freeholders: Political Practices in Washington's Virginia.* Chapel Hill: University of North Carolina Press.

Tarr, Joel A. 1985. "Building the Urban Infrastructure in the Nineteenth Century: An Introduction." In *Infrastructure and Urban Growth in the Nineteenth Century,* 61–85. Chicago: Public Works Historical Society.

———. 1988. "Sewerage and the Development of the Networked City in the United States, 1850–1930." In *Technology and the Rise of the Networked City in Europe and America,* ed. Joel A. Tarr and Gabriel Dupay, 159–85. Philadelphia: Temple University Press.

Taylor, E. G. R. 1930. *Tudor Geography 1485–1583.* London: Methuen & Co.

———, ed. 1935. *The Original Writings and Correspondence of the Two Richard Hakluyts.* Hakluyt Society, 2d ser., no. 76–77, 2 vols. N.p.: Hakluyt Society.

Taylor, Graham Romney. 1915. *Satellite Cities: A Study of Industrial Suburbs.* New York: Appleton.

Taylor, Peter J. 1999. *Modernities: A Geohistorical Interpretation.* Minneapolis: University of Minnesota Press.

Teaford, Jon C. 1997. *Post-Suburbia: Government and Politics in the Edge Cities.* Baltimore: Johns Hopkins University Press.

Teece, David J. 1992. "Competition, Cooperation, and Innovation: Organizational Arrangements for Regimes of Rapid Technological Progress." *Journal of Economic Behavior and Organization* 18: 1–25.

Tellier, L.-N. 1995. "Projecting the Evolution of the North American Urban System and Laying the Foundations of a Topodynamic Theory of Spatial Organization." *Environment and Planning A* 27: 1109–1131.

Temin, Peter. 1969. *The Jacksonian Economy.* New York: Norton.

Temin, Peter, and Barrie A. Wigmore. 1990. "The End of One Big Deflation." *Explorations in Economic History* 27: 483–502.

Tepass, Michael. 1992. "Resolving Extraterritoriality Conflicts in Antitrust: Two Case Studies and Proposals of Solution." *Connecticut Journal of International Law* 15: 565–623.

Thomas, George M. 1989. *Revivalism and Cultural Change: Christianity, Nation Building, and the Market in the Nineteenth-Century United States.* Chicago: University of Chicago Press.

Thompson, Wilbur R. 1965. *A Preface to Urban Economics.* Baltimore: Johns Hopkins University Press.

Thunen, Johann Heinrich von. 1930 [orig. 1842, 1850]. *Der isolierte staat in Beziehung and Landwirtschaft und Naturaläokonomie.* Jena: Fischer.

Trevor-Roper, Hugh. 1992. *From Counter-Reformation to Glorious Revolution.* Chicago: University of Chicago Press.

Trubowitz, Peter. 1997. "Sectionalism and American Foreign Policy: The Political Geography of Consensus and Conflict." *International Studies Quarterly* 36: 173–90.

Trubowitz, Peter, and Brian E. Roberts. 1992. "Regional Interests and the Reagan Military Buildup." *Regional Studies* 26: 555–67.

"Urban Sprawl." 1999. *The Economist,* August 21: 24–25.

U.S. Bureau of the Census. 1975. *Historical Statistics of the United States from Colonial Times to the Present.* 2 pts. Washington, D.C.: U.S. Government Printing Office.

———. 1991. *State and Metropolitan Area Data Book 1991.* Washington, D.C.: U.S. Government Printing Office.

———. 1997. *Statistical Abstract of the United States: The National Data Book,* 117th ed. Washington, D.C.: U.S. Government Printing Office.

———. 2000. *Statistical Abstract of the United States: The National Data Book.* 119th ed., 1999. Washington, D.C.: U.S. Government Printing Office.

———. 2001. *State and Metropolitan Area Data Book 2001.* Washington, D.C.: U.S. Government Printing Office.

U.S. Congressional Record. 1933. H10048. Washington, D.C.: U.S. Government Printing Office.

U.S. Department of Commerce. 1930. *Statistical Abstract of the United States 1930.* Washington, D.C.: Government Printing Office.

———. 1998. *The Emerging Digital Economy.* Washington, D.C.: U.S. Government Printing Office.

U.S. Department of Commerce and Labor. 1909. *Industrial Districts: 1905: Manufactures and Population.* Bulletin 101. Washington, D.C.: U.S. Government Printing Office.

U.S. Department of Transportation. 1997. *Transportation Statistics: Annual Report 1997: Mobility and Access.* Washington, D.C.: U.S. Government Printing Office.

U.S. Seventy-sixth Congress. 1939. *Federal Ownership of Real Estate and Its Bearing on State and Local Taxation.* House Doc. No. 111. Washington, D.C.: U.S. Government Printing Office.

Usher, A. P. 1928. "Colonial Business and Transportation." In *Commonwealth History of Massachusetts,* ed. Albert B. Hart, 2: 386–418. New York: States History Company.

Vagts, Detlev F. 1970. "The Multinational Enterprise: A New Challenge for Transnational Law." *Harvard Law Review* 83: 705–39.

Vatter, Harold G. 1967. "Has there been a Twentieth-Century Consumer Durables Revolution?" *Journal of Economic History* 27: 1–16.

von Erde, Eleanor, and Thomas Weiss. 1993. "Consumption of Farm Output and Economic Growth in the Old Northwest, 1800–1860." *Journal of Economic History* 53: 308–18.

von Hoffman, Alexander. 1996. "Weaving the Urban Fabric: Nineteenth-Century Patterns of Residential and Real Estate Development in Outer Boston." *Journal of Urban History* 22: 191–230.

Wacquant, L. 1993. "Urban Outcasts: Stigma and Division in the Black American Ghetto and the French Urban Periphery." *International Journal of Urban and Regional Planning* 17: 366–83.

Walker, Richard. 1995. "Regulation and Flexible Specialization as Theories of Capitalist Development: Challengers to Marx and Schumpeter? In *Spatial Relations: Critical Explorations in Social Theory*, ed. Helen Liggett and David C. Perry, 167–208. Thousand Oaks, Calif.: Sage.

Walker, Ruth. 2001. "Does NAFTA Trump Countries' Laws?" *Christian Science Monitor*, April 3: 1–3.

Wallace, Anthony F. C. 1978. *Rockdale: The Growth of an American Village in the Early Industrial Revolution*. New York: Knopf.

Wallis, John Joseph. 1998. "The Political Economy of New Deal Spending Revisited, Again with and without Nevada." *Explorations in Economic History* 35: 140–70.

Walsh, Lorena S. 1999. "Summing the Parts: Implications for Estimating Chesapeake Output and Income Subregionally." *William and Mary Quarterly*, 3d ser., 56: 53–94.

Walton, Gary M., and James F. Shepherd. 1979. *The Economic Rise of Early America*. Cambridge: Cambridge University Press.

Ward, David. 1971. *Cities and Immigrants: A Geography of Change in Nineteenth-Century America*. New York: Oxford University Press.

Warntz, William. 1964. "A New Map of the Surface of Population Potentials for the United States, 1960." *Geographical Review* 54: 170–84.

———. 1967. "Macroscopic Analysis and Some Patterns of the Geographical Distribution of Population in the United States, 1790–1950." In *Quantitative Geography*, Studies in Geography 14, ed. William L. Garrison, 191–218. Evanston, Ill.: Department of Geography, Northwestern University.

———. 1981. "*Geographia Generalis* and the Earliest Development of American Academic Geography." In *The Origins of Academic Geography in the United States*, ed. Brian Blouet, 245–63. New York: Archon.

Warren, Donald I. 1969. "Neighborhood Structure and Riot Behavior in Detroit: Some Exploratory Findings." *Social Problems* 16: 464–84.

Washburn, Wilcomb E. 1957. *The Governor and the Rebel: A History of Bacon's Rebellion in Virginia*. Chapel Hill: University of North Carolina Press.

Weber, Alfred. 1969 [orig. 1929]. *Theory of the Location of Industries*, introduction and notes by Carl J. Friedrich. Chicago: University of Chicago Press.

Weidenbaum, Murray. 1988. *Rendezvous with Reality: The American Economy after Reagan*. New York: Basic Books.

Weinstein, Bernard L., and Robert E. Firestine. 1978. *Regional Growth and Decline in the United States: The Rise of the Sunbelt and the Decline of the Northeast*. New York: Praeger.

Weintraub, Sidney. 1995. "The Depth of Economic Integration between Mexico and the United States." *Washington Quarterly* 18: 173–84.

Weiss, Thomas. 1994. "Economic Growth Before 1860: Revised Conjectures." In *American Economic Development in Historical Perspective*, ed. Thomas Weiss and Donald Schaefer, 1–27. Stanford, Calif.: Stanford University Press.

Wertenbaker, Thomas J. 1940. *Torchbearer of the Revolution: The Story of Bacon's Rebellion and its Leader*. Princeton, N.J.: Princeton University Press.

Westbrook, Jay Lawrence. 1990. "Extraterritoriality, Conflict of Laws, and the Regulation of Transnational Business." *Texas International Law Journal* 25: 71–97.

Wheeler, James O., and Raymond Greene. 1999. "Recent Employment Changes in Major Metropolitan Areas in the United States." *Geographical Bulletin* 41: 26–36.

Wiebe, Robert. 1967. *The Search for Order: 1877–1920*. New York: Hill & Wang.

Willan, T. S. 1959. *Studies in Elizabethan Foreign Trade*. Manchester, U.K.: Manchester University Press.

Williams, Basil. 1939. *The Whig Supremacy, 1714–1760*. Oxford: Clarendon.

Williams, William Appleman. 1969. *The Roots of the Modern American Empire*. New York: Random House.

Williamson, Jeffrey G. 1965. "Regional Inequality and the Process of National Development: A Description of the Patterns." *Economic Development and Cultural Change* 13: 3–45.

Wills, Garry. 1999a. *A Necessary Evil: A History of American Distrust of Government*. New York: Simon & Schuster.

———. 1999b. "Signs of the Times in Seattle." *The Advocate* [Baton Rouge, La.], December 11: 12b.

Wilson, Charles. 1965. *England's Apprenticeship, 1603–1763*. New York: St. Martin's.

Wilson, Franklin. 1987. "Metropolitan and Nonmetropolitan Migration Streams: 1935–1980." *Demography* 24: 211–28.

Wilson, William J. 1996. *When Work Disappears: The World of the New Urban Poor*. New York: Knopf.

Wolff, Edward N. 1995. *Top Heavy: The Increasing Inequality of Wealth in America and What Can Be Done about It*. New York: New Press.

Wood, Gordon S. 1969. *The Creation of the American Republic, 1776–1787*. Chapel Hill: University of North Carolina Press.

———. 1987. "Interests and Disinterestness in the Making of the Constitution." In *Beyond Confederation: Origins of the Constitution and American National Identity*, ed. Richard Beeman, Stephen Botein, and Edward C. Carter II, 69–109. Chapel Hill: University of North Carolina Press.

Wood, Peter H. 1974. *Black Majority: Negroes in Colonial South Carolina from 1660 through the Stono Rebellion*. New York: Knopf.

World Trade Organization. 1996. *Trade Policy Review: United States 1996*. Geneva: Author.

———. 1997. *WTO Annual Report 1997: International Trade Statistics*, vol. 2. Geneva: Author.

———. 1998. *WTO Annual Report 1998: International Trade Statistics*, vol. 2. Geneva: Author.

———. 1999. *WTO Annual Report 1999: International Trade Statistics*, vol. 2. Geneva: Author.

Wrigley, E. A., and R. S. Schofield. 1981. *The Population History of England, 1541–1871*. Cambridge, Mass.: Harvard University Press.

Wyly, Elvin K. 1999. "Continuity and Change in the Restless Urban Landscape." *Economic Geography* 75: 309–38.

Yamakawa, Ryuichi. 1992. "Territoriality and Extraterritoriality: Coverage of Fair Employment Laws after *EEOC v. ARAMCO*." *North Carolina Journal of International Law* 17: 71–119.

Yapa, Lakshman. 1977. "Green Revolution: A Diffusion Model." *Annals of the Association of American Geographers* 67: 350–59.

———. 1982. "Innovation Bias, Appropriate Technology, and Basic Goods." *Journal of Asian and African Studies* 17: 32–44.

Yarbrough, Beth V., and Robert M. Yarbrough. 1994. "Regionalism and Layered Governance: The Choice of Trade Institutions." *Journal of International Affairs* 48: 95–117.

Young, James P. 1996. *Reconsidering American Liberalism: The Troubled Odyssey of the Liberal Idea*. Boulder, Colo.: Westview.

Zevin, Robert. 1972. "An Interpretation of American Imperialism." *Journal of Economic History* 32: 316–60.

Zuckert, Michael P. 1994. *Natural Rights and the New Republicanism*. Princeton, N.J.: Princeton University Press.

Index

About the Author

Carville Earle is Carl O. Sauer Professor of Geography at Louisiana State University, past editor of the *Annals of the Association of American Geographers* (1994–1996), and formerly chair of the Department of Geography at Miami University and the Department of Geography and Anthropology at Louisiana State University. He served on the editorial boards of the *Annals of the Association of American Geographers,* the *Journal of Cultural Geography,* and *Historical Geography,* on the executive board of the Social Science History Association, and as chair of the Historical Geography Specialty Group of the AAG and the Historical Geography Network of the SSHA. He was Charles Warren Fellow at Harvard University, distinguished visitor in the Department of Geography at Cambridge University, and designated as Distinguished Scholar in Historical Geography by the Historical Geography Specialty Group of the Association of American Geographers. Professor Earle is the author of *The Evolution of a Tidewater Settlement System* (1975), *The Pursuit of Liberty* (1984), and *Geographical Inquiry and American Historical Problems* (1992), and the co-editor of *Concepts in Human Geography* (1996). He has published fifty or so articles in scholarly journals and books on the historical geography of the United States from the colonial period to the twentieth century on topics including colonization, rural and urban settlement, agriculture, frontier expansion and regional development, and the geography of labor and industrial relations.